THE PRENTICE-HALL SERIES IN MARKETING

Philip Kotler, Series Editor

SERVICES MARKETING

Text, Cases, & Readings

CHRISTOPHER H. LOVELOCK
Graduate School of Business Administration
Harvard University

Prentice-Hall, Inc., Englewood Cliffs, New Jersey 07632

Library of Congress Cataloging in Publication Data

LOVELOCK, CHRISTOPHER H.
  Services marketing.

  1. Marketing. 2. Professions—Marketing.
3. Service industries. I. Title.
HF5415.122.L68 1984   658.8   83-555
ISBN 0-13-806786-4

Editorial/production supervision and interior design: Esther S. Koehn
Cover design: Barbara Shelley, 20/20 Services, Inc.
Manufacturing buyer: Ed O'Dougherty

Printed in the United States of America

10 9 8 7 6 5 4 3 2 1

ISBN 0-13-806786-4

Prentice-Hall International, Inc., *London*
Prentice-Hall of Australia Pty. Limited, *Sydney*
Editora Prentice-Hall do Brasil, Ltda., *Rio de Janeiro*
Prentice-Hall Canada Inc., *Toronto*
Prentice-Hall of India Private Limited, *New Delhi*
Prentice-Hall of Japan, Inc., *Tokyo*
Prentice-Hall of Southeast Asia Pte. Ltd., *Singapore*
Whitehall Books Limited, *Wellington, New Zealand*

*To my brothers, Roger and Jeremy, and
my sister, Rachel—all of whom
work in the service sector*

Contents

II

Developing Frameworks for Understanding Services Marketing

49

CASES

READINGS

III

Positioning The Service Organization in the Marketplace

133

CASES

V

Managing Demand

279

CASES

READING

VI

Managing the Service Marketing System

339

CASES

─────────────── **VII** ───────────────

Planning, Organizing,
and Implementing the Marketing Effort
413

Preface

The service sector of the economy, which in the United States is more than twice as large as the manufacturing sector, is today in a state of turmoil. Deregulation, changes in professional association standards, the growing application of computer technology, and the continued expansion of franchise chains are combining to produce dramatic changes in the environment of many service industries. Perhaps the most significant trend—representing both a threat and an opportunity—is the increasingly competitive nature of the marketplace. This development requires a new emphasis on marketing for services as diverse as airlines and accounting, hotels and hospitals, and banking and real estate brokerages.

Until now, few managers of service businesses have accorded the marketing function as much importance as have their counterparts in manufacturing. In today's marketplace a marketing orientation is becoming essential to competitive survival. But a policy of simply drafting marketers from manufacturing firms, outfitting them in service costumes, and expecting them to succeed by pursuing the same marketing tactics and strategies as before is likely to fail.

The theme of this book is that service organizations differ in many important respects from manufacturing businesses, requiring a distinctive approach to marketing strategy development and execution. By this I don't mean to imply that services marketing is uniquely different from goods marketing. If that were true, it would undercut the whole notion of marketing as a coherent management function. Rather, I am stressing the importance of *understanding service organizations in their own terms* and then tailoring marketing goals and strategies accordingly. In the process, I believe we can enrich our understanding of the marketing discipline in general.

Development of this book began in 1979, when the Division of Research at the Harvard Business School, under its then director, Richard S. Rosenbloom, agreed to provide funding for development of a new MBA course entitled Marketing of Services, which was inaugurated in fall 1980 and has been taught at Harvard five times.

Building on earlier work undertaken at the Marketing Science Institute, I worked with research assistants to study marketing problems and practices across a broad array of service industries. Although the subjects of this research were drawn primarily from the private sector, they also include public and nonprofit organizations. It is important to recognize, I think, that most public agencies and nonprofit organizations are service institutions that have many characteristics in common with for-profit service businesses.

Both the structure and contents of the book have been influenced by advice and suggestions from a great many people. Particular thanks are due to my colleagues at the Harvard Business School, especially E. Raymond Corey, director of the Division of Research; Theodore Levitt; James L. Heskett; John A. Quelch; Robert D. Buzzell; David H. Maister; W. Earl Sasser, Jr.; and Daryl D. Wyckoff. My thinking has also been shaped in important ways by Stephen A. Greyser of the HBS faculty (formerly executive director of the Marketing Science Institute); by Alden R. Clayton, MSI's managing director; as well as by class discussions with participants in Harvard's MBA, doctoral, and executive programs. Outside the Harvard family, I want to acknowledge the intellectual and other contributions of my own family, especially those of my wife, Molly. Valuable insights have also been provided by Charles B. Weinberg of the University of British Columbia, Adrian B. Ryans of the University of Western Ontario, Ben M. Enis of the University of Southern California, Leonard L. Berry of Texas A&M University, William R. George of Rutgers University, John E.G. Bateson of the London Business School, and Eric Langeard and Pierre Eiglier of the Université d'Aix-Marseille.

In developing the cases for this book I was fortunate to have the help of several research assistants and Harvard Business School students: Terrie F. Bloom, Jeffrey S. Kahn, Robert J. Kopp, Penny Pittman Merliss, Jeffrey J. Sherman, and Lawrence H. Wilkinson. I'm very grateful to them for their splendid contributions. I am sure that they will not feel slighted if I single out Penny Merliss, my full-time research assistant and associate for more than a year, for her outstanding work in helping me to develop the Marketing of Services course.

My thanks are also due to the many other authors of articles and cases in this book, as well as to their publishers for permission to reprint their work here. Their names and affiliations appear on the title pages of their contributions.

Finally, I'd like to acknowledge the assistance of all those who helped bring this book into being. They include my present and former secretaries, Beverly Outram and Ellen Robinson; the staff of the Word Processing Center at the Harvard Business School; Karen Lindsey, who was responsible for the copy editing; and, of course, the editorial and production staff at Prentice-Hall, who transformed the manuscript into published form.

SERVICES MARKETING

I

Distinctive Aspects of Service Marketing

Some 200 years ago the British army was besieged by its American and French opponents at Yorktown, Virginia, in what was to prove the final major encounter of the American Revolutionary War. In losing the siege, the British lost the war. But in the face of defeat, the British bandmaster retained his sense of humor. As the British officers surrendered their swords to the commander of the Continental army, their regimental bands played in the background. The tune selected by the bandmaster—"The World Turned Upside Down"—offered a wryly appropriate commentary on the outcome of the war.

Today, a different world is being turned upside down—the world of services management. How managers in the service sector respond to the dramatic changes presently affecting it will determine whether their organizations survive and prosper or go down in defeat.

THE TOPSY-TURVY WORLD OF SERVICES

Like the factors that led to the American Revolution, some of the origins of today's service-sector revolution go back a number of years, whereas others reflect relatively recent events. Their key ingredients include:

- *A decline in government regulation,* especially in the United States, which has already eliminated or reduced many constraints on competitive activity in such major industries as securities, airfreight, passenger airlines, railroads, and trucking.[1]

- *Changes in professional association standards,* particularly as these relate to advertising and promotion, which are introducing a new element of competition to services supplied by members of such professions as medicine, law, accounting, and architecture.

- *Computerization and technological innovation,* which are radically altering the ways in which many service organizations do business with their customers (as well as what goes on behind the scenes). Retail banking, airfreight, and health care have been among the most affected industries.

- *The growth of franchising,* which is seeing large franchise chains displace or absorb a vast array of atomistic Mom-and-Pop service businesses in fields as diverse as real estate brokerage, quick service restaurants, muffler repair, plumbing, and haircutting.

Few of the eclectic group of industries composing the service sector find themselves untouched by any of these factors. In many industries, notably transportation and

1

financial services, several elements are converging—like a gale, a new moon, and heavy rains—to produce a flood tide that will wreck organizations whose management seeks to maintain the status quo. Other managers with more foresight recognize, like Shakespeare's Brutus, that a tide taken at the flood can lead to fortune. Leaving their competitors "bound in shallows and in miseries," they seek to ride the current. But where does this current lead and what does it imply for the role of marketing in the service sector?

Opportunities Resulting from Fewer
Regulations and Professional
Restrictions

The end result of government regulation or professional association prohibitions against advertising has been restraint of competition. Regulations have had the threefold effect of confining individual service businesses—such as banking and transportation—to specific geographic areas and product categories, of restraining price competition, and of establishing obstacles to new market entrants. Professional associations, by prohibiting or severely restricting the use of advertising and other communication tools, made it very difficult for newcomers to grow rapidly through innovation in service features and delivery systems, since new entrants had to rely on referrals and personal contacts to reach prospective customers.

The net effects of reduced regulation and changes in professional standards include

- Easier entry to specific product markets
- More freedom to compete on price
- Removal of many geographic restrictions on service delivery
- Incentives to differentiate services in meaningful ways

- The ability to use the mass media to promote professional services

Marketing Opportunities Arising
from New Technology

New technology (or more sophisticated use of existing technology) offers service businesses a variety of ways to improve their competitive stance. These include

- Creation of new or improved services. A good example is the Merrill Lynch Cash Management Account, which uses computerization to combine brokerage with a checking service and a debit card, automatic investment of surplus cash in a money market fund, plus an integrated monthly statement of all transactions.[2]

- More involvement of customers in operational tasks by providing self-service systems. Examples include automatic teller machines in banks, self-service gasoline pumps, airline ticket dispensers, and travelers' check dispensing machines. In many instances, these services can now be made available 24 hours a day at new locations where a full-service facility would be infeasible.

- Creation of centralized customer service departments backed up by computerized file systems and reached by toll-free telephone calls. Examples include airlines, credit firms, and car rental businesses. These departments may enable multisite service operations to maintain higher standards for providing information, taking reservations, and handling problems and complaints than when such responsibilities are assigned to individual local service outlets. Federal Express is among the firms that are leading the way in using technology to improve direct interactions between customers and the company. Service has been redefined to include "all actions and reactions that customers perceive they have purchased."[3]

• Recording customer information in easily accessible data banks. This offers several major advantages. Knowledge of customer usage patterns may suggest new ways of grouping customers into market segments, help improve pricing decisions, and lead to better targeted selling and advertising efforts. There may also be opportunities to personalize direct mail communications and customer-machine interactions. As noted by a Citibank executive, "Customers want to deal with people they know and that's not possible any more. But there's no reason why a [computer] terminal can't know more about you than a person can."[4]

Growing Impact of Franchising

The creation of franchise chains is transforming industries previously characterized by small unit size, local orientation, and absence of professional management skills. Even though franchisees retain some of the characteristics of individual entrepreneurs, many key marketing tasks are now in the hands of a professional staff at the chain's central offices. Certain activities, previously unnecessary or beyond the scope of an individual entrepreneurship, have become important as well as feasible. For example,

• Service features and prices are standardized and codified.

• Brand names, symbols, and uniforms are developed to ensure systemwide recognition and standardization.

• Mass media advertising is employed to create awareness and brand preference across the entire geographic market area served—regional, national, or international.

• For services that specialize in matchmaking—such as realtors and employment agencies—creation of centralized data banks increases the scope of the services offered and improves the chances of achieving a good match across geographic distances. Century 21, for instance, has recently been running advertisements in national magazines promoting its ability to find beachfront California property for Kansas residents, or New England fishing cottages for folks in Arizona. Few of the previously independent realtors who make up this franchise chain could ever have offered such services on their own.

• The economies of scale provided by a chain allow for creation of a centralized marketing research function. This is valuable for internally monitoring the results of existing operations (and thereby highlighting examples of good and poor practice by franchisees), for formulating pricing strategy, and for evaluating the effectiveness of advertising campaigns. Perhaps even more significant is the input provided to strategic market planning, including information on competitive positioning, identification and evaluation of new product opportunities, and appraisal of alternative distribution strategies.

Implications for Management

Few, if any, service businesses are likely to find themselves simultaneously facing all the marketing opportunities noted above. It is just as true, however, that few will find themselves entirely unaffected by the changes now racing through the service sector. Comfortable barriers to competition are being swept away in many instances, allowing the entry of aggressive, innovative upstarts. Consider, for instance, the effects competition has had on the older U.S. domestic airlines. Customer loyalty to established service businesses is proving quite fickle in the face of price-cutting, product differentiation, and provision of more convenient delivery systems. And old product-market boundaries—as between the banking and securities industries—are breaking down.

In short, not only is competition intensifying but the rules of the competitive game are changing just as quickly. In the process, there is more of a premium being placed on effective marketing. The ability to run a good operation, while as important as always, is no longer sufficient. The service product must be tailored to customer needs. More specifically, new market entrants are positioning their services to appeal to *specific* market segments, rather than trying to be all things to all people. Pricing, communication efforts, and service delivery systems are also being tailored to specific segments.

All these actions require development or acquisition of marketing skills that are more broadly defined than just "advertising and public relations." In their search for more sophisticated marketing techniques, senior executives of service businesses often turn to the manufacturing sector. A widely recognized source of marketing talent is packaged goods firms, which have honed their skills to a remarkable sharpness over the past three decades.

Are the marketing skills developed in manufacturing companies *directly* transferable to service organizations? I think not. It is my contention that marketing management tasks in the service sector differ from those in the manufacturing sector in several important respects.

BROAD DIFFERENCES
BETWEEN SERVICES AND GOODS

Among the characteristics distinguishing services marketing from goods marketing are the nature of the product, the greater involvement of customers in the production process, greater difficulties in maintaining quality control standards, the absence of inventories, the relative importance of the time factor, and the structure of distribution channels.[5] Let's look briefly at each, while recognizing that not all of these generalizations apply with equal force to all services.

• *Nature of the product.*[6] Leonard Berry in his article "Services Marketing Is Different," which is included in this section, captures the distinction well when he describes a good as "an object, a device, a thing," in contrast to a service which is "a deed, a performance, an effort." Marketing a performance (which in the case of rental services may involve an object like a power tool or a car) is very different from attempting to market the physical object itself. For instance, in automobile rentals, customers usually reserve a particular category of car, rather than a specific model, paying more attention to such elements as location and appearance of pickup and delivery facilities; availability of inclusive insurance, cleaning, and maintenance; provision of free shuttle buses at airports; availability of 24-hour reservations service; hours when rental locations are staffed; and quality of service provided by customer-contact personnel.

• *Customer involvement in production.* Performing a service involves assembling and delivering the output of a mix of physical facilities and mental or physical labor. Often customers are actively involved in helping to create the service product—either by serving themselves (as in a fast-food restaurant or laundromat) or by cooperating with service personnel in settings such as hair salons, hotels, colleges, or hospitals. Like all performances, services are timebound and experiential, although they may have lasting consequences.

• *Quality control problems.* Since many services are consumed as they are produced, final assembly must take place under real-time conditions. People, both service personnel and other customers, often become an integral part of the experience. These factors make it hard for service organizations to control quality and offer a consistent product. As a former packaged goods marketer—now a Holiday Inn executive—observed, "We can't control the quality of our product as well as a Procter and Gamble control engineer on a production line can. . . . When you buy a box of Tide, you can reasonably be 99 and 44/100ths percent sure that this stuff will work to get your clothes clean. When you buy a Holiday Inn room, you're sure at some lesser percentage that it will work to give you a good night's sleep without any hassle, or people banging on the walls and all the bad things that can happen in a hotel."[7]

• *No inventories for services.* Because a service is a deed or performance rather than a tangible item that the customer keeps, it cannot be inventoried. Of course the necessary equipment, facilities, and labor can be held in readiness to create the service, but these simply represent productive capacity, not the product itself. Unused capacity in a service business is rather like having a running tap in a sink with no plug: The flow is wasted unless customers (or possessions of theirs requiring servicing) are present to receive it. And when demand exceeds capacity, customers are likely to be sent away disappointed, since no inventory is available for backup. An important task for service marketers, therefore, is to find ways of smoothing demand levels to match capacity.

• *Different distribution channels.* Unlike manufacturing firms, which require physical distribution channels for moving goods from factory to customers, service businesses either use electronic channels (as in broadcasting or electronic funds transfer) or else combine the service factory, retail outlet, and point-of-consumption into one. In the latter instance, service firms often find themselves responsible for managing customer-contact personnel (rather than contracting out the retailing task to intermediaries). They may also have to manage the consumption behavior of their own customers to ensure that the operation runs smoothly and that one person's behavior doesn't irritate other customers who are present at the same time.

Consumer Needs and Management Tasks

In many instances, of course, services compete in the marketplace with goods that offer broadly similar benefits. For instance, buying a service may be an alternative to doing it yourself. Examples range from lawn care and babysitting to janitorial services and industrial equipment maintenance. Too, using a rental service is frequently an alternative to owning a good. The Yellow Pages in any large city includes listings for a wide array of rental services, ranging from trucks to typewriters and from furniture to formal wear. Figure I–1 shows how, in certain instances, three different types of services may compete with ownership and use of a good.

But just because a good and a service may be close competitors does not mean that the marketing management tasks for each are the same. A packaged foods marketer is likely to come to grief using strategies similar to those of fast-food restaurant marketers; a successful automobile marketer will not necessarily find it easy to replicate that success in the rental car business; a marketing executive for a manufacturer of heavy electrical equipment will need to develop a new managerial style—as well as new strategies—if transferred to the same company's equipment servicing division.

FIGURE I–1

Services as Substitutes for Owning and/or Using Goods

	OWN A PHYSICAL GOOD	RENT THE USE OF A PHYSICAL GOOD
PERFORM THE WORK ONESELF	• Drive own car • Type on own typewriter	• Rent a car and drive it • Rent a typewriter
HIRE SOMEONE TO DO THE WORK	• Hire a chauffeur to drive car • Hire a typist to use typewriter	• Hire a taxi or limousine • Send work out to a typing agency

On the other hand, the nature of many services is such that no reasonable alternative exists for average consumers to "do it themselves" or "own it themselves." Thus, few people are wealthy and skilled enough to fly their own jet aircraft across the Atlantic or to own accommodations in all cities they visit. Moreover, there are many industries where the service does *not* compete with a physical good that offers similar benefits and when customer performance of the service is not a realistic option. Insurance services, for instance, are predicated on the principle of sharing risks among numerous participants; "self-insurance" means assuming the risks oneself and entails going without coverage. Similarly, many health problems cannot be self-treated and require the services of medical professionals.

One reason why marketers from the manufacturing sector often run into difficulties in the service sector is that the working environment is typically quite different. In manufacturing firms, production takes place in factories that consumers normally never see; marketers provide the link between customers and the company. In service businesses, operations has traditionally been the key function, responsible for both product execution and customer contact. To receive service, customers may have to come directly to the "factory" where the service is created and delivered.

Marketing, being a relatively new func-

tion, is often perceived by operations managers as an "add-on" at the staff level. But if the term *marketer* is used in its broadest sense to include all service personnel whose responsibilities extend to managing customer interactions and relationships, then it is clear that many operations managers *already* have marketing responsibilities. The challenge is to execute these responsibilities in ways that will strengthen the competitive posture of the firm. This may require retraining existing managers, hiring new marketing executives from outside (and then acculturating them to the nature of the service operation in question), or both.

SCOPE OF THE BOOK

The book is divided into seven sections, of which the first consists of this introduction and three readings that discuss the extent to which services marketing is distinctively different from goods marketing.

The six remaining sections of the book are as follows:

- Section II—Developing Frameworks for Understanding Services Marketing
- Section III—Positioning the Service Organization in the Marketplace
- Section IV—Managing the Customer Mix
- Section V—Managing Demand

- Section VI—Managing the Service Marketing System
- Section VII—Planning, Organizing, and Implementing the Marketing Effort

Each of these sections consists of a discussion of the subject at hand plus several cases and readings related to the subject. An appendix at the end, "Studying and Learning from Cases," suggests how to obtain the best insights from the 20 case studies in the book. Let us briefly look at an overview of Sections II through VII.

Section II: Developing Frameworks for Understanding Services Marketing

The service sector is enormously diverse. It includes both for-profit and not-for-profit organizations varying widely in the size and scope of their activities. This diversity makes it difficult to come up with useful generalizations concerning marketing practices in service organizations. Historically, relatively few managers (or researchers, for that matter) have gone beyond basic industry classifications in searching for managerial insights that might have value to different service entities.

The theme of Section II is that service organizations need to be classified in ways that reflect the nature of the marketing problems faced by management. Accordingly, six classification schemes are developed that transcend narrow industry boundaries. These show how seemingly unrelated service businesses may have important characteristics in common that enable them to gain marketing-relevant insights from studying one another's activities.

Section III: Positioning the Service Organization in the Marketplace

As service industries become more competitive, it becomes increasingly necessary for the management of each organization to develop a good understanding of the characteristics of its own product, how these relate to the needs of different market segments, and how the product compares to competing services.

Understanding the concept of product positioning—the process of developing and maintaining a distinctive "niche" in the market—is critical to developing an effective competitive posture. Positioning strategy is certainly not limited to services; in fact, it had its origins in marketing consumer-packaged goods. But, as shown in Section III, positioning is a powerful concept for forcing service marketers to think explicitly about product characteristics as these relate to both consumers' needs and competitive offerings. Translating vague terms such as *service* and *convenience* into more tightly defined and more easily measurable product attributes is a particularly important task for service businesses that have historically defined the product internally according to operational standards, rather than externally according to consumer choice criteria.

Section IV: Managing the Customer Mix

All marketers need to be concerned about who their customers are. As emphasized in Section IV, this concern takes on added dimensions for services in which customers become a part of the service product. This is most likely to occur when customers have a high level of contact with the service organization and share the service facilities with many other customers. The marketing challenge here is to ensure that the mix of customers attracted will reinforce the desired positioning of the service rather than contradict it. A related task is to minimize incompatibility among customers who use the service.

The problem of managing the mix of customers takes on added significance under conditions of limited capacity and fluctuating demand. In such situations, the challenge for the service marketer is to develop strategies for attracting the most profitable segment available at any point in time, so that relatively less profitable customers do not crowd out more desirable ones at times when demand for the service exceeds capacity.

Section V: Managing Demand

As noted earlier, one of the characteristics of most service businesses is that their products are highly perishable and cannot be produced for inventory. This is a significant problem for services with high fixed costs and relatively fixed capacity if customer demand fluctuates widely over time.

Section V explores marketing strategies for bringing demand into balance with capacity, in contrast to operational strategies for managing capacity to match demand. Among the issues raised are the need to separate predictable from random demand fluctuations and to determine the underlying causes of such fluctuations. Without such understanding, there is a risk that the marketing strategies developed to manage demand may address the symptom rather than the cause.

Section VI: Managing the Service Marketing System

Services are often described as intangible, ephemeral, and experiential. This is true in as much as one cannot buy all the elements of a service, wrap them up, and take them home for future consumption. But a whole host of features in a service business is quite evident to one or more of a customer's senses. In many instances, the customer actually encounters the service production process in operation. These operational elements thus become part of the service product and are therefore relevant to marketers.

Section VI is concerned with identifying and managing all the different ways in which the service organization (or information about it) touches current and prospective consumers. Managing the service marketing system brings service marketers into much closer contact with their counterparts in operations than is true of marketing and production managers in a manufacturing firm. To ensure consistency across all the service elements may require carefully developed "internal marketing" strategies, so that operations personnel understand how their work affects customer satisfaction and recognize what is expected of them.

In services that require frequent interactions with customers in terms of answering queries, taking orders, and responding to complaints or other problems, a new, professionalized management function is emerging—customer service. A case can be made for establishing this as an independent department, complementing the efforts of operations and sales rather than being under the direction of either.

Section VII: Planning, Organizing, and Implementing the Marketing Effort

Much of the content of this book is concerned with analysis and strategy development. But a strategy is only a blueprint for action: Getting results is another matter. Section VII focuses on translating marketing plans into reality in service businesses.

Marketing managers who move from manufacturing firms to service businesses are often surprised to find how different the managerial environment is between their current and former jobs. In part, this reflects the traditional dominance of the operations function in service firms, as contrasted with marketing's usual status as a relative newcomer. But it is also true that marketing and operations managers need to work together much more closely than do marketing and manufacturing executives. The text, readings, and cases in Section VII consider the type of organizational design that makes the most sense for different kinds of service firms. The section addresses three issues: developing marketing plans, deciding how the marketing function in service businesses should be organized, and determining how it should relate to operations in terms of creating and implementing marketing strategies in a timely and effective fashion.

NOTES

1. Note that government regulations pertaining to service industry practices have historically been more stringent in the United States than in many other industrialized nations.

2. Clever use of computer technology and electronic funds transfer systems has enabled Merrill Lynch to circumvent regulations designed to prevent nonbanks from offering banking services.

3. See the case in Section VI entitled, "Federal Express: Customer Service Department, I."

4. Cited in "Toward Service Without a Snarl," *Fortune*, March 23, 1981, 58–66.

5. The extent and implications of these differences are discussed in more depth in the three readings reprinted in this section.

6. I use the term *product* in this book to include both goods and services; however, readers should note that some authors still equate the word *product* with manufactured goods.

7. Quoted in Gary Knisely, "Greater Marketing Emphasis by Holiday Inn Breaks Mold" (reprinted in the Section I of this book).

READINGS

Comparing Marketing Management in Package Goods and Service Organizations

GARY KNISELY

After four decades of experience that have firmly established the marketing discipline in the consumer package goods industry, experienced marketers are invading the consumer service industry, bringing with them a new set of skills developed through trial, error, and refinement. How successful will they be? What is the likelihood of marketing alter-

Gary Knisely is a principal of the consulting firm of Johnson, Smith, and Knisely, Inc., New York. Reproduced with permission from the January 15, 1979; February 19, 1979; March 19, 1979, and May 14, 1979 issues of *Advertising Age*. Copyright © 1979 by Crain Communications, Inc.

ing the service sector as fundamentally as it has the consumer products industry?

The answers to these and other questions can perhaps best be given by managers who have served successfully in senior marketing positions in both consumer-package goods and consumer service organizations. This reading reproduces four interviews with marketers who have experienced firsthand what can and cannot cross the barrier between the two areas.

Greater Marketing Emphasis by Holiday Inn Breaks Mold

The first interview is with James L. Schorr, then executive vice president–marketing, Holiday Inns Inc. Mr. Schorr previously held positions in account management with Ogilvy & Mather and in brand management with Procter & Gamble. Prior to joining Holiday Inns in 1975, he served in a succession of senior marketing positions with the U.S. Postal Service and as a special consultant to the President of the U.S. on energy communications. Mr. Schorr's responsibilities at the time of the interview included planning, product development, sales, advertising and promotion activities of the Holiday Inn system of hotels throughout the world.

Knisely: You've marketed soap, postal services, and now hotel rooms. What's the difference between what you were doing five years ago and now, in terms of managing the marketing process?

Schorr: Essentially what I did at Procter & Gamble (or with General Foods when they were my client) and at the Postal Service and here was that in each instance I simply used what we call marketing tools to persuade somebody to do something that I wanted them to do. Whether it's to purchase a service or purchase a product, there really isn't as much difference as a lot of people think—tactically, yes; but not strategically.

Knisely: Convincing me to stay at a Holiday Inn seems more complex than getting me to choose one brand of soap or another. It's a more complex decision from my standpoint, if for nothing more than there are more actions involved in it.

Schorr: Well, I suppose a major difference between product marketing and service marketing is that we can't control the quality of our product as well as a P&G control engineer on a production line can control the quality of his product. When you buy a box of Tide, you can reasonably be 99 and 44/100% sure that this stuff will work to get your clothes clean. When you buy a Holiday Inn room, you're sure at some lesser percentage that it will work to give you a good night's sleep without any hassle, or people banging on the walls and all the bad things that can happen to you in a hotel.

Holiday Inns really brought the brand name into the hotel business. Back in the 50s, the only brand name in the business was Hilton with a lot of downtown aging properties. Today, Holiday Inns is 10 times bigger than the Hilton chain. We brought the brand name concept to the business by providing a uniformity of experience and certain standards that the customer can depend on.

But that's still a far cry below the kind of

quality control that manufacturers can put on their products.

Knisely: How do you define a "service" business *vis à vis* a "product" business?

Schorr: Simply defined, in our terms, a product is something a consumer purchases and takes with him or consumes, or otherwise uses. If it is not physical, not something that they can take away or consume, then we call it a service.

Knisely: What about a McDonald's, where most people say it's the fast-foods *service* business?

Schoor: I don't agree with that. I think McDonald's sells products. They sell french fries and hamburgers—products. They're also selling the service with which they provide those products, but very few people go to McDonald's for service.

Knisely: Let's talk about the room part of the business. When you think of what somebody is buying, what are those elements you think of?

Selling an Experience

Schorr: What I am really selling, in terms of what people are buying, is a hotel experience. I'm selling the room, the way they treat you at the front desk, the way the bellman treats you, the way the waitress treats you—it's all mixed together in a consumer's mind when he makes a hotel decision. I could go out and convince everybody in the world that I had the world's most superior rooms and it probably wouldn't have much impact on my business, even though that's obviously the most important thing I've got. My sale is much more a service sale and much more a people-on-people sale.

Knisely: How do you sell people-on-people? Are advertising and some of the standard marketing tactics of selling a package goods product as applicable to this business as they are to P&G or General Foods?

Schorr: No. Such tactics are not as directly efficient for us as for somebody who can control the quality of their product or service better than we can. Half of our efforts are in product development, which is part of the marketing organization here. Very unusual. Even in a sophisticated company like P&G, product development is not part of the marketing operation.

I am famous here for what's called the Bucket Theory of Marketing in the service business. I say you've got to think of marketing as a big bucket. It's what the sales programs, the advertising programs, and the other programs do that shovels business into the top of that bucket. When the bucket's full, that's 100% occupancy. And we keep building new programs and accelerating existing programs to shovel more and more business into that bucket.

There's only one problem. There's a hole in the bottom of the bucket. When we run our business really well, when we control the quality of our product, then the hole is very small and the business falls out much more slowly than I throw it in at the top.

But when we run weak operations, when our experience, our people contact, our systems, or our rooms degrade or deteriorate, then that hole gets bigger. When I'm in a period of declining occupancy, what's happening is I'm losing them out of the bottom of that bucket faster than I can bring in new ones at the top. Those two functions—product quality and selling—*that* is marketing.

Knisely: Give me some examples of the kinds of things that that bucket theory gets you involved in.

Schorr: Take our rules of operation, which every Holiday Inn has to follow if they want to have the sign out front and if they want to have a Holidex machine at the front desk, which fills up half the rooms every night before they do anything. We'll unplug the sign, we'll unplug the Holidex machine, if they don't live by our rules of operation.

It used to be those rules were written by people who would define standards in technical terms. There was almost no consumer orientation in our rules. Our rules now are very consumer oriented. In another six months to nine months, they will be totally consumerized in terms of setting priorities for the inns on what the most important things are and what they must do.

We run test inns here, where we try a number of new programs. The customers at those inns don't know they're in the test inns, but they are guinea pigs for things so we can work out operational glitches and also screen things that people really didn't like before we expand nationally.

Difficult to Test

Knisely: Is market research more difficult in this business than when you're selling a product in a box?

Schorr: Much more difficult. Also much more rewarding. No one else does much of it in the industry but us. You have most competitors flying by the seat of their pants. We are taking the techniques that have been developed in the package goods industry and then putting those techniques to work in this industry.

Knisely: Do you have to fiddle with them to make them work here?

Schorr: Invariably. Things that are applicable to the package goods business are only somewhat applicable here.

The best example would be something we run called "travel audit." That would be this industry's version of a Nielsen, except that only Holiday Inns has it.

Knisely: What about more attitudinal marketing research—qualitative? Are you looking at demographics and psychographics?

Schorr: We don't do much qualitative research. Most of it is quantitative, even the attitudinal research.

We do something annually here that basically splits our market down into whether or not people are traveling to a property as a destination or as an overnight pit stop. Then that splits out by business versus leisure travel. Then we go into the usage of hotel chains by these categories and the attitudinal reasons why. It's very similar to national brand usage studies conducted by a major package goods company.

Knisely: What about the functional linkages? In the classic package goods terms, there are certain relationships between manufacturing, R&D, distribution, etc. What about your linkages?

Schorr: What do you mean by linkages?

Knisely: Who reports to whom—who calls the shots—who has the real power. In the soap business, marketing tells manufacturing, "We want it to be white with blue dots; it should smell a certain way with a certain package"—and it comes out that way. In many of the service businesses, banking particularly, it is operations that calls the shots.

Closely Linked

Schorr: In a service business, marketing and operations are more closely linked than they are in a manufacturing business. My eye is on the same target as the eye of the guy who runs operations. As a result, we tend to walk hand-in-hand.

There's an awareness in the company about marketing. Marketing is not subservient to operations and neither is operations subservient to marketing. If there is a conflict, theoretically the president of the company resolves it.

In the structure of this corporation, there tend not to be the conflicts between operations and marketing. I may go into operations, for example, and say, "Hey, listen, I've got this idea on something we ought to do." His response to me may be, "Sounds nifty, but it would be a nightmare if I did that." My response is, "I know it would be a nightmare, but let's see if we can figure out a way to do it. Put it in our test inns and we'll see if everybody stumbles over themselves and what the customer thinks of it, and what he's going to pay for it."

That's a very easy way to work things out, so you quickly find out first of all if it is a good marketing idea, and secondly if it is an operational infeasibility—it just can't be done.

Knisely: You've worked in two organizations now where you've had to recruit a lot of people from the package goods industry. Did you find that there are certain mind sets that might have come along that make it difficult for them to adapt to this way of thinking? Were there certain surprises that hit a lot of people that they just never thought about?

Schorr: That's the best question you've asked. There definitely are certain kinds of people who should never make the move. There are some that certainly could make it, and should. After all, the service industries are the growth sectors of the U.S. economy.

The biggest difference is that—let's go back to package goods companies. There are essentially two kinds of people. There is the kind who gets his marketing plan from last year, who gets an assignment to ship 8% more cases next year and who develops the marketing plan to do that. And that's a certain mind set that functions very well inside of P&G. That person should probably never leave the package goods industry.

On the other hand, there is a kind of person who is somewhat more pioneering, a person who wants to take those skills that heretofore have not been applied to that industry and to see something dramatic happen, more dramatic than 8%.

They're Pioneers

I think every one of the persons [from package goods] we attracted to Washington when I was there [and now here at Holiday Inns] really comes because his mind set is a little more pioneering, more innovative, more of "I don't want to do that same thing for the next 30 years of my life," and "I want to have a little more fun" and "innovate a little more," to be a builder of things at least as much as a manager.

Knisely: What's the most important skill that ought to be brought from the package goods industry?

Schorr: The most important skill is the creativity and the judgment involved in the ability to recognize when something will be persuasive to people. Successful marketing people, no matter what industry they're in, are people who have a mix of skills that enable them to identify when something will be persuasive to people and who will be able to persuade them to do something.

If you have that skill, then what the package goods industry has done is to identify some 87 media through which you can execute. A guy simply brings a knowledge of "continuity promotions" versus "trial promotions" versus "repurchase promotion" versus "trial incentive" versus "discounts." He's learned all these categories and learned all the different ways to do it and they are all very valuable. I think they apply equally in both industries.

But the successful guys would have the persuasion skills and be able to succeed in either.

Knisely: Are there more surprises here than in package goods?

Schorr: Yes. One of the things I've learned is the difference between our kinds of businesses—tactical, not strategic, but it makes a big difference.

In the process of learning differences about the hotel business, there have been a lot of surprises. I came in believing the classical marketing tactics and I've learned that only about half of the so-called classical beliefs are immutable truths. For example, I was taught by Procter that in marketing you fish where the fish are: In periods of high consumption, that's when you advertise the most.

Well, that's ridiculous in this industry. For example, in periods of high consumption, I'm full. I don't have any rooms to sell. This is not the time that I want to spend all my marketing money. Yet, classical theory would have me spend 40% of my marketing effort in that three-month period to stimulate that activity; I have a capacity problem, so I don't spend any of my marketing funds during that period of time.

There have been, I suppose, a dozen little surprises like that where you just can't operate out of rote. It means a little more open mindedness, a little less moving by rote.

Knisely: Is part of it that you just don't have all the data available that you had at P&G?

Schorr: We have, in the last three years, generated more base data in terms of consumer aspects of the lodging market than P&G possesses in the soap business and the consumer aspects of the soap market. It has to, because as you said earlier, our customer has a more complex purchasing decision.

Can't Transplant P&G

It's not the possession of the data or the rote application of the data. Most of the guys that I've seen come out of P&G who failed someplace else and just really died in the service industry were guys who tried to reinvent P&G wherever they went. The classic way failed. It is not reinventable. P&G has *evolved* to where it is. You cannot walk into any com-

pany—I don't care if it's General Foods—and plant your P&G system. It will never work. It took years and years and generations and a lot of personnel and manpower, fine tuning, and training to get where they are.

Lesser Role

So a guy has to be able to go in without the crutches of a P&G media staff department, P&G promotional development staff department, where he was almost unable to fail; he has to be able to throw those crutches away and be willing to operate without that kind of staff support.

There's one other big difference. In service industries, people aren't oriented to the marketing concept; marketing is not as important in the service industry as in the package goods industry. Most organization charts of the service industry show the head of marketing is not the equal of the head of operations; he just doesn't have as much horsepower.

There are several service companies—Holiday Inns is, I think, foremost—which are organized to pay real attention to marketing and to innovate multi-million-dollar annual investments and manpower and staff. They bring in the best marketing people they can find to help them.

I won't say to you that marketing has the acceptance as it has at P&G, but I would say at Holiday Inns that it's maybe 80% of the way there. My image of the service industry, in general, is that it's somewhere around 20% of the way there. But there are service companies that are breaking out of the traditional operations mold and becoming much more marketing oriented.

Listening to Consumer Is Key to Goods or Service Marketing

The second interview is with Thomas R. Engel, then product group manager, Lever Bros., New York.

Thomas R. Engel's position at the time of the interview included both established brands and test market brand management respon-

sibilities within Lever's Household Products Business Unit.

He was part of the original consumer package goods team brought into the U.S. Postal Service to develop a marketing operation. In his senior marketing management capacity there, he directed marketing behind a wide-ranging group of new postal products and services.

He started his career in account management with the J. Walter Thompson Co., working on Lever Bros. business.

Knisely: What, to you, is the thing that most distinguishes product marketing from the marketing of services?

Engel: Probably, the most distinguishing thing is where the attention is devoted. In product marketing, you fight tooth and nail from one footline to another footline. Everybody is intensely interested in everything that occurs. Once you get that plan approved, you're pretty much on your own and you've got to be able to muster the resources—business and personal—to make it happen.

From my experience both in consumer package goods and consumer services, I can see that the two are enormously different. Those differences are twofold.

The first is the nature of the organization and what they believe to be most important. In most product companies, marketing is the number one action spot. The upper reaches of people managing a service company—whether it's a lodging company which sells beds, the Postal Service which sells mail services, or a bank which sells financial services—typically prize other disciplines as much or more so than marketing.

The second is the massive difference—and one must grasp how massive it is—that emerges *vis-à-vis* customer interface with your product. On the product marketing side, we obviously must ensure we have the spanking best product on the shelf, but the sale is between the eyes of the consumer and our marketing and our product.

A service company typically introduces a third party who is an intermediary between the customer and the service. The Postal Service, up until 1973, had an enormously profitable business called stamps—$40,000,000 worth, with extremely profitable margins. If you sell a stamp for collection purposes, that's all profit, period. However, in taking that business into competition in the leisure time category, eyeball to eyeball with Parker Bros. and with bowling and other hobbies, we have a very different situation than that faced by product marketers. We had to grasp the fact that all the brilliant marketing, product development, and financial leverage planning comes to a screeching halt if Mrs. Jones goes to buy $10 worth of stamp collecting products and she meets a clerk who says, "I'm sorry, I'm closed. Go to the other window." And that happened.

Knisely: Why did it take so long to learn that?

Engel: Because it's difficult to teach an old dog new tricks. The concept of direct customer service is foreign to a product marketer. At the Postal Service, I joined a group of people who had been recruited from private industry, principally from package goods companies. Not in all the years of experience of people coming out of the companies did we think in terms of a dialog with your customer—which is a crucial point in making the sale in most service businesses.

Revamp System

I had a colleague who was head of product development at the Postal Service. We had to ensure that services we were considering introducing into the marketplace were fully deliverable. We came to the conclusion that we could not conduct over-the-counter marketing until we had wholesale restructuring and training of the over-the-counter customer service situation.

We found that we were driving people to the counter and then driving them away because clerks were not fully aware of the product line. And among those who were aware, there was no sophistication by way of skillful trading up: "Okay, here's a stamp collecting kit. Have you thought about a commemorative stamp of the United Nations?"

Once one grasps the enormous difference at the point of sale, you have grasped the enormous difference between service and product marketing.

Knisely: Did that translate back into the structure of the marketing-management function?

Engel: Yes, it did. In package goods marketing, the marketing management group doesn't have anything to do with managing checkout clerks. When marketing people went to the Postal Service, they set up marketing management that wasn't focused enough on that person at the counter. And the backlash was enormous. It was like throwing a bucket of ice on our heads.

Early on, we realized we could bring a level of expertise in three areas: Isolate where the most pronounced market demand was, for a range of products and services; develop plans which would capitalize on that market development, and execute those plans. All of which we knew how to do because that's what we had done for a living. However, what we didn't know how to do, but soon learned had to be done, was to gain leverage at the point of sale.

Knisely: Step back a little—different perspective. What did you find were the transferable skills? We talked about one that was there—the idea of managing the service aspect of it, delivery. Did you find that everything else was transferable and needed and could be used almost in the same way?

Engel: That's a very good question. Let me frame it this way. We found that most of the things we knew how to do in a product marketing capacity were not only needed, tremendously needed, but also that the organization realized that the concept of marketing management made a lot of sense.

What I think was not easily transferable was more mental than technical. And mental meaning a preoccupation with excellence and

a real intensity to build, to grow, to make things happen.

If you think about some of the most successful service marketing companies, you've got to ask yourself whether things are bought or whether things are sold. In product marketing, things are sold. In service marketing, things are sold also. People don't rush out and buy insurance per se. But, frequently, in the lodging industry, rooms are bought and, in the postal system, things were typically bought as commodity items.

But we realized that there was a demand influence that could be utilized—we could build in consumer end benefits and product superiorities and create a pull as well as just a buy. That's something that product marketeers have been interested in for a long time.

We did run into some real brick walls. One in particular—that was in the area of using marketing as a leverage point for reducing operating costs.

Reducing Costs

We went through a massive business analysis of all the services we were marketing and new services under consideration. Then out of nowhere, some very bright folks in the finance department said, "Hey, listen, I don't know whether you guys can do anything about it, but we've got lots and lots of costs that we should get rid of."

Keep talking, we said. "Well, for example, each year the Postal Service incurs somewhere in the neighborhood of $350,000,000 in potentially avoidable labor costs. Roughly 20,000,000 Americans move each year. People move; their mail comes in to their old post office; it can't be delivered; it's reshuffled and pushed onto their new post office, if we're lucky; otherwise, people go scurrying around trying to find their new address. And every time they touch a piece of mail twice, that's twice the cost, half of which is avoidable."

So we started thinking that what we had was a marketing problem and what was missing was a service. The marketing problem is that consumers are missing the opportunity to get improved service from their mail because there is a lack of service geared to that. So we said we'll introduce a new service called "the change of address kit."

And it was very simple: Mrs. Engel would be given a change of address kit, with lots of change of address notices to send to friends, businesses, etc. That would prevent her mail from going to the old post office and shoot it right on to the new post office. We went throughout the building and throughout the work force and they said, "Are people really going to do that? All they're going to do is give us the notice, if they get around to it—and in the meantime, we're getting months and months of their mail and we'll just get the clerks to schlepp it on to the new place."

We said you may be right. You also may be wrong. And if you're wrong, you're losing the opportunity of reducing those costs. After a tremendous amount of sweat and agony, we went into test markets. What we discovered was that in setting forth the moving public's benefit—getting mail on time, no hassles, arriving in a new home, and having their mail right there—we could gain an enormous amount of cooperation. In turn, we could reduce operating costs in those markets by millions of dollars. That plan was approved for national expansion based on successful test results. And it's now a national service.

There's another thing, and this is what I consider the enormous excitement of service marketing. Specifically, all mail is not equal. Household-to-household mail is not time sensitive, but business-to-business mail, or business-to-household mail is incredibly time sensitive. And yet, prior to several years ago, mail was basically mail whether it took General Motors three days to get the contract from here to Honolulu or 24 hours. But it was determined that there was a primary demand for speed. Out of this emerged Express Mail, a highly successful service introduced by the new Postal Service.

Secondly, mail is not mail, *vis-à-vis* reliability. The marketing group determined that the securities industry had an overwhelming need for secured theftproof mail, absolute. So a product line was developed called "Control Pak," which we would literally carry from origin to destination.

Knisely: So you really have product differentiation?

Focus on Consumer

Engel: Certainly. The bar soap business is broken down into a number of subsegments, soap for washing your face, for washing your total body, for cosmetic purposes, for deodorant purposes. Likewise, with mail. Some mail is time sensitive, some isn't; some mail is security mail, some of it isn't. All potential customers have different needs, and it's essential you groom your services to meet these different demands.

I think what service marketing can most learn from product marketing is that it's most important to focus not on what the company wants, but on what the consumer wants, to orient the focus against consumer wants and needs as they exist today or as they can be developed. And I would encourage anybody in service marketing who may not have been in a product marketing environment to listen carefully to the product marketing people and follow what they are saying as it related to consumers and their wants.

Interface

Secondly, what product marketing people going into the service marketing environment must know and must learn is the concept of customer service and customer interface.

What I suggest is that a mechanism be developed whereby the product marketer going into a service organization can share in customer interface to the point literally of getting behind the counter for a week, a month, three weeks—watching, listening, and coming away with a very clear and obvious grip on the one final step that exists in making the sale that has never existed in consumer marketing.

Knisely: A lot of people who have had

package goods experience and tried out the service market were driven out of the field.

Engel: Yes.

Knisely: Why do you suppose that is?

Engel: Why? The primary reason is because you feel less loved and less needed.

You've got to have a zealous missionary spirit. You also have to have resiliency.

Different Mentality

Let me give you a practical example of the difference in mentality. Here I am every day—it's like the city room of the *New York Times*—the place is very active—8 in the morning til 5:30 at night and people are saying, "Let's go; tell us, tell us." In a service company which has perhaps been built on skills and disciplines that have not included large doses of marketing, you're selling—you're saying "listen to me" as opposed to "tell me, tell me."

Another thing is that you have to learn to speak a different language if you are marketing in a service company.

It's one thing when you're an assistant brand manager, talking to a brand manager who has been there, who's selling to a group who has been there, who is selling to a president of the division who has worked up this line. Then you can easily talk with him about positioning, share of market, image versus whatever.

The issue is one of language, ensuring we're not speaking in a foreign language. For example, in Washington, we wouldn't talk about our marketing plans, we talked about programs—an innocuous term, program, which is a popular term in Washington. We wouldn't talk about regional strategies, we'd talk about field programs. We wouldn't talk about measuring the net effectiveness of this campaign, we'd talk about what happens.

More Variables

The determination of profitability for a particular program in a service company is more difficult. There are too many related functions. If you introduce a new soap, there may be some cannibalization to your existing products, but it doesn't change the other products. Whereas in the service area, if you put in product "A," it will change what product "B" is.

This is what many product marketing guys find enormously challenging until they burn themselves out. They're frustrated by it all and feel very unloved. In many respects, it is or can be a much more sophisticated marketing area, if for no other reason than there are frequently a lot more variables flying around than in product marketing.

Selling Stamps

The Postal Service had a long-standing stamp collecting business which was about as orthodox as anything we handled. We had products; you could touch them; you use them; you derive benefit from them.

However, there's a striking difference in the customer interface. If you're marketing Widget soap, you know a customer will frequently walk up to that shelf, pick it up, look at it, and because fragrance emits from bar soap packages, smell it. In effect, there is a practical means for the consumer to interface with what you're selling. However, for us, no product could go out of the vault—stamps, money orders, anything—for overriding security reasons. We found it was extremely difficult to get our product in the hands of our consumers. We couldn't hand it to them in a letter and say, look at it. Or even hang it on their doorknobs.

In this one, we made an end run. A sales promotion consultant was hired to go out and figure a way, in effect, to develop in-store trial. We developed kiosks. You've probably seen them in your post office; they look like three-tiered things, with all our products displayed. You can't touch them, but you can come as close to touching them as you could conceivably imagine.

In product marketing, assuming your research is well focused and disciplined, you can narrow down and get a very clear isolated grip on the ultimate consumer end benefits. But you can't really ever totally understand what a service means to the customer, the user, as you can find out what the use of a product is to the customer.

Ultimate Benefits

It's much more efficient in product marketing to isolate ultimate user end benefits than it is, in my judgment, in service marketing. That's why I think service marketing, in the main, can oftentimes be more sophisticated or demanding.

Knisely: Perhaps more of an art than a science.

Engel: Yes.
One other point. Whether you're marketing a beauty product or a risk-free financial service or a good tasty meal, ultimately, whatever strategies you develop, they should be based on listening to the consumer and be derived from knowing what the consumer wants and needs. That is the key.

Financial Services Marketers Must Learn Package Goods Selling Tools

The third interview is with Rodney Woods, then group marketing officer at United States Trust Co. of New York, responsible for the marketing of all personal services lines.

He began his career in the United Kingdom with the Unilever Organization. Subsequently, he spent over 10 years on the advertising agency side of the business. This experience began with Young & Rubicam in London, continued with Leo Burnett in Toronto, and concluded with nearly seven years with Doyle Dane Bernbach in New York. During that time, he worked on a number of package goods accounts, including Pillsbury, Procter & Gamble, Bristol–Myers, and Johnson & Johnson.

Prior to joining U.S. Trust, he spent two and a half years with Merrill Lynch, managing a group responsible for new products/services development.

Knisely: Rodney, how has your job changed coming out of package goods into services marketing?

Woods: I think the first impression when you move into the service area is that there really are no formulas. Additionally, there isn't a very good reporting system so you don't know exactly how well you're doing month by month and you can't adjust as fast to competitive pressures.

Overall, I think there are a number of proven disciplines that as package goods marketers we employed to launch, rejuvenate, reposition, maintain, and even wind down a brand. There's an established management system of checks and balances. It's really quite difficult for a single brand manager to dramatically change the course of his brand's marketing or promotional strategy, and consequently, there's a large amount of repetition in running a major brand in a well-established category.

In service marketing, that's not the case. Further, the number of variables involved in the marketing mix is normally larger in a service business than for a stable product. The real intangible is the human element, which, with the best will in the world, most of us cannot control to anywhere near the same degree that a product manager controls the formulation of a beauty soap, for example.

Marketing, *per se*, is such a new discipline to most service organizations that they're only just beginning to learn the need for a management information system. Even in organizations committed to that discipline, often the system is incomplete, some of the data inaccurate, and worse, a great deal of the obsolescent input renders a lot of the information not much good in terms of projecting future market potential or competitive weaknesses.

Knisely: But are there fundamental differences in how you market products versus services?

Woods: While I believe there are substantive differences between the marketing of products and services, I think it's a question of degree. It's affected by your particular vantage point and at what level you are involved in the marketing of a service.

In my opinion, most marketing directors, whether they are involved in products or services, are engaged in marketing a range of services or a number of brands and are employing proven business disciplines that, to some extent, are common.

However, there are a number of definite differences at the individual brand level. These would include distribution, pricing strategy, "brand" nomenclature, and competitive data. One is most conscious of problems in transition when a new product manager or account team at the agency begins working on a service after they've transferred from a major package goods account.

Lack of Hard Data

Perhaps the principal difference that is immediately apparent is the lack of real data on the "brand." In the soap category, for example, there are well-established track records for the major brands going back, in some instances, for decades. Not only do you have a great historical perspective, but every two months you have the benefit of an extremely detailed Nielsen.

In most services categories, there is an almost complete lack of historical competitive data. And, to some extent, the reports that are filed regularly by your own sales force or even research studies that may be undertaken on your behalf are considerably less accurate and obviously way less detailed than is the case in package goods.

Therefore, the product manager and his agency are not able to monitor the progress of their marketing efforts as tightly. Neither can they track the results of their promotional efforts with the same degree of accuracy.

Similarly, it is not very easy to recommend to senior management that they increase spending within a particular category because you're unable to design, much less measure the results of, an extra spending test.

Knisely: What kind of marketers are making the transition to the services area?

Woods: A couple of years ago, we were looking for some marketing people to join a group working on new product development at a major company in the financial services field. In the space of two weeks, I saw a number of senior people who had worked on well-established package goods brands, either at the client or on the agency side. These included Procter & Gamble, General Foods, Lever, American Home, Nabisco, etc.

All of these people had been through the annual budget process on established brands a number of times and were anxious to work in an environment which gave them a little more flexibility. However, significant to us was that each one was considerably nervous about venturing into a category where, first, marketing as a discipline was still suspect; two, there hadn't been much of a precedent for the kind of work they were about to do, and three, without Nielsen, how do you document your contribution?

Frankly, I had to agree with their estimate of how difficult it would be to convince senior management to fund this work on an ongoing basis. Nevertheless, the people we hired found it a lot less hide-bound and, in some cases, infinitely more challenging. One told me later, "You even have to be creative in your management presentations."

Knisely: What other surprises hit them when they come on board?

Woods: A major stumbling block to most product marketing professionals concerns the marked difference in distribution. Obviously, in food or toiletries most of the majors enjoy near optimum distribution. A new brand rides in on the coattails of your established franchise, leaving you to concern yourself with packaging, pricing, copy, and whatever deal you arrange with the trade or a couponing effort against the consumer.

In a service category, your distribution network, which is normally wholly owned, can be extensive, such as the major brokerage houses with literally hundreds of offices, or extremely limited, like our own with only three. However, even in a multi-branch distribution system, the product manager cannot safely assume that the potential client will be exposed to his "brand" within each of those outlets.

That will depend on first, the manager's endorsement of that product; second, whether the sales force will feel comfortable selling it, and, third, a number of time factors that might affect adequate presentation of the attributes of that particular service to the customer.

The contrast is dramatic. In package goods, you know the product is in stock, that it has at least X number of facings in the soap section of that particular chain, that it will be kept stocked up and the potential consumer will be pushing a shopping cart past those shelves.

In a lot of service situations, the product manager is competing for the space within the salesmen's mental inventory of services. Without sufficient priority in that individual's mind, the product story will be inevitably weakened or ignored.

You are also unable to influence that situation entirely through increased spending on consumer advertising. If the individual account executive does not particularly like the offering for whatever subjective reasons, the advertising is unlikely to make a consumer so vehement in his desire for that particular product/service that he can persuade the salesmen to let him have the opportunity of buying it.

The Role of Pricing

Knisely: Where does pricing enter the equation?

Woods: Perhaps the most critical factor that differs in marketing services and products is the pricing structure. In a lot of product situations, particularly package goods, the unit price is relatively small and frequency of purchase is high, with inherent willingness on the customer's part to try new brands.

By comparison, in financial services for example, many people have deep-seated habitual loyalties that mitigate against their changing suppliers. Also, the appeal of a lower initial price in stimulating trial is less effective and may affect long-term positioning.

Even in the most frequent banking services, checking, one can remember disastrous price wars in some parts of the nation over free checking. I'm thinking of one market where free checking began as a service to those maintaining a balance of $1,000, rapidly went down through $500, $200, $150, to the point where the entire local banking community was giving checking away, only, of course, to realize that there was a fixed cost for providing checking services to clients.

Essentially, the pricing of your service may in itself be a critical element in the positioning of the service. To tamper with that pricing mechanism as a promotional device may alter the perception of your service in the potential consumer's mind.

Another factor that frequently comes into the pricing equation in service marketing concerns the costs of a sales call and the profit generated by individual services. Some of the more frequently used services have very narrow margins, which means that if the sales are limited to that level of service, then it will take some time to recover the cost of the sale.

Therefore, cross selling becomes critically important and the desirability of closing a customer on some of the less frequent, but more profitable, services is obvious. Further, given the rather infrequent purchase of these higher profit services, any degree of "brand loyalty" that can be generated for that type of activity is obviously extremely positive in terms of the bottom line.

Knisely: In a P&G or General Foods as examples, there's a brand management organization that has established relationships to manufacturing, R&D, distribution, sales, etc.— it's been set up over the years and seems to work. What happens when you come into an organization where there is a structure that has never had a marketing group *per se* as part of it?

Woods: It's an evolving situation. When I originally went into financial services, we were considered internal consultants, with no responsibility in terms of product sales and not really a great deal of interaction with the field force. Since that time, it's been up to each marketing person to build an equity with those people in the organization who have product responsibilities.

What has gradually evolved is that the staff group has been called upon more and more to help in the marketing of any new product/service. In a lot of cases, these new entries may be a relaunch or repositioning of an existing service.

As you probably know, the unbundling of services and the generation of fees for some elements that were historically free has been critical in recent years on Wall St. as companies attempt to move away from the cyclicality of commission revenues. In the pricing structure that the product group put together for these unbundled services, we didn't just worry about what the customer is going to pay, or whether that is strictly competitive with other companies, but that, plus how we were going to pay the account executive.

It's very critical to get the account executive to sell the new entry enthusiastically since his behavior pattern over the years has been to give these extras away. While that ensured good client relations in the days when fixed commissions were universal, it doesn't make sense in an environment of discounted commissions.

Knisely: Do you find there was a learning process to go through in terms of how to sell to your internal market?

Buzz Words Arrive

Woods: Yes, to some extent. But being essentially sales-oriented, financial services management recognizes an attractive concept. Five years ago, there was a growing awareness of the marketing terms, a slow arrival of some of the same buzz words. People didn't talk about categories in quite the same way. Nor product segments, nor customer segmentation.

Although we don't have brand managers, we have people who are responsible for certain products areas. Some of these people could almost be called service managers who are responsible for the component parts of a particular package. What they are involved in doing is delivery of vehicles to the sales force that will satisfy specific customer segments, not by the normal demographics that one uses in a package goods sense—i.e., age, income, family size, in very neatly defined categories—but more into professional/life-style requirements and attitudes.

That's a key difference. There's a psychological attitude involved in just about every one of the markets we approach. Take guys who are within the same professional category. They may make roughly the same amount of money, they may be in the same socio-economic group, but they have vastly different investment objectives simply because of their characteristics.

Some are speculators; some are not; some are very cautious, independent decision makers, they don't want somebody else taking that away from them; others are delegators, the professional people.

Knisely: Do you find that you have to be more sensitive to the "factory" here than at a package goods company?

Woods: Oh yes, definitely, if you can very loosely equate operations with manufacturing. You have to sell the benefits of a service to the operations group, too.

In a package goods company, when you say we need X quantity of Y by Sept. 1, and we want the fragrance permutations to be 1–2–3, that's a direct order.

If you were to adopt the same mentality in financial services, you would be amazed how many times the support systems would be down or nonfunctioning. You somehow have to get that side of the house, particularly, to think from a marketing standpoint and not just internal efficiency.

I mean, their performance criteria is: How do we do this quicker, faster, with fewer corrections? That's the only criteria they employ. And to get those people to focus their attention on what you're actually delivering outside to the ultimate consumer is a new discipline for them.

Knisely: Let's talk about new product development.

Woods: I guess most new products in our industry are provoked or developed as a result of either changes in consumer habits or consumer needs, and, to an extent, influenced by new legislation that may restrict one area or open up another.

New Product Problems

Although not strictly a new product, the recent legislative action that allowed one bank account—i.e., transfers from savings to checking—may be illustrative of some of the problems in this service environment.

A number of banks have recently launched campaigns that talk in terms of offering transfers from savings to checking accounts. But as a recent article in *The Wall Street Journal* pointed out, a number of these accounts are subject to certain minimums being maintained in either the checking or savings account.

We do have more aware consumers and, in an inflationary environment, there is evidence to suggest that they resent not receiving income on uninvested funds or deposits. In this instance, the way in which these new accounts have been introduced has not always communicated to the individual the price for this new service. In fact, some of these arrangements offer little benefit to the customer compared to his normal checking account because the fees leveled on the new account exceed any interest earned, particularly when you consider the after-tax consequences.

Some organizations are attempting to rectify the situation that evolved from possibly making the wrong decision on free checking accounts. Now they're seen to be penalizing the client for patronizing their institution and, in some instances, there have been distinctly unhappy clients as a result.

In essence, you are seeing evidence of the difficulty of making a marketing decision on pricing when most organizations are not able to determine their costs.

This confusion is even more acute in New York state where Congress allowed NOW accounts to be offered. Clearly, no one had been prepared for this move, and there still appears to be a great deal of reluctance on the part of many banks to offer this service where interest is paid on checking account balances.

The reasons for the reluctance are predictable. Earlier experience in New England showed that it is very difficult to make money on that particular product offering. To draw a comparison with a package goods situation, here you have all the major competitors forced into a product where the test market experience has clearly shown it's a bust.

However, if you are a factor in the retail banking business today, it is difficult to imagine how you can stay out of this particular line of business. Again, it reinforces the need for effective cross-selling if you are to realize an over-all profit.

This leads me to the last and often ignored, but to my mind significant, difference between products and services. That is, the branding nomenclature or the strategic difference between selling an independent brand rather than one service within the range of a major service organization.

Some of the most successful package goods

marketers, including P&G, pay little attention to corporate identity, preferring instead to establish independent brands that will stand alone within a specific category. Not only does that allow them to have multiple entries in the same horse race, but any failure with an individual brand does not carry overtones for the remainder of the range.

I once worked on a toiletry brand that P&G withdrew from the marketplace (one of very few that I know of) and almost no one outside the test market cities was even aware of the brand's existence. Even within the test market cities, the failure of that product in no way handicapped other toiletry brands or products from the same organization.

In a service situation, one of the things that you are selling is the over-all stature and imagery of the organization. Rarely can you justify creating a separate brand of subsidiary to market a particular line of business.

Even when you do, as in the case of the brokerage industry, recently there is a great deal of awareness among your public that the subsidiary belongs to the parent organization. Thus, differentiation between those services is difficult to maintain, and any test program that fails immediately hurts client perception of other lines.

Knisely: What about the ability of your competition to replicate your newly developed services?

No Secrecy in Services

Woods: Well, that's a real concern. If you do something with a bar of soap, for example, that gives it a unique fragrance; if you decide that's consistent with the position you want as a beauty bar soap, your competitors can't duplicate that because there's inherent secrecy in the formulation. It's patentable.

Now in our situation, it isn't. It's very difficult to build proprietary products, because it's based on perception rather than reality. I guess that probably is the one fundamental difference between products and services. It's all perception, really.

Knisely: What do you perceive the state of the marketing art to be in your business today versus five years ago?

Woods: We have come a fair way, but in my opinion, marketing within most service industries is still too narrowly confined. In a great number of situations, marketing is equated to just advertising and sales promotion. Many of the people within our industry, for example, feel that a new promotional campaign is the way one undertakes a marketing assignment.

I think we are moving in the right direction, but it is obviously going to be some considerable time before we will have all the tools necessary to do a thoroughly effective job. In my opinion, it is essential that we continue to work hard to translate some of the disciplines that have worked well in the product environment into service industries, because, without that methodology, we will not be able to attract the right kind of marketing talent to our organizations.

Service Business Is People Dealing with Other People

This interview is with Robert L. Catlin, then senior vice-president—management supervisor at N. W. Ayer ABH International, New York, *responsible for the AT&T account. He started his career with the Vick Chemical Co. in sales, sales management, and product management* and then moved to Benton & Bowles as an account manager.

He subsequently spent more than seven years in the airline business, first as advertising director with TWA, then as vice-president at American Airlines with responsibility for advertising and sales promotion and marketing development.

Prior to joining Ayer, he worked at Chase Manhattan Bank as vice-president–corporate marketing/advertising and vice president–retail bank marketing.

Knisely: You've sold mouthwashes, acne medications, cereals, vitamins, throat lozenges, artificial sweeteners, airlines, and banks. What's the difference between marketing products and services?

Catlin: There are numerous differences *and* similarities. First, the state of the marketing art is different between the two. I think that this is most evident in two areas: (1) Consumer orientation . . . knowledge of consumer needs and dedication to satisfying them and (2) consistent application of marketing planning disciplines. Product marketing is ahead in both areas. But service marketing is coming on.

There is also a tremendous difference in quality control between the two. When I was working on products, I knew exactly what the product was made of and, as a consequence, what it would do. So as I was trying to develop the appeals, the thrusts, the strategies to communicate to the consumer, I knew that every product that I was dealing with, every unit of that product, predictably would do certain things.

In a service business, you find that you're dealing with something that is primarily delivered by people—to people. Your people are as much of your product in the consumer's mind as any other attribute of that service. People's performance day in and day out fluctuates up and down. Therefore, the level of consistency that you can count on and try to communicate to the consumer is not a certain thing.

Knisely: What's your first approach to that kind of problem?

Catlin: My hypothesis is that, generally, people tend to use products because they believe they work. People tend to use services because they believe they like them. And, that "liking" is a very complex kind of thing. Some of it may be rational and tangible and much of it may be totally emotional.

Knisely: Don't some products have those same kinds of emotional appeals?

Catlin: Yes. And, as time goes on, products may in many respects be becoming more like services. They are being bought more by people who have built up an image of them in their own minds, an image which is becoming more operative because true product differences are becoming less discernible. And I don't think there's any question that there is a conscious effort on the part of product manufacturers to go that route.

But that is more recent—say, in the last five to ten years. Prior to that, manufacturers were more able to produce products that did something that wasn't being done (or wasn't being done well) by the competition. Now the maneuvering room for products to excel, to be unique, to be discernibly better and superior, has been reduced to the point that a lot of appeal is being made on a more emotional basis.

If service businesses have a major opportunity to improve their marketing today, it is in the more consistent, more effective use of research to understand consumer segments.

State of the Art

Knisely: Is that because it is a service? Or is it just because of the state of the art?

Catlin: I think it's because of the state of the art. I don't think it's because it's a service. The decision-making process as one opts for one service versus another is a fantastically complex one from the consumer standpoint.

Traditional kinds of attitude and behavior research may not be discerning enough, insightful enough to help the market understand just exactly what is going on. That's compounded by the fact that many of the service marketers have tended to go into research with a list of questions and attributes. They start with what they believe the consumer cares about, and then they try to get some order of magnitude, sense of value, about those attributes.

That may be a major mistake for most service marketers. They should start with the assumption that they don't really understand what is going on in the consumer's mind and, furthermore, that the consumer probably doesn't consciously understand it either, and therefore can't tell them. Their research technique is going to have to utilize some of the more sophisticated statistical means to get the real salient needs and wants revealed.

If you're going to differentiate yourself from the other guy, when you're basically selling a commodity like airline seats, you will have to raise the level of expectations about airline "X" higher than that of airline "Y." It gets to be a matter of what areas you raise the level of expectations in and how specific those expectations are.

For a long period, the airlines waged the great menu wars. But that's not the main reason people fly. And if what you do is try to differentiate yourself with something that is really unimportant in the consumer's eye, you may be changing this total image of you in a negative way.

Knisely: Some airlines like American have done a phenomenal job of selecting stewardesses, uniforms, interiors, exteriors, to project an image that sets them apart. Were those marketing decisions? Or were they intuitive?

Catlin: At American, it was a marketing decision made way back when C. R. Smith recognized that the businessman was providing the bulk of customers for air transportation. He made a concerted effort to cater to the businessman. He was eminently successful and much of that excellent reputation with businessmen still lives today.

I think the competition has, over the years, been catching up, simply because American

can become only so excellent. The biggest problem that somebody like American and some of the other heavily business-oriented airlines had to face up to was that although they may have been carrying a majority of passengers for business reasons (a stable piece of business that was essentially nonseasonal, paying top dollar, and terribly important) nonetheless, in a relatively short period of time, the leisure side of the market started producing more dollars than the business side.

Reasons Different

What we began to realize was that the reasons somebody wants to use an airline will be different depending on *why* he or she is traveling. For instance, the business traveler who is a $50,000 a year executive and flies first class to Chicago once a week isn't going to look at the airline the same way when he pays out of his own pocket for the flight from here to California on two weeks' vacation with his wife and four kids. He's not going to go first class, he's going to be worried about seat comfort in coach, about the cost, about flexibility to move about once he's there, about a lot of things he wasn't worried about when he was traveling for business.

Knisely: From a marketing standpoint, what are the kinds of things that you can fiddle with to cover those bases?

Catlin: You go back to the basics. You examine what you know about the decision-making process in your particular service business. What do people consider to be important? What do they consider to be differentiating? What are they unhappy about? What are their lukewarm buttons? (Because I don't think there are hot ones.)

I don't think there's any one answer. Research is not going to reveal some panacea. What it's going to do is give you greater insights and greater understanding.

Given that insight and understanding, you can develop appeals which are relevant despite what anybody else is doing. Over a period of time, you will open up the distance between you and the competition. You must understand what the target audience considers relevant to its problems and needs. You must be in that marketplace—testing, listening, probing, evaluating, with a set of hard eyes.

Product Positioning

Then, you've got to translate that consumer knowledge into relevant marketing activity, from the type of personnel you hire, to the kind of training that you give those personnel, to the kind of involvement that you bring with your top management, to the type of image that you get projected in editorial content, to the bottom-line performance that you get, to the kind of advertising that you run.

No one single thing is going to be the key. What happens is that you get a number of variables all working together to address some things that you have reason to believe are more important than other things to the target audience that you are trying to reach.

The better you know your customer, the better chance you have of doing things that will be meaningful to him or her. And if you're consistently more meaningful, more relevant, than your competitors, you're going to do better over the long haul.

Maybe 50 years later, you get to the product versus product situation: Blind taste test, no difference; identify them and one wins—4 to 1, 7 to 1. Why? It is not just the product anymore. It's a thing that's happened over a long period of time, and no single advertising campaign, single marketing program, or single promotion is going to change it overnight.

Knisely: You're suggesting the difference between airlines, either American or TWA, is no different than the difference between, say, Coke and Pepsi?

Catlin: No, I'm suggesting this. That a key thing for Americans to have perceived back in the late 1960s, early 1970s, was that when somebody flies on a vacation, you are no longer selling a ride on an airplane. You are selling a dream fulfillment in an economically attractive way. And, incidentally, fulfillment happens to include a ride on our airline.

For the airline, that meant that what you really ought to promote and push for summer vacation travel wasn't the destinations, it was the fly/drive packages. Why fly/drive packages? Because research suggested that the family who was going across the country really didn't want to go to a resort and stay for a week or two weeks. It was a big expense, they wanted to make as much of it as they could, to see as much as they could see, but they didn't want to have to pay an arm and a leg to do so. If you could offer something that was attractive and offered flexibility for a package price, that gets to be very appealing to them.

Knisely: Let's talk about product positioning. Have the service companies consciously researched their niches?

Catlin: I don't think consciously. Well, that's not fair. Airlines and banks have not all consciously done it. Quite a number of them are positioned by virtue of things that they have or have not done. Their problem now is to articulate what that position is, to understand it and how it relates to competitors, and then to decide whether or not they're going to reinforce it or whether they would like to change it, and, if so, what they would like to change it to.

However, I would like to go back and say that TWA ran one of the best airline marketing programs. Starting with a problem and a perception that was not helping them fulfill their business objectives, and going through a calculated series of moves—coordinated, integrated, and supported—TWA changed its image over a period of time.

The research TWA did showed they got very high marks as an international airline, they had a very good first class service, that when their service was good it was absolutely spectacular, but that the quality level of their service tended to fluctuate up and down widely. The customer never really knew which level he would get.

Also, a characteristic of international carriers was that their on-time performance wasn't very good. They tended to leave late, take a long time to process passengers in and out. Passengers did not look upon TWA as a really viable short-haul business carrier because of the perceptions of the weaknesses of international carriers, despite the fact that TWA serviced more domestic U.S. cities than American.

So what did TWA do? They changed the internal configuration of their aircraft, changed the decor and the seats so you could almost turn a coach seat into a first-class kind of seat, moved their scheduling on the short hauls up 15 minutes and made something of leaving before the traffic. They put on carry-your-own luggage; they made much of the various types of food service in terms of the basic staples a businessman was inclined to like and packaged the whole thing.

Then, they told that story in very straightforward terms in their advertising in a way businessmen could readily relate to.

We sat at American and watched them take market share. We looked at our research and saw business traveler perceptions changing.

Knisely: Let's go back to product control. In product quality control, you can measure it as something that comes off the production line. You don't even have to go out of the plant to control quality. But in services, quality is purely in the perception of the customer.

Catlin: It is, after the fact. What is required, unlike package goods, is a lot more thought to performance levels and the fluctuations of those levels. You must try to dampen the fluctuations in your performance levels. You must recognize very early, with a great deal of sensitivity, where you may be creating an expectation that you cannot deliver on. If you think you may do that, don't.

I think that's the biggest message in service marketing. It is far easier to create a customer expectation that you have no possibility of satisfying. If you do that, you're going to have "X" number of unsatisfied customers. Once you've got an unsatisfied customer, you've got a tough person to ever sell again. It doesn't take a lot to go from black ink to red ink in many service

businesses, particularly when they are both capital and labor intensive. If a small percentage of your customers decides not to use you anymore, you're in big trouble. What it suggests to me is that rarely in service marketing is the best solution the "big idea."

What I'm saying is that a "big idea" almost *has* to be inherently controversial. If you're in a business where you're in big trouble if relatively few people don't like that idea, it seems to me a better way to go is with less spectacular, but better wearing appeals, ones with longer-term relevance to the target audience.

Strive for consistency in your appeals, relevance to consumer needs, and execute them so as to achieve and enhance a good, solid image of you in the consumer's mind.

In the service business, people deal with people they like. And they like people for all kinds of funny reasons. One of the reasons is because they come to expect certain things will happen when they use that service. If you're different every year, I don't think their expectation can be anything but "I don't know what I'm going to get this time."

Why use an unpredictable service if there's another which is predictable?

There's evidence that says people don't seek out the one that's really good or super, as much as they avoid the one they've had a problem with. So if you don't give them problems and you give them a satisfaction—maybe not 100%, but consistently 80%—that's better than the guy who gave them 100% this time and 10% the last.

We talked about applying that approach with meals in the airlines. Meals—always a big problem. The idea was to see if we could identify those dishes that were most acceptable to the largest number of people, design and develop menus with them which could be put through the reconstituting ovens and come out tasting, maybe not great, but good and hot.

The thought was to go for a rotating menu lineup that had the least chance of being unsatisfactory and the most chance of being acceptable. Now if you get off a flight where the meal was hot, tasted good, and satisfied you, one variable—a poor meal—has been eliminated which could have caused dissatisfaction.

If you go the fancy, but more difficult to

prepare well, meal route, believing you were going to get significantly larger numbers of people, and in the process 10% of them thought that that fancy food was terrible, what are those 10% going to do the next time around?

Marketing Leverage

Knisely: Do you think the leverage of marketing is as high in the service business as it is in the product business?

Catlin: I think that the leverage can be as high or higher. But, I think it's a much slower thing. I don't think you can afford mistakes in service marketing. Once you have put in play a number of forces designed to cause the marketplace to see you and have certain kinds of reactions and experiences with you, if you have been wrong—if you've got to change that process—it's going to take a lot of time. You will have lost ground by competitive standards.

I think ultimately marketing in services will be just as important, maybe more important, than marketing in products.

It is exactly the consistent application of the disciplined marketing process that is ultimately going to give you a certain positioning, a certain image, a certain appeal, to either a broad or limited market segment, depending upon what you're trying to do. Because of the nature of the time element involved, I'm inclined to think you're not going to get all that many cuts at it in service businesses.

You can back away from a bad product positioning. You've seen it happen. Somebody brings out a cosmetic, prices it at 89¢ and it dies. Take the same formula, charge $1.89, put it in a different package and bring it out again under a different name, and it goes.

You can't do that with a bank. The bank's got the same brand name on everything it sells. That's not to say you can't change a bank's positioning or image. You can. But, it takes longer. For that very reason—the longer time element involved in changing basic consumer perceptions and images of a service business—I think marketing is all the more important to those businesses.

The disciplines of marketing planning, knowledge of consumer needs through research, recognition of the effects of people-performance on the perception of your products or services, and avoidance of trying to be all things to all people will help service businesses more effectively sell themselves to consumers. I see a great deal of progress already being made in service business marketing. It won't be long before they're all on equal footing with package goods marketers, in my judgment.

Services Marketing Is Different

LEONARD L. BERRY

Services are relatively intangible, produced and consumed simultaneously, and often less standardized than goods. These unique characteristics of services present special challenges and strategic marketing opportunities to the services marketer.

In 1978 $600 billion was spent by Americans for services—for airline tickets, electricity, rent, medical care, college tuition, sports entertainment, automobile repair, and so forth. Today, in excess of 45% of the average family's budget is spent on services.[1]

Leonard L. Berry is Professor of Marketing at Texas A & M University. Reprinted by permission from *Business* Magazine, May-June 1980. Copyright by the College of Business Administration, Georgia State University, Atlanta.

Despite the importance of the services sector in the American economy, services marketing has only recently attracted the attention of academic marketers. As a result, far more research and writing has been done on how to market goods than on how to market services. This would not really matter if the problems encountered in services marketing were identical to those encountered in goods marketing, but such is not the case. This article examines some of the special characteristics of services and suggests some of the marketing strategy implications that arise from them.

CHARACTERISTICS OF SERVICES

Although service industries are themselves quite heterogeneous (ranging from beauty salons to electric utilities), there are some characteristics of services about which it is useful to generalize. Three of the most important of these characteristics are discussed here.

More Intangible Than Tangible

A good is an object, a device, a thing; a service is a deed, a performance, an effort. When a good is purchased, something tangible is acquired; something that can be seen, touched, perhaps smelled or worn or placed on a mantel. When a service is purchased, there is generally nothing tangible to show for it. Money has been spent, but there are no additional clothes to hang in the closet and nothing to place on the mantel.

Services are consumed but not possessed. Although the performance of most services is supported by tangibles—for instance, the automobile in the case of a taxi service—the essence of what is being bought is a performance rendered by one party for another.

Most market offerings are a combination of tangible and intangible elements.[2] It is whether the essence of what is being bought is tangible or intangible that determines its classification as a good or a service. In a restaurant the acquisition of supplies, the preparation and serving of meals, and the after-meal clean-up (or some combination thereof) is performed for the consumer by another party. Hence, we think of the restaurant industry as a service industry. This is so even though there are tangibles involved—for example, the building, interior decor, kitchen equipment, and food.

The concept of intangibility has two meanings, both of which present challenges for marketing:

- That which cannot be touched, impalpable.
- That which cannot be easily defined, formulated, or grasped mentally.[3]

Addressing the marketing problems that intangibility presents is generally a matter of far more concern to the services marketer than to the goods marketer.

Simultaneous Production and Consumption

Services are generally produced and consumed in the same time frame. The college professor produces an educational service while the student consumes it. The telephone company produces telephone service while the telephone user consumes it. The babysitter produces a baby-sitting service while the children and parents consume it.

Generally, goods are produced, then sold, then consumed. Services on the other hand are usually sold first, then produced and consumed simultaneously.

Simultaneous production and consumption means that the service provider is often physically present when consumption takes place. Whereas a washing machine might be manufactured in Michigan and consumed in Virginia, the dentist is present when examining a patient; the singer is present when performing a concert; the airline stewardess is present when serving an in-flight meal.

What is important to recognize about the presence of the service provider is that the "how" of service distribution becomes important. In the marketing discipline, great stress is placed on distributing goods where and when customer-prospects desire them to be distributed—that is, to the "right place" and at the "right time." With services, it often is important to distribute them in the "right way" as well. How automobile mechanics, physicians, lawyers, teachers, and bank tellers conduct themselves in the presence of the customer can influence future patronage decisions. Washing machines can't be rude or careless or thoughtless, but people providing services can be and sometimes are. And when they are, the result may be a search for a new service supplier.

Less Standardized and Uniform

Service industries tend to differ on the extent to which they are "people-based" or "equipment-based."[4] That is, there is a larger human component involved in performing some services (for example, plumbing) than others (for example, telephone communications). One of the implications of this distinction is that the "outcomes" of people-based service operations tend to be less standardized and uniform than the outcomes of equipment-based service- or goods-producing operations. Stated differently, the extensive involvement of people in the production of a service introduces a degree of variability in the outcome that is not present when machines dominate. This is an important consideration, given the vast number of service industries that are labor-intensive.

The ever-present potential for variability in a labor-intensive service situation is well known in the marketplace. Whereas consumers expect their favorite breakfast cereal to always taste the same, and to almost always hear a dial tone when picking up a telephone receiver, expectations are far less certain on the occasion of getting a haircut. This is why consumers look at their hair in a mirror before the hair-cutting service is concluded. The outcome is uncertain and more service production may be needed, even when the barber or beautician has had long experience with the consumer.

The growing use of automatic-teller machines (ATMs) by the financial-services industry makes the point. The net effect of the ATM is to transform the delivery of certain traditional banking services from a human delivery mode to a machine delivery mode. This transformation does not mean that all consumers will like or use these machines. It does mean, however, that those who do use ATMs will find far less variability in the services rendered than if human tellers were used. A banker can paint a smile on an ATM and call it Tillie; except when not working properly, the machine will perform uniformly for all customers regardless of how these customers are dressed, the time of day, or the length of the queue waiting for service. Such is not the case with the human teller who may have a bad day, get tired, or become angry with a supervisor, co-worker, or customer. Moreover, human tellers differ among themselves in their customer-relation and technical skills, their personalities, and their attitudes toward their work. In short, bankers cannot paint a smile on a human being.

MARKETING SERVICES

The special characteristics of services present a number of implications concerning their marketing. Although many marketing concepts and tools are applicable to both goods and services, the relative importance of these concepts and tools, and how they are used, are often different. This section suggests a number of strategic marketing opportunities of particular importance to service industries.

Internal Marketing

In what Richard Chase calls "high-contact" service businesses, the quality of the service is inseparable from the quality of the service provider.[5] High-contact businesses are ones in which there is considerable contact between the service provider and the customer, e.g., health care, financial services, and restaurants. Human performance materially shapes the service outcome and hence becomes part of the "product."

Just as goods marketers need to be concerned with product quality, so do services marketers need to be concerned with service quality, which means—in labor-intensive situations—special attention to employee quality and performance. It follows that in high-contact service industries, marketers need to be concerned with internal, not just external, marketing.

Internal marketing means applying the philosophy and practices of marketing to the people that serve the external customer so that (1) the best possible people can be employed and retained and (2) they will do the best possible work. (Technically the phrase "internal marketing" can be applied to any form of marketing inside an organization, for example, marketing an idea to a superior. In this article, the phrase concerns marketing to employees.) More specifically, internal marketing is viewing employees as internal customers, viewing jobs as internal products, and (just as with external marketing) endeavoring to design these products to better meet the needs of these customers.[6]

Although most executives are not accustomed to thinking of marketing in this way, the fact is that people do buy jobs from employers, and employers can and do use marketing to sell these jobs on an initial and ongoing basis. To the extent that high-contact service firms use the concepts and tools of marketing to offer better, more satisfying jobs, they upgrade their capabilities for being more effective service marketers.

The relevance of marketing thinking to personnel management is very real. The banks and insurance companies (among others) adopting flexible working hours are redesigning jobs to better accommodate individual differences, which is market segmentation.[7] The Marriott Corporation is noted for its commitment to employee attitude monitoring, but what it really is doing is marketing research.[8] Indiana National Bank's recent "Person-to-Person" advertising campaign featuring its own personnel was designed to motivate employees as well as external customers and prospects. Aggressive investment in behalf of employee quality and performance is a hallmark of many of America's most successful service companies, including Delta Airlines,[9] Bank of America,[10] and Walt Disney.[11]

Importantly, the crucial matter is not that the phrase "internal marketing" come into widespread use, but that the implication of the phrase be understood; i.e., by satisfying the needs of its internal customers, an organization upgrades its capability for satisfying the needs of its external customers. This is true for most organizations and is certainly true for high-contact service organizations. As one recent article pointed out, "the successful service company must first sell the job to employees before it can sell its services to customers."[12]

Customizing Service

The simultaneous production and consumption characteristic of services frequently provides opportunities to "customize" service. Some service organizations take full advantage of this opportunity within the boundary of productivity requirements, but many do not.

Since a fundamental marketing objective is to effect a good fit between what the customer-prospect wants to buy and what the organization has to sell, the potential for tailoring service to meet the precise desires of individual customers should not be taken lightly. The possibilities for service customization are far greater than first meet the eye. Free Spirit Travel Agency, headquartered in Boulder, Colorado, completes information forms for first-time customers indicating travel patterns and preferences. The marketing potential of such a customer-information system is significant—for example, automatically sending notices on travel specials to Japan to those customers expressing an interest in that country. Automotive Systems, a Decatur, Georgia, automotive repair and maintenance firm, provides explicit notes on its customer bills indicating what still needs to be done with the car and the degree of priority. A growing number of financial institutions have implemented training and incentive programs to encourage tellers to refer to customers by name during transactions. Wendy's designed its hamburger production line to accommodate individual preferences in the makeup of a hamburger and, in the process, to capitalize on the limited flexibility of the McDonald's system.

One of the key strategic issues for many service marketers is to determine the circumstances under which customization should apply and the circumstances under which standardization should apply. This issue is at the heart of an interesting trend in the banking industry toward the use of "personal bankers." Banks fully implementing personal banking assign to each retail customer a specific banker who opens new accounts and compiles information for future reference, makes loans and provides financial consultation, cuts red tape when problems arise, and in general is available when service of a nonroutine nature is needed. In short, personal bankers function on a client basis in much the same way as public accountants or attorneys function.[13]

Banks that have adopted a personal-banker mode of organization have, in effect, established a system in which customers can on appropriate occasions get individualized service from a trained banker with whom they have dealt before. For routine transactions, the customer continues to use the teller station or ATMs that provide more standardized services. Although neither inexpensive nor easy to implement, personal banking is growing because it facilitates the custom packaging and hence the cross-selling of financial services; because it helps banks attract more affluent customers who value personalized and competent service; and because it is a way for larger institutions— a Wachovia, Harris Bank, or Irving Trust, for example—to credibly position themselves in the market as personalized institutions.[14]

Managing Evidence

Because goods are tangible and can be seen and touched, they are generally easier to evaluate than services. The intangibility of services prompts customer-prospects to be attentive to tangibles associated with the service for clues of the service's nature and quality.

A prime responsibility for the service marketer is to manage these tangibles so that the proper signals are conveyed about the service. As one author convincingly writes on this subject:

> Product marketing tends to give first emphasis to creating *abstract* associations. *Service* marketers, on the other hand, should be focused on enhancing and differentiating "realities" through manipulation of *tangible* clues. The management of evidence comes first for service marketers.[15]

There are a number of ways service marketers can manage evidence, as the following sections indicate.

Physical Services Environment. The physical environment in which services are purchased generally provides an important opportunity to tell the "right" story about a given service. Fortunately, service marketers are frequently in a position to shape the environment to their specifications because they distribute the service they produce.

There are many examples of service marketers capitalizing on this opportunity to manage evidence. A Richmond, Virginia, pediatrician decorated his office with bright, multi-colored carpeting, pictures of Disney characters on the walls, a huge balloon Superman suspended from the ceiling in one of the examining rooms, a play area in a corner of the waiting room, and an after-visit toybox from which each child could select an inexpensive toy to take home. Braniff Airlines not only painted the exteriors of its planes a variety of bright colors but also furnished the interior with leather seats and wall murals. Hyatt with its daring hotel designs, Walt Disney with its spectacular theme parks, and TransAmerica with its pyramid-like headquarters building are three service companies that have succeeded notably in making architecture a centerpiece of their marketing strategy.

Appearance of Service Providers. The appearance of service providers is another tangible that can be managed. Fitness consultants at Cosmopolitan Health Spas often wear white "doctor" smocks and are rarely flabby. The Richmond pediatrician referred to earlier wore bright shirts and oversized bow ties rather than the traditional smock, which would have signaled "doctor" to the child. Braniff stewardesses wear designer outfits to complement the striking decor of the planes. Disney goes to great lengths to assure that theme park employees appear "freshly scrubbed," neatly groomed, and unfailingly cheerful.

Service Pricing. The tendency for customer-prospects to use the price of a product as an indicator of its quality is well known. Some researchers suggest that this tendency is even more pronounced for services. They argue that the relative absence of material data with which to appraise services makes price a potentially important index of quality.[16]

It follows that setting the right price is especially critical in circumstances where there is reason to expect differences in service quality from one supplier to another, and where the personal risk of buying a lower quality service is high. Lawyers, accountants, investment counselors, consultants, convention speakers, and even hair stylists can contradict signals they wish to communicate about quality by setting their prices too low. In short, price can be a confidence builder; price is a clue.

Tying Services Marketing to Goods Marketing. Sometimes increased credibility concerning a service's quality can be gained by distributing it through a goods-marketing organization that already has credibility. The automotive-service and insurance business lines at Sears have undoubtedly benefited greatly from the association with the Sears' name and reputation.

A recent paper illustrates the potential benefits of tying services marketing into a goods-marketing organization with a hypothetical scenario involving an established department store adding a health spa:

> The store's strengths include a loyal market of middle age, upper middle class, upper income customers . . . a reputation for quality; and an image of progressive merchandising. . . . The

health spa industry, in general, has a poor image which includes high pressure selling tactics, poor quality personnel, and inattention once the sale has been made. The new offering's intangibility allows the store to use its positive image to reduce the uncertainty and perceived risks for potential users of the spa. In addition to revenues generated from the spa services, there are many possibilities for cross-selling other store lines such as sporting goods, sportswear, and health food products.[17]

Interestingly, the process can work the other way with well-known and well-regarded service companies moving into goods marketing. The key of course is where the credibility and access to the customer-prospect lies. In the preceding scenario, it lies with the department store. In the case of service enterprises like American Express and TWA, it lies with them.

Making the Service Tangible

Earlier it was indicated that intangibility has two meanings: that which cannot be touched; that which cannot be easily grasped mentally. Marketing advantage usually is to be gained if the service can be made more "touchable" and more easily grasped mentally. This involves attempting to make the service more tangible.[18]

Sometimes it is possible to make a service more palpable by creating a tangible representation of it. This is what has occurred with the development of the bank credit card. By representing the service with a specially encoded plastic card that, when used, triggers the service, Visa and others have been able to overcome many of the handicaps normally associated with marketing an intangible. The existence of the plastic card has allowed Visa to physically differentiate the service through color and graphics and to build and even extend a potent brand name, e.g., Visa travelers checks. Moreover, institutions distributing bank charge cards can extend their trading areas because once the card is obtained by consumers (often by mail), credit purchases can be made without going to the bank.

Just as service marketers should consider whether there are opportunities to develop a tangible representation of the service, so should they look for opportunities to make the service more easily grasped mentally. For example, the insurance industry has made it easier for consumers to perceive what is being sold by associating the intangible of insurance with relevant tangible objects. Consider the following:

- "You are in good *hands* with Allstate."
- "I've got a piece of the *rock*."
- "Under the Traveler's *umbrella*."
- "The Nationwide *blanket* of protection."

Hands, rocks, umbrellas, and blankets are used to more effectively communicate what insurance can provide people: they are devices used to make the service more easily grasped mentally.

Synchronizing Supply and Demand. Because services are performances, they cannot be inventoried. This is a significant fact of life in a service business because demand peaks cannot be accommodated simply by taking goods off a shelf. If an airline has 40 more flight-reservation requests than capacity permits, some business will likely be lost. Conversely, if an airliner takes off with 40 empty seats, the revenue that those seats could have produced, had they been filled, is lost forever. One of the crucial challenges in many service industries is to find ways to better synchronize supply and demand as an alternative to recurring conditions of severe overdemand and underdemand. This is easier said than done. Demand peaks can occur during certain times of the day (airlines, restaurants), during certain days of the week (movies, hair styling), and during certain months of the year (income tax services, beach resorts).[19]

The service marketer interested in better synchronizing supply and demand may attempt to reshape demand and/or supply patterns for the service.[20]

Reshaping Demand. All elements of the marketing mix are potentially available to help bring demand more in line with supply constraints. Delta Airlines, for example, has used pricing incentives to encourage travelers to fly during the early morning hours ("Early Bird" flights) and late evening hours ("Owly Bird" flights). Differential pricing to encourage demand during nonpeak periods is also commonly used by rental-car companies, movie theaters, and bars, among others. Through intensive promotion, the U.S. Postal Service has persuaded many customers that it is beneficial to them and their addressees to mail Christmas cards and packages early.[21] By adding a breakfast product line, McDonald's and other fast-food companies have been able to make productive use of previously under-utilized facilities. Many banks have been able to lessen lobby traffic during peak hours through the use of automatic-teller machines.

Importantly, demand-altering marketing actions can only have an impact when customer-prospects have control over their demand patterns. One recent article discusses the failure of the Boston rapid transit system to attract significant numbers of new riders between 10:00 A.M. and 2:00 P.M. by reducing the normal $.25 fare to $.10 (promoted as "Dime Time"). A key problem was that most rush-hour riders were commuting to and from work and had little control over work schedules. More recent efforts by the transit system have centered on helping area employers understand the benefits of staggered and flexible working hours and how to implement them.[22]

Reshaping Supply. Another option available to the service marketer is to attempt to alter supply capacities to better match demand patterns. The possibilities are many and include the following:

- Using part-time employees and performing only essential tasks during peak demand periods.
- Training employees to perform multiple jobs so they can switch from one to another as demand dictates.
- Using paraprofessionals so that professionals can concentrate on duties requiring their expertise, e.g., parabankers who do legwork, solve routine problems, and handle clerical duties.

- Substituting equipment for human labor to make the service system more productive, e.g., automated car washes and computer-prepared income tax returns.

Obviously there are limits to how much supply capacity can be modified to fit demand requirements. The use of part-time personnel may be a variable cost, but the space they use when they come to work is a fixed cost. Nevertheless, the bottom-line potential from finding new ways to mesh supply capacity with demand is significant, and we can expect considerable innovation in this area during the 1980s. The same should be true for demand management as well. Indeed, America's best-managed service firms can be expected to vigorously work both sides of the street by seeking ways to reshape demand *and* supply patterns.

SUMMARY

Services differ from goods in some very important ways, and these differences present special challenges to the services marketer. The importance of the services sector in the American economy suggests the advisability of learning more about these differences and their marketing implications.

Services are more intangible than tangible, are produced and consumed simultaneously, and in many cases are less standardized and uniform than goods. These characteristics heighten the importance of certain marketing approaches that are usually not considered priorities or even applicable in goods marketing. These important services-marketing approaches include internal marketing, service customization, managing evidence, making the service tangible, and synchronizing supply and demand patterns.

In the academic discipline, services marketing has long been a stepchild to goods marketing, although progress has been made in recent years. It is time to do some serious catching up in terms of marketing thought. Perhaps the 1980s will be the decade in which this occurs.

NOTES

1. Fabian Linden, "Service, Please," *Across the Board*, August 1978, p. 42.

2. For a good discussion of this point see G. Lynn Shostack, "Breaking Free from Product Marketing," *Journal of Marketing*, April 1977, pp. 73–80.

3. *New World Dictionary of the American Language*, 1974, p. 731.

4. Dan R. E. Thomas, "Strategy Is Different in Service Businesses," *Harvard Business Review*. July–August 1978, pp. 158–165.

5. Richard B. Chase, "Where Does the Customer Fit in a Service Operation?" *Harvard Business Review*, November–December 1978, pp. 137–142.

6. Thomas W. Thompson, Leonard L. Berry, and Phillip H. Davidson, *Banking Tomorrow—Managing Markets Through Planning* (New York, Van Nostrand Reinhold, 1978), p. 243.

7. See, for example, Warren Magoon and Larry Schnicker, "Flexible Hours at State Street Bank of Boston: A Case Study," *Personnel Administrator*, October 1977, pp. 34–37; and Charles A. Cottrell and J. Mark Walker, "Flexible Work Days:Philosophy and Bank Implementation," *Journal of Retail Banking*, December 1979, pp. 72–80.

8. See G. M. Hostage, "Quality Control in a Service Business," *Harvard Business Review*, July– August 1975, pp. 104–105.

9. See "Delta's Flying Money Machine," *Business Week*, May 9, 1977, pp. 84–89.

10. See "Listening and Responding to Employee Concerns—An Interview With A. W. Clausen," *Harvard Business Review*, January–February 1980, pp. 101–114.

11. See N.W. Pope, "Mickey Mouse Marketing," *American Banker*, July 25, 1979, pp. 4 and 14; and

N.W. Pope, "More Mickey Mouse Marketing," *American Banker*, September 12, 1979, pp. 4–14.

12. W. Earl Sasser and Stephen P. Arbeit, "Selling Jobs in the Service Sector," *Business Horizons*, June 1976, p. 64.

13. Leonard L. Berry, "The Personal Banker," *Bankers Magazine*, January–February 1978, pp. 54–55.

14. See Thomas J. Stanley, Leonard L. Berry, and William D. Danko, "Personal Service versus Convenience: Perceptions of the High-Income Customer," *Journal of Retail Banking*, June 1979, pp. 54–61.

15. Shostack, "Breaking Free from Product Marketing," p. 78.

16. Pierre Eiglier and Eric Langeard, "A New Approach to Service Marketing," in Eiglier, et al., *Marketing Consumer Services: New Insights* (Cambridge, Massachusetts, Marketing Science Institute, 1977), p. 41.

17. William R. George, "The Retailing of Services—A Challenging Future," *Journal of Retailing*, Fall 1977, pp. 88–89.

18. This section draws heavily from James H. Donnelly, Jr., "Service Delivery Strategies in the 1980s—Academic Perspective," in Leonard L. Berry and James H. Donnelly, Jr., eds., *Financial Institution Marketing: Strategies in the 1980s* (Washington, D.C., Consumer Banker Association, 1980), pp. 143–150.

19. W. Earl Sasser, "Match Supply and Demand in Service Industries," *Harvard Business Review*, November–December 1976, p. 138.

20. Ibid., pp. 137–140.

21. Christopher H. Lovelock and Robert F. Young, "Look to Consumers to Increase Productivity," *Harvard Business Review*, May–June 1979, p. 176.

22. Ibid., p. 173.

Breaking Free from Product Marketing

G. LYNN SHOSTACK

*Service marketers urgently require concepts and strategies that are relevant to their actual situations. Traditionally, the marketing discipline has been overwhelmingly oriented to practices in the manufacturing sector, especially mass-produced, packaged consumer goods. The theme of this article is that many insights from goods (or "product") marketing are not directly transferrable to the service sector.**

New concepts are necessary if service marketing is to succeed. Service marketing is an uncharted frontier. Despite the increasing dominance of services in the U.S. economy, basic texts still disagree on how services should be treated in a marketing context.[1]

The heart of this dispute is the issue of applicability. The classic marketing "mix," the seminal literature, and the language of marketing all derive from the manufacture of physical goods. Practicing marketers tend to think in terms of products, particularly mass-

G. Lynn Shostack is senior vice president, Bankers Trust Company, New York. Reprinted by permission from *The Journal of Marketing*, April 1977. © 1977 by the American Marketing Association, Chicago.
Editor's note: Marketing academics and practitioners increasingly use the word *product* as a generic term to describe both goods and services. In this article, however, the author equates the word *product* with *manufactured good.*

market consumer goods. Some service companies even call their output "products" and have "product" management functions modeled after those of experts such as Procter and Gamble.

Marketing seems to be overwhelmingly product-oriented. However, many service-based companies are confused about the applicability of product marketing, and more than one attempt to adopt product marketing has failed.

Merely adopting product marketing's labels does not resolve the question of whether product marketing can be overlaid on service businesses. Can corporate banking services really be marketed according to the same basic blueprint that made *Tide* a success? Given marketing's historic tenets, there is simply no alternative.

Could marketing itself be "myopic" in having failed to create relevant paradigms for the service sector? Many marketing professionals who transfer to the services arena find their work fundamentally "different," but have a difficult time articulating how and why their priorities and concepts have changed. Often, they also find to their frustration and bewilderment that "marketing" is treated as a peripheral function or is confused with one of its components, such as research or advertising, and kept within a very narrow scope of influence and authority.[2]

This situation is frequently rationalized as being due to the "ignorance" of senior management in service businesses. "Education" is usually recommended as the solution. However, an equally feasible, though less comforting, explanation is that service industries have been slow to integrate marketing into the mainstream of decision making and control because marketing offers no guidance, terminology, or practical rules that are clearly *relevant* to services.

MAKING ROOM FOR INTANGIBILITY

The American Marketing Association cites both goods *and* services as foci for marketing activities. Squeezing services into the Procrustean phrase, "intangible products,"[3] is not only a distortion of the AMA's definition but also a complete contradiction in terms.

It is wrong to imply that services are just like products "except" for intangibility. By such logic, apples are just like oranges, except for their "appleness." Intangibility is not a modifier; it is a state. Intangibles may come with tangible trappings, but no amount of money can buy physical ownership of such intangibles as "experience" (movies), "time" (consultants), or "process" (dry cleaning). A service is rendered. A service is experienced. A service cannot be stored on a shelf, touched, tasted, or tried on for size. "Tangible" means "palpable," and "material." "Intangible" is an antonym, meaning "*im*palpable," and "*not* corporeal."[4] This distinction has profound implications. Yet marketing offers no way to treat intangibility as the core element it is, nor does marketing offer usable tools for managing, altering, or controlling this amorphous core.

Even the most thoughtful attempts to broaden the definition of "that which is marketed" away from product synonymity suffer from an underlying assumption of tangibility. Not long ago, Philip Kotler argued that "values" should be considered the end result of "marketing."[5] However, the text went on to imply that "values" were created by "objects," and drifted irredeemably into the classic product axioms.

To truly expand marketing's conceptual boundaries requires a framework which accommodates intangibility instead of denying it. Such a framework must give equal descriptive weight to the components of "service" as it does to the concept of "product."

THE COMPLEXITY OF MARKETED ENTITIES

What kind of framework would provide a new conceptual viewpoint? One unorthodox possibility can be drawn from direct observation of the marketplace and the nature of the market "satisfiers" available to it. Taking a fresh look, it seems that there are really very few, if any, "pure" products or services in the marketplace.

Examine, for instance, the automobile. Without question, one might say, it is a physical object, with a full range of tangible features and options. But another, equally important element is marketed in tandem with the steel and chrome—i.e., the service of transportation. Transportation is an *independent* marketing element; in other words, it is not car-dependent, but can be marketed in its own right. A car is only *one* alternative for satisfying the market's transportation needs.

This presents a semantic dilemma. How should the automobile be defined? Is General Motors marketing a *service*, a service that happens to include a *by*-product called a car? Levitt's classic "Marketing Myopia" exhorts businessmen to think in exactly this generic way about what they market.[6] Are automobiles "tangible services"? It cannot be denied that both elements—tangible and intangible—exist and are vigorously marketed. Yet they are, by definition, different qualities, and to attempt to compress them into a single word or phrase begs the issue.

Conversely, how shall a service such as airline transportation be described? Although the service itself is intangible, there are certain very real things that belong in any description of the total entity, including such important tangibles as interior decor, food and drink, seat design, and overall graphic continuity from tickets to attendants' uniforms. These items can dramatically affect the "reality" of the service in the consumer's mind. However, there is no accurate way to lump them into a one-word description.

If "either-or" terms (product versus service) do not adequately describe the true nature of marketed entities, it makes sense to explore the usefulness of a new *structural* definition. This broader concept postulates that market entities are, in reality, *combinations of discrete elements* which are linked together in molecule-like wholes. Elements can be either tangible or intangible. The entity may have either a tangible or intangible nucleus. But the whole can only be described as having a certain dominance.

MOLECULAR MODEL

A "molecular" model offers opportunities for visualization and management of a total market entity. It reflects the fact that a market entity can be partly tangible *and* partly intangible, without diminishing the importance of either characteristic. Not only can the potential be seen for picturing and dealing with multiple *elements*, rather than *a thing*, but the concept of dominance can lead to enriched considerations of the priorities and approach that may be required of a marketer. Moreover, the model suggests the scientific analogy that if market entities have multiple elements, a deliberate or inadvertent change in a *single* element may completely alter the entity, as the simple switching of FE_3O_2 to FE_2O_3 creates a new substance. For this reason, a marketer must carefully manage all the elements, especially those for service-based entities, which may not have been considered previously within his domain.

DIAGRAMMING MARKET ENTITIES

A simplified comparison demonstrates the conceptual usefulness of a molecular modeling system. In Exhibit 1, automobiles and airline travel are broken down into their major elements. As shown, these two entities have different nuclei. They also differ in dominance.

Clearly, airline travel is intangible-dominant; that is, it does not yield physical ownership of a tangible good. Nearly all of the other important elements in the entity are intangible as well. Individual elements and their combinations represent unique satisfiers to different market segments. Thus:

- For some markets—students, for example— pure transport takes precedence over all other considerations. The charter flight business

EXHIBIT I
Diagram of Market Entities

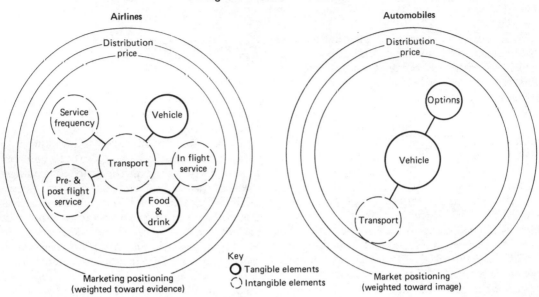

Airlines · Automobiles

Distribution price · Distribution price

Service frequency · Vehicle · In flight service · Transport · Pre- & post flight service · Food & drink · Options · Vehicle · Transport

Key
○ Tangible elements
◌ Intangible elements

Marketing positioning (weighted toward evidence) · Market positioning (weighted toward image)

was based on this element. As might be expected during lean economic times, "no frills" flights show renewed emphasis on this nuclear core.

- For business travelers, on the other hand, schedule frequency may be paramount.
- Tourists, a third segment, may respond most strongly to the combination of in-flight and post-flight services.

As the market entity of airline travel has evolved, it has become more and more complex. Ongoing reweighting of elements can be observed, for example, in the marketing of airline food, which was once a battleground of quasi-gourmet offerings. Today, some airlines have stopped marketing food altogether, while others are repositioning it primarily to the luxury markets.

AIRLINES VERSUS AUTOMOBILES

In comparing airlines to automobiles, one sees obvious similarities. The element of transpor-

tation is common to both, as it is to boats, trains, buses, and bicycles. Tangible decor also plays a role in both entities. Yet in spite of their similarities, the two entities are not the same, either in configuration or in marketing implications.

In some ways, airline travel and automobiles are mirror opposites. A car is a physical possession that renders a service. Airline travel, on the other hand, cannot be physically possessed. It can only be experienced. While the inherent "promise" of a car is service, airline transportation often promises a Lewis Carroll version of "*product*," i.e., *destination*, which is marketed as though it were physically obtainable. If only tropical islands and redwood forests *could* be purchased for the price of an airline ticket!

The model can be completed by adding the remaining major marketing elements in a way that demonstrates their function vis-à-vis the organic core entity. First, the total entity is ringed and defined by a set value or price. Next, the valued entity is circumscribed by its distribution. Finally, the entire entity is encompassed, according to its core configuration, by its public "face," i.e., its positioning to the market.

The molecular concept makes it possible to describe and array market entities along a continuum, according to the weight of the "mix" of elements that comprise them. As Exhibit 2 indicates, teaching services might be at one end of such a scale, *intangible* or *I-dominant*, while salt might represent the other extreme, *tangible or T-dominant*. Such a scale accords intangible-based entities a place and weight commensurate with their true importance. The framework also provides a mechanism for comparison and market positioning.

In one of the handful of books devoted to services, the author holds that "the more intangible the service, the greater will be the difference in the marketing characteristics of the service."[7] Consistent with an entity scale, this axiom might now be amended to read: "The greater the weight of intangible elements in a market entity, the greater will be the divergence from product marketing in priorities and approach."

IMPLICATIONS OF THE MOLECULAR MODEL

The hypothesis proposed by molecular modeling carries intriguing potential for rethinking and reshaping classic marketing concepts and practices. Recognition that service-dominant entities differ from product-dominant entities allows consideration of other distinctions which have been intuitively understood, but seldom articulated by service marketers.

A most important area of difference is immediately apparent—i.e., that service "knowledge" and product "knowledge" cannot be gained in the same way.

A *product* marketer's first task is to "know" his product. For tangible-dominant entities this is relatively straight-forward. A tangible object can be described precisely. It is subject to physical examination or photographic reproduction or quantitative measure. It can not only be exactly replicated, but also modified in precise and duplicate ways.

EXHIBIT 2
Scale of Market Entities

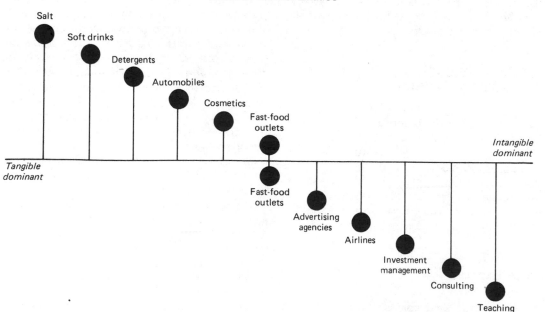

It is not particularly difficult for the marketer of *Coca-Cola*, for example, to summon all the facts regarding the product itself. He can and does make reasonable assumptions about the product's behavior, e.g., that it is consistent chemically to the taste, visually to the eye, and physically in its packaging. Any changes he might make in these three areas can be deliberately controlled for uniformity since they will be tangibly evident. In other words, the marketer can take the product's "reality" for granted and move on to considerations of price, distribution, and advertising or promotion.

To gain *service* "knowledge," however, or knowledge of a service element, where does one begin? It has been pointed out that intangible elements are dynamic, subjective, and ephemeral. They cannot be touched, tried on for size, or displayed on a shelf. They are exceedingly difficult to quantify.

Reverting to airline travel, precisely what *is* the service of air transportation to the potential purchaser? What "percent" of airline travel is comfort? What "percent" is fear or adventure? What *is* this service's "reality" to its market? And how does that reality vary from segment to segment? Since this service exists only during the time in which it is rendered, the entity's true "reality" must be defined experientially, not in engineering terms.

A NEW APPROACH TO SERVICE DEFINITION

Experiential definition is a little-explored area of marketing practice. A product-based marketer is in danger of assuming he understands an intangible-dominant entity when, in fact, he may only be projecting his *own* subjective version of "reality." And because there is no documented guidance on acquiring service-knowledge, the chances for error are magnified.

Case Example

One short-lived mistake (with which the author is familiar) occurred recently in the trust department of a large commercial bank. The department head, being close to daily operations, understood "investment management" as the combined work of hundreds of people, backed by the firm's stature, resources, and long history. With this "reality" in mind, he concluded that the service could be better represented by professional salesmen, than through the traditional, but interruptive use of the portfolio manager as main client contact.

Three salesmen were hired, and given a training course in investments. They failed dismally, both in maintaining current client relationships and in producing new business for the firm. In hindsight, it became clear that the department head misunderstood the service's "reality" as it was being experienced by his clients. To the clients, "investment *management*" was found to mean "investment *manager*"—i.e., a single human being upon whom they depended for decisions and advice. No matter how well prepared, the professional salesman was not seen as an acceptable substitute by the majority of the market.

Visions of Reality

Clearly, more than one version of "reality" may be found in a service market. Therefore, the crux of service-knowledge is the description of the major *consensus realities* that define the service entity to various market segments. The determination of consensus realities should be a high priority for service marketers, and marketing should offer more concrete guidance and emphasis on this subject than it does.

To define the market-held "realities" of a service requires a high tolerance for subjective, "soft" data, combined with a rigidly objective attitude toward that data. To understand what a service entity is to a market, the marketer must undertake more initial research than is common in product marketing. More important, it will be research of a different kind than is the case in product marketing. The marketer must rely heavily on the tools and skills of psychology, sociology, and other behavioral sciences—tools that in product marketing usually come into play in determining *image*, rather than fundamental "reality."

In developing the blueprint of a service entity's main elements, the marketer might find, for instance, that although tax return preparation is analogous to "accurate mathematical computation" within his firm, it means "freedom from responsibility" to one segment of the consuming public, "opportunity for financial savings" to another segment, and "convenience" to yet a third segment.

Unless these "realities" are documented and ranked by market importance, no sensible plan can be devised to represent a service effectively or deliberately. And in *new* service development, the importance of the service-research function is even more critical, because the successful development of a new service—a molecular collection of intangibles—is so difficult it makes new-product development look like child's play.

IMAGE VERSUS EVIDENCE— THE KEY

The definition of consensus realities should not be confused with the determination of "image." Image is a method of *differentiating* and *representing* an entity to its target market. Image is not "product," nor is it "service." As was suggested in Exhibit 1, there appears to be a critical difference between the way tangible- and intangible-dominant entities are best represented to their markets. Examination of actual cases suggests a common thread among effective representations of services that is another mirror-opposite contrast to product techniques.

In comparing examples, it is clear that consumer product marketing often approaches the market by enhancing a physical object through abstract associations. *Coca-Cola*, for example, is surrounded with visual, verbal, and aural associations with authenticity and youth. Although *Dr. Pepper* would also be physically categorized as a beverage, its *image* has been structured to suggest "originality" and "risk-taking"; while *7-up* is "light" and "buoyant." A high priority is placed on linking these abstract images to physical items.

But a service is already abstract. To compound the abstraction dilutes the "reality" that the marketer is trying to enhance. Effective service representations appear to be turned 180° *away* from abstraction. The reason for this is that service images, and even service "realities," appear to be shaped to a large extent by the things that the consumer can comprehend with his five senses—tangible things. But a service itself cannot be tangible, so reliance must be placed on *peripheral* clues.

Tangible clues are what allow the detective in a mystery novel to surmise events at the scene of a crime without having been present. Similarly, when a consumer attempts to judge a service, particularly before using or buying it, that service is "known" by the tangible clues, the tangible evidence, that surround it.

The management of tangible evidence is not articulated in marketing as a primary priority for service marketers. There has been little in-depth exploration of the *range* of authority that emphasis on tangible evidence would create for the service marketer. In product marketing, tangible evidence is primarily the product itself. But for services, tangible evidence would encompass broader considerations in contrast to product marketing, *different* considerations than are typically considered marketing's domain today.

Focusing on the Evidence

In *product* marketing, many kinds of evidence are beyond the marketer's control and are consequently omitted from priority consideration in the market positioning process. Product marketing tends to give first emphasis to creating *abstract* associations.

Service marketers, on the other hand, should be focused on enhancing and differentiating "realities" through manipulation of *tangible* clues. The management of evidence comes first for service marketers, because service "reality" is arrived at by the consumer mostly through a process of deduction, based on the total impression that the evidence creates. Because of product marketing's biases, service marketers often fail to recognize the unique forms of evidence that they *can* normally control and fail to see that they should be part of marketing's responsibilities.

MANAGEMENT
OF THE ENVIRONMENT

Environment is a good example. Since product distribution normally means shipping to outside agents, the marketer has little voice in structuring the environment in which the product is sold. His major controllable impact on the environment is usually product packaging. Services, on the other hand, are often fully integrated with environment; that is, the setting in which the service is "distributed" *is* controllable. To the extent possible, management of the physical environment should be one of a service marketer's highest priorities.

Setting can play an enormous role in influencing the "reality" of a service in the consumer's mind. Marketing does not emphasize this rule for services, yet there are numerous obvious examples of its importance.

Physicians' offices provide an interesting example of intuitive environmental management. Although the quality of medical service may be identical, an office furnished in teak and leather creates a totally different "reality" in the consumer's mind from one with plastic slipcovers and inexpensive prints. Carrying the example further, a marketer could expect to cause change in the service's image simply by painting a physician's office walls neon pink or silver, instead of white.

Similarly, although the services may be identical, the consumer's differentiation between "Bank A Service" and "Bank B Service" is materially affected by whether the environment is dominated by butcher-block and bright colors or by marble and polished brass.

By understanding the importance of evidence management, the service marketer can make it his business to review and take control of this critical part of his "mix." Creation of environment can be deliberate, rather than accidental or as a result of leaving such decisions in the hands of the interior decorators.

Integrating Evidence

Going beyond environment, evidence can be integrated across a wide range of items.

Airlines, for example, manage and coordinate tangible evidence, and do it better than almost any large service industry. Whether by intuition or design, airlines do *not* focus attention on trying to explain or characterize the service itself. One never sees an ad that attempts to convey "the slant of takeoff," "the feel of acceleration," or "the aerodynamics of lift." Airline transport is given shape and form through consistency of a firm's identification, its uniforms, the decor of its planes, its graphics, and its advertising. Differentiation among airlines, though they all provide the same service, is a direct result of differences in "packages" of evidence.

Some businesses in which tangible and intangible elements carry equal weight emphasize abstractions and evidence in about equal proportions. McDonald's is an excellent example. The food *product* is associated with "nutritious" (two all-beef, etc.), "fun" (Ronald McDonald) and "helpful" ("We Do It All for You," "You Deserve a Break Today"). The main *service* element, i.e., fast-food preparation, is tangibly distinguished by uniformity of environment, color, and style of graphics and apparel, consistency of delivery (young employees), and the ubiquitous golden arches.

Using the scale developed in Exhibit 2, this concept can be postulated as a principle for service representation. As shown in Exhibit 3, once an entity has been analyzed and positioned on the scale, the degree to which the marketer will focus on either tangible evidence or intangible abstractions for market positioning will be found to be *inversely related to the entity's dominance.*

The more intangible elements there are, the more the marketer must endeavor to stand in the consumer's shoes, thinking through and gaining control of *all* the inputs to the consumer's mind that can be classified as material evidence.

Some forms of evidence can seem trivial until one recognizes how great their impact can be on service perception. Correspondence is one example. Letters, statements, and the like are sometimes the main conveyers of the "reality" of a service to its market; yet often these are treated as peripheral to any marketing plan. From the grade of paper to the choice

EXHIBIT 3
Principle of Marketing Positioning Emphasis

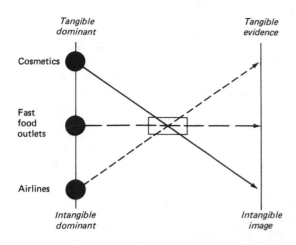

of colors, correspondence is visible evidence that conveys a unique message. A mimeographed, nonpersonalized, cheaply offset letter contradicts any words about service quality that may appear in the text of that letter. Conversely, engraved parchment from the local dry cleaner might make one wonder about their prices.

Profile as Evidence

As was pointed out in the investment management example, services are often inextricably entwined with their human representatives. In many fields, a person is perceived to *be* the service. The consumer cannot distinguish between them. Product marketing is myopic in dealing with the issue of *people as evidence* in terms of market positioning. Consumer marketing often stops at the production of materials and programs for salesmen to use. Some service industries, on the other hand, have long intuitively managed human evidence to larger ends.

Examples of this principle have been the basis for jokes, plays, and literature. "The Man in the Grey Flannel Suit," for example, was a synonym for the advertising business for many years. Physicians are uniformly "packaged" in smocks. Lawyers and bankers are still today known for pin-stripes and vests. IBM representatives were famous for adhering to a "White Shirt" policy. Going beyond apparel, as mentioned earlier, McDonald's even achieves age uniformity—an extra element reinforcing its total market image.

These examples add up to a serious principle when thoughtfully reviewed. They are particularly instructive for service marketers. None of the above examples were the result of deliberate market planning. McDonald's, for instance, backed into age consistency as a result of trying to keep labor costs low. Airlines are the single outstanding example of consciously-planned standards for uniformity in human representation. The power of the human evidence principle is obvious, and the potential power of more deliberately controlling or structuring this element is clear.

Lest this discussion be interpreted as an advocacy of regimentation, it should be pointed out that management of human evidence can be as basic as providing nametags to service representatives or as complex as the "packaging" of a political candidate, whose very words are often chosen by committee and whose hair style can become a critical policy issue. Or, depending upon what kind of service "reality" the marketer wishes to create, human representation can be encouraged to display *non*conformity, as is the case with the "creative" departments of advertising agencies. The point is that service marketers should be charged with tactics and strategy in this area, and must consider it a management responsibility.

SERVICES AND THE MEDIA

As has been previously discussed, service elements are abstract. Because they are abstract, the marketer must work hard at making them "real," by building a case from tangible evidence. In this context, media advertising presents a particularly difficult problem.

The problem revolves around the fact that media (television, radio, print) are one step removed from tangibility. Media, by its McLuhanesque nature, abstracts the physical.

Even though product tangibility provides an anchor for media representation because a product can be *shown*, media still abstract products. A photograph is only a two-dimensional version of a physical object, and may be visually misleading. Fortunately, the consumer makes the mental connection between seeing a product in the media and recognizing it in reality. This is true even when a product is substantially distorted. Sometimes, only part of a product is shown. Occasionally, as in recent commercials for *7-up*, the product is *not* shown. However, the consumer remembers past experience. He has little difficulty recognizing *7-up* by name or remembered appearance when he sees it or wants to buy it.

Thus, media work *with* the creation of product image and *help* in adding abstract qualities to tangible goods. Cosmetics, for example, are often positioned in association with an airbrushed or soft-focus filmed *ideal* of beauty. Were the media truly accurate, the wrinkles and flaws of the flesh, to which even models are heir, might not create such an appealing product association.

Making Services More Concrete

Because of their abstracting capabilities, the media often make service entities more hazy, instead of more *concrete*, and the service marketer must work *against* this inherent effect. Unfortunately, many marketers are so familiar with product-oriented thinking that they go down precisely the wrong path and attempt to represent services by dealing with them in abstractions.

The pages of the business press are filled with examples of this type of misconception in services advertising. In advertisements for investment management, for instance, the worst examples attempt to describe the already intangible service with *more* abstractions such as "sound analysis," "careful portfolio monitoring," "strong research capability," etc. Such compounded abstractions do *not* help the consumer form a "reality," do *not* differentiate the service and do *not* achieve any credibility, much less any customer "draw."

The best examples are those which attempt to associate the service with some form of *tangible evidence*, working against the media's abstracting qualities. Merrill Lynch, for instance, has firmly associated itself with a clear visual symbol of bulls and concomitant bullishness. Where Merrill Lynch does not use the visual herd, it uses photographs of *tangible physical booklets*, and invites the consumer to write for them.

Therefore, the final principle offered for service marketers would hold that effective media representation of intangibles is a function of establishing nonabstract manifestations of them.

CONCLUSION

This article has presented several market-inspired thoughts toward the development of new marketing concepts, and the evolution of relevant service marketing principles. The hypotheses presented here do not by any means represent an exhaustive analysis of the subject. No exploration was done, for example, on product versus service pricing or product versus service distribution. Both areas offer rich potential for creative new approaches and analysis.

It can be argued that there are many grey areas in the molecular entity concept, and that diagramming and managing according to the multiple-elements schema could present considerable difficulties by virtue of its greater complexity. It might also be argued that some distinctions between tangible and intangible-dominant entities are so subtle as to be unimportant.

The fact remains that service marketers are in urgent need of concepts and priorities that are relevant to their actual experience and needs, and that marketing has failed in evolving to meet that demand. However unorthodox, continuing exploration of this area must be encouraged if marketing is to achieve stature and influence in the new post-Industrial Revolution services economy.

NOTES

1. See, for example, E. Jerome McCarthy, *Basic Marketing: A Managerial Approach*, 4th ed. (Homewood, IL: Richard D. Irwin, 1971), pg. 303, compared with William J. Stanton, *Fundamentals of Marketing*, 3rd ed. (New York: McGraw-Hill, 1971), pg. 567.

2. See William R. George and Hiram C. Barksdale, "Marketing Activities in the Service Industries," *Journal of Marketing*, Vol. 38, No. 4 (October 1974), pp. 65–70.

3. *The Meaning and Sources of Marketing Theory*, Marketing Science Institute Series (New York: McGraw-Hill, 1965), pg. 88.

4. *Webster's New Collegiate Dictionary* (Springfield, MA: G & C. Merriam Company, 1974).

5. Philip Kotler, "A Generic Concept of Marketing," *Journal of Marketing*, Vol. 36, No. 2 (April 1972), pp. 46–54.

6. Theodore H. Levitt, "Marketing Myopia," *Harvard Business Review*, Vol. 38 (July–August 1960), pp. 45–46.

7. Aubrey Wilson, *The Marketing of Professional Services*, (New York: McGraw-Hill, 1972), pg. 8.

II

Developing Frameworks
for Understanding Services Marketing

Developing professional skills in marketing management requires the ability to look across a broad cross section of marketing situations to understand their differences and commonalities and to identify appropriate marketing strategies in each instance. In the manufacturing sector, many experienced marketers have worked for a variety of companies in several different industries, often including both consumer goods and industrial firms. As a result, they have a perspective that transcends narrow industry boundaries.

Nevertheless, exposure to marketing problems and strategies in different industries is still quite rare among managers in the service sector. Not only is the concept of a formalized marketing function still relatively new to most service firms, but management personnel in service industries have historically been somewhat inbred. The majority of railroad managers, for instance, have spent their entire working lives within the railroad industry—even within a single company. Most hoteliers have grown up in the hotel industry. And most hospital or college administrators have remained within the confines of health care or higher education, respectively. The net result of such narrow

exposure is that it restricts a manager's ability to identify and learn from the experience of organizations facing parallel situations in other service industries and, of course, from marketing experience in the manufacturing sector.

Conversely, marketers from the manufacturing sector who take positions in service businesses often find that their past experience has not prepared them well for working on some of the problems that regularly challenge service marketers.[1]

ACADEMIC RESEARCH IN SERVICES

Marketing scholars have been discussing services and how they differ from physical goods since the issue of distinguishing the two was first raised in marketing circles over 15 years ago.[2] However, although the importance of services for the national economy has been recognized for more than a decade, it has only been in the past five years or so that enough literature has accumulated on the subject to constitute a critical mass, and that research into services marketing has begun to acquire any degree of sustained commitment.[3]

49

Perhaps one reason why services marketing has traditionally received so much less attention than goods marketing has been the problem of definition. Basically the range of services is too broad to allow meaningful, in-depth analysis of the entire field. The opposite extreme of focusing on a single industry has taken place in areas like transportation, banking, and insurance. But such an approach fails to generate the insights gained from comparing and contrasting marketing applications in several related industries.

I believe that development of greater sophistication in services marketing will be aided if we can find new ways to group services other than current industry classifications. A more useful approach may be to segment services into clusters that share certain marketing-relevant characteristics in common, and then to examine the implications for marketing action.

After briefly reviewing the value of classification schemes in marketing, this section summarizes past proposals for classifying services, followed by a discussion of six classification schemes. In each instance, examples are given of how various services fall into similar or different categories, and an evaluation is made of the resulting marketing insights and what they imply for marketing strategy development.

THE VALUE OF CLASSIFICATION IN MARKETING

Although classification schemes have their limitations, they can offer important insights for both practitioners and researchers.[4] Various attempts have been made in the past by marketing theorists to classify goods into different categories. One of the most famous and enduring is Copeland's classification of convenience, shopping, and specialty goods.[5] Not only did this help managers obtain a better understanding of consumer needs and behavior, it also provided insights into the management of retail distribution systems.

Another major classification has been between durable and nondurable goods. Durability is closely associated with purchase frequency, which has important implications for development of both distribution and communications strategy. Yet another classification is consumer goods versus industrial goods; this classification relates both to the type of goods purchased (although there is some overlap) and to product evaluation, purchasing procedures, and usage behavior. Recognition of these distinctions by marketers has led to different types of marketing strategy directed at each of these groups. Through such classifications, the application of marketing management tools and strategies in manufacturing has become a professional skill that transcends industry divisions.

By contrast, service industries remain dominated by an operations orientation that insists that each industry is different. This mindset is often manifested in managerial attitudes that suggest that the marketing of (say) airlines has nothing at all in common with that of (say) banks, insurance, motels, hospitals, or household movers. But if it can be shown that some of these services do share certain, marketing-relevant characteristics in common, then the stage may be set for some useful cross-fertilization of concepts and strategies.

HOW MIGHT SERVICES BE CLASSIFIED?

Various attempts have been proposed in the past for classifying services.[6] But developing classification schemes is not enough.

If they are to have managerial value, they must offer strategic insights. Thus, it is important to develop ways of analyzing services that highlight the characteristics they have in common and then to examine the implications for marketing management.

Let's examine some of the characteristics of services that transcend industry boundaries and that affect the way marketing is practiced. Such characteristics can be understood by answering the following questions:

1. What is the nature of the service "act"?
2. What type of relationship does the service organization have with its customers?
3. How much room is there for customization and judgment on the part of the service provider?
4. What is the nature of demand for the service?
5. How is the service delivered?
6. What are the attributes of the service product?

We'll examine each question in turn, with a view to suggesting classification schemes that will yield strategic marketing insights and encourage thinking about problems in service marketing across industry boundaries.

What Is the Nature of the Service Act?

A service has been described by Berry as a "deed, act, or performance."[7] Two fundamental questions are: At whom (or what) is the act directed? And is this act tangible or intangible in nature?

As shown in Table II–1, these two questions result in a four-way classification scheme, involving (1) tangible actions to people's bodies, such as airline transportation, haircutting, and surgery; (2) tangible actions to goods and other physical possessions, such as air freight, lawn mowing, and janitorial services; (3) intangible actions directed at people's minds, such as broadcasting and education; and (4) intangible actions directed at intangible assets, such

TABLE II–1

Understanding the Nature of the Service Act

WHAT IS THE NATURE OF THE SERVICE ACT?	WHO OR WHAT IS THE DIRECT RECIPIENT OF THE SERVICE?	
	People	Things
TANGIBLE ACTIONS	(1) Services directed at people's bodies Health care Passenger transportation Beauty salons Exercise clinics Restaurants Haircutting	(2) Services directed at goods and other physical possessions Freight transportation Industrial equipment repair and maintenance Janitorial services Laundry and dry cleaning Landscaping/lawncare Veterinary care
INTANGIBLE ACTIONS	(3) Services directed at people's minds Education Broadcasting Information services Theaters Museums	(4) Services directed at intangible assets Banking Legal services Accounting Securities Insurance

as insurance, investment banking, and consulting.

Sometimes a service may seem to spill over into two or more categories. For instance, the delivery of educational, religious, or entertainment services (directed primarily at the mind) often entails tangible actions such as being in a classroom, church, or theater; the delivery of financial services may require a visit to a bank to transform intangible financial assets into hard cash; and the delivery of airline services may affect some travelers' states of mind as well as physically moving their bodies from one airport to another. But in most instances the core service act is confined to one of the four categories, although there may be secondary acts in another category.

Insights and Implications. Why is this categorization scheme useful to service marketers? Basically it helps answer the following questions:

1. Does the customer need to be *physically* present?
   a. throughout service delivery
   b. only to initiate or terminate the service transaction (for example, dropping off a car for repair and picking it up again afterward)
   c. not at all (the relationship with the service supplier can be at arm's length through the mails, telephone, or other electronic media).
2. Does the customer need to be *mentally* present during service delivery? Can mental presence be maintained across physical distances through mail or electronic communications?
3. In what ways is the target of the service act "modified" by receipt of the service? And how does the customer benefit from these "modifications"?

Because services are intangible, it is not always obvious what the service is and what it does for the customer. By identifying the target of the service and then examining how it is "modified" or changed by receipt of the service act, we can develop a better understanding of the nature of the service product and the core benefits that it offers.

If customers need to be physically present during service delivery, then they must enter the service "factory" (whether it be a train, a hairdressing salon, or a hospital at a particular location) and must spend time there while the service is performed. Their satisfaction with the service will be influenced by the interactions they have with service personnel, the nature of the service facilities, and also, perhaps, by the characteristics of other customers using the same service. Questions of location and schedule convenience assume great importance when a customer has to be physically present or must appear in person to initiate and terminate the transaction.

Dealing with a service organization at arm's length, by contrast, may mean that a customer never sees the service facilities at all and never meets the service personnel face-to-face. In this sort of situation, the outcome of the service act remains very important, but the *process* of service delivery may be of little interest, since the customer never goes near the "factory." For instance, credit cards and many types of insurance can be obtained by mail or telephone.

For operational reasons, it may be very desirable to get the customer out of the factory and to transform a "high-contact" service into a "low-contact" one.[8] The chances of success in such an endeavor will be enhanced when the new procedures also offer customers greater convenience. Many services directed at *things* rather than at people formerly required the customer's presence, but they are now delivered at arm's length. Certain financial services have long used the mails to save customers the inconvenience of personal visits to a specific office location. Today, new electronic distribution channels have made it possible to offer instantaneous delivery of financial services to a wide array of alternative locations. Retail banking provides a good example, with its growing use of electronic delivery systems such as automatic teller machines in airports or shopping centers, pay-by-phone bill paying, or on-line banking facilities in retail stores.

By thinking creatively about the nature of their services, managers of service organizations may be able to identify opportunities for alternative, more convenient forms of service delivery or even for the transformation of the service into a manufactured good. For instance, services to the *mind,* such as education, do not necessarily require attendance in person since they can be delivered through the mails or electronic media. (Britain's Open University, which makes extensive use of television and radio broadcasts, is a prime example.) Two-way communication hookups can make it possible for a teacher and student physically distant from one another to interact directly whenever it is necessary to the educational process. (One recent Bell System advertisement featured a chamber music class in a small town being taught by an instructor several hundred miles away.) Alternatively, lectures can be packaged and sold as books, records, or videotapes. And programmed learning exercises can be developed in computerized form, with the terminal serving as a Socratic surrogate.

What Type of Relationship Does the Service Organization Have with Its Customers?

With very few exceptions, consumers buy manufactured goods at discrete intervals, paying for each purchase separately and rarely entering into a formal relationship with the manufacturer. (Industrial purchasers, by contrast, often enter into long-term relationships with suppliers and some-

times receive almost continuous delivery of certain supplies.)

In the service sector, both household and institutional purchasers may enter into ongoing relationships with service suppliers and may receive service on a continuing basis. This offers a way of categorizing services. We can ask, Does the service organization enter into a "membership" relationship with its customers, as with telephone subscriptions, banking, and the family doctor? Or is there no formal relationship? Is the service delivered on a continuous basis, as in insurance, broadcasting, and police protection? Or is each transaction recorded and charged separately? Table II–2 shows the matrix resulting from this categorization, with some additional examples in each category.

Insights and Implications. The advantage to the service organization of a "membership" relationship is that it knows who its current customers are and, usually, what use they make of the services offered. This can be valuable information for segmentation purposes if good records are kept and the data are readily accessible in a format that lends itself to computerized analysis. Knowing the identities and addresses of current customers enables the organization to make effective use of direct mail, telephone selling, and personal sales calls—all highly targeted methods of marketing communication.

The nature of service relationships also has important implications for pricing. Whenever service is offered on an ongoing basis, there is often just a single periodic charge covering all contracted services. Most insurance policies fall in this category, as do tuition and board fees at a residential college. The big advantage of this package approach is its simplicity. Some memberships, however, entail a series of separate and identifiable transactions with the price paid being tied explicitly to the number and type of such transactions. While more complex to

TABLE II-2

Relationships with Customers

NATURE OF SERVICE DELIVERY	TYPE OF RELATIONSHIP BETWEEN THE SERVICE ORGANIZATION AND ITS CUSTOMERS	
	"Membership" Relationship	No Formal Relationship
CONTINUOUS DELIVERY OF SERVICE	Insurance Telephone subscription College enrollment Banking American Automobile Association	Radio station Police protection Lighthouse Public highway
DISCRETE TRANSACTIONS	Long-distance calls from subscriber phone Theater-series subscription Travel on commuter ticket	Car rental Mail service Toll highway Pay phone Movie theater Public transportation Restaurant

administer, such an approach is fairer to customers (whose usage patterns may vary widely) and may discourage wasteful use of what are perceived as "free" services. In such instances, "members" may be offered advantages over casual users—for instance, discount rates (telephone subscribers pay less for long-distance calls made from their own phones than do pay phone users) or advance notification and priority reservations (theater subscriptions).

Some memberships offer certain services (such as rental of equipment or connection to a public utility system) for a base fee and then make incremental charges for each separate transaction above a defined minimum.

Profitability and customer convenience are central issues in deciding how to price membership services. Will the organization generate greater long-term profits by tying payment explicitly to consumption, by charging a flat rate regardless of consumption, or by unbundling the components of the service and charging a flat rate for some and

an incremental rate for others? Telephone and electricity services, for instance, typically charge a base fee for connection to the system and rental of equipment, plus a variety of incremental charges for consumption above a defined minimum. On the other hand, Wide Area Telephone Service (WATS) offers the convenience of unlimited long-distance calling for a fixed fee. How important is it to customers to have the convenience of paying a single periodic fee that is known in advance? Members of the American Automobile Association (AAA) can obtain information booklets, travel advice, and certain types of emergency road services free of additional charge. Such a package offers elements of both insurance and convenience to customers who may not be able to predict their exact needs in advance.

Where no formal relationship exists between supplier and customer, continuous delivery of the product is normally found only among those services that economists term "public goods"—for instance, broadcasting, police protection, lighthouse services, and public highways—which are continuously available, financed from tax revenues, and available free of charge. Discrete transactions—when each usage involves a payment to the service supplier by an essentially "anonymous" consumer—are typical of many transportation services, restaurants, movie theaters, shoe repairs, and so forth. The problem for marketers of such services is that they tend to be less informed about who their customers are and what use each customer makes of the service than are their counterparts in membership-type organizations.

Membership relationships usually result in customer loyalty to a particular service supplier. (Sometimes, however, there is no choice, because the supplier has a monopoly.) As a marketing strategy, many service businesses seek ways to develop formal, ongoing relations with customers in order to ensure repeat business and/or ongoing financial support. Public radio and television broadcasters, for instance, develop membership clubs for donors and offer monthly program guides in return; performing arts organizations sell subscription series; transit agencies offer monthly passes; airlines create clubs for high-mileage fliers; and hotels develop "executive service plans" offering priority reservations and upgraded rooms for frequent guests. The marketing task here is to determine how it might be possible to build sales and revenues through such "memberships," while avoiding a formal membership requirement that would result in freezing out a large volume of desirable casual business.

How Much Room Is There
for Customization and Judgment?

Relatively few consumer goods nowadays are built specially to order; most are purchased "off the shelf." The same is true for a majority of industrial goods, although by permutating options, it is possible to give the impression of customization. Once they have purchased the goods, of course, customers are usually free to use them as they see fit.

The situation in the service sector, by contrast, is sharply different. Because services are created as they are consumed, and because the customer is often actually involved in the production process, there is far more scope for tailoring the service to meet the needs of individual customers. As shown in Table II–3, customization can proceed along at least two dimensions: (1) how much the characteristics of the service and its delivery system lend themselves to customization and (2) how much judgment customer-contact personnel are able to exercise in defining the nature of the service received by individual customers.

Some service concepts are quite standardized. Public transportation, for instance, runs over fixed routes on predetermined schedules. Routine appliance repairs typically involve a fixed charge, and the customer is responsible for dropping off the item at a given retail location and picking it up again afterward. Fast-food restaurants have a small, set menu; few offer the customer much choice in how the food will be cooked and served. Movies, entertainment, and spectator sports place the audience in a relatively passive role, albeit sometimes a noisy one.

Other services offer customers a wide range of options. Each telephone subscriber enjoys an individual number and can use the phone to obtain a broad array of different services—from receiving personal calls from a next-door neighbor to calling a business associate on the other side of the world, from data transmission to dial-a-prayer. Retail bank accounts are also customized, with each check or bank card carrying the customer's name and personal code. Within the constraints set down by the bank, the cus-

TABLE II-3

Customization and Judgment in Service Delivery

EXTENT TO WHICH CUSTOMER-CONTACT PERSONNEL EXERCISE JUDGMENT IN MEETING INDIVIDUAL CUSTOMER NEEDS	EXTENT TO WHICH SERVICE CHARACTERISTICS ARE CUSTOMIZED	
	High	Low
HIGH	Legal services Health care/surgery Architectural design Executive search firm Real estate agency Taxi service Beautician Plumber Education (tutorials)	Education (large classes) Preventive health programs
LOW	Telephone service Hotel services Retail banking (excl. major loans) Good restaurant	Public transportation Routine appliance repair Fast-food restaurant Movie theater Spectator sports

tomer enjoys considerable latitude in how and when the account is used and receives a personalized monthly statement. Good hotels and restaurants usually offer their customers an array of service options from which to choose, as well as considerable flexibility in how the service product is delivered.

In each of these instances, the role of the customer contact personnel (if, indeed, there is any) is somewhat constrained. Other than tailoring their personal manner to the customer and answering straightforward questions, contact personnel have relatively little discretion in altering the characteristics of the service they deliver: Their role is basically that of operators or order takers. Judgment and discretion in customer dealings is usually reserved for managers or supervisors who will normally not become involved in service delivery unless a problem arises.

A third category of services gives the customer-contact personnel wide latitude in how they deliver the service, yet these individuals do not significantly differentiate the characteristics of their service between one customer and another. For instance, educators who teach courses by lectures and give multiple-choice, computer-scored exams may offer a distinctly different course from colleagues teaching on the same topic, yet within each class all students are exposed to a similar experience.

However, there is a class of services that not only involves a high degree of customization but also requires customer-contact personnel to exercise judgment concerning the characteristics of the service and how it is delivered to each customer. Far from being reactive in their dealings with customers, these service personnel are often prescriptive: Users (or "clients") look to them for advice as well as for customized execution. In this category, the locus of control shifts from the user to the supplier—a situation that some customers may find disconcerting. Consumers of surgical services literally place their lives in the surgeon's hands (the same, unfortunately, is also true of taxi services in many cities). Professional services, such as law, medicine, accounting, and architecture, fall within this category. They are all white-collar, "knowledge" industries, requiring extensive training to develop the requisite skills and judgment needed for satisfactory service delivery. Also within this category are found service deliverers such as taxi drivers, beauticians, and plumbers. Their work is customized to the situation at hand, and in each instance the customer purchases the expertise required to devise a tailor-made solution.

Insights and Implications. To a much greater degree than in the manufacturing sector, service products are "custom-made." Yet customization has its costs. Service management often represents an ongoing struggle between the desires of marketing managers to add value and the goals of operations managers to reduce costs through standardization. Resolving such disputes—a task that may require arbitration by the general manager—requires a good understanding of consumer choice criteria, particularly as these relate to price-value trade-offs, and competitive positioning strategy. At the present time, most senior managers in service businesses have come up through the operations route; hence, participation in executive education programs may be needed to give them the necessary perspective on marketing to make balanced decisions.

Customization is not necessarily important to success. As Levitt has pointed out, industrializing a service to take advantage of the economies of mass production may actually increase consumer satisfaction.[9] Speed, consistency, and price savings may be more important to many customers than customized service. In some instances, such as spectator sports and the performing arts, part of the product experience is sharing the service with many other people. In other instances, the customer expects to share the service facilities with other consumers, as in hotels or airlines, yet still hopes for some individual recognition and personal treatment. Allowing customers to reserve specific rooms or seats in advance, having service personnel address them by name (it's on their ticket or reservation slip), and providing some latitude for individual choice (room service, morning wake-up calls, drinks, and meals) are all ways to create an image of customization.

Generally, customers like to know in advance what they are buying, what the product features are, and what the service will do for them. Surprises and uncertainty are normally not popular. Yet when the nature of the service requires a judgment-based, customized solution—as in a professional service—it is not always clear to either the customer or the professional what the outcome will be. Frequently, an important dimension of the professional's role is diagnosing the nature of the situation and then designing a solution.

In such situations, those responsible for developing marketing strategy would do well to recognize that customers may be uneasy concerning the uncertainty about the outcome. Customer-contact personnel in these instances are not only part of the product, but they also determine what that product should be.

One solution to this problem is to divide the product into two separate components—diagnosis and implementation of a solution—that are executed and paid for separately. Although the outcome of the diagnosis cannot always be accurately predicted, the customer at least has the reassurance of knowing that he or she need not proceed immediately with the proposed solution; indeed, there is always the option of seeking a second opinion. The solution "product," by contrast, can often be spelled out in detail beforehand, so that the customer has a good idea of what to expect. Even then, there may still be some uncertainty, as in legal actions or medical treatment, but the range of possibilities should be narrower by this point, and it may be feasible to assign probabilities to alternative outcomes.

Marketing efforts may need to focus on the *process* of client-provider interactions. It will help prospective clients make choices between alternative suppliers (especially where professionals are concerned) if they know something of the organization's (or individual's) approach to diagnosis and problem solving, as well as their client-relationship style. These considerations transcend mere statement of qualifications in an advertisement or brochure. Sometimes it may be appropriate to allow prospective customers time for a free interview before any commitments are made. Such a "trial" encounter has the advantage of allowing both parties to decide whether or not a good match exists.

What Is the Nature of Demand for the Service?

Manufacturing firms can inventory supplies of their product as a hedge against fluctuations in demand. This enables them to enjoy the economies derived from operating plants at a steady level of production. Service businesses can't do this, because it is not possible to inventory the finished service. For instance, the potential income from an empty seat on an airline flight is lost forever once that flight takes off, and each hotel room-night is equally "perishable." Likewise, the productive capacity of an auto repair shop is wasted if no one brings a car for servicing on a day when the shop is open. Conversely, if the demand for a service exceeds supply on a particular day, the excess business may be lost. Thus, if someone can't get a seat on one flight, another carrier gets the business, or the trip is cancelled or postponed. And if an accounting firm is too

busy to accept tax and audit work from a prospective client, another firm will get the assignment.

But demand and supply imbalances are not found in all service situations. A useful way of categorizing services for this purpose is shown in Table II–4. The horizontal axis classifies organizations according to whether demand for the service fluctuates widely or narrowly over time; the vertical axis classifies them according to whether or not capacity is sufficient to meet peak demand.

Organizations in box 1 could use increases in demand outside peak periods, those in box 2 must decide whether to seek continued growth in demand and capacity or to continue the status quo, and those in box 3 may need temporary demarketing until capacity can be increased to meet or exceed current demand levels. Service organizations in box 4, however, face an ongoing problem of trying to smooth demand to match capacity, which involves both stimulation and discouragement of demand.

Insights and Implications. Managing demand is a task faced by nearly all marketers, whether offering goods or services. Even when the fluctuations are sharp and inventories cannot be used to act as a buffer between supply and demand, it may still be possible to manage capacity in a service business, by hiring part-time employees or renting extra facilities at peak periods, for instance. But for a substantial group of service organizations, successfully managing demand fluctuations through marketing actions is the key to profitability.

To determine the most appropriate strategy in each instance, it is necessary to seek answers to some additional questions:

1. What is the typical cycle period of these demand fluctuations?
   a. Demand is predictable and varies by hour of the day, day of the week or month, and season of the year.

TABLE II–4

What Is the Nature of Demand for the Service Relative to Supply?

EXTENT TO WHICH SUPPLY IS CONSTRAINED	EXTENT OF DEMAND FLUCTUATIONS OVER TIME	
	Wide	*Narrow*
PEAK DEMAND CAN USUALLY BE MET WITHOUT A MAJOR DELAY	1 Electricity Natural gas Telephone Hospital maternity unit Police and fire emergencies	2 Insurance Legal services Banking Laundry and dry cleaning
PEAK DEMAND REGULARLY EXCEEDS CAPACITY	4 Accounting and tax preparation Passenger transportation Hotels and motels Restaurants Theaters	3 (Services similar to those in 2 but which have insufficient capacity for their base level of business.)

b. Demand is random and there is no apparent pattern to demand fluctuations.

2. What are the underlying causes of these demand fluctuations?
   a. Customer habits or preferences? (Could marketing efforts change these?)
   b. Actions by third parties, for instance, employers set working hours? (Can marketing efforts usefully be directed at those employers?)
   c. Nonforecastable events, such as health symptoms, weather conditions, acts of nature, and so forth? (Marketing can do only a little about these, such as offering priority service to "members" and disseminating information about alternative services to other people.)

One way of smoothing the ups and downs of demand is through strategies that encourage customers to change their plans voluntarily, such as offering special discount prices or added product value during periods of low demand. Another approach is to ration demand through a reservation or queuing system, which basically inventories demand rather than supply. Alternatively, to generate demand in periods of excess capacity, new business development efforts might be targeted at prospective customers with a countercyclical demand pattern. For instance, an accounting firm with a surfeit of work at the end of each calendar year might seek new customers whose financial year ended on June 30 or September 30.

Determining what strategy is appropriate requires an understanding of who or what is the target of the service (as previously discussed). If the service is delivered to customers in person, there are limits as to how long a customer will wait in line; hence strategies to inventory or ration demand should focus on adoption of reservation systems.[10] But if the service is delivered to goods or to intangible assets, then inventorying demand should be more feasible, unless the good is a vital necessity such as a car, in which case reservations may be the best approach.

How Is the Service Delivered?

Understanding distribution issues in service marketing requires that two basic issues be addressed. The first relates to the method of delivery. Is it necessary for the customer to be in direct physical contact with the service organization (customers may have to go to the service organization or the latter may come to the former), or can transactions be completed at arm's length? And does the service organization maintain just a single outlet or does it serve customers through multiple outlets at different sites? The outcome of this analysis can be seen in Table II–5, which consists of six different cells.

Insights and Implications. The convenience of receiving service is presumably lowest when a customer has to come to the service organization and must use a specific outlet. Offering service through several outlets increases the convenience of access for customers but may start to raise problems of quality control, especially as this relates to the consistency of the service product delivered. For some types of services, the service comes to the customer. This is, of course, essential when the target of the service is some immovable physical item, such as a building that needs repairs, an apartment that requires pest-control treatment, or a garden that needs landscaping. Since it is usually more expensive to take service personnel and equipment to the customer, the trend

has been away from this approach—for example, doctors no longer like to make house calls. In many instances, however, direct contact between customers and the service organization is not necessary; instead, transactions can be handled at arm's length by mail or electronic communications. Through the use of toll-free telephone numbers, many service organizations have found that they can bring their services as close to the nearest telephone, yet obtain important economies from operating out of a single physical location.

Although all services cannot be delivered through arm's-length transactions, it may be possible to separate certain components of the service from the core product and to handle them separately. This suggests an additional classification scheme—categorizing services according to whether transactions such as obtaining information, making reservations, and making payment can be separated from delivery of the core service. If so, then the question is whether or not it is advantageous to the service firm to allow customers to make these peripheral transactions through an intermediary or broker. For instance, information about airline flights, reservations for such flights, and purchases of tickets can all be made through a

TABLE II–5

Method of Service Delivery

NATURE OF INTERACTION BETWEEN CUSTOMER AND SERVICE ORGANIZATION	AVAILABILITY OF SERVICE OUTLETS	
	Single Site	*Multiple Sites*
CUSTOMER GOES TO SERVICE ORGANIZATION	Theater Barbershop	Bus service Fast-food chain
SERVICE ORGANIZATION COMES TO CUSTOMER	Lawncare service Pest control service Taxi	Mail delivery AAA emergency repairs
CUSTOMER AND SERVICE ORGANIZATION TRANSACT AT ARM'S LENGTH (MAIL OR ELECTRONIC COMMUNICATIONS)	Credit card company Local TV station	Broadcast network Telephone company

travel agent as well as directly through the airline. For those who prefer to visit in person rather than conduct business by telephoning, this greatly increases the geographic coverage of distribution, since there are usually several travel agencies located more conveniently than the nearest airline office. Added value from using a travel agent comes from the "one-stop–shopping" aspect of travel agents—the customer can inquire about several airlines and make car rental and hotel reservations during the same call. Insurance brokers and theater ticket agencies are also examples of specialist intermediaries that represent a number of different service organizations. Consumers sometimes perceive such intermediaries as more objective and more knowledgeable about alternatives than the various service suppliers they represent. The risk to the service firm of working through specialist intermediaries is, of course, that they may recommend use of a competitor's product!

What Are the Attributes of the Service Product?

One of the distinctive characteristics of services, discussed in some depth in Section I, is their intangibility. However, many of the elements which go to make up certain services are highly tangible, including building interiors and exteriors, seats, meals, vehicles, equipment, printed materials, and, of course, service personnel. Thomas has suggested that useful management insights can be gained from dividing services into those that are primarily equipment-based and those that are primarily people-based.[11] While it is true that service personnel can sometimes be substituted for equipment and vice versa, this broad distinction is perhaps too simplistic for considering how consumers may perceive and evaluate service characteristics.

An alternative approach shown in Table II–6 recognizes that a service may vary in its emphasis on either people or equipment at-

TABLE II–6

Understanding the Characteristics of the Service Product

EXTENT TO WHICH EQUIPMENT-/FACILITY-BASED ATTRIBUTES FORM PART OF THE SERVICE PRODUCT[a]	EXTENT TO WHICH PEOPLE-BASED ATTRIBUTES[b] FORM PART OF THE SERVICE PRODUCT		
	High	Medium	Low
HIGH	Five-star hotel Hospital	Passenger airline Car rental	Subway Retail banking (with ATMs)
MEDIUM	Dentist Live theater College education	Retail banking (with human tellers)	Freight transportation Movie theater
LOW	Corporate banking Management consulting Public accounting	Tax preparation	"Easy listening" radio[c]

a Could also include such other physical attributes as food and drink.
b These could be service personnel, other customers, or both.
c Equipment (a radio receiver) is needed to receive broadcasts but is not part of the service itself.

tributes, or both. Further, the service may expand the "people" dimension to include other customers as well as service personnel, and it may expand the "equipment" dimension to include the physical facilities where (or in which) the service is delivered. Our interest here is in consumer perceptions of the product. Such a perspective inevitably excludes equipment and personnel working behind the scenes, since they are not normally in evidence as part of the product unless there is some form of breakdown in the system.

Using this scheme, a radio station that broadcasts nothing but music (with minimal commentary) would be categorized as "low" on both people and physical attributes, whereas a good hotel might be categorized as "high/high." A management consulting firm would probably be categorized as "low" on equipment and facility attributes, but "high" on people, whereas for subway transportation, the classification might be reversed—"high" on equipment and facilities, but "low" on people.

Insights and Implications. One of the classification schemes discussed earlier in this chapter addressed the issue of how the service was delivered. We saw that one alternative was for the customer to go to the service organization, another was for the organization to come to the customer, and a third possibility was for customer and organization to transact at arms' length through mail or electronic communications. The closer the degree of interaction between customer and service organization, the more likely service personnel and equipment or facilities are to form an important part of the service product. In short, the *process* of service delivery becomes part of the customer's experience in obtaining service.

The classification scheme presented in Table II–6 can help marketers zero in on what types of attributes are dominant in the

service package, so that they can then, perhaps, seek insights from other service businesses with a similar facilities/people emphasis. Thus Rice, Slack, and Garside suggest that a hospital chain corporation might usefully look to well-run hotels for marketing insights, or a public accounting firm might consider the marketing strategies employed by a successful management consulting firm.[12] Alternatively, this type of analysis may show that services provided by the same industry—such as highway motels and resort hotels, or retail banking and corporate banking—prove to have relatively little in common with each other from the perspective of their relative emphasis on facilities and people attributes. The implication here is that the marketing strategies employed by one type of service in the industry may not be generalizable to other services offered by that same industry.

Service businesses that are high on people attributes tend to be more difficult to manage than those that are primarily equipment-based. Of particular concern to marketers is the fact that consistency of product execution is hard to achieve. Some service businesses, like retail banking, are switching from labor-intensive distribution systems, such as services delivered by bank tellers, to self-service systems in which customers operate equipment such as automatic-teller machines. As shown on Table II–6, a change in the nature of delivery procedures may alter the characteristics of the service product. Unless customer service personnel are available to provide assistance, a user who is having difficulties with an automatic teller must either contact an anonymous person at the other end of a telephone or ask a fellow customer for help. The switch to self-service represents a significant trend in many service businesses today and involves industries such as banking, retail gasoline stations, quick service restaurants, as well as purchases of travelers' checks and train or airline tickets.[13] In some instances, equipment replaces personnel; in other cases, customers' own efforts replace service personnel for certain tasks, such as retrieval of food from the kitchen and clearing of tables after a meal in a fast-food restaurant. In the latter instance, customers still retain contact with service personnel, but instead of dealing with waiters or waitresses, they are now dealing with kitchen staff.

CONCLUSION

Widespread interest in the marketing of services among both academics and practitioners is a relatively recent phenomenon. Possibly this reflects the fact that marketing expertise in the service sector has significantly lagged behind that in the manufacturing sector. Up to now, most academic research and discussion has centered on the issue, "How do services differ from goods?" As we saw in Section I, a number of authors, including Shostack and Berry, have argued that there are significant distinctions between the two and have proposed several broad generalizations for management practice. Yet others, such as Enis and Roering, remain unconvinced that these differences have meaningful strategic implications.[14]

Rather than continue to focus on this broad dichotomy, it seems preferable to offer insights that are more specific to particular types of service marketing problems yet are not confined to a single industry. The classification schemes proposed in this chapter can contribute usefully to management practice in two ways. First, by addressing each of the six questions cited above, marketing managers can obtain a better understanding of the nature of each service product, the types of relationships their service organizations have with customers, the factors underlying any sharp variations in demand, and the characteristics of service delivery systems. This understanding should help them identify how these factors shape marketing problems and opportunities, thereby enabling them to affect the nature of the marketing task. Second, by recognizing which characteristics their own service shares with other services—often in seemingly unrelated industries—managers will learn to look beyond their immediate competitors for new insights into how to resolve the marketing problems that they face.

These classification schemes should also be of value to researchers, to whom they offer an alternative to the broad-brush research approach into services and the industry-by-industry approach. Instead, they suggest a variety of new ways of looking at service businesses, each of which may offer opportunities for focused research efforts. Recognizing that the products of service organizations that have previously been considered as "different" actually face similar problems, or share certain characteristics in common, can yield valuable managerial insights. Innovation in marketing, after all, often reflects a manager's ability to seek out and learn from analogous situations in other contexts.

NOTES

1. See, for instance, the following three readings in this book: G. Lynn Shostack, "Breaking Free from Product Marketing" in Section I; Gary Knisely, "Comparing Marketing Management in Package Goods and Service Organizations" in Section I; and Christopher H. Lovelock, "Why Marketing Management Needs to Be Different for Services" in Section VII.

2. See, for instance, Robert C. Judd (1964), "The Case for Redefining Services," *Journal of Marketing* 28 (January), 59; John M. Rathmell (1966), "What Is Meant by Services?" *Journal of Marketing* 30 (October), 32–36; John E. G. Bateson (1979), "Why We Need Service Marketing," in O. C. Ferrell, S. W Brown, and C. W. Lamb, eds., *Conceptual and Theoretical Developments in Marketing*, Chicago: American Marketing Association, 131–146; and Leonard L. Berry (1980), "Services Marketing Is Different," *Business* (May–June), 24–29 (reprinted in Section I of this book).

3. See, for instance, John A. Czepiel (1980), *Managing Customer Satisfaction in Consumer Service Businesses*, Cambridge, MA: Marketing Science Institute; James H. Donnelly and William R. George, eds. (1981), Marketing of Services, Chicago: American Marketing Association; Pierre Eiglier, Eric Langeard, Christopher H. Lovelock, John E. G. Bateson, and Robert F. Young (1977), *Marketing Consumer Services: New Insights*, Cambridge, MA: Marketing Science Institute; Eric Langeard, John E. G. Bateson, Christopher H. Lovelock, and Pierre Eiglier (1981), *Services Marketing: New Insights from Consumers and Managers*, Cambridge, MA: Marketing Science Institute; and G. Lynn Shostack (1978), "The Service Marketing Frontier," in G. Zaltman and T. Bonoma, eds., *Review of Marketing 1978*, Chicago: American Marketing Association, 373–88.

4. Shelby D. Hunt (1976), *Marketing Theory*, Columbus, OH: Grid.

5. Melvin T. Copeland (1923), "The Relation of Consumers' Buying Habits to Marketing Methods," *Harvard Business Review* 1 (April), 282–89.

6. For a review of previous attempts to classify services, see Christopher H. Lovelock (1980), "Towards a Classification of Services," in C. W. Lamb and P. M. Dunne, (eds.), *Theoretical Developments in Marketing*, Chicago: American Marketing Association, 72–76.

7. Berry, as in Note 2 above.

8. Richard B. Chase, "Where Does the Customer Fit in a Service Operation?" (reprinted in Section VI of this book).

9. Theodore Levitt (1972), "Production Line Approach to Service," *Harvard Business Review* 50 (September–October), 41; and (1976) "The Industrialization of Service," *Harvard Business Review* 54 (September–October), 63–74.

10. W. Earl Sasser, "Match Supply and Demand in Service Industries" (reprinted in Section V of this book).

11. Dan R. E. Thomas (1978), "Strategy Is Different in Service Businesses," *Harvard Business Review* 56 (July–August), 158–65.

12. James A. Rice, Richard S. Slack, and Pamela A. Garside, "Hospitals Can Learn Valuable Marketing Strategies from Hotels" (reprinted in Section II of this book).

13. Langeard et al., as in Note 3 above.

14. Shostack, as in Note 1 above; Berry, as in Note 2 above; Ben M. Enis and Kenneth J. Roering, "Services Marketing: Different Products, Similar Strategy" in J. H. Donnelly and W. R. George (1981), *Marketing of Services*, Chicago: American Marketing Association, 1–4.

---------- *CASES* ----------

RYDER SYSTEM, INC.

A national truck rental firm offers trucks on both long-term leases and short-term rentals, serving both commercial users and consumers. Management recognizes that the needs of these segments are not entirely

This case was prepared by Roberta N. Clarke, assistant professor of marketing at Boston University, and Martin V. Marshall, the Henry R. Byers professor of business administration at the Harvard Business School.

*similar and wonders how best to take this fact into account in design-
ing marketing strategies for future growth.*

"We are a growth company. We are not just a leasing company any more. Most leasing companies have multiples far lower than Ryder's. Wall Street now takes a much broader view of us, particularly because of our spectacular growth." These sentiments were voiced by Ryder System executive Chris Gibbs, presently the director of marketing for Ryder Schools, who was examining the marketing strategies of the various operating subsidiaries of Ryder System, Inc. The discussion focused on the problems of implementing marketing strategies to various market segments, and on what might be done to improve implementation.

COMPANY BACKGROUND

In 1972, Ryder System was composed of a truck leasing and rental division, which the previous year had accounted for 71 percent of Ryder's revenue ($126 million from leasing, $86 million from rental); a specialized transportation division whose contract carriage services for General Motors and the Chrysler Corporation provided 24 percent of Ryder's revenue; a chain of trade and technical schools which brought in 4 percent of the revenue; and a number of other small divisions (1 percent of the revenue). Exhibit 1 contains financial data for 1966 through 1971.

The Ryder System was started in 1933 when James A. Ryder formed the Ryder Trucking Company and built up a small local drayage business in Miami, Florida. In 1938, Mr. Ryder sold a beer distributor on the then new idea of leasing his delivery trucks. Ryder provided his first customer with five units, plus servicing, and from that point on, he saw his company grow to truck leasing sales in excess of $52 million in 1960 and to total sales of $298 million in 1971.

In 1952, Ryder bought the Great Southern Trucking Company, the largest motor freight carrier in the Southeast. He continued to acquire and operate other freight companies, including T.S.C. Motor Freight Lines, Loo-Mac Freight Lines, and Ryder Tank Lines (a bulk commodity carrier). This complex of subsidiaries placed Ryder System among the nation's top ten trucking operations, operating approximately 39,000 tractors, trailers, and trucks in 1972.

Ryder System, Inc., parent of the subsidiary operating companies, was formed in March 1955 with Mr. Ryder as president and chairman of the board. In 1961, Ryder System experienced a loss due to the unprofitable operations of its nontruck and nonleasing businesses, of which it soon divested itself.

In 1967, however, Ryder System again began to diversify by offering short-term one-year leases and contract carriage services. In 1968, it acquired a group of technical and trade schools and entered the proprietary education field. And in July 1968, Ryder entered the one-way consumer rental market. Commercial short-term rental services had always existed, but had not played an important part in the company's operations. According to Chris Gibbs, who had been hired by Ryder System in June 1969 on graduation from Harvard Business School to help implement the marketing plans for Ryder one-way consumer rental, the company went on to commit substantial resources to this new market, and discovered that a great deal more of management time than expected was required to develop and build the new business. Due to the difficulty experienced in entering the one-way consumer truck rental market, Ryder System found the years 1969 and 1970 to be somewhat traumatic. Nevertheless, by 1971, sales from consumer rentals were $31 million.

From 1969 through 1972, Ryder System continued to diversify in accordance with two company policies: (1) enter fields that would help Ryder System to maintain its growth goals of 15 to 20 percent increase in profits and revenues per year and (2) never enter an area that was not complementary to Ryder System's existing divisions. Acquisitions made during this period included a mobile home operation, a warehouse-computer network, and a large truck-stop operation, which they had plans to expand at a fairly rapid pace.[1] Net earnings in 1971 had increased 58.5 percent over the previous year's earnings and were expected to increase at least as much again in 1972.

THE TRUCK LEASING INDUSTRY

Leasing was a means of obtaining the use of equipment without resorting to existing capital or the raising of new capital. Since payment was made from current earnings, advocates of leasing claimed that it placed equipment on a "pay-as-it-earns" basis. Rental was a term of convenience used to differentiate short-term contracts—such as by the hour, day, or week—from long-term leases.

There were several types of truck leasing arrangements. Full-service leasing provided everything except the driver. The contract was tailored to the customer's needs, omitting any functions the latter wished to provide. Thus, the leasing firm offered painting, lettering, washing, lubrication, tires, gasoline and oil, complete maintenance, insurance, license fees, road service, substitute trucks, if needed, and driver safety programs. The lessee gained better truck engineering and release of working capital, avoided maintenance headaches, saved on executive and clerical time, and gained flexibility for emergencies or peak period requirements. Ryder System was the largest full-service leasing and truck (not car) rental company in the industry.

Financial leasing differed from full service in that the customer controlled the vehicles and took care of all fleet costs, maintenance, etc., but the leasing company purchased and licensed the vehicles. Capital leasing differed from financial leasing in that the lessee, at the end of the lease, owned the vehicles; in other words, it was a conditional sales contract.

Less than 6 percent of the 17 million commercial vehicles in the United States in 1971 were in the leasing industry. However, because of rapidly rising transportation costs, industry spokesmen contended that primary demand for leasing, particularly for full-service leasing, was growing and that the proportion of leased commercial vehicles was rising.

Because they were buying vehicles, fuel, and other supplies in huge quantities, full-service leasing firms believed that they were able to provide savings in transportation costs which normally would not be available to the individual truck operator. In 1971, for example, Ryder spent $141,512,220 on fuel, tires, repairs, housing of trucks, and other truck-related costs, in order to maintain its fleet of 17,000 full-service leased vehicles, plus an additional 20,000 rental vehicles for which it provided maintenance at 370 company-owned and operated locations throughout the United States and Canada.

Ryder's Competition

A number of transportation modes other than trucking represented indirect competition for Ryder; each, however, had its disadvantages. Railroads, for example, were less dependable and air freight more expensive than trucking, so that other leasing companies were Ryder's primary competitors. Competition for local leases—where the truck made short-distance hauls, remained within a relatively restricted area and could always be serviced at the same Ryder maintenance center—was stiff, with Hertz, Avis, and many small Mom-and-Pop operations as prime contenders.

There was far less competition, on the other hand, for over-the-road or long-distance haul leases. This was the market in which Ryder did most of its leasing and which it felt best prepared to serve. Ryder System believed it had a competitive edge over the other large leasing firms (Saunders, Hertz, Avis, Leaseway, Rollins, Pepsico) because of two factors which characterized many of their competitors: franchised maintenance/service outlets and geographically limited outlets.

Chris Gibbs explained why he believed that company-owned operations, such as Ryder's, were superior to the franchised operations and outlets characteristic of some of the competition.

> We have company policies that are standardized throughout the country. Franchised dealers are independent businessmen operating under a corporate trademark. They are not dependent on each other around the country from a policy standpoint—as are our dealers—because they are all individual companies. So the level of attention and consistency of service varies much more than when you have control of your own people and facilities. We believe that franchised dealers tend to provide poorer service.

> It is judgmental, really; it is the attitude of your customers toward a Hertz versus a Ryder, when they have had actual experience leasing from us. Ryder has had far greater growth than Hertz or Avis in leasing. This must be the result of successful operations over the years. We feel that company control has contributed to our growth more than if we had gone the franchise route.

The second factor which Ryder executives believed gave Ryder System a competitive edge was its widespread geographical representation, in the form of 370 truck service centers distributed throughout the U.S. and Canada (Exhibit 2). Because of its extensive national network of service outlets, which one Ryder representative stated was superior to any service network offered by the competition, Ryder lessees were relatively unlimited in the areas to which they could go and still expect service. As one of Ryder's advertising slogans said: "You're never more than a 10¢ phone call from the nearest Ryder location."

National Network

This national network of service outlets, or the interbranch system, as it was called by most Ryder people, was considered unique in that it created a common dependency of the 370 branches upon each other for their over-the-road accounts. Said Gibbs: "Over-the-road tractors that operate in more than one location

account for 70 percent or more of our revenue from leasing in Ryder Truck Rental. That is our special niche in the market; we have that network for interdistrict traveling."

Under this system, Branch A would rely totally on Branch B to provide maintenance and servicing when Branch A's (leased) truck was in Branch B's district. For example, if a truck, leased in upstate New York and traveling to Oregon broke down in Des Moines, Iowa, that truck would receive first priority in repairs and service from the Des Moines branch. It was a strictly enforced company policy that first priority should be given to other branches' vehicles. Thus, any maintenance or repair problem, no matter where in the United States, would not detain a Ryder truck more than a few hours; if a truck could not be repaired within a few hours, a new truck would be provided so as to avoid lengthy delays. Therefore, the truck leased in upstate New York could expect the same immediate service in Iowa—or in Michigan, Montana, or Oregon—that it received in its home location of upstate New York. The servicing branch (Des Moines, in this case) would be fully reimbursed for labor and given a markup on fuel and parts, all of which was charged to the branch whose truck it was (upstate New York).

Lease Customer Profile

Mr. Gibbs provided a generalized profile of a Ryder leasing customer:

> Our customer does not lease because he needs the capital or because he cannot afford to buy. He must have a good Dun and Bradstreet rating; we want to know that he can meet our payments. One-seventh of the *Fortune* 500 lease from Ryder, although no one account produces greater than 2 percent of Ryder's leasing and rental revenue. Our customer recognizes the complexity of running a trucking system. He says: "Trucking is a necessary evil of my business. I can depend on Ryder to keep my trucks running." He is someone who has a hard enough time finding competent professionals in his primary business, let alone in a different industry—transportation. He sees the ineffi-

ciencies of running his own transportation system.

Ryder's leasing customers varied from small local businesses with limited transportation needs to large, national, multiplant corporations with complex transportation and distribution systems. Although a greater proportion of Ryder's leasing business was coming from national or geographically dispersed companies rather than from local businesses, Ryder's average lease account still called for between two and ten tractor-trailers.[2] That is, a single plant of a national multiplant company generally required much the same number of tractor-trailers as a local small business.

National Accounts

While the desirability of local lease accounts, on which Ryder had originally built its business, was rarely a topic of discussion, the attractiveness of national accounts was frequently discussed. The company believed that it would have to handle an increasing number of national accounts in order to stay abreast of the trend toward larger, interdistrict accounts; small businesses were expanding into new markets, big companies were getting bigger, and the feeling at Ryder was that if it did not fill the demand, someone else would. Gibbs observed,

> These very large companies need professional advice, need to look at their total transportation and distribution system. Therefore, in 1970, we formed a consulting group that advises large companies on their transportation needs. The consulting group does not always recommend using Ryder, but when it does, it sells to these companies on a corporate level and coordinates a national transportation plan because a Ryder district account manager is not equipped to analyze a national account's total transportation needs. Additionally, a national account requires the coordination of many of our district facilities, which many of our district account managers are not prepared to oversee.

The district managers preferred to have a one-district (local) contract rather than an interdistrict contract, because they had better control over the contract (including the price set for the services specified by the contract) if they were handling it alone. The loss of a one-district contract was also less damaging to the company than the loss of a regional or national one. If one district manager was inattentive to an interdistrict contract, it could affect the other districts involved in that contract; managing these relationships could therefore become quite difficult.

Bill Denight, regional manager of Ryder's largest region (New England and New York State, excluding New York City) said that he and many other district and regional managers were extremely uncomfortable with the way in which national accounts had been administered by Ryder in the past.

> The handling of national accounts is finally beginning to change. It used to be thought by the salespeople that it was highly important to "have the image," to lease to the big companies. The national sales office would dance on buttercups for a national account; show us one hundred trucks and we would become outright prostitutes.

Although Ryder was eager to obtain national accounts, it accepted no account that did not meet the minimum profit requirements of Ryder overall. The theory was that Ryder would take a little less profit in one area of the country and make it up in another in order to get a national contract. However, many districts were not happy with this arrangement, not only because certain districts had higher minimum profit requirements than did Ryder overall, but also because local operating conditions of customers' fleets were not always adequately analyzed. These districts had found that national accounts could dilute their profitability, which determined bonuses such as cash and stock options. Because they could lessen a district's control over profits and diminish profitability itself, national accounts were sometimes viewed as a direct threat to bonus potential.

In the past, when Ryder's corporate office in Miami was contacted by a prospective national account, the office would ask the districts to complete rate sheets such as shown in Exhibit 3. In order not to have to take on a national account, which they feared might be less profitable than their local accounts, the districts would often adjust their rates too high. Said Bill Denight,

> We have gotten away from abuses such as these in the field and in Miami. National deals used to be made on the customer's terms. In the future, they will be made on our terms. A national account is now handled at the individual district location, and a district has the option to refuse acceptance or to drop its part of the contract with a national account.

Ryder Lease Contract Maintenance and Sales Activities

"We spend at least 75 percent of our time," stated Denight, "with existing accounts, due to problems of poor service, to our screwing up." He continued,

> We try to train our account managers not to do too much hand-holding with our existing accounts, for we would rather have them go out and sell. Our best source for new business, however, is existing accounts who want to add new trucks to their leases, so we want to keep our present customers happy, happy enough to expand their leases. For small companies with little growth potential, we aim for a minimum of hand-holding. We hope that we shall have as little contact with this type of customer as possible. The personal relationships that we form with small businesses, however, are very similar to those we form with the local representatives of our national accounts.
>
> Once a contract is signed, a customer is brought in and introduced to those people with whom he will be having contact: the service manager, the office manager (for matters of billing), the safety supervisor (in regard to accidents), and the account manager (for generally poor service). We do not want the account manager to waste his time on a problem that is

supposed to be handled by someone else nor do we want the customer to spin his wheels when he has a problem. The customer is introduced to these guys so he knows who to call for what.[3]

Ryder took a number of steps to generate new customers. When entering a new city, numerous cold calls were made to officers of prospective companies, since the decision maker on a lease was usually a top executive. Ryder corporate offices, meantime, undertook direct mail, promotional, and advertising campaigns targeted at top management.

According to one district manager, "The biggest part of our business calls us and requests to see us." An account manager, sent in response to a customer request, would spell out the services provided by Ryder. If the customer were still interested, the account manager would make a proposal stating costs and services. If this met with approval, the customer would sign a contract specifying the mutual obligations of both parties and detailing all financial aspects. Once the customer's financial statements, banking references, and company drivers had been approved by Ryder, then the lease agreement was completed and the leased units were delivered to the customer. From that day on, the vehicle was in service.

Gibbs explained that the hardest people to propose a lease to were those who knew the least about their transportation costs. "You have to educate them to understand their present costs before they can talk about future leasing costs," Gibbs stated. Because of the need to educate a prospect and draw up a specific transportation plan, it took an average of nine months from initial contact to when revenue was generated by the lease.

Other sources for new leases were companies which frequently rented from Ryder; because leasing rates were substantially lower than renting rates for the equivalent unit of time, it was sometimes less costly for a frequent renter to enter into a lease agreement rather than to rent a truck on many separate occasions. Another source was companies which had made use of the Ryder tractor-trailer pool. The pool came into existence in 1970 because many customers had temporary seasonal demands for tractor-trailers. The districts were reluctant to purchase a large number of these vehicles when demand was likely to last only a short period of time, because they were partially evaluated on return-on-assets. To meet this seasonal demand, Ryder formed a tractor-trailer pool. In 1971, it had produced $14 million in revenues. The 750 tractors and 1,300 trailers in the pool were considered corporate assets and were rented wholesale to the districts. The pool often resulted in new customers because it provided a trial period to test Ryder's vehicles and maintenance service.

Lease Contract Terminations

Estimates of the proportion of lease contracts terminated annually varied from 25 to 40 percent. According to Bill Denight, the number of leases terminated by Ryder roughly equaled the number terminated by customers. Reasons for termination were many. A customer could have been promised more service than was being delivered, or might have been provided with the wrong equipment (Ryder would replace it if the customer did not first break the contract). A customer might also terminate because of perceived poor service or because a competitor offered a lower rate. For its part, Ryder would terminate leases on the basis of a bad driver accident record, poor treatment of equipment by drivers and freight loaders, or a customer's failure to make lease payments.

Another possible cause of broken contracts was high turnover of account executives, resulting in poor and disrupted communications between Ryder and its customers. The caliber of management which Ryder sought was high and therefore very scarce. Said Gibbs,

> Management scarcity is a great constraint on Ryder's growth. Because the markets we should be in are opening up faster than we can find competent new managers, we cannot give account and branch managers enough experience before they are made district managers. And by promoting these managers so frequently, we are forced to upset the relationship between the lessee and the Ryder representative with whom the lessee has been dealing.

Leasing Advertising and Promotion

Ryder advertised in business-oriented magazines, such as *Business Week*, *Wall Street Journal*, and *Forbes*, and at trade shows, such as those of the American Trucking Association and the Postal Forum. In 1972, Ryder also bought 8 to 10 spots on National Football League television, which represented a considerable outlay. The company had achieved much success recently with direct mail followed by presentations to chief executive officers of companies which used trucks in their operations. Gibbs attributed 80 percent of Ryder's leasing business directly to its own sales development efforts.

THE TRUCK RENTAL INDUSTRY

Truck rentals fell into two categories: commercial and consumer. These two categories differed considerably. Consumer or one-way rentals tended to be seasonal, with the vast majority taking place between June and September. Most consumer rentals were one-way, with the renter picking up the truck in one location and dropping it off in another. Commercial rentals, on the other hand, were generally made between September and June, and tended to be local, with vehicles being picked up and dropped off at the same location.

Competition also differed for the two types of rentals. Occasional renters, who were usually noncommercial customers, perceived a rented truck as an undifferentiated product. They were mainly interested in convenience, accessibility of the rent-a-truck location, price, available vehicle sizes, and destinations allowed; they were unlikely to view service as a selling point. By contrast, local commercial renters were likely to rent more frequently, to better recognize—and desire—service and reliability, and to be somewhat less price sensitive.

Industrywide, the total number of vehicles available for the commercial and one-way markets was 50,000 to 60,000. U-Haul was the industry leader in both these markets; it had three times as many dealers (6,000) and trucks (33,000) as Ryder System, the number two in the industry. U-Haul was more accessible all over the United States, and thus allowed one-way renters a greater choice of destination drop-off locations. Following U-Haul and Ryder in terms of share of the consumer rental market were Easy-Haul and Hertz. Competitors in the commercial market included the above four companies plus thousands of Mom-and-Pop operations. The consumer fleet renters also faced competition from professional movers. Much of the public had not yet been educated to the advantages of do-it-yourself moving and used moving firms in spite of their greater cost, inconvenience, damage rates, and delays.

Ryder Commercial Rental

Ryder district managers were, and always had been, asset-responsible for their commercial local fleet, which produced 64 percent of the rental revenue. There had recently been great growth in Ryder's commercial fleet; it had lost money for a number of years, but after Ryder entered the consumer rental market, management saw the need for greater truck utilization and began a rental blitz. They would obtain a list of truck users in a given area and over a three-day period make hundreds of cold calls to inform them about Ryder rental. This sales effort had been phenomenally successful, and Ryder management attributed most of the success to personal selling. Because commercial rentals were generally sold to males, advertising spots were bought on televised Monday night football games. Direct mail was also used, but personal selling allowed Ryder to rifle in on the decision maker, who, in commercial rental, was often the driver.

Ryder Consumer Rental

Perceiving a demand for one-way truck rentals, Ryder created its consumer rental service in July 1968. By January 1969, the consumer fleet had 1,300 trucks in service and had committed itself to have 7,600 trucks in service by the following May, an investment of $40 million. By 1972 the fleet comprised 11,000 trucks with a value of $60 million.

When the consumer fleet first came into existence, the districts were not made asset-responsible for the operating costs of the fleet, because the high start-up cost of entering this new market would reflect unfairly on the districts' profit and loss statements. Due to the continual shortage of Ryder mechanics to service the trucks for which they were asset-responsible (these being the leased and commercial rental trucks), district managers found it more desirable to send consumer rental trucks to outside service stations for repairs. Even though this increased the costs greatly, the consumer rental costs did not impact upon their district's performance as evaluated by Ryder headquarters.

To combat this wholesale farming out of consumer truck repairs to non-Ryder outlets, Ryder assigned each district a bogey inventory (potential to rent). Each district was then assessed a fixed charge based upon the bogey inventory and a variable charge based on the actual number of vehicles present. The districts were then evaluted on the basis of the consumer fleet margin (revenue from consumer fleet less variable operating costs = the money remaining to cover fixed costs and profits).

One of Ryder's major marketing efforts for consumer truck rentals was directed at creating awareness that Ryder rented trucks of all sizes. Selected markets were hit with newspaper and television advertising. Ryder also tried to create awareness by getting as many Ryder rental trucks out on the road as possible so that people would see the Ryder name on the vehicles. However, the Yellow Pages, of which Ryder was the second largest user in the industry, was considered to be the most important form of consumer advertising. It was estimated that 70 percent of Ryder's rental inquiries resulted from advertisements in the Yellow Pages.

Flow and Utilization Problems

Much management time had been spent trying to solve the questions raised by the consumer fleet. One question was how to control the flow. If too many trucks were dropped off in Great Falls, Montana, such that more trucks were there than were likely to be rented, a utilization problem was created. An under-utilized truck did not pay its own way. Ryder's answer to this problem, stated Gibbs, was to "close down the dealer, or exclude him from the dealer list—so that customers don't know that they can drop off a truck in Great Falls, Montana—or to add a surcharge to cover the cost of transferring the vehicle to a better dealer. Or charge so much that the customer goes to U-Haul. We won't lose him as a potential customer because, the next time, he will be shopping for price."

Greater utilization resulted in a greater need for repairs. When there was a shortage of Ryder mechanics (as there usually was), the consumer rental truck was always the vehicle to be sent to non-Ryder people for servicing, because the consumer fleets were the only vehicles for which the district was not totally asset-responsible. Non-Ryder servicing resulted in higher operating costs, meaning that greater utilization sometimes resulted in proportionately even greater operating costs.

Increased utilization also brought about higher insurance costs, because the incidence of physical damage and liability increased. The more consumer trucks rented, the less selective Ryder could be about drivers, and thus the less qualified were the drivers. The total result was a greater need for repairs, which resulted in more downtime for trucks. Ryder attempted to correct some of these problems by excluding overhead damage from the insurance policy, by collecting the $100 deductible written into the insurance contract (a practice not rigorously followed previously), by improving driver selection, and by telling the drivers where trucks could not be driven.

One further question posed was how to capture the one-way demand without depleting a dealer's inventory of rental trucks. If a consumer rented a truck for a one-way trip, the dealer would receive the revenue for that one trip, but would accrue no more revenue from that truck, as it was no longer there to rent. When trucks were in short supply, dealers sometimes turned down one-way requests so as not to lose the truck. To compound matters, one-way rentals were often very profitable for Ryder. For instance, if 20 percent of the rentals were one-way, they might contribute as much as 50 percent of the total rental revenue. Ryder sought to deal with this problem by setting up a central reservations agency in each district which would have full knowledge of how many trucks were at which dealers. Making the decision on rentals at central reservations meant that the dealer was eliminated from the decision-making process. With the advent of central reservations, which received top priority listing, most individual dealers were no longer listed in the Yellow Pages.

Non-Ryder Dealers

Although the districts were responsible for the marketing and operating costs of the consumer rental fleet, they distributed many consumer trucks through such non-Ryder outlets as gas stations, car rental offices, and rental yards, which rented other types of equipment. These non-Ryder dealers received 16.5 percent of gross rental revenues, 13.25 percent of which was a regular commission, the remaining 3.25 percent being paid to the dealership if it reported regularly, on time, with the money owed to Ryder. The commission was paid to these dealers to keep the vehicle clean and secure, to know the administrative requirements, and to carry on point-of-sale promotion. Dealers also checked the vehicles in and out, checked the conditions of the trucks, and did minor maintenance.

Ryder management felt that it was necessary to have non-Ryder dealers because they believed most customers would not travel more than 3 miles to rent a truck, so that it was imperative to have many dealers in order not to make accessibility a problem.

Dealer turnover was about 25 percent per year; about half of this number were terminated by Ryder for failure to live up to company standards. Ryder management also decided that they could not list any but the most established dealers in the Yellow Pages, because most dealers were not good salesmen and did not provide the prospective customer with a good initial contact with Ryder. Therefore, central reservations was set up. A customer who called now spoke to a Ryder-trained person rather than to a high-school–aged gas station attendant who frequently did not know if that station rented Ryder trucks, let alone what the rates were and where to find the keys.

Commenting on the central reservation system, Denight remarked,

> Central reservations protects our image; it gives us the ability to direct the customer to the location where we want him and to give him good information (pricing changes, availability of truck sizes). We try to push our Ryder-owned locations first so that we do not have to pay 16.5 percent to the non-Ryder dealer. We have closed approximately 8,000 dealers since 1968. We did not police the dealers in the beginning; they stole money from us and were rude to our customers. A big dealer (ten or more trucks) does not steal because he is making too much money legitimately to make the risk of stealing worth it. We want dealers but we want good dealers.

Referring to the dealers, another Ryder executive familiar with the rental operation stated,

> It is inconsistent with company policy to pay someone who does not even break even, but we do. Isn't there some way, as we build a stronger dealer organization, to motivate dealers to break even? To evaluate them on a minimum performance standard? We would like to eliminate the small truck dealers (who own one to two trucks) with little potential, but still want enough dealers to be able to compete with U-Haul.

DISCUSSION OF LEASE VERSUS RENTAL

When asked whether Ryder management might ever consider separating rental and leasing into two divisions, Gibbs responded,

> No, it really does not make sense to separate them since we service them in the same facilities, and all our office administration is geared up to handle both lease and rental. The difference between them is only a matter of the length of time of use of the vehicle.
>
> In a lease, you work out a price to a customer based on the estimated miles that the vehicle is going to operate and your price has profit built into it. In rental, you never know from one day to the next who and how many are going to use your truck. You estimate the utilization you are going to get out of the vehicle, build in your profit, and work to achieve that utilization or better. In leasing, we have a certainty of income flow and we price accordingly. In rental the customer must pay the price of uncertainty—of not knowing day in and day out who is going to rent the truck. Therefore, if we bought two equal tractors for $25,000, it would cost significantly more to rent it than to lease it.
>
> Our whole theme is that we rent trucks—for six hours, one week, five weeks, one year, or three years. It just depends upon how the customer wants to use the vehicle.

NOTES

1. Truck stops are restaurant-hotel-maintenance-retail shop complexes designed for drivers on long hauls. All Ryder truck stop services could be signed for by the driver of a Ryder-leased truck, thus relieving the driver of the need to carry large amounts of money on long hauls.

2. Ryder leased three types of vehicles: (1) trucks, in which the power and cargo carrying units were all one unit; (2) tractors (power units only); and (3) trailers (cargo carrying units only). Tractors and trailers tended to be leased together.

3. See Exhibit 4 for details of district management responsibilties.

EXHIBIT 1

Financial Summary 1966–1971

(Dollar Amounts in Thousands Except per Share Figures)

	1971	1970	1969	1968	1967	1966
RESULTS FOR YEAR						
Revenue from						
Vehicle leasing and services	$212,615	166,698	133,222	101,775	86,898	76,578
Specialized motor transportation	70,787	43,179	17,074	7,102		
Technical and trade schools	10,949	7,330	3,768			
Other	4,198	3,784	2,715	1,550	1,242	880
Total	$298,549	220,991	156,779	110,427	88,140	77,458
Income before interest and taxes	$ 38,655	28,121	23,662	14,938	9,968	8,326
as % of revenue	12.9	12.7	15.1	13.5	11.3	10.7
as % of average capital employed	13.7	11.6	13.9	14.3	11.4	10.6
Interest charges	$ 15,214	14,672	9,615	4,875	3,859	3,443
Income taxes:						
Current	$ 2,836	507	3,528	2,084	239	462
Deferred (includes def. inv. tax credits)	8,084	5,038	1,872	1,590	1,995	1,472
Total	$ 10,920	5,545	5,400	3,674	2,234	1,934
Net earnings	$ 12,521	7,904	8,647	6,389	3,875	2,949
as % of average tangible share-holders' equity	21.7	16.5	29.1	25.9	17.6	15.4
Earnings per common share:						
Primary	$ 2.23	1.40	1.81	1.42	1.00	.80
Fully diluted	$ 1.99	1.34	1.66	1.28	.88	
Dividends—common and preferred	$ 3,507	3,384	2,344	1,772	1,181	938
Dividends per common share	$ .50	.50	.50	.425	.325	.275
Capital expenditures	$ 99,663	113,910	93,544	59,627	33,687	35,034
Average capital employed	$283,119	242,382	170,554	104,712	87,715	78,269
FINANCIAL POSITION AT YEAR END						
Working capital[1]	$ 31,491	40,905	35,765	15,714[2]	16,371	12,317
Property and equipment—less accumulated depreciation	$247,397	223,258	156,252	108,241	79,610	72,152
Capital employed:						
Debt	$207,055	205,266	152,674	91,644	65,349	60,728
Tangible shareholders' equity	65,402	52,284	34,614	26,278	26,043	21,622
Deferred taxes and inv. tax credits	24,853	16,393	9,646	7,686	6,337	4,151
Total	$297,310	273,943	196,934	125,608	97,729	86,501
Debt as % of capital employed	70	75	78	73	67	70
Shares outstanding						
Common	5,250,067	5,050,851	4,859,969	4,483,810	4,082,254	3,713,886
Preferred A	179,734	186,329				
Preferred B	9,090	9,090				
OTHER DATA						
Vehicles at year end	39,209	37,245	28,896	19,081	15,223	14,849
Employees at year end	7,418	6,373	4,483	3,687	2,360	2,241
Payroll—excluding benefits	$ 61,712	55,913	37,103	24,534	17,840	16,576

[1] Exclusive of equipment obligations due within one year.
[2] Exclusive of short-term financing of $10 million for acquisitions.

EXHIBIT 2

Either the United States has measles or Ryder is showing off its locations again.

What do you do if your phone rings at three o'clock in the morning and one of your truck drivers tells you he's broken down 50 miles outside of Magnolia, Arkansas?

We'll tell you what happens if it's a Ryder-leased truck. You don't get a call at three in the morning.

Ryder gets the call.

See all those spots in this picture? Each one is a Ryder-owned truck service center. Not a franchise or licensee, but a company owned location. And each one has ironclad orders: take care of out-of-town trucks first. So Ryder gets out to your truck fast. And Ryder fixes your truck fast. We don't pass the buck to a local truck dealer who may be booked up four days ahead. We fix that truck ourselves. Or we get you a replacement truck fast. Your load is moving again within four hours or there is such hell raised within the Ryder organization that it reaches right up to the head man. Your trucks roll or our heads roll. (Not shown on this map are another 600 Ryder contract stations where your drivers can charge fuel, oil and even repairs when necessary.)

So if the thought of one of your trucks breaking down at three in the morning makes you feel a little sick, take another look at our spots. Then find out about our road service and all the other advantages of a Ryder full service lease. Call Ryder Truck Rental.

EXHIBIT 3

76

RYDER RATE SHEET

VEHICLE NO. _____

CUSTOMER INFORMATION

LEGAL NAME OF PROSPECT
EXECUTIVE CONTACTED
RADIUS OF OPERATION

	D AND B RATING	ANNUAL MILES	TYPE OF BUSINESS	ADDRESS		GUARANTEED MILES		STOPS PER DAY

INSURANCE LIMITS | DEDUCTIBLE PHYS. DAMAGE | FIXED FUEL COST
INSURANCE COVERED BY
PAST INSURANCE EXPERIENCE

TYPE OF DRIVERS | MANAGEMENT ATTITUDE AFFECTING SAFETY

	YEAR	MAKE	MODEL	W/B	C/A	TYPE AND BODY LENGTH	GEAR RATIO
NO. OF UNITS							

	SIZE	PLY	CHASSIS WEIGHT	BODY WEIGHT	PAYLOAD	GVW	GCW
NO. OF TIRES							

VEHICLE INVESTMENT

DETAILS	USED	DETAILS	NEW	USED
CHASSIS OR TRAILER		BODY		
NET COST		NET COST		
PAINTING		SHELVING		
LETTERING		REPAIRS		
SERVICING CHARGE		SALES TAX		
FIFTH WHEEL		TOTAL		
AUX. FUEL TANK		REFRIGERATION		
MIRRORS		NET COST		
FLARES·FUSEES		REPAIRS		
FIRE EXTINGUISHERS		SALES TAX		
TIRE—B.F.—INV.—MFR.		TOTAL		
SALES TAX		LIFT GATE		
		NET COST		
		REPAIRS		
		SALES TAX		
		TOTAL		
REPAIRS		AMORTIZATION		
TOTAL		NET INVESTMENT		

DEPRECIATION AND SCHEDULE "A" VALUES

		BOOK VALUES				SCHEDULE "A" VALUES				
EQUIPMENT	NET INVESTMENT	RESID. VALUE	AMOUNT TO DEPR.	ANNUAL DEPR.	MOS. OR YRS.	SCH."A" VALUE	RESID VALUE	AMOUNT TO DEPR.	NO. WKS.	WKL'Y DEPR. AMOUNT
NEW — CAB & CHASSIS										
BODY										
OTHER										
TOTALS										
USED — CAB & CHASSIS										
OR BODY										
T/O OTHER										
AMORTIZATION										
TOTALS										

REMARKS

DISTRICT			DATE
UNIT NOS. ASSIGNED			
PREPARED BY		APPROVED BY	DM

RYDER RATE SHEET

NEW VEHICLE INVESTMENT	ANNUAL MILES	TAKEOVER VEHICLE INVESTMENT	VEHICLE NUMBER

ANTICIPATED NEW VEHICLE CONTRACT LIFE

COST PROJECTION

RUNNING COSTS

	COST PER MILE		ANNUAL COST OF FIXED SERVICES	AMOUNT

FUEL
_____ % RYDER
_____ % HOME @ _____ CPG
_____ % INT. DIST. @ _____ CPG
RYDER FUEL CPG _____ ÷ _____ MPG=
_____ % OUTSIDE _____ ÷ _____ MPG=
FUEL TAX: EST. UNRECOVERED CPG _____ ÷ _____ MPG=
TOTAL FUEL COST PER MILE
REFRIGERATION FUEL

FIXED COSTS:
DEPRECIATION
INTEREST (From Table _____ % X _____ Investment)
LICENSE
PERSONAL PROPERTY TAX
HIGHWAY USE TAX (Category _____)
BI & PD INSURANCE
PHYSICAL DAMAGE
REPAINTING AND RELETTERING
TOTAL ANNUAL FIXED COSTS

OIL

MARGIN SECTION

REPAIRS:
LABOR
PARTS
OUTSIDE
REFRIGERATION
TOTAL REPAIRS

DIRECT COSTS:
TOTAL FIXED COSTS
TOTAL RUNNING COSTS
TOTAL DIRECT COSTS
FACTOR FROM MARGIN TABLE
X _____

ADD _____ % TO REPAIR RATE (Used or Takeover)
TIRE REPLACEMENT
WASHING
TOTAL COST PER MILE

ADDITIONAL OVERHEADS:
PLUG-IN SERVICES—REFRIG.
FUEL PERMITS

TOTAL MARGIN REQUIRED
TOTAL FIXED COSTS AND MARGIN

TOTAL ANNUAL RUNNING COST RECAP

ANNUAL MILES X TOTAL COST PER MILE
RUNNING COST SERVICES NOT SOLD:

SUB. _____ % TOTAL FIXED & MARGIN
TOTAL COST OF FIXED SERVICE
COST OF FIXED SERVICES NOT SOLD:

LESS TOTAL
ANNUAL MILES X ADJUSTED COST PER MILE

LESS TOTAL
ADJUSTED COST OF FIXED SERVICES

REVENUE AND MARGIN PROJECTION

RATE SOLD	AMOUNT	REVENUE REQUIRED	AMOUNT

FIXED $ _____ X 52 WEEKS
MILE $ _____ X _____ MILES
HOUR $ _____ X _____ HOURS
OR
GUARANTEED MILES _____ X _____ RATE
EXCESS RATE _____ DEFICIT RATE _____
TOTAL ANNUAL REVENUE SOLD

FIXED $ _____ X 52 WEEKS
MILE $ _____ X _____ MILES
HOUR $ _____ X _____ HOURS
TOTAL ANNUAL REVENUE REQUIRED

REV. SOLD MINUS REV. REQ. = MARGIN VARIANCE (+ OR –) ÷ INVESTMENT = PERCENT VARIANCE (+ OR –) _____ %
TOTAL MARGIN REQUIRED (FROM MARGIN SECTION) ÷ TOT. ANN. REV. REQ. = REQUIRED MARGIN _____ %
MARGIN SOLD (MARGIN VARIANCE PLUS MARGIN REQ.) ÷ TOTAL ANNUAL REV. SOLD = MARGIN SOLD _____ %
FIXED COSTS CONVERTED TO MILE RATE $ _____ ÷ REQUIRED MARGIN % = _____ % OF MARGIN

REPLACEMENT VEHICLE RATE COMPARISON: OLD VEHICLE NO. _____ MODEL & TYPE _____
CURRENT BILLING RATE: $ _____ PER WEEK, $ _____ RATE _____ PER MILE, $ _____ PER HOUR OR
GUARANTEED MILES _____ EXCESS RATE _____ DEFICIT RATE _____

9-1 (4/76)

EXHIBIT 4

Ryder District Organization

District manager					
Rental manager (commercial)	Account manager (leases)	Service manager	Dealer manager (consumer)	Office manager	Safety supervisor
Responsible for return on assets on commercial rental. No bogey inventory. Salary and bonus based on asset return.	Responsible for general servicing of his existing accounts, for return on assets of his existing accounts, and for new lease sales.	Responsible for all servicing and maintenance of Ryder vehicles for which district is asset responsible, for Ryder leased vehicles from other districts and, in some form, for the consumer rental fleet.	Responsible for merchandising effectiveness operating costs, training and opening up of new dealers. Salary and bonus based on revenues/truck-week of his dealers, and on margin.	Essentially the district office controller. Bonus based on district performance.	Oversees insurance and accidents of district's vehicles. Bonus based on district's performance.

KCTS—CHANNEL 9, SEATTLE

The director of programming for an innovative public television station is making selections for the following season's program schedule. He must evaluate findings of an audience poll and other research studies, making trade-offs between audience preferences, financial constraints, and the number of program hours available.

The difference between transmission and broadcasting is that the latter requires an audience. Transmitter operators simply mind their machines. You don't become a broadcaster until you relate to the people in your audience and are concerned about how they respond to your programs.

A PBS executive

"The response has been fantastic!" exclaimed Burnill F. Clark, director of programming and operations at KCTS, as he surveyed the ballots submitted for Channel 9's *Viewers' Choice 1976.* "We've received sacks of mail from members and nonmembers, regular and occasional KCTS/9 viewers, all anxious to state what kind of programs they want to see on television."

This case was prepared by Christopher H. Lovelock, associate professor of business administration at the Harvard Business School, and Lawrence H. Wilkinson, a member of the Harvard MBA Class of 1976.

Channel 9, the Seattle area's major public television station, had developed a strong reputation for its community orientation. Mr. Clark saw the innovative *Viewers' Choice* project, conducted in February 1976, as a way to increase the viewing public's input into programming decisions. He planned to use the ballot responses as one of several inputs when making purchases of program series from the PBS[1] Station Program Cooperative.

Program selection and scheduling, the director indicated, was a complex process involving a great many tradeoffs. He would have to decide how much emphasis to give the viewers' ballots in making his selection.

PUBLIC BROADCASTING IN THE UNITED STATES

In the mid-1970s, the United States was unusual in having a commercially dominated broadcast industry. In some countries—such as Britain and Canada—long-established, state-owned broadcasting corporations financed by receiver license fees or by tax monies faced highly regulated commercial competitors. But in most countries the state broadcasting system had a monopoly.

Public broadcasting in the United States presented a very different picture. Although noncommercial broadcasters had operated in some numbers since the first "sign-on," nationally organized public broadcasting was a relative newcomer. The federal government provided partial funding but did not own or operate any facilities.

Historically, noncommercial TV in the United States had been termed "educational television" regardless of its purpose. Until the 1960s there was no networking, and most programming was locally produced. In 1958, the federal government became involved in funding, awarding substantial grants for research and experiments in educational TV. In 1962, it authorized $32 million for construction of educational stations in the form of 50–50 matching grants against funds provided by state and local sources. That same year, the National Educational Television and Radio Center (NET) established a national program service during prime-time evening hours for all 57 existing stations.

After intensive study, the presidentially appointed Carnegie Commission on Educational Television concluded in 1967,

A well-financed and well-directed educational television system substantially larger and far more pervasive and effective . . . must be brought into being if the full needs of the American public are to be served.

The report distinguished two types of noncommercial operations, "public" and "instructional," centering its recommendations on the former. It proposed establishment of a federally financed Corporation for Public Broadcasting (CPB) to facilitate both local and national programming, encourage technical and personnel development, and provide network interconnection.

In November 1967, Congress passed the Public Broadcasting Act, establishing CPB as an independent, nonprofit corporation funded by yearly Congressional appropriations. CPB established a national TV land line interconnection and created the Public Broadcasting Service (PBS) to manage this distribution system. National Public Radio was formed in 1970 on similar lines. PBS took responsibility for running the interconnection and also for scheduling and coordinating national programming, subject to joint review with CPB. It also provided other support services, including legislative lobbying. In 1975 CPB provided some 40 percent of PBS's $25 million budget.

The total budget for public broadcasting in the U.S. in 1975 was $353 million. Funding came from federal, state, and local appropriations, plus foundation grants and corporate and individual donations. The Ford Foundation's decision to phase out its longstanding grants to public TV, together with the budgetary constraints facing local school boards, emphasized the need for station fundraising. Corporate funding was often sought for underwriting specific programs (". . . made possible by a grant from Mobil Oil"), while many stations pursued an aggressive and frequently criticized policy of on-air fund-raising.

By late 1975, 26 percent of the 962 television stations on the air in the U.S. and 31 percent of the 2,571 FM radio stations were operating noncommercially. About 40 percent of the TV stations transmitted on VHF (Channels 2–13), where the commercial network stations were generally located; the balance transmitted on UHF (Channels 14–38), which was often difficult to receive, although increasing use of cable TV was helping to resolve this problem. It was estimated that public TV signals reached about 84 percent of the nation's homes.

There were four types of licensees—community-supported (26 percent of total), colleges and universities (34 percent), state agencies (17 percent), and public school systems (12 percent). Community stations tended to be quite audience conscious, reflecting both their community governance and their dependence on viewer donations for financial support. Some of the stations licensed to colleges and universities had adopted a broader community mandate and reflected that in their operations policies and fundraising activities. Seattle's KCTS was such a station.

THE SEATTLE AREA

Seattle, seat of King County and the largest city in the Pacific Northwest, had a metropolitan population of some 1.4 million in 1976, making it the twentieth largest metro area in the United States. The nonwhite population represented about 14.4 percent of the total, comprising Blacks, Chicanos, American Indians, and Asian-Americans of Chinese and Japanese descent.

An attractive city, Seattle was built on seven hills between Puget Sound on the west and some large, freshwater lakes on the east. Travel around the area afforded striking views of both mountains and shorelines; on a clear day, one could see the snow-capped summit of Mount Rainier over 50 miles away. Local residents enjoyed excellent fishing and sailing year-round, and Seattle boasted the highest per capita boat ownership of any major city in the country. Water skiing was invented there, and snow skiing was a popular winter sport, with good slopes as close as one hour's drive from the city.

The city had achieved international prominence with its 1962 World's Fair. One legacy was the Seattle Center, a 74-acre convention and family entertainment center, dominated by the 607-foot Space Needle and connected to the downtown area by monorail service.

By 1976, the region's economy was recovering from a prolonged slump in the aerospace industry, which had caused high local unemployment from 1969 to 1972. Economic diversification had been aided by Seattle's excellent maritime location and relative proximity to Alaskan oil development and Far East ports.

Seattle was home to a number of arts organizations, including the Seattle Symphony Orchestra, Seattle Opera Association, Seattle Repertory Theatre, Seattle Art Museum, and ACT Theatre. College and amateur groups provided a variety of other cultural offerings.

Spectator sports in the area included major league baseball, soccer, football, and horse racing. The opening of the huge Kingdome (King County domed stadium) in early 1976 had provided a new site for large spectator events.

Seattle Area Media

Greater Seattle was well served by print and broadcast media. The city had two major dailies, the *Seattle Times* (circulation 219,000) and the *Seattle Post-Intelligencer* (circulation 183,000), as well as numerous local papers and periodical magazines. There were 21 AM radio stations and 19 FM radio stations on the air in the region, including four public FM stations.

Viewers had a good choice of television stations, although reception was uncertain in some locations. Eight stations were broadcasting in the Seattle-Tacoma television market in early 1976, six on VHF and two on UHF. According to the 1975 edition of *Broadcasting Yearbook*, there were 768,400 TV households in the "Area of Dominant Influence," 606,000 of these being located in King County and in adjoining Pierce and Snohomish Counties.

The Seattle-Tacoma TV market was dominated by the three commercial network affiliates operating in Seattle. The oldest station in the area was an NBC affiliate, KING-TV (Channel 5), which had begun operation through an earlier license in 1948. The owners, King Broadcasting Co., also operated stations in Spokane and Portland. KOMO-TV, an ABC affiliate, dated from 1953 and was operated on Channel 4 by a company which also owned a station in Portland. The CBS affiliate, on the air since 1958, was KIRO-TV (Channel 7). This station was a subsidiary of the Bonneville International Corporation, owned by the Mormon Church, which administered numerous other broadcast properties. The fourth commercial station in this market was KSTW (Channel 11) in Tacoma, an "independent" owned by the Oklahoma Publishing Company.

In addition to KCTS, there were three public TV stations in the Seattle-Tacoma area. Two of these were licensed to the Clover Park School District in Lakewood Center, south of Tacoma. Clover Park had operated a UHF station, KPEC-TV (Channel 56), for a number of years; recently it had also acquired the license for Channel 13, an independent commercial station, redesignated KCPQ. Although this station's resources were limited, Channel 13 had a strong signal and was seen as a potential competitor by Channel 9 management. Another UHF station, KTPS (Channel 62), was licensed to a Tacoma school district and specialized in educational programming.

THE DEVELOPMENT OF KCTS

KCTS was licensed to the University of Washington, a state institution, and transmitted a powerful signal on Channel 9. Aided by microwave links and cable systems, its signal extended from the Oregon border in the south up through British Columbia in the north, and from the Cascades in the east to the Pacific Ocean (Exhibit 1). KCTS had an authorized power of 275 kw visual and 55 kw aural, exceeding that of two of the three commercial TV network affiliates in Seattle. Although reception was generally good, Seattle's hilly terrain made it difficult to view KCTS transmissions from some parts of the city.

In many respects, KCTS epitomized the evolution of public television over the years. From a low budget, local educational outlet, Channel 9 had developed into a technically sophisticated station with a high community profile, broadcasting more national than local material, and ambitious to see its own productions achieve nationwide distribution.

KCTS History, 1954 to 1972

KCTS first went on the air in December 1954 and was the eighth noncommercial television station to begin broadcasting in the United States. Its initial objective was to provide educational broadcasting for the schools of Seattle and surrounding King County. The station's offices and studios were housed by the University of Washington, while monetary support came initially from public schools and institutions of higher education.

During its early years, Channel 9 employed a dozen staff members—all state employees—and broadcast 20 hours weekly, Monday through Friday. Most of the programs were locally produced, although some films were obtained from outside agencies. Daytime instructional programming for use by teachers was combined with limited evening broadcasts of "telecourses" and community-oriented programs.

In 1962, NET's establishment of national program service during prime evening time increased KCTS's programming hours and broadened the range of programs available. A more powerful transmitter improved Channel 9's geographic coverage, as did the growth of cable and microwave links. In 1969, the PBS interconnect further extended the station's programming capabilities. Despite these improvements, Channel 9 operated only on weekdays and was perceived by most people as a local educational station.

New Management

In 1972, Channel 9's first station manager retired after 17 years. Later characterized by a journalist as a "quiet, don't-rock-the-boat sort of man who tended to think of educational TV as dealing with academic education," this individual had consistently maintained a low personal profile.

His successor, who joined the station in July 1972, was entirely different. Dr. Richard J. Meyer, then aged 38, came to KCTS from WNET in New York, one of the best known public TV stations in the country, where he had been a producer and vice-president.

Meyer, portrayed by a local journalist as "bearded, curly haired, exuberant, and energetic," inherited what some described as "a stodgy and stuffy old educational television station, the channel nobody watched [unless they wanted] to sit through awful panel discussions featuring erudite but inarticulate professors or watch [someone] explain the intricacies of hemstitching under water."[2]

When Meyer arrived in Seattle, he immediately set about making changes, cancelling much of Channel 9's local programming, making staff changes and seeking the active involvement of the local community.

His credo, he said, was to involve public television in all areas of contemporary life: "The public is what public TV is really all about and that is why I like it." Commenting on his ambitions for the station, he observed,

> The background of Channel 9 is fascinating because it was one of the first public TV stations in the nation, starting out on a par with WNET in New York, WGBH in Boston, and KQED in San Francisco. But while they progressed, Channel 9 stayed just about the same. My goal is to try to make it equal again. I would like to make Channel 9 one of the nation's flagship stations for public broadcasting.

Initiating an aggressive fund-raising policy in fall 1972, he took the station from zero to 25,000 supporters in less than two years. By the end of 1975, KCTS boasted some 30,000 individuals and families in Washington State and British Columbia who gave annually towards the station's operating expenses. About one-third of these "members" were Canadian. On average, 80 percent of current members renewed again the following year.

The staff also grew rapidly as new technical and managerial expertise was added. In September 1975, many of them were rehoused in another building owned by the University, freeing up additional production space at the studios. By early 1976, KCTS employed a staff of 50.

The general manager hoped to give KCTS the capacity to produce programs of sufficient quality and caliber that the station could market them nationally through PBS. "We're not likely to receive any production grants," he said, "until we have the equipment that will allow us to do a first rate job. We already have the talent."

Color transmissions of films and slides started in December 1973, and in late 1975, KCTS began purchasing the new equipment long coveted by Dr. Meyer. This included state-of-the-art color cameras and recorders, a mobile unit and microwave to permit live outside telecasts, plus major improvements in studio lighting and audio systems. Meyer saw these improvements as central to his goals of technical excellence, local programming which reflected Seattle's needs and problems, and development of major production capabilities. An 18-month installation period was anticipated. Financing came from public contributions, a capital grant from the University, and matching federal funds.

ORGANIZATION AND FINANCING

The upper levels of the KCTS organization reflected the station's dual identity as both a university and community station. Since the license was held by the University of Washington, all legal authority and responsibility rested with this institution through its vice-president for university relations.

As a practical matter, executive authority rested with a 30-member "Advisory Board." Ten of these individuals represented institutions providing financial support to the station, while the remaining 20 were drawn from the community at large. In the language of its by-laws,

> The present board is charged to make recommendations and to advise on matters relating to finance, development, ascertainment, and education.

These by-laws specifically excluded programming from the board's domain.

Station Management

After Meyer was hired as general manager, he initiated a reorganization of the station's management, upgrading the position of director of programming and adding a director of development. Exhibit 2 shows a partial organization chart, reflecting a further reorganization in early 1976 when the director of programming, Burnill F. Clark, assumed additional responsibilities in operations and was named assistant general manager.

Clark had joined KCTS in May 1975 after ten years' experience with Nebraska Educational Television, a state network, where his most recent position had been assistant network program manager. At Channel 9, he handled local program conceptualization and planning, program selection and scheduling, as well as overseeing production and studio operations. He also worked closely with the station's research director.

The development director, Hope S. Green, had first come to KCTS in 1974, after six years at WGBH in Boston. She headed up fundraising activities for Channel 9; these included on-the-air and mail membership solicitation, foundation and government development, and corporate underwriting. Green also coordinated the activities of Channel 9's volunteer group.

Other senior staff members at Channel 9 who reported to the general manager included the directors of administration, engineering, and community involvement.

Financial Matters

Funding for KCTS had historically come from public school districts and from the University of Washington. Beginning in 1972, fundraising had been directed toward the community at large.

Public contributions had jumped from $215,000 in 1972–1973 to a projected $600,000 in the current year. From 1974 onwards, efforts had also been made to attract local underwriting for specific programs. Four local firms donated $43,000 in 1974–1975, and in 1975–1976 seven firms, including the telephone company, a local restaurant, a department store, a regional oil company, and the *Seattle Post-Intelligencer* had collectively donated almost $70,000 to underwrite programs on Channel 9. Exhibit 3 traces the growth and changing composition of KCTS's operating income and expenditures from 1970–1971 through 1975–1976.

The FY 1976 budget projected an annual deficit of almost $360,000,[3] as compared with a $178,000 surplus the previous year. Underlying this change in financial circumstances were increased operating expenses, noncapitalized equipment purchases, and a projected $250,000 cut in the school district levies payable to KCTS. Station management was concerned about the implications of this cut for the future of school programming.

University support was being increased in the present budget, but some members of KCTS management expressed frustration at the relative inflexibility imposed by Channel 9's relationship to the University of Washington. The latter's biennial funding, voted by the state legislature, was one problem. Another was the slow, complicated process of hiring personnel, involving civil service salary regulations and other procedures. Only a few station personnel were exempt, and management was concerned that these procedures made it difficult not only to hire and fire, but also to pay competitive salaries.

Development activity was seen as an important means of improving the station's financial situation and its flexibility. Said Green, "I'm interested in increasing the percentage of viewers who are donors." Her goal was to obtain 10 percent of the viewing audience as subscribers. Nielsen data indicated that approximately 280,000 households in the Seattle-Tacoma area (about 40 percent of the total) watched a KCTS program for at least 15 minutes in any given week.

Green conceded that there had been some negative reaction to KCTS's increased emphasis on fundraising. "There's a large faction," she remarked, "not only in this station, but everywhere, that considers fundraising 'philistine.'"

Pledge weeks, known in 1975–1976 as "Festival Weeks" at most PBS stations, occurred four times annually; previously fundraising evenings had been scattered throughout the year. Green indicated that an effort was made to include particularly high quality programs during Festival Weeks. "What we try to do" she said, "is to get all those people who tune in just once in a while to tune in during pledge week." A station auction was also planned, beginning in November 1976. Clark felt strongly that individual programs should not be interrupted for pledge breaks and Green agreed: "I really think that what we're selling is uninterrupted service."

PROGRAMMING

In early 1976, KCTS was broadcasting daily, 100 hours a week. In addition to presenting nationally distributed shows from PBS and some local interest programs, KCTS devoted more than a third of its air time to instructional programming.

Meyer discussed the broader interpretation of "educational" broadcasting shown by public television in recent years:

There's nothing that says that educational or public television has to be dry and uninterest-

ing. I feel that if we can inform and educate in an interesting way we should do it. Today's television viewers look for good quality entertainment and fine productions. My philosophy is that our programming should be just as excellently produced and just as entertaining.

Everything we do is educational in some way, but it's no longer the old and deadly image of Miss Johnson standing in front of her blackboard and throwing an eraser at someone. . . .

What we have to remember is that public television tends to be a collection of "minority" programs that commercial stations can't afford to run. For instance, in summer 1973, we carried the Spassky-Fisher "world championship" chess match, and we had viewers watching that thing on little portable sets all over the city. That's one example of what I mean by a "minority" program, appealing to a minority or numerically small audience. There are many other examples.

However, KCTS was also interested in broadening its appeal. Clark emphasized that one of his programming objectives was to increase public awareness of Channel 9:

Public television involves the public. It is *their* station, and we've got to have large numbers of people watching us in order to meet the mandate that I see.

In analyzing the situation when I arrived here, it occurred to me that the best way to make people aware of us and what we're trying to do is to get the best damn schedule we can. So we want to do a number of high visibility programs at this stage in our development.

As an example of high visibility, Clark cited an upcoming programming on "redlining" in the Seattle area, which coincided with a mayor's task force on that problem in the city.[4]

Sources of Programming

In-school programming on KCTS originated locally. Approximately one-third was produced at KCTS or at another station supported by an overlapping school district. The balance came from instructional programming services, such as American Instructional Television and the Great Plains National Instructional Television Library.

Public programming, which accounted for some 60 broadcast hours weekly, was "sourced" in several ways. About 5 percent consisted of programs produced locally at KCTS, mostly focusing on topics of interest to one or more segments of the Seattle community. Other programs came from public TV stations in the state, independent distributors, the Eastern Educational Network, or PBS. In a typical week, PBS-distributed materials accounted for 50 broadcast hours.

Programs taken from the PBS national interconnection were made available to stations in one of four ways. Shows which had been underwritten—with costs covered in advance by a foundation, a corporation, CPB, or a government agency—were offered to affiliates "free of charge." A station's decision on whether or not to carry them was based on their content.[5]

Many unfunded or only partially underwritten shows were offered through the Station Program Cooperative. The SPC was an arrangement whereby PBS affiliates "bid" the programming dollars they intended to spend next year through PBS on series or individual programs. Many of the shows offered were still only in pilot or concept form, being submitted by producing stations in the hope that their costs could be spread. Since 1976 marked the Cooperative's third year, the upcoming effort was referred to as "SPC III." There were several rounds of SPC bidding, after each of which shows with insufficient "votes" were dropped. The costs of those shows which survived the entire process were apportioned among the stations bidding. SPC bids thus involved a commitment to pay an unknown amount (subject to a predetermined maximum) determined after each round by the number of stations bidding on a specific program. These shows could only be carried by stations which had previously bid and paid for them.[6]

The SPC III offerings totalled some 1,000 hours of programming. It was planned that the first round of bidding should take place in early March. Clark's goal was to purchase 500–550 hours. His budget for SPC use was $102,700, of which $36,000 was nonmatching funds contributed by the Ford Foundation and CPB.

The Station Acquisition Market (SAM) was another PBS vehicle for station programming. SAM was created to deal in existing programs (e.g., a BBC series packaged for American distribution). SAM shows were offered at a fixed price, keyed to the size of the station, and program directors had only to vote "yes" or "no."

The fourth source of PBS programming was the Station Independence Project (SIP). This was a PBS service which in 1975–1976 provided special shows for two weeks each year, aimed at helping participating stations with fundraising and membership drives.

Program Selection and Scheduling

Balancing content and cost to fill the desired number of broadcast hours was a complicated task, Clark indicated.

It's a tough choice when I have limited dollars to spend and three 90-minute shows of the caliber of "American Musical Theater" will cost me $30,000, versus ten series of thirty programs each for the same price. Everyone says "buy quality," but then you have to fill up that schedule.

I think there are a lot of misconceptions among people within public television stations—as well as among the general public—as to what it really costs to do a local show, what it costs to buy a program. It's expensive!

I'm not sure that the people who watch us really understand that it costs us $1,500 a week to have "Nova" in the schedule. So we told them, "The program you just watched costs $1,500 a week. We have to have your support in order to show those kinds of programs." I think that sort of honesty will pay off in the long run.

To me, it's tremendously important to clear up some misconceptions, not only on their part, but also on ours. Our overhead at this station for the programming department is $200,000 in salaries, and we pay $100,000 for SPC programs and $30,000 more for acquisitions. So that's a third of a million already without producing one show out of that studio ourselves!

It was necessary, Clark emphasized, to invest a certain amount of money in acquisitions.

We have to give our program schedule variety. We need to get a number of acquisitions so that we don't duplicate constantly what Channel 13 and Channel 62 are airing.

Research, he indicated, played a significant role not only in deciding what programs to broadcast, but also *when* to schedule them. It was vital to promote the program schedule and specific shows so that viewers knew what KCTS would be offering and were encouraged to watch.

Promotional Activities

Patti Parson, promotion director, reported to the director of development. However, she noted that half her time was spent on production and program promotion—"anything that helps production helps fundraising."

Her activities comprised a range of promotional, PR, and communications tasks. In a typical week she prepared and distributed 10 to 15 press releases to 160 periodicals and appropriate special interest groups. Almost all were related to specific programs, but general station activities were mentioned, too. She also prepared the monthly news and program guide, *Nine*, mailed to all subscribers, and compiled program listings for *TV Guide* and daily and weekly newspapers. Parson was critical of PBS's frequent failures to send out press materials on time for national shows, and noted that underwriters' advertising agencies could not always be relied upon to promote their clients' shows in local media.

Listings and press releases were supplemented by newspaper advertising and by on-air promotion on KCTS. Advertising had several objectives in addition to encouraging people

to watch a specific show. For instance, promotion of specific programs tended to help fundraising, while advertisements in smaller newspapers were believed to generate good will and to improve the station's chances of receiving editorial coverage in these papers' entertainment sections.

On-air promotion of a forthcoming show was seen as an excellent way to increase viewing. Said Parson, "It doesn't build a new audience, but it solidifies the audience you already have. Instead of getting them for one show, you get them to watch your schedule." Recent rating improvements at KCTS were ascribed in part to heavy on-air promotional activity, and it was planned to conduct new research to test this hypothesis.

Other promotional activities included parties to introduce new shows to the press and local underwriters. These often included a visit from one of the stars of the show in question. Meantime, leaflets were used to reach specific target segments, such as an insert promoting "Classic Theatre" in the printed programs of a local theater group.

Although no scientific attempt had been made to measure the effectiveness of promotional efforts, some insights were obtained from a review of clippings, the level of mail and phone calls received, the amount of donations, and the trend of Nielsen ratings.

On local productions, Parson made suggestions on the choice of title and general tone. Clark also sought her input when considering schedule changes, with a view to determining their implication for promotional activities.

Research

Research at KCTS was the responsibility of the programming department. The staff used ratings and internally generated data to assess the station's effectiveness at reaching general and specific audiences, as well as to plan future programming strategy.

For the past three years, KCTS had selected a part-time research director from among doctoral candidates at the University of Washington School of Communications. This individual worked 20 hours a week (and often more) at the station, being paid through a CPB grant at the standard rate for a graduate research assistant.

Patricia Harris, research director in 1975–1976, was working closely with Clark on a number of studies, as well as interpreting research data and presenting it in an intelligible form for other station personnel. KCTS subscribed to the Nielsen Station Index rating service. Each rating period, Harris digested the data received and distributed it in a format which included the ratings obtained for the same time slot in the same week of the previous year (Exhibit 4).

The rating data were used to evaluate the performance of individual shows and to make scheduling decisions. Attempts were made to maximize "audience flow," by juxtaposing programs in such a way that an audience attracted to one show would find it followed by another calculated to appeal to them. The Nielsen indexes provided some insights into Channel 9's success in building and holding audiences in this way.

The ratings of competing shows were another input into scheduling decisions, especially when the shows being compared were similar. In such instances, Clark sometimes "counter programmed." For instance, he placed an entertainment show on Channel 9 during the time slot when Channel 7 presented the CBS News magazine, "60 Minutes," anticipating that a KCTS public affairs program would be wasted in that slot. On the other hand, like many public TV stations, he often scheduled movies at the "network standard" time of 9 p.m.; viewers expected movies to start then and were believed to evaluate all the films offered by different stations before choosing one of them.

In addition to purchasing syndicated research, KCTS also collected its own data. For the past three years, using a CPB grant, the station had conducted "viewer profile" research; this involved detailed studies of KCTS viewer characteristics, with a comparison of their program interests against those of non-KCTS viewers. In the 1975 study, which in-

volved a mail survey, the sample was segmented by (1) KCTS members in Washington State and in British Columbia, (2) KCTS viewers who were not members, and (3) non-KCTS television viewers. Demographic findings are summarized in Exhibit 5, while Exhibit 6 highlights program interests for the different segments.

Harris had instituted other, more specialized studies. Convinced, for instance, that Nielsen figures did not adequately represent the viewing habits of the college and teen audience, she conducted a simple poll of students in three area schools. These comprised an undergraduate psychology class at the University; a high school located in a predominantly white, middle-class neighborhood; and a high school containing a large percentage of Black and Asian-American students from relatively low socio-economic backgrounds.

The subject of her study was KCTS's Tuesday night schedule, planned by Clark to attract and hold younger viewers. Her findings suggested that the schedule was somewhat successful, but that this success was not reflected in the Nielsen ratings (where the research techniques did not measure such phenomena as viewing in college dorms). One unexpected finding was the discovery that Channel 9 reception was poor in the neighborhood of the minority high school.

Harris regularly evaluated unsolicited mail and phone comments from viewers. She also participated in the station's ascertainment efforts, helping Channel 9 to identify community problems and needs. In this, she was joined by Sharon Maeda, director of community involvement, who worked with a consultant to ensure that KCTS obtained inputs from all segments of the Seattle community. Maeda spent much of her time with representatives of ethnic and other groups to determine their programming concerns and interests.

Viewers' Choice 1976

In late 1975, Channel 9 conceived the idea of seeking viewers' opinions of program offerings. Arrangements were made to preempt all regular programming on the evening of Friday, February 2, 1976. Between 7:00 p.m. and 10:00 p.m. that day, pilot segments were shown of 18 potential new series for Channel 9's fall season. These shows were a representative sampling of programs which public TV stations across the country were thinking of purchasing through the PBS Station Program Cooperative. At 10:00 p.m. there followed a half-hour "kaleidoscope" of 22 series previously shown on KCTS which could be purchased again for rebroadcast in the fall.

Ballots were printed in *Nine*, *TV Guide*, and the two major Seattle newspapers (Exhibit 7). Further publicity was generated by press releases. Viewers were reminded to complete and return their balots through on-air promotional messages (Exhibit 8). Additionally, 450 community leaders and organizations were contacted individually and urged to participate. Complementing this activity, Channel 9's consultant for community involvement hosted a preview of ethnically oriented SPC programming at his home on February 1; national programs available to PBS stations were grouped into four ethnic categories and shown to individuals and representatives of interested organizations.

The results of *Viewers' Choice* greatly exceeded expectations. Within less than two weeks, over 4,500 completed ballots had been returned. Surprisingly, $3,800 was received in unsolicited donations—more than covering the $3,000 cost of *Viewers' Choice*. Another side benefit was generation of many new names for Channel 9's mailing list. The overall feeling at the station was that considerable good will and favorable publicity had been generated by this project.

PLANNING THE FALL PROGRAM SCHEDULE

Within a few weeks, all *Viewers' Choice* ballots had been tabulated and the responses analyzed. Exhibit 9 shows the percentage of respondents voting for each program pilot. Burnill Clark had earlier ranked each pilot in the order he expected viewers to respond. Although quite closely correlated, there were a few significant discrepancies. "World Press" and "Prism" (a science program) had been ranked by viewers rather higher than Clark had predicted. By contrast, "Sesame Street"— which, according to Nielsen data, had consistently been the station's most popular program—was ranked fourteenth by the viewers. The profile of *Viewers' Choice* respondents indicated that they were primarily evening viewers of public TV, and tended to be older and living in one- or two-person households. Hence their relative lack of interest in children's programming. Clark also recognized that the interests of minorities and infrequent public TV viewers would be under-represented in the ballot results. To compensate for this, he had received inputs from the special preview of ethnically oriented SPC III programs; among those which had been particularly well received by representatives of ethnic groups were "Realidades," "Black Film Festival," and "Black Perspectives on the News."

In early March, 83 program proposals had been presented to member stations for the preliminary "bidding" round in the SPC III selection process. Some of these programs were subsequently withdrawn. Underwriting had been obtained for "In Search of the Real America" and "Grand Prix Tennis" so that they could be distributed by PBS free of charge, while CPB had decided to fund "Realidades" and "Black Film Festival" to make them widely available. By April, a number of programs which had fared poorly in preliminary rounds of SPC bidding had been eliminated, due to lack of sufficient station support.

In mid-April 1976, Clark and Harris were reviewing the list of programs remaining in the SPC III catalogue (Exhibit 10). Less than half the original offerings remained, and Clark believed that many of these commanded insufficient support to survive. In a few days, KCTS would be asked to make its selection for an SPC "purchase" round. Program selections made on this occasion would become irrevocable purchase commitments if prices did not increase beyond the predetermined maximum.

In addition to making SPC selections for

KCTS's fall schedule, Clark also had to decide on how to address the programming concerns voiced by ethnic minority groups, as well as the criticism raised by some observers that Channel 9 still did not provide enough local programming.

A related concern was the competition posed by KCPQ, Channel 13, in Lakewood Center, now that this public TV station was operating on its powerful new VHF transmitter. As usual, Clark had prepared an overview of the projected spring series schedule for KCTS, KCPQ, and the three commercial network affiliates, and he was wondering what programming and scheduling strategy his own station should adopt towards Channel 13. As far as SPC III selections were concerned, he believed that KCPQ had a budget of about $50,000, was seeking to buy about 500 hours of SPC pro-

gramming, and would only have to pay about 60 percent of the program prices charged to KCTS. Clark could foresee three basic options: to ignore KCPQ completely, to compete directly, or to work with them in planning complementary schedules.

Conclusion

As he reviewed the overall situation, Clark recognized that KCTS had many different constituencies. A strategy directed at satisfying the needs of one group might result in losing the support of others. In the light of past experience and recent research findings, Clark had to decide where his station should place its priorities in making programming selections for the current year.

NOTES

1. Public Broadcasting Service.

2. "The Old Place Ain't What It Used to Be," by Ed Sullivan. *Seattle Business*, February 11, 1974.

3. This deficit, made possible by the size of the station's reserves, was planned as a one-time–only situation. By February 1976, it appeared that the deficit would, in fact, be much smaller than originally projected.

4. *Redlining* is a practice allegedly followed by many banks, whereby red lines are drawn on a map around certain urban neighborhoods considered poor loan risks. Refusal to make loans for home

purchases or improvements in the "redlined" areas thus contributes to urban decay.

5. Examples of such underwritten programs in 1976 included "Masterpiece Theatre" (underwritten by Mobil Oil) and "Black Journal" (Pepsico).

6. The SPC bidding process was actually somewhat more complex than depicted in this case, involving bidding rounds to determine the level of support, elimination rounds to get rid of the least popular programs, and finally purchase rounds. Presentation of the SPC selection process has been simplified here for the purposes of case analysis.

EXHIBIT I

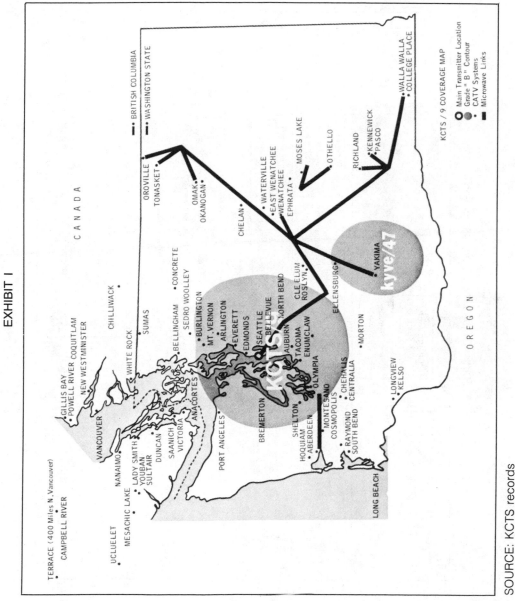

SOURCE: KCTS records

EXHIBIT 2

KCTS: Partial Organization Chart, March 1976

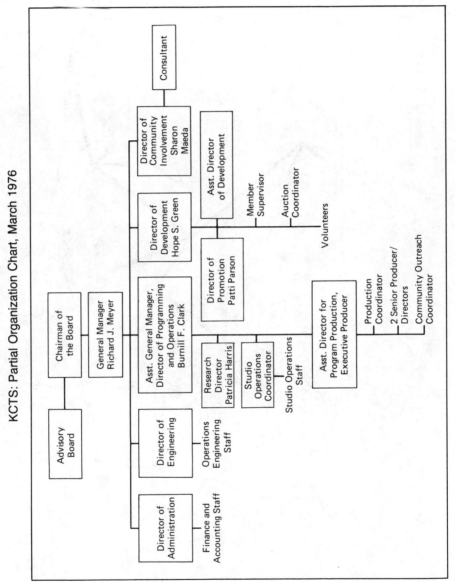

SOURCE: KCTS records

EXHIBIT 3

KCTS: Income and Expense Statement FY 1971–FY 1976

	1970–71	1971–72	1972–73	1973–74	1974–75	BUDGET 1975–76
REVENUES						
University of Washington	$225,050	$133,797	$135,855	$142,606	$162,426	$267,432
Schools, institutions of higher education	412,248	347,799	353,612	348,194	446,621	133,000
Public contribution	0	0	215,856	348,627	467,267	600,000
Grants	0	0	180,289	173,873	201,829	165,000
Interest	0	0	0	16,325	18,610	10,000
Underwriting	0	0	0	0	43,609	69,500
Other	53,364	80,857	31,824	73,361	29,828	11,000
Total Revenues	$690,662	$562,453	$917,386	$1,102,986	$1,370,190	$1,255,932
EXPENSES						
Programming, education, development, and administration	$203,156	$199,920	$253,346	$298,804	$410,380	$568,666
Engineering	164,477	124,283	168,934	242,693	280,792	418,562
Other operating expenses	187,391	145,337	299,526	333,334	494,982	419,488
Total Operating Expenses	$555,024	$469,540	$721,806	$874,831	$1,186,154	$1,406,716
Noncapital equipment purchases[1]	0	0	15,574	212,276	6,347	208,646
Total Expenses	$555,024	$469,540	$737,380	$1,087,107	$1,192,501	$1,615,362
Net increase (decrease) in funds	135,638	92,913	180,006	15,879	177,689	(359,430)
Beginning fund balance	104,343	239,981	332,894	512,900	528,779	706,468
Ending fund balance	$289,891	$332,894	$512,900	$528,779	$706,468	$347,038

[1] In 1975, KCTS planned to use $1.8 million in specially earmarked funds (of which $1.5 million was coming from the University of Washington) for the purchase of new capital equipment.
SOURCE: KCTS records

EXHIBIT 4

Digest of Nielsen Data for KCTS Programs

4-WEEK PERIOD ENDING NOVEMBER 26, 1975

TIME (PM)	MONDAY	TUESDAY	WEDNESDAY	THURSDAY	FRIDAY	SATURDAY	SUNDAY
6:30–7	HUMAN SEXUALITY (-.3)1^{10}	COSMOLOGY (-.3)-.3	HUMAN SEXUALITY (-.3)1^{6}	COSMOLOGY (-.3)-.3	PEACEMAKERS (-.3)-.3	SCENE 1 TAKE 1 (1)-.3	CHAPLIN SHORTS (1)2^{15}
7–7:30	CLASSICAL PREVIEW (-.3)1^{6}	LILIAS YOGA (1)-.3	LILIAS YOGA (-.3)-.3	ASCENT OF MAN (1)3^{21}	FIRING LINE (-.3)2^{11}	WASHINGTON WEEK (-.3)2^{13}	WORLD PRESS (1)2^{11}
7:30–8	WORLD PRESS (1)-.3	VARIOUS (1)1^{5}	BOOK BEAT (-.3)1^{7}	ASCENT OF MAN (2)3^{24}	FIRING LINE (1)1^{11}	WALL ST. WEEK (-.3)1^{8}	LOWELL THOMAS (2)2^{16}
8–8:30	VARIOUS (WOLF TRAP) (2)2^{13}	VARIOUS (3)2^{12}	TRIBAL EYE (1)2^{15}	ROMANTIC REBELLION (1)1^{9}	WASHINGTON WEEK (2)3^{20}	RIVALS OF SHERLOCK HOLMES (1)2^{23}	SYMPHONY (2)2^{17}
8:30–9	VARIOUS (WOLF TRAP) (2)3^{25}	RIVALS OF SHERLOCK HOLMES (2)2^{14}	TRIBAL EYE (1)2^{18}	CLASSICAL PREVIEW (1)1^{10}	WALL ST. WEEK (2)2^{18}	RIVALS OF SHERLOCK HOLMES (2)2^{23}	SYMPHONY (5)1^{8}
9–9:30	VARIOUS (1)2^{20}	RIVALS OF SHERLOCK HOLMES (2)2^{19}	JENNIE (2)6^{41}	CLASSICAL THEATRE (-.3)3^{24}	MASTERPIECE THEATRE (2)2^{20}	SILENT YEARS (1)1^{7}	MASTERPIECE THEATRE (5)3^{29}
9:30–10	VARIOUS (1)2^{17}	MONTY PYTHON (1)4^{26}	JENNIE (2)5^{40}	CLASSICAL THEATRE (-.3)3^{24}	MASTERPIECE THEATRE (2)2^{19}	SILENT YEARS (1)1^{5}	MASTERPIECE THEATRE (3)4^{26}
10–10:30	FIRST CHURCHILLS (1)2^{12}	SOUNDSTAGE (1)2^{14}	SAY BROTHER (2)1^{7}	CLASSICAL THEATRE (1)3^{20}	VARIOUS (1)1^{5}	SILENT YEARS (1)-.3	ASCENT OF MAN (1)1^{9}
10:30–11	FIRST CHURCHILLS (1)2^{14}	SOUNDSTAGE (2)2^{11}	SAY BROTHER/JAZZ (1)1^{4}	CLASSICAL THEATRE (-.3)3^{19}	VARIOUS (-.3)1^{9}	SILENT YEARS (1)-.3	ASCENT OF MAN (1)1^{9}

KEY: (1)2̲14 — — — — — Total No. of Households / Current Rating / Nov. 1974 Rating

Note: The large number (current rating) and the small subscript in parentheses (November 1974 rating) represent the percentage of Seattle area homes watching TV in that time slot which are tuned in to Channel 9. The convention -.3 is traditionally used to denote a viewership which is too small to measure. The small superscript denotes the number of homes (in thousands) actually watching Channel 9 at the time.

Research conducted for PBS in 1974–1975 showed that *nationally*, public TV achieved an average rating of 1.0. Ratings nationally varied from an average of 1.5 for "arts" programs to 0.7 for "public affairs." A rating of 5 was considered extremely good.

SOURCE: KCTS records

EXHIBIT 5

Demographic Characteristics of KCTS Viewing Groups

Demographic Characteristics of Sample Groups

	NON-KCTS VIEWERS	KCTS VIEWERS	AMERICAN KCTS MEMBERS	CANADIAN KCTS MEMBERS
	(n = 93)	(n = 211)	(n = 243)	(n = 236)
EDUCATION OF RESPONDENT				
12 years or less	49.5%	28.4%	13.2%	24.6%
13–15 years	20.4	23.2	20.6	22.0
16 years or more	30.1	48.3	66.3	54.4
AGE OF RESPONDENT				
Under 30 years	26.9%	27.0%	12.3%	6.8%
30–59 years	43.0	46.4	53.9	59.7
60 years or over	30.1	26.5	33.7	33.5
SEX OF RESPONDENT				
Male	50.0%	52.4%	50.0%	56.0%
Female	50.0	47.6	50.0	44.0
OCCUPATION OF RESPONDENT				
Blue or white collar worker	30.8%	22.5%	12.7%	18.5%
Skilled worker, business	20.9	25.0	19.1	24.0
Professional	9.9	18.1	28.0	19.7
Housewife	11.0	12.7	16.1	12.0
Student	22.9	28.6	3.0	4.3
Not working	18.7	16.7	21.2	21.5
CHILD UNDER 12 YEARS IN HOUSEHOLD				
No	52.7%	65.4%	65.4%	65.7%
Yes	47.3	34.6	34.6	34.3
RACE				
White	88.9%	96.6%	98.8%	98.7%
Black	4.4	1.0	.4	0
Other	6.7	2.4	.8	1.3
DAILY HOURS OF TV VIEWING				
0–2 hours	17.1%	16.6%	18.5%	21.9%
3–5 hours	44.7	55.6	50.6	54.8
Over 5 hours	37.8	28.3	30.7	23.4

	NONMEMBER (VIEWERS + NONVIEWERS)	MEMBERS	CANADIANS
	(n = 279)	(n = 226)	(n = 223)
WEEKLY HOURS OF KCTS VIEWING BY ADULTS IN HOUSEHOLD			
0 hours	15.8%	2.2%	.9%
1–5 hours	56.6	41.1	41.7
Over 5 hours	27.7	56.7	57.3
WEEKLY HOURS OF KCTS VIEWING BY CHILDREN IN HOUSEHOLD[a]			
0 hours	47.2%	26.3%	21.4%
1–5 hours	29.1	35.6	37.1
Over 5 hours	23.7	38.1	51.5

[a] Includes only those households who reported having children in families.
SOURCE: KCTS records

EXHIBIT 6

Program Interests of KCTS Viewing Groups

(A) Programs on KCTS/9 That Respondents Enjoy Viewing: Open-Ended Responses

KCTS/9 PROGRAM TITLES	CATEGORY	AMERICAN KCTS MEMBERS (n = 243)	CANADIAN KCTS MEMBERS (n = 236)	NONMEMBER KCTS VIEWERS (n = 211)
Masterpiece Theatre	Drama	63.3%	77.5%	34.1%
Ascent of Man	Instructional/Cultural Affairs	33.7	42.0	18.9
Washington Week in Review	News/Public Affairs	29.9	19.5	12.2
Nova	Documentary (Science)	28.4	30.0	19.9
Bill Moyers	News/Public Affairs	25.8	13.9	11.3
Wall Street Week	Public Affairs (Economics)	22.6	16.1	9.0
Firing Line	News/Public Affairs	21.8	21.1	10.9
America	Instructional/Cultural Affairs	15.6	21.2	11.2
Evening at Pops	Music	14.4	21.5	11.3
Sesame Street	Children's	12.0	6.3	14.1
Classical Music (unspec.)	Music (Classical)	9.8	10.9	13.2
Theater in America	Drama	9.3	7.6	3.3
World Press	News/Public Affairs	9.1	5.9	5.2
Romantic Rebellion	Instructional/Cultural Affairs	8.9	16.9	5.8
Electric Company	Children's	8.1	5.0	7.5
Mr. Rogers	Children's	7.8	3.3	7.5
Public Affairs (unspec.)	News/Public Affairs	7.7	5.8	9.9
In Performance at Wolf Trap	Music	7.0	4.2	1.9
Movies (unspec.)	Movies	6.8	8.4	9.8
Zoom	Children's	6.1	5.0	4.7
Feeling Good	Health	6.0	2.0	3.8
The Japanese Film	Movie	5.6	6.3	5.6
Plays (unspec.)	Drama	4.9	9.7	6.6
Popular Music (unspec.)	Music	4.4	5.9	6.1
Book Beat	Cultural Affairs	4.0	3.7	.9
The Silent Years	Movie	4.0	3.3	1.9
Nana	Drama	4.0	2.4	2.4
Behind the Lines	News/Public Affairs	3.2	1.2	1.0
Yoga	Health (Yoga)	2.8	3.7	2.9
Bridge	Recreation	2.8	2.5	3.2
Watergate	News/Public Affairs	2.4	2.9	1.9
Science-Nature (unspec.)	Instructional/Science	2.4	2.8	4.6
Hollywood TV Theater	Drama	2.4	2.0	.9
Roads to Freedom	Cultural Affairs	1.6	3.6	1.4
Contemporary Scene (unspec.)	Instructional/Cultural Affairs	1.6	2.4	3.7
Black Journal	Public Affairs (Black)	1.6	.8	1.9
Health Programs	Health	1.6	2.1	5.1
Assignment America	News/Public Affairs	1.6	0	.9
Ballet	Cultural Affairs Performance	.8	4.2	1.4
Soundstage	Music (Rock and Jazz)	.4	0	1.9
Great Performances	Drama	1.2	1.6	0
Evening at Symphony	Music (Classical)	.4	.4	.9

EXHIBIT 6 (continued)

(B) Commercial Programs That Respondents Enjoy Viewing: Open-Ended Responses[a]

COMMERCIAL PROGRAM CATEGORY	AMERICAN KCTS MEMBERS (n = 243)	CANADIAN KCTS MEMBERS (n = 236)	NONMEMBER KCTS VIEWERS (n = 211)	NON-KCTS VIEWERS (n = 93)
News-Public Affairs	58.4%	38.1%	41.2%	24.7%
Situation Comedy	43.6	42.8	43.1	32.3
Documentary	37.4	38.1	30.8	15.1
Drama	29.2	13.1	32.2	30.1
Sports	27.2	24.6	26.5	18.3
Travel-Nature	24.7	25.8	24.6	12.9
Movies	21.8	24.6	29.9	11.8
Crime	19.3	26.3	31.8	26.9
Game	14.4	7.2	15.6	15.1
Variety-Talk	9.9	5.5	13.7	8.6
Music	8.6	9.3	10.4	4.3
Variety-Comedy	8.5	9.7	7.0	7.1
Children's	2.1	1.7	2.8	1.1
Western	1.6	.8	4.3	2.2
Soap	1.6	.4	3.3	8.6
Religion	.4	0	.5	2.2
Other	11.5	36.4	8.5	3.2

[a] Open-ended responses, multiple responses permitted.
SOURCE: KCTS records

EXHIBIT 7

Ballot for *Viewers' Choice 1976*

(Actual Size Published on TV Listings Page of Seattle Times, *Monday, February 2, 1976*

Was Four Times this Size)

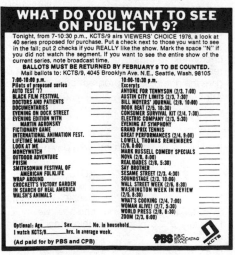

EXHIBIT 8

On-Air Promotion for *Viewers' Choice 1976*

Production: Viewers' Choice 1976—*Opening Segment (3:30)*
Producer/Director: Lee Olson

VIDEO	AUDIO
FADE UP ON SLIDE: Logo	For the next 3½ hours, we are pre-empting all regular programming to bring you *Viewers' Choice 1976.* This special presentation will give you an opportunity to say what you want to see on Public TV 9. With *Viewers' Choice 1976,* we become one of the first television stations in the country to give its viewers a chance for input into programming decisions. Starting in a few minutes, we will show you excerpts of 40 national programs available for purchase by Public TV 9.
DISSOLVE TO SLIDE: Ballot in *Nine* Magazine—*Nine* logo and date	You will be able to mark your preference on ballots which can be found in the February issue of *Nine* magazine.
CUT TO SLIDE: Ballot in *TV Guide*—logo and date	The January 31 issue of *TV Guide.*
CUT TO SLIDE: Ballot in newspaper—*PI* and *Times* logos and dates	And the February 2 editions of the *Seattle Post-Intelligencer* and the *Seattle Times.*
DISSOLVE TO SLIDE: Station Program Cooperative	The programs you can select from are national series that Public TV 9 is considering buying from the Station Program Cooperative. This cooperative is made up of all Public Broadcasting Service member stations who wish to acquire PBS programs for local use. Each station is invited to submit programs and then to purchase from the pool. If enough buyers are found for a specific show, it becomes part of the PBS broadcast schedule. However, each station can air only those programs that it has purchased specifically.
DISSOLVE TO SLIDE: CU of left side of ballot	The first selection of segments you will see tonight is listed on the left side of your ballot. They are short pilots of 18 potential new series to air in the fall. This is not the complete list of program pilots which will be offered to Public TV 9 for consideration. But it is a representative sampling of those pilots available for broadcast at this time. Your reaction to them will tell us the kinds of programs you are interested in. This group of pilots will run for 3 hours.
DISSOLVE TO SLIDE: CU of right side of ballot	Then, from 10:00 to 10:30 tonight, we will broadcast a sample of 22 series that are listed on the right side of the ballot. These are shows that have been carried recently or are currently on Public TV 9. And they are available again to be purchased for broadcast in the fall. Not included in this list are certain PBS shows, like "Masterpiece Theatre," which we do not buy through the Station Program Cooperative.
DISSOLVE TO SLIDE: CU hand with pen making check marks on ballot	We invite you to watch each of these segments, and then to vote by putting a check next to those you want to see on Public TV 9 this fall. Put 2 checks if you really like the show. For your convenience in identifying the program pilots, we will give the name of the program both before and after each segment.
DISSOLVE TO SLIDE: CU hands cutting out ballot over table top. Addressed envelope seen on table	After you have voted, cut out your ballot, and mail it to the address given.
DISSOLVE TO SLIDE: mailing address	If you do not have a ballot, write down your preferences on a piece of paper, and mail it to: KCTS/9 Box 5028 Seattle, Washington 98105
DISSOLVE TO SLIDE: "Deadline: February 9"	In order to process your choices, we must have the ballots in our hands by February 9. So please get them ready, so they can be mailed first thing in the morning.
DISSOLVE TO SLIDE: "Pilots of Proposed New Series"	Now we begin *Viewers' Choice 1976* with the 18 pilots of proposed new series.

SOURCE: KCTS records

EXHIBIT 9

Result of *Viewers' Choice 1976*
(Percentage of Respondents Voting for Each SPC Pilot)

PROGRAM	CATEGORY	PERCENTAGE OF RESPONDENTS
Nova	Documentary (Science)	78.7
Documentaries	Documentary (Miscellaneous)	69.5
Great Performances	Drama	67.3
Evening at Symphony	Music (Classical)	64.8
Bill Moyers' Journal	News/Public Affairs	63.2
Washington Week in Review	News/Public Affairs	53.8
World Press	News/Public Affairs	50.5
Outdoor Adventures with Lute Jerstad	Documentary (Nature)	49.6
Crockett's Victory Garden	Nature	48.9
Evening Edition: Martin Agronsky	News/Public Affairs	46.1
Walsh's Animals	Nature/Children's	45.4
Prism	Documentary (Science)	45.4
Wall Street Week	Public Affairs (Finance)	44.8
Sesame Street	Children's	44.4
Moneywatch	Public Affairs (Economics)	44.2
Book Beat	Public Affairs (Books)	43.0
Lowell Thomas Remembers	Public Affairs (Travel)	42.2
Evening at Dock Street	Drama	42.1
Doctors and Patients	Health	41.9
Smithsonian Festival	American Cultural Heritage	41.7
Consumer Survival Kit	Public Affairs (Economics)	40.0
Anyone for Tennyson?	Drama (Poetry)	38.9
International Animation Festival	Movies	38.1
Autotest '77	Consumer Report/Automobiles	38.0
In Search of the Real America	Public Affairs (Commentary)	34.1
Lifetime Magazine	Programming for Elderly	30.3
Soundstage	Music (Rock and Jazz)	30.3
Electric Company	Children's	28.8
Mark Russell Comedy Specials	Variety (Comedy)	27.5
What's Cooking?	Cooking	27.4
Wraparound	Lifestyle "Magazine"	27.1
Fictionary Game	Game Show (Adults)	25.6
Grand Prix Tennis	Sports	22.8
Zoom	Children's	21.0
Look at Me	Public Affairs (Parents)	20.7
Black Film Festival	Movies (Black)	18.2
Woman Alive	Public Affairs (Women)	17.8
How We Got Here	Documentary (Ethnic Immigrants)	16.7
Realidades	Spanish Language Programming	14.0
Austin City Limits	Music (Country)	10.3
Say Brother	Programming for Blacks	7.2

SOURCE: KCTS records

EXHIBIT 10

Program Catalogue for SPC III, April 1976

SERIES TITLE	CATEGORY	FORMAT (Minutes)	NUMBER OF PROGRAMS	TOTAL HOURS	PURCHASING POWER[a] (Percent)	NUMBER OF STATIONS SELECTING	ESTIMATED COST TO KCTS (MAX.) ($000)
Washington Week in Review	News/Public Affairs	30	52	26	97	150	2.3
Evening at Symphony	Music	60–90	13	15	95	148	2.1
Wall Street Week	News/Public Affairs	30	52	26	94	146	2.5
Sesame Street	Children's	60	130	130	93	145	16.7
Great Performances	Drama	60–180	25	37½	92	142	8.5
Electric Company	Children's	30	130	65	91	142	9.7
Nova	Documentary (Science)	60	20	20	86	134	11.3
The Age of Uncertainty	Documentary (Economics)	60	13	13	80	120	6.3
Consumer Survival Kit	Public Affairs (Economics)	30	26	13	80	132	4.2
Soundstage	Music (Rock and Jazz)	60	12	12	75	124	2.9
Black Perspectives on the News	News/Public Affairs	30	52	26	75	112	3.3
Anyone for Tennyson?	Drama (Poetry)	30	15	7½	66	112	2.7
Woman	Public Affairs (Women)	30	46	23	65	104	2.0
Special Events	News/Public Affairs	30–60	40	25	65	92	10.6
Mark Russell Specials	Comedy	30	4	2	64	102	0.6
Crockett's Victory Garden	Gardening	30	34	17	62	96	2.1
Lowell Thomas Remembers	News/Public Affairs (Nostalgia)	30	39	19½	60	96	9.0
The Best of Ernie Kovacs	Variety-Comedy (Nostalgia)	30	10	5	54	88	2.6

Program	Category						
Opera Theatre Presents	Music/Drama	60–150	5	10	53	80	4.4
World Press	News/Public Affairs	30	52	26	51	82	5.0
Parent Effectiveness	Public Affairs (Parents)	30	13	6½	50	76	2.3
Scenes from a Marriage	Drama	60	6	6	48	65	6.6
Zoom	Children's	30	66	33	46	70	4.1
Book Beat	Public Affairs (Books)	30	45	22½	46	75	2.7
Lilias, Yoga and You	Health (Yoga)	30	52	26	45	82	1.5
Bill Moyers' Journal	News/Public Affairs	60	6	6	44	66	12.2
Front and Center	Public Affairs (Pollution)	30	20	10	37	51	7.6
Walsh's Animals	Children's	30	10	5	37	56	4.7
Studio See	Children's	30	26	13	35	60	3.9
At the Top	Music (Jazz)	60	13	13	35	63	3.7
International Animation Festival	Movies	30	11	5½	32	51	5.3
Austin City Limits	Music (Country)	60	10	10	27	47	4.4
Evening Edition: Martin Agronsky	News/Public Affairs	30	60	30	23	41	17.9
Mother's Little Network	Variety-Comedy	30	10	5	23	30	15.9
Say Brother	Public Affairs (Black)	30	13	6½	22	28	7.1
Max Morath: Illustrious Past	Music (Nostalgia)	30	10	5	17	27	5.1
Autotest '77	Consumer Report/Automobiles	60	3	3	15	20	4.9
The Highest Court	Public Affairs (Law)	30	20	10	13	18	36.2
Mancini	Music	30	12	6	10	16	43.7
What's Cooking?	Cooking	30	13	6½	10	16	5.6

a Since larger stations were assessed at a higher rate for program costs, they had more purchasing power than small stations. The "purchasing power percentage" was thus a more significant measure of the support for a program (and its chances for success) than the total number of stations bidding. Clark believed that a program which commanded less than 25 percent of purchasing power support at this time was unlikely to survive, and that a program with less than 45 percent had, at best, an even chance.
SOURCE: KCTS records

COOLIDGE BANK AND TRUST COMPANY

A fast-growing, retail-oriented bank, Coolidge owes its growth to aggressive management and an iconoclastic approach to banking. But now the innovator has been outstripped. Thrift institutions such as savings and loans are promoting NOW accounts, similar to checking accounts but with the added advantage of paying interest on the outstanding balance. Should Coolidge follow suit and offer NOW accounts too?

Milton Adess, president of the Coolidge Bank and Trust Company of Watertown, Massachusetts, was debating whether or not his bank should introduce NOW accounts.

Although modest in size, Coolidge had gained a national reputation for its innovative approach to banking. Among other things, it had pioneered development of no-service-charge checking accounts. In 1972, however, a mutual savings bank in Worcester, Massachusetts, had begun offering negotiable order of withdrawal (NOW) accounts, which were effectively interest-bearing checking accounts. This concept was soon adopted by a number of other banks in Massachusetts. In the spring of 1974, Coolidge management recognized that some of their bank's large personal checking depositors were taking their business to NOW accounts at competing banks.

BANKING IN MASSACHUSETTS

Studies by the Federal Reserve Bank of Boston identified the existence of eight major banking markets in Massachusetts in the early 1970s. The largest of these, the Boston market, covered nearly all of eastern Massachusetts, extending from a few towns in southern New Hampshire, whose residents worked in the Boston area, down to the neck of Cape Cod. The wide geographic expanse of this market reflected Boston's position as the cultural and economic hub of New England as well as its role as the governmental center of the Commonwealth of Massachusetts.

Observers described the Boston retail banking market as "very competitive." This growing market had been the scene of active developments in recent years. The city of Boston was the home of a number of large and powerful banking organizations, headed by the First National Bank of Boston, the nation's tenth largest correspondent bank. As commuting into metropolitan Boston from the outlying areas had increased, banks located in this area had become alternative sources of banking to more people.

While the population of metropolitan Boston was approximately 2.8 million in 1974, that of the Boston banking market was estimated by the Federal Reserve Bank at 3.8 million. The total population of Massachusetts was 5.8 million.

State banking laws in Massachusetts restricted the operations of individual commercial banks to a single county. Banks were not allowed to open new branches or merge with other banks outside the county in which the home office was located. However, subject to regulatory approval, a bank holding company could acquire another bank anywhere in the state. This provided a means of circumventing the county branching restrictions. Many large, Boston-based banks had recently formed holding companies which allowed them to take advantage of this situation, although subsidiary

---

This case was prepared by Christopher H. Lovelock.

banks retained separate identities in each county. In the long run, observers anticipated that banking laws would be amended to permit statewide branch banking in Massachusetts.

The Boston banking market covered major portions of 5 of Massachusetts' 14 counties. Suffolk County was composed of the cities of Boston, Revere, Winthrop, and Chelsea; Essex County comprised the so-called "North Shore" communities running up to the New Hampshire border; Middlesex, the most populous county in the state, included Cambridge, Watertown, and a large number of towns and cities west of Boston; gerrymandered Norfolk County included Brookline and many communities south and west of Boston; Plymouth County extended south of Norfolk down toward Cape Cod (Exhibit 1).

Although not direct competitors in all commercial bank services, thrift institutions[1] in Massachusetts competed vigorously with commercial banks for savings deposits and were also important lenders of consumer credit. The introduction of NOW accounts by mutual savings banks in 1972 had enabled them to offer a substitute for commercial bank demand deposits (checking accounts). In January 1974, the right to offer NOW accounts was extended to savings and loan associations, cooperative banks, and also commercial banks.

In mid-1974, there were 167 mutual savings banks operating in Massachusetts, plus 179 savings and loan associations and cooperative banks. These institutions controlled approximately $18.8 billion in total deposits, exceeding the total deposits of the state's 153 commercial banks.

COMPETITION IN RETAIL BANKING

Prior to the advent of "free" checking in the mid-1960s, retail banking institutions in Massachusetts and other states had avoided any significant price competition.

It was generally assumed that customers selected their banks primarily on the basis of convenience and, to a lesser extent, image. An article in the *New England Economic Review* noted,

Many banks have found that they can draw a larger volume of customers by increasing the accessibility of their facilities, for example, by establishing branch offices in convenient locations, by adding parking space or opening drive-in windows, or by extending banking hours. Advertising is also an important mode of competition. Through creative use of the media, some banks have achieved an attractive image, stressing their friendly or personal services, or their status as a small bank underdog—trying harder, of course. Advertising campaigns are often combined with such gimmicks as baby photo contests, washing the windshields of customers' cars, or a wide variety of promotional giveaway offers to new customers, ranging from flatware to thermal blankets. Building attractive offices, adopting modern logos, and offering "beautiful" checks are other items in the repertoire of appeals to retail customers.[2]

Price competition, by contrast, was rare. In any given region, the prices of retail banking services (e.g., loan rates, checking account service charges, and other fees), had tended to settle at a competitive rate that was relatively uniform among all banks in the area, with only minor deviations in evidence. Price competition on a broad scale was restrained not only by a plethora of state and federal regulations designed to protect bank solvency, but also by customary industry practices and a widespread distaste for "price-cutting" in banking circles. Coolidge Bank had shattered this situation in 1964 by introducing, and vigorously promoting, the concept of no-service-charge checking accounts.

THE GROWTH OF COOLIDGE BANK

The Coolidge Bank and Trust Company received its charter from the Commonwealth of Massachusetts in July 1960. It was founded by a group of merchants and businessmen who, dissatisfied with the quality of service provided by the local bank in Watertown (a suburb of Boston), resolved to start their own. They named the bank after one of the seventeenth century founders of Watertown.

The leader of this group, Milton Adess, became president of the new bank. Adess himself had no previous banking background. As a young man during the Depression, he had worked as a Fuller Brush salesman. From there, he went into retailing and subsequently built up a successful hardware business.

Coolidge Bank opened for service in a former store in December 1960 with a staff of 12 people. Initially, the operation was managed by the executive vice-president, a former Rhode Island banker with 21 years' experience who had been recommended by one of the large Boston banks. However, after a year, this individual left Coolidge and Adess, in his own words, "offered to come in and just watch the store."

Looking back, many years later, Adess discussed the background he brought to banking.

> I didn't know a thing about banking. I took a few AIB courses at night and learned a little bit about the language, but I certainly don't claim—even today—to have a strong banking background. I know a little about operations, but my forte is really marketing and loans. It's more of a straight businessman's view of what should be done.

Over the years, the president said, Coolidge had built up a strong professional management group with skills complementing his own. Regarding the bank's philosophy, he observed,

> We look at banking as another business and money as another commodity. We have one color to offer—green. And it's very much like selling any other commodity: we're selling money. And I've always been convinced that the individual or company who brings the best product to the public at the lowest possible price usually does very, very well.

The challenge during the bank's first years was to develop an asset base, since—as Adess noted—the bank's lending ability was limited by the size of its capital.

> I devoted half my time in the first formative year to just making cold calls. Strangely enough, a couple of my directors who are among our largest customers came as a result of those cold calls. We went out and knocked on doors, we got all our friends and cousins and everyone we [could] possibly grasp by the lapels and drag into the bank to open up an account of one sort or another, either savings or business.

> For the convenience of the public, we immediately started opening at 8 o'clock in the morning, rather than 9. And we extended the hours of banking. We were the first commercial bank to open Saturday mornings. We felt that Saturday mornings were times when the public, as a whole, had their leisure hours and were able to do their banking or sit down and talk to a bank loan officer.

Other early innovations for Coolidge included becoming the first bank in the Boston area to pay interest on Christmas Club accounts as well as the first to pay postage both ways for bank-by-mail accounts. Coolidge also reduced service charges for business checking accounts by one-third. Reproductions of billboards advertising these and later innovations are shown in Exhibit 2.

No-Service-Charge Checking

From total assets of $4 million at the end of its first year, "which was quite amazing to our friendly competitors and bankers in Boston," Coolidge Bank's asset base grew steadily, reaching some $12 million by the end of 1964. However, this still left Coolidge a very small bank by the standards of the major Boston banks, whose assets were in the hundreds of millions and higher.

During 1964, Coolidge began testing a radical departure in banking practice—no-service-charge (NSC) personal checking. Coolidge management had decided that the way to compete with the giants was, in Adess's words, "by trying to use our old hardware efforts— bring the best product to the people at the lowest possible cost." Commented the president,

> After doing an in-depth statistical study, we decided that service charges on personal checking accounts were really not necessary to operate a bank successfully. I didn't think that the profit picture of a bank required service charges—and still don't!
>
> I thought it was a little unusual, really, that for all these years banks had been charging *you* for the privilege of leaving *your* money in *their* bank so that they could lend it out and make money on it. Now if you're going to be good enough to deposit your money with us, and we can make money on your money, why should we charge you for that privilege?
>
> Well, I thought of a plan in 1963, and it took me close to a year and a half to convince my Board, because it was really breaking all existing banking principles. And when our friendly competitors in Boston heard about our plan, their reaction was one of amazement. I received many telephone calls with gloomy forecasts that eliminating service charges on personal checking accounts would result in disaster. They said, "Do you realize what service charges amount to in banks?" And my response was, "Look, I don't know what your service charges amount to, but I know that mine don't mean too much because we haven't got very many customers."

After preliminary testing, Coolidge adopted NSC checking for all personal checking accounts in 1965, requiring a $100 minimum balance. After promoting this concept through billboards and newspapers, a limited advertising budget was assigned to WEEI, a talk-show radio station. The response to the radio advertising was described as "astounding." Coolidge Bank started getting accounts from "every city, town, and hamlet in the state," and at one point, before the competition began following suit, was opening up to 200 accounts a day.

Many other banks soon followed Coolidge's lead, and within a few years NSC checking had become widespread in the Boston area. In 1969, Coolidge went one better, becoming the first to offer genuinely free checking by dropping its $100 minimum balance requirement.

A subsequent survey by the Federal Reserve Bank of Boston indicated that Coolidge's success in attracting new accounts as a result of its NSC plan had been replicated by many other banks in New England, mostly fairly new ones, which had been the first to offer NSC accounts in their local area.

Other Marketing Activities at Coolidge

Other innovations promoted by the bank included a program to market the American Express Gold Card—which carried a $2,000 credit line and was issued only through banks—to graduating MBA students with verified job offers. Coolidge promoted this concept to business school students nationwide (and later to medical and dental students), and before long became the second largest retailer of such cards in the United States.

Beginning in late 1971, Coolidge introduced its "Cool Cash" concept by installing automated banking consoles, termed *Cool-O-Mats*, outside certain branches. These machines effectively provided 24-hour, 7-day banking transaction services for customers and were more sophisticated than existing cash dispensing machines (which had been in use in Britain since 1967 and in the U.S. since 1969). Coolidge was the first bank in the Boston area to install automatic "total tellers," capable of performing the same range of banking transactions as a human teller. It promoted them aggressively, and by 1973 its Harvard Square machines were the most heavily used in the country.

Despite some early mechanical problems, later resolved, the Coolidge machines had generally performed well. Adess conceded that there had been occasional vandalism. "We've had some strange people in the Harvard Square area who poured bottles of Coke into the machines, but security has not been a problem." Viewed overall, he saw automatic tellers as a major opportunity to offer the public greater convenience.

Over the years, Coolidge had experimented

with a number of communications approaches, including on-campus representatives, direct mail ("very expensive"), television ("outlandishly expensive"), newspapers, billboards, and radio. Commented Adess,

> I found that the greatest response came from radio. We checked this. Every new account was asked, "How did you happen to open an account at Coolidge?" And the greatest response came from talk programs. At one time, we were on three or four stations in the Boston area.
>
> We haven't had a direct mail piece now for years. We went out of the newspaper business. Our response from local newspapers has been minimal. Large Boston newspapers are very expensive and you're competing with some very big people in there.
>
> When you buy that minute on the radio, that's yours. And if that man—or woman—is driving in his car, or listening to that program at home, you've got his ear. And the results for us have been really great. Very, very good.

Stimulated by a combination of innovative approaches to banking and aggressive advertising, Coolidge's deposits and assets grew rapidly (Exhibit 3). Although it had organized a holding company, First Coolidge Corporation, in 1970 to acquire the assets of Coolidge Bank and Trust Company, no attempt had been made to acquire subsidiaries outside Middlesex County. Nevertheless, Coolidge had succeeded in drawing some deposits not only from other parts of Massachusetts but from throughout the United States and even from depositors resident abroad.

Partly responsible for the growth in Coolidge assets and deposits were two mergers and the addition of several new offices. Branches were opened in Watertown in 1962 and in Cambridge in 1964, 1967, and 1970. In 1970 the bank also opened an attractive new four-story headquarters in Watertown Square, replacing its existing office there. 1971 was a particularly busy year for expansion. In April, Coolidge acquired the Industrial Bank and Trust Company of Everett, and in July it acquired the Arlington National Bank, with offices in Arlington, Lexington, and Bedford. In that same year, the bank moved its Harvard Square, Cambridge, office from a temporary location in a large trailer into a gaily painted former garage. In Adess's words, this was all part of Coolidge's attempt to "get away from that cold, granite-faced banker image that banking seems to have acquired over the years."

COOLIDGE BANK IN 1974[3]

By mid-1973, the First Coolidge Corporation ranked as the ninth largest commercial banking organization in the Boston banking market (Exhibit 4). Its operating income in 1973 exceeded $9 million and net income was some $668,000 (Exhibit 5), while year-end assets stood at $127 million (Exhibit 6).

In early 1974, the Coolidge Bank and Trust Company had a total staff of 201. There were 37 officers of the bank, headed by the president and executive vice-president. Most of the senior officers had over 15 years professional banking experience.

Five of the bank's nine offices were located in the densely populated cities of Cambridge and Watertown. Although five-sixths of its personal checking account holders in the Boston area were resident in Middlesex County, Coolidge also drew a number of accounts from residents of neighboring counties, notably Suffolk. This was true of savings accounts too.

Coolidge had in the vicinity of one hundred thousand accounts of all categories. About 70 percent of these were personal checking accounts, while 23 percent were regular savings accounts held by individuals. There were no charges for transactions in either type of account. Savings account holders maintained a small passbook which was updated every time they made a deposit or withdrawal, and they received 5% interest on the outstanding balance. Management believed that a high proportion of their savings account holders also maintained checking accounts at Coolidge. Other types of consumer deposits included 90-day notice savings accounts and longer-term savings certificates of deposit, all of which paid higher interest rates. Coolidge was more retail oriented than most commercial banks, and accounts held by businesses represented only a small proportion of the total; however, the value of their deposits was quite substantial (Exhibit 7).

One significant difference between demand and time deposits was the reserve requirements. Under Massachusetts law, not more than 85 percent of demand deposits (i.e., checking accounts) could be reinvested by banks, whereas they were free to reinvest 100 percent of time and savings deposits.[4] NOW accounts were treated as time and savings deposits. Like most banks, Coolidge maintained cash balances and deposits with other banks exceeding this legal minimum. The treasurer indicated that, as of mid-1974, Coolidge was realizing an average yield on loans and securities of around 9½ percent.

THE COMPETITIVE SITUATION

Coolidge was one of 32 commercial banks and some 60 thrift banks in Middlesex County. Management saw the principal competition as banks with branches in the southeastern part of the county. A 1973 survey showed that Coolidge and two other commercial banks— Harvard Trust Company ($264 million assets and 13 branches) and Middlesex Bank N.A. ($302 million assets and 29 branches)—each had approximately 11 percent of the personal checking account market in Middlesex. Another significant competitor was Newton-Waltham Bank and Trust Company ($236 million assets and 21 branches) with an estimated 8 percent of this market. These three competing banks were all subsidiaries of the Baystate Corporation, a Boston-based bank-holding company. A fourth competitor, County Bank N.A., which had 11 branches and $171 million in assets, was a subsidiary of the Shawmut Association, Inc. Another Shawmut subsidiary, Community National Bank, was not viewed as a direct competitor since most of its branches were located in the western part of the county.

Profiles of the personal checking customer base served by Coolidge and other selected Middlesex banks are shown in Exhibit 8.

Where savings accounts were concerned, competition was much stronger, coming from both thrift institutions as well as other commercial banks. Coolidge's market share of regular savings accounts was believed to be between 1 percent and 2 percent for the county as a whole. Thrift institutions had an advantage in that they could pay 5¼ percent on passbook savings versus the 5 percent legal maximum payable by commercial banks. Many of the thrift banks had multiple branches and a number were active in marketing their services.

Most of the locations served by a Coolidge branch were populated by several competing banks. The extreme example was at Harvard Square in Cambridge, where, including Coolidge, four commercial banks and three thrift banks could be found within a 200 yard radius.

Bank Consumers

A large-scale consumer survey in the Boston area found that nearly 82 percent of respondents maintained a checking account, while some 87 percent had savings accounts. However, there were significant variations in the pattern of checking and savings account ownership among households with different demographic characteristics (Exhibit 9).

In general, the survey found that respondents were more satisfied with their savings account bank than they were with their checking account bank. "Need better hours" and "poor personnel" were the principal complaints for both types of banks. About 10 percent of respondents had switched their accounts to different banks during the past year, but moving house was given as a reason more frequently than dissatisfaction or ability to obtain a "better deal" at another bank. "Good service" was the most frequently cited reason for recommending a checking account bank, while "good rates" was cited most often for savings account banks (Exhibit 10).

In terms of location, branches close to

home were preferred to those nearer to work. 50 percent of respondents with personal checking accounts said that the branch they used most often was closer to home than to work; 24 percent said the opposite; 16 percent said it was about equidistant, while 10 percent said they banked by mail. People in lower income and educational brackets were somewhat more likely to use a branch nearer home, while single people showed a greater tendency to patronize a bank near their workplace or to bank by mail than the sample as a whole.

THE ADVENT OF *NOW* ACCOUNTS

Negotiable order of withdrawal (NOW) accounts originated as a device to expand the ability of mutual savings banks to attract deposits.

The first attempt to obtain regulatory approval of NOW accounts in the United States was made in July 1970 by the Consumers Savings Bank of Worcester, Massachusetts. The bank filed a plan with the state banking commissioner to allow its savings account customers to withdraw funds by means of a negotiable order, similar to a check, instead of presenting a passbook. Although the commissioner denied this application, a suit brought by Consumers Savings later resulted in a ruling in the bank's favor by the Massachusetts Supreme Judicial Court.

On June 12, 1972, Consumers Savings began offering NOW accounts, paying the maximum legal interest rate of 5¼ percent and charging 15¢ for each withdrawal order. Ten other mutual savings banks followed suit in August 1972. The following month, after it had been established that New Hampshire law was similar to Massachusetts law, savings banks in New Hampshire began offering their own version of NOW accounts, paying a 4 percent interest rate but making no charge for withdrawals.

NOW accounts were soon adopted by other mutual savings banks in the two states and attracted significant deposits. However, commercial banks saw these accounts as an unfair advantage in competing for household deposits, especially since they were prohibited by federal law from offering NOW accounts themselves. Although the commercial banks lobbied hard for abolition, state and federal regulatory agencies were unable to reach agreement on control of NOW accounts.

The issue was then brought to Congress where, after further debate, a compromise was reached. Public Law 93–100, signed in August 1973, extended authorization to issue NOW accounts to commercial banks, savings and loans, and cooperative banks, but limited such accounts to Massachusetts and New Hampshire.

The various regulatory agencies then authorized commercial banks, S & L's and cooperative banks to begin offering NOW accounts from January 1, 1974, setting a maximum interest rate of 5 percent on these accounts for all institutions, including mutual savings banks. Advertising efforts were limited to media aimed primarily at residents of the two states. Although individuals and nonprofit organizations were allowed to hold NOW accounts, businesses were prohibited from doing so.

Coolidge Bank and NOW Accounts

Coolidge management had followed the development of NOW accounts closely. Despite his bank's reputation for innovation, Adess's attitude toward them had, initially, been quite negative. As he explained,

> To take away service charges, pay postage both ways, and give everything free—that's one thing. But to start paying 5 percent on top of that—now that's something else. That could become a real financial problem.

Coolidge held back in January 1974, when commercial banks first became entitled to issue NOW accounts. In that month, 11 of 153 commercial banks and 12 of the 179 S & L's and cooperative banks in Massachusetts began offering the accounts. Some 75 mutual savings banks in the state already offered NOW accounts prior to 1974, and by the end of January the figure had jumped to 85, more than 50 percent of all such banks in the state. Data collected each month by the Federal Reserve Bank of Boston showed a steady increase in the number of banks offering NOW accounts, as well as in new accounts opened and the volume of deposits (Exhibit 11). By May 1974, 13 percent of all commercial banks offered NOW accounts, as compared to 45 percent of all thrift banks. However, not all commercial banks offering NOW accounts advertised the fact, although thrift institutions did so vigorously. The only commercial banks actively promoting these accounts in the Boston area were some small and medium-sized banks in Essex County.

Many of the new accounts were opened by existing customers of the same bank and quite a significant volume of the funds deposited in these NOW accounts represented transfers from existing demand deposits or time and savings deposits at the same institution.

By June, Adess had noticed "quite a few decent-size, personal checking accounts" leave Coolidge for NOW accounts at nearby competing thrift institutions. He had also received "more than a few" calls from longstanding Coolidge customers, who had historically carried "decent balances" in their personal checking accounts, explaining the dilemma that they faced. Although they felt kindly disposed toward Coolidge for the innovative banking services that it had provided them over the years, they were nevertheless strongly tempted to move their checking business to other banks offering interest-bearing NOW accounts. The president felt that the time had come for the board to reassess the bank's position.

If Coolidge management decided to offer such accounts, then one issue would be what terms to offer. It was evident from the Federal Reserve Bank reports that significant variations existed between banks in the terms attached to NOW accounts, especially in the service charges levied per draft. Although most commercial banks charged 15 cents per draft, many thrift banks charged only 10 cents and fully one-third of them had no charge at all.

As further inputs to this decision, management was aware of the size distribution of existing demand and time deposits at Coolidge (Exhibit 12). The treasurer estimated that the direct cost to the bank of servicing a checking account transaction averaged around 10 cents, with overhead costs about the same. The costs for savings account transactions were substantially higher, due to the greater labor input required, particularly by tellers. However, the number of savings account transactions each month was only a tiny fraction of those by checking accounts. Also available was additional Federal Reserve Bank data on NOW account activity concerning the number of drafts issued by individual accounts each month (Exhibit 13).

"The priority," Adess told his fellow directors at the executive committee meeting called to discuss the NOW account issue, "is to hold the accounts that we have. We've taken a good hard look at every account we've lost or are afraid of losing and it's the better ones—like the over $1,000 average monthly balance accounts—not the 'garbage' accounts averaging $50."

NOTES

1. The term *thrift institutions* comprised mutual savings banks, savings and loan associations, and cooperative banks. These were distinguished from commercial banks in that only the latter had authority to accept demand deposits (i.e., checking accounts) or make commercial loans. The three types of thrift institutions fulfilled essentially similar banking functions, and the primary differences between them lay in the source of their charters and whether they were regulated and insured by state or federal authorities.

2. Steven J. Weiss, "Commercial Bank Price Competition: The Case of 'Free' Checking Accounts," *New England Economic Review*, September–October, 1969.

3. Certain nonpublished data in the balance of the case are either disguised or approximations.

4. Demand deposit reserve requirements were 20 percent in the city of Boston. Commercial banks which were members of the Federal Reserve System (Coolidge was not) had a 3 percent reserve requirement on time and savings deposits.

EXHIBIT 1
Cities and Counties in Eastern Massachusetts

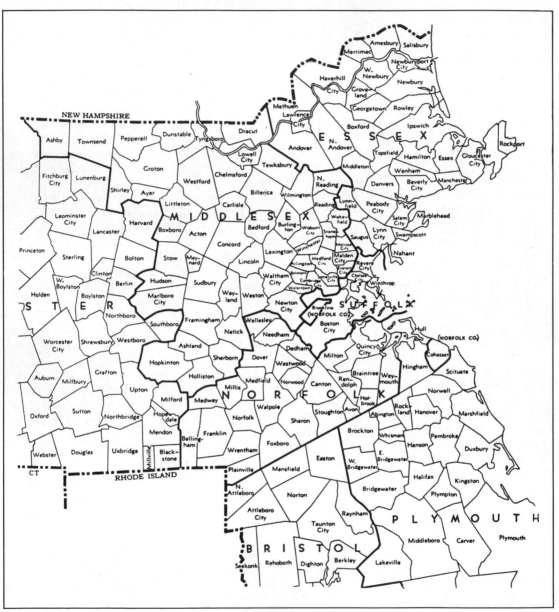

EXHIBIT 2
Coolidge Bank Billboards, 1960–1970

A DECADE OF INNOVATION A key to the dynamic growth of Coolidge Bank is its innovative approach to banking. The billboards on this page chronicle ten years of our bank's "firsts" in the Boston area.

we close Sundays! AT COOLIDGE BANK

1960 — Our first innovation, giving our customers Saturday banking.

xmas interest ALL YEAR AT COOLIDGE BANK

1960 — First to pay interest on Christmas Club Accounts.

we give business a break CHECK OUR LOW-COST BUSINESS CHECKING AT COOLIDGE BANK

1960 — Coolidge offered one-third reduction on service charges for Business Checking Accounts.

we pick up and deliver POSTAGE – FREE BANKING AT COOLIDGE BANK MEMBER F.D.I.C.

1961 — Coolidge was first to pay postage, both ways, in bank-by-mail accounts.

fnscpca! MEANS FREE CHECKING AT COOLIDGE BANK

1964 — Coolidge led the industry in No-Service-Charge Personal Checking.

we're loners... GET REFUND-A-LOANS ONLY AT COOLIDGE BANK

1966 — Coolidge rewards in cash, those who repay their loans in full and on time.

no money down WITH FREE NO-SERVICE-CHARGE CHECKING AT COOLIDGE BANK

1969 — First to offer No-Minimum-Balance, No-Service-Charge Checking.

we love m. b. a.'s AT COOLIDGE BANK

1970 — A "head-start" credit program for Business School Graduate students.

WHAT'S THE NEW GENERATION COMING TO? COOLIDGE BANK, THAT'S WHAT!

1970 — Members of the younger generation, from 50 states and 26 foreign countries, bank with Coolidge.

if you'd grown like we have, you'd need a new home too. COOLIDGE BANK MEMBER F.D.I.C.

1970 — Coolidge Bank's new headquarters at Watertown Square opens its doors.

Coolidge Bank gives you credit for being successful. Call 926-1400

1970 — With American Express, Coolidge extended credit to professional people.

coolidge bank comes to kendall BADGER BUILDING, CAMBRIDGE MEMBER F.

1970 — Our fifth branch office opens at Kendall Square, Cambridge.

EXHIBIT 3

Coolidge Bank and Trust Company
(*Year-End Deposits, 1960–1973*)

($ million)

	DEMAND DEPOSITS[a]	TIME DEPOSITS[a]	TOTAL DEPOSITS[b]
1960	$ 0.4	$ 0.2	$ 0.8
1961	1.9	1.0	3.5
1962	2.7	1.9	5.7
1963	3.8	3.0	8.0
1964	4.2	3.9	10.2
1965	6.7	5.4	13.9
1966	9.3	7.6	18.9
1967	16.2	10.7	29.8
1968	24.2	15.8	44.3
1969	25.4	11.1	44.3
1970	27.9	22.5	61.2
1971[c]	43.1	29.9	84.8
1972	51.7	32.5	94.2
1973	54.5	46.1	113.6

[a] Deposits of individuals, partnerships, and corporations.

[b] Total deposits included deposits of the U.S. Government ($1.7 million in 1973), of states and political subdivisions ($9.6 million in 1973), and of commercial banks, as well as certified and officers' checks.

[c] Coolidge acquired two other banks in 1971.

SOURCE: Year End Reports by Coolidge Bank to FDIC

EXHIBIT 4

Boston Banking Market
(June 30, 1973)

ORGANIZATION	NO. OF OFFICES	TOTAL DEPOSITS		DEMAND DEPOSITS < $20,000 (6/30/72)	
		($ million)	Percent	($ million)	Percent
1. First National Boston Corp.	42	3,137.8	30.7	202.3	15.3
2. Shawmut Association Inc.	104	1,520.5	14.9	191.3	14.5
3. State Street Boston Financial Corp.	34	1,169.2	11.4	103.8	7.9
4. Baystate Corp.	125	1,138.4	11.1	239.9	18.2
5. New England Merchants Company, Inc.	17	921.2	9.0	72.7	5.5
6. Arltru Bancorporation	14	242.5	2.4	26.0	2.0
7. Multibank Financial Corp.	35	199.1	1.9	46.5	3.5
8. Essex Bancorp	14	118.2	1.2	26.4	2.0
9. First Coolidge Corp.	9	94.9	.9	28.5	2.2
10. UST Corp.	9	93.3	.9	21.6	1.6
11. Framingham Financial	15	87.2	.9	19.4	1.5
12. Charterbank, Inc.	13	78.2	.8	19.4	1.5
13. Atlantic Corp.	5	73.2	.7	7.9	.6
14. Hancock Group	14	68.3	.7	21.5	1.6
15. Rockland Trust	15	68.2	.7	22.7	1.7
16. Massachusetts Bay Bancorp	8	67.5	.7	10.4	.8
17. Security National Bank	9	66.1	.6	14.4	1.1
18. Harbor National Bank	3	65.1	.6	4.4	.3
19. Commonwealth National Corp.	8	57.9	.6	11.3	.9
20. New England Bancorp.	15	53.4	.5	12.9	1.0
Next 60 bank organizations	150	900.5	8.8	225.1	17.0
	658	$10,220.7	100.0	$1,328.4	100.0

SOURCE: Federal Reserve Bank of Boston, Research Report 59

EXHIBIT 5

First Coolidge Corporation/Consolidated Statement of Income
(For the Years Ended December 31, 1973 and 1972)

	1973	1972
Operating income:		
Interest on loans	$7,952,215	$6,210,930
Interest and dividends on securities		
U.S. Government securities	304,233	277,300
Obligations of state and political subdivisions	199,672	332,103
Other securities	59,601	10,331
Other operating income	732,947	587,376
Total	9,248,668	7,418,040
Operating expenses:		
Salaries	1,895,640	1,705,963
Other employee benefits	159,723	203,117
Interest	2,471,277	1,790,298
Occupancy expense of bank premises	435,340	461,532
Loan loss provision	626,228	451,860
Other operating expense	2,476,142	2,268,194
Total	8,064,350	6,880,964
Income before income taxes and securities gains	1,184,318	537,076
Less applicable income taxes		
Current	178,229	(508,588)
Deferred	340,169	425,703
	518,398	(82,885)
Income before securities gains	665,920	619,961
Securities gains, less applicable income taxes of $2,158 and $41,785	1,843	35,737
Net income	$ 667,763	$ 655,698
Earning data per common share (based on 1,435,180 shares):		
Income before income taxes and securities gains	$ .83	$ .37
Applicable income taxes	(.37)	.06
Income before securities gains	.46	.43
Securities gains, less applicable income taxes	.01	.03
Net income	$ .47	$ .46

SOURCE: First Coolidge Corporation, Annual Report, 1973

EXHIBIT 6

First Coolidge Corporation/Consolidated Statement of Condition
(December 31, 1973 and 1972)

	1973	1972
ASSETS		
Cash and due from banks	$ 14,175,427	$ 12,911,111
Investment securities		
United States government obligations	5,009,926	5,049,377
Obligations of state and political subdivisions	8,949,981	3,516,426
Other securities	1,237,556	686,252
Total investment securities	15,197,463	9,252,055
Loans	89,803,957	78,335,088
Federal funds sold	—	800,000
Bank premises and equipment	4,247,813	4,254,904
Customers' liability under letters of credit	2,528,392	3,404,040
Accrued interest receivable	657,558	375,564
Other assets and deferred charges	558,277	1,726,388
Total	$127,168,887	$111,059,150

EXHIBIT 6 (continued)

	1973	1972
LIABILITIES AND CAPITAL		
Demand deposits	$ 60,944,902	$ 57,722,105
Time deposits	52,576,676	36,186,015
Federal funds purchased	—	2,000,000
Unearned income	1,965,975	1,804,323
Letters of credit outstanding	2,528,392	3,404,040
Other liabilities	804,708	1,637,124
Total liabilities	118,820,653	102,753,607
Reserve for loan losses	882,989	882,989
Capital funds:		
Capital debentures	190,000	241,000
Stockholders equity:		
Common stock, $0.60 par value		
2,000,000 shares authorized		
1,435,180 shares issued and outstanding	861,108	861,108
Surplus	5,645,020	5,645,020
Undivided profits	769,117	675,426
Total stockholders' equity	7,275,245	7,181,554
Total capital funds	7,465,245	7,422,554
Total	$127,168,887	$111,059,150

SOURCE: First Coolidge Corporation, Annual Report, 1973

EXHIBIT 7

Distribution of Accounts by Type
and Deposit Volume

Mid-1974

CATEGORY	PERCENT OF ACCOUNTS	PERCENT OF $ DEPOSITS
Checking:		
Government	*	2
Business	4	22
Personal	70	26
Savings:		
Regular savings	23	24
Notice savings	*	3
Savings certificates of deposit	3	11
Commercial certificates of deposit	*	12
	100%	100%

Asterisk (*) indicates less than 1 percent.
SOURCE: Coolidge Bank records (disguised data)

EXHIBIT 8

Consumer Account Holder Profiles of Boston Area Banks, Coolidge Bank and Selected Competitors

	INCOME ($ 000)					AGE					
	<5	5–10	10–15	15–25	>25	18–24	25–34	35–44	45–54	55–64	65+
ALL BOSTON AREA CHECKING ACCOUNTS	9.5%	25.4%	32.1%	24.4%	8.7%	12.6%	27.3%	20.2%	18.7%	11.5%	9.7%
Individual Bank Profiles:											
Coolidge Bank	13.6	21.4	31.4	25.7	7.9	19.1	47.1	15.3	10.2	5.7	2.5
Harvard Trust	12.0	28.0	22.7	28.7	8.7	17.9	31.5	19.1	14.2	8.6	8.6
Middlesex Bank	10.2	32.3	37.8	17.3	2.4	10.6	17.7	25.5	20.6	14.2	11.3
Newton-Waltham Bank	4.0	20.8	29.7	30.7	14.9	11.7	20.7	26.1	19.8	9.9	11.7
Community National Bank	1.5	22.7	34.8	33.3	7.6	12.7	35.2	26.8	14.1	8.5	2.8
ALL BOSTON AREA SAVINGS ACCOUNTS	10.9	26.7	31.6	23.0	7.8	12.8	25.5	19.4	18.9	12.6	10.9

	MARITAL STATUS			EDUCATION				
	Married	Single	Other	Some High School	High School Graduate	Some College	College Graduate	Post Grad Work
ALL BOSTON AREA CHECKING ACCOUNTS	70.3%	18.4%	11.3%	6.8%	25.5%	25.3%	21.3%	21.0%
Individual Bank Profiles:								
Coolidge Bank	57.6	32.9	9.5	3.8	14.0	17.2	23.6	41.4
Harvard Trust	64.6	26.8	8.5	3.0	12.2	23.8	19.5	41.5
Middlesex Bank	77.3	10.6	12.1	10.0	40.0	23.5	13.6	12.9
Newton-Waltham Bank	73.2	13.4	13.4	7.2	17.1	23.4	27.9	24.3
Community National Bank	80.3	8.5	11.3	1.4	25.4	26.8	25.4	21.1
ALL BOSTON AREA SAVINGS ACCOUNTS	69.5	18.3	12.1	9.1	27.6	24.9	19.9	18.6

SOURCE: Survey conducted for Coolidge Bank and Trust Company, mid-1973

EXHIBIT 9

Possession of Checking and Savings Accounts in the Boston Area by Demographic Segments

(Do you and your family currently have a checking account/savings account?)

	PERCENT RESPONDING YES	
	Checking Account	*Savings Account*
All Boston Area	81.8%	86.9%
Age:		
19–24	78.1	83.8
25–34	87.7	86.7
35–44	85.6	87.2
45–54	82.6	88.9
55–64	78.7	90.8
65+	69.0	83.9
Marital Status:		
Married	84.9	89.1
Single	79.1	84.0
Other	69.5	80.2
Education:		
Not high school graduate	55.1	78.0
High school graduate	72.6	83.6
Some college	85.5	88.9
College graduate	92.6	91.6
Postgraduate work	96.7	90.7
Income:		
< $5,000	59.8	73.2
$5,000–10,000	73.2	81.6
$10,000–15,000	87.3	91.2
$15,000–25,000	95.1	94.7
$25,000 +	98.8	94.7

SOURCE: Survey conducted for Coolidge Bank, mid-1973

EXHIBIT 10

Coolidge Bank: Selected Responses to Boston Area Consumer Banking Survey

	CHECKING ACCT. BANK	SAVINGS ACCT. BANK
What would you say is the most irritating characteristic of your Checking Account Bank/Savings Account Bank?		
Need better hours	4.2%	3.8%
Poor personnel	4.0	2.3
Want free checking	3.8	0.1
Long lines	2.2	2.0
Hidden charges	2.0	0.5
Bookkeeping errors	1.8	0.5
Slow bookkeeping	1.7	0.2
Low interest	0.1	1.0
Bad location/parking	0.8	0.5
Other complaints	5.2	2.7
No complaints cited	74.2	86.4
	100.0	100.0
Have you switched your account from another bank within the last year?		
Yes	10.3%	9.3%
No	89.7	90.7
	100.0	100.0
If yes, what was the major reason you switched your account?		
Moved	35.6%	35.1%
Dissatisfied with former bank	23.0	26.0
Better deal at new bank	9.2	15.6
Proximity to home or work	6.9	9.1
Other	25.3	14.3
	100.0	100.0
Why would you recommend this bank for Checking Accounts/Savings Accounts?		
Own experience*	10.7%	9.9%
Proximity*	8.6	10.6
Good service	35.1	24.0
Helpful, friendly personnel	10.5	10.6
Word of mouth	3.4	2.7
Good rates (chkg. or svgs.)	14.1	28.2
Full service	5.1	3.9
More branches	2.6	1.4
Liberal on loans	0.5	0.4
Large, stable	1.5	1.9
Good hours	1.5	1.4
Other	6.4	5.1
	100.0	100.0

* Note: If respondent answered "own experience" or "proximity," the interviewer was instructed to probe why the experience was good and circle another category if valid.

SOURCE: Survey conducted for Coolidge Bank, mid-1973

EXHIBIT 11

NOW Account Activity in Massachusetts by Type of Bank, 1974

	JAN.	FEB.	MAR.	APR.	MAY
COMMERCIAL BANKS					
Number of new accounts—existing customers	917	409	478	799	461
new customers	347	557	642	613	774
Number of accounts closed	5	18	34	37	89
Total number of accounts at month end	1,259	2,207	3,293	4,668	5,814
Deposits ($ million)	2.5	2.3	4.0	6.0	6.7
Withdrawals ($ million)	0.2	0.8	1.9	3.5	5.9
Balance at month end ($ million)	2.3	3.8	5.9	8.5	9.3
MUTUAL SAVINGS BANKS					
Number of new accounts—existing customers	4,660	4,061	4,960	4,784	5,033
new customers	3,360	3,715	4,157	4,021	4,860
Number of accounts closed	1,379	1,753	1,489	1,599	1,730
Total number of accounts at month end	95,677	101,701	109,365	116,618	124,822
Deposits ($ million)	57.0	49.0	62.7	72.7	76.5
Withdrawals ($ million)	59.8	45.9	53.8	70.8	75.9
Balance at month end ($ million)	134.8	138.5	147.8	150.3	151.5
SAVINGS AND LOANS, COOPERATIVES					
Number of new accounts—existing customers	784	809	1,242	1,499	1,355
new customers	464	763	1,043	739	1,077
Number of accounts closed	8	8	27	36	57
Total number of accounts at month end	1,240	2,831	5,166	7,394	9,820
Deposits ($ million)	1.0	2.3	4.3	7.3	8.8
Withdrawals ($ million)	0.1	0.8	2.4	4.7	6.9
Balance at month end ($ million)	0.9	2.3	4.3	6.9	8.9

SOURCE: Research Department, Federal Reserve Bank of Boston

EXHIBIT 12

Coolidge Bank and Trust Company:
Distribution of Personal Checking and Savings Accounts by Size of Average Monthly Balance

AVERAGE MONTHLY BALANCE	PERSONAL CHECKING ACCOUNTS		REGULAR SAVINGS ACCOUNTS	
	Percent of Accounts	*Percent of Deposits*	*Percent of Accounts*	*Percent of Deposits*
$50 and under	22.4%	1.4%	4.4%	0.1%
$51–$100	29.9	5.6	2.1	0.2
$101–$250	16.4	7.2	2.2	0.7
$251–$500	11.3	10.6	13.2	7.3
$501–$1,000	11.2	21.1	70.5	59.3
$1,001–$2,500	7.6	30.3	4.0	7.0
$2,501–$5,000	0.7	7.1	1.8	6.3
$5,001–$10,000	0.4	7.0	1.3	9.7
$10,001–$20,000	0.1	5.6	0.4	6.3
$20,000 +	*	4.1	0.1	3.1
	100.0%	100.0%	100.0%	100.0%

* Denotes less than 0.1 percent.
SOURCE: Coolidge Bank records (disguised data)

EXHIBIT 13

Volume of Drafts Issued by NOW Accounts in Massachusetts *1974*

	JANUARY	FEBRUARY	MARCH	APRIL	MAY
COMMERCIAL BANKS					
Total volume of NOW drafts ('000)	3.2	4.7	11.1	19.2	25.1
% Distribution of NOW accounts by number of drafts per account:					
0 Drafts	51.8%	55.0%	47.8%	43.9%	44.5%
1–9 Drafts	46.1%	34.7%	39.1%	41.4%	39.6%
10–20 Drafts	2.0%	9.0%	10.7%	11.7%	12.2%
>20 Drafts	0.2%	1.3%	2.5%	3.0%	3.7%
Average number of drafts per active account	5.4	4.7	6.4	7.3	7.7
MUTUAL SAVINGS BANKS					
Total volume of NOW drafts ('000)	493.7	498.2	598.5	708.8	757.5
% Distribution of NOW accounts by number of drafts per account:					
0 Drafts	25.1%	27.2%	26.9%	27.2%	26.6%
1–9 Drafts	56.5%	55.7%	56.3%	53.2%	52.9%
10–20 Drafts	14.6%	12.2%	13.5%	15.3%	15.5%
>20 Drafts	3.8%	0.9%	3.3%	4.3%	4.9%
Average number of drafts per active account	6.8	6.7	7.4	8.3	8.2
SAVINGS AND LOANS, COOPERATIVES					
Total volume of NOW drafts ('000)	2.1	9.9	25.5	46.8	66.4
% Distribution of NOW accounts by number of drafts per account:					
0 Drafts	59.5%	30.0%	36.0%	25.7%	20.0%
1–9 Drafts	37.6%	57.5%	44.0%	47.2%	49.1%
10–20 Drafts	2.9%	11.2%	15.9%	20.7%	23.1%
>20 Drafts	—	1.3%	4.1%	6.4%	7.8%
Average number of drafts per active account	4.2	5.0	7.7	8.5	8.4

SOURCE: Research Department, Federal Reserve Bank of Boston

READINGS

Hospitals Can Learn Valuable Marketing Strategies from Hotels

JAMES A. RICE

RICHARD S. SLACK

PAMELA A. GARSIDE

Hospitals have certain important characteristics in common with hotels. Managers of hospitals and hospital chains will find it to their advantage to study the marketing precepts and strategies developed by hotel chains and then to adapt these to their own situations.

Hospitals and multihospital systems can strengthen their marketing activities by selectively borrowing ideas from other service industries such as the hotel industry. Although no analogy is perfect, there are several similarities between multihospital systems and hotel chains, as well as between individual hospitals and hotels. These similarities suggest a number of useful ideas for marketing by multihospital systems during the 1980s.

The hotel and hospital industries offer interesting similarities, including the following:

• Their basic business is focused on overnight occupancy of rooms, but much of their net operating revenue is derived from ancillary services.

• They are developing a keen interest in diversifying into synergistic new lines of business.

• Operating costs are labor-intensive.

• They deal with intermediate "purchasers" of service—namely, travel agents and physicians.

• Competition for certain relatively stable markets is increasing.

• They must give careful attention to physical facility amenities.

Certain descriptive statistics also indicate parallels between the two industries, as summarized below:

• While the number of individual hotels and hospitals has remained relatively stable or declined slightly, the average size of each unit has increased.

• Individual units are coalescing into significantly larger chains; 70 percent of all hotel rooms and about 40 percent of all hospital beds are operated within chains.

• Occupancy is in the low 70 percentiles (hospitals have experienced a decline).

• Hospitals and hotels have increased their labor intensity, but hospitals have a considerably higher number of employees per unit and a higher rate of increase in that number.

James A. Rice is vice-president corporate planning and development, and Richard S. Slack and Pamela A. Garside are planning associates, Health Central System, Minneapolis. Reprinted by permission from *Hospitals* (Vol. 55, No. 22), copyright November 16, 1981, American Hospital Publishing, Inc.

• Increases in room rates have exceeded the Consumer Price Index (CPI).

Hotels and hotel chains compete aggressively for several diverse markets, including business travelers, family vacationers, and convention groups. They assign differing priorities to each market, but they acknowledge keen competition in each one. This competition has stimulated an increase in the importance of marketing and market research for hotel chains. Approximately 3 to 7 percent of their operating budgets are allocated to marketing, with the younger, growth-oriented chains spending more than the larger, established chains. As marketing received increasing attention during the 1970s, the hotel chains established formal marketing departments that perform sales, research, and marketing planning functions. The training, experience, and compensation of the staff members of these departments also increased. Hotel chains organized their marketing functions within three areas: (1) market research, (2) marketing planning, and (3) targeted marketing strategies. All activities within these three functions are guided by the following basic precepts:

• The customer is the central focus of the organization's mission and ultimate profitability.

• Marketing is not a cluster of techniques so much as it is an *orientation* and a *process* that attempt to systematically study, plan, and manage exchange relationships between customers and hotels. (In an exchange relationship, two parties trade something of value to receive something of value, believe that they benefit from the interaction, and may assign differing values to the items exchanged. The items exchanged may include money, information, power, prestige, patients, or services.)

• Marketing is behavior-oriented; therefore, effective marketing research, planning, and strategies deal with factors that influence human behavior. For example, to achieve optimum exchange relationships, two-way behavior modification often is required—that is,

changes in the behavior of customers as well as changes in the behavior of the provider regarding scope of service, hours of operations, price, quality, and so forth.

• Marketing is oriented to key publics and to fostering of positive exchange relationships with these publics. This orientation must permeate all levels of the organization. When all units and employees are aware of and effective in their efforts to serve the key publics, the organization is more vital and prosperous.

Marketing by the hospital industry is a relatively new phenomenon that has been caused, in part, by increasing competition in the field. In multihospital systems, marketing is undertaken at two levels, and each level addresses significantly different target publics or customers.

At the *institutional* level, marketing is concerned with services to be provided by an individual hospital; specialties to be represented on its medical staff; types of patients to be attracted to the hospital; and promotional methods to be used to enhance the hospital's image and attractiveness to physicians, patients, and the community-at-large. The primary target groups are patients and physicians, and the primary objective generally is to effect more appropriate institutional utilization.

At the *corporate* level, marketing is concerned with which services the corporation should offer at which prices to which geographic markets. The primary objectives of marketing at this level are to secure hospital units for management services or acquisition, to attract investors, and to attract and retain essential clinical or managerial personnel.

Several investor-owned hospital chains have invested heavily in formal market research and market development activities at the individual hospital level. For example, Humana has organized hospital-level market research and marketing training programs.[1] Individual not-for-profit hospitals, which have more localized markets, generally have been less active in marketing and advertising and have maintained their traditional reliance on annual reports, community events, local news media, and service club activities of their managers in order to develop recognition.

At the system level, the growth of investor-owned companies and their need to promote their names and reputations in the physician, hospital, and financial markets have fueled the growth of marketing activity. Similarly, not-for-profit systems' desire for growth has led them to seek wider public and provider recognition. Their corporate marketing strategy has been to promote the advantages of systems in general and to enhance their own corporate recognition among hospitals that could become members or affiliates of their systems. In addition, some not-for-profit systems offer marketing assistance as an unbundled service to nonmember hospitals and also are developing formal marketing programs for corporate services.

Considering that competition among multihospital systems for sale of shared services, for acquisitions, and for management of hospitals is increasing, it can be anticipated that marketing activities by both investor-owned and not-for-profit systems will continue to grow in intensity and sophistication. This trend is already being exhibited by the establishment of marketing departments both at the hospital level and the corporate level and by the development of staff specialists in marketing. The hotel industry underwent the same developments during the 1970s.

Market research by hotel chains involves various methods designed to answer six key questions:

- Who are our customers—that is, what markets are we serving?

- Why are these customers using us rather than our competitors?

- What do the customers want from a hotel?

- What changes should we make to better meet the wants of our existing customers or of customers we would like to have?

- What messages should we use to best communicate with our customers?

- What media should we use and how in order to ensure that our messages are understood and believed by our customers?

As multihospital systems adopt methods to answer similar questions for their communities and clients, they will learn, as hotel chains did, that market research need not always be expensive or highly quantitative. For example, it need not be a new survey. Hotel chains have found that the most cost-effective research, in fact, focuses on existing data from routine operations, such as demographic and seasonal use trends from registration data, data on units and costs of services from billing systems, and information on customer satisfaction from check out procedures. Similarly, hospital systems can rely on such existing data from their operations to establish and maintain the following marketing information systems:

- *Market analysis*, which determines the size, the location, and other characteristics of existing markets.

- *Sales analysis*, which provides information on sales volume trends within each market segment.

- *Motivation research*, which determines why customers use products or services.

- *Advertising or communications research*, which determines which communications are working with selected groups of customers and why.

In hotel chains, responsibility for designing and conducting such research is shared by the individual hotels and the corporate offices.

In the hospital industry, market research has been developed largely as an adjunct to planning systems. The type of research that has been conducted at the individual hospital level has been based on standard information that has been available for planning purposes, such as patient origin and utilization data, and, more recently, on information that has been generated specifically for marketing through targeted surveys, such as community needs surveys conducted in the locale of individual hospitals. Sales analysis, motivation research, and communications research are not yet well-developed in the hospital industry, particularly not in the not-for-profit sector. Therefore, rapid growth can be expected in these areas, particularly at the corporate level, as hospital systems strengthen their use of marketing.

Hotel chains launch their marketing planning by generation of a "fact base" of market research and trend data. The unique strengths and weaknesses of each hotel in a chain for specific target markets are identified by their local managers through analysis of this fact base. Specific objectives for the next operating period are then established by the corporate staff with input from the local managers, and specific corporate and local strategies as well as related activity schedules and management responsibilities are defined for each marketing objective. Advertising is one component of marketing that might be conducted at either the corporate or the local level.

The corporate offices provide guidance for this process by issuing a pro forma marketing plan that defines the steps in the marketing planning process, and the essential forms of data analysis to be performed. The individual hotels prepare their marketing plans within these guidelines and submit them to the corporate offices for review. The corporate staff also periodically conducts on-site audits of each hotel's marketing planning process and performance. It is expected that similar support and evaluation roles will be developed in both the investor-owned and the not-for-profit multi-hospital systems.

Hotel marketing strategies pay particular attention to two types of customers—(1) the guest or basic purchaser and (2) the intermediate purchaser, the travel agent. Useful analogies may be drawn to a hospital's patients as guests and to physicians as the intermediate decision makers on purchasing of services, and hospital systems may identify a variety of provocative marketing ideas for these customers.

To patients, service amenities are tantamount to the quality of care. In evaluating price/value relationships, patients judge their hospital experiences on the basis of features that they feel qualified to evaluate—on the food, the room, the bed, personalized treatment from the staff, and so forth—more than the basis of the technical quality of professional care that they receive. Therefore, if a hospital wants to be the patients' hospital-of-choice, it has a legitimate management priority to provide facilities and services that meet patients' needs and expectations regarding amenities.[2] Table 1 demonstrates key points of guest contact both in hospitals and in hotels that may affect the guests' experiences.

Marketing programs also may be developed for the intermediate purchasers of services—the travel agents and the physicians. Table 2 describes a current, three-stage, three-year marketing program developed by the Radisson Corporation and shows how its basic elements can be applied in a hospital marketing program. This program was developed and targeted for the travel agent market when market research showed that only 18 percent of U.S. travel agents were directing business to Radisson hotels.

Marketing strategies and programs in the hospital industry are less well developed than are those in the hotel industry. One reason is that, despite the parallels between the two industries, hospitals and hospital systems serve an additional client group—the community—for which there is no direct corollary in the hotel industry. The community is not strictly a consumer group but, instead, also has an ownership or stewardship role vis-a-vis hospitals. This added dimension renders a certain uniqueness to marketing in the health care sector. At the system level in the hospital industry, marketing strategies have been targeted specifically to this group largely through contacts with hospital trustees. These contacts range from advertising to direct-mail techniques.[3]

At the corporate level, advertising is the most visible marketing effort of hospital systems. All investor-owned systems use national print media to reinforce their corporate images, to place their names and growth histories before potential shareholders, and to recruit new employees and medical staff members.

TABLE 1 (continued)

TABLE 1

Factors Affecting Guest/Patient Experience in Hotel/Hospital

HOTEL	HOSPITAL
TRANSPORTATION	

Impression of car, van, or limousine service
  cleanliness
  age of vehicle
  appearance of driver
  attitude and knowledge of driver
	May not apply except for elderly patients or patients who arrive by ambulance

BUILDING AND LOCATION	
Design	Design
Parking	Parking
Cleanliness of grounds	Cleanliness of grounds
Maintenance impression	Maintenance impression

Doorman
  availability
  appearance
  attitude and actions
  ability to help
	Receptionists or information desk
	  personnel available
	  appearance
	  attitude and actions
	  ability to help

Signage	Signage
Guest directory	Guest directory
CHECK IN	
Visual impression of front desk	Visual impression of front desk

Personnel at desk
  attitude
  appearance
  efficiency
  knowledge of facility
  ability to orient guest
	Personnel at desk
	  attitude
	  appearance
	  efficiency
	  knowledge of facility
	  ability to orient patient

Bellman
  attitude
  appearance
  efficiency
  knowledge of facility
  ability to orient guest
	Attention to others in party
	  lounge
	  child care

	Assistance to room
	  nurse
	  aide
	  orderly
	  none
	  ability to orient patient

ROOM	

Employee-guest interactions
  attitudes
  orientation to room
	Employee-patient interactions
	  attitudes
	  orientation to room

Cleanliness	Cleanliness

Bed
  size
  quality
	Bed
	  size
	  quality

TABLE 1 (continued)

HOTEL	HOSPITAL
Appropriateness of decor	Appropriateness of decor
View	View
Amenities	Amenities
Directory to facility available	Directory to facility available
FACILITY EXPERIENCE	

Meeting space	Food and beverage
	  availability
	  pricing
	  menu variety
	  food quality
	  personnel attitudes

Food and beverage
  availability
  pricing
  menu variety
  food quality
  personnel attitudes	

Maintenance impression	Maintenance impression
Cleanliness	Cleanliness

Special features
  pool, gym, gift shop, so forth
	Special features
	  lounges for visitors

Entertainment
  lounge
  TV
  gift shop
	Entertainment
	  visiting hours
	  TV
	  reading materials

Directory to facility or information desk	Directory to facility or information desk

Basic entertainment center
  games
  sports
  playground	

CHECK OUT	
Visual impression of desk	Visual impression of desk

Personnel at desk
  attitude
  appearance
  efficiency
	Personnel at desk
	  attitude
	  appearance
	  efficiency

Presentation and explanation of bill	Presentation and explanation of bill

Follow up
  systematic attempt to assess quality of stay
	Follow up
	  patient education
	  personal attention
	  home visit or call
	  orientation to subsequent therapy

Not-for-profit chains are considerably less active in nationwide advertising, using communications media primarily for recruiting key medical, nursing, and managerial personnel. It is anticipated that this pattern will change as

TABLE 2

Marketing Program for Intermediate Purchasers of Services of Hotels and Hospitals

HOTELS/ TRAVEL AGENTS	HOSPITALS/ PHYSICIANS
STAGE 1: BUILDING AWARENESS	
Message	
Emphasize that Radisson is a hotel company	Emphasize existence and mission of hospital
Medium	
Car give-away to travel agent who directs most business to Radisson	Direct-mail campaign to physicians
Direct-mail campaign to travel agents	Presentations at meetings of local medical society
Public relations releases	Hospital newsletters sent to physicians
Mail stuffers in travel agents' commission checks	
STAGE 2: DIFFERENTIATION OF SERVICES	
Message	
Emphasize price, quality, accomodations, locations, and other features	Emphasize hospital's unique facility, staff, training, quality of nursing care, positive public image
Medium	
Direct-mail campaign to travel agents	Direct-mail campaign to physicians that features testimonials from nurses, other physicians, and patients
Public relations releases	
Mail stuffers in travel agents' commission checks	Presentations at meetings of local medical society
	Hospital newsletters sent to physicians
	Practice management seminars convened at no cost to physicians
STAGE 3: SOLICITATION OF BUSINESS	
Message	
Emphasize that it is logical to direct business to Radisson in light of new awareness and understanding of its services that travel agents now should have	Encourage admissions in light of new awareness and understanding of the hospital that the physicians now should have
Medium	
Direct-mail campaign to travel agents	Provision of reasonably priced medical office space, parking, and staff facilities
Public relations releases	

TABLE 2 (continued)

HOTELS/ TRAVEL AGENTS	HOSPITALS/ PHYSICIANS
Mail stuffers in travel agents' commission checks	Computer printouts on status of each physician's admitted patients and quarterly summary activity reports
	Presentations at meetings of local medical society
	Hospital newsletters sent to physicians
	Staff picnics

not-for-profit systems become more aggressive in the marketplace.

Direct-mail programs increasingly are being used by both investor-owned and not-for-profit systems and are being targeted to specific groups of hospital trustees, such as those of local government hospitals or of hospitals owned by religious groups. The promotional material often is accompanied by educational information on current issues in the health care industry in order to dilute the hard sell approach.

This examination of the marketing experiences of hotel chains and the state of the art of marketing by multihospital systems leads us to offer the following predictions concerning the future of marketing activities by multihospital systems:

• Hospital systems will add to their existing planning staffs members who have special capabilities in market research and marketing planning. These special staff members will be recruited from other service industries and will be compensated attractively.

• Computer-assisted analysis packages will be used to centralize certain ongoing market research that is conducted by corporate staff on behalf of individual hospitals' managers. Control over what research is initiated by whom, when, how, and at what cost will be shared by the individual hospitals and the corporation according to each system's operating philosophy.

• Hospital systems will facilitate sharing of the costs associated with periodic research studies that are designed to test patients' and physicians' attitudes and preferences.

• They will develop and issue "pro forma" guides on how individual hospitals should conduct local market research, planning, and promotion.

• Funds will increasingly be invested to develop corporate marketing themes and advertising campaigns that can be used at the hospital level to feature the image and the strength of both the systems and of the individual hospitals.

• Systems will provide their member hospitals with technical assistance for the development of their local marketing plans.

• They also will monitor the individual hospitals' marketing performance by conducting periodic marketing audits.

The hotel industry is only one of the service industries from which multihospital systems can borrow management practices. It is hoped that this article will stimulate study of additional ways in which hospitals and multihospital systems can adapt marketing and planning techniques from service industries such as banks and bank holding companies, public utilities, and airlines.

NOTES

1. G. Kinkead, "Humana's Hard-Sell Hospitals," *Fortune*, Nov. 17, 1980, pp. 68–70, 76, 81.

2. D. E. Johnson, "Hospitals Emphasize Guest Relations," *Modern Healthcare.* 10:42, December 1980.

3. S. L. Tucker, "Introducing Marketing as a Planning and Management Tool." *Hosp. and Health Serv. Admin.* 22:37, Winter 1977.

The Marketing of Professional Services—25 Propositions

EVERT GUMMESSON

Professional service firms are becoming increasingly interested in marketing, despite previous barriers against employing marketing tools and strategies in many professional fields. This article raises a number of important marketing issues for such firms and provides guidelines for effective planning and implementation.

This paper consists of 25 propositions on the marketing of professional services. The propositions constitute an effort to apply research on service marketing to practical guidelines for the professional service firm:

1. To point out, in a condensed form, important marketing issues—new ones and old ones—that are particularly relevant to professional services.

2. To inspire the professional service firm to audit its own marketing and ask vital questions such as

Evert Gummesson is with the Stockholm Consulting Group, Stockholm, Sweden. Reprinted by permission from *Marketing Services*, eds. James H. Donnelly and William R. George, the American Marketing Association (Chicago, 1981).

"Is proposition X relevant to us? If so, what are the consequences to our firm? What action should we take to improve our marketing?"

Apart from my own practical experience the propositions are based on findings from a recent research project which I carried out in Sweden.

This paper is concentrated on professional services offered to industry and other organizations (*producer services* as opposed to *consumer services*, see Fig. 1). The groups of professionals whom I have studied are advertising agencies, public relations consultants, market research institutes, management consultants, consultants in the computer field, auditors, lawyers, architects and the other consultants in the building and construction field, and, finally, groups of consultants working with various aspects of technology.

There is no commonly accepted definition of a professional and a professional service. When I use the term professional service in this paper I refer primarily to the above professionals. A more general definition includes the following criteria:

- A professional service is qualified, it is advisory and problem-solving, even though it may also encompass some routine work for clients.
- The professionals involved have a common identity as, for example, management consultants or lawyers, and such professionals are regulated by traditions and codes or ethics.
- The service on offer, if accepted, involves the professional in taking on assignments for the client and those assignments are themselves the limit of the professional's involvement. Such assignments are not undertaken merely as overtures to sell hardware or other services.

However, the propositions presented here may also be of use to others. Among them: *public organizations*, e.g., weather forecasting institutes, export and trade promotion authorities, central statistical bureaus, and institutes that provide testing facilities of various kinds. Such bodies often have the capacity to undertake more work but do not market their services (some even put off potential customers by their rigid and unhelpful responses to inquiries). Similarly trade associations may offer a set of services to their members (often within the yearly fee) but could also provide tailor-made extras (even for nonmembers) at special fees.

Systems selling is becoming an important strategy for many firms who traditionally worked with single commodities. A system is a package composed of hardware and software, where the ability to provide the software may constitute the unique competitive advantage. The software may to some extent consist of professional services concerning construction,

FIGURE 1

Professional services can be divided into *consumer services* (sold to households) and *producer services* (sold to firms and other organizations).

FIGURE 2

The figure illustrates the relation between *goods, services, professional services* (P), and *systems* (S). A system is a package composed of commodity products (hardware) and related services (software) which may be to some extent professional services.

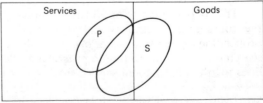

management, training, etc. (See Fig. 2.) Thus today, the *manufacturing firm* could also profit from a knowledge of professional services marketing.

Proposition 1—Marketing is more than getting orders. A professional service firm which has a full workload today may not feel spontaneously the need for marketing; there is no direct need to go out and acquire new clients. However, marketing strategy considerations are always significant: Which services should we offer the market ("our service line"), which types of clients shall we aim at ("segmentation"), what should our price level be, shall we prepare for growth, the establishment of new local offices, start up international operations, join another professional firm? These questions are a part of marketing as are analyses of the market, marketing planning and organization. All these problems need constant or at least periodical consideration—when the firm is in trouble it is too late to begin; the options within the available time scale are too few.

Proposition 2—It is necessary to actively market professional services. It is dangerous to believe that a good service will sell itself. Professional service firms sometimes have a mental block against efficient marketing; in some professional groups, marketing is actively resisted, looked down upon, and considered below the dignity of the professional man. You can stick to the strategy of no marketing as long as your services are scarce and as long as there is restricted entry to your profession. When these conditions are not fulfilled you either go under with an impeccable reputation among your peers or you change to a strategy of active marketing.

Proposition 3—Most professionals are not born salesmen. They become it if they want to. Professionals need to use effective sales techniques just like any other salesmen. They should also learn what it means to lead a sales force with regard to planning, motivation, and remuneration. However, they have to adjust the techniques to the specif-

ic features of professional service marketing. To learn sales techniques properly it is necessary to combine various media: Training courses where film and TV is used, on-the-job training visiting clients together with professionals who are good salesmen, and practising on one's own.

Proposition 4—The client's need is the basis of successful selling. The salesman starts by identifying the *needs* of the prospect and goes on to make clear if his firm is the right one to *satisfy* the need. The concluding step is to communicate to the prospects the professional's ability to satisfy the need in the best possible way—i.e., he starts *selling*. To start argumentation for a service that the prospect does not need is poor salesmanship.

Proposition 5—A large number of activities are available to the professional services marketer. By *marketing mix* is meant a combination of various means and activities. One well-known classification is the 4 P's: *product* (the professional service), *price* (the professional's fee), *promotion* (ways of communication), and *place* (where the services can be offered). The third P—promotion—includes some forty activities that can be carried out to influence the market. Each professional service firm should actively seek its own *promotional mix*, combining those activities that the firm finds suitable, as follows:

A. Activities that require personal contact with prospects: sales calls on own initiative; sales calls on inquiry. Proposals: current contacts with certain important customers and prospects, current contacts with suppliers or others who may influence sales; surveying activities and events in the market; developing know-how on individual prospects.

B. Advertising: advertisements in daily newspapers; advertisements in trade journals; other types of advertisements: telephone directories, year books, etc.; brochures; direct mail; participation in advertising arranged by trade associations.

C. Public relations and other promotional activities: conferences, symposiums, seminars, courses, etc., arranged by the professional firm; participation in conferences, etc., arranged by a trade association or someone outside the professional firm; participation as lecturer, seminar leader, etc.; membership of associations; dinners, lunches, and other forms of entertainment; invitations, e.g., to the professional firm's office; exhibitions; reference assignments; references to persons; introductions; participation in professional contests; arranging contests; awarding fellowships; publication of articles; reprints of articles; publication of books; product sheets; annual reports; publishing a magazine for clients; slides, films, etc.; billboards and name-plates; press releases; press conferences, interviews; gifts; Christmas greetings, anniversary greetings, etc.

Proposition 6—The cheapest way to get assignments is through inquiries. The most costly way is personal sales calls. In order to get the prospect to make an inquiry, the professional service firm must be known in its particular *market segment*. The activities in B and C above serve primarily to *generate inquiries*. By actively building the *image* of the firm the probability of inquiries is enhanced.

Proposition 7—It is often an advantage if the relationship between the professional and the client remains stable for a longer period of time. But sometimes it can be desirable that a relationship is broken. Getting new assignments continuously or at regular intervals naturally is a wish from the professional: It gives him a stable workload and it keeps his marketing costs down. In Sweden ad agencies usually keep their clients for several years, public auditors seem to keep them forever, [but] management consultants are changed quite often. A long relationship may however go from stable to rigid. A certain amount of change may be necessary to bring in novel approaches.

Proposition 8—Marketing tasks are performed by all who have client contact—i.e., all professionals in the firm. But often the professionals do not realize *this and therefore do an inferior marketing job.* Professional services are produced in close contact with the client. At one time the marketing of professional services was often handled exclusively by the directors of the firm (see the old organizational model in Fig. 3). In times when competition is tougher, another organization model has to be used: everybody takes responsibility for attracting business (the new model in Fig. 3). Why is this more efficient? The reasons are these:

• The client prefers to negotiate the assignment with someone who is going to carry out the job.

• Every professional, in the operation of the assignment, is in contact with clients and can then see new needs for assistance.

• Social contact between the individual professional and the client is important. Mutual understanding and trust, which are crucial for the long-term development of the firm, are fostered by the interaction of work and social relationships.

• Every professional has contacts who can give him information on what is going on in the market. From his friends or from fellow members of associations he may learn of potential clients. This multitude of contacts cannot be achieved by a marketing director or some salesmen.

Proposition 9—The marketing department is only one part of the marketing function. If a professional service firm grows it may have a special marketing department. This department can only handle part of the marketing function, mainly advertising, planning, and coordination. In the large professional service firms, the marketing department may have a full-time staff; in smaller firms it may be a professional working part time with marketing. The marketing department does not replace the individual professional's marketing activities; it is complementary.

Proposition 10—The professionals should wear "marketing glasses." What does it mean to wear "marketing glasses"? Our

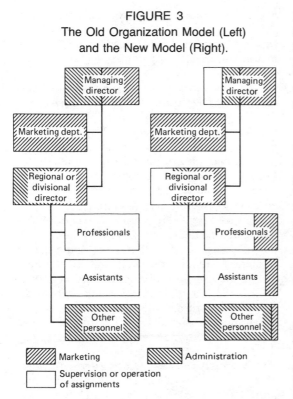

FIGURE 3
The Old Organization Model (Left)
and the New Model (Right).

Marketing

Administration

Supervision or operation
of assignments

way of perceiving what happens around us is restricted by our interests and attitudes—*our perception is selective.* By seeing the world through "marketing glasses," the professional will discover ideas and opportunities when reading the newspaper and *Fortune* magazine, watching television, driving his car, discussing with friends, etc. One can be trained with the ability to see opportunities. For instance, the architect reads about a corporation's new strategy within which investment in a new plant will be made, the management consultant hears about a firm's low profits, the ad man sees a bad sales campaign. . . . Such information may initiate contact with a prospect.

Proposition 11—It is usually easier to turn a professional into a marketing man than to hire a marketing man and get him to understand the professional service firm's business. The one who sells a service is also expected to take part in its production.

Professional services are often complex: to plan a firm's public relations, to study consumer attitudes of a new product, to reorganize a corporation, to design a new housing area. Only those who have learned the service and the service firm from within can meaningfully present it to a prospect.

Proposition 12—A professional service firm that wants to develop its marketing must be prepared to invest in planned efforts. To get the marketing function of a professional service firm operating, it is necessary to establish a development program with long-term objectives. "Happenings" every now and then such as an occasional sales conference, a sales film, or a seminar seldom give more than pleasure (or aggravation) for a couple of hours.

Proposition 13—The time to negotiate an assignment can be drawn out, even several years. Therefore, seeds must be sown now in order to harvest during the coming years. Even if the professionals have a full workload now, they must not forget to create contacts and spread knowledge about their capabilities. There are many examples of how firms have engaged themselves in one or two large assignments and when these ended they had no jobs in the pipeline.

Proposition 14—Marketing requires time and money. It is essential to decide upon an adequate budget for marketing activities. In order to maintain a certain volume of work, a professional service firm can estimate that a certain marketing effort is necessary. The effort consists of time spent by the staff, the expenses of advertising, public relations and sales promotion, and finally the cost caused by specific sales situations (e.g., travel expenses). Efforts that cause outlays are easy to calculate; the problem is to evaluate the time spent by the professional. If the workload is full, then, in the short run, there is an opportunity cost, i.e., the fee lost by not working for an existing client. However, it is necessary also to look ahead: I have to abstain from today's fees in order to obtain tomorrow's fees. Sometimes, in professional service firms, an attitude against marketing costs is developed: We want to increase our marketing but it must not cause any costs. This attitude will slow down or hinder marketing orientation.

Proposition 15—One can never compensate inferior services with hard selling and advertising techniques. Simply stated, you have two boxes at your disposal. In the left box you have your services, in the right box the media to communicate with and influence the market. Both these boxes must be filled with a good content in order to create balance.

Proposition 16—A warning: Professionals may sometimes become too insistent marketers and may then be a nuisance to the client. Sometimes a client may feel that a professional service firm never leaves him alone. For instance, a swarm of management consultants or ad men invades his firm and constantly finds new areas for investigation. This may be profitable in the short run but will make the client tired and it may backfire. Instead, try and find the balance: See the client's needs, recommend projects, sell them, but do not take over the client's business.

Proposition 17—Professional service firms must also engage in "product" development. If the services are not developed there is a great risk that in three to five years, the professionals may lag behind. Service development mainly takes place in the following form:

• In assignments where the professional can try his know-how on real problems, discover his strengths and weaknesses.

• In marketing services when he may detect the client's changing needs and adjust his services accordingly.

• Through his education, reading, participating in associations, etc.

• In planned development projects. In these projects you sum up know-how from the above three sources and experiences. Development projects that are not closely tied to actual experiences with clients often become academic and commercially frustrating.

Proposition 18—If a professional service firm is to flourish, the members of the staff must look upon themselves as professionals and strive to become better professionals. Internal administration and hierarchical structure should be kept at a minimum. In the cases I have come across, where the professional is restricted to marketing, developing, or administering services, results have been poor. A professional who does not take part in the carrying out of assignments suffers after some time a reduction in his professional effectiveness. Therefore, as is indicated in the new organization model in Fig. 3, a professional should not stay away from actual operating for too long. Often in professional service firms the responsibility for the management of the firm rotates.

Proposition 19—Make sure you negotiate assignments with the right person. It is not always easy to identify the people who influence the selection of professionals. There exist a large number of models of organizational buyer behavior which can be helpful. In one of the best-known models (Webster and Wind) five roles are defined and one individual can play more than one of these roles:

• *The decider* has the formal authority or informal power to make the final decision in selecting the professional.

• *Influencers* are those who influence the decision in some way, e.g., by special know-how on the subject. A product manager may influence the selection of an advertising agency while the marketing director is the decider.

• *The buyer* is the one who administrates the purchase. Professional services are not usually bought by a purchasing department or a specialized buyer (an exception is often found in building and construction which affects consulting engineers).

- *The user* of the service may have important views on the selection, e.g., a management consultant may be working with the personnel in a certain department to reorganize for better efficiency.

- *The gate-keeper* may be a secretary who lets some professionals get through to her boss; it may be a buyer who prefers to recommend some firms for the job while others are excluded at an initial stage.

Proposition 20—The client is often insecure when buying professional services and wants to reduce his risk. The professional should be aware of this and help the client reduce his risk and uncertainty. The uncertainty is greatest when the client is a new buyer or when he has an unsuccessful purchase behind him. As it is difficult to assess the quality of the service, both beforehand and afterwards, the client feels uncertain and may react to reduce his risk in the following ways:

- Loyalty to his existing suppliers of professional services, i.e., the stability of relations becomes important.

- He makes sure that others in the organization are involved in the choice (large buying center), so that he can feel secure and not be criticized.

- He puts in extensive resources in time, people, and costs in order to make sure he is buying the right professional.

- He treats the problem as a gambler would and takes a chance.

- He lowers his demands on the professional to well within a realistic level, thus increasing the chance of reaching expected results.

Proposition 21—Many clients do not care about the professional service firm; they buy the individual. Assignments are usually carried out in close cooperation with the client. This means that the professional and the client must match each other, not only professionally but also in personality. Therefore, what the service firm sells is often individuals or teams rather than an assortment of services.

Proposition 22—Usually there is no objective measure of the quality of a professional service. The client, therefore, is buying confidence. Quality is an elusive concept. Assignments are often assessed as producing only indirect, although positive, effects, and they are only one of several factors that influence the situation of the client. Occasionally it is possible to specify the effects on the profitability of the client's business by assessing revenue increase, cost reduction or capital reduction, or some combination of these that gives a net result which, compared with the initial state, shows an improvement. One such case is a business lawyer helping his client to a favorable solution of a contract dispute. A consulting engineer may recommend a layout of a new plant that is economical both to build and to operate. However, one rarely knows whether another professional would have done a better or worse job. Quality, therefore, becomes a matter of a subjectively perceived quality which is also influenced by the professional's ability to sell himself and to sell his results.

Proposition 23—A professional is expected to solve problems. His ideas may be alien to the client; they may even annoy the client. Therefore, solutions must be "sold" in a way that the client gets a fair chance to evaluate their merits. A good solution can easily be killed by a bad presentation. In my experience clients ask for new approaches but when they get them they become insecure. Most people are not prepared for innovations and creative recommendations. The professional, therefore, should test his ideas on the client gradually and learn about the client's way of receiving them.

Proposition 24—Professionals are more often than not seen as investigators and advisers. Often it is desirable that the professional takes part in implemen-

tation—this may substantially raise the quality of service. Ad agencies and public relations consultants usually carry out their recommendation, e.g., a campaign. An architect may not take part in the actual building process; this is left to a contractor. It may, however, be valuable for him to be around until the building is ready. His intentions may have been misinterpreted in some respects; he may have suggested impractical or expensive designs. By joining the implementation phase, the professional can test the validity of his recommendations and improve his skills.

Proposition 25—Marketing literature has a lot to offer professionals. Although little has been written directly on the marketing of specific professional services, there are other areas of marketing that are partly relevant. These other areas are: service marketing in general, marketing management and marketing mix, industrial marketing, systems selling, organizational buying behavior, sales techniques, and marketing audit.

FINAL COMMENT

Small professional service firms cannot be operated the same way as big ones, local U.S. firms not the same way as multinationals, consulting engineers not as ad agencies, etc. The propositions above should be viewed as a basis for discussion. Read them, consider them constructively and without prejudice, and assess if they fit your own firm. It is not until an idea is applied and tried in practice that it starts living.

BIBLIOGRAPHY

GUMMESSON, EVERT, *Marknadsföring och inköp av konsult-tjänster,* with summary in English, Stockholms Universitet/MTC/Akademilitteratur, Stockholm, 1977.

———, "Toward a Theory of Professional Service Marketing," *Industrial Marketing Management,* vol. 7, no. 2, April 1978.

———, "Models of Organizational Buying Behaviour—Their Relevance for Professional Service Marketing," in *Proceedings of the 5th International Research Seminar in Marketing,* Institut d'Administration des Entreprises, Université d'Aix-Marseille, Senanque Abbey, 1978, pp 233–251.

———, "The Marketing of Professional Services—An Organizational Dilemma," *European Journal of Marketing,* vol. 13, no. 5, 1979.

———, *Models of Professional Service Marketing,* Marknadstekniskt Centrum (MTC)/Liber, Box 6501, S-113 83 Stockholm, Sweden, 1979.

———, "Vad är det man köper när man köper reklambyrátjänster," in *Klara besked om 110 reklambyráer,* Sveriges Reklambyråförbund, Stockholm, Sweden, 1979, pp 10–12.

———, "How Professional Services Are Bought," in *Marketing Handbook,* Gower Press, London, 1981.

———, "25 pàstàenden om marknadsföring och inköp av konsulttjänster," in Arndt, J. (ed) and Friman, A. (ed) *Marknadsföring av'tjänster,* Liber, Malmö, Sweden, 1981.

III

Positioning the Service Organization in the Marketplace

Ask a group of managers from different service businesses how they compete, and the chances are high that many will say, "on service." Press them a little further and they may add, "value for money," "our people are the key," or "convenience."

None of these phrases is very informative to a marketing specialist who is trying to develop strategies to help a particular organization compete more effectively in the marketplace. At issue is what makes consumers or institutional buyers select one service supplier over another. Terms such as *service* typically subsume a variety of specific characteristics ranging from the speed with which a service is delivered to the quality of interactions between customers and service personnel; from the avoidance of errors to the provision of desirable "extras" supplementing the core service. Likewise, *convenience* could refer to a service that is delivered at a convenient location, available at convenient times, or easy to use. Without knowing the product features that consumers are specifically concerned about, it is hard for a marketing manager to evaluate performance and develop an appropriate strategy.

Goods can usually be touched and examined visually prior to purchase. Samples on display sometimes can be tasted, listened to, or smelled. As a generalization, many of the attributes of a consumer good are readily apparent *prior* to use. This makes it easier to understand the nature of the product, to compare it with competing products, and to predict its performance in advance.

It is not easy to make such assessments with most services. Although service facilities and personnel are tangible enough, these are simply the production elements. The actual service is a deed or performance that cannot be wrapped up and taken home. As a result, it is relatively more difficult to define the nature of service products and to evaluate them against competing alternatives.

The purpose of this section of the book is to help readers gain a good understanding of the components that make up a service, to recognize how these various components (or attributes) are valued by customers, and to develop appropriate competitive strategies in the marketplace.

Competition is intensifying in the service sector—reflecting factors such as the reduction of government regulation, the advent of new technologies, the breakdown of traditional product-market boundaries, and the absorption of independent service units by large chains.

Understanding the concept of product positioning is the key to developing an effective competitive posture. This concept is certainly not limited to services—indeed it had its origins in packaged goods marketing—but it does offer valuable insights by forcing service marketers to provide specific answers to the questions: What is our product? How well does it meet the needs of customers in different market segments?

WHAT IS POSITIONING?

Positioning is the process of establishing and maintaining a distinctive place in the market for an organization and/or its individual product offerings. *Repositioning* involves changing one's existing position, such as when Telex sought to position itself as an inexpensive, urgent message service competing with Express Mail, Federal Express, long-distance phone calls, and telecopying services, rather than maintain its position as a slightly old-fashioned telecommunications service. In a competitive marketplace, a "position" reflects how consumers perceive the product's (or organization's) performance on specific attributes relative to that of competitors.

Many marketers associate positioning primarily with the communication element of the marketing mix. This reflects the widespread use of advertising in packaged goods marketing to create images and associations for branded products in order to give them a special distinction in the consumer's mind. Examples include the visual imagery created for a major cigarette brand by the Marlboro man and the positioning of Seven-up as an alternative to cola products through the use of the term *unCola*. Comparable use of communications for position-

ing purposes in the service sector is found in the use of the distinctive "bullish" theme by Merrill Lynch, the underdog claim of Avis ("We're only number 2. . . . We try harder"), or the "finger-lickin good" appeal of Colonel Sanders' Kentucky Fried Chicken.

Our concern here is with the role of positioning in guiding development of marketing mix strategy for services that compete on more than just imagery. This entails decisions on substantive attributes that are known to be important to customers and that relate to product performance, price, and service availability (distribution). The primary task of communication—advertising, personal selling, and PR—in such instances is to ensure that prospective customers accurately perceive the way in which the service is positioned in terms that are important in making choice decisions. Additional excitement and interest may be created by evoking certain images and associations in advertising, but these are likely to play only a secondary role in customer choice decisions unless competing services are perceived as virtually identical on performance, price, and availability.

Role of Positioning in Marketing Strategy

Positioning plays a pivotal role in marketing strategy, since it links market analysis and competitive analysis to internal corporate analysis. From these three—market analysis, competitive analysis, and corporate analysis—a position statement can be developed that enables the service organization to answer the questions, What is our product, what do we want it to become, and what marketing actions must we take to get there? The following table summarizes the principal uses of positioning in marketing management.

Developing a positioning strategy can

TABLE 1

Principal Uses of Positioning in Marketing Management

---

1. Provides a useful diagnostic tool for defining and understanding the relationships between products and markets:
   a. How does the product compare with competitive offerings on specific attributes?
   b. How well does product performance meet consumer needs and expectations on specific performance criteria?
   c. What is the predicted consumption level for a product with a given set of performance characteristics offered at a given price?
2. Identifies market opportunities for:
   a. Introducing new products
      (1) What segments to target?
      (2) What attributes to offer relative to the competition?
   b. Redesigning (repositioning) existing products
      (1) Appeal to the same segments or to new ones?
      (2) What attributes to add, drop or change?
      (3) What attributes to emphasize in advertising?
   c. Eliminate products that
      (1) Do not satisfy consumer needs
      (2) Face excessive competition
3. Making other marketing mix decisions to pre-empt, or in response to, competitive moves:
   a. Distribution strategies
      (1) Where to offer the product (locations, types of outlet)?
      (2) When to make the product available?
   b. Pricing strategies
      (1) How much to charge?
      (2) What billing and payment procedures to employ?
   c. Communication strategies
      (1) What target audience(s) are most easily convinced that the product offers a competitive advantage on attributes that are important to them?
      (2) What message(s)? (Which attributes should be emphasized and which competitors—if any—should be mentioned as the basis for comparison on those attributes?)
      (3) Which communication channels—personal selling versus different advertising media? (Selected not only for their ability to convey the chosen message(s) to the target audience(s), but also for their ability to reinforce the desired image of the product.)

take place at several different levels, depending on the nature of the marketing organization involved. Among multisite, multiproduct, service businesses, a position might be established for the entire organization, for a given service outlet, or for a specific service offered at that outlet. It is particularly important that there be some consistency between the positions held by different services offered at the same location, since the image of one may spill over onto the others.

Because of the intangible, experiential nature of many services, an explicit positioning strategy is valuable in helping prospective customers to get a "mental fix" on a product that would otherwise be rather amorphous.

Failure to select a desired position in the marketplace and to develop a marketing action plan designed to achieve and hold this position may result in one of several possible outcomes, all undesirable:

1. The organization (or one of its products) is pushed into a position where it faces head-on competition from stronger competitors.
2. The organization is pushed into a position which nobody else wants because there is little customer demand there.
3. The organization's (product's) position is so fuzzy that nobody knows what its distinctive competence really is.
4. The organization (product) has no position at all in the marketplace because nobody has ever heard of it.

Steps in Developing a Positioning Strategy

Figure III–1 identifies the basic steps involved in identifying a suitable market position and developing a strategy to reach it.

Market analysis is needed to determine factors such as the overall level, trend, and geographic location of demand. Then alter-

FIGURE III–1
Developing a Market Positioning Strategy[a]

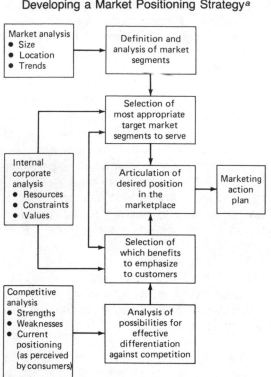

[a]Developed from an earlier schematic by Michael R. Pearce.

native ways of segmenting the market should be considered and an appraisal made of the size and potential of the different segments. Additional research may be required to generate insights into the needs and preferences of prospective customers within each of the different segments, and how they perceive the competition.

Internal corporate analysis requires identifying the organization's resources (financial, human labor and know-how, and physical assets), the limitations in these areas as well as other constraints, and the values of its management. Based on the insights gained from this analysis, the organi-

zation is now able to select a limited number of target market segments that it is able and willing to serve with new or existing services.

Finally, through identification and *analysis of competitors* (both direct and generic)[1] a marketing strategist can gain a sense of strengths and weaknesses, which, in turn, suggest opportunities for product or organizational differentiation. Relating these insights back to the internal corporate analysis should suggest which benefits to offer to which target market segments.

The outcome of integrating these three forms of analysis is a *position statement* that articulates the desired position of the organization in the marketplace and, if desired, that of each of the component services offered. Armed with this understanding, the marketer should then be able to develop a specific marketing action plan. The cost of implementing this plan must, of course, be related to the expected payoff.

Issues in Research and Analysis

Research is needed to identify (1) what attributes of a given service are important to specific market segments, and (2) how different individuals perceive several competing service organizations as performing against these attributes. But strategists should recognize that the same individuals may set different priorities for attributes according to

1. The purpose of using the service
2. The timing of use (time of day, week, or season)
3. Whether the individual is using the service alone or with a group
4. The composition of that group

Consider the criteria you might use when choosing a restaurant for dinner while on a

---

[1]*Direct competitors* are those that offer a similar way of achieving the same benefits (e.g., the case of Ryder, another full-service truck leasing firm). *Generic competitors* are those that offer a different way of achieving similar benefits (for example, truck manufacturers, motor carriers, or railroads offer generic competition to a truck rental firm).

vacation with friends or family compared with one for an expense account lunch at which you are meeting a prospective customer of your company. Given a reasonable selection of alternatives, it is unlikely that you would choose the same type of restaurant in each instance.

It is also important to identify *who* is making the decision to select a specific service. In the case of a hospital, it could be the end user (a patient), or some intermediary (a doctor, for instance). If the latter, the marketer's task is to determine (1) what attributes are important to the customer in choosing the intermediary and (2) what attributes are important to the intermediary in selecting the service provider.

Consumers usually make their choice between alternative service offerings on the basis of perceived differences between them. But the most important attributes are not always those that distinguish competing services from one another. For instance, most travelers rank "safety" as their number-one consideration in air travel. But since major U.S. airlines are generally all perceived as equally safe (unless one has recently had a well-publicized crash), safety is not usually an attribute that influences consumer choice between several major domestic carriers. *Determinant attributes* (that is, those that *do* determine choice) are often somewhat down the list of product characteristics that are important to consumers, but these are the attributes where significant differences between competing alternatives are apparent to consumers. Food and beverage service on board or courtesy of reservations personnel are examples of such distinguishing characteristics. The researcher's task is to identify which attributes are determinant, since they can be used to form the basis of a positioning campaign.

One further issue in evaluating service characteristics and establishing a positioning strategy is that some attributes are easily quantified, whereas others are qualitative and highly subjective. Price, for instance, is a straightforward, quantitative measure. Punctuality of transportation services can be expressed in terms of the percentage of trains, buses, or flights arriving within so many minutes of the scheduled time. Both of these measures are easy to understand and therefore generalizable. But characteristics such as a hotel's ambiance or degree of luxury are more qualitative and therefore are subject to individual interpretation, although consumers may trust the evaluations of an independent rating service, such as the *Mobil Travel Guide* or the AAA.

DEVELOPING POSITIONING MAPS

Developing a "positioning map" is a useful way of representing consumers' perceptions of alternative products in a graphic fashion. A map is usually confined to two attributes (although three-dimensional models can be used to portray three attributes). When more than three dimensions are needed to describe product performance in a given market, then a series of separate charts needs to be drawn for visual presentation purposes. A computer model, of course, can handle as many attributes as are relevant.

Information about a product's or organization's position relative to any one attribute can either be inferred from market data, derived from ratings by representative consumers, or both. The risk in using the first method is that consumers may perceive the situation differently and make their choices accordingly. (If consumer perceptions of product characteristics differ sharply from "reality" as defined by management, then marketing efforts may be needed to change these perceptions.)

Figure III–2 illustrates a hypothetical arrangement of how six airlines might be positioned on a map relating to quality of in-flight food service and speed of baggage recov-

FIGURE III–2
Hypothetical Airline Positioning Chart

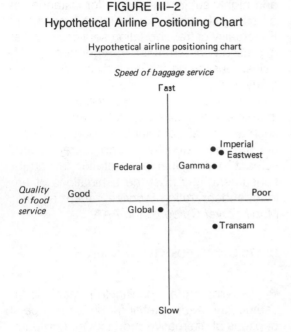

Hypothetical airline positioning chart

ery at the terminal. Assuming these to be important attributes, the figure suggests that Federal is probably doing the best all-around job and TransAm the worst, with Imperial, Gamma, and EastWest almost indistinguishable on these two dimensions. Alternative strategies for any one of these three are to improve food to compete with Federal or to improve baggage handling and be known as the fastest in the business. If Global decides to compete directly with Federal, it will have to improve its baggage service; an alternative position would be to maintain the speed of baggage service at its present level and improve its food service significantly. This will give the airline a distinctive position ("the best food") and offer it a chance to be the number-one choice of business travelers flying with take-on bags. Two questions for consideration by Global management are: (1) Which is easier to control systemwide—baggage handling speed or food quality? and (2) Which set of improvements would cost the most to implement and yield the best revenue-cost tradeoffs?

A positioning chart is, of course, only as good as the quality of the information used in constructing it (see the discussion above under the heading Issues in Research and Analysis). Often more than two attributes need to be evaluated, thus requiring two or more maps. Additionally, maps will need to be redrawn to reflect the dynamic nature of the marketplace. New market entrants and repositioning of existing competitors may mean that an organization's position has ceased to be distinctive.

Moreover, there may be occasions on which different maps need to be drawn for different market segments if research shows that there are sharp variations in perceptions between segments. Some services, such as hotels at destination resorts, deliberately seek different positions during different seasons of the year. For instance, in the winter, a Colorado ski resort hotel might appeal to singles and couples on skiing vacations; in the summer, the same hotel might be positioned to appeal to families on their summer vacations. Not only might the perceptions of these two segments be different, but they might also have different priorities in terms of which attributes are more important to them.

As a generalization, graphic representations of product positions are much easier to grasp than tables of quantitative data or paragraphs of prose. They enable management to understand the nature of competitive threats and opportunities; they can highlight gaps between how customers (or prospects) see the organization and how management sees it; and they can help confirm or dispel beliefs that a service—or its parent organization—occupies a unique niche in the marketplace.

CONCLUSION

The concept of positioning is a potentially valuable one for service marketers since it forces explicit recognition of product characteristics. Combining an analysis of market product needs on a segment-by-segment basis with an understanding of competitive offerings enables the marketer to identify opportunities for serving a particular segment's needs better than anyone else. If offering such a service is seen as compatible with the organization's resources and values, then the firm should be able to develop a profitable niche for itself in the marketplace.

CASES

HARRIS–JOHNSON ASSOCIATES

An architectural partnership is in financial difficulties and needs to obtain more business. What sorts of clients should it seek to serve and what types of projects should it try to obtain? The partners invite an MBA student to advise their firm on what strategy to adopt and how to go about developing a marketing program for a small professional firm such as theirs.

"So we thought you'd have some ideas for us, Beth," said architect Leslie Harris as he finished describing his firm's financial problems.

Beth Brigham, an MBA student whose brother Gary worked for Harris and his partner, Leonard Johnson, mentally reviewed what the architect had just told her. The firm's expenses were increasing with inflation, clients were delaying payments, and the bank had refused to increase the line of credit that was customarily used to meet payroll.

"We've always gotten by somehow," added Johnson. "We borrowed a little more or laid off employees. That's just the way architecture is if you're not hacks."

Harris said, "I think we've got to do something about marketing."

"What do you mean?" asked Brigham.

"Well, we're not invited to enough interviews for jobs," he replied.

"Yes, but when we do interview, we get jobs," said Johnson. "Look at last year—five interviews and three jobs. I'm not sure marketing is the answer. We don't know anything about it; we wouldn't know where to start. And who would do the work? I'm not sure we can afford to hire someone—if we could find someone qualified. And I don't think you or I can—or want to—take time out from architecture. . . ."

Harris nodded. "That's a good point, Len. But why don't we have lunch, Beth, and we can tell you more about how we operate. Maybe then you can figure out what's wrong."

THE ARCHITECTURAL PROFESSION

In 1980, most architectural firms were small. A management consultant to the profession estimated 71 percent of the firms had 10

This case was prepared by Linda Carlson, a member of the Harvard MBA Class of 1980, and Christopher H. Lovelock.

or fewer members; 26 percent had between 10 and 40, and only 3 percent had more than 40 employees.

The basic services an architectural firm offered included schematic design, where the design concept was illustrated; design development, where the schematics were used to create more detailed drawings; and construction drawings, the final set of detailed working drawings and technical specifications from which the project was built.

Often the architect also helped the client negotiate a contract for the building's construction and supervised the construction. Some firms also did site analysis and selection; land-use studies; economic feasibility analysis; land-use and master planning; landscape, interior, and graphic design. Two other services were programming, which involves studying how the building would be used and what provisions for foot traffic, offices, meetings, equipment, and the handicapped, etc. must be made; and second, construction management, where a member of the architect's staff managed the construction of the project.

Business Development

Few firms had formal marketing programs. Like other professionals, many architects had vague ideas that marketing was neither appropriate nor necessary. "Do good work and people will find you" was the traditional attitude. Many architects also perceived themselves as artists and expected to struggle financially; they resisted the idea of "selling" their creativity in the same manner in which packaged goods manufacturers sold soap and cake mixes.[1]

Although most firms did some promotion, such activities were often limited to entering awards programs. Winners in these programs received extensive publicity in the professional press (for example, in *Architectural Record*, *Progressive Architecture*, and the *AIA Journal*, the three leading architectural publications), but seldom much coverage in daily newspapers, the business press, or magazines serving such related trades as construction.

Many observers of the profession were encouraging architects to do more marketing. In the January 1980 issue of *Progressive Architecture*, editor John Morris Dixon wrote,

> Marketing of professional services has become not only respectable in recent years, but essential. Architects can no longer depend on previous work—or social connections—to get commissions. In the 1980s, marketing will do much to determine which firms flourish and how they work.

It was estimated that only about 10 percent of the country's architectural firms had marketing coordinators. These people might write proposals for jobs, maintain lists of leads on jobs, and prepare staff résumés and information on projects. Other responsibilities included organizing slide shows and photograph files, writing brochures and newsletters, and supervising general public relations. Such staff coordinators usually had little client contact.

Even fewer firms had marketing or "business development" directors. These people usually worked with a firm's principals to develop marketing strategies and plan integrated campaigns. In contrast to marketing coordinators, marketing directors often made presentations to prospective clients with or on behalf of principals. The firms that did not have full-time marketing coordinators often had someone—perhaps a secretary—who worked part-time on public relations.

Finding staff members experienced in marketing was difficult. Industry experts agreed that the demand for trained professionals far exceeded the supply. There were no formal academic curricula in marketing design services and only a few short programs for practitioners. As a result, most people hired to do marketing or even public relations for architectural firms had to train themselves. Some started with design training or architecture degrees; others had liberal arts degrees, writing skills, and an interest in design. Some marketing directors had public relations or media experience; many marketing coordinators had started as secretaries in architectural offices.

A 1979 Society for Marketing Professional Services survey showed that the average salary for marketing coordinators in firms with fewer than 15 members was $15,000. Harris suspected a more accurate estimate for New York City was $18,000 to $20,000. Compensation for marketing directors was substantially higher. At a recent luncheon Harris had been seated next to a consultant who told him that marketing directors in larger firms might earn $60,000 plus profit-sharing and bonuses. "You have to pay for experience—and you have to give a marketing person your complete support," she told him. "Otherwise you're wasting time and money."

Few architectural firms advertised. Although the American Institute of Architects (AIA), the professional association to which many registered architects belonged, had lifted its ban on members' advertising in 1978, AIA members were still prohibited from using pictures of their work in advertisements.

Generally, architects obtained clients in one of three ways—by contacting potential clients themselves, by waiting for clients to contact them, or by using an intermediary like a friend, former client, or consultant. Writing in *Architectural Record*, Bradford Perkins pointed out that virtually every successful firm used all three methods. "And there are neither ethical nor business reasons to favor one method over another," he added.

Architects usually were commissioned through direct selection, comparative selection, or a design competition. In the first instance, someone planning a construction project would hire an architect on the basis of the architect's reputation, personal acquaintance, or recommendations from the architect's former clients. The selection process often involved only informal noncompetitive interviews and a slide presentation of the architect's work.

By 1980, the most common way of hiring an architect was comparative selection. A client would invite several firms to submit information about their experience, qualifications, special abilities, and personnel. Government agencies required architects to use standard forms for submissions. A few firms, usually the three to six that appeared most qualified, would be invited to interview. Often these interviews involved elaborate presentations. Once the client firm had selected the architectural firm it preferred, the two firms negotiated a budget.

A third means of selecting an architect was the design competition, in which architects were asked to submit solutions to a particular problem. For example, in early 1980 the city of Portland, Oregon, was holding a competition for Pioneer Courthouse Square, part of its downtown renovation work. The winner of the competition would automatically be awarded the design contract for the project. Such competitions were infrequent and also expensive to enter, because of the need to prepare scale models in addition to the time cost of design development.

FIRM BACKGROUND

Harris–Johnson Associates (HJA) was established in 1974 when Leonard Johnson joined the architectural firm Leslie Harris had opened in 1964.

A New York City native, Harris had attended Rensselaer Polytechnic Institute and served in the military before moving to Cambridge, Massachusetts, where he worked for the prestigious firm, The Architects Collaborative.

After a few years, he returned to graduate school at Yale. As he was completing his studies, he began to design medical buildings commissioned by a family friend. After graduation, Harris returned to New York City to continue work on the projects, which were to be built on Long Island. Later he taught at the Pratt Institute and at the City College of New York while working part time for other architects. He opened his own office in his studio apartment when he received two commissions—his brother-in-law's dental office and a family friend's Fire Island vacation home. (The fee on the latter project, which Harris was still collecting in 1980, was use of the house one weekend every year.) In 1964, his first year of full-time practice, Harris hired a draftsman and billed about $20,000. He lived and worked in the studio until 1965, when he converted all the space to offices. In 1966, with a staff of four, he was forced to find larger office facilities.

In his first six years of practice, Harris received several state and national awards for his work from professional magazines and associations.[2] Features on many of his projects were published in leading journals. He did not order reprints of those stories because of the reprints' cost. As he admitted later to Beth Brigham,

> I didn't even think of marketing myself. I thought all I had to do was good work and someone would discover me.

In that period Harris also met Billy Brown, a brash young developer for whom he designed office buildings and 3,000 multifamily housing units in three Northeastern states. These jobs gave Harris the opportunity to move out of small projects like single-family houses and into site development. Remembering Brown, the architect said, "He wasn't too honest, but he had all the intuition of a builder; he knew how to get financing and he had the guts to build even without money."

This association, which ended when the developer failed to pay bills, was followed by commissions from the 40-year-old heir to a multinational conglomerate. Although trained in law, this man wanted to start a development company. Harris's work for this client, who demanded high quality, resulted in several design awards. However, most of the projects were never constructed. "He had the money to pay for studies and design but not the guts to build," the architect said.

The partnership with Johnson resulted when Harris realized he would have to offer equity in the firm to attract talented, responsible people. He was impressed with the way Johnson's technical skill complemented his emphasis on design. Both men believed the partnership had allowed them to grow, giving them experience on very different projects.

The partners had been invited to merge their organization into large, prestigious New York firms, but had always declined. They feared the loss of their autonomy. They also believed their skills—for example, their expertise in housing and in solar energy—would be exploited. Harris and Johnson had invited a landscape architect with whom they worked closely to join the firm, but he had declined because of the same desire for autonomy. The men had no plans to expand the firm by offering partnerships to current staff members.

Both Harris and Johnson were now in their forties, with children entering college. Both had been recognized by their colleagues. Harris, who still taught part time at a New York architectural school, had been elected to the College of Fellows of the AIA in 1979. Johnson, who had worked in two nationally known architectural firms before joining Harris, had just concluded a lecture series at the Smithsonian Institution on the future of architecture. A graduate of the Pratt Institute, Johnson frequently testified on solar energy collection systems before members of state governmental agencies and spoke on energy to students and groups like the New York City Chamber of Commerce.

Both partners worked on every project which came into the office. Their general interests were the restoration and reuse of buildings and city areas, energy conservation, and land use. Their work had included the conversion of a Brooklyn candy factory into studio apartments for artists, multifamily housing in rural areas, and downtown revitalization projects like malls. Most of their work had been done in the Northeast, but both partners were certified by the National Council of Architectural Registration Boards, so they easily could be registered to practice in other states. The partners emphasized life-cycle costing[3] and they worked to relate their projects to the surroundings, whether rural or urban.

Staffing

Headquartered high in a New York City luxury hotel, the firm in early 1980 included the two partners, four design professionals, and a secretary. An accountant and a book-keeper worked part time. The designers each made between $15,000 and $25,000. Harris, who was the senior partner, and Johnson, who was buying a third of the firm, would together draw $100,000 out of HJA in 1980.

The design staff included three associates: Oscar Weston, Jon Random, and Anton Paulac. The title "associate" meant that employees were one step away from partnership, but as Harris pointed out, "it's a very large step." At HJA, employees were usually named associates after two years, once they were registered and ready to serve as project architects. Through the years, the firm had had about six other associates; most were practicing on their own by 1980. Gary Brigham, who had graduated from college the previous year, was the junior staff member.

Oscar Weston, 49, had joined the firm in 1974, shortly after the partnership was formed. He was a former colleague of Johnson's who had also worked for Skidmore, Owings, Merrill, one of the largest architectural firms in the U.S. Weston came to HJA because he was tired of large firms and internal politics. "I knew my design philosophy fit with Len's and Leslie's, and I knew I'd have more responsibility and more direct involvement here," he said. Weston, who was not a registered architect, had no plans to open his own office. Harris and Johnson assumed Weston was one of the employees who would be interested in partnership if it were offered.

Although Weston had no experience in marketing, he believed the firm should be doing more promotion. Recently he had told Harris that the associates could handle more of the routine work to free the partners for marketing. The first marketing task the firm should tackle was a brochure, he suggested. "It's been at least a year in the works; we need something that tells the client what we're all about."

Weston also recommended the firm consider every way in which it presented itself. "For example, look at this conference room," he exclaimed. "I'd start by cleaning the carpet!" On the other hand, he emphasized, the firm should not have a luxurious office because clients might assume the staff could not work with limited budgets.

Anton Paulac, 45, recently had returned to the firm after two years in Paris with the French office of an international firm. Previously he had spent 14 years working in New York City, including two with HJA. Born in Hungary and educated there and in France, Paulac was a confirmed Manhattanite. "I won't even live in one of the other boroughs," he often said. Because of the expense of opening an office of his own in Manhattan, Paulac expected to stay with Harris and Johnson as their firm grew. Although he had no experience or training in marketing, he had been quick to respond to Beth Brigham's questions about business development, noting,

> We need lots of contacts in every direction to help us. We're not dynamic enough about making contacts; we need to spend more time with former and potential clients.

Paulac believed the time spent to get projects featured in magazines was worthwhile, but he also felt that architects shouldn't concentrate on publications read only by their peers. "Getting a story in *Progressive Architecture* is excellent for our reputation with other architects," he remarked, "but it doesn't help us reach business people." Like Weston, Paulac believed that anyone hired to do public relations or marketing for the firm needed an architectural background. "That person has to understand the design process and has to be able to stimulate our clients' imaginations, too," he said.

The third associate, Jon Random, 27, had recently received his license. He had spent two years with the firm, and now frequently served as a project architect (the individual in charge of a project). Some staff members described him as "good with people"; others said he was sometimes less cooperative than desired.

Gary Brigham, 23, had spent the summer before college graduation as an unpaid intern in the office. He had selected the firm because he enjoyed the staff's concern with design. "It's not a bunch of hacks," he said. Hired upon graduation, he had received an unusual amount of responsibility for someone so inexperienced because the office was so small. He had even served as the project architect on a very small job. Brigham hoped to begin graduate school in autumn, 1980. If he was not accepted at the school of his choice, he was considering staying with HJA for a few more years. Discussing the firm, he told his sister,

> This office is better than 95 percent of the others in the city . . . though I would like to see how the other 5 percent operate. But there's a lot to learn here. For example, sometimes the partners call everybody together and we discuss a problem with a project. It's almost like school . . . and when you have a problem, the partners take the time to teach you how to handle it. But the variety of opinions in the office—and the strength of each one—don't create an efficient system for getting work completed.

Evonne Rhodes, the office secretary, had joined the firm in 1978 after working for several years in government and publishing both in New York City and in Europe. She held a graduate degree in education. When Harris had mentioned hiring someone to handle marketing, she had expressed interest in the position.

The first part of the office to be seen by visitors was the entry, where Rhodes worked. The area was decorated with posters and a large calendar; several framed award certificates were hung on the wall, but they were difficult to see during regular business hours when the main door was open and against the wall. The adjoining conference room overlooked Central Park. One wall was covered with a soft panel that could be used as a bulletin board, another was dominated by a large abstract photograph. The paint on the high ceiling was peeling. The space, which was leased until April 1984 on very reasonable terms, would accommodate as many as 20 professionals. Harris hoped the staff, which had never exceeded 15, could be increased to 25 or 30 within the next five years. "Then we'd have the skills to do almost anything. And we'd still be small enough that Len and I would be in touch with every project."

The partners' ideas about geographic expansion differed. Johnson wanted work outside New York City limited to very large jobs (for example, where construction cost exceeded $5 million) or to smaller projects done for very important clients who had other work in the immediate area. "Because we're a small firm, we have to use our time efficiently," he said. Harris, in contrast, was interested in international work and in a branch office in the growth areas of the Southwest.

THE FIRM'S SERVICES

Although HJA's promotional material listed site planning, interior and graphic design, programming and construction management among the services offered, the firm generally hired or associated itself with specialists (usually called consultants) in professions like structural engineering, lighting, and interiors. Harris was trained in related fields like graphics, but he preferred to subcontract the work to specialists because he believed they usually did better work than he could. To handle the job site responsibilities of construction management commissions, the partners would have to hire another architect.

The firm was neither a "full service" office with staff people who could handle every step of the design and building process, nor a "specialist" firm that concentrated on medical buildings, banks, schools, or other specific institutions. "We're really too general, considering our small staff," Harris explained, "but we're interested in several different kinds of projects and services." Because of this general approach, the firm had only done a few projects of each type. (See Exhibit 1 for representative jobs by HJA.) Harris hoped that the firm's billings—which in the late 1970s had ranged from $200,000 to $400,000 per year—might reach $600,000 in 1980. Reflecting delayed payments from clients, the firm's receipts from fee income in 1979 had amounted to only $231,000 (Exhibit 2). Accounts and advances receivable amounted to over $200,000 at the end of 1979 (Exhibit 3).

Architects were usually compensated in one of three ways. A widely used method, percentage of construction cost, assumed a correlation between project size and the architect's effort. New York State paid architects by this method, so HJA was penalized for projects that came in under budget. Architects might also be paid by the hour; this method was designed to compensate them for every hour spent on the project plus overhead and a reasonable profit. By 1980, HJA was trying to do most of its work on this basis. A third payment method was lump sum or fixed fee; it was often used by government agencies. The receipt of revenues on a long job could be erratic. For instance, it might be established as 25 percent after delivery of the working drawings, 50 percent when construction was half done, and 25 percent on completion of the building.

One problem with government work was that both New York City and the State of New York were very slow to pay fees that were due. On one job for the state, it had taken two years for HJA to receive full payment because of funding problems.

To improve both their billings and their profits, both partners wanted to do more work for corporations. "That's the only time we make any money," Harris said. "But I don't know how to get corporate clients . . . I don't have any access to them." However, he had a friend who worked for a law firm representing many *Fortune* 500 firms, and several of his former classmates worked for major corporations. Johnson, too, had contacts in government agencies that commissioned architecture.

Harris was ambivalent about some types of projects, especially housing. He and Johnson believed they should be interested in multi-family housing because they had designed award-winning projects that had been very successful financially. But working with developers could be difficult because the builders often paid poorly. "Single-family housing? We do it for fun," Harris said. "You can't possibly make money on it."

The partners were interested in institutional work like libraries and college campuses. Because Harris believed that buildings (what he called "the built environment") could help solve social problems, the firm was trying

to obtain a jail commission. Such a job would be time-consuming because it would involve not only design but supervision, requiring monthly—even weekly—inspection visits as construction proceeded. However, he and Johnson did not want to restrict themselves to public sector clients.

Market Conditions

To give Beth Brigham an idea of HJA's best opportunities for work in the next few years, Harris showed her a collection of recent newspaper and magazine articles.

A recent *Wall Street Journal* report had noted that many architectural firms had not been affected by the slump in construction. According to the article, major firms in San Francisco were expanding by 10 to 15 percent. In New York, business was described as "less brisk," but many firms were still growing through diversification. The managing partner of one firm with a staff of 100 told the *Journal*, "Only about half of our work is tied to new construction; the rest is related to renovation and interior design."

In "A View of the 1980s," *Progressive Architecture* said, "Energy considerations beyond any doubt, will have a greater impact on architectural design in the 1980s than any other factor. . . . Life-cycle cost will be the measure of building economy."

Architectural Record, in its November 1979 issue, had discussed the changing market for institutional buildings. Because of demographics, which had caused a decline in educational building construction, and because of the dependence on public financing, the magazine's editors did not expect a strong institutional construction market. Rehabilitation of existing structures was the best potential market, they suggested.

Building Design & Construction also cited the market for reuse in November 1979; a mortgage company official pointed out that the trend toward reviving choice inner-city residential areas had become a stampede. James W. Rouse, whose firm was involved in inner-city development in Baltimore, Philadelphia, and Boston (where its work included Quincy Market), agreed. In the January 7, 1980, issue of *Builder*, he wrote that people and industry were moving back to cities because of young couples' changing life styles, improved public transportation, and the financial difficulty in buying a single-family house in the suburbs.

Marketing at HJA

Harris knew HJA could not compete with full-service firms unless a prospective client had had unpleasant experiences with large firms where the client did not receive the partners' attention. He admitted,

> Our only real strength is that Len and I are working principals; we offer our abilities, our experience, our involvement in the jobs. What we have to sell is our personal work on every project. But our problem is getting interviews. We simply don't go after enough work.

In 1979 the partners had been invited to five interviews for specific jobs. They did not solicit any of the invitations. The firm received commissions for three of the five jobs for which the partners interviewed. At the third interview, it received the commercial job in question—and also was asked to renovate an apartment for the client. A fourth commission was lost because HJA would not cut its fee. The final job, a single-family house, was rejected because Harris and Johnson did not like the prospective clients. "The couple would have been a nuisance to work with . . . and we wouldn't have made any money anyway."

The partners had made a sixth presentation to officials of the New York State Corrections Agency. Harris and Johnson had not been applying for a specific job; they wanted their firm considered when architects for each of several proposed new jails were selected. They did not expect to hear about the first of several jobs until spring.

The firm had not had a brochure since 1968, when Harris printed, but never distributed, an informational packet on his work.

For the last year, the partners had been trying to collect photos for a new brochure and agree on text and design. At least two graphic artists had been commissioned to design brochures; neither one's work had satisfied the partners. Because no brochure existed, the partners did not respond to most inquiries about their work. For example, they had not even written to a group in Rochester, New York, that wanted information on mall design.

For HJA's few formal presentations, the secretary custom-bound existing photographs, prepared photocopies of newspaper stories about the firm's work, and typed descriptions of the staff and their projects.

As a service to the consultants with whom they worked—these were specialists in engineering, landscape architecture, graphics, and interior design—the partners distributed copies of their consultants' brochures to help them obtain work. If HJA had a brochure, Johnson said, he would ask the consultants to do the same for his firm. Harris agreed that consultants had been an unexpectedly valuable source of work.

> We've gotten about 10 percent of our work because of introductions to potential clients by our landscape architects, through our graphic designers and through our engineers. But I've never expected them to promote us . . . although, of course, they're in a good position to give clients a fair assessment of how different architects work.

The firm frequently had its work featured in magazines, newspapers, and professional journals. But these stories were seldom initiated by the partners or their staff. Two HJA projects were to be featured in architectural journals in spring 1980; both stories had resulted from the photographer's contact with the editors. (Architectural photographers usually owned all reproduction rights to their work, being paid every time a picture was published. For this reason, most photographers tried to interest editors in projects that had already been photographed.)

One project had been featured in the January issue of a magazine for developers because a consultant had sent in the story. The same project recently had been described in the *New York Times* because Harris had called an editor he knew. Johnson was also interested in having the firm's work mentioned in the business— not the design—pages of the *New York Daily News*. "An article there on an apartment we'd designed with solar energy brought lots of calls," he noted. Harris admitted the firm had done no followup on the inquiries.

Although HJA sometimes ordered reprints of magazine stories, it never used these as part of a mailing program. In fact, the firm had no mailing list. Even Christmas cards were addressed and mailed sporadically, as the partners thought of people who should receive cards. The firm did no advertising. Nor did it do any business entertaining, despite the attractive location of the office. "We could do some entertaining, though," said Harris. "People love to come to this hotel."

The partners belonged to no clubs for business and did not attempt to make clients of any former college classmates, neighbors, or other social contacts. Neither partner believed social contacts were necessary in obtaining work. "Although I do know people who get work through their friends," added Harris.

All of HJA's work resulted from personal contacts—but these were strictly business associations. As Harris observed,

> Because of our contacts, our potential clients hear about us from many different sources . . . and we need that to get a job. For example, our presentation is one source of information, a reprint of a magazine article is another, and a consultant's comment is a third.

A recent project in Brooklyn was typical of the way in which a variety of HJA's contacts could generate a commission. A member of the New York City mayor's staff had friends in Trenton, New Jersey, where Harris had designed a mall several years earlier. Having seen the Trenton work, the mayor's assistant called Harris and Johnson to suggest that they and an engineering firm submit a proposal. While preparing their presentation, the architects called an architect on the mayor's staff whom they knew slightly. They also called the staff members who would select an architect.

"You find excuses to call them," said Harris. "Often you can try out different combinations of consultants with them . . . you know, ask them what they think of a particular graphic artist or an engineer. . . ."

Before their interview with the mayor's staff, Harris and Johnson also called firms who had consulted with them on other projects and asked these firms' principals to call colleagues on the mayor's staff. Neither of the partners believed they had enough experience with such marketing "campaigns"; Harris believed they sometimes neglected to determine what was necessary for goodwill from the decision-makers. "For example," he said, "one of the most important groups in the state corrections agency is headed by a minority woman who likes to see firms that have minority staff members or consultants. We don't have any."

Sometimes, he added, corporate bureaucracies were so complex that determining the decision-makers was difficult. "We work with one corporation that has many different departments," he said. "Each department has its favorite architect. Our project overlaps at least two departments . . . so the selection of an architect becomes a power struggle between the groups."

Harris rarely had difficulty with those who initiated the contact ("they have a vested interest in seeing you get the job") or with those who influenced the selection decision. "I usually call people outside the client organization who might be able to help . . . I don't feel awkward doing that . . . I guess they just know I may be able to help them some day." He believed the real problem was the lack of a system for finding out about work and requesting interviews. "And we need someone to do the followup," he said.

HJA had once subscribed to *The Coxe Letter*, one of a few monthly bulletins describing forthcoming architectural jobs and marketing techniques. "But we never followed up on any of the leads, so I dropped the subscription," said Harris. "If I had a brochure I'd subscribe again because I could develop a systematic way to use the leads." (Exhibit 4 shows estimated costs for the newsletter, brochures, magazine reprints, and other marketing-related activities.

Johnson, however, questioned the value of such newsletters, noting, "By the time you've decided to follow up the lead, it's too late. Someone else's already got the job." To learn about possible work, Johnson said he would prefer to call the firm's consultants and the architects who worked in purchasing for large corporations like American Telephone & Telegraph Co., General Electric, and IBM.

HJA'S PROBLEMS

Back at her apartment, Beth Brigham cleaned out her briefcase and described her day at HJA to her roommate, Sue Adams, a fellow MBA student.

"Sue, I don't know what I'm going to tell them. They're both such nice guys and their work is terrific, but they don't know anything about marketing. And I'm not sure they really want a marketing program, at least one where they have to do the work themselves."

"So why don't they hire someone?" asked Adams.

"First, they can't afford to. And secondly, people who are commissioning architecture want to work with the people who will do the design. That's one of the strengths of this firm: What you see is what you get," replied Brigham.

"But that doesn't solve my problem," she went on. "How do I—a student with no experience in architecture—tell these men that they don't seem to know what they want to sell? And that they don't really seem too interested in the selling task? And then what kind of recommendations do I make? Where should they start?"

NOTES

1. However, some architects had always appreciated the importance of business development. In *Architectural Record*, this story was told about the well-known nineteenth-century architect H. H. Richardson, designer of Trinity Church in Boston and Harvard University's Sever and Austin halls. A mother implored Richardson to advise her son, who wanted to be an architect. "What," she asked, "is the most important thing in architectural practice?" "Getting the first job!" Richardson replied. "Of course that is important," she agreed, "but after that what is important?" "Getting the next job!" was Richardson's gruff response.

2. Such awards (not to be confused with those in design competitions) could be particularly helpful to young architects, since they conferred credibility, as well as publicity and introductions to editors of publications.

3. Life-cycle costing, in contrast to initial or construction cost, considers all of the costs of operating a building during a fixed period, usually the length of the mortgage. Because life-cycle costing includes maintenance, interest, and fuel costs, it became a popular theme in construction after the first energy shortage in the early 1970s.

EXHIBIT 1

Representative H.J.A. Projects

PROJECT	CLIENT	TOTAL CONTRACT AMOUNT	CONTRACT SIGNED	STATUS (1980)	ARCHITECTS' COMMENTS
Bronx hospital roof repair	New York State	$150,000	September 1974	Under construction	Bread and butter job
Brooklyn school	New York City	$105,000	First contract signed in 1974; work interrupted by fiscal crisis. New contract in February 1980	Final steps on working drawings to be started soon	Great project
Brooklyn mall, second phase	New York City	$131,500	To have been signed in September 1979; now expected in Spring 1980	Phase 1 under construction; Phase 2 to be designed	Another great project, but working with NYC is difficult
Planned community, suburban New Jersey	Private	$50,000	Expected soon	No work started	Will be a feasibility study
Corporate exhibit in New York City	Private	$80,000	1979	Just completed	Great job—and may result in several other jobs for same client
Queens hospital restoration	New York State	$100,000	Phase 1, 1977 Phase 2, 1978 Phase 3, 1979	Phase 2 under construction, Phase 3 (interiors) in design	Bread and butter; but allowed use of innovative system for completing working drawings
Library and mall, suburban New York	City	$225,000	January 1975	Just completed	LJ: not sure the aggravation was worth the rewards. LH: gave us a chance to work on so many areas of interest . . . but the political climate was the worst we've encountered.

(continued)

149

EXHIBIT 1 (continued)

PROJECT	CLIENT	TOTAL CONTRACT AMOUNT	CONTRACT SIGNED	STATUS (1980)	ARCHITECTS' COMMENTS
Pine Meadows multi-family housing	Private (project designed for one client and completed for another)	$170,000	1975	Under construction	Very good housing project. Client for whom job was finished took some short cuts.
					Model for project took months to build, is valued at $20K. Was rented to builder for marketing purposes for $2,500 for a year.
Microwave station, New Jersey	Private	$150,000	November 1979	Design work cannot start until zoning commission approves	One of few corporate clients with whom we have good working relationship. A technically interesting project.
Nuclear plant emergency control center, suburban New York	Private utility	$50,000	On retainer	Design work starting	We're "no nuke" people, but the safety issue is challenging . . . and we want to keep client.
Bronx office building (30,000 square feet in existing building)	Same utility	$150,000	On retainer	Design work starting	Interior renovation
White Plains office (5,000 square feet in storefront)	Same utility	$40,000	On retainer	Under construction	Another interiors job
Planned community, Patterson, NJ	Private	$50,000	No contract yet; made proposal in early 1980		Would be a master plan for housing, church, shopping center.

SOURCE: HJA records

EXHIBIT 2

Income Statement for Year Ending December 31, 1979

Income from fees		$231,664
Cost of services		
Direct project salaries	$63,895	
Other direct costs	34,472	98,367
Gross profit		133,297
General expenses		
Officers' compensation	61,360	
Office salaries	10,920	
Rent	15,417	
Taxes	9,639	
Interest	3,770	
Depreciation	802	
Subscriptions, dues, etc.	2,973	
Office supplies	3,635	
Telephone	3,144	
Insurance	9,847	
Employee hospitalization and major medical	4,680	
Auto and travel	8,796	
Cleaning	768	
Product brochures and proposals	3,391	
Postage	306	
Professional fees	500	
Reproduction and copying	2,062	142,010
Net profit (loss)		($8,713)

SOURCE: HJA records

EXHIBIT 3

Balance Sheet
December 31, 1979

ASSETS

Current Assets

Cash	$ 1,720	
Accounts receivable[a]	186,685	
Advances receivable	27,254	
Due from officers (borrowed from HJA)	33,000	
Total Current Assets		$248,659

Fixed Assets

Furniture, fixtures, and equipment (less accumulated depreciation of $6,606)		15,000
Total Assets		$263,659

LIABILITIES AND SHAREHOLDERS' EQUITY

Current Liabilities

Accounts payable	$ 19,500	
Note payable (line of credit)	35,000	
Payroll taxes payable	9,394	
Total Current Liabilities		$ 63,894

Equity

Capital stock	15,000	
Paid-in surplus	21,606	
Retained earnings	163,158	
Total Equity		199,764
Total Liabilities and Equity		$263,659

[a] Harris said most of the firm's receivables were at least 60 days old. Many were at least six months old. There was no provision for bad debts.
SOURCE: HJA records

EXHIBIT 4

Estimated Costs for Marketing-Related Projects

Brochure (500 copies)	$10,000[a]
Envelopes for mailing brochure, special order	Unknown
Photography of finished projects	$1,000–$3,000 per project[b]
Black-and-white prints for newspaper publicity and awards program entry books	$15 each
Mounted enlargements of photographs for office display	$300 each[c]
The Coxe Letter	$85 per year
Reprints of magazine features	$500–$700 per 1,000 copies
Awards program entry fees	$25–$100 per program

[a] This was a typical price paid by architectural firms for a brochure.
[b] Many magazine editors expected architects to pay for the photography of projects that were to be described in the publications. Although architectural photography was usually available for about $750 per day in 1980, HJA preferred to use one of the most expensive photographers in the New York area. Fees did not include film, processing, prints, or reprint rights.
[c] HJA had its enlargements (usually about 20 inches square) mounted by the same craftsman who mounted photographs for museums.

THE PARKER HOUSE

Capitalizing on its downtown location, the management of a famous old hotel has rescued it from bankruptcy, repositioned it, and restored the hotel to profitability. But now several new hotels are being planned for the city. What is the best position for the Parker House against this future competition?

Yervant Chekijian, group director of operations for the Classic Hotels division of Dunfey Hotels, didn't mince words. "Business at the Parker House has never been better—but our biggest challenge may be right around the corner."

Robert McIntosh, general manager of the Parker House, Boston's oldest hotel, watched as Chekijian picked up a newspaper clipping dated April 1979 and headlined, "Hotels Bring Jobs to Boston, Tax Money to State."

"This story in the *Globe*," he continued, "confirms what we've suspected for some time—that within five years, as many as five or six brand new hotels may open within three miles of the Parker House. Business travelers in this town are going to have more atriums, swimming pools, and king-size beds than they know what to do with. Our mission statement outlines the market position we want for the Parker House; now we need to establish how each department of the hotel will contribute to that position."

McIntosh nodded in agreement. "We'll need more than old-world charm to hold on to our market share," he observed. "What we're really talking about is competition-proofing the Parker House."

HISTORY OF THE PARKER HOUSE

The Parker House, the oldest continuously operating hotel in America, opened on October 8, 1855, and was immediately popular with Bostonians and visitors alike. Charles Dickens, the most popular English novelist of the nineteenth century, was a regular visitor to the Parker House during his American tours and in 1867 described it to his daughter as "an immense hotel, with all manner of white marble public rooms. I live in a corner high up and have a hot and cold bath in my bedroom." Dickens was unusually well qualified to judge the merits of his bath, having fallen into it fully dressed one night after enjoying the Parker House wines.

The founder of the hotel, Harvey Parker, was a former stableboy from Maine who began his career in the hospitality industry by operating a moderately priced lunchroom in Boston's Courthouse Square. After opening his new hotel, Parker directed his energies toward food and beverage development and was the first hotelkeeper in the world to offer a formal American Plan: lodging plus three meals daily at a single price. His French chef, hired for $5,000 in a day when many hotel cooks earned about $500 annually, created lavish banquets that brought additional fame to the hotel; Boston cream pie was first served at the Parker House, and the soft, crustless Parker House rolls created by the hotel's German baker were shipped as far west as Chicago.

Refurbished and enlarged throughout the nineteenth century, the Parker House was almost totally rebuilt in 1927. Constructed from yellow-gray brick, the 14-story building stood on the corner of Tremont and School streets, both busy, narrow thoroughfares in the heart of Boston. The Boston Common, a large public park established as a cow pasture by the Puritans, was two blocks away.

This case was prepared by Robert J. Kopp, a doctoral candidate at the Harvard Business School; Penny Pittman Merliss, a former research associate at Harvard; and Christopher H. Lovelock.

Although the exterior of the Parker House resembled an office building more than a grand hotel, the wood-paneled lobby with its rich carpeting, framed eighteenth century engravings, and ornate brass elevator doors created an aura of elegance which was reflected in the handsome first floor dining room and the other public rooms on the second floor. In 1927 the newly built hotel contained a total of over 550 guest rooms and suites, and throughout the 1920s and 1930s continued to attract the rich and famous.

But the following decades were not kind to the hotel. During the 1950s and 1960s Boston's waterfront and many of the downtown streets which bordered it fell into decay, and new shopping and commercial areas grew up in the suburbs and the Back Bay. With its main entrance tucked away on a narrow side street and its facade growing darker with age, the Parker House failed to catch the eye of many tourists and corporate travelers. By 1969, occupancy was down to 35 percent, and the former grand old lady of Boston had fallen into bankruptcy.

The Parker House was brought back to life in 1969 by Dunfey Family Hotels, a privately owned, regional lodging chain which at that time operated 11 hotels and inns in the northeast U.S. The company was founded in 1954 by six Dunfey brothers and their mother. To finance further expansion following the purchase of the Parker House, the Dunfey family sold the company to Aetna Life Insurance in 1970. Five years later, Jon Canas, formerly head of international marketing for the Sheraton Corporation, joined the company as vice-president of sales and marketing. In 1976, Aer Lingus, the national airline of Ireland, acquired Dunfey from Aetna and arranged to lease the hotel properties through a subsidiary. Throughout these changes of ownership, Jack Dunfey remained chief executive officer of Dunfey Hotels Corp.

Initial Renovations

In February 1973, as a major step in their effort to revive the Parker House, the Dunfeys hired Yervant Chekijian, who had managed the prestigious Mayflower Hotel in Washington, DC, as general manager. Chekijian arrived in Boston to discover a city in renaissance. The huge Prudential Center, a network of apartments, shops, hotel, and plazas built on the former railroad yards in the Back Bay area of Boston, had ignited redevelopment in 1959. Next came Government Center, a 60-acre project planned by I. M. Pei, which transformed shabby Scollay Square into an open plaza surrounded by two large government office towers, a sweeping curve of retailing and office space, and other government buildings. The focal point of the project was a dramatically modern City Hall, which one architectural critic considered "as fine a building for its time and place as Boston has ever produced." Nearby was Boston's financial district, where banks and other financial firms were building new 30- and 40-story office towers.

Dunfey management could see that the Parker House's location now offered the hotel a distinctive advantage over its major competitors. Built in a day when many business travelers in the city still preferred to walk to their destinations, the Parker House was closer to Boston's corporate, legal, and financial offices than any other hotel in town. Three rapid transit stations lay within a five-minute walk; Logan Airport was only 2½ miles away, and could be reached by taxi in half the time it took to travel there from any other downtown hotel. Although the Parker House did not have its own parking garage, guest parking was available within one block.

Impressed by the hotel's distinguished history, the Dunfeys saw a chance to rebuild its dominant position by catering to corporate and professional travelers and discriminating tourists rather than large groups of conventioneers. They knew that much individual business was booked locally, since travelers frequently relied on those whom they were visiting to make lodging arrangements. The key to rebuilding wide demand for the Parker House, they decided, was reestablishing the hotel's image within Boston itself.

The first public area of the Parker House to be renovated in 1973 was The Last Hurrah, an informal bar and restaurant in the basement, created from a former grillroom. The Last Hurrah offered moderately priced drinks and meals and (beginning in 1977) one of the only live swing bands in Boston. Decorated with photographs depicting figures from Boston's colorful political past, The Last Hurrah soon attracted a loyal lunch and after-work following from City Hall, the state legislature, and the financial district.

Total renovation of most of the Parker House guest rooms and corridors was the second stage of the repositioning of the hotel. During 1973–74 walls were stripped, repainted, and repapered; new furniture and carpets purchased; new bathroom fixtures installed and bathtubs reglazed; and new lighting and mirrors added. Additionally, the entire hotel was rewired and individual heating and air-conditioning controls (costing approximately $2,500 per room) were installed in each bedroom. "Not one piece of old furniture was left in the renovated rooms," Chekijian recalled. "Our objective was to create a first-class facility that would not offend any top-of-the-line traveler; by adding a very high level of service to this new physical plant, we could then market the Parker House as a luxury hotel."

In 1975, Dunfey management renovated the hotel's once-elegant dining room, used as a meeting room since 1969. Reopened as Parker's Restaurant, it was furnished with overstuffed sofas and large wingback chairs, its brown and beige color scheme accented by spectacular floral arrangements. Its warm atmosphere and mixture of French and American cuisine soon made Parker's one of the most popular fine restaurants in town: Readers polled by *Boston* magazine considered it one of the top ten in the city and felt that Parker's service was second only to that of the Ritz. Bostonians were particularly fond of Parker's Sunday brunch; diners were served from a buffet line as a harp played softly in the background. Adjoining Parker's Restaurant was Parker's Bar, which had been transformed into a quiet, luxurious piano lounge.

"This was the key to our repositioning effort," Chekijian commented. "It's important to sell a dining room to the local community, since local residents, not those who are visiting, usually make dining decisions. We saw the dining room as a window onto us for the community, and we wanted to create a room which would define the hotel."

The total cost of renovations through 1975 exceeded $5 million. The following year, the south wing of the hotel, which had been closed off since 1969, was completely renovated at a cost of $500,000, adding another 51 guest rooms and giving the Parker House a total of 546 rooms. Occupancy rose from 52 percent in 1973 to 83 percent in 1976, when Chekijian was promoted to a new position at Corporate Headquarters.

By 1979, the only restaurant to remain substantially unrenovated was the Revere Room, a 108-seat coffee shop serving breakfast and lunch. A holdover from Dunfey's early days at the hotel, when management had instituted a colonial theme, the Revere Room was prominently located near the Tremont Street entrance. It offered fast, reasonably inexpensive meals in what management conceded was a rather dull and conventional setting.

THE DUNFEY ORGANIZATION

The rising popularity of the Parker House mirrored the growing success of the Dunfey corporation as a whole. Revenues had doubled since 1977, when Jon Canas became executive vice-president. Chainwide occupancy rates leaped from 56 percent in 1975, below industry average, to a projected 76 percent in 1979. By late 1979, the company, now known as Dunfey Hotels, owned or managed 23 hotels and inns. These properties were divided into six distinct groups, among which was the Classic Hotels division, consisting of the Parker House, the Ambassador East in Chicago, and the Berkshire Place in New York City.

The Dunfey Management Process

The character of Dunfey inns and hotels varied widely; within the Boston area alone, Dunfey-managed facilities included a 275-room executive inn and a 120-room suburban motor inn in addition to the Parker House. Accordingly, the corporation made it a point to maintain clear distinctions in planning, pricing, and promotion between the Classic hotels and other Dunfey properties.

The foundation of the Dunfey management process, established by Jon Canas, was the annual mission statement developed for each hotel. Responsibility for this detailed planning document was shared between corporate marketing and operations executives and the Executive Operating Committee (EOC) of each individual property. The Parker House EOC included Robert McIntosh, general manager; the director of sales; the resident manager for food and beverage; the resident manager for rooms; and the personnel director. Working closely with Yervant Chekijian, they attempted, through the mission statement, to specify what kind of customer, at what time of year, at what rate, was most desirable for the hotel. After this "ideal business mix" (IBM) had been determined, objectives could be set for the Rooms Division and the Food and Beverage Division, capital needs established, and a marketing plan designed.

Through this marketing plan, based on the mission statement, detailed strategic blueprints covering four-month and twelve-month periods could be devised for each hotel. Essential to the plan in each case was a supply/demand analysis for each major revenue-producing area (rooms, banquets, à la carte operations, lounges). Such a study showed demand by market segment; it also analyzed the features of the competition and the hotel's competitive advantages and disadvantages vis-à-vis the needs of each market segment. The mission statement expressed the desired market position of the hotel; the supply/demand analysis provided data through which a plan designed to achieve that position could be constructed.

THE CLASSIC HOTELS

Each Dunfey Classic hotel was considered a unique facility with a character and tradition all its own. This individuality was reflected in the hotels' decorating schemes: Manhattan's Berkshire Place, acquired in 1978, was furnished in a sophisticated contemporary mixture of marble, plants, oriental rugs, and overstuffed furniture; the decor of Chicago's Ambassador East, acquired in 1977, blended eighteenth-century antiques with contemporary accessories; and the Parker House evoked a wood-paneled comfortable club.

Like the Parker House, the Ambassador East and the Berkshire Place were restorations of old, centrally located hotels. Such restorations were advantageous to Dunfey for several reasons. It was faster and less expensive (on a per-room basis) to restore an old hotel than to construct a new one. In the long run this could produce a relative cost advantage for Dunfey Classic hotels challenged by newly constructed competitors. Moreover, the location of such hotels—in the heart of the downtown business district—was often difficult for a new property to duplicate.

The history and physical facilities of the Classics also created an atmosphere which many Dunfey executives felt was missing in more modern hotels. As the company's newsletter stated:

> Our Classic hotels have a tangible quality and an intangible ambience . . . much like an older, cultured, grand lady whose very presence exudes charm, sophistication, and prestige. We believe that many travelers seek an escape, an oasis from the sterile sameness of some national hotel chains. Even in the newer, plush megastructures of modern hotels, there is the risk of being lost in a sea of conventioneers, of experiencing impersonal service. We know there is a growing market for hotels where guests are treated as individuals in distinctive settings.

On the other hand, hotels constructed during an era when guests frequently traveled with their servants generally had many bedrooms considerably smaller than those offered by more modern competitors; 50 rooms at the Parker House, for example, were too small to include a full bathtub and contained only showers. Even after renovation, the rooms of older hotels tended to vary widely in size and location, a potential source of annoyance to guests charged the same rates for "different" rooms. Repair and maintenance costs were higher than for new hotels.

Pricing Policy

As Jon Canas described it, "pricing is the exteriorization of your marketing position"; with this philosophy in mind, Classic hotel rates were customarily set to fall within the top 10 percent of local competition. Local rates could also be an inhibiting factor: Although Parker House management felt that the hotel's high average occupancy rate had given them substantial pricing leverage, Boston hotel rates in general were much lower than those in New York. Yervant Chekijian summarized the situation as follows:

> Right now, at the Parker House, we're running $53 to $65 single and $63 to $75 double. Personally, I'd like to see these rates brought closer to parity with New York, where the Berkshire, for instance, is charging $85 single. But local custom heavily influences pricing. In Chicago, when a number of hotels began offering substantial discounts to their corporate customers, we had to lower rates at the Ambassador East to match competition.

On the other hand, continuing inflation in construction and furnishings costs meant that rates charged by new hotels generally had to be set higher than prevailing rates in the same area. The average rate for Massachusetts hotels in 1979 was projected to reach about $42. Discussing this figure, Chekijian noted:

> The average rate, even for a luxury hotel, can appear surprisingly low. It's important to remember that heavy seasonal and day-of-the-week variations give a hotel much flexibility in discounting. The average room rate is thus the result of sales to many different market segments at significantly different rates.

According to Dunfey management, any hotel operating at 85 percent room sales efficiency or above needed a rate increase. Room

sales efficiency (RSE) was a standard used throughout Dunfey Hotels to measure the occupancy-price performance of an operation in which substantial discounting was common; RSE was defined as the ratio of total room sales revenues achieved during a specific period divided by the sum of the maximum revenues that could have been obtained if all available rooms had been sold at full (or "rack") rates during the same period. For example, if occupancy was 90 percent and the average room rate obtained was 90 percent of the full rate, the RSE would be 81 percent.

Room sales accounted for close to three-fifths of the hotel's departmental revenues in 1978 (Exhibit 1); because the incremental costs of room rental were relatively low, the hotel's high occupancy meant a substantial profit margin in that department—72 percent in 1978. The margin for food and beverage, by contrast, could be as low as 18 percent. The Parker House's earnings (Exhibit 1), like the earnings of every Dunfey hotel, returned to the corporation for distribution.

Advertising and Sales Efforts

National and major regional advertising for each Classic hotel was supervised by Dunfey's director of advertising and public relations, who was based at the head office in Hampton, New Hampshire. In addition to placing ads for individual Classic properties in such periodicals as *The New Yorker* and *Forbes* (Exhibit 2), the advertising department was developing an advertisement which would promote the Classic hotels as a group in such print media as *Business Week*, *Sports Illustrated*, and *Time*. Total national advertising for the Classics was budgeted at about $784,000 for 1979.

As well as creating demand for rooms at the three Classic properties, the promotional campaign was designed to meet two other objectives: first, to create awareness of Dunfey Classic hotels as a group in order to pave the way for expansion of the division in other key metropolitan areas; and second, to establish a favorable institutional image for the corporation as a whole. Obtaining management contracts for prime properties from third-party owners was a continuing part of Dunfey's plans for expansion.

Local advertising for the Parker House was supervised by McIntosh, working with the hotel's director of sales, and was used primarily to promote Parker's Restaurant and The Last Hurrah (Exhibit 2). A Boston public relations firm also worked closely with McIntosh in achieving local visibility for the hotel. Sales department expenditures totalled $371,769 in 1978, of which 52 percent went to salaries and wages, 38 percent to advertising, and 10 percent to sales and promotions. Newspaper advertising, which totalled about $51,000 in 1978, was budgeted at almost $130,000 in 1979.

Although most hotels segmented their guests into two or three categories (tourists, corporate travelers, and groups), the Parker House identified eleven major segments. The three most important—individual professionals and executives, corporate groups, and professional or special-interest associations—were contacted regularly by the Parker House sales staff. The hotel did not have space to accept large conventions. "Customers contribute to the atmosphere or hotel experience," declared one Dunfey executive. "You should choose your clientele selectively to match your mission."

Two Parker House salespeople represented the hotel's Executive Service Plan (ESP) sales effort, targeted toward individual business travelers; they had a weekly quota of 40 sales calls to Boston-based organizations. According to McIntosh, no other hotel in the city carried out an equivalent direct sales campaign. In a further effort to attract ESP guests, who were always charged rack rate, the hotel offered an unlisted telephone number for reservations, larger rooms, express check-out, complimentary newspapers, and free weekend accommodations for an ESP guest's spouse. Other Parker House sales representatives solicited business from associations and groups in or near Boston. Obtaining bookings from companies, associations, and tour groups outside the Boston area was the responsibility of Dunfey's corporate sales department.

The Parker House in 1979

In May 1979, the 546 Parker House guest rooms were divided into the eight categories shown in Exhibit 3. Rooms were classified according to size, location (i.e., whether the room had an outside view), and quality of furnishings and appointments. The hotel's 36 Patriot rooms were the smallest it offered, accommodating only single occupancy, and were located in the interior of the building, overlooking a central airshaft. These rooms were sold at a substantial discount to government employees; similar, somewhat larger rooms were sold, by annual contract, to airline personnel. Standard and Deluxe rooms were larger than Patriot rooms, possessed an outside view, had better quality furniture, and contained such amenities as color television and an AM-FM clock radio. Top of the Line rooms were more spacious still and had king-size beds. Suites consisted of one or more very large rooms—often constructed by combining two smaller rooms—with superior appointments; many suites had kitchen facilities such as a sink or wet bar.

In addition to its guest rooms, the Parker House contained a variety of facilities for meetings, including three small "board rooms" accommodating 8 to 15 people; ten meeting rooms accommodating 25 to 200; and one ballroom accomodating 350. Duplicating machines, blackboards, and audio-visual equipment were available to groups at a small fee. Opening off the main lobby were a gift shop, a bank, a small shop selling newspapers, magazines, and sundries, and an Aer Lingus ticket office. A barber shop was located on the basement level. Laundry/valet service, airport limousines, and rental cars could all be requested through the hotel's front desk.

Occupancy rates at the Parker House, in keeping with the upward trend enjoyed by the city's hotels at large, had risen sharply in recent years. However, Dunfey executives realized that these figures were averages, in which the high weekday occupancy balanced out significantly lower weekend levels. As the corporation's director of sales explained:

The Parker House is favored with a very heavy demand on Monday, Tuesday, and Wednesday nights. Management still has to stretch the Sunday night arrivals that are staying through the week. On Thursday, Friday, and Saturday nights, the hotel is not favored with a tremendously high turnaway. The ideal, of course, would be to have people coming in Sunday, checking out Friday, and followed by a heavy weekend influx. That's still not true for the Parker House.

At the same time, the hotel had also shown an improvement in room sales efficiency. Published room rates at the Parker House had risen at least once each year; the most recent increases had been posted on December 1, 1977; September 1, 1978; and April 1, 1979. Exhibit 4 shows occupancy rates, room sales efficiency index, and room, food, and beverage sales figures at the Parker House for calendar year 1978 and early 1979.

THE BOSTON HOTEL MARKET

The average occupancy rates for Boston hotels had been considerably higher than the national average for a number of years (Exhibit 5). The city offered many diverse attractions to visitors. In addition to its status as a financial and commercial center, the Boston area boasted the greatest concentration of colleges and universities in the world, including both Harvard University and the Massachusetts Institute of Technology. Known as the "Medical Mecca" of the United States, Boston was also home to the Massachusetts General Hospital and a host of other renowned medical centers and research institutions. The Museum of Fine Arts and the Boston Symphony Orchestra were world famous, and the area's many colonial historic sites also attracted a substantial number of tourists.

A major Atlantic seaport, Boston had a very accessible airport and one of the most extensive public transportation systems in the U.S. But driving in the city could be difficult; many downtown streets followed the meandering patterns of colonial cow paths, and parking was scarce and expensive. Driving was particularly a problem in winter, when heavy snow falls and illegally parked cars (Bostonian drivers, according to a *New York Times* article, were notorious scofflaws) rendered some streets almost impassable. The city's most pleasant season, many felt, was fall, when tourists flocked to the area on their way to view autumn foliage.

The city had not always been so popular; between 1930 and 1955, not a single new hotel room was built in Boston. Although construction resumed during the 1960s, many hoteliers put aside plans for expansion following the recession of 1974–1975. Between 1930 and 1960, the city posted a net decrease of 4,938 hotel rooms.

With a restricted supply of hotel rooms, the city's economic revival pushed occupancy rates steadily higher (Exhibit 5). In 1978, average occupancy rates exceeded 80 percent during six months out of twelve, reaching a peak of 90 percent in September and October. Since weekend occupancy tended to drop sharply, this meant that many hotels were fully booked Monday through Thursday for several months of the year.

The supply/demand imbalance in Boston had reached what many city officials described as a crisis by early 1979, when two major national organizations called off plans to hold conventions in the city, citing lack of space. Hynes Auditorium, located in the Prudential Center, was Boston's only major convention center and contained only 150,000 feet of floor space; although Boston was the eighth largest population area in the nation, 30 other cities could accommodate larger conventions. It was estimated that the loss of major conventions, plus straight business and tourist turnaways, was costing the city and state $30 million annually.

Despite Boston's severely limited convention facilities, convention visitors composed 31 percent of local hotel guests in 1978. Tourists accounted for 20 percent, and business travelers, 49 percent. Business demand was expected to reach 5,683 rooms by 1985, a 67 percent increase over 1978.

According to a recent study conducted for the mayor of Boston by the Boston Redevelopment Authority (BRA), the city was noted for possessing an unusually large concentration of what the BRA defined as "luxury" hotels. More than half of the town's 6,925 rooms were classed as luxury by the BRA; one third were classed as moderately priced; and less than 10 percent were categorized as inexpensive. Exhibit 6 presents the BRA's analysis of Boston's hotel stock by class and major use.

Competition

Visitors to Boston could choose from approximately a dozen major hotels, as well as several lesser ones, located within a three-mile radius of the central city (Exhibit 7). The Boston hotel stock was positioned to absorb the cream of hotel demand, leaving the adjacent metropolitan region to accommodate the overflow of convention delegates and tourists (an additional 2,883 rooms were located outside the city in Cambridge and other suburbs).

McIntosh and Chekijian agreed that the Parker House's most significant competitors were the Ritz Carlton, the Copley Plaza, and the Hyatt Regency (the latter located across the river in Cambridge). Built in 1927 by a Harvard graduate who for decades admitted guests according to his evaluation of their social status, the Ritz never suffered the temporary decline that blighted the Parker House. Ninety percent of its guests were repeat visitors, and though its dining room was felt to have slipped somewhat in recent years, it was still considered one of the best restaurants in town. After its owner's death in 1961, the Ritz had been sold to a local real estate investor, and several senior employees resigned in the ensuing years, stating, it was reported, that the hotel's rigorous standards had declined. (One chef, for example, expressed indignation over the presence of frozen food in the kitchen.)

Nevertheless, the Ritz remained a formidable competitor. Its Back Bay location, between Newbury Street and Commonwealth Avenue, was some distance from Boston's congested financial center, but very convenient to the city's shops, theatres, and galleries; the public rooms and many guest rooms offered a fine view of the Boston Public Garden, situated across the street from the hotel's main entrance. Guest rooms were also equipped with working fireplaces, and the hotel's average ratio of 0.7 rooms per staff member was the lowest in town (Exhibit 8). Although one industry expert interviewed by *Boston* magazine in 1977 considered the Ritz somewhat "tired looking," he nevertheless declared that "if there were a list of great hotels in the United States, and a hotel in Boston had to be on it, the Ritz is the only Boston hotel that would make it." A tower extension to the Ritz was presently under construction and scheduled to open in 1981. This addition would add 50 new rooms and a ballroom to the hotel; the remainder of the tower would be divided into condominiums.

Discussing the Hyatt Regency, opened in 1976, Chekijian commented,

> Although the Cambridge location is a bit isolated and thus somewhat of a disadvantage, this is our toughest competition. They have a unique physical plant, the freshest rooms, and a beautiful view of Boston across the Charles River. Food and beverage is very good, and there is a wide selection of room configurations in the hotel. They are well managed and have the highest rates in town, as well as a national identification. All in all, a customer who doesn't like the Parker House will probably go to the Hyatt Regency.

The Hyatt offered visitors a swimming pool, a revolving rooftop restaurant, and an exotic lobby described by one local journalist as

> nothing short of spectacular, a soaring brick atrium built on the scale of a railroad station . . . the main attractions here are four glass-enclosed elevators that glide aloft to the revolving Spinnaker lounge and swoop swiftly down to a thrilling splashdown in the fountain.

The Hyatt also offered special "Regency Club" service, reserved for guests on the tenth floor of the hotel, who enjoyed the full-time attention of their own concierge in the private Regency Club lounge. Industry observers estimated that occupancy at both the Hyatt and the Ritz would reach 80 to 85 percent for 1979.

The Copley Plaza, located a few blocks from the Ritz in the Back Bay, had been built in 1912. According to Chekijian, "The Copley's physical plant is beautiful—as you approach from the outside, you know it's a luxury hotel." Like the Parker House, however, the Copley had suffered a long eclipse; during the 1940s it was bought by the Sheraton Corp. and renamed the Sheraton Plaza. The neighboring John Hancock Life Insurance Company bought the Copley in 1972, and in 1974, when the hotel regained its former name, many rooms were lavishly redecorated with Chippendale chairs, bronze and marble chests, and ornate mirrors—what one local magazine called "the only truly rococo grand-hotel-style chambers in Boston." But the same writer went on to say that some of the rooms, particularly those on the "inside" overlooking the hotel's maintenance plant, were "cramped and dingy." Occupancy was estimated at 75 to 80 percent for 1979.

The remaining large hotels in the city, according to Chekijian, were less attractive than the Parker House and its three serious competitors:

The Colonnade has an exceptional physical plant, built in 1971. It's not in a particularly convenient location, but President Ford stayed there when he visited Boston for the Bicentennial.

The Park Plaza was formerly the Statler Hilton, which fell on hard times and closed in November 1976. The building was renovated and reopened in February 1977. Its location is fairly convenient, but the neighborhood is somewhat unattractive. They only compete with us for the discount segments, where they do an exceptional job.

The Sheraton Boston is a typical large Sheraton. Everything about this hotel is middle-of-the-road: food and beverage, rooms, and its location on the far side of the Prudential Center. The Sheraton attracts conventioneers and tour groups.

Howard Johnson's 57 has an excellent physical plant, built in 1972. The location is convenient but not very desirable—right on the edge of the adult entertainment district. Their restaurant is fairly good, and they have a movie house in the building. I think the Howard Johnson name and chain image negates the market position they're striving for.

Finally, there's the Holiday Inn. They have the highest occupancy rate in town because of their proximity to Massachusetts General Hospital. They have relatively spacious rooms and average, predictable Holiday Inn standards. In addition to visitors to the hospital, they get federal, city, and state government travelers, plus the people who always stay in a Holiday Inn.

Exhibit 8 summarizes key statistics for 20 hotels and motor inns in Boston and immediately adjacent suburbs. Exhibit 9 presents a selection of competitive hotel advertisements.

Plans for New Construction

According to the Boston Redevelopment Authority, future business expansion would generate the need for almost 6,000 new rooms in Boston by 1985 (Exhibit 6) plus more than 4,000 additional rooms between 1985 and 1990. However, some observers viewed these forecasts as optimistic. They pointed out that much of the new demand was projected to result from projects not yet approved—the construction of a second convention center and the expansion of existing convention facilities. Others pointed to the likelihood of a slowdown in demand resulting from the recession which economists had forecast for late 1979 or early 1980.

Developers and hotel chains alike had nevertheless become very interested in new hotel construction in Boston. By 1979, no fewer than 17 new hotels were in various stages of planning, although informed observers doubted that all proposed would actually be built. (Exhibit 7 shows the location of selected current and proposed hotels.) A plan to convert the liner *United States* to a hotel (known as S. S. Boston) and moor it next to Commonwealth Pier appeared particularly unlikely to materialize.

In the view of Bob McIntosh and his associates, the greatest threats to the Parker House would come from the proposed Marriott Hotel, the Meridien, the Inter-Continental Boston, and the hotel planned for Copley Place. The first three would all be located within a ten-minute walk of the Parker House. Architects' sketches of Marriott's Long Wharf Hotel showed a dramatically modern, low-rise design on a wharf jutting into Boston Harbor. It was rumored that construction on the 400-room property in the city's attractive new Waterfront area would begin in early 1980, and that the hotel would open in late 1981 or early 1982.

The shell of the elegant old Federal Reserve Bank building in the heart of the financial district was being converted into a new luxury hotel by Meridien Hotels of Paris, a subsidiary of Air France. Preliminary work had already begun. The 330-room hotel, to be called the Hotel Meridien, would be joined via a glass atrium to a new 40-story office tower. Construction was scheduled to begin in late 1979, with the opening expected in mid-1981. Plans called for the hotel to appeal primarily to the executive and luxury markets. The architect's design included large suites and guest rooms (some on two levels), ornate board rooms, a ballroom for banquets and conferences, and specialty retail shops on the ground floor.

Inter-Continental Hotels, a worldwide chain and wholly owned subsidiary of Pan American World Airways, planned to build a 21-story, 500-room hotel, scheduled to open in late 1982, as a major element of Lafayette Place. This proposed new complex in Boston's reviving downtown retail area would include retail stores, a large circular public mall, and a parking garage for 1,300 cars. The hotel would contain a swimming pool, sun terrace, and health club as well as a large outdoor terrace for open-air receptions. Convention facilities, equipped with four simultaneous translation booths, could accommodate 1,000 people.

The proposed Copley Place complex, to be built over the Massachusetts Turnpike next to the Prudential Center, would be located near the Copley Plaza hotel on the fringe of the Back Bay, an area whose shops and art galleries already attracted many tourists and city residents. An 800-room luxury hotel was planned for Copley Place, in addition to enclosed parking for 1,500 cars; a two-level retail center; a five-story, mixed-income apartment building; and four connecting seven-story office buildings, each located on top of a two-level shopping mall. There was talk of the plans being revised to include a second hotel. The Copley Place project had generated considerable community opposition and had not yet been approved; the earliest completion date was seen as 1984.

The only other new hotel scheduled to open before 1985 was a 160-room tourist hotel near the waterfront; this was not considered major competition by Parker House management.

It was estimated that the average construction cost per room for each of the four new luxury hotels would range from $80,000 to $100,000. The pricing rule of thumb followed by the hotel industry in opening new properties was that the initial daily "rack rate" per room (i.e., the maximum published rate established by hotel management) should be set at one dollar for each thousand dollars of construction cost.

Contemplating the competitive challenge he would be facing in the next five years, McIntosh summarized his position:

> Unless we get a significant amount of corporate capital invested in substantial renovations for the Parker House, we'll be offering our guests fairly well-worn rooms that haven't been significantly redecorated since 1974. Faced with this or the chance to try out a brand-new luxury property, which do you think they're going to choose?

EXHIBIT 1

Operating Statements
1979 Budget versus 1978 Actual

	1978	1979 (Budgeted)[a]
DEPT. REVENUES		
Rooms	$ 6,273,078	$ 6,865,270
Food	2,829,678	3,078,900
Beverage	1,454,066	1,560,600
Food and Bev. (Misc. Income)	53,852	59,100
Telephone	251,655	259,480
Valet and Guest Laundry	39,677	34,700
Other Income	16,129	11,400
Check Room	5,149	11,500
Operated Dept. Revenues	10,923,554	11,880,950
PROFIT OR (LOSS)		
Rooms	4,682,429	5,198,601
Food and Beverage	824,007	962,096
Telephone	(153,007)	(122,730)
Valet and Guest Laundry	13,209	11,880
Check Room	(9,952)	(5,070)
Operated Dept. Profit	5,356,686	6,044,777
Other Income	16,129	11,400
Gross Operating Income	5,372,814	6,056,177
DEDUCTIONS		
Administrative and General	701,310	657,214
Marketing	371,769	471,854
Energy Costs	695,385	815,961
Property Operation	531,079	892,617
Total Deductions from Inc.	2,299,543	2,837,646
House Profit	3,073,750	3,218,531
Commercial Rental[b]	190,479	173,580
Gross Operating Profit	3,263,750	3,392,111
Property Tax and Fire Ins.	813,544	712,000
Operating Rentals[c]	59,379	59,640
Operating Profit	2,390,827	2,620,471
Depreciation and Amortization	1,342,000	1,435,000
Hotel Earnings	1,048,827	1,185,471

[a] "Budgeted" amounts were a low estimate for financial purposes and did not represent what was expected of management.
[b] Derived from shops approached through the Parker House lobby.
[c] Cost of rented color television sets in rooms.
SOURCE: Company records

Advertising in National Print Media

For People Who Appreciate the Classics.

Classic Accommodations   Classic Service

In Boston

PARKER HOUSE

A DUNFEY CLASSIC HOTEL

Tremont & School Sts., Boston, MA 02107   617/227-8600
Reservations 800 228-2121

Advertising in Boston-Area Print Media

A lot of Boston restaurants are simply replicas of Boston's best.

There is only one great Boston night spot with authentic turn-of-the-century atmosphere, delicious traditional fare, moderate prices, free garage parking by valet, no cover charge and nightly dancing to the delightful sound of the Winiker Swing Orchestra.

The others can only try their best.

THE LAST HURRAH

At The Parker House
Dining/Dancing/Sunday Brunch
Tremont & School Streets/
Boston/Reservations
227-8600

PARKER'S

Dine exquisitely on Boston's favorite dishes, American and continental cuisine. Serving lunch, dinner and Sunday Brunch.

PARKER'S BAR

Our cosmopolitan lounge adjoining Parker's restaurant. Perfect for light lunch at noon. Cocktails till closing.

THE LAST HURRAH

Come eat, drink, dance and be entertained in a plush turn-of-the-century place. Open at 11:30 a.m. to 2 a.m.

PARKER HOUSE
A DUNFEY CLASSIC HOTEL
School & Tremont Street
Boston

EXHIBIT 3

Room Categories at the Parker House, 1979

ROOM TYPE	NUMBER	DAILY RATE	
		Single	*Double*
Patriot	36	$ 35	(none)
Airline	117	47	(none)
Standard	151	53	$63
Deluxe	168	57	67
Top of the Line	23	65	75
Mini-Suites	33	75	85
Suites	17	110	
Deluxe Suite	1	210	

EXHIBIT 4

Selected Performance Measures at the Parker House
1978–1979

PERIOD	ROOM NIGHTS	OCCUPANCY RATE	ROOM SALES EFFICIENCY	ROOM SALES	FOOD SALES	BEVERAGE SALES
Total 1978	160,062	80%	68%	$6,273,077	$2,829,678	$1,454,066
January 1978	11,565	68	53	411,868	194,618	106,487
February	11,402	75	59	418,806	177,638	105,908
March	12,944	77	63	489,657	247,263	141,023
April	13,710	84	72	541,328	250,043	120,689
May	13,863	82	70	547,462	242,681	119,742
June	13,598	83	71	545,280	220,276	105,067
July	12,638	75	63	496,233	168,230	81,632
August	15,081	89	76	598,732	217,394	101,655
September	14,516	89	76	577,712	254,965	125,853
October	15,495	92	79	623,768	316,894	142,092
November	13,659	84	75	573,061	260,021	135,576
December	11,591	69	56	449,170	279,655	168,162
January 1979	13,244	78	61	522,829	234,525	132,179
February	11,741	77	60	463,630	208,382	118,915
March	14,809	87	73	624,512	275,125	154,401
April	14,527	89	80	661,863	280,206	139,566

SOURCE: Company records

EXHIBIT 5

Average Hotel Occupancy Rates in Boston by Month
1965–1978

	1965	1966	1967	1968	1969	1970	1971	1972	1973	1974	1975	1976	1977	1978	WEIGHTED AVERAGE 1965–1977
January	61.9	59.3	69.8	68.7	62.6	58.6	53.3	53.8	59.7	53.9	49.8	51.4	56.6	59.3	57.8
February	65.0	63.7	73.0	75.0	70.8	60.8	57.8	58.3	57.0	58.1	51.6	54.8	57.2	64.1	61.1
March	67.9	66.4	75.5	78.9	73.1	66.7	62.6	68.0	63.3	68.0	55.1	62.9	65.7	73.5	70.2
April	69.6	71.3	82.3	79.6	80.5	80.1	66.7	78.3	71.1	72.6	68.5	69.8	74.8	80.3	73.9
May	66.0	79.6	78.9	84.2	79.5	71.9	69.4	68.5	73.0	76.1	75.6	74.9	76.1	83.6	74.7
June	68.6	80.7	83.4	82.4	83.1	77.4	72.2	78.3	78.5	80.8	74.7	81.7	81.8	87.6	78.7
July	56.7	67.5	75.0	73.1	74.6	63.5	66.9	67.3	67.4	69.9	61.7	72.3	67.8	76.8	68.0
August	65.3	76.0	82.0	80.2	77.8	77.6	75.3	71.6	72.6	78.1	68.3	76.9	78.3	87.1	75.3
September	73.1	82.0	88.0	80.9	80.6	74.2	77.2	75.6	76.5	73.9	74.2	80.4	84.8	90.1	78.4
October	77.4	91.0	85.5	90.1	85.4	81.6	83.9	87.7	84.8	82.3	83.7	84.1	88.6	89.9	85.1
November	65.5	71.5	72.2	72.3	67.1	62.5	63.0	69.1	64.2	62.4	62.0	59.6	67.6	75.1	65.8
December	50.0	53.6	56.6	52.4	58.3	51.3	47.3	51.9	50.3	43.9	43.4	55.1	52.8	58.7	51.1
Total	66.7	72.2	76.8	76.5	74.4	68.9	66.4	68.9	68.3	68.3	64.1	68.9	71.2	77.1	69.9
National Averages	71.3	72.2	74.6	73.6	73.3	67.6	64.1	65.0	66.3	65.8	62.5	65.9	67.7	N.A.	

SOURCE: Cited in *Hotel and Convention Center Demand and Supply in Boston*, Boston Redevelopment Authority, March 1979, pp. IV–4.

EXHIBIT 6

Current Hotel Stock and Projected Demand in Downtown Boston by Class and Major Use

Spring 1979

	CLASS A LUXURY HOTEL ROOMS			CLASS B MODERATELY PRICED HOTEL ROOMS		
	Current Stock	*1985 Demand[a]*	*1985 Stock[a]*	*Current Stock*	*1985 Demand[a]*	*1985 Stock[a]*
Business Visitor	2,169	3,845	4,019	1,003	1,536	1,487
Tourist	518	1,321	1,123	599	1,342	949
Convention	1,294	2,487	3,894	720	1,234	720
Total	3,981	7,653	9,036	2,322	4,112	3,156

	CLASS C INEXPENSIVE HOTEL ROOMS			TOTALS		
	Current Stock	*1985 Demand[a]*	*1985 Stock[a]*	*Current Stock*	*1985 Demand[a]*	*1985 Stock[a]*
Business Visitor	211	302	221	3,393	5,683	5,727
Tourist	296	642	296	1,413	3,305	2,378
Convention	105	148	105	2,119	3,869	4,719
Total	622	1,092	622	6,925	12,857	12,814

[a] Projections
SOURCE: Boston Redevelopment Authority study, 1979

EXHIBIT 7

Location of Major Existing and Proposed Hotels in the Boston Area, 1979

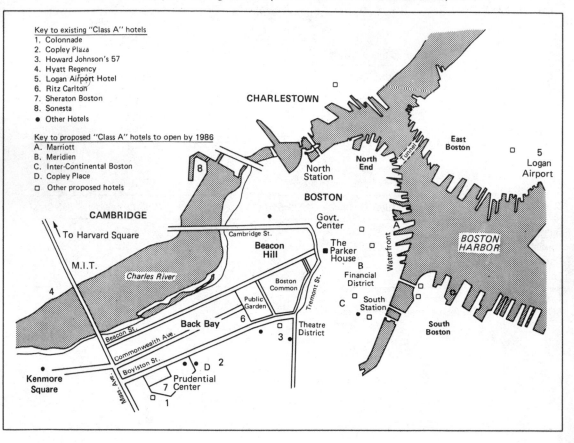

Key to existing "Class A" hotels
1. Colonnade
2. Copley Plaza
3. Howard Johnson's 57
4. Hyatt Regency
5. Logan Airport Hotel
6. Ritz Carlton
7. Sheraton Boston
8. Sonesta
● Other Hotels

Key to proposed "Class A" hotels to open by 1986
A. Marriott
B. Meridien
C. Inter-Continental Boston
D. Copley Place
□ Other proposed hotels

EXHIBIT 8

Characteristics of Hotels Competing in the Central Boston Market

HOTEL	OPENING DATE	NUMBER OF ROOMS	1979 PRICE RANGE ($)		CLASS a	MAJOR USE b	EMPLOYEES	ROOMS PER EMPLOYEE	PERMANENT RESIDENTS
			Single	Double					
Boston Park Plaza	1927	1,100	32–42	38–50	B	C	375	2.1	0
Bradford Hotel	1927	322	24	29	C	T	70	4.6	7
Children's Inn	1968	82	31	33	B	B	75	1.1	0
Colonnade Hotel	1971	306	58–64	66–72	A	B	260	1.2	0
Copley Plaza Hotel	1912	450	41–58	49–66	A	B	420	1.1	4
Copley Square Hotel	1895	160	28–32	32–38	B	T	45	3.6	15
Essex Hotel	1900	300	21–27	27–32	C	B	45	6.7	60
Fenway Boylston	1956	94	29	37	B	B	50	1.9	0
Holiday Inn	1968	300	41	45	B	B	175	1.7	0
Howard Johnson's 57	1972	400	44	52	A	B	225	1.8	0
Howard Johnson's Kenmore Square	1963	178	30–32	38–42	B	B	130	1.4	0
Hyatt Regency (Cambridge)	1976	478	45–73	58–75	A	B	600	0.8	0
Lenox Hotel	1900	220	34–46	40–54	B	C	140	1.6	0
Logan Airport Hilton	1975	600	42	52	A	B	270	2.2	0
Midtown Motor Inn	1961	161	42	49	B	T	90	1.8	0
Parker House	1927	546	53–65	63–75	A	B	432	1.3	0
Ramada Inn-Logan	1972	209	39	47	B	B	150	1.4	0
Ritz-Carlton Hotel	1927	250	60–78	65–78	A	B	350	0.7	8
Sheraton Boston	1965	1,428	35–58	59–70	A	C	1,000	1.4	1
Sonesta Hotel (Cambridge)	1963	200	48–52	53–60	A	B	150	1.3	1

a Class: Luxury (A), Moderate (B), Inexpensive (C).
b Major Use: Tourist (T), Business Visitor (B), and Convention (C).
SOURCE: Boston Redevelopment Authority study, 1979 (Cambridge hotel data added separately)

169

EXHIBIT 9

Selected Competitive Advertising

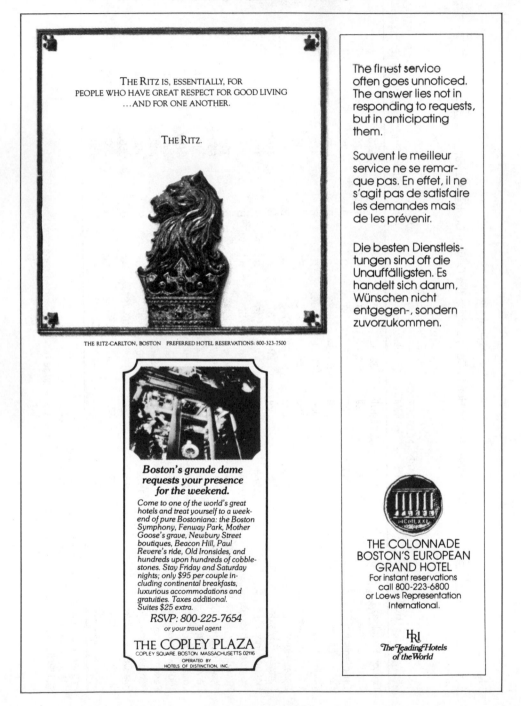

THE RITZ IS, ESSENTIALLY, FOR
PEOPLE WHO HAVE GREAT RESPECT FOR GOOD LIVING
...AND FOR ONE ANOTHER.

THE RITZ.

THE RITZ-CARLTON, BOSTON   PREFERRED HOTEL RESERVATIONS: 800-323-7500

*Boston's grande dame
requests your presence
for the weekend.*

Come to one of the world's great
hotels and treat yourself to a weekend of pure Bostoniana: the Boston
Symphony, Fenway Park, Mother
Goose's grave, Newbury Street
boutiques, Beacon Hill, Paul
Revere's ride, Old Ironsides, and
hundreds upon hundreds of cobble-
stones. Stay Friday and Saturday
nights; only $95 per couple in-
cluding continental breakfasts,
luxurious accommodations and
gratuities. Taxes additional.
Suites $25 extra.

RSVP: 800-225-7654

or your travel agent

THE COPLEY PLAZA
COPLEY SQUARE BOSTON MASSACHUSETTS 02116
OPERATED BY
HOTELS OF DISTINCTION, INC.

The finest service
often goes unnoticed.
The answer lies not in
responding to requests,
but in anticipating
them.

Souvent le meilleur
service ne se remar-
que pas. En effet, il ne
s'agit pas de satisfaire
les demandes mais
de les prévenir.

Die besten Dienstleis-
tungen sind oft die
Unauffälligsten. Es
handelt sich darum,
Wünschen nicht
entgegen-, sondern
zuvorzukommen.

THE COLONNADE
BOSTON'S EUROPEAN
GRAND HOTEL
For instant reservations
call 800-223-6800
or Loews Representation
International.

HRI
The Leading Hotels
of the World

HEALTH SYSTEMS INC.

A growing consulting firm specializing in work for hospitals and other health care organizations seeks to strengthen its competitive posture. Management is considering opening one or more branch offices and wonders what types of clients the firm should be seeking to serve and in which geographic areas it should concentrate its efforts.

Kelly Breazeale, vice-president of Health Systems Incorporated (HSI), a Boston-based consulting firm, tilted his chair back from his desk, gazed at his calendar for April 1980 and shook his head. The airline tickets on his left meant another trip to Michigan this week. The neat 18-inch stack of papers placed in a corner by his secretary was an insistent reminder of the "certificate of need" required before the State of New Hampshire would approve the construction project planned for the Mary Hitchcock Medical Center in Hanover, New Hampshire. Heaped at the back of his desk was a pile of notes for the 55-page hospital consolidation proposal due to be presented in suburban Woburn, Mass., on Thursday afternoon. It occurred to him suddenly that by skipping lunch and dinner for four days, a consultant could add one extra eight-hour working day to his week. Just as he was mulling over the consequences of this rather austere regimen, there was a knock at the door.

"Morning, Kelly." Robert DeVore, HSI's president, stuck his head in the doorway. "I finished reading the Baptist Hospital report—it looks OK to mail. And I've arranged a meeting next week to discuss possible locations for our new office. We also need to talk about how we market HSI and how a branch office would affect our marketing. Can you give it some additional thought over the weekend?"

COMPANY BACKGROUND

Health Systems Inc. had been founded in 1970 by DeVore, an architect, and Robert Bland, a venture capitalist, who had been classmates at college. The partners split almost half of the stock of the new venture between themselves and agreed that DeVore, because of his architectural experience and entrepreneurial inclination, would serve as chief executive officer; Bland took the title of executive vice-president in charge of project management, serving as consultant to health care construction projects. Their goals, DeVore recalled, were threefold: to have fun, to make money, and to make a social contribution in health care planning and policy.

DeVore and Bland were convinced that market analysis, project and operating cost models, and elaborate forecasting could be applied to public and nonprofit health care projects as well as to private sector construction. At the same time, they considered it essential to recognize the unique needs of health care facilities in design, capital construction, and financing.

Originally Health Systems was organized to offer design, engineering, construction, and financial expertise in a single package; unfortunately, such broad positioning resulted in a severe competitive handicap, as HSI, which was not a contractor, found itself competing against both architects and contractors for jobs. As DeVore himself later remarked, describing the company's early struggles: "We made the classical marketing error of running in 20 different directions at 20 different times."

From his present office on the twenty-second floor of a downtown Boston skyscraper with a view of the harbor, DeVore could laugh as he recalled HSI's early days:

Bland and I rented this great office above,

This case was prepared by Penny Pittman Merliss, a former research associate at the Harvard Business School, and Christopher H. Lovelock.

would you believe, a Goodwill store. I had a plywood desk, and there was a rug merchant downstairs who would lend us a rug if somebody big was going to come by. If a really big potential client was supposed to come over, I'd take a van and go around town the night before, collecting good furniture from everybody who worked for us. We'd put it in the office, and we'd also get all our friends to come in the next day, spread papers around on some desks, and look busy. What business we had came from personal contacts. We were barely surviving.

Typical of the firm's early days was a project management job for a hospital in Viro Beach, Florida. The stakes were high: a $10,000 job at a time when the company's total annual income was about $40,000. HSI threw all its resources into the proposal, and came out second-best. Afterward the chairman of the board of trustees commented frankly to DeVore: "We know you boys can do a better job. But if I pick you, and you fail, I'll be killed for giving the job to a small, unknown firm. If the other guys fail, no one can blame us for choosing them."

In desperation, DeVore and Bland decided to reposition HSI. Rather than competing for projects at major medical centers across the nation, they decided in 1972 to 1973 to concentrate on the design and construction of doctors' office buildings and ambulatory care (outpatient) centers in the Northeast, an area they knew well. Their reasoning was that a small company could defeat the "big boys" for small jobs by putting its best people into the project and assimilating more information about the client's needs, objectives, and environment than large competitors were willing to pursue for a proposal. Almost immediately the new strategy paid off, as HSI won contracts for medical office buildings in Marlborough, Massachusetts, and Rochester, New York, defeating much larger design firms.

In 1973 Health Systems commissioned a detailed analysis of the company's past, present, and future marketing directions. The consultant's report recommended that the firm focus its efforts on clients in heavily regulated New England and mid-Atlantic urban areas (particularly Baltimore, Philadelphia,

Buffalo, and New York) who were planning doctors' office buildings, ambulatory care centers, and hospital garages. Accordingly HSI sought, and won, contracts in Baltimore and Schenectady, New York.

In 1974, the company came close to disaster in an abortive attempt to develop a medical office condominium in Houston. The absence of any real roots in Texas was a significant problem in the venture; as everyone came to realize, "we weren't good old boys." As he spent more and more time trying to salvage what he could in Houston, DeVore was increasingly unavailable for other projects, and the firm's income dropped. Finally Houston was written off, and Bland later summed up the whole episode in a pungent sentence: "It costs lots of money to go to school."

HSI recovered by 1977, when professional fees more than doubled over those earned the previous year. As contracts began to flow into the firm, DeVore made another crucial decision: HSI was not in the business of architecture. Design would be subcontracted in the future, as would a few smaller services originally offered by the company. Government regulation of health care was mushrooming in the mid-1970s, especially in Massachusetts, and DeVore was convinced that the firm's future lay in management, financial planning, and construction cost control.

By 1980, HSI's revenues appeared to justify his decision: Professional fees topped $900,000 in fiscal 1979—a 55 percent increase over 1978 (Exhibit 1). Fees were projected to reach $1.4 million for the year ending July 31, 1980, and net income after tax was projected to rise to $140,000. By the end of its first decade of operations, the company employed 15 professionals and 9 supporting staff. The backgrounds and experience of HSI professionals varied widely, ranging from hospital administration to real estate development to health care regulation.

Organization

The Management, Planning, and Financial Services (MPFS) Group, headed by Kelly Breazeale, was the fastest growing segment of the company. This group accounted for 67 percent of HSI's revenues in 1979. Among the services offered by MPFS were strategic planning, multi-institutional work (involving mergers, consolidations, or sharing of facilities between two or more institutions), and financial feasibility studies (often projecting the results of planned expansion or cutbacks in services). Facility master planning, another MPFS service, included marketing studies as well as operations and management analysis. Certificates of Need (CON) were also handled by this group. The CON process, a series of lengthy regulatory hearings designed to curb unnecessary hospital spending, was a legal prerequisite in many states to hospital construction, expansion, or introduction of new services.

Marketing studies produced by MPFS could lead to long-range planning projects for the same clients; a CON contract frequently followed. The CON jobs in turn could produce projects for HSI's Project Management Group. In general, Breazeale noted, "any small-scale specialty study can lead to a long-term relationship with a client in a variety of ways." Current MPFS work included joint planning and consolidation studies for the Choate and Symmes hospitals, near Boston. By the end of 1980, HSI expected to bill almost $350,000 on this project. Breazeale saw it not only as a major income producer but as an opportunity for the firm to offer innovative solutions to some of the most important problems facing hospitals in the 1980s. MPFS had recently completed a long-range market plan for Episcopal Hospital in Philadelphia. This project, billed at $46,500, was considered important as an entree for HSI to the Philadelphia market; it had already produced an invitation to compete for planning work at another hospital.

The Project Management Group, headed by Bob Bland, handled management, financing, and construction of building projects for hospitals, nursing homes, clinics, and other health care facilities, including doctors' offices and institutional garages. This group accounted for 27 percent of HSI revenues in 1979. Among other tasks, Bland and his consultants assisted clients in the selection of architects, engineers, and general contractors; established

detailed project cost models; submitted frequent reports describing progress toward performance standards and work deadlines; and advised clients in the preparation of documents for regulatory agencies. Projects ranged from a $500,000 office building for Goodall Hospital in Sanford, Maine, to a $32 million ambulatory care center for the Massachusetts General Hospital (MGH) in Boston.

The ongoing MGH job was the largest in HSI's history, with $220,000 in billings anticipated by July 1980, and $650,000 over its full duration. It had been awarded following a CON project for MGH. DeVore had personally supervised this initial project, which he regarded as a watershed in HSI's development. By planning an ambulatory care center for one of the most prestigious medical centers in the country, DeVore believed HSI had achieved visibility and credibility in addressing a problem that would be faced by almost every major medical center in the 1980s. The CON study for MGH had led directly to similar CON-project management work for Tufts–New England Medical Center, also in Boston. A later recommendation from an MGH administrator led to a feasibility study and strategic plan for ambulatory care at the University of Michigan Medical Center. HSI expected to be competing for project management of the satellite clinic that the MPFS Group had subsequently recommended for Michigan.

The Housing Programs and Facilities Development Group, formed in 1978, did not involve health care consulting as such. At the end of 1979, housing development activities accounted for 6 percent of HSI's revenues. Exhibit 2 shows a divisional breakdown of HSI projects for fiscal years 1977 to 1979.

THE HEALTH CARE CONSULTING ENVIRONMENT

By 1980 health care, once the province of apothecaries, snake oil salesmen, and village healers, was consuming almost one out of every ten dollars of the U.S. gross national product. "Nobody looked and there it was, the third largest industry in the nation," said Hale Champion, Undersecretary of Health, Education and Welfare, in spring of 1978.[1] At that time, only food and construction generated more spending than health care. In 1929 medical costs (for hospitals, physicians, and laboratory tests) had amounted to $3.5 billion in the United States; by spring of 1979 a total medical bill of $206 billion (9.1 percent of GNP) was predicted. Few laughed when the president of a California medical society warned: "We are now in a position to spend the entire national budget on medical tests and procedures."[2]

Since government programs like Medicare or Medicaid, or employer-subsidized private insurers like Blue Cross/Blue Shield, paid the vast majority of American hospital bills (94 percent in 1979), there was little grassroots effort to check costs. Moreover, because the federal government and most independent insurers based their reimbursements on cost rather than fixed rates, neither hospitals nor doctors had any incentive to streamline operations and lower fees. Expenditures of all U.S. hospitals totaled $70.9 billion in 1978, an 11.5 percent increase over 1977 and up from $19.1 billion in 1968. (See Exhibits 3 and 4 for data on hospital size, distribution, expenses, and regulation.)

Following the enactment of Medicaid and Medicare in the mid-1960s, the government share of total expenditures for personal health care began to increase sharply, reaching 40 percent in 1977. Federal and state interest in controlling health care spending rose simultaneously. By 1979, in states like Massachusetts where regulation had reached an advanced stage, hospitals were subjected to state and federal investment controls, rate-setting by state commissions, utilization review (to prevent unnecessary or overly long hospital stays) by federally sponsored Professional Standards Review Organizations (PSROs), and a variety of other checks on independent decision making. HSI consultants considered Connecticut, Maryland, Massachusetts, Michigan, New Jersey, New York, Ohio, and Washington the nation's most heavily regulated states. By comparison, a state like Florida, which ranked forty-seventh in the state support for Medicaid, was relatively "wide open."

By 1980, the cost and complexities of health care administration placed a premium on top management skills. One industry journal predicted that "operations research modeling, trade-off analysis, and decision gameplaying will become commonplace in hospital decision making . . . supplemented by the use of outside consultants as task complexity increases."[3]

Competitive Activity

Many U.S. health care consulting firms still employed fewer than 15 people in 1980 and offered HSI no significant competition. More important competitors could be divided into three major groups:

1. Large general management consulting or accounting firms with branches throughout the U.S. (revenues over $10 million).
2. Specialized health care consulting firms offering at least one of the services offered by HSI (revenues usually under $500,000).
3. For-profit hospital management and ownership firms.

Health care, initially disregarded by many large consulting firms because it had been viewed as a service function managed by nonprofit institutions, had begun to attract considerable interest from general management consultants by 1980. Arthur D. Little, headquartered in Cambridge, Massachusetts, was particularly active in the field. ADL was the nation's largest management consultant, with billings of $121 million in 1978, and over 2,500 employees. The firm maintained an international consulting practice in health care, and between 1974 and 1978 published 13 reports on the industry. A typical recent project was the development of an entire system of hospitals in Brazil. Booz, Allen and Hamilton, in 1978 the second largest American management consultant, with billings of $115 million, based its health and medical division in Chicago.

By 1980, according to *Business Week*, specialization would become a necessity for any general management consulting firm seeking to maintain market share.[4] The importance of specialization in consulting was underlined by the growing importance of accounting firms; the management advisory services (MAS) divisions of six on the "Big 8" accounting firms placed among the nation's top ten consultants in annual billings for 1978. The most important accounting firm active in health care consulting was Laventhol and Horwath (L & H), based in Philadelphia. L & H's MAS division served about 2,500 clients annually in health care and accounted for 12 percent of company revenues in 1978. The firm maintained 35 offices in the U.S. and 62 abroad; industry observers estimated that it ranked within the top 15 accounting firms in the U.S.

As HSI entered its second decade, Bob DeVore felt that only ADL and Booz, Allen offered the firm any real competition in providing creative, contemporary solutions to clients' problems. Even so, DeVore commented,

> They lack the follow-through in project management that we offer. It's also an advantage that they're not really interested in the small hospitals. We're not in a position yet to compete regularly with Booz or ADL on a national basis, but we can regionally. By selectively focusing our market efforts, I'll know more about that market than anyone else. HSI will do more homework and apply more principals' time to the job. Actually I love to compete with these guys, because they charge huge fees and we can creep right underneath them. Our close ratio against the big firms is better than 70 percent—but we compete against them selectively, not all over the country.

DeVore dismissed Laventhol and Horwath: "They still think like auditors—I guess a risk-averse client might choose them. Most of their clients now are audit clients." Nevertheless, he considered the potential threat of the Big 8 firms and general management consultants more serious than the challenge posed by any of the specialized health care consulting groups.

In evaluating competition among the specialized groups, most of whom had revenues from $1 to $2 million in 1979, several HSI consultants identified the TriBrook Group, based in Illinois, as their most significant rival. Tri-Brook, unlike most of the other firms, offered project management as well as strategic planning, CON assistance, merger studies, and other services to its clients. Founded in 1972, TriBrook maintained offices in Oak Brook, Illinois; Birmingham, Alabama; Walnut Creek, California; and Vienna, Virginia (a suburb of Washington, D.C.). Washington-based Ryan Advisors also duplicated almost all of HSI's services, and had branch offices in Rome and Singapore. Other competitors included Anthony J. J. Rourke of White Plains, New York, and Hamilton Associates of Minneapolis.

Most of the firms in this group, according to DeVore, had been established by

> . . . the old-line hospital consulting firms, who did exactly what doctors and hospital administrators wanted in the days when there were no regulators or tough financial modes and the government was encouraging hospitals to expand. I don't consider them competitors in the spheres where HSI operates. TriBrook, for instance, closed its New England offices because the regulatory environment here is too tough.

Breazeale disagreed:

> I think they *are* competition. They are old-line firms with traditional solutions to problems, and we beat them routinely, but that is not to say that they're not competition. Potential clients respond very well to very senior people who've really been around—they don't always realize that the solutions that were good 20 years ago don't work anymore.

The final factors in the competitive equation were the for-profit hospital management and ownership corporations, whose steadily rising revenues had reached $10 billion in 1978. The industry averaged a 30 to 35 percent profit gain in 1979, and a 20 to 25 percent advance was predicted for 1980. Originally investor ownership of hospitals had been limited primarily to small, local groups, often established by doctors; as costs rose and planning and regulation became more complex, national management and ownership chains were formed. By mid-1979, 1,000 of the 7,000 hospitals in the U.S., accounting for 108,000 of the nation's 1.4 million beds, were owned by local or national organizations and operated for profit.

Through management contracts, typically lasting two to five years, the hospital management firms provided purchasing, cost-saving, and revenue-producing assistance to some 300 independent hospitals (triple the number managed in 1975). Under the usual contract, the management corporation assumed total responsibility for the hospital's day-to-day operations and received a fee based on a percentage of gross revenue, plus incentive. One major firm listed 40 services available in its management package, including budgeting and finance, CON, construction, community relations, laboratory operations, long-range planning, personnel, and third-party reimbursement.

Management services—as well as outside ownership—attracted the interest of a significant portion of small- and medium-sized hospitals. Almost 40 percent of hospitals owned by national for-profit chains were in the 100- to 199-bed category; only 2 percent contained over 400 beds. The distribution of hospitals owned by chains varied significantly by region. The chains owned 11 percent of the hospitals in the six New England states and only 9 percent of the hospitals in Delaware, New Jersey, and New York. On the other hand, they owned 80 percent of all hospitals (94 percent of all beds) in the Colorado-Idaho-Montana-Utah-Wyoming area and owned 62 percent of all hospitals in Alabama, Florida, Georgia, Mississippi, the Carolinas, and Tennessee.

Unlike professional consulting firms, the management corporations advertised their services vigorously, in media ranging from professional periodicals like *Hospital Financial Management* or *Modern Healthcare* to local daily newspapers and the *Wall Street Journal*. Appraising their relation to HSI, Breazeale commented:

> We do different things. Most of our business is in helping clients understand what problems they have and tailoring solutions to those problems. Health care management firms sell a solution. "The solution to your problem is, hire us and we'll solve your problem."

HSI did occasionally compete for projects at privately managed hospitals, but such invitations were unusual.

PROJECT DEVELOPMENT AT HSI

As of 1980, DeVore's extensive personal contacts and reputation as a consultant were still HSI's most important source of new business. This personal network was augmented as new professionals with their own contacts in health care were brought into the firm. One HSI project manager described the evolution of a proposal as follows:

> A job usually begins for us with a letter or phone call from a potential client, presenting a problem. We respond by having at least two people, one of them a potential project manager or better yet a principal in the firm, set up an appointment and go to see them and find out informally what's on their minds. That's really a marketing strategy in two ways: One is to leave an impression with them of how we do business; the other is to show them that we're there to find out more than just what was in the letter.

If the results of that visit appeared promising, the future project manager would write a draft of a proposal, send it to the client, and follow up with a second personal visit, asking for reactions. HSI took preliminary work very seriously; it was not unusual for the company to spend $7,000 to $10,000 up front developing a major proposal, "custom-tailored to clients 100 percent."

After the second visit the proposal was rewritten and resubmitted, and the HSI project manager returned for another visit, this time often accompanied by a junior member of the staff. Negotiations followed: A client group, for example, might feel that they couldn't afford HSI's assistance on the whole project and would ask for advice on how to do one or more segments themselves. Following final revisions, a formal presentation to a board or governing committee was required in 80 percent of HSI's jobs. The nature of the board varied according to the size and mission of the institution. Community hospitals, for example, usually recruited both their board and their administrators locally. The board of a major academic medical center, in contrast, consisted of well-known business, professional, and public leaders drawn from across the nation.

Usually the company was allowed 1 to 2 hours to present a proposal, frequently in a highly pressured situation where competitors' presentations preceded and followed HSI's. Communication skills were considered an essential part of the consultant's job. According to Breazeale,

> One of the goals of the firm is to hire 100 percent presentable people: We don't want people who only sit in their office and crank around numbers. Everyone who's hired in the firm is hired with the notion that they either are currently or are capable of becoming a project manager—articulate, carrying themselves well, and relating well to other people. We don't have people who are not capable of client relationships.

Proposals had five major elements. First, HSI's understanding of the client's problem, as constructed from interviews and conversations. Second, the scope of the effort, including an analysis of possible solutions. Third, a detailed time schedule; sometimes a critical path schedule. Fourth, the résumés of the people who would work on the project. (These included descriptions of previous jobs.) The final component was an estimate of fee. Project work was subdivided in detail and hours of work in each job category were figured for each participant, then multiplied times that person's hourly rate. What the client saw was a flat fee, stating that HSI would do the job in a certain time for a certain amount. Said one manager:

> I think that makes an incentive contract; it forces us to look at the market, and say if we go there with a $100,000 fee, that's way out of the league of this particular institution. We can also look at it and say, this is a risky deal, or market conditions ought to make that a more expensive study. In that case we could go from

$100,000 to $120,000 without touching the scope of the job.

Depending on how well they knew the client, the HSI team tried to follow up a presentation before a decision was made. These calls and letters were considered a marketing device, to show the firm's continued interest and willingness to change if a presentation had not met the client's needs. The time elapsed from first contact with a client to a signed contract usually exceeded four months.

Professional Life Style

The typical project lasted 5 to 7 months, though complex or highly regulated contracts could require 1 to 2 years. It was company policy never to locate consultants at a site; all business was conducted out of the HSI office in Boston. Usually 10 percent of total fees for a project were budgeted for expenses. In the case of the ongoing University of Michigan Medical Center project, an $80,000 contract initiated in October 1979, which had grown out of a strong recommendation from a top administrator at MGH, $12,000 had been budgeted for expenses; this included $8,800 for air fares and $800 for lodging.

Breazeale was not sure whether HSI's lack of branch offices had caused the firm to lose business:

> I accept the notion that we are so successfully competitive in New England because we live here and we understand it better. I find it difficult to believe that you can understand an area and carry out successful indirect, informal marketing when you don't live there. I can also say that none of us like the idea of making 40 round trips to Michigan in order to do a project the way we want to do it. So our desire to set up a branch office is motivated as much by our need to do the work in a *manner* we deem satisfactory as it is by our need to get the work.

The average HSI project manager or senior consultant worked about 55 hours a week. Because of the firm's regional base, even project managers rarely spent more than six nights a month away from home. Breazeale estimated that about 40 percent of his time was spent on "billable" projects, either in planning jobs for which he had primary responsibility or in formally helping others bring their projects along. Approximately 30 percent of his average week went to marketing: conferring with his staff, developing proposals, making presentations, and meeting with prospective clients. General administration of the MPFS group and recruitment and support of new consultants accounted for the remainder of his time. HSI had no formal recruitment or training program.

Breazeale enjoyed the variety and intellectual stimulation of the constant problem-solving which consulting required. His feelings were shared by the other senior members of the firm—each of whom, shaped by his own temperament, also saw disadvantages to the job. DeVore's entrepreneurial zest made it very difficult for him to settle down to desk work; he wanted new continents to conquer. For Bland there was a disconcerting aspect to consulting—the need to jump constantly from one set of problems to another. It often occurred to him, he said, that it might be pleasant to work for one institution with one set of problems, one environment, one kind of politics—facing questions that could be known and anticipated.

Communication Efforts

In spring of 1979, *Business Week* noted that many professional service firms were beginning to market their skills aggressively through brochures, advertisements in trade journals, and sponsorship seminars. Nevertheless, many more traditional, established members of the profession agreed with those consultants who stated, "People find us, we don't find them." On DeVore's personal insistence, HSI paid for no advertisements or professional listings. Business came solely through referrals, and by 1980 it was still a point of pride to DeVore that the company had "never made a cold call." He refused to join either of the two major professional organizations in his field:

They're a marketing device for old-timers. Some people have told me that joining might help HSI establish a base outside New England, but I don't want any identification with that group. If I get in their pack I'm one of them, and then I'm one of twenty.

DeVore felt that his refusal to join was not just a philosophy but a marketing strategy in itself: "HSI's uniqueness is an absolutely essential part of its image." Though very wary of any promotional schemes that might demean HSI's professional status, DeVore was not opposed to promotion if appropriately conducted. He made it a point to speak frequently before groups of hospital administrators and other professionals who might provide contacts. "Marketing is an area where I lack some sophistication," he admitted. "I need to learn more about it."

Until 1979 HSI had no promotional material to send even to institutions which had expressed an interest in negotiating a contract with the firm. In spring of that year, a new consultant was hired who insisted that HSI have a brochure, and he was given the responsibility for producing one. A 7½ by 11, full-color brochure was developed, ten pages in length (including four full-page photographs and four pages of text). It identified the principals of the firm, described HSI's organization, listed several recent projects for each division, and included extensive quotations from four principals. The brochure was customarily taken to the first, informal visit with a client; DeVore referred to it as an "expanded calling card—it says, here's our image, here's what we want you to think of Health Systems." When a new associate joined the HSI staff, he or she often wrote letters to friends and colleagues announcing the news and including the brochure.

At present there was some debate in the office as to how far the marketing efforts of a professional group like Health Systems could go. Kelly Breazeale commented:

I personally believe that we are missing the opportunity to do some acceptable "cold" marketing. What I would like to see the firm produce is a newsletter or periodic publication of some kind. My "test" comes from the success of the Ryan Report. A number of years ago, the head of Ryan Advisors started publishing a newsletter just for his clients. It's a little too newsy-chatty for my taste, not so much an elegant statement of style and image, but it's a lot of information. It was so successful that he had people from all over the country writing him and asking to get on his list. This is his major marketing device, and now people are actually paying for it—$12 yearly subscription. Yet he's really a consultant, and he's selling himself every time he puts it out.

Some argument had arisen over the cost of Breazeale's proposal. One staff member had urged a relatively low budget, particularly in the absence of substantial research into the project. "At the least," he commented, "let's not put a lot of money into paper and mailing." Breazeale disagreed, insisting that the newsletter "should stand out as being in the top 1 percent of the mail someone receives." Discussions with designers and printers indicated that Breazeale's ideas could be implemented for a total budget of $6,000, not including the time spent by HSI staff in writing articles. On the other hand, a cheap version of the project with a minimal design standard could be produced for about $1,500. Initial readership was estimated at 1,000.

PLANNING COMPANY GROWTH

By early 1980, HSI's senior staff generally agreed that, as Bob Bland put it, "the health care environment is so tightly knit that we can only do so much work in Boston—even in Massachusetts—before we run into conflict-of-interest problems from serving so many competing institutions." (Exhibit 5 indicates HSI's activities in the New England market.) But Bland urged caution in any expansion. The company had only recently added a housing division, and he was concerned that HSI might spread itself too thin and sacrifice quality. Already his Project Management Group was

turning down jobs, and he had almost no time available for recruiting.

One option open to the company was acquisition. DeVore had looked at two smaller health care consulting firms on the East Coast, but was not enthusiastic about the idea.

The firms that were buyable that I knew about were either old-line firms that were declining, or their offshoots. I did not want the association of any of those old-timers or their derivatives. I don't like what they do—besides, I can't market-differentiate myself in one breath and then be a businessman and buy them out in the next breath.

Others in the firm had pointed out the problems of acquiring bad staff, as well as good, when a whole firm was purchased. Currently, the greatest general interest centered on opening an HSI branch. Company projections indicated that one-time start-up costs of a new office would total about $26,000; ongoing expenses like salaries, overhead, and commuting between Boston and the branch office were estimated at $165,000 annually. Washington, Atlanta, Philadelphia, Cleveland, and Detroit had all been mentioned as possible sites.

The head of HSI's Housing Group strongly favored Atlanta:

Atlanta is a boom town. The whole state of Georgia is just getting started—and has lots of growth potential. Labor and materials are still fairly cheap. Housing projects down there are two-thirds to three-fourths the cost of jobs in New England. Atlanta is the metropolis and sophisticated hub of the whole Southeast—but as far as housing development or health care goes, it's just beginning to have and handle the kind of problems we've been dealing with up here. In Boston our competition is fierce—but there's a drastic drop in the competitive level of expertise out of state. I say let's maximize that advantage while it lasts.

Breazeale disagreed:

Where we're likely to do poorly is in places where our style and Boston-based credibility are not a factor. I'd like to see us have a chance to reestablish these roots quickly in any move—that's why I support a relatively similar environment like Philadelphia or Washington.

Breazeale felt it important that the firm consider a third expansion site simultaneously with a second; he didn't want HSI to pin itself geographically into a corner that might make further expansion difficult.

DeVore as yet was undecided. He preferred to think of possible expansion sites as spheres of influence or regional medical networks rather than specific cites. Just as HSI's Boston office reached out to New England and upstate New York, he felt that a Washington office, for example, could reach out to suburban Maryland and Virginia, Philadelphia, and national projects. Alternatively, he felt,

> . . . through an Atlanta office HSI could move north to Kentucky and Tennessee, where the coal mining industry could provide a lot of projects related to both health care and housing. Ohio is also a real possibility: seven cities of over one million population, decaying urban areas, hospitals located downtown. I think regulation is moving fast into Pennsylvania; a location there could take full advantage of a Boston-type market.

Offices west of the Mississippi had not yet been considered in any detail. New York City was dismissed as a "nightmare," whose health care regulation was so intricate and so area-specific that it would not be profitable to locate a regional office there. "New York City and the rest of New York State are completely different regulatory spheres," said one HSI consultant.

Market Positioning

Another subject of internal debate was the problem of positioning. Most HSI professionals were well aware of views similar to those expressed by an industry observer:

> The health care consulting firm seeking to survive against the giants moving into the field is going to have to position itself very carefully. The key is to target the kinds of hospitals most

likely to need its services, identify the size and location of the jobs it can most successfully bid for, and concentrate its efforts on those jobs.

DeVore, in contrast, insisted that HSI had a mission to serve a wide range of institutions: small rural hospitals as well as large academic medical centers. (See Exhibit C for the scope and distribution of recent HSI projects.) Breazeale went further:

> What motivates people at HSI is interesting work, having fun, the thrill of discovery. Much of our work will always be "typical" projects, which are not much fun for high-caliber people once they've learned how to do them. Variety and growth are absolutely essential.

A recent disappointment suffered by the company in rural northern Maine had brought the issue of positioning to the fore. Seven small hospitals seeking a long-range plan had asked HSI and two competitors for presentations. Follow-up phone calls indicated a favorable response to HSI's proposal—but after ten days there was still no word from the hospitals. HSI made four more phone calls. In each case, the company was told that its proposal was too expensive—though each respondent conceded that HSI had the best proposal, the best staff, and the best chance of success on the project. Further investigation uncovered a second explanation for HSI's failure: the hospital decision makers did not want to risk real change. Apparently what had been desired was a pro forma study, and the winning proposal had come from a 73-year-old freelance consultant whose ideas for change promised to be essentially cosmetic.

The experience had led to an internal debate: Should HSI bid at all in a situation where the company might appear too high-powered for the client? What would this mean for DeVore's desire to meet the needs of rural and smaller hospitals as well as the needs of major national medical centers? As a former hospital administrator himself, Breazeale was well aware of the arrogant image sometimes presented by consultants. One expert in the field had pointed out that each group of clients had its own "absorption capacity"—its own limit to the scope, pace, and range of innovation it could absorb from a consultant. To what extent, he wondered, should HSI be modifying its image for individual clients? How would a move to a new geographic area affect the answer to that question?

DeVore listened to Breazeale's concerns with interest and added several of his own. "Our problem," he declared at the meeting called to discuss HSI's expansion, "is to devise a marketing strategy for the next five years that will maintain an annual growth target of 30%. For at least three years, 80% of that growth must come from health care. It seems to me that we have several important questions to answer. What kind of image do we want to project? What kind of client do we want to serve? Where are those clients located? And, within the constraints imposed by our professional status, how can we convince those clients to choose HSI?"

NOTES

1. "Soaring Price of Medical Care Puts a Serious Strain on Economy," *New York Times*, May 7, 1978.

2. "Health Costs: What Limit?" *Time*, May 28, 1979, p. 60.

3. Jerold A. Glick, "The Hospital: How Will It Survive?" *Hospital Financial Management*, January 1979, pp. 13–14.

4. "The New Shape of Management Consulting," *Business Week*, May 21, 1979, pp. 98–102.

EXHIBIT I

Comparative Income and Retained Earnings (Deficit) Statements

	YEAR ENDED JULY 31, 1979		YEAR ENDED JULY 31, 1978		YEAR ENDED JULY 31, 1977	
Professional fees earned		$908,583		$581,151		$464,435
Direct expenses						
Salaries and wages of professionals	$220,920		$156,644		$ 95,092	
Consulting fees	147,454		74,047		105 015	
Material and travel	41,931		28,498		16 626	
	410,305		259,189		216,733	
Decrease (increase) in unbilled costs inventory	—		—		16,461	
Gross profit		410,305		259,189		233,194
		498,278		321,962		231,241
General and administrative expenses						
Depreciation	2,941		4,590		-,067	
Dues, subscriptions, and registrations	6,639		4,861		247	
Insurance:						
Hospitalization, group life and disability	15,948		9,032		4,057	
Officers' life insurance	1,575		872		842	
General	1,367		2,901		2,696	
Interest	—		151		4,634	

Marketing and promotion:[a]						
Salaries and wages	58,889		18,686		8,190	
Material and travel	26,103		4,785		4,877	
Office supplies and expense	27,984		24,455		5,539	
Professional fees	4,834		7,361		7,535	
Profit sharing trust contributions	20,000		21,000		—	
Rent, space	42,294		20,372		9,299	
Reprocuction expense	1,223		2,754		2,213	
Salaries and wages of supporting staff	143,721		79,039		19,274	
Taxes, payroll	23,734		11,634		6,470	
Taxes, state and local	11,626		10,873		13,570	
Telephone	16,661	405,539	10,797	234,163	7,613	98,123
Net income (loss) for year from operations		92,739		87,799		133,118
Non-operating income and expense						
Interest income	7,587		6,081		—	
Less recognition of loss on real estate venture	—	7,587	—	6,081	6,502	(6,502)
Net income (loss) before federal income tax		100,326		93,880		126,616
Federal income tax		20,916		27,417		6,300
Net income (loss) for year		79,410		66,463		120,316
Retained earnings (deficit), beginning of year		51,211		(15,252)		(135,568)
Retained earnings (deficit), end of year		$130,621		$ 51,211		$ (15,252)

[a] Reflects professional time spent on (1) exploratory meetings and entertainment; (2) nonbillable aspects of ongoing projects; (3) development of specific proposals.

SOURCE: Company records

EXHIBIT 2

Dollar Value of HSI Projects in Progress at Year End[a]

Fiscal Years 1977–1979, in $000

CLIENT CATEGORY	Strategic Planning			Multi-institutional Work			Financial Feasibilities			Certificates of Need			Facility Master Planning			Project Management		
	1977	1978	1979	1977	1978	1979	1977	1978	1979	1977	1978	1979	1977	1978	1979	1977	1978	1979
Large teaching hospitals (400 or more beds)	10	85	133							132	49			5	17	41	59	386
Community hospitals (150–400 beds)	79	126	70	23	37	149			6	47	71	89				3	9	40
Small hospitals (50–150 beds)			16								37						31	46
Government work		14	3															

Management, Planning, Financial Services

DIVISION

Hospital-based physicians														43	17	9
Community physicians' offices		2	8				5							51	51	12
Neighborhood health centers									5	42	9					
Nursing homes		1					7			2	15	1		7	11	18
Annual totals	91	225	231	23	37	149	12	6	184	164	150	6	17	145	178	511

[a] Excludes projects by Housing Group.
SOURCE: Company records

EXHIBIT 3

U.S. Community Hospitals: Regional Analysis[a]

U.S. CENSUS DIVISION[b]	TOTAL HOSPITALS	NUMBER OF BEDS							TOTAL PERSONNEL	TOTAL EXPENSES ($000)	PERCEIVED LEVEL OF REGULATION[c]
		6–99	100–199	200–299	300–399	400–499	500+			
1. New England	379	142	90	52	41	19	35	221,593	4,831,735	1
2. Middle Atlantic	820	167	211	161	86	47	148	617,732	13,955,961	1
3. South Atlantic	1,014	405	256	137	78	50	88	511,767	10,472,487	3
4. East North Central	1,076	368	271	152	93	73	119	627,709	13,773,808	2
5. East South Central	543	289	128	45	21	26	34	199,177	3,769,030	4
6. West North Central	898	567	153	54	36	26	62	273,565	5,451,453	3
7. West South Central	961	592	196	71	28	23	51	306,248	6,019,251	4
8. Mountain	446	296	68	31	29	8	14	133,723	2,802,418	4
9. Pacific	878	439	217	101	50	32	39	388,717	9,851,047	2

[a] Excludes veterans and other government hospitals, psychiatric hospitals, convalescent (long-term) hospitals, TB hospitals, and hospital units of nonhospital institutions.
[b] States composing these regions are indicated in Exhibit 4.
[c] Varies from 1 (stringently regulated) to 4 (loosely regulated).
SOURCE: Hospital Statistics, 1979 and HSI records

EXHIBIT 4
United States Census Regions and Divisions

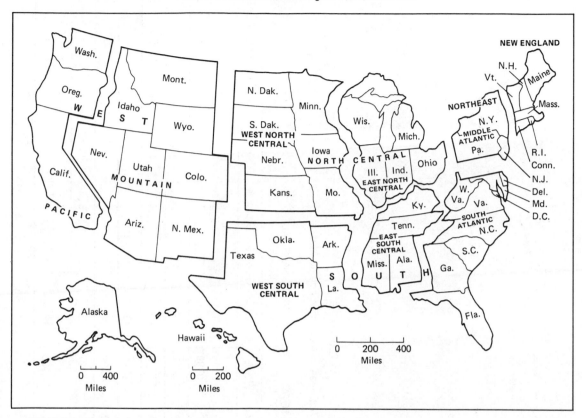

SOURCE: Department of Commerce

EXHIBIT 5

HSI Activities in the New England Market

	TOTAL HOSPITALS		TOTAL HOSPITALS BY BED SIZE			HSI PROJECTS			TOTAL HSI BEDS
	Number	Beds	Group C 50–150	Group B 150–400	Group A 400+	Group C	Group B	Group A	
Massachusetts (by county)									
A. Eastern counties (including Greater Boston)*									
Essex	21	3709	11	9	1	1	2	1	1267
Middlesex	37	11,452	10	22	5	3	7	1	3458
Suffolk	36	10,339	12	16	8	2	4	5	4584
Norfolk	21	3,024	14	7	0	1	1	0	262
Plymouth	9	2,519	5	2	2	0	1	0	322
Bristol	9	2,227	3	3	3	0	1	0	220
B. Central and Western counties									
Worcester	24	4,720	12	9	3	0	1	0	226

Franklin	2	285	1	1	0	1	1	0	285
Hampshire	8	2,673	4	1	3	0	0	0	0
Hampden	11	2,963	5	4	2	0	0	0	0
Berkshire	5	836	3	2	0	0	0	0	0
C. Cape Cod and The Islands Barnstable	3	400	2	1	0	0	0	0	0
Nantucket	1	50	1	0	0	0	0	0	0
Duke's	1	80	1	0	0	0	0	0	0
Maine	50	5577	37	11	2	4	2	1	1326
New Hampshire	30	4352	19	10	1	2	2	0	679
Vermont	16	2246	12	3	1	1	0	0	100
Rhode Island	19	4837	8	7	4	0	0	1	494
Connecticut	51	15,132	19	19	13	1	2	1	1386

* Figures include five projects at mental health care facilities, accounting for 3,674 beds.
SOURCE: Company records

EXHIBIT 6

Geographic Distribution of HSI Projects in Progress at Year's End, Fiscal Years 1978 and 1979[1]

(Number of Ongoing Projects Inside[2] and Outside[3] New England at Year End)

DIVISION

Management, Planning, Financial Services

CLIENT CATEGORY	Strategic Planning 1978 NE	1978 Other	1979 NE	1979 Other	Multi-Institutional Work 1978 NE	1978 Other	1979 NE	1979 Other	Financial Feasibilities 1978 NE	1978 Other	1979 NE	1979 Other	Certificates of Need 1978 NE	1978 Other	1979 NE	1979 Other	Facility Master Planning 1978 NE	1978 Other	1979 NE	1979 Other	Project Management 1978 NE	1978 Other	1979 NE	1979 Other
Large teaching hospitals 400+ beds	1	1[a]	2	1[a]									2				1		2	1[a]	2		1	1[c]
Community Hospitals 150–400 beds	7		5		1		2				1		3		6						2		3	
Small hospitals 50–15 beds			2												1						2		2	
Government work	1		1																					
Hospital-based physicians																							2	
Community physicians' offices			1												1						3	1[b]	3	1[b]
Neighborhood health centers													1		1									
Nursing homes			1										1		2		1				1		1	
Annual totals	9	1	12	1	1		2				1		7		10		2		2	1	12	1	12	2

[1] Excludes Housing Division projects
[2] NE = Maine, New Hampshire, Vermont, Massachusetts, Connecticut, and Rhode Island
[3] a = Philadelphia; b = Baltimore; c = Cincinnati
SOURCE: Company records

READING

How Consumer Evaluation Processes Differ between Goods and Services

VALARIE A. ZEITHAML

It is harder for consumers to evaluate services than goods. This is because services are intangible and nonstandardized and because consumption is so closely intertwined with production. This article proposes a framework for isolating the differences between consumer evaluation processes for goods and services and then suggests some strategic implications for service marketers.

According to projections, services will account for more than half of the nation's economic activity by the end of the 1980s (*Business Week*, March 17, 1980). Providers of medical and legal services, haircuts, day care, entertainment, and education, among others, will proliferate to meet the growing demands for leisure and spending which accompany the United States' rising standard of living. The primary objective of these service producers will be identical to that of all marketers: to develop and provide offerings that satisfy consumer needs, thereby ensuring their own economic survival.

To achieve this objective, service providers will need to understand how consumers choose and evaluate their offerings. Unfortunately, most of what is known about consumer evaluation processes pertains specifically to goods. The assumption appears to be that services, if not identical to goods, are at least similar enough in the consumer's mind that they are chosen and evaluated in the same manner. This paper proposes to refute this assumption by showing that services' unique characteristics necessitate different consumer evaluation processes from those used when assessing goods.

SERVICES: SEARCH VERSUS EXPERIENCE VERSUS CREDENCE PROPERTIES?

One framework for isolating differences in evaluation processes between goods and services is the classification of qualities of goods proposed by economists Philip Nelson (1970) and Darby and Karni (1973). Nelson distinguishes between two categories of qualities of consumer goods: *search qualities*, attributes which a consumer can determine prior to purchasing a product; and *experience qualities*, attributes which can only be discerned after purchase or during consumption. Search qualities include attributes such as color, style, price, fit, feel, hardness, smell, while experience qualities include characteristics such as taste, wearability, purchase satisfaction. Some goods (e.g., clothing, furniture, and jewelry) are high in search qualities, for their attributes can be almost completely determined and evaluated prior to purchase. Other goods and services (e.g., vacations and restaurant meals) are high in experience qualities, for their attributes cannot be known or assessed until they have been purchased and are being consumed. Darby and

Valarie A. Zeithaml is assistant professor of marketing at Texas A & M University. Reprinted with permission from *Marketing of Services*, eds. James H. Donnelly and William R. George, American Marketing Association (Chicago, 1981).

Karni (1973) add to Nelson's two-way classification system a third category of qualities of goods, *credence qualities*, which are characteristics which the consumer may find impossible to evaluate even after purchase and consumption. Examples of offerings high in credence qualities include appendix operations and brake relinings on automobiles. Few consumers possess medical or mechanical skills sufficient to evaluate whether these services are necessary or are performed properly, even after they have been prescribed and produced by the seller.

Figure 1 arrays goods and services high in search, experience, and credence qualities along a continuum of evaluation ranging from "easy to evaluate" to "difficult to evaluate." At the left end of the continuum are goods high in search qualities, easiest to evaluate even before purchase. In the center are goods and services high in experience qualities, more difficult to evaluate because they must be purchased and consumed before assessment is possible. At the right end of the continuum are goods and services high in credence qualities, most difficult to evaluate because the consumer may be unaware of or may lack sufficient knowledge to appraise whether the offerings satisfy given wants or needs even after consumption.

The major premise of this paper is that most goods fall to the left of this continuum, while most services fall to the right due to three distinguishing characteristics. These distinguishing characteristics—intangibility, nonstandardization, and inseparability of production and consumption—make services more difficult to evaluate than goods. Difficulty in evaluation, in turn, forces consumers to rely on different cues and processes when evaluating services.

Several scholars detail the characteristics which distinguish services from products (Bessom 1973, Rathmell 1974, Eiglier et al. 1977). *Intangibility* pertains to the inability of services to be seen, felt, tasted, or touched in the same manner in which goods can be sensed. Services cannot be displayed, physically demonstrated or illustrated; therefore, they possess few search qualities and many experience qualities. *Nonstandardization* entails the inability of a producer to provide consistent performance and quality with a service. Since services cannot be inventoried, performance depends to some extent on level of demand; in periods of high demand, a service provider may not spend as much time or exert as much effort as in periods of low demand. Quality also may change from day to day because different employees perform the service, or because each employee's skills and moods vary. Nonstandar-

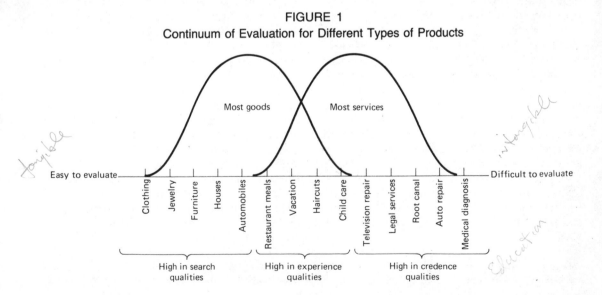

FIGURE 1
Continuum of Evaluation for Different Types of Products

dization results in high experience qualities, for consumers cannot be certain about performance on any given day, even if they use the same service provider on a regular basis. *Inseparability of production and consumption* constitutes the final characteristic which distinguishes goods and services. While tangible goods are produced, sold, and then consumed, services are sold, then produced and consumed simultaneously (Regan 1963). Because of this inseparability, the buyer usually participates in producing the service, thereby affecting the performance and quality of the service. A doctor's accurate diagnosis, the desired haircut, from a salon, effective stain removal from a drycleaner—all these depend on the consumer's specification, communication, and participation in the production of the service. The quality of most services, and their ability to satisfy the consumer, depend not only on how well the service provider performs, but also on how well the consumer performs.

In sum, the inseparability, nonstandardization, and tangibility of services lead them to possess few search qualities and many experience qualities. Credence qualities also dominate in many services, especially those provided by professionals and specialists. While consumers may find it easy to evaluate the performance of everyday services (e.g., restaurant meals, housekeeping, or lawn care) prior to consumption, they may find it impossible to judge those performed by professionals and specialists with extensive training or experience in a specialized skill (e.g., medical diagnosis, television repair, or estate settlement).

SERVICES: SOME HYPOTHESES ABOUT CONSUMER EVALUATION PROCESSES

Because experience and credence qualities dominate in services, consumers may employ different evaluation processes than those they use with goods, where search qualities dominate. Specific areas where characteristics of services may lead to divergent evaluation processes are: information search; evaluative criteria; size and composition of the evoked set of alternatives; perceived risk; adoption of innovations; brand loyalty; and attribution of dissatisfaction.

Information Search (w/407)

Consumers obtain information about products and services from personal sources (e.g., friends or experts) and from nonpersonal sources (e.g., mass or selective media). When purchasing goods, consumers employ both personal and nonpersonal sources since both effectively convey information about search qualities.

When purchasing services, on the other hand, consumers may seek and rely to a greater extent on personal sources for several reasons. First, mass and selective media can convey information about search qualities but can communicate little about experience qualities. By asking friends or experts about services, however, the consumer can obtain information vicariously about experience qualities. Second, nonpersonal sources may not be available because: (1) many service providers are local, independent merchants with neither the experience nor the funds for advertising; (2) "cooperative" advertising, or advertising funded jointly by the retailer and the manufacturer, is used rarely with services since most local providers are both producer and retailer of the service; and (3) professional associations banned advertising for so many years that both professionals and consumers tend to resist its use even though it is now permitted. Third, since consumers can discover few attributes prior to purchase of a service, they may feel greater risk to be associated with selecting an alternative. Given this risk, they may depend to a greater extent on sources such as word-of-mouth which they may perceive to be more credible and less biased.

Researchers suggest that personal sources might be more appropriate in situations where experience qualities dominate. Robertson (1971) claimed that personal influence becomes pivotal as product complexity increases and when objective standards by which to evaluate the product decrease (i.e., when experience qualities are high). Eiglier and Langeard et al. (1977) revealed that managers in four service industries believe word-of-mouth to have a great influence in services. Finally, many researchers (among them Perry and Hamm 1969, Cunningham 1967, Arndt 1967) confirmed that the credibility of personal sources encourages their use in situations of high perceived risk.

> *Hypothesis 1:* Consumers seek and rely more on information from personal sources than from nonperson sources when evaluating services prior to purchase.

Consumers may find post-purchase evaluation more essential with services than with goods because services possess experience qualities which cannot be adequately assessed prior to purchase. The dissonance-attribution model of audience response to communication (Ray 1973) describes the situation which frequently occurs when consumers select services: (1) The consumer selects from among virtually indistinguishable alternatives; (2) through experience, the consumer develops an attitude toward the service; and (3) after the development of an attitude, the consumer learns more about the service by paying attention to messages supporting his choice. In contrast both to the learning response model and the low-involvement model (Ray 1973), where consumers seek information and evaluate products prior to purchase, as they do with tangible goods, the dissonance-response model represents the case of services where most evaluation succeeds purchase.

> *Hypothesis 2:* Consumers engage in greater post-purchase evaluation and information seeking with services than with products.

> *Hypothesis 3:* Consumers engage in more post-purchase evaluation than pre-purchase evaluation when selecting and consuming services.

Criteria for Evaluating Quality

When purchasing goods, the consumer employs multiple cues to judge quality, among them style, color, label, feel, package, brand name, and price. When purchasing services, the consumer is limited to a small number of cues; in many cases, the only cues available on which to judge quality are the service's price and the physical facilities which house the service.

Plumbing, housecleaning, and lawn care are examples of services where price may be the only pre-purchase indicator of quality. Research (Tull 1964, Olander 1970, McConnell 1968) demonstrates that when the price is the only information available, consumers use it to assess quality.

With other services (e.g., haircuts, legal aid, dental services, and weight reduction), consumers may base decisions about quality on the tangible evidence of the services: the physical facilities. Thus they may examine the offices, personnel, equipment, and paraphernalia used to perform the service in order to evaluate quality. The importance of physical facilities for this purpose has been emphasized by Eiglier et al. (1977), Bessom (1973) and others.

> *Hypothesis 4:* Consumers use price and physical facilities as the major cues to service quality.

Evoked Set

The evoked set of alternatives, that group of products which a consumer considers acceptable options in a given product category, is likely to be smaller with services than with goods. One reason for the reduced set involves differences in retailing between goods and services. To purchase goods, consumers generally shop in retail stores which display competing products in close proximity, clearly demonstrating the alternatives from which a consumer may select. To purchase services, on the other hand, the consumer visits a retail establishment (e.g., a bank, a dry cleaner, or a hair salon) which offers only a single "brand" for sale. A second reason for the smaller evoked set is that consumers are unlikely to find more than one or two stores providing the same services in a given geographic area, whereas they may find numerous retail establishments in that same area carrying the identical manufacturer's product. A third reason for a smaller evoked set is the difficulty of obtaining adequate pre-purchase information about services.

Faced with the difficult task of collecting and evaluating experience qualities, consumers may satisfice by selecting the first acceptable alternative rather than maximize by considering and evaluating all available alternatives.

> *Hypothesis 5:* The consumer's evoked set of alternatives is smaller with services than with products.

For nonprofessional services, consumers' decisions often entail choices between performing the services for themselves and hiring someone else to perform them. Working wives may choose between cleaning their own homes or hiring housekeepers, between altering their families' clothes or taking them to a tailor, even between staying home to take care of the children or engaging a day care center to provide child care. Many other services, including lawn care, tax preparation, and restaurant meals, involve decisions where consumers may consider themselves as sources of supply.

> *Hypothesis 6:* For many nonprofessional services, the consumer's evoked set frequently includes self-provision of the service.

Innovation Diffusion

The rate of diffusion of an innovation depends on consumers' perceptions of the innovation with regard to five characteristics: elative advantage, compatibility, communicability, divisibility, and complexity (Rogers 1962). A product which has a relative advantage over existing or competing products, that is compatible with existing norms, values, and behaviors, that is communicable, and that is divisible (i.e., that can be tried or tested on a limited basis) diffuses more quickly than others. A product which is complex, i.e., difficult to understand or use, diffuses more slowly than others.

Considered as a group, services are less communicable, less divisible, more complex, and probably less compatible than goods. They are less communicable because they are intangible (e.g., their features cannot be displayed, illustrated, or compared) and because they are often unique to each buyer (as in a medical diagnosis or dental care). Services are less divisible because they are usually impossible to sample or test on a limited basis (e.g., how does one "sample" a medical diagnosis? a lawyer's services in settling a divorce? even a haircut?). Services are frequently more complex than goods because they are composed of a bundle of different attributes, not all of which will be offered to every buyer on each purchase.

Finally, services may be incompatible with existing values and behaviors, especially if consumers are accustomed to providing the services for themselves. As an illustration, consider a novel day care center which cooks breakfast for children so that parents can arrive at work early. Mothers accustomed to performing this service for their children may resist adopting the innovation because it requires a change in habit, in behavior, even in values.

> *Hypothesis 7:* Consumers adopt innovations in services more slowly than they adopt innovations in goods.

Perceived Risk

Eiglier et al. (1977) report that French managers believe the level of perceived risk to be higher for consumers purchasing services as opposed to physical goods. While some degree of perceived risk probably accompanies all purchase transactions, more risk would appear to be involved in the purchase of services than in the purchase of goods because services are intangible, nonstandardized, and are usually sold without guarantees or warranties.

First, the intangible nature of services and their high levels of experience qualities imply that services generally must be selected on the basis of less pre-purchase information than is the case for products. Since research (Cox and Rich 1967, Spence et al. 1970, and others) suggests that a decrease in the amount and/or quality of information usually is accompanied by a concomitant increase in perceived risk, the purchasing of services may involve more perceived risk than the purchasing of goods.

Second, consumers may perceive more risk to be associated with the purchase of services because they are nonstandardized. Even though a consumer may have purchased the same service (e.g., haircut) in his or her lifetime, there will always be recurring uncertainty about the outcome and consequences each time the service is purchased.

Third, service purchases may involve more perceived risk than product purchases because, with few exceptions, services are not accompanied by warranties or guarantees. The dissatisfied service purchaser can rarely "return" a service, since he has already consumed it by the time he realizes his dissatisfaction.

Finally, many services (e.g., medical diagnosis or pest control) are so technical or specialized that consumers possess neither the knowledge nor the experience to evaluate whether they are satisfied, even after they have consumed the service.

Hypothesis 8: Consumers perceive greater risks when buying services than when buying products.

Brand Loyalty

The degree to which consumers are committed to particular brands of goods or services depends on a number of factors: costs of changing brands, the availability of substitutes, the perceived risk associated with the purchase, and the degree to which they have obtained satisfaction in the past. Because it may be more costly to change brands of services, because it may be more difficult to be aware of the availability of substitutes, and because higher risks may accompany services, consumers may tend to be more brand loyal with services than with goods.

Greater search costs and monetary costs may be involved in changing brands of services than in changing brands of goods. Because of the difficulty of obtaining information about services, consumers may be unaware of alternatives or substitutes to their brands, and may be uncertain about the ability of alternatives to increase satisfaction over present brands. Monetary fees may accompany brand switching in many services: Physicians often require complete physicals on the initial visit; dentists sometimes demand new X-rays; and day care centers frequently charge "membership fees" at the outset to obtain long-term commitments from consumers.

If consumers perceive greater risks with services, as is hypothesized above, they probably depend on brand loyalty to a greater extent than when they purchase products. Bauer (in Cox, 1967) stated that brand loyalty is a "means of economizing decision effort by substituting habit for repeated, deliberate decisions," and suggested that it functions as a device for reducing the risks of consumer decisions. He predicted a strong correlation between degree of perceived risk and brand loyalty, and his prediction has been supported by research in perceived risk (Cunningham 1967, Roselius 1971, Sheth and Venkatesan 1968).

A final reason why consumers may be more brand loyal with services is the recognition of the need for repeated patronage in order to obtain optimum satisfaction from the seller. Becoming a "regular customer" allows the seller to gain knowledge of the consumer's tastes and preferences, ensures better treatment, and encourages more interest in the consumer's satisfaction. Therefore, a consumer may exhibit greater brand loyalty in order to cultivate a satisfying relationship with the seller.

Hypothesis 9: Brand switching is less frequent with services than with products.

Attribution of Dissatisfaction

When consumers are disappointed with purchases—because the products did not fulfill the given needs, because they did not perform satisfactorily, or because they were not worth the prices—they may attribute their dissatisfaction to a number of different sources, among them the producers, the retailers, or themselves. Because consumers participate to a greater extent in the definition and production of services, they may feel more responsible for their dissatisfaction when they purchase services than when they purchase goods. As an example, consider a female consumer purchasing a haircut; receiving the cut she desires depends in part upon her clear specification of her needs to the stylist. If disappointed, she may blame either the stylist (for lack of skill) or herself (for choosing the wrong stylist or for not communicating her own needs clearly).

The quality of many services depends on consumer definition: a doctor's accurate diagnosis requires a conscientious case history and a clear articulation of symptoms; a dry-cleaner's success in removing a spot depends on the consumer's knowledge of its cause; and a tax preparer's satisfactory performance relies on the receipts saved by the consumer. Failure to obtain satisfaction with any of these services may not be blamed completely on the retailer or producer, since the consumer must adequately perform his or her part in the production process also.

With products, on the other hand, a consumer's main form of participation is the act of purchase. The consumer may attribute failure to receive satisfaction to her own decision-making error, but she holds the producer responsible for product performance. Goods usually carry warranties or guarantees with purchase, emphasizing that the producer believes that if something goes wrong, it is not the fault of the consumer.

> *Hypothesis 10:* Consumers attribute some of their dissatisfaction with services to their own inability to specify or perform their part of the service.

> *Hypothesis 11:* Consumers may complain less frequently about services than about products due to their belief that they themselves are partly responsible for their dissatisfaction.

SERVICES: STRATEGIC IMPLICATIONS FOR MARKETERS

If research confirms the hypotheses about services, service providers may need to alter their marketing mixes to recognize different consumer evaluation processes. The high levels of experience and credence qualities postulated to be characteristic of services require alternative approaches to information provision, pricing, new service introduction, and other marketing strategies.

Information provision. If consumers employ personal sources more frequently than nonpersonal sources when seeking information about services prior to purchase, the marketer's task may be to reduce the proportion of advertising in the promotional mix. Alternatively, the marketer may want to use advertising to stimulate and simulate word-of-mouth communication (e.g., through testimonial advertisements or by developing advertising high in conversational value) (Kotler 1980). If consumers seek more post-purchase information with services, the marketer's task may be to concentrate communication efforts to reduce dissonance after purchase.

Quality image. The potential importance of price and physical facilities as indicators of service quality suggests that the marketer should manipulate these cues to his own advantage. If the marketer desires to position his service as a high-quality offering, for example, he may need to set a price above that of competing services. He might also want to match his physical facilities to the desired impression of quality (Bessom 1973) so that the tangible evidence of the service provides the appropriate atmosphere.

The consumer as competitor. Non-professional service providers today must recognize that they often replace or compete with the consumer, which may imply more exacting standards from the consumer and more individualized, personal attention from the service provider. Consumers know what they expect from providers of housecleaning or lawn care or day care because they know what they are accustomed to providing for themselves. The alert service marketer will be certain to research consumers' expectations and demands in such situations.

Innovation diffusion. Marketers may need to concentrate on incentives to trial when introducing new services. The awareness-interest-evaluation stages of the adoption process may best be bypassed because of the difficulty and inefficiency of communicating information about intangibles. Offering free visits, dollars off coupons, and samples may be appropriate strategies to speed diffusion of innovations in services.

Reduction of perceived risk. The hypothesized increase in perceived risk involved in purchasing services suggests the use of strategies designed to reduce risk. Where appropriate, guarantees of satisfaction may be offered. To the extent possible, service providers should emphasize employee training and other procedures to standardize their offerings, so that consumers learn to expect a given level of quality and satisfaction.

Implications of strong brand loyalty. The fact that one's own customers may be brand loyal with services is not a problem;

the fact that the customers of one's competitors may be difficult to capture, however, may create special challenges. The marketer may need to direct communications and strategy to the customers of competitors, emphasizing attributes and strengths which he possesses and his competitor lacks.

SUMMARY AND CONCLUSION

Service's unique characteristics of intangibility, nonstandardization, and inseparability lead them to possess high levels of experience and credence properties, which, in turn, make them more difficult to evaluate than tangible goods. Eleven specific hypotheses about differences in consumer evaluation processes between services and goods were offered, accompanied by strategic implications for marketers.

REFERENCES

ARNDT, J. (1967), "Word-of-Mouth Advertising and Information Communication," in *Risk Taking and Information Handling in Consumer Behavior*, D. F. Cox, ed., Boston, MA: Division of Research, Harvard University.

BESSOM, R. M. (1973), "Unique Aspects of Marketing Services," *Arizona Business Bulletin*, 9 (November), 8–15.

COX, D. F. AND S. U. RICH (1967), "Perceived Risk and Consumer Decision Making—The Case of Telephone Shopping," in *Risk Taking and Information Handling in Consumer Behavior*, D. F. Cox, ed., Boston, MA: Division of Research, Harvard University.

CUNNINGHAM, S. M. (1967), "Perceived Risk in Information Communications," in *Risk Taking and Information Handling in Consumer Behavior*, D. F. Cox, ed., Boston, MA: Division of Research, Harvard University.

DARBY, M. R. AND E. KARNI (1973), "Free Competition and the Optimal Amount of Fraud," *Journal of Law and Economics*, 16 (April), 67–86.

EIGLIER, P., E. LANGEARD, C. H. LOVELOCK, J. E. G. BATESON, AND R. F. YOUNG (1977), *Marketing Consumer Services: New Insights*, Cambridge, MA: Marketing Science Institute.

KOTLER, P. (1980), *Marketing Management: Analysis, Planning and Control*, Englewood Cliffs, N.J.: Prentice-Hall, Inc.

McCONNELL, J. D. (1968), "Effect of Pricing on Perception of Product Quality," *Journal of Applied Psychology*, 52 (August), 300–303.

NELSON, P. (1970), "Advertising as Information," *Journal of Political Economy*, 81 (July–August), 729–54.

OLANDER, F. (1970), "The Influence of Price on the Consumer's Evaluation of Products," in *Pricing Strategy*, B. Taylor and G. Wills, eds., Brandon/Systems Press.

PERRY, M. AND B. C. HAMM (1969), "Canonical Analysis of the Relationship Between Socioeconomic Risk and Personal Influence in Purchase Decisions," *Journal of Marketing Research*, 6 (August), 351–4.

RATHMELL, J. M. (1974), *Marketing in the Service Sector*, Cambridge, MA: Winthrop Publishers, Inc.

RAY, N. L. (1973), "Marketing Communications the Hierarchy-of-Effects," unpublished research paper 180, Stanford University (August).

REGAN, W. J. (1963), "The Service Revolution," *Journal of Marketing*, 27 (July), 57–62.

ROBERTSON, T. S. (1971), *Innovative Behavior and Communication*. New York: Holt, Rinehart & Winston.

ROSELIUS, T. (1971), "Consumer Rankings of Risk Reduction Methods," *Journal of Marketing*, 35 (January), 56–61.

ROGERS, E. M. (1962), *Diffusion of Innovations*, New York: The Free Press.

"SERVICE INDUSTRIES: Growth Field of '80's" (1980), *U.S. News and World Report* (March 17), 80–84.

SHETH, J. N. AND M. VENKATESAN (1968), "Risk-Reduction Processes in Repetitive Consumer Behavior," *Journal of Marketing*, 5 (August), 307–310.

SPENCE, H. E., J. F. ENGEL, AND R. D. BLACKWELL (1970), "Perceived Risk in Mail-Order and Retail Store Buying," *Journal of Marketing Research*, 5 (August), 307–310.

TULL, D., R. A. BORING, AND M. H. GONSOIR (1964), "A Note on the Relationship of Price and Imputed Quality," *Journal of Business*, 37 (April), 186–191.

IV

Managing the Customer Mix

What sort of customers should we seek to serve? Market segmentation is at the root of this question, but unfortunately all too few service businesses respond to the question with the precision that it merits.

In both the service and manufacturing sectors, segmentation analysis plays a key role in creation of an effective positioning strategy, helping the marketer resolve such questions as:

- In what ways can the market for our service be segmented?
- What are the needs of the specific segments that have been identified?
- Which of these segments best fits our institutional mission and capabilities?
- In each instance, what are the competitive advantages and disadvantages of our service?
- Which specific segment(s) should we elect to serve?
- How should we differentiate our marketing efforts from those of the competition?

Market segmentation is, of course, central to most professionally planned and executed marketing programs. Through careful analysis, the marketer can decide which markets to serve and then develop strategies to attract and retain customers within specific segments. But segmentation strat-

egy assumes added dimensions for two types of services—those that involve a high level of customer contact and those that frequently experience capacity constraints. In the former, careful segmentation is important because the customers themselves become a part of the product; in the latter, managers must think carefully about which customer segments they will choose to serve at specific points in time.

CUSTOMERS AS PART OF THE PRODUCT

Of particular interest where segmentation strategy is concerned are those services which are not only delivered to the customer in person but which also require each user to share the same facility with many other users. Examples of these high-contact, shared services include theaters, restaurants, hotels, airlines, and retail stores. The composition of the customer base has important implications for both the image of the service organization and the nature of the service "experience."

Marketers of many goods and services try to associate their products with particular types of users, often defined in demographic or life-style terms. Since this positioning is primarily achieved through advertising, the

201

actual mix of customers is not always clear to a user.

In the case of high-contact, shared services, however, the nature of the client base is readily apparent. Any observant customer can quickly determine whether a service such as a hotel, theater, or airline is well or poorly patronized and what sorts of people are using the service—their appearance, age range, apparent income bracket, dress (formal or casual), and whether they appear to have come alone, in couples, or in groups. Also apparent—sometimes obtrusively so—is how these other customers are behaving: Are they quiet or noisy, slow or active in their movements? Do they appear glum or cheerful, rude or considerate toward others?

Recognizing that customers contribute strongly to the atmosphere of many high-contact services, marketers need to ensure, first, that they attract customers from the most appropriate market segments, and second, that these individuals know the appropriate dress and behavior. A coffee shop that thrives on business from casually dressed undergraduates would probably not seek middle-aged people in business attire. A hotel that is trying to build up a clientele of business executives may be concerned about how they will react to the presence in the lobby or dining room of large tour groups on vacation. Similarly, in banking, a high mix of retail business on the floor may discourage business patronage. Airlines don't normally care how their passengers dress (within reason), but passengers who want to read, work, or sleep usually try to avoid an airline that has a reputation for on-board rowdiness. Audience members at a symphony concert are expected to be quiet during the performance lest they disturb others' enjoyment of the music. By contrast, active audience participation usually adds to the pleasure of attending a rock concert.

Many service marketers would probably like to be able to refuse admission to prospective customers who do not fit the market position sought by the organization. However, although there are ways to discourage unwanted persons from requesting services, for instance, by insisting on certain standards of dress, outright refusal to admit someone to a service facility may be viewed as illegal or unethical if that person has the ability to pay.

One of marketing's roles is to inform prospective customers in advance about the specific nature of a service, so they know what to expect. This increases the chances of a satisfactory "fit" between customers and organization. Sometimes, however, friction develops between customers and staff or between different customers, and management may have to play police officer and either resolve the problem or ask the offending individuals to leave. Failure to do this quickly and efficiently may seriously damage the impression that other customers have of the service, destroying the chances of obtaining repeat business from them.

Homogeneity of the customer base is not always possible or even desirable for many service organizations. Two or more distinct market segments may each contribute importantly to the organization's success, yet they may not mix well. Ideally, potentially conflicting segments should be separated in their use of the facility; that is, they should use the facility sequentially rather than jointly, so that they never encounter each other. If this isn't possible, then it may be possible to adopt a strategy of physical separation. Examples include separating airline passengers into first class and economy cabins, placing conventioneers on a different floor of a hotel from other guests, and assigning bank customers with substantial accounts a separate entrance and transaction area from holders of more modest accounts.

CAPACITY-CONSTRAINED ORGANIZATIONS

Service organizations often experience significant variations in demand over time. This is particularly true of those services involving tangible actions to the consumer in person or to the customer's physical possessions. When demand is low relative to capacity, then any business might seem welcome, but when demand exceeds capacity, then some business will have to be turned away or put on a waiting list.

Does it matter whether there are sharp variations in the customer mix between periods of high and low demand? If the off-peak business is financially profitable, can be handled effectively by the service organization, and is not going to hurt the latter's image, then it is presumably worth taking. Little harm is probably done to an airline's positioning strategy if it uses its aircraft for charter flights when business demand is low. But if a hotel or restaurant gains a reputation for attracting a totally different type of customer in the off season, there is a risk that this may negate its desired high-season image, particularly if a few high-season customers visit at another season expecting the same types of customers and service levels as before. One way of resolving this problem is to be quite explicit about the different positioning strategies. Thus, in the winter months, Boston's Symphony Hall offers classical concerts by the Boston Symphony Orchestra (BSO), with high-priced seats sold to discriminating music lovers. In the spring and early summer, the BSO season is replaced by the Boston Pops. Prices are reduced; tables and chairs replace the orchestra-level seats; and concerts of popular music are played to sociable audiences who talk, drink, and eat as the concert proceeds. The overlap between BSO and Pops audiences is probably quite small, and the distinctions between the two series are generally well known.

ASSET UTILIZATION AND REVENUE GENERATION

Private sector services are in business to make a profit. Most capacity-constrained organizations have a high fixed-to-variable-cost ratio, reflecting the presence of expensive physical facilities and equipment plus a pool of full-time personnel. In effect customers "rent" the use of service facilities and personnel. Assuming for the moment that the costs associated with serving different segments remain constant, then the higher the rent and the greater the volume of usage, the greater the profits. However, different customer segments vary in their ability and willingness to pay for use of these services and also in their potential to use the full breadth of services offered on a single occasion. To complicate matters further, the volume of demand from a specific segment and even the price sensitivity of that segment may vary sharply over time.

Many capacity-constrained service organizations use percentage of capacity sold as a measure of operational efficiency. For instance, transportation services talk of the "load factor" achieved, hotels of their "occupancy rate," and hospitals of their "census." But, by themselves, these percentage figures tell us little of the relative profitability of the business attracted, since high utilization rates may be obtained at the expense of heavy discounting.

What is needed, then, is a measure of the extent to which the organization's assets are achieving their full revenue-generating potential. This must take into account the relationship between the average price actually obtained per unit of service and the maximum price that might potentially have been charged—what might be termed the *price efficiency rate.* By multiplying the capacity utilization rate by the price efficiency rate, we can derive an index of *asset revenue generating efficiency* (ARGE). For example, a hotel has 400 rooms with a maximum posted price of $100 each. If only 70 percent (280) of the rooms is occupied one night—140 at $100 and 140 at $60—then the price efficiency rate is 80 percent and the ARGE is 56 percent (70 percent multiplied by 80). Another way to arrive at the ARGE is to divide total revenues received ($22,400) by the theoretical maximum revenues that could have been obtained by selling all rooms at the highest price ($40,000).

The value of the ARGE approach to performance measurement is that it forces explicit recognition of the opportunity cost of accepting business from one segment when another might subsequently yield a higher rate. Consider the following problems facing sales managers for different types of service organizations:

- Should a hotel accept an advance booking from a tour group of 200 room-nights at $50 each when these same room-nights might possibly be sold later at short notice to business travelers at the full rack rate of $75?

- Should a railroad with 30 empty freight cars at its disposal seek an immediate shipment worth $300 per car, or should it hold the cars idle for a few more days in the hope of getting a priority shipment that would be twice as valuable?

- How many seats on a particular flight should an airline sell in advance to tour groups and passengers traveling at special excursion rates?

- Should an industrial repair and maintenance shop reserve a certain proportion of productive capacity each day for emergency repair jobs that offer a high contribution margin and the potential to build long-term customer loyalty, or should it simply follow

a strategy of making sure that there are sufficient jobs, mostly involving routine maintenance, to keep its employees fully occupied?

- Should a computer service bureau process all jobs on a first-come, first-served basis, with a guaranteed delivery date for each job, or should it charge a premium rate for "rush" work, and tell customers with "standard" jobs to expect some variability in completion dates?

Good market information supported by good marketing sense is the key to making appropriate decisions in such instances. The decision to accept or reject business should not be based on the flip of the coin. Rather, that decision should represent a realistic estimate of the probabilities of obtaining the higher rated business, together with a recognition of any incremental costs involved.

Based upon past experience and an understanding of current market conditions, prices can be set that reflect the demand curves of different market segments. At the same time, "selective sell" targets can be assigned to advertising and sales personnel, reflecting how management expects to allocate available capacity among different market segments *at a specific point in time.* These allocations by segment also constitute vital information for reservations personnel, since they tell them when to stop accepting reservations from certain segments. To simplify their task, different segments can be assigned different phone numbers or mailing addresses for making reservations.

Figure IV–1 shows how capacity might be allocated by a hotel over one week in the high season and one in the low season. As can be seen, this chart allocates available room capacity to different categories of guests, with day-of-the-week and week-of-the-year variations. These capacity allocations represent forecasts of the customer mix that might potentially be obtained, based

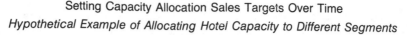

FIGURE IV–1

Setting Capacity Allocation Sales Targets Over Time
Hypothetical Example of Allocating Hotel Capacity to Different Segments

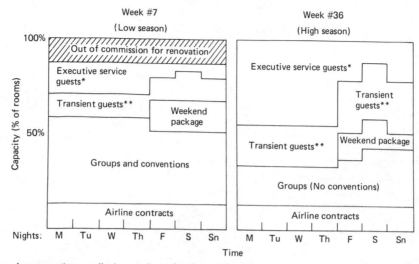

* Employees of corporations called upon by sales force (pay full price and book rooms through special reservations line).

** Individual customers paying full price but reserving rooms via publicized telephone number or by just "walking in."

upon an analysis of demand levels by the various segments at different times of year and an assessment of competitive activity. Prices can be assigned to each category, also based upon demand-and-supply analyses for different days of the week and different seasons of the year. If there are substantial differences in the costs of serving the various segments, then it may be necessary to use unit contribution rather than unit price in the calculation of the ARGE index. Some segments, such as individual corporate customers whose firms provide repeat business, can be charged the full rate. Others, such as groups and weekenders, are probably more price-sensitive and may be offered substantial discounts at times of low demand, such as during the low season and on weekends.

Similar types of capacity allocation charts could be developed for most other capacity-constrained businesses. In some instances, capacity is measured in terms of

seats; in others it may be in terms of machine time, labor time, vehicle units, or cubic capacity—whichever is the scarce resource. Unless there is the option for easy diversion of business from one facility to a similar alternative, allocation planning decisions have to be made at the level of geographic operating units. Thus, each hotel, repair and maintenance center, or computer service bureau may need its own plan. For service operations where speed of turnaround or ability to respond to emergencies are important, a good understanding of the time value of the service to customers is a necessary ingredient to development of profitable pricing strategies.

Transportation operations pose a particular problem in that their productive assets are mobile. Hence the relevant unit of analysis is the number of seats, vehicles, or cubic feet of carrying space of a particular type available at a particular location on a given day. A decision to accept a one-way load must be evaluated not only on the basis of the relative attractiveness of that load, but also with reference to the opportunities for obtaining a profitable back haul; the effect of taking that return load on the firm's ability to attract and hold particular classes of customers should also be evaluated.

Some of these tasks may sound like the responsibility of operations, and traditionally they have been, often with limited regard for the relative profitability of accepting different mixes of business. Hence the need for injecting a strong marketing orientation and for developing a balance between operational and marketing considerations.

The Role of Marketing

Marketing's task in helping maximize ARGE is sixfold. It involves the following procedures:

1. Identifying the principal market segments that might be attracted to the service facility and that are consistent with its capabilities or its mission.

2. Forecasting the volumes of business that might be obtained from each segment at specific price levels (through supply-and-demand analysis).

3. Recommending the "ideal business mix" at each specific point in time in terms of maximizing net revenues, which may not, in fact, be the same as maximizing capacity utilization.

4. Providing the sales force with specific sales targets on specific dates for each segment. This information may also be useful for planning advertising and related communication efforts.

5. Providing guidelines for the prices to charge each segment at specific points in time. For some segments, these guidelines should be adhered to rigorously; in other instances they may simply provide targets for negotiation.

6. Monitoring performance over time, evaluating

the reasons for achieving a higher or lower than predicted performance on the ARGE index, and modifying future strategy accordingly. For instance,

a. A consistently high ARGE index may indicate the need for a price increase.

b. A below-target ARGE may reflect failure to achieve the business mix anticipated, due to poor forecasting or unanticipated changes in the environment. In this case, changes will have to be made in the ideal business mix at specific points in time.

c. Alternatively, a poor ARGE performance could be due to sales or reservation personnel overriding the business mix targets or charging lower prices than recommended in the plan.

Clearly, the adoption of customer mix sales targets that may vary from day to day— or even from hour to hour—puts a premium on accurate market analysis and forecasting. But the economic and strategic benefits are likely to greatly outweigh the planning and research costs involved. Setting specific sales targets by segments, with recommended prices for each segment, reduces the risk that (1) business will be booked in advance at a discount when there is a high probability of later obtaining business for the date in question from a higher-paying segment or that (2) potential business from lower-rated segments will be turned away in the hope of obtaining a higher priced sale when the chances of obtaining the latter are actually very small. Similarly, operations personnel will be better able to plan service levels, staffing, and availability of special features if they have a good idea of the business mix that is likely to be obtained on specific dates.

Constraints

One possible constraint on management's desire to maximize ARGE in the short term is the need to maintain good customer relations, especially with customers that provide extensive repeat business or use substantial capacity during periods of low demand. In the former instance, perceived price gouging during peak periods may alienate customers and result in bad word-of-mouth publicity. In the second instance, it may sometimes be necessary to take low-rated business in the peak period in order to ensure continued patronage by that organization during off-peak periods. Each case should be taken on its own merits, with careful assessment being made of who needs whom the most—the buyer or the seller.

The pricing strategy outlined earlier presumes that the marketer is in a position to charge different customer segments different prices at the same point in time. This, in turn, presumes no legal restraints against such a strategy and general acceptance of such practices as discounts for bulk purchases or premiums for providing emergency service at short notice. If different segments are being charged different prices for similar service under more or less identical conditions and the higher-paying segment learns of this price differential, then ill will may result. Such a strategy may only be feasible, therefore, when the different segments are unlikely to share information with each other.

In many instances prices have to be advertised up front and equal treatment provided to all parties (or certainly to all individual purchasers). This does not alter the need to adjust price to reflect variations in demand over time—a topic that we return to in Section V. Nor does it mean that the customer mix may not vary significantly over the time cycle. Hence, it may still be appropriate for the marketer to identify the most likely sources of business at a specific point in time and to direct sales and advertising efforts accordingly.

CONCLUSION

All marketers need to be concerned about who their customers are, but this concern takes on added dimensions for certain types of services. When customers have a high level of contact with the service organization and with one another, the customer mix helps to define the character of the organization, since customers themselves become a part of the product. Marketers must be selective in targeting the desired customer segments, and guidelines must be established for customers' behavior while they are using the service.

For services that are capacity constrained, the marketer's task is not only to balance supply and demand but also to obtain the most desirable types of customers at a particular point in time. This may require targeting different segments at different times. For profit-seeking businesses, a key issue is which segments will yield the greatest net revenues. Public and nonprofit organizations, while not ignoring financial issues, need to consider which segments will help them best fulfill their nonfinancial objectives. In all instances, accurate market analysis and forecasting assume great importance in guiding marketing strategy.

CASES

BRIDGER BOWL SKI AREA

The general manager of a Western ski area is evaluating alternative product improvements. Considerations include the possibility of competition from a new ski resort and the conflicting interests of local and out-of-state skiers.

INTRODUCTION

Early in August 1975, Bob Macdonald, general manager of Bridger Bowl Ski Area, was planning for next year's operation. Macdonald had just completed his first year with Bridger Bowl, having held similar positions with ski areas in the Northeast and Northwest during the past six years. Because it was summer, only a skeleton crew of seven was employed for general maintenance and secretarial duties, leaving the general manager some time at last to consider long-range strategy and operations. Last year had been particularly hectic because of several factors but now some order and planning time prevailed.

BACKGROUND

Bridger Bowl was a medium-sized (by Western standards) ski area located 16 miles northeast of Bozeman, Montana. Bozeman was the center of a largely agricultural community but also enjoyed the presence of one of the state's branch universities having an enrollment of nearly 9,000. Total population and other descriptive statistics for both Bozeman and Montana are presented in Exhibit 1.

The average ski season at Bridger Bowl began in late November and ran an average of 125 days to mid-April. The area received over 400 inches of snow annually and had 17 runs between elevations of 6,000 to 8,500 feet. Its longest run was over 2 miles long. Conditions usually ranged from fresh powder to packed snow on beginner to expert runs. Approximately 30 percent of the terrain and lift capacity was classed as novice, 40 percent intermediate, and 30 percent advanced-expert. (Although opinions varied, industry guidelines recommended a breakdown of 20 percent, 60 percent, and 20 percent of terrain and lift capacity for beginner, intermediate, and advanced-expert skiers, respectively.) Temperatures (highs) ranged from 15° to 25°F. throughout the season.

Three double chairlifts, a T-bar, and two pony lifts (wire ropes with handles for beginning skiers) were in operation last year. Total lift capacity for the chairs was 2,800 skiers per hour with total daily capacity about 2,300 skiers. The latter figure was arrived at by industry-supported methods, allowing average lift waiting lines of no more than 10 minutes. Seldom had Bridger Bowl ever experienced more than 2,300 skiers in a single day but intermediate skiers had experienced 15- to 20-minute waits during peak periods (Christmas vacation and weekends in February).

Two chalets, one at the base of the chairlifts and one midway on the south side of the area, provided 6,900 and 2,100 square feet of space, respectively. Services in these chalets included: two cafeterias, warming areas, "brown-bag" tables, restrooms, ski school office, ski lockers, and ski patrol headquarters. Outside both chalets were sun decks.

This case was prepared by James E. Nelson, assistant professor of marketing at the University of Colorado at Denver, and James B. Lee, associate professor at Montana State University.

Located close to the base chalet were separate buildings for offices, lift ticket purchases, equipment rental and purchases, bar and gourmet restaurant, and lodging. The last three services were provided by firms outside Bridger Bowl's organization who usually cooperated and agreed with the ski area's management. A parking lot capable of holding 700 cars was also located close to the base chalet.

Lodging for approximately 50 people was available at the area. However, most of Bridger Bowl's out-of-state skiers stayed in the 12 motels and hotels in Bozeman. A Ramada and Holiday Inn complex provided near 300 rooms with independent operators in the town accounting for approximately 500 more.

Bozeman was well served by public transportation and Interstate 90 bypassed the city. The airport was used by both Northwest and Frontier Airlines with all-jet direct service to Minneapolis, Denver, and Salt Lake City with connections to most major western cities. Amtrak provided daily service to Bozeman from Minneapolis and Chicago on the east and from Spokane and Seattle on the west. Avis, Hertz, National, and local firms operated rental car services, and Bridger Bowl itself provided twice daily shuttle bus service between various motels and the area.

Bridger Bowl had been in operation since 1960 and last year at the height of the season employed over 100 people. Financial and other operational data are presented in Exhibit 2.

In Macdonald's mind, the fact that Bridger Bowl was a nonprofit corporation did not distinguish it from many Western ski areas. Many such areas failed to show a profit but *not by design* (as was the case with Bridger Bowl and this, perhaps, made it unique). Bridger Bowl had incorporated as a nonprofit corporation and was exempt from federal and state income taxes. Its articles of incorporation provided that no part of its income or profit be distributed to its members, directors, or officers.

As originally conceived, Bridger Bowl was to be a "family ski area" primarily for local residents. Rates were to be minimal, non-family-oriented amenities discouraged, and "frills" downplayed for basic skiing enjoyment. The corporation had largely followed this philosophy and, by most measures, seemed successful at it.

Lately, however, the rapid rise in all costs of skiing had made Bridger Bowl more attractive to out-of-state families and students. While little accurate data existed, surveys conducted during the 1973 and 1974 seasons indicated about one-sixth of all skier days were accounted for by out-of-state skiers. Excluding weekends, out-of-state skiers accounted for roughly one-fourth of all skier days. Both proportions were likely to grow in the near future, Macdonald thought, especially if intermediate skiing terrain and lifts were expanded.

COMPETITION

Until the 1973 season, little close competition existed for the local market of Bridger Bowl. The nearest areas were at least 3 to 4 hours away and were mostly "destination" or resort areas with higher prices (30 to 50 percent) and more amenities.

The picture changed in 1973 with the opening of Big Sky of Montana, Inc. some 40 miles away or about a 70-minute drive south of Bozeman. Big Sky was a multi-million-dollar ski resort area which attracted skiers from a nationwide market. Local skiers also used Big Sky, but, if anything, the net effect of Big Sky was thought to be complementary to Bridger's operations. Casual observation had suggested that many skiers spent some time at Bridger either on their way to or returning from Big Sky.

Big Sky seemed to contain all that the destination ski resort should. Lift capacity was 5,200 skiers per hour on mostly intermediate terrain. To date, this capacity had seldom been approached, even during peak periods. On-site ski shops, lodges, condominiums, hostels, restaurants, bars, a guest ranch, convention facilities, and other services were provided with a resort atmosphere. Long-term expansion was also planned to increase intermediate and advanced-expert terrain and lifts.

Further competition, but perhaps also complementary, might be expected within the next 5 years from Ski Yellowstone, Inc. This organization had recently released information about an area similar to Big Sky some 50 miles south of Big Sky. If realized, the Ski Yellowstone complex would turn the whole area into a Colorado-like section because of Ski Yellowstone's proximity to Jackson Hole, Wyoming, Grand Targhee, and Sun Valley, Idaho, all destination ski resort areas located about 2 to 3 hours further away.

THE PLANNING COMMITTEE REPORT

The Board of Directors of Bridger Bowl had authorized the formation of a Planning Committee in December 1973. The action seemed wise because: (1) the planning function was previously unassigned and largely sporadic; (2) opportunities as well as problems created by Big Sky seemed certain; and (3) present Bridger Bowl capacity appeared to have been approached or exceeded during peak periods in the last few years.

The planning committee had organized itself into four subcommittees: mountain, base, finance, and marketing. Each had met numerous times by itself both on and off the area and with consultants. Each had summarized its work with recommendations in a report by September 1974. Macdonald understood that, while there was some difference of opinion among board members, most recommendations were received at least favorably. Some recommendations were, in fact, put into operation for the 1974 season.

MOUNTAIN SUBCOMMITTEE REPORT

Briefly summarized, the mountain subcommittee recommended expansion of the area in four stages to a capacity of about 7,000 skiers per day (sufficient property was available to accommodate this number of skiers). Stage one recommendations included:

1. Renovating the beginner's T-bar
2. Altering two chair-lifts by lowering the distance between lift and ground to lessen wind problems

3. Moving the midway loading station of a chair-lift downhill to make a longer intermediate run (from the top of the lift to the loading station)
4. Building a new chair-lift for intermediate skiers leading to previously little-used terrain (lift A)
5. Building a new chair-lift for intermediate skiers leading to new terrain (lift B)
6. Building a short T-bar lift at the end of an existing chair-lift for expert skiers to reach the top of the mountain, previously reached only by foot (lift C)
7. Obtaining 3 acres of novice terrain and building a short T-bar lift here (lift D)
8. Constructing a new uphill chalet at the base of lift A with a minimum of 9,000 square feet and expansion potential to 15,000 (Chalet A)

Recommendations 1, 2, and 3 were completed prior to the start of the 1974 season.

Stage two recommendations included:

1. Building two new chair-lifts for intermediate skiers to reach new terrain (lifts E and F)
2. Building a short T-bar lift for expert skiers uphill from the terrain served by lifts E and F (lift G)
3. On demand, building a new chalet complex with or without parking at the base of lift E (Chalet B)
4. On demand, enlarging the old base and mid-way chalets

Stages three and four concerned further lift expansion. All stages of expansion are summarized in Exhibit 3.

Stage two expansion, as well as stages three and four, cost proportionately more per skier than stage one, because of extra land clearing and other construction costs.

BASE SUBCOMMITTEE REPORT

The base subcommittee made several immediate recommendations to ease crowding at the old base chalet, which were largely implemented before the 1974 season began.

A detailed comparison of the subcommittee's new chalet recommendations with existing chalet facilities is found in Exhibit 4. The new chalet facilities recommended were consistent with the mountain committee's recommendations. The base subcommittee further recommended establishing a new maintenance area complex for equipment, located from public view but near Chalet B. A parking lot for 1,500 cars at Chalet B was also planned.

By first completing Chalet A, the base subcommittee felt that sufficient chalet area would be available for services to a total of 3,000 skiers per day. Beyond this number, Chalet B or other unplanned expansion would be needed. Of course, several years of overcrowding or under utilization of chalets and mountain might reasonably be expected, Macdonald reasoned, because of demand fluctuations and scale economics. Having food service available at all chalets would create some unnecessary duplication and management problems, he thought, but the subcommittee felt that food was a break-even service and really not a profit opportunity.

FINANCE SUBCOMMITTEE REPORT

The finance subcommittee's recommendations, in contrast to those of the mountain and base groups, were primarily short run in orientation. Beyond providing estimates of expansion costs (Exhibit 3), little other long-term financial planning was undertaken.

Rather, the finance subcommittee focused on providing financing for the immediate mountain and base subcommittee's recommendations ($125,000) and for the restructuring of present debt. Bridger had two loans due in April 1976 and one in April 1977, balances of which totaled approximately $240,000. Payments on these three loans were over $80,000 annually. Due in 1987 was a $225,000 loan on which payments of $25,000 were being made annually.

With the aid of the finance committee and local bankers, the loans due in 1976 and a new loan for $125,000 were consolidated into one. Annual payments for this loan were $43,000, bringing total annual debt servicing requirements to approximately $80,000.

In addition to long-term debt servicing, Bridger usually borrowed approximately

$60,000 to provide for summer operations. This type of loan had frequently been needed in the past and was always paid back from season pass sales by early December.

While not actively investigating sources of long-term debt, the subcommittee thought it realistic that 20-year loans could be obtained at each stage of expansion. Interest rates might be as high as 10 percent, given the economy and Bridger's relative lack of owner's equity in the balance sheet. If this were the case, annual payments for each $100,000 borrowed would be approximately $12,000. No accurate estimate was made of the increase in skier days needed to provide for this repayment.

With regard to recommendations 4 through 8 of stage one expansion and the recommendations of stages two, three, and four, the finance committee largely adopted a "wait-and-see" position. This would allow time to:

1. Establish sound budgeting and forecasting methods
2. Study the impact of Big Sky on Bridger operations
3. Reduce existing debt
4. Examine long-range funding sources
5. Strengthen Bridger's marketing program and determine its effectiveness in attracting more midweek or balanced usage

Consistent with this position, the finance committee recommended that Macdonald initiate a budgeting system based on seasonal and 5-year objectives. This Macdonald had done with extraordinary success for his first year. Actual revenue and expenses for the 1974 season had varied less than 3 percent of his predicted figures calculated last fall.

MARKETING SUBCOMMITTEE REPORT

The marketing subcommittee's report was limited in comparison to the other three. Little was done other than to recognize the need for more accurate forecasts of usage and attempt definition of Bridger's market segments. A whole set of questions regarding promotion budgets, media, targets, appeals, and effectiveness measures were noted but unanswered with respect to recommendations.

Because of the time and effort put into the planning reports and the positive reaction by the board of directors, Macdonald knew the report formed, in effect, a master plan for expansion. His opinions and recommendations relative to their content and approximate timing were expected by the board; Macdonald was not sure yet exactly what his position was in these matters.

THE CONSUMER

Conforming to Macdonald's experience, several national studies characterized skiers as "young, married, having attended college, and employed in a professional, managerial, or supervisory position with an above average income." Many skiers, however, were students with incomes less than $6,000 per year.

Resident skiers in Montana were typically

1. In their early twenties and males (60 percent)
2. Living within 75 miles of a ski area
3. From a household with two skiers in it
4. Averaging $13,000 in household income
5. An intermediate to advanced ability skier
6. Skiing 5 hours per ski day, 20 days per season locally
7. Skiing 4 days away from local areas
8. Taking no lessons in the past five years

The general manager had received this information from a study of four Montana ski areas, including Bridger Bowl, performed by the Advertising Unit of the Montana Department of Highways in 1973.

The same study characterized Montana's nonresident skiers as

1. At least in their mid-twenties and male (55 percent)
2. Living in a household of four or more, three of whom were skiers
3. Averaging near $19,000 household income

4. More an intermediate skier
5. Spending about 6 hours per ski day skiing
6. Skiing 11 to 14 days per season with 3 to 8 days away from home
7. Taking skiing lessons

Macdonald thought the above data were fairly accurate in describing Bridger Bowl's users. Nonresidents were reported as accounting for about one-third of all skier days at Bridger Bowl, which was perhaps high, given the other survey data mentioned earlier which was collected at Bridger Bowl over the past three years.

During the past three seasons, usage and demographic questions had been asked of about 900 Bridger Bowl day-ticket skiers over 8 weekends and holidays and 10 weekdays each year. Days were randomly selected and respondents approached at the base chalet for their cooperation. Obviously, noncooperating skiers represented somewhat of a bias, although interviewers reported a high cooperation rate because of their friendly approach. To minimize interview bias and save time, the interview form was printed on a computer card and given only to day-ticket skiers who were instructed to leave the completed card with any Bridger Bowl chalet employee. Findings are summarized in Exhibit 5.

It was Macdonald's impressions that out-of-state skiers at Bridger Bowl were not the sort of skiers who skied the more famous and expensive Colorado areas. Rather, they appeared to be middle- and lower–middle-class families, interested in Western skiing at lower prices.

Less was known about season-pass skiers who skied primarily on weekends. Almost certainly the season-pass skier lived within 30 miles of the area and was an above-average skier in terms of ability. Skiing was extremely popular as a winter sport in Bozeman, and Macdonald was aware of estimates that upwards of one-fourth of the local population skied.

Likely the season-pass skier was more "loyal" to Bridger Bowl than day-ticket skiers. The general manager reasoned that the price of the season pass served to keep pass holders at Bridger Bowl while day-ticket skiers were more free to travel and visit other areas.

During the past year, Macdonald had spent much time talking to local skiers. It seemed that their feelings about expansion and nonresident skiers were of two schools. Many felt expansion to be desirable and that the increased variety in terrain and attractions thus presented to out-of-state skiers would keep costs to local skiers down and benefit the community.

An equally, if not more, vocal group desired zero growth or at least limited unpublicized growth to keep Bridger Bowl for Bozemanites. Whether it was a matter of local pride, fear of change and increased prices, or Montana chauvinism, Macdonald did not know. He did know of several instances where out-of-state skiers had been rudely treated by younger, local skiers and this disturbed him.

Such treatment was unsettling because of the desirable use characteristics believed typical of out-of-state skiers being primarily during midweek. Some overcrowding was present on weekends and during the Christmas holidays, however, and out-of-state skiers were particularly noticed at these times. The problem existed at other areas, Macdonald knew, but this did not make the situation any better.

Especially disturbing were studies which showed out-of-state skiers relying primarily on word of mouth in selecting new areas. Satisfied previous skiers, one study reported, were the source of information nearly four times more frequently than was advertising to first-time skiers at an area.

DIRECTOR'S MEETING

A director's meeting was scheduled for August 15 and the general manager knew his opinions would be expected. Specifically, he had to summarize his views on expansion and provide recommendations for the upcoming season.

EXHIBIT 1

Selected Characteristics of Bozeman and Montana Residents

	BOZEMAN	MONTANA
AGE (YEARS)		
Under 18	4,594	253,125
18–24	6,554	76,673
25–34	2,187	79,879
35–49	2,112	113,660
50–64	1,727	102,336
65 and over	1,496	68,736
Total Population (includes college students)	18,670	694,409
Median Age (Years)	22.7	27.1
Median Years of School (Completed)	13.2	12.3
Persons per Household	2.50	3.10
Median 1969 Household Income	$8,776	$8,512
Unemployment Rate 1970	5.3%	6.1%

Note: Estimates of 1975 Bozeman population would be approximately 1.5 times each figure above.
SOURCE: U.S. Census of Population, 1970

EXHIBIT 2

Summary of Bridger Bowl Financial and Operational Data

	SEASON					
	1969–70	*1970–71*	*1971–72*	*1972–73*	*1973–74*	*1974–75*
GROSS INCOME	$233,200	$339,300	$316,500	$362,100	$420,000	$521,000
EXPENSES	164,000	221,600	264,700	358,900	445,200	515,000
NET INCOME	$69,200	$117,700	$51,800	$3,200	$(25,200)	$6,000

1974–75 Season Detailed Income Statement[a]
Balance Sheet, as of June 30, 1975

INCOME		CURRENT ASSETS	
Season Pass	$147,100	Cash	$2,400
Lift Tickets	260,200	Accounts Receivable	2,100
MSU Ski School	13,400	Inventory—Food Supplies	3,300
Ski School	18,000	Total Current Assets	$7,800
Food Income	70,400	FIXED ASSETS (NET OF DEPRECIATION)	
Bus Income	10,500	Land	$82,000[b]
Other Income	1,400	Buildings	88,000
Total Income	$521,000	Lifts	380,000
EXPENSES		Mobile Grooming Equipment	75,000
Salaries and Wages	$213,900	Sewer System	3,500
Repairs and Maintenance	22,700	Ski Run Construction	22,400
Insurance	27,600	Gun Mounts	8,000
Light, Power, Fuel	26,900	Power Lines	12,000
Rent	6,000	Total Fixed Assets	670,900
Payroll Taxes	22,900	Total Assets	$678,700
Ski Patrol Supplies and Expenses	9,100		
Advertising, Promotion, Dues	31,700	CURRENT LIABILITIES	
Security	2,600	Accounts Payable	$4,100
Interest	22,600	Mortgage Payable	80,000
Miscellaneous	18,800	Taxes Payable	2,900
Office Supplies and Expenses	6,600	Total Current Liabilities	$87,000
Operating Supplies	10,000	LONG-TERM DEBT	
Professional Fees	9,700	Mortgage	$250,000
Taxes, Licenses, Telephone, Travel	12,900	Bank Notes	228,300
Long-Range Planning	1,100	Total Long-Term Debt	479,100
Ammunition for Avalanche Control	2,800	Total Liabilities	$566,100
Bus Expenses	3,500	NET WORTH	
Ski School	2,200	Contributed Capital	$20,000
Depreciation	61,400	Surplus	86,600
Total Expenses	$515,000	Income Year to Date	6,000
Net Income	$6,000	Total Net Worth	112,600
		Total	$678,700

1974 Lift Rates and Usage Summary (119 Days Operation)

TICKET	CONSUMER COST	SKIER DAYS[c]	SEASON PASSES SOLD
Adult All-Day	$ 6.50	25,800	
Junior All-Day	2.50	11,700	
Adult Half-Day	5.00	12,600	
T-Bar Only	2.00	1,500	
MSU Ski School	1.50	6,700	
Complimentary	0.00	1,200	
Adult Season Pass	90.00	21,100	965
High School Season Pass	50.00	7,400	500

EXHIBIT 2 (continued)

1974 Lift Rates and Usage Summary (119 Days Operation)

TICKET	CONSUMER COST	SKIER DAYS[c]	SEASON PASSES SOLD
Junior High and Under Season Pass	$25.00	12,200	717
Mid-Week Season Pass	55.00	4,400	317
Employee Complimentary Season Pass	0.00	1,900	108

1973 Lift Rates and Usage Summary (130 Days Operation)

TICKET	CONSUMER COST	SKIER DAYS[c]	SEASON PASSES SOLD
Adult All-Day	$ 6.00	22,300	
Junior All-Day	1.50	16,000	
Adult Half-Day	3.50	18.500	
T-Bar Only	2.00	1,600	
MSU Ski School	1.50	7,500	
Complimentary	0.00	5,800	
Adult Season Pass	80.00	23,400	1,318
High School Season Pass	40.00	8,600	496
Junior High and Under Season Pass	20.00	11,600	668
Employee Complimentary Season Pass—No Record			

[a] 1974–75 income statement is for the first three-quarters of the fiscal year. Additional summer operation expenses of approximately $30,000 were expected before the fiscal year ended on September 30, 1975.

[b] Bridger Bowl conducted its operations primarily on leased U.S. Forest Service land. Some privately held property adjacent to Forest Service land had been purchased for parking and other uses.

[c] A skier day is defined as one skier using the facility for one day of operation.

EXHIBIT 3

Summary of Proposed Expansion

LIFT EXPANSION	SKIER CLASS SERVED	INCREASE IN DAY SKIER CAPACITY	ESTIMATED COST
Stage 1			
A	Intermediate	600	$300,000
B	Intermediate	360	200,000
C	Advanced-Expert	250	100,000
D	Novice	50	50,000
Stage 2			
E	Intermediate	450	350,000
F	Intermediate	600	450,000
G	Advanced-Expert	160	100,000
Stage 3			
H	Advanced-Expert	400	300,000
I	Intermediate	600	450,000
J	Intermediate	1,100	700,000
Stage 4			
K	Intermediate	450	400,000
Total		5,020	$3,400,000
Chalet A (16,000 sq. ft. area)			480,000
Chalet B (8,000 sq. ft. area)			280,000
Enlarged Base Chalet (12,000 sq. ft. area)			180,000
Enlarged Midway Chalet (10,000 sq. ft. area)			240,000

EXHIBIT 4

Chalet Facilities and Recommendations

	ENLARGED BASE	ENLARGED MIDWAY	NEW CHALET (A)	NEW CHALET (B)
SITE SPACE (ACRES)				
Parking and Roads	20 +			5
Open Space	10	5	5	5
CHALET SPACE (SQUARE FEET)				
Sun Decks*	1,000	3,000	5,000	2,000
Cafeteria	2,000	6,000	10,000	2,000
"Brown Bag" Room	750	2,000	3,500	1,000
Commercial Area†	25,000			
Ski Racks*	500	1,500	2,500	1,000
Administration	2,250			
Forest Service Administration	1,000			
Ticket Sales*	300			300
Warming Space	250	750	1,250	500
Nursery	150			150
Chapel*	300			
Ski Patrol and First Aid	4,000	1,000		2,000
Ski School (Gathering and Lockers)	500			500
Ski Shop†	10,000			
Bier Stube†	15,000			
Public Toilets	500	600	1,000	500
Change Room and Lockers	900			1,000
Chalet Space Requirements (Skiers and Related Uses)	12,300	10,350	15,750	7,650
CHALET SPACE NOW AVAILABLE:	Lower Chalet		6,900 sq. ft.	
	Deer Park Chalet		2,100 sq. ft.	

* Not in chalet totals.
† Commercial, ski shop, and bier stube requirements of 50,000 sq. ft. not in chalet totals.

EXHIBIT 5

Residence Distribution of Day-Ticket Skiers

	1974 (n = 985)			1973 (n = 964)			1972 (n = 634)
RESIDENCE	Weekends	Weekdays	Total	Weekends	Weekdays	Total	Weekends
Bozeman	22.4%	20.6%	21.8%	30.0%	18.9%	26.1%	32.3%
Butte	7.7	1.1	5.2	10.6	1.8	7.6	7.7
Missoula	2.9	1.1	2.2	2.5	0.0	1.7	3.6
Great Falls	1.3	.3	.9	2.9	1.5	2.4	3.1
Helena	16.9	7.2	13.2	10.6	0	7.0	12.7
Billings	7.2	1.8	5.2	6.0	3.3	5.1	6.1
Other, In-State	8.2	2.4	6.0	5.1	5.1	5.1	8.3
Minneapolis/St. Paul[a]	11.3	16.5	13.2	6.2	27.3	13.5	4.5
Fargo[a]	5.1	9.9	6.9	7.3	12.0	8.9	2.0
Other, Out-of-State[a]	7.0	26.8	14.5	6.5	21.6	11.7	7.9
College Students	10.0	12.3	10.9	12.4	8.4	10.1	11.5

[a] Approximately 50% of all out-of-state skiers were skiing at Bridger Bowl for the first time.

AMERICAN REPERTORY THEATRE

A repertory theatre has moved to a new city and is planning its first season there. The management has conducted a detailed mail survey of potential attendees and seeks to use the resulting responses to help it in setting ticket prices, designing subscription packages, and promoting the initial season of performances.

It was 9:15 in the morning, and already the phone was ringing in the office of Sam Guckenheimer, comptroller of the American Repertory Theatre (ART) in Cambridge, Massachusetts. Guckenheimer grabbed the receiver from across a pile of computer printouts and strained to listen as voices and typewriters chattered behind him. "Could you speak up, please?" he asked his caller. "I'm in the middle of four conversations, one of them with a machine."

Depending on the time of day, Guckenheimer could be found wearing any one of several hats. After finishing college, he had attended the Yale School of Drama for two years and, as ART's comptroller, was in charge of budgeting and finance. He had also majored in slavic languages and literature as an undergraduate and was presently at work on a new translation of Gogol's *The Inspector General*, the fourth play of ART's spring 1980 repertory. But at the moment, his most pressing task was designing ART's first direct-mail subscription offer, to be mailed to a test group of 25,000 potential subscribers within 30 days.

BACKGROUND

The seeds of the American Repertory Theatre were sown in 1966 when Robert Brustein was invited to create a professional resident repertory theatre at the Yale School of Drama in New Haven, Connecticut. Brustein, an actor and theatre scholar who was also one of America's leading drama critics, was named dean of the school. His resident company, the Yale Repertory Theatre, became renowned for the quality and originality of its productions; drama critic Clive Barnes described the Yale Rep in 1978 as "one of the finest theatre companies in the English-speaking world." The company's repertory was eclectic, ranging from new interpretations of foreign and American classics to premieres of works by relatively unknown playwrights.

From the outset, the threatre was conceived as a not-for-profit, subsidized operation. As Brustein commented:

> The profit motive requires an appeal to the lowest common denominator for the widest possible audience . . . the more serious artist does not always make his or her appeal known immediately. It takes some time before the audience catches up in some cases. In other cases, the audience is ahead. But what do we do about our James Joyces and our Stravinskys and our Picassos and our Ibsens and our Brechts until they've become absorbed into the culture and become more popular? We have to serve them, we have to subsidize them, we have to support them. And that's why some institutions exist.

Brustein's emphasis on professional performance and production standards aroused some opposition on campus, particularly among undergraduates seeking more stage time for amateur productions. In 1978, A Bartlett Giamatti was appointed president of Yale. After months of conflict, Giamatti, a supporter of undergraduate theatre, informed Brustein that he

This case was prepared by Penny Pittman Merliss, a former research associate at the Harvard Business School, and Christopher H. Lovelock.

would be replaced as dean of the drama school. Following intense negotiation, Brustein and his company—renamed the American Repertory Theatre—announced their intention to move to the Loeb Drama Center in Cambridge, Massachusetts, under the sponsorship of Harvard University.

The Loeb Drama Center

Harvard had long encouraged undergraduate extracurricular theatricals, a tradition which culminated in the development of the Loeb Drama Center. The $1.8 million building, funded by a $1.5 million gift from John L. Loeb, an investment banker, was opened in 1960.

Located on the edge of an upper-income residential area, the Loeb was a five-minute walk from Harvard Square, a busy retail area next to the University. The Harvard Square neighborhood contained many specialty stores, including more bookstores within a half-mile radius than any other area of its size in the world; some remained open till almost midnight. A newsstand adjoining the Square subway stop boasted that it offered the world's most extensive stock of international newspapers and periodicals. Local restaurants were equally cosmopolitan, offering visitors a choice of Chinese, Italian, French, Arabic, Spanish, Mexican, Swiss, Cuban, German, Indian, Brazilian, and Vietnamese cuisine, in addition to fast food and vegetarian cooking. Three movie theatres were within easy walking distance of the Square, and several bars and coffeehouses in the area scheduled regular performances of jazz and folk music.

The Loeb had no parking lot for patrons, and on-street parking was limited. The nearest public parking lots, four blocks away, charged a flat rate of $2 for evening parking. Public transportation service to the area, however, was extensive. Harvard Square was the terminus of the MBTA subway system's Red Line and a major subway-bus transfer point. Downtown Boston could be reached by train in 10 minutes.

Praised by one Boston theatre critic as a "magnificent facility," the Loeb's main auditorium contained a fixed bank of 402 comfortable seats, rising in the rear of the house. The remaining 154 seats were mounted on two motorized platforms, resting on hydraulic lifts, which could be banked to produce a traditional proscenium stage, an arena, or an Elizabethan apron. Sightlines were excellent.

Yet with the exception of a summer theatre and occasional special attractions (often one-person shows or small dance troupes), the Loeb's main stage was dark for much of the year. In 1978–1979, student productions occupied the main stage for a total of only 14 weeks (56 performances), leading one observer to refer to the Loeb as a "Rolls Royce without a chauffeur."

THE BOSTON THEATRE ENVIRONMENT

Their expectations aroused by Boston's reputation as "the Athens of America," many newcomers to the city were surprised to discover how rarely Boston was exposed to theatre and dance of the first rank. Only four legitimate theatres survived downtown in 1979, all of them located only a block from the notorious "Combat Zone."[1] Boston contained only one auditorium large enough to accommodate first-class ballet troupes; this was also the city's major convention facility, and the acoustics were so bad that no ballet company comparable to the New York City Ballet or the Bolshoi had visited the city in years. The internationally respected Boston Symphony Orchestra (BSO), founded in 1881, enjoyed the highest earned income of any orchestra in the U.S., but was the only professional performing arts institution in the city with a permanent home until Sarah Caldwell's Opera Company of Boston finally managed to purchase a theatre in 1978.

Financial Problems

Some observers felt that a general lack of funds was the real reason why Boston had failed to establish itself nationally as a center for the performing arts. Although Massachusetts ranked third among the 50 states in number of artists and arts organizations (after New York and California), it ranked fifteenth in per capita state spending on the arts.

Unlike New Yorkers, Bostonians could look to only a few large local businesses for corporate support. The problem was exacerbated, according to some observers, by the fact that large donors to the arts did not always achieve the immediate social prominence they found in other cities. As *Time* magazine once put it: "Boston has class that is bred on Beacon Hill, not bought with hefty contributions to the arts."

Response to Repertory

Failure to develop a permanent, professional resident theatre company was not a problem unique to Boston, however. Philadelphia, Atlanta, Houston, and even New York City lacked a company comparable to ART. Several explanations for this deficiency had been advanced. Although repertory companies offered performers regular employment and a chance to perform against "type," the physical and emotional demands of repertory acting could be severe. Since plays ran in rotation, actors might find themselves performing three or four major parts in different plays within the same week—or rehearsing one play while they took leading roles in another. Salaries, though they conformed to union standards for a theatre of the Loeb's size ($239 per week minimum through June 1980), did not approach the pay offered by motion pictures, television, or major Broadway work, and repertory theatres were rarely able to use stars to attract the public. Even more important to many actors than salary was the loss of national exposure which they might suffer by working outside New York or Hollywood.

In addition to a relatively long-term commitment from performers, successful repertory theatre, it was generally agreed, also required the presence of a loyal audience willing to support a variety of plays ranging from traditional to experimental. Carolyn Clay, arts critic for *The Boston Phoenix*, distinguished two disparate theatre audiences in the Boston community. The first was a group located primarily in the suburbs who would come downtown to large commercial theatres like the Shubert, the Wilbur, and the Colonial for proven hits and big stars. Boston had once been well known as a tryout town for Broadway-bound plays, and, according to the press agents questioned by Clay, was still considered a better barometer of New York taste than Washington, D.C. Nevertheless, Clay noted:

> Most of the people I spoke with agreed that Boston, which used to be more adventuresome in its capacity for Broadway-bound hopefuls, would rather see a show that had already made it in New York.

The prices charged by downtown theatres (up to $22.50 for a top seat at a musical in 1979) were seen by some as motivating this customer preference for guaranteed appeal.

The other major school of taste in Boston, Clay felt, was represented by more intellectual theatregoers, many residing in Cambridge. This audience patronized improvisational revues like those offered by the Next Move Theatre in Boston and was relatively more likely to support college or experimental productions. Shows like British actor Alec McCowen's reading of St. Mark's Gospel, performed at the Loeb in 1978 following a successful run in London, also appealed to this group. Even McCowen's show, however, was far from obscure; it had received rave reviews in British publications and *The New Yorker* before reaching the Loeb.

The most successful plays in Boston were those that managed to bring these two audiences together. The consensus among the professional theatre people interviewed by Clay was that "recognizability" was essential in selling theatre to Bostonians; even the managing director at the Loeb admitted that the audience for truly avant-garde theatre was "wildly limited" in Boston. Moreover, the college student population, which helped to support a number of repertory and art cinemas in the area, was rarely visible at legitimate theatre productions.

Anticipating ART's arrival, Clay concluded,

There *is* an audience here for weighty and adventuresome, if not for radical, theatre. Perhaps, if we acquire such a company for ourselves, and it feeds us a reasonably steady diet of quality laced with controversy, we'll learn to take pot luck.[2]

ART management had discovered some preliminary statistics which appeared to support this view. Previous national research sponsored by The Ford Foundation had indicated that people with at least some college education were more than three times as likely to attend the theatre as people with high school education or less; the Boston Standard Metropolitan Statistical Areas (population 2.7 million) had a proportion of college graduates and professionals over 50 percent above the national mean.

On the other hand, despite the widely held opinion that Boston would welcome a company of ART's standing, no theatre in the city had developed a consistent, loyal audience. Two previous attempts to develop a lasting audience for repertory theatre in Boston had both failed eventually. The Charles Street Playhouse disbanded its repertory company in 1968 after five years; the Boston Repertory Theatre had disbanded in 1978 after ten years. Many people had ideas about what Boston audiences liked, but no one really knew—and no one in any of the city's arts organizations had carried out detailed market research studies over an extended period.

PLANNING THE FIRST SEASON

Brustein and his company came to Boston knowing they would need to undertake a major fund-raising effort. It has been estimated that an initial 14-week season of four plays (112 performances) would cost roughly $1 million.[3] Harvard would contribute $163,000 of this sum in cash, as a grant from the Faculty of Arts and Sciences. (It would also provide maintenance and utilities and allow ART the use of the University's accounting, billing, and other miscellaneous services totaling about $175,000 in value.) In return for this contribution, ART planned to offer full-season student pass subscriptions to Harvard/Radcliffe undergraduates at $10 per pass. Students would be asked to pick up their tickets at the box office beginning two weeks before each production opened, after full-price subscription sales had concluded; subject to box office discretion, they could be seated anywhere in the house. No other special offers were planned for the Harvard community, which ART management considered a captive audience. ART had raised $214,000 for 1979–1980 from government agencies and national foundation grants; over 60 percent of the first season's budget would have to come from community contributions and ticket sales.

Management stated that, as was customary for the company, the repertory for the first Cambridge season had been chosen without regard to commercial appeal (although the first play, Shakespeare's *A Midsummer Night's Dream*, had been a hit at Yale in 1975). The original New Haven production of this tale of magic, romance, and slapstick was being revived for ART's Cambridge premiere, with designers, director, and several actors recreating their original work. Music would be provided by Boston's "Banchetto Musicale," a group of early music specialists whose instruments were copies of restorations of seventeenth- and eighteenth-century models. According to Brustein, beginning the season with a revival would give a sense of continuity to the work of the transplanted company and show new audiences what ART had done in the past. *A Midsummer Night's Dream* was scheduled to open on March 21, 1980.

The second play of the season was *Terry by Terry*, written by Mark Leib, a student at the Yale Drama School. It had been performed in workshop in New Haven and would receive its professional premiere on April 4. *Terry by Terry* was a two-part play within a play. The first act presented a Kafkaesque parable of a young boy who refused to talk; the second depicted the anger, alienation, and comic protest of the young playwright who wrote the parable.

Happy End, a comic musical melodrama

with book and lyrics by Bertolt Brecht and music by Kurt Weill, was the company's third offering, opening April 25. Set in Chicago in 1919, the play combined bumbling gangsters with "Salvation Army lasses" and was more overtly humorous than Brecht and Weill's famous *Three-Penny Opera. Happy End* had been presented at Yale in 1972 and 1975, but would be performed in Cambridge as a totally new production.

The last play of the season, Gogol's *The Inspector General*, was scheduled to open May 22. This satire of petty bureaucracy had attracted a good deal of attention when Brustein announced that it would be directed by a Harvard senior, many of whose controversial undergarduate productions had received excellent critical reviews in Boston. *The Inspector General* had been presented at Yale in 1970 to a relatively unfavorable critical and public reception. It too would receive a completely new production—as well as a new translation—for the first Cambridge season.

Reviewing the upcoming repertory, Guckenheimer commented:

> As you can see, it's far from a line-up of greatest hits. We did have to come in and sell very well as soon as possible—that's one reason we chose *A Midsummer Night's Dream*. Yet, from a broader perspective, we tried to assemble a season that is very characteristic of the range of plays we have done and continue to do—one premiere, one Shakespeare, one neglected modern play, one translated European classic.

The company's need for strong subscriber-contributor support was exacerbated by the very nature of repertory theatre. Because plays ran in rotation for fixed periods of time, a repertory company could not "milk" a successful production indefinitely, as a Broadway theatre might. Nor could a flop be closed before its appointed time. On the other hand, successful repertory productions like *A Midsummer Night's Dream* could be packaged, stored, and re-presented. ART had over 80 plays in its repertory, and planned to draw on these for at least two of its six productions during 1980–1981.

In Search of an Audience

Sam Guckenheimer had begun to explore the notion of building a subscriber-contributor base with the aid of market research during the spring of 1979, when he was a student in theatre administration at the Yale School of Drama and the company was preparing for its move to Cambridge. Convinced from his experience as an undergraduate at Harvard that the city would welcome an organization of ART's caliber, Guckenheimer began to assemble studies produced by other arts groups in an effort to develop his own audience survey for Boston. Robert Orchard, ART managing director, listened to Guckenheimer's ideas with interest and hired him shortly thereafter, charging him with the task of defining ART's new audience.

From the beginning, everyone involved in the project shared the conviction that ART should not use the results of market research to shape the company's offerings. As Guckenheimer phrased it:

> We were going to do a certain kind of theatre no matter what people wanted. Our task was to find the people who wanted our kind of theatre.

Evaluating Previous Research

One of the difficulties of the project was the lack of reliable existing research; only one significant national survey of theatre audiences had ever been conducted. In 1974 The Ford Foundation had sponsored an extensive study designed to measure the size and characteristics of audiences for all the performing arts. Five hundred telephone interviews were conducted on a random sample of the population in each of 12 cities; all cities were regionally dispersed locations in which the performing arts were especially active.[4] Selected results are reproduced in Exhibits 1 and 2.

The previous studies undertaken by individual arts organizations varied widely in complexity, ranging from nonspecific one-page questionnaires to intricate lists of essay questions probing likes and dislikes. In none of the 10 examples which Guckenheimer examined had respondents been contacted by name (one theatre began its cover letter: "Dear Washington-Area Friend of the Performing Arts"). Many questionnaires were simply handed out to audiences after performances, rather than mailed to any particular area or group. After reviewing these previous efforts, Guckenheimer felt more strongly than ever the need for a detailed, methodologically rigorous survey on which to build ART's marketing strategy:

> There have been very few situations in the arts where a calculated expectation of return has determined the design of a marketing campaign, where the regional audience has been clearly segmented and analyzed in advance, or where a new theatre has been able to scale its house and schedule its season according to a prior knowledge of the local market.[5]

Although ART management had had some experience with subscription mailings to New Haven, the Yale Rep had not undertaken research or testing of subscription offers prior to sending them out. In its most recent Yale season, the company had sent out three mailings. The first went to 1,200 households, accounting for 2,500 existing subscriptions, and resulted in 1,500 subscription renewals. The second, sent to a mailing list of 17,000 names which management had compiled, yielded 400 subscriptions. The third mailing, which went out to a large number of purchased lists totalling 150,000 names, yielded a mere 600 new subscribers.

In committing themselves to the survey, Guckenheimer and Orchard faced some opposition. A Ford Foundation consultant who specialized in arts marketing urged that the money be used for direct-mail advertising instead. But Guckenheimer's support for the survey never wavered:

> How else would we have the information necessary to design the test mailing, except by going by the seat of our pants—or following the advice of the local publicists, each of whom disagrees with everybody else?

He also supported extensive use of direct mail as opposed to newspaper or other media advertising, noting:

> You cannot, in a newspaper ad, in a cogent way, convey enough information to sell someone a subscription. You can sell a pair of tickets for a single night, but not a series of plays, or a range of prices, or a whole institution, unless you want to take out a full-page ad.

> Moreover, if you look at the kinds of things that are sold in newspaper ads—or the kinds of behavior that are encouraged—the promoters try to get you into a store for a sale, or get you to go to a movie, or get you to watch TV. Few can convey a message the way we want to—with color, glossy paper, and sophisticated graphics. We want to tell people that there will be a new life for the theatre in Boston, beginning on the first day of spring, 1980. How do you do that in a newspaper ad?

"Newspapers are not cheap, either," Guckenheimer commented, pointing out that though they might offer a good way to reach huge numbers of people and convey a small amount of information ("this product will be available next week in your grocer's freezer"), "they are not a good medium through which to communicate a large amount of information to a small number of people." A full-page ad in the Sunday *New York Times*, widely read by ART's target audience, Guckenheimer observed, would cost $19,000 and reach every Sunday *Times* reader in the U.S. By contrast, a four-page, four-color 8½-by-11 flyer stuffed into the Boston editions of the Sunday *Times* would reach 50,000 readers for a total printing and stuffing cost of $5,000.

Designing the Survey

Guckenheimer's objectives for the survey were twofold. First, in the absence of concrete experience, he wanted to predict how many people would come to ART, how much to charge them, and how best to attract them. Second, he wanted to establish an information system to monitor ART's audience over time. By examining data on the changing size and characteristics of this audience, he hoped to be able to predict its responsiveness to new programs and promotional campaigns.

Work began on the survey in New Haven during April 1979. Sponsored by a grant from Theatre Communications Group, Inc., Jan Geidt, ART's Director of Press and Public Relations, was sent on a tour of four well-known regional theatres across the country to examine their marketing efforts. She returned with several observations:

> We were strongly urged to identify our potential audience in terms of demographics—i.e., geography, age, profession, education. Efforts to reach this audience, I was told, should include everything from social activities to paid and nonpaid advertising, billboards along travel routes, handout information, bus displays, and anything else to saturate these specific locales.

> As the director of marketing at the American Conservatory Theatre in San Francisco expressed it: "Establish as a base those natural pockets of the population where support is most likely to come from, and keep gearing your efforts to those supporters."

> The staff of the Seattle Rep, which is 92 percent subscribed this year, told me that there is still room, and need, for the single ticket buyer; one of their concerns is dispelling the idea that their performances are always sold out. On the other hand, Seattle's managing director pointed out that careful control of seats is the key to early success. He believes we should plan only so many performances (or subscription series) as we realistically believe can be filled. This ensures a look of success—and from this solid base we can expand.

> All these audiences share one of our constant problems: how to keep productions that remain in a repertory for several months "newsworthy" over a period of time.

Technical advice for the project was given by a Cambridge management consultant, who warned that the survey should contain only those questions whose answers would affect actual decisions: "It's very easy to fall into the game of 'it would be nice to know,'" he said. Accordingly, questions were designed with three criteria in mind: maximum information

yield for management decisions; maximum intelligibility for respondents; and ease of conversion into numerical data for processing and statistical analysis. Originally a telephone survey had been planned, but it was discarded because of the relatively low incidence of regular theatregoers (estimated at 3 to 5 percent) in the population; constructing a sample from the phone book and completing interviews by telephone with 400 theatregoers would have cost approximately $15,000. In contrast, the entire cost of the mail survey, including consulting fees ($8,000) and the expenses associated with coding, keypunching, programming, and computer time ($4,000) came to approximately $20,000.

The questionnaire was pretested three times on friends, relatives, and business associates of the ART staff (but not on a sample of the mailing group). Several questions posed initially were radically changed or rejected as too complicated; for example, one question, which asked how much respondents would pay to see each of six different kinds of productions, offered a choice of 13 responses in each category.

Guckenheimer had identified four key variables to examine: price sensitivity, attendance patterns, exposure to different media, and voluntary contribution patterns. Questions on these categories, plus others on subscription preferences, artistic preferences, location, and personal background of respondents, composed the final version of the questionnaire.

By the beginning of June 1979, Guckenheimer had completed the questionnaire design and was planning a cover letter. ART asked Kitty Dukakis, who was well known both for her interest in the arts and as the wife of the previous Massachusetts governor, to sponsor this letter. The final versions of the letter and the questionnaire (reproduced with percentage response disributions) are shown in Exhibit 3.

Developing the Sample

The mailing list for the survey was drawn from two sources. A group of 2,023 names was drawn from 7 of the 12 Boston-area census tracts which had the highest median educational level and the highest incidence of professional and managerial workers in the labor force. Of these 12 original tracts, seven were located in Cambridge. Guckenheimer had chosen the seven tracts needed for his mailing list by selecting two tracts from Cambridge and all five tracts outside Cambridge. These names were supplied by a broker. Another 2,235 names were obtained from the mailing lists of ten arts-related organizations in Boston, each of which had been asked to supply a random sample of up to 300 names.

In describing ART's potential audience, Robert Brustein had stated: "Our audience is anybody who can enjoy our work, and I think that means it can come from any class, any sex, any race, any part of town." Neither Orchard nor Guckenheimer saw any contradiction between this definition of audience and the survey sample. Orchard pointed out:

> The goal of the mailing was to identify people who would respond and subscribe without ever having seen an ART production. This group was almost by definition high education and high income, up on the threatre scene, aware of Brustein's reputation, or generally supportive of the arts.

Guckenheimer added:

> The theatre's goal in its first year is to bring income to a dependable level as quickly as possible; then we can go after less responsive groups. Any other policy would be like building the computers before reaping the grain.

Included in the final mailing package (addressed to respondents by name) were the cover letter; the questionnaire; and a prepaid reply envelope, to be returned by first class mail.

The survey was mailed as scheduled on July 5. Over 1,200 responses had been received by August 3, when keypunching began; 1,343 were ultimately tabulated. Approximately 300 of the pieces directed to census tract addresses were returned to Guckenheimer as undeliverable. A breakdown of response rates from each organization contributing names to the mailing list is presented in Exhibit 4. Although response rates varied by sample, subsequent analysis revealed no significant differences between responses from the census tract group and those from the arts organizations group.

ANALYZING THE RESULTS

After the survey results were tabulated (see Exhibit 3), Guckenheimer's consultant suggested that he undertake a further analysis of the data in order to look for characteristics that might identify ART's target audience. In particular, Guckenheimer was interested in segmenting survey respondents in terms of the subscription benefits they desired. He did not expect the survey results to produce concrete answers, but hoped to be able to use the data to uncover "possibilities" which he could convert to concrete sales.

Guckenheimer's most immediate need was to determine what sources he should use to compile ART's first subscription solicitation mailing list. Potential lists of addresses that he had identified included five possible sources: (1) Individuals residing in targeted census tracts (information available at a cost of about $20 per thousand names). If mailings were restricted to census tracts having a median education level of at least 16 years—four or more years of college—then the list for Greater Boston would total 17,000 names; if the median were lowered to 14 years and up, the total would amount to 63,000 names. (2) Members of, or subscribers to, other local arts organizations (cost about $35 per thousand);[6] this could generate a total of up to 25,000 names if all available sources were used, but an estimated 8,000 of these would be multiple listings. (3) Subscribers to specialized publications such as *Massachusetts Lawyers Weekly* (17,000 names in the Greater Boston area, available at a cost of $60 per thousand) or to *Bon Appetit*, a gourmet cooking magazine with 22,000 subscribers in Greater Boston (cost about $35 to $40 per thousand). (4) Up to 70,000 charge account customers from expensive retail stores in the Boston area (about $55 to $60 per thousand). (5) Five thousand buyers of expensive small appliances, notably food processors (available from a corporation which processed warranty cards for the appliances and searched out income data; cost, about $80 per thousand).

Eventually ART management hoped to send enough subscription solicitations—at an average unit cost for printing, stuffing, and mailing of about 28¢ each—to sell out the season. General experience suggested that ART could expect to sell an average of 2.0 to 2.5 seats per subscriber. The entire subscription campaign, including advertising, was budgeted at $70,000, including the $20,000 already spent on the survey. Because both Guckenheimer and Orchard wanted the theatre to be sold out for all subscription performances, the length of each play's run would not be determined until a significant number of subscription orders had come in. ART planned to offer 10 to 16 weeks of subscription performances, followed by approximately four weeks of non-subscribed performances whose seats would be easier to promote than an equivalent number of seats spaced out over the full 16 weeks.

Ticket prices presented another problem. ART's goal was to maximize box office income while simultaneously maximizing attendance. According to Guckenheimer:

> Our prices should be high enough so that anyone who can and will pay a lot to attend will do so. At the same time, anyone who really wants to come should be able to.

There were other constraints on pricing. ART management felt it important to have a top ticket price "high enough to distinguish us from the church basement productions," as Guckenheimer put it; "but on the other hand, we do depend on outside funding, and for that reason we can't be out for blood like the commercial theatres." At Yale, the company's top ticket price (for the most desirable seats on Friday and Saturday nights) had been $8; bottom price (for the least desirable seats for matinees, Monday nights, and previews) had been $3.50. Guckenheimer expected to raise these prices at the Loeb, following interpretation of the survey results and a review of the ticket press and subscription plans offered by other Boston arts organizations (Exhibit 5).

The final task Guckenheimer faced was designing a subscription offering for potential ART subscribers, based on the information furnished by the survey. Freelance designers would produce the brochure describing the season's repertory; it was Guckenheimer's job to draw up a subscription coupon. How many different kinds of subscription packages should ART offer, he wondered, and how should they be distinguished from each other? What benefits might a subscription include, and how could they best be communicated on the coupon? To whom should he mail the different types of offers? What prices should he charge for the various subscriptions? And would it be possible to ask subscribers for a contribution to ART at the same time? At Yale, contributions had never been solicited from individuals in or outside of the subscription campaign. However, the technique of adding a contribution line had been used successfully for subscription renewals by several opera and ballet companies. Guckenheimer had heard that this approach could add 5 to 10 percent in contributions over the total dollar value of all renewals.

With a mixture of anticipation and apprehension, he began to leaf through the pile of computer printouts on his desk. He had run a series of cross-tabulations (Exhibit 6) on the survey data, relating willingness to pay certain ticket prices (survey question 10) to a variety of other variables (questions 6, 7, 11, 12, 13, 14, 15, 20 c–e). These results, Guckenheimer hoped, would clarify the relationship between each of the various factors that would encourage people to subscribe and the activities they might combine with a visit to the theatre. Once the subscription offering had been mailed, he would also use the survey results to develop a strategy for promoting sales of individual seats for approximately 35 nonsubscription performances in midsummer.

NOTES

1. An eight-block area (referred to by city officials as the "adult entertainment district") that contained most of the city's pornographic bookstores, cinemas, and stage shows.

2. Carolyn Clay, "Beyond the Theatre Fringe," *The Boston Phoenix*, December 5, 1978, p. 12.

3. Performances were scheduled for six evenings (Tuesday–Sunday) and two afternoons (Saturday–Sunday) weekly. It was estimated that extending the initial season would cost roughly $30,000 per week. Costs for the following six-play season, running from September to June 1980–1981, were estimated at $1.7 million.

4. Cities surveyed included Boston, New York, Philadelphia, Chicago, Cincinnati, Minneapolis, Atlanta, Washington, Houston, Seattle, San Francisco, and Los Angeles.

5. "Scaling the house" consists of setting varying ticket prices according to time of performance and location of seats.

6. In the future, these names might also be obtained by trading ART's list for that of other local arts organizations.

EXHIBIT 1

American Repertory Theatre's Exposure to Professional Performance of the Arts During the Past Year, 1974[a]

ART FORM	LOCATION OF RESPONDENTS	EXPOSED ONCE ONLY	EXPOSED TWO OR MORE TIMES PER			TOTAL EXPOSED	TOTAL NOT EXPOSED
			Year	Month	Week		
1. Movie on television	Boston	3%	16%	34%	37%	90%	10%
	12 U.S. Cities	4	17	30	41	93	7
2. Movie in movie theatre	Boston	6	44	15	1	66	34
	12 U.S. Cities	6	45	16	2	69	31
3. Live professional play	Boston	6	7	0	0	13	87
	12 U.S. Cities	5	10	*	0	16	84
4. Live professional Broadway musical	Boston	9	8	*	0	17	83
	12 U.S. Cities	8	9	*	0	18	82
5. Live professional jazz, rock, or folk music	Boston	6	13	2	1	22	78
	12 U.S. Cities	8	15	2	1	25	75
6. Live professional symphony	Boston	3	5	*	0	8	92
	12 U.S. Cities	4	5	*	0	10	90
7. Live professional opera	Boston	1	*	0	0	1	99
	12 U.S. Cities	2	2	0	0	4	96
8. Live professional ballet	Boston	1	1	0	0	2	98
	12 U.S. Cities	3	2	0	0	4	96

[a] All numbers are rounded to the nearest percent. If literally none of the respondents was exposed, "0" is used. If a marginal number of respondents (fewer than one-half of one percent) was exposed, an asterisk (*) is used.
SOURCE: *The Finances of the Performing Arts*, a report to the Ford Foundation, 1974

EXHIBIT 2

Findings from 1974 Ford Foundation Study

A. EXPOSURE TO LIVE PROFESSIONAL PERFORMANCES OF FOUR ARTS, 1974

AMONG THOSE WHO ATTENDED	PERCENT WHO ALSO ATTENDED:				ATTENDED NO OTHER ARTS
	Theatre	Symphony	Opera	Ballet	
Theatre		31	13	19	63
Symphony	45		27	27	36
Opera	50	75		25	25
Ballet	60	60	20		20

B. TOTAL PERCENT EXPOSED DURING PAST YEAR BY INCOME, 1974

	MOVIE	THEATRE	MUSICAL	JAZZ	SYMPHONY	OPERA	BALLET
Up to $7,500	47	7	8	17	4	2	3
$7,500 to $15,000	72	14	15	24	8	3	3
$15,000 to $25,000	83	25	28	32	16	6	6
$25,000 and over	83	38	44	36	28	13	13

C. TOTAL PER CENT EXPOSED DURING PAST YEAR BY EDUCATION, 1974

	MOVIE	THEATRE	MUSICAL	JAZZ	SYMPHONY	OPERA	BALLET
Some high school	57	7	9	20	5	2	2
High school graduate	71	12	15	22	5	2	2
Some college	81	23	25	35	14	6	7
College graduate	81	39	39	31	26	11	13

D. TOTAL PERCENT EXPOSED DURING PAST YEAR BY OCCUPATION, 1974

	MOVIE	THEATRE	MUSICAL	JAZZ	SYMPHONY	OPERA	BALLET
Executive-managerial	75	24	27	26	14	6	4
Professional	83	28	25	33	18	5	9
Teaching	84	35	36	28	27	10	11
Student	93	17	19	49	15	6	6
Housewife	59	13	15	14	7	3	3
White collar	75	19	23	28	11	4	5
Blue collar	63	10	11	20	4	1	2
Retired	37	9	11	8	7	4	4

E. INCOME COMPOSITION OF AUDIENCES OF FOUR PERFORMING ARTS, 1974

	THEATRE	SYMPHONY	OPERA	BALLET
Up to $7,500	13%	12%	15%	20%
$7,500 to $15,000	40	37	34	32
$15,000 to $25,000	33	34	32	30
$25,000 and over	14	17	19	18
	100%	100%	100%	100%

F. EDUCATIONAL COMPOSITION OF AUDIENCES OF FOUR PERFORMING ARTS, 1974

	THEATRE	SYMPHONY	OPERA	BALLET
Some high school	18%	21%	20%	18%
High school graduate	26	18	18	16
Some college	23	24	24	26
College graduate	33	37	38	40
	100%	100%	100%	100%

SOURCE: *The Finances of the Performing Arts,* a report to the Ford Foundation, 1974

Kitty Dukakis

July 5, 1979

J.M. Johnson
55 Willard St.
Cambridge, MA 02138

Dear J.M. Johnson,

I am writing to you on behalf of the American Repertory Theatre
Company (A.R.T.C.)--a non-profit, professional resident theatre
scheduled to open in Boston next spring--to ask for your opinions.
For this purpose we have enclosed a brief questionnaire on cultural
activities in the Boston area.

This study will assist the A.R.T.C. in serving the interests and
needs of the metropolitan area's residents, and the results will
be shared with many arts organizations around Boston. We have
sent the questionnaire to a limited number of people, some selected
randomly, others by their involvement with the various cultural
institutions in the area.

Please show your interest by filling out the questionnaire and
returning it in the postage-paid envelope provided no later than
Wednesday, July 18. In order for the A.R.T.C. to obtain an accurate
cross-section of views on the cultural activities of Boston, it
is very important that we receive your responses.

Your answers will, of course, be anonymous. However, if you would
like to request further information about the cultural organizations
that have helped us prepare this study, we have enclosed a separate
postcard which offers you this option.

We hope that you will find these questions interesting and that
they might further stimulate your thinking about cultural activities
in the Boston area. Thank you very much for your assistance.

Sincerely yours,

Kitty Dukakis

KD:sg
encls

EXHIBIT 3 (continued)

Survey Questionnaire[a]

This survey is being sponsored by the American Repertory Theatre Company (A.R.T.C.) to understand the interests and opinions of the residents of Greater Boston on the region's cultural activities. Your answers to this questionnaire will help the A.R.T.C. and other local arts organizations better serve the needs of the metropolitan area's residents.

The questionnaire should take you about 15 minutes to complete. Of course, your responses will be anonymous. Please answer all of the questions to the best of your ability. There are no right or wrong answers, but for statistical purposes, it is important that we receive complete responses.

When you have finished the questionnaire, please return it in the postage-paid envelope provided, no later than **July 18.**

Thank you very much.

[a] As reproduced here, the questionnaire includes the percentage distributions for responses to each question.

EXHIBIT 3 (continued)

ATTENDANCE

1. Have you ever attended a live theatre performance? *(Check one.)*

	Yes	No	Not sure
	☐ 99.6	☐ 0.4	☐

2. In the past year, have you attended any live performances of:
    (For each category, check the box next to the appropriate answer.)

	Yes	No	Not sure
a symphony orchestra?	☐ 77.6	☐ 21.9	☐ 0.6
chamber music?	☐ 58.1	☐ 40.9	☐ 1.0
an opera?	☐ 46.5	☐ 52.9	☐ 0.6
a ballet?	☐ 60.7	☐ 38.4	☐ 0.9
modern dance?	☐ 43.8	☐ 54.5	☐ 1.7
musical on a Broadway tour?	☐ 61.3	☐ 37.9	☐ 0.8
drama on a Broadway tour?	☐ 60.9	☐ 37.5	☐ 1.6
production at a professional regional theatre?	☐ 64.4	☐ 33.9	☐ 1.7
university theatre production?	☐ 57.5	☐ 41.4	☐ 1.0

3. During the past two or three years, how often have you been to performances at the following places:
    (For each performance hall, check the box next to the appropriate answer.)

	Not at all	Once or twice	Three or four times	Five or more times	Not sure
Symphony Hall?	☐ 16.1	☐ 28.5	☐ 16.1	☐ 39.2	☐ 0.2
Boston Shakespeare Company?	☐ 75.8	☐ 13.9	☐ 4.4	☐ 5.8	☐ 0.1
Loeb Drama Center?	☐ 43.6	☐ 25.7	☐ 10.9	☐ 19.2	☐ 0.5
The Shubert Theatre?	☐ 24.5	☐ 42.0	☐ 15.4	☐ 16.3	☐ 1.8
The Colonial Theatre?	☐ 28.3	☐ 40.9	☐ 14.8	☐ 13.9	☐ 2.1
The Wilbur Theatre?	☐ 30.1	☐ 40.5	☐ 15.0	☐ 11.4	☐ 3.1
The Music Hall?	☐ 32.7	☐ 40.1	☐ 13.9	☐ 10.7	☐ 2.5
The Next Move?	☐ 75.6	☐ 18.8	☐ 4.5	☐ 0.6	☐ 0.5
Trinity Square Repertory Company? *(Providence)*	☐ 93.0	☐ 4.5	☐ 0.4	☐ 1.9	☐ 0.2
Charles Street Playhouse?	☐ 51.0	☐ 36.3	☐ 9.1	☐ 2.8	☐ 0.7
Savoy Theatre?	☐ 70.0	☐ 11.7	☐ 7.7	☐ 7.2	☐ 3.4

EXHIBIT 3 (continued)

B. SUBSCRIPTIONS

4. A list of performing arts institutions is shown below. Please check the name(s) of those to which you have subscribed for a full season or series of performances. *(Check as many as apply.)*

32.4 ☐ Boston Symphony Orchestra   ☐ Opera Company of Boston   ☐ Shubert Subscription Series 12.5

26.0 ☐ Boston University Celebrity Series   ☐ Theatre Guild 23.2 12.6   ☐ None of these   27.7

21.0 ☐ Loeb Special Series   ☐ Boston Ballet 17.8   ☐ Not sure   0.8

5. Many cities now have professional resident repertory theatres, where a permanent acting ensemble produces a season of several plays from the broad range of dramatic literature. The productions alternate performances in repertory, and one actor may appear in two or three plays in a given week. If such a repertory theatre were established in Boston, is it likely that you would: *(Check one.)*

     ☐ Not attend at all?   5.8

     ☐ Probably attend just one performance?   13.4

     ☐ Probably subscribe to a four-play half season?   21.4

     ☐ Probably subscribe to a full eight-play season?   8.4

     ☐ Probably attend more than one performance, but not subscribe?   51.0

6. What two or three factors would **encourage** you most to subscribe to a theatre season or series of performances? *(Check up to **three** items which you consider to be most important.)*

55.0 ☐ Discount ticket prices   ☐ Membership newsletters/calendars   9.7

10.8 ☐ Restaurant or parking discounts   ☐ Greater likelihood of attending regularly   19.8

35.7 ☐ Guaranteed priority seating   ☐ Desire to support the institution   16.1

17.4 ☐ Guaranteed ticket availability   ☐ Ability to attend with friends more easily   8.5

28.2 ☐ Ease of ordering tickets   ☐ Desire to attend many performances by one particular group   3.4

17.3 ☐ Special ticket exchange privileges   ☐ Interest in a particular selection of performances   52.9

     ☐ Other: *(Please specify.)* _____

7. What two or three factors would **discourage** you most from subscribing to a theatre season or series of performances? *(Check up to **two** items which you consider to be most important.)*

34.2 ☐ Too much money to commit at once   ☐ Unfamiliarity with performance group   31.4

32.4 ☐ Too much advance planning required   ☐ Limited interest in attending so many performances of one ensemble 16.6

                         ☐ Limited interest in the particular selection of performances   52.6

18.5 ☐ Too inconvenient *(live too far away, takes too long to get there, difficulty leaving the house at night, etc.)*

     ☐ Other: *(Please specify.)* _____

8. When is it most convenient for you to attend a live theatre performance? *(Check your two most preferred times.)*

8.9 ☐ Weekday matinees   ☐ Weekday evenings   53.7

13.6 ☐ Saturday matinees   ☐ Friday - Saturday evenings   62.0

23.4 ☐ Sunday matinees   ☐ Sunday evenings   18.1

1.1 ☐ Not sure/Don't attend

EXHIBIT 3 (continued)

C. PRICING

9. If you were going to one production at **a resident repertory theatre**, what would you be willing to pay? *(Check one.)*

☐ $6.00 or less	☐ $8.00	☐ $10.00	☐ $12.00	☐ $14.00	☐ $16.00	☐ More than $16.00	☐ Not sure
22.2	31.2	22.5	10.3	3.5	1.2	1.1	8.0

10. If you were going to a series of eight plays at a resident repertory theatre, what would you be willing to pay **per play**? *(Check one.)*

☐ $6.00 or less	☐ $8.00	☐ $10.00	☐ $12.00	☐ $14.00	☐ $16.00	☐ More than $16.00	☐ Not sure
45.8	26.5	11.4	3.9	1.0	1.1	0.5	9.7

D. CONTRIBUTIONS

11. Have you ever contributed to any of the following institutions: *(For each institution, check the appropriate answer.)*

	Yes	No	Not sure
Boston Symphony Orchestra?	☐ 40.2	☐ 57.8	☐ 1.9
Opera Company of Boston?	☐ 23.2	☐ 74.7	☐ 2.1
Boston Ballet?	☐ 20.4	☐ 78.7	☐ 0.9
Boston Shakespeare Company?	☐ 8.3	☐ 90.4	☐ 1.3
Museum of Fine Arts?	☐ 50.1	☐ 47.4	☐ 2.5
Loeb Drama Center?	☐ 17.7	☐ 80.8	☐ 1.5
Fogg Art Museum?	☐ 16.6	☐ 81.7	☐ 1.7
WGBH (Channel 2)?	☐ 77.3	☐ 21.4	☐ 1.3

E. MEDIA

12. How do you usually find out about the plays which you attend? *(Check the two most frequent sources you use.)*

☐ TV Commercial	4.3	☐ TV Review	8.8
☐ Radio Commercial	3.9	☐ Radio Review	3.7
☐ Newspaper Ad	50.8	☐ Newspaper Review	50.9
☐ Mail Brochure	33.4	*Which critics:*	27.0% completed this
☐ Poster in MBTA	0.9		
☐ Poster elsewhere	2.0		
☐ Recommendation from a friend	35.4		
☐ Shubert Subscription Series	9.2	☐ Newspaper Story	9.5
☐ Theatre Guild Membership	8.1	☐ Not sure	0.9

☐ Other motivating factors: *(Please specify.)* _____ 7.9% completed this _____

EXHIBIT 3 (continued)

13. The names of several newspapers and magazines available in the Boston area are listed below. How frequently do you read each of these journals? *(For each publication, check the appropriate box to indicate frequency of reading.)*

	Never	Less than half the issues	More than half the issues	Almost every issue	Not sure
Weekday Boston Globe?	☐ 10.3	☐ 27.0	☐ 8.4	☐ 53.3	☐ 0.9
Sunday Boston Globe?	☐ 11.4	☐ 18.9	☐ 7.9	☐ 61.1	☐ 0.7
Weekday Herald American?	☐ 71.8	☐ 14.8	☐ 1.4	☐ 11.4	☐ 0.6
Sunday Herald American?	☐ 78.6	☐ 9.2	☐ 1.3	☐ 10.2	☐ 0.7
Weekday New York Times?	☐ 45.1	☐ 33.0	☐ 6.1	☐ 14.4	☐ 1.4
Sunday New York Times?	☐ 32.6	☐ 30.1	☐ 6.5	☐ 29.7	☐ 1.1
Christian Science Monitor?	☐ 79.1	☐ 13.5	☐ 1.5	☐ 4.5	☐ 1.3
The Boston Phoenix?	☐ 52.0	☐ 34.1	☐ 6.1	☐ 6.3	☐ 1.5
The Real Paper?	☐ 52.2	☐ 33.8	☐ 6.9	☐ 5.6	☐ 1.5
Boston Magazine?	☐ 48.1	☐ 26.5	☐ 6.2	☐ 17.9	☐ 1.3
Time?	☐ 34.6	☐ 28.2	☐ 7.7	☐ 28.0	☐ 1.5
Newsweek?	☐ 42.7	☐ 28.3	☐ 5.7	☐ 21.1	☐ 2.2

14. What are the local radio stations to which you listen regularly? *(Please list up to three by name [call letters] or dial numbers.)*

Name_____ Dial Number_____ AM_____ FM_____

Name_____ Dial Number_____ AM_____ FM_____

Name_____ Dial Number_____ AM_____ FM_____

15. How much television do you usually watch? *(Check one.)*

☐ Less than 10 hours per week 68.1   ☐ 10 - 20 hours per week 26.9   ☐ More than 20 hours per week 5.0

F. ARTISTIC PREFERENCES

16. The names of some artistic leaders and their respective institutions are listed below. Would artistic direction by any of these people make you more inclined to attend the performances of a particular organization: *(For each person listed, please check the appropriate answer.)*

	Yes	No	Not sure
Seiji Ozawa? *(Boston Symphony Orchestra)*	☐ 63.1	☐ 26.5	☐ 10.4
Sarah Caldwell? *(Opera Company of Boston)*	☐ 55.9	☐ 29.3	☐ 14.8
Arthur Fiedler? *(Boston Pops)*	☐ 49.1	☐ 41.9	☐ 9.0
Robert Brustein? *(Yale Repertory Theatre)*	☐ 34.6	☐ 31.7	☐ 33.7
Adrian Hall? *(Trinity Square Repertory Co.)*	☐ 15.2	☐ 41.8	☐ 43.1
E. Virginia Williams? *(Boston Ballet)*	☐ 22.1	☐ 45.4	☐ 32.4

EXHIBIT 3 (continued)

17. How interested are you in seeing any of the following kinds of plays: *(Check one answer for each category.)*

	Very interested	Somewhat interested	Not very interested	Not at all interested	Not sure
Musical comedies	☐ 40.6	☐ 34.7	☐ 17.3	☐ 7.2	☐ 0.2
Comedies	☐ 43.6	☐ 45.9	☐ 8.6	☐ 1.3	☐ 0.6
Dramas	☐ 64.3	☐ 30.7	☐ 3.5	☐ 0.8	☐ 0.8
American classics	☐ 43.0	☐ 44.1	☐ 10.3	☐ 1.4	☐ 1.1
Shakespeare or other English classics	☐ 43.0	☐ 38.1	☐ 15.0	☐ 3.3	☐ 0.6
Translated European classics	☐ 30.9	☐ 38.8	☐ 20.8	☐ 6.8	☐ 2.6
New plays ·	☐ 38.3	☐ 45.7	☐ 11.3	☐ 2.1	☐ 2.7
Light operas	☐ 21.0	☐ 34.7	☐ 23.9	☐ 19.1	☐ 1.3

G. LOCATION

18. The Loeb Drama Center is a 550-seat theatre on Brattle Street off Harvard Square. Are you familiar with it?

    ☐ Yes 79.8   ☐ No 18.6   ☐ Not sure 1.6

19. Have you ever attended a performance at the Loeb?

    ☐ Yes 67.4   ☐ No 31.2   ☐ Not sure 1.4

20a. If you heard about an interesting professional theatre production at the Loeb, would you be likely to attend?

    ☐ Probably 88.1
    (Please continue to questions b-f.)

    ☐ Probably not 11.9
    (If you have checked this box, then please skip ahead to question 21.)

  b. What means of transportation might you use to go to the Loeb?

    ☐ MBTA 19.2   ☐ Car 62.8

    ☐ Taxi 1.6   ☐ Foot or Bicycle 15.1   ☐ Not sure 1.2

  c. Would you be likely to go out to eat **before** the performance?

    ☐ Probably 53.0   ☐ Probably not 47.0

  d. Would you be likely to go out to a cafe/bar/restaurant **after** the performance?

    ☐ Probably 42.3   ☐ Probably not 57.7

  e. Would you spend part of the evening shopping or browsing around Harvard Square?

    ☐ Probably 39.2   ☐ Probably not 60.8

  f. What would be the most convenient evening performance time for theatre at the Loeb? *(Check one time on each of the two lines.)*

	7:00 or earlier	7:30	8:00	8:30	9:00 or later	Not sure
Sunday-Thursday	☐ 10.8	☐ 30.6	☐ 45.7	☐ 10.5	☐ 1.0	☐ 1.5
Friday-Saturday	☐ 5.7	☐ 16.4	☐ 51.0	☐ 21.7	☐ 3.9	☐ 1.2

21. What factors might keep you from attending the Loeb?

_____

_____

EXHIBIT 3 (continued)

H. BACKGROUND

22. What is your age?

☐ 18 or under	☐ 19-25	☐ 26-35	☐ 36-45	☐ 46-55	☐ 56-65	☐ 66 or over
1.3	6.9	30.0	20.6	19.1	13.2	8.9

23. Are you: ☐ Female? ☐ Male?

      55.8   44.2

24. Are you: ☐ Single? ☐ Married?

      42.7   57.3

25. What is the last grade in school or college that you completed?

☐ Grade School	☐ High School	☐ Technical or Vocational Training	☐ Some College	☐ College Degree	☐ Some Graduate School	☐ Graduate Degree
0.4	3.5	1.4	11.7	18.2	15.1	49.7

26. What is your zipcode at home? _____

27. What is the zipcode of your place of employment? _____

28. What is your occupation? _____

29. What is the occupation of the head of your household *(if different)?*

_____

30. And for statistical purposes only, which of the following broad categories represents your household's annual income?

☐ Under $10,000	☐ $10,000 -19,999	☐ $20,000 -29,999	☐ $30,000 -49,999	☐ $50,000 or over
7.3	21.1	21.0	27.6	23.0

Thank you very much for your time and interest. If you would like to receive more information about the arts organizations that have helped the American Repertory Theatre Company prepare this study, please return the prepaid reply postcard when you return this questionnaire.

EXHIBIT 4

Breakdown of Returns from Organizations
Contributing Names to the Survey Mailing List

SOURCE	PERCENTAGE OF TOTAL RETURNS	NET RESPONSE[a]
Geographic[b]	30.3%	22%
Ideas Associates[c]		
Individuals	4.6	48
Groups	3.7	25
Shubert Subscribers	7.9	39
Opera Company Subscribers	8.4	50
Friends of The Loeb	5.2	56
Boston Ballet Subscribers	4.9	30
Boston Shakespeare Company Subscribers	4.9	30
Friends of The Fogg (Art Museum)	8.6	45
Loeb Subscribers	13.6	64
Boston University Celebrity Series Subscribers	9.3	40
	100.0%	

[a] Net Response = Returns expressed as a percentage of questionnaires mailed less undeliverable pieces.
[b] Represents individuals targeted through census tracts.
[c] An organization serving as a ticket broker to both groups and individuals within the Boston area.
SOURCE: ART records

EXHIBIT 5

Representative Subscription Plans Offered by Performing Arts Organizations in the Boston Area[a]

ORGANIZATION	STATUS	HALL	SEATING CAPACITY	TYPE OF OFFERING	INDIVIDUAL TICKET PRICES		SUBSCRIPTION PLANS	PERCENTAGE OF OCCUPIED SEATS SOLD BY SUBSCRIPTION
					High	Low		
1. Boston Ballet	Non-profit	Music Hall John Hancock Hall	4,200 1,200	Classical ballet "Choreographers' Showcase"; premieres of new works (once a year)	$17.00	$4.00	Two plans. First offers entire season's repertory of 4 productions at 33% savings. Second, mailed in December, offers subscriptions to last two productions of year, at 33% savings.	45%
2. Boston Pops	Non-profit	Symphony Hall	2,625	Three-part programs featuring light classical music, soloists, and popular music. For Pops performances (May–July), orchestra seats of Symphony Hall removed and replaced by tables seating 5 people; light meals and alcoholic beverages sold during performance. 85% to 90% sold to groups.	$11.00	$3.50	None. Most seats sold in blocks of 50–2,000 to corporations, universities, charitable organizations, and other large groups.	0%
3. Boston Symphony Orchestra	Non-profit	Symphony Hall	2,625	Classical and modern music	$16.00 Rush (½ hour before performance, Friday–Saturday): $3.50	$5.00	14 plans, ranging from full season of 22 concerts to shorter series and open rehearsals. Also, covers concerts given in Providence, R.I., and New York City. Discount: 5%.	85%–90%
4. Boston Shakespeare Company	Non-profit	BSC Theatre	320	Shakespeare; occasional revivals	$8.50 Student rush (½ hour before performance): $4.00	$4.00	8 plans, each offering a selection of 5 plays from a play season. Discounts range from 7% to 20%.	50%–60%
5. Boston University Celebrity Series	Non-profit ("profits" sent to B.U. scholarship fund)	Symphony Hall Jordan Hall John Hancock Hall Music Hall Berklee Performance Center	2,625 1,019 1,200 4,200 1,226	Wide variety of classical music, dance, jazz, solo performers. No rock or popular music.	Only subscriptions available; $66.50	$45.50	35–40 plans. Patrons choose 7 productions from a list of about 50, at discounts of up to 33%.	Varies; has reached 100%

(continued)

EXHIBIT 5 (continued)

ORGANIZATION	STATUS	HALL	SEATING CAPACITY	TYPE OF OFFERING	INDIVIDUAL TICKET PRICES		OCCUPIED SEATS SUBSCRIPTION PLANS	PERCENTAGE OF OCCUPIED SEATS SOLD BY SUBSCRIPTION
					High	Low		
6. Charles Street Playhouse	For profit	Main stage Cabaret	525 175–200	Primarily Broadway hits reaching Boston for the first time—always cast in New York. Infrequently, hosts Broadway-bound tryouts. A "four-wall rental" theatre; each production brings in its own managerial staff.	$12.95 (varies)	$8.00	None. Theatre hopes to acquire non-profit status, develop a repertory company, and offer subscriptions by January 1981.	0%
7. Chateau de Ville	For profit	Three locations in suburbs adjoining Boston	NA	Well-known light comedies, musicals, often revivals; revues, including burlesque; occasional solo performers. Dinner available before the show at extra charge (varies).	$22.95[b]	$7.95	None	0%
8. Colonial Theatre	For profit		1,658	Broadway (or Broadway-bound) plays and musicals	musical $20/$10	drama $16.50/$9	None. Through Show-of-the-Month Club, mails notices of coming attractions to 30,000 people. Show-of-the-Month discounts range from 0%–15%.	20%–80% sold through Show-of-the-Month, depending on New York reputation of the show.

	Type	Capacity	Repertoire	Prices	Subscription	Subscribers
9. Shubert Theatre	For profit	1,698	Broadway (or Broadway-bound) plays and musicals	musical $22.50/$10; drama $20/$9	1 plan; requires subscribers to attend entire season and offers no discounts. Benefits: preferred seating, prior notification of productions	Varies widely; subscribers compose about 33% of house for first two weeks of play's run
10. Wilbur Theatre	For profit	1,200	Broadway (or Broadway-bound)plays and musicals; occasional dance troupes	$18.50/$14.50; $16/$9	None. Uses Show-of-the-Month (see above)	Less than 50% sold through Show-of-the-Month
11. Harvard/Radcliffe Dramatic Club	Student	556	Wide variety of dramas, comedies, musicals; both classic and modern plays	$4.50; $3.50 Rush (½ hour before performance): $2; $1 discount to Harvard students	1 plan; offers season of 3 plays for 33% discount	25%
12. Next Move Theater	Non-profit	186	Next Move Theater Premieres and plays new to Boston, ranging from musical adaptations of classical comedies to satirical revues to new productions of twentieth-century classics	$9.50; $7.50 Student rush (20 minutes before performance): $4.50	3 plans, first offered in 1979–80. Subscribers choosing Wed./Thurs./Sun. nights receive 33% discount; those choosing Fri./Sat. pay full price. Subscription covers season of 4 shows, plus free admission to one additional revue.	18%
13. Opera Company of Boston	Non-profit	2,700	Primarily well-known classical operas with major stars; some modern works, occasional premieres	$27.00; $8.00	1 plan; offers season of 4 operas for discounts of 8%–22%	80%

[a] Excludes most college productions and smaller groups like the Boston Camerata or Boston Repertory Ballet.
[b] The top price shown here was obtained when big name soloists were performing.

239

EXHIBIT 6

Cross Tabulations of Price Sensitivity Against Other Variables[a]

		Q10: PRICE WILLING TO PAY PER PLAY (FOR A SERIES OF 8 PLAYS) AT REPERTORY THEATRE				NUMBER OF POSITIVE RESPONSES
		$6 or Less	$8	$10	$12 or More[b]	
Q6:	Factors encouraging subscription					
	Discount ticket prices[c]	73%	45%	32%	24%	629
	Guaranteed priority seating	30	38	45	57	407
	Guaranteed ticket availability	13	21	21	27	192
Q12:	Media used to find out about plays					
	Radio commercials	5	2	1	6	43
	Shubert Theatre subscription series	4	9	21	21	97
	TV review	8	10	3	15	92
Q13:	Newspaper read more than half the time					
	Weekday *Boston Globe*	56	64	72	72	677
	Sunday *Herald American*	7	12	20	21	104
	Weekday *New York Times*	18	23	23	37	200
	Boston *Phoenix*	14	10	14	13	123
	Real Paper	16	9	13	7	123
Q20d and e:	Activities before/after show					
	Go to cafe/bar/restaurant *after*	41	48	57	55	533
	Shop/browse in Harvard Square	41	35	31	28	428

[a] Shown here are those items in Questions 6, 12, 13, and 20d and e where a statistically significant difference ($p < .05$) existed between the responses given in each of the four price categories. (Please refer to Exhibit 3 for exact wording of questions.)

[b] Combines $12, $14, $16, and more than $16 categories; "not sure" responses have been excluded.

[c] Interpret the data as follows: 73% of those saying they would be willing to pay $6 or less (in Question 10) checked discount ticket prices as one of the factors (in Question 6) that would most encourage them to subscribe, whereas only 45% of those saying $8 checked this factor, 32% of those saying $10, and 24% saying $12 or more.

BURNHAM VAN SERVICE, INC.

Following partial deregulation of the U.S. trucking industry, the management of a medium-sized but rapidly growing trucking company is trying to decide where to focus its marketing efforts. Which market segments to serve, how much business to seek from each, and how to organize the firm's marketing efforts are among management's major concerns.

"This industry has been doing things much the same way for fifty years," remarked Ray E. Crowley, president and chief executive officer of Burnham Van Service, Inc. "But with deregulation now a fact, there are going to be some changes taking place." Crowley and sev-

This case was prepared by Jeffrey J. Sherman, a former research assistant at the Harvard Business School, and Christopher H. Lovelock.

eral of Burnham's senior executives were discussing future strategy for the Georgia-based moving company in fall 1980, soon after passage of legislation reducing government regulation of the trucking industry in the United States.

"Last year," continued Crowley, "our gross sales were $38.5 million. We expect to be over the $100 million mark within the next four to five years. Some of this growth will come from diversification outside the moving industry, but much will be contributed by our basic business."

James B. Herndon, the vice-president responsible for marketing, pointed towards a large wall map of the United States. "We have 195 agencies and 15 branches," he said, "located in 34 states. We serve three distinct market segments. Where we focus our marketing efforts and how we organize those efforts are going to play a major role in determining whether we meet the revenue goals that Ray has outlined." He paused, then added: "It's also going to help determine whether or not Burnham continues to outperform its competitors in terms of profitability."

COMPANY BACKGROUND

Burnham Van Service, Inc., was founded in 1921 by L. R. Burnham, a furniture dealer who began using his delivery truck to move household goods. The company gained an early reputation as an innovator, and it established one of the industry's first formal training programs for van operators. In the early 1940s, Burnham handled the first shipment of household goods via air transit. The company pioneered the movement of computers and other high-value commodities in the 1950s, using specially designed "air-ride" vans. In the 1960s and 1970s, the firm handled many sensitive shipments for the American space program.

The company had its headquarters in a handsome white office and warehouse building next to a major highway just outside Columbus, Georgia, about 110 miles southwest of Atlanta. Parked around the premises at any given time were a number of trucks, flatbed trailers, and vans.[1] On a typical day, five or six vans, painted in white with bright red lettering, could be seen backed into the loading docks in the rear of the building. The vast warehouse area contained rows of crates stacked halfway to the two-story ceiling, but a large amount of space remained available for other shipments. Just inside the drivers' entrance stood a life-size male mannequin, smartly dressed in dark blue pants, a royal blue shirt with "Burnham Van Service" embroidered in red on the pocket, a blue hat, and polished black shoes.

Ray Crowley had joined Burnham as chief executive officer in 1974. At that time, the company was in serious financial trouble. It had moved into a new building, purchased an expensive computer system, and increased other operating expenses, but had been unable to increase its revenues sufficiently to cover its enlarged budget. In 1974, it lost $181,000 on revenues of $23.1 million. The firm's bankers and owners, concerned about Burnham's viability, brought in Crowley, who had held senior executive positions at General Mills and Royal Crown Cola, to manage a turnaround. He recalled,

> I took the job because it gave me the chance to implement so many new ideas. Whenever someone said we couldn't do something, I became interested, because it usually meant he hadn't tried. My turnaround strategy was concerned with Burnham's people, financial condition, and operating concept—in that order. Morale was our biggest problem, so I concentrated first on showing our employees how they could work better.

The new CEO attacked the firm's financial problems by implementing a system of management encompassing tight controls, collection of accounts receivable, cost reductions, and general retrenchment prior to attempting new growth. He improved Burnham's operating methods by focusing the firm on giving premium service, believing that this was the best way a small van line could reestablish a favorable reputation in the marketplace. "Commitment to Excellence" was the theme of Crowley's new program, which enabled the company's employees to increase the value of the services they provided by developing improved work procedures and support systems.

The firm established a national 24-hour, 7-day WATS line to encourage customers to call with questions or complaints. Constantly updated computer printouts kept the telephone agent informed of where every truck and shipment was located in the system. Most van lines only gave out this information during the normal work week. By using the telephone (in lieu of letters) to handle customer problems, the average claims settlement time at Burnham dropped from 17 days in 1976 to 10 days in 1979—the best in the industry.

Burnham's revenues grew rapidly, reaching $38.5 million in 1979; net income after tax stood at $2.1 million (Exhibit 1). The company had ranked fourteenth in size among national van lines in 1976; by 1979 it had moved up to eighth position (Exhibit 2). Its national market share during these three years increased from 1.6 to 2.2 percent.

By mid-1980, Crowley's emphasis had shifted from rebuilding the firm to preparing for the decade that lay ahead. Considerable changes were occurring in the moving industry. The larger van lines were expanding to handle an increasing amount of the industry's volume. Rising fuel prices and other costs were putting severe pressure on many carriers' operating margins. And in the latter part of the year, President Carter signed into law acts that brought a substantial measure of deregulation to the United States trucking industry.

THE UNITED STATES MOVING INDUSTRY

The movement of household goods represented just one component of the U.S. trucking industry. In signing the deregulation legislation into law, President Carter noted that "there is no other nation on earth that depends so heavily on motor transportation for its economic life's blood."

The trucking industry could be divided into two broad segments, private and for hire.

Private carriers transported their products or merchandise in their own or rented vehicles. The trucking-for-hire segments, which had annual revenues of some $30 billion, was regulated according to the nature of the products carried and the carrier's relationship to the shipper. Certain goods, such as unprocessed agricultural products and selected commodities, were exempt from regulation and could be carried by anyone. But a license from the Interstate Commerce Commission (ICC) was needed before a carrier could haul other goods. There were two types of licensee: common carriers, which could carry specific classes of goods for any shipper; and contract carriers, which could haul only for a limited number of designated shippers. Burnham was licensed as a common carrier.

Recognizing the different types of vehicles needed to carry different products, the ICC identified 15 commodity specializations—ranging from refrigerated solids to liquid petroleum to forest products to household goods. Two additional, residual classifications were "general freight"—usually shipped in less-than-truckload (LTL) volumes—and "specific commodities not subgrouped," otherwise known as "special products," which usually were shipped by the truckload. Common carriers had to obtain separate licenses for each of these 17 groups.

Like a number of other moving companies, Burnham had ICC operating authority to carry both household goods and special products. The latter consisted of goods such as electronic equipment, new furniture, and displays, which required special handling. Most of the larger van lines cultivated special products business because it provided a steady revenue base, commanded a premium price, and was more geographically balanced than household goods.

In 1980 the moving industry consisted of over 4,000 carriers with ICC authority to carry household goods and a variety of special products. Only 49 of these carriers had annual revenues over $1 million, and only 19 could claim to have any form of national presence. The 10 largest van lines accounted for $1.27 billion of total industry sales of $1.54 billion in 1979, with the top six lines representing 72 percent of this total (Exhibit 2)—up from 57 percent of industry sales of $728 million in 1970. However, although industry revenues had grown at an average annual rate of 17 percent between 1975 and 1979, rate increases had not kept pace with inflation.

According to Mr. Crowley, there was no clear indication that a particular form of ownership or even size significantly affected service levels, which, he said, were more a function of management systems and personnel quality. The profitability of the ten largest moving companies varied widely. Burnham had the lowest operating ratio (operating expenses divided by operating revenues) of any of these carriers in 1979 (Exhibit 2).

Industry Structure

Four distinct entities composed the basic structure of the moving industry: agents, truck operators, national organizations, and their branches. Each played a defined role in a typical interstate move.

Agents were usually privately owned moving operations located in a single city (or in some cases, a single state). They frequently had their own trucks and drivers, but because interstate operating authority had been difficult to obtain from the ICC, they usually serviced only a small geographic area. Agents employed their own service representatives who provided most of the customer-interface services involved in a move. For example, an agent at the originating end of a move might sell the moving service to a customer, estimate the cost, prepare all necessary documents, and, through a service representative, supervise the packing and loading. At the receiving end, another agent would arrange warehousing (if necessary) and coordinate unloading, delivery, and (sometimes) unpacking of the goods. Each of these operations commanded a certain percentage of the total revenue to be received for a move. The actual split was determined by agreement with the national van line that the agent represented.

Agents were divided into one of four ICC-approved classes, according to the services they contracted to perform. Class I agents were full-service businesses that handled both household goods and special products, and provided all origin/destination services. Class II agents handled all services except military bookings. Both Class I and Class II agents were legally required to represent a single van line exclusively. Class III agents, which handled only special products, might represent more than one van line. This was also true of Class IV agents, which were located near military bases and specialized in shipping household goods owned by military personnel.

Moving companies also had service contractors which packed or received goods, completed documents and held storage-in-transit; however, they did not book shipments on behalf of the van line. Many service contractors were simply warehouses which offered additional services, and most were located in thinly populated areas.

Truck operators picked up shipments at their origin (or sometimes at an agency warehouse) and delivered them to the final destination or to a receiving agent's facility. About 50 percent of the truckers in the moving industry were independent owner/operators who contracted out their services. Some worked with large agents, but the vast majority contracted with national van lines; they were generally paid 53 percent of the total revenue for a move. (See Exhibit 3 for a further explanation of how moving fees were typically divided.) Other operators were employees of an agent or national van line, which paid them a wage to drive a company-owned truck.

National van lines were the central operating organizations. They provided billing services, dispatching, national marketing, interstate operating authority, and claims-processing for their agents. Some lines owned their own trucks and hired drivers, while others contracted with independent owner/operators. Many firms did both.

Branches: Some investor-owned national van lines opened their own local branch facilities, usually in areas where they had no agents. Branches provided the same services as an agent, but offered the van line greater operating control and revenue. Industry opinion was mixed as to the role branches should play. Agents opposed the branch concept, and competed vigorously against those that were opened in their areas of operation. Some lines found branches to be quite profitable, especially in locations where they were unable to obtain a good agent and needed a facility to handle incoming business. Of the six major van lines, only Bekins operated a branch network. Burnham had been expanding its branch network and now had 15.

Changes in the Regulatory Environment

Van lines operating across state lines had historically been regulated by the ICC in matters of rates, entry areas served, exits, services, reporting, and financing. Only companies granted ICC authority were permitted to transport household goods and special products between states. Approximately 24 major van lines had authority which allowed them to operate anywhere in the 48 contiguous states.

Two pieces of legislation were enacted in 1980 to reduce government regulation of the trucking industry and make it more competitive. These were the Motor Carrier Act and the Household Goods Act. This legislation reduced barriers to entry, allowed more flexibility in rate setting, curbed certain existing restrictions on operating rights, and sought greater protection for consumers.

Reducing barriers to entry would encourage existing firms to expand by taking on new routes, and would make it simpler for new van lines to enter the market. One concern of many large moving companies was expressed by Herndon of Burnham Van Service:

> Some of the local agents are pretty big, booking anywhere from $3 million to $17 million of business per year. Since interstate operating authority will now be easy to get, they may decide to go out on their own. They'll no longer have to pay a commission to the national organization to use its broader operating authority for interstate shipments. Thus, we may see the birth of

some new national van lines, and perhaps a shifting of concentration in the industry.

Herndon anticipated that attempts by major agents to operate as independent carriers would be characterized by lower quality service, because they lacked experience in managing operations across an area as large as 10 to 20 states.

Rates in the trucking industry had historically been set by industry rate bureaus which had immunity from antitrust prosecution. Collective rate-making had led to a cumbersome tariff approach to pricing (a specific rate for a given weight of a particular commodity between two specified points). As a result, pricing had not been used much as an element in marketing strategy. The new legislation, however, created a 10 percent zone of rate flexibility, either side of these basic rates, within which price variations did not need to receive ICC approval. One moving company president saw this as the beginning of real price competition, and stated that his company had been preparing for it by doing a lot of work in management information, costing, and market research. "We'll have to become much better at analyzing routes," he noted, "in order to determine where our money is made and whether we can afford to compete on price."

Burnham management believed that the changes in price regulation would allow the company to simplify its rate structure, and felt that this in itself could prove to be a competitive advantage.

One industry observer pointed out that deregulation not only permitted price competition but would also allow carriers to charge different rates to different shippers. He believed that this could be particularly beneficial to contract shippers, enabling them to undercut the rates charged by common carriers and thus skim the cream off the most profitable traffic.

Finally, the Household Goods Act attempted to make sure that the consumer had better information in selecting moving companies and established procedures for settlement of shippers' disputes with a company.

While recognizing that the new legislation

offered some important opportunities for his company, Mr. Crowley noted that the industry remained a regulated one. "The term *deregulation* is really a misnomer," he cautioned. "In fact, we'll continue to see an increase in regulation in the next 3 to 5 years, with an emphasis on consumerism. But there should be a slackening of regulations as it relates to paperwork."

BURNHAM VAN SERVICE IN 1980

The company had been run by members of the Burnham family since its founding. After Mr. Crowley became chief executive officer, B. LeRoy Burnham and Otis B. Burnham (both sons of the founder) continued to serve with Crowley on an executive committee which made most of the firm's policy decisions. In October 1980, Burnham had some 500 employees, of whom approximately 60 percent were based in the 15 branch locations. These branches served as regional sales and distribution centers, and as geographic focal points for controlling traffic.

Crowley was concerned that maintaining the company's fast expansion pace might tax the abilities of each of the operating units on which it was dependent. He was confident that Burnham's traffic operations group could handle this growth, but was unsure about its network of agents, truck operators, and branches. Since each of these would play an important role in the company's marketing strategy for the 1980s, he monitored their progress closely.

Traffic Operations Department

All requests for service passed through Traffic Operations, heart of the company's service-delivery system, which was managed by John Riddle, director of traffic. Customers could call the company directly, or they could call one of its agents or branches, but in either case the move was managed by this central group. Riddle noted,

Our most difficult task has been to balance the demands of our customers and agents with the supply of available drivers and vans. Competent professional truck operators are in short supply during the industry's peak season, and this puts great pressure on my staff. Booking requests jump from an average of 75 per day in the winter season to almost 200 per day during the summer. Although we contract for extra drivers and trucks, 80 percent of which come from our agents, our fleet was not sufficient last summer to handle all the business we were offered. I had to refuse almost five million pounds of shipments, and I'm certain that another five million pounds weren't offered to us because shippers knew that we couldn't handle the load.

Agents put great pressure on Traffic Operations to accept every load they were offered, particularly during the summer season. Many agents relied on a successful summer to carry them for the rest of the year. Owner/operators were vocal in their demands for balanced loads, long runs, and an occasional trip near their homes. Said Riddle,

We try to be fair with each agent and account. Much of the business we turned down last summer was military transfers offered by agents located near army bases, but that was because we receive a disproportionate amount of requests from that sector during the summer. In general, we allocate our resources fairly across the entire customer base.

Riddle's group usually accepted a load from an agent or branch if it weighed 1,500 lbs. or more and could be picked up at a time suitable to Burnham and the shipper. Department objectives were to pick up an average of 80 percent of shipments direct (without using an agent's truck and having to store goods in transit), and to deliver 90 percent of shipments on schedule. An agent received $1.50 per hundred pounds to make a pick-up and store a shipment. Traffic Operations would not move a truck until it had a minimum 85 percent of capacity, unless it was forced to deadhead a unit back from a delivery location. The deadhead budget for 1980 was $75,000.

Although Traffic Operations was hard

pressed to satisfy all demands placed upon it, Burnham's performance statistics were among the industry's best, particularly in relation to on-time shipments. Crowley gave Traffic Operations much of the credit and felt it had played an important role in the company's turnaround.

Agents

The moving industry had become increasingly dominated by the six largest van lines, which, according to Crowley, put some constraints on Burnham's ability to attract agents.

> Theoretically, because we are the number eight van line in terms of size, we should have the number eight agent in any given location. This isn't always true, of course, since we have been able to maintain some very good agents in many cities. But it does account for some of the agency firms we are forced to do business with.

The quality of each agent and its relation to Burnham were critical to the success or failure of the company in any given location. "You are your agent" was a general industry maxim, and each van line strove to develop the best network of quality agents. It was not unusual for larger van lines to lure agents away from the smaller lines since they could offer greater shipment volume, more storage in transit,[2] and other comparable incentives. A large agent typically had a force of three to five salespeople and might spend up to $50,000 a year on local advertising, including direct mail. By contrast, small agents might have no representation and limit publicity to a listing in the Yellow Pages.

Burnham management could cite situations from the company's past where it had worked to develop an agent in a particular location who, just as business began to grow, left to join another van line—usually taking their local business with them. In 1979, Burnham lost 21 agents and gained 43 new ones. During the first nine months of 1980, losses totaled 22

and gains 42. In some instances, Burnham was able to replace a small agent by a larger booking/hauling agent.

In October 1980, Burnham had agreements with 195 agents: 96 Class I, 48 Class II, 9 Class III, and 42 Class IV. These agents varied in gross sales revenue from $50,000 to $3 million per year. There was no pattern among them with respect to financial and operating characteristics. Expenses varied widely depending upon the functions the agency performed (booking new moves, hauling long and/or short distances, storage, etc.). Some of the better agents produced profits in excess of 10 percent before taxes, while others operated at breakeven or even lost money. A number of agents had ICC authorization to work only in a single city, while others moved intrastate, and still others shipped to a number of states on their interstate authority. The company was also represented by 70 service contractors, together employing 82 service reps. However, Burnham had no agency representation at all in 16 states, mostly in the north central area of the country; shipments into and out of those states were consequently low (Exhibit 4). Two regional managers were assigned to coordinate the efforts of current agents and to acquire new ones.

Burnham's relationship with its agents was a mutually cooperative one. The company employed a detailed reporting system which monitored their performance. All drivers were required to call in daily to report their status and receive routing information. Large-volume booking agents were telephoned by Burnham on a regular schedule to record orders and discuss operations. Smaller agents called Burnham on its WATS line as they booked business.

In turn, the company provided a number of services for its agents. Bulletins were issued weekly summarizing ICC directives and changes. Each agent was sent a weekly commission statement showing all debits and credits to its account. Specific communications arrangements were established for accident and claim reporting and handling. Burnham also published statements showing shipments and revenue received on a monthly and yearly basis. Another service the company offered its agents and truck operators was maintenance of many of the registrations and permits needed to operate in their highly legalized environment. The company also held frequent seminars designed to help agents improve the various aspects of their operations. Every 18 months company executives met with all of their agents to discuss general business conditions and operating problems.

Burnham had previously tried to set revenue goals for each of its agents, but had met with little success. The company set minimum standards regarding operating and financial performance, cleanliness, maintenance, and so forth. However, agents did not always comply with them, and management had no way to enforce these standards short of terminating an agent.

Truck Operators

At Burnham, approximately 90 percent of the drivers handling interstate shipments were independent owner/operators. The company competed vigorously with the other national van lines for competent professional operators, recruiting only experienced contractors. The great majority of Burnham's owner/operators owned and drove one truck. About 5 percent owned two or more, and hired their own drivers to haul loads for Burnham.

Most new drivers entering the trucking business began as assistant operators, gained experience, and then purchased their own trucks using their savings from prior employment. A few van lines loaned money for this purpose; Burnham did not. Purchasing a truck was comparable to purchasing a home, with new owners required to put down 10 to 20 percent of the purchase price.

In fall 1980, Burnham had 100 tractors and 100 smaller trucks, plus some 400 vans and 10 flatbed trailers. The company expected to pay roughly $45,000 for a new tractor, including such options as air conditioning, power steering, AM–FM radio, a power window on the passenger side, and air-ride seats.

These vehicles, known as "fleet trucks," were approximately ten feet high with engine sizes ranging from 270 to 330 horsepower. Fuel consumption varied, but most fleet trucks averaged 4.5 miles per gallon, depending upon terrain and weather.

Independent owner/operators were often known to spend a great deal more for tractors—as much as $70,000 in some instances. They took great pride in their vehicles and dressed them with many additional features, including customized paint and chrome, oversize engines, musical horns, extra lights, and other options. Industry experts felt that such vehicles were often overpowered and overspecified for the jobs they performed.

Burnham operators usually drove ten and a half months per year, ten hours per working day. They were paid on a weekly basis, receiving 53 percent of the total revenue obtained from a move, plus extra money for related services such as loading and unloading (Exhibit 3). In 1979, the typical operator drove 63,000 miles per year, spent $48,000 on vehicle operating costs, and made a net annual income of $21,000.

The average van could carry 20 rooms of furniture (22,000 pounds) and generate almost $9,000 in revenue for a move from New York to California. Thus, it was important to an independent truck operator to be affiliated with a van line which could provide full furniture loads for most trips. Trucks traveling empty (deadheading) were paid 30¢ per mile by the van line for any distance over 100 miles. This rate covered only fuel costs. Drivers unable to obtain furniture loads on their return trip from a delivery destination would try to haul whatever was available, including unregulated goods such as sealed perishables. However, this was not a very profitable business since agricultural products were generally shipped in units of 60,000 pounds, and the rate structure was not lucrative.

The bigger van lines attempted to lure away Burnham's best operators by promising them more full loads and a larger number of trips near their homes. Burnham tried hard to develop loyalty among its operators to protect itself against this. It was flexible in its scheduling and attempted to satisfy drivers' route requests whenever possible. In 1980, Burnham had 280 drivers. It had added 120 drivers that year and lost 70.

Branches

Mr. Crowley's strategy was to establish company branches in areas which offered substantial amounts of special products business (as opposed to household goods) that could potentially be used as a base to guarantee immediate revenue. The number of branches had increased from 8 in 1978 to 15 by the fall of 1980.[3] Burnham tried not to locate them in cities where the firm already had agents. Mr. Herndon's responsibilities included coordinating the selling activities of a total of 16 sales managers and sales consultants within all these branches. Overhead and operating costs at the average "special products" branch ranged from $85,000 to $100,000 per month, about 80 percent of sales. Most of this money was spent on rent, salaries, and operation of smaller trucks used for deliveries in the local area. In 1980, branch managers received a salary of $30,000 to $35,000 with bonuses ranging from 10 to 20 percent of the base pay. In some instances, the branch manager doubled as a sales manager, but in other instances this task was assigned to a separate individual. Each branch spent approximately $700 per month for display advertising in the Yellow Pages (in addition to a listing there).

The company had not been particularly successful in developing branches catering to household goods business. Burnham could have used these in cities where it had trouble contracting with good agents; it was caught in the dilemma of being unable to lure an agent with a large incoming volume, yet having to turn away business because it did not have an agent in that city. However, the expense of maintaining a branch in a new area, coupled with the intense competition from local agents every time it entered a city in this manner, had been somewhat discouraging. Other national organizations faced a similar problem.

According to Herndon, finding and retaining good people to manage the branches was one of Burnham's most difficult problems. Individuals with the sales and operating skills needed to run a successful unit appeared to be scarce. For example, a manager was required to supervise the daily movement of products through each branch, including those shipments which arrived in the late evening and early morning. The branch manager was also responsible for selling the firm's services to a wide variety of customers—from sophisticated business executives to nervous homeowners—and monitoring expenses and revenues on a daily basis. Said Herndon, "Most of those whom we hire terminate with us and seek less demanding employment elsewhere."

PRINCIPAL MARKET SEGMENTS

For marketing purposes, Herndon segmented Burnham's customer base into three types of accounts, divided according to who paid for the move: COD accounts, government (or military) accounts, and national accounts. Industrywide, these represented 41, 12, and 47 percent, respectively, of all linehaul traffic in household goods. Exhibit 5 shows changes in the composition by market of the household goods business carried by Burnham and six other major van lines between 1975 and 1979. Exhibit 6 summarizes Burnham's operating experience in each of the three markets in 1979, including the division of bookings between agents and Burnham branches' head office.

The COD Market

Consisting mainly of private individuals moving household goods at their own expense, this market was called "Cash on Delivery" (COD) because the ICC required shippers to submit cash or a certified check to a moving firm before their goods were unloaded at the new location.

This was a very seasonal business which found most van lines capacity-constrained during the summer season (May 15 to September 15) and suffering from overcapacity during the rest of the year. Contributing to this pressure was the fact that more household goods moves originated in the northeast and traveled west or south than came from the other direction. Burnham's state-by-state analysis of its inbound and outbound shipments in 1978 (Exhibit 4) demonstrated the extent of the problem, and was typical of the general industry imbalance.

This market was large but growing relatively slowly. It was dominated by the six major carriers, which advertised on a seasonal basis in consumer-oriented media and enjoyed broad visibility through the widespread presence of their trucks. Success required a strong local agency or branch selling effort focused on discovering new customers and convincing them of a moving company's ability to satisfy their requirements. A large network of agents and/or branches was desirable to meet the needs of customers moving to widely scattered locations. A moving company's operations department had to be flexible to handle the busy peak season effectively and then adjust capacity to ride out the slower months.

Once a potential COD mover was identified, personal selling was required to book the move. A timely, accurate estimate of the moving expense, a packet of information preparing the customer for what to do and expect, a mutually agreeable delivery schedule, and constant reassurance were all necessary to complete the sale. Competition came not only from other carriers but also from "drive-it-yourself" truck and trailer rental firms, such as U-Haul and Ryder, whose one-way rental services appealed to those on tight budgets or with a limited amount of personal possessions to ship. Most moving companies believed that interstate COD moves were traumatic events for the individuals involved. Consequently, it was easy to disappoint a COD mover even if the company fulfilled all basic tasks as agreed.

Consumers had complained in the past about delays and other service shortcomings during the summer season. In 1978, the ICC had issued regulations requiring van lines to give each type of account—COD, military, and national—equal treatment and service on all business accepted. Some observers believed that past advertising practices had increased consumers' expectations of service quality beyond most carriers' ability to deliver.

Burnham left major responsibility for marketing to COD accounts with its local agencies and branches. The company supported them with a variety of brochures, booklets and promotional materials. Exhibit 7 shows an example of one of the brochures. The basic marketing tool was an advertisement in the local Yellow Pages directory; the firm believed that most people used this as their initial source of information. Some Burnham agents supplemented this with mail campaigns, newspaper advertising, and other promotional efforts. Creative agents developed selective marketing plans directed toward specific moving accounts, such as graduating business school students at local universities.

Although some of Burnham's better agents were very active, most of the firm's agents were not sophisticated marketers and many of their sales representatives had a difficult time selling the company's relatively unknown name. Consequently, agents suffered a high turnover rate among their salespeople, and relied on limited local advertising to solicit business.

The Government Market

This market consisted of moving the household goods of transferred military personnel. It was seasonally oriented, although to a lesser degree than the COD market. A van line needed a network of agents and/or branches at important military locations to compete effectively.

The military had an elaborate "Carrier Evaluation and Reporting System" (CERS) to determine which van lines received business. Grades were given to carriers for every part of each move, and penalty points assessed for failure to meet standards. A minimum number of points were needed to remain qualified to obtain business, but excellent performance against a number of operational criteria was no guarantee of additional shipments, since price was the ultimate determinant. Poorly performing van lines could rise to the top of an evaluation list simply by cutting their rates. Some van lines catered to this business, offering discounts of as much as 30 percent from the normal military fees. They tended to be smaller regional carriers, a number of which had gone bankrupt trying to implement this strategy.

Burnham let responsibility for marketing to the military lie with its local agencies and branches, but they did very little to promote themselves. Agents near bases solicited business, and Burnham carried such loads to keep its vans filled. Some of the company's managers would have preferred not to handle military goods, because of the low rates at which they traveled. The military was still attractive, however, because of its very large volume; it represented almost 50 percent of Burnham agents' bookings.

The National Account Market

National accounts were composed of companies, institutions, and other organizations that used van lines on a regular basis and were extended credit. Many had established relationships with more than one line. The market was divided into household goods and special products.

Household goods involved moving the possessions of individuals who had been transferred by their employers. This business was somewhat seasonal with peak demand occurring in the summer; but demand did not fluctuate as widely as in the COD segment.

Personnel and/or traffic managers at a prospective customer evaluated a van line's entire system before deciding whether or not to place business with it. They looked at operating ratios (see Exhibit 2), ICC performance indicators, agency and branch locations, the types of equipment owned, and a firm's ability to put together corporate moving packages. A moving company's task was to convince the prospect that it had the ability to serve as the carrier between two given locations, that it had

competent people at both ends, and that it would handle every detail to the employee's satisfaction. Since customers frequently moved people between points other than their headquarters city, Burnham executives felt that most accounts preferred to deal with the van line's national staff rather than with the agent in the HQ city. All six major van lines had a corporate sales group and regional sales managers.

Competition was aggressive, since each large account could provide a substantial amount of business, especially when it was relocating its headquarters or a major office. Moving companies strove to differentiate themselves by offering a variety of special services. Many helped companies design moving policies, either by showing what other firms did or—as in Burnham's case—asking specific questions so that it might customize a policy for each account. Some prepared informative film strips or slides to explain their capabilities and wrote booklets describing destination cities in great detail. A few firms held periodic national forums to bring corporate traffic managers together to discuss changes in the industry.

Herndon, who was responsible for advertising, sales, and customer relations, worked primarily on developing national account household goods business at Burnham. His department included Donald Oakley, director of sales, and a secretary; its budget in 1980 amounted to some $325,000 including travel and lodging expenses, salaries, fringe benefits, advertising, and sales aids. Advertising and public relations expenditures accounted for $80,000 of this total, with $8,000 being allocated for the Yellow Pages listings nationwide, $54,000 for direct mail and novelty items, and $18,000 for local PR in the Columbus market.

Herndon and Oakley segmented the market for employee transfers very broadly. They believed that personal selling was the best way to obtain business, and would solicit any corporation with the potential for 100 or more transfers per year; Herndon felt that this was the minimum level needed to justify the expense of a personal sales visit. Over 20% of Herndon's time and almost all of Oakley's was spent in traveling to potential and existing accounts making presentations or maintaining relationships. Hiring of new account executives was under consideration. The total cost in each instance, including salary, benefits, overheads, and travel amounted to approximately $70,000 per year.

Herndon had developed three mailing lists of current and prospective accounts. First was a list of 250 major accounts with which Burnham did $10,000 or more business per year. He or Oakley each tried to visit half of these on a regular basis. Another 400 accounts, identified as having recognizable potential but which had not placed significant business with the firm, were also targeted for potential visits. In addition, 200 future accounts had been identified as having good potential, but thus far Herndon's department had lacked the resources to visit them. The companies on each of these three lists represented a broad cross section of American business, with no industry or group of companies predominating.

Because the number of potential accounts was so large and Burnham's resources were limited, Herndon focused on obtaining "mass moves" (office relocations) and *Fortune 100–* company employee transfer business in those areas where Burnham's agents were particularly strong. Some of the better agents helped Herndon in this effort by establishing and maintaining relationships with national account offices located near them. They were quite helpful with moves into or out of their service areas, but could provide little help with a move between two distant locations.

Herndon sometimes turned down requests for moves to certain locations if he was not confident in his company's ability to obtain return loads. This occasionally created difficulty with customers, although most firms understood Burnham's constraints.

Special products referred to the shipment of goods on the part of the manufacturer or marketer. In an attempt to break out of the seasonal cycle of household goods moving, LeRoy Burnham—the founder's son—had begun cultivating certain special products business when he traveled for the firm. He was among the first to recognize the unique needs

and growth potential of the computer and copy machine industries.

Ray Crowley continued this emphasis on computer and electronics shipments when he took over. In particular, he catered to IBM's needs. Borrowing a method developed by United Parcel Service (and later used by Federal Express), Burnham established four "hubs" in a constantly flowing network of trucks to and from IBM's factories and customers. Truckloads of weekly shipments flowed from the plants into certain Burnham branches where they were sorted, grouped by geographic destination, and loaded in outbound trucks.

This operation guaranteed the movement of fully loaded vehicles, enabling IBM to ship complete systems—although components might have been manufactured in separate factories—and providing for continuous, scheduled service. The system worked well because most new computer sales replaced existing equipment; so instead of unprofitable empty backhauls, Burnham trucks carried used units on the return to the hubs, where they were loaded onto trucks headed back to IBM plants or warehouses. As this business grew, Crowley began to build company branches near his customer's manufacturing locations, facilitating equipment handling at that end (by October 1980 there were six branches near IBM plants). In 1979, the IBM account represented some 22 percent of Burnham's total revenues.

Frequently, special products shipments demanded special equipment and handling, regularly scheduled runs, or some other feature. Yet, customers were very cautious about placing such business, because the carrier's performance could substantially affect the shipper's relations with its own customers.

Burnham had found this market to be well suited to its capabilities because customers appreciated the firm's operating statistics, performance history, reputation, and distribution system. Herndon had been exploring the possibility of handling other products to complement the firm's successful electronics business; earlier he had obtained ICC permission to carry new furniture from factories to dealers, golf carts from manufacturers to golf courses, and equipment for rock groups across the country to their performance locations. Deregulation opened up a number of new possibilities, although he wasn't quite sure where to concentrate.

The company's existing operating strategy encouraged him to search for those loads which encompassed the following characteristics:

- *Heavy material*, to maximize the amount of weight that would fit in the firm's limited capacity, specially designed furniture vans;
- *Loaded at one location*, to run full trucks as much as possible;
- Having a *single unloading point*, for the same reason;
- *Handled in bulk*, to reduce loading and unloading time; and to take advantage of the firm's other material handling equipment.

Herndon was also interested in developing business that would fit the existing route structure. The company had an imbalance of household goods shipments to California and Florida, and many trucks returned empty or with a low-profit load. He tried to find accounts with shipments moving east and/or north, especially during the peak season, to alleviate this problem.

Burnham's personal selling efforts to national accounts were accompanied by a limited amount of advertising and public relations. Herndon used direct mail to contact those accounts which had not been visited in the recent past, as well as those which he was particularly interested in cultivating. He retained a marketing consulting firm to design promotional brochures, to write occasional press releases describing awards received by the company and other successes, and also to publish a company newspaper.

Traditionally, Burnham had done no national advertising, but in 1980 it began a small campaign in *Transport Topics*, an industry periodical. A half-page advertisement (Exhibit 8) was being run six times between January and December 1980 at a total cost of $6,000. It was designed primarily to attract agents interested in switching national affiliations, but there had been very little response to these advertisements thus far.

FUTURE DIRECTIONS

Although Burnham was profitable and growing rapidly, management was concerned about where to focus the firm's marketing efforts. Some executives could see good reasons for targeting all household goods business—COD, military and national account—as well as catering to special products opportunities. They felt that Burnham should not limit itself to one or more particular market areas, and should continue trying to outperform its larger competitors. One executive confessed,

> The question of geographic expansion bothers me. We have to try to get all the business we can in each new area in order to lure a good agent or cover the overhead of a branch. We can't expect both to grow geographically and limit ourselves to specific markets.

Other managers felt that specialization had its advantages, particularly if Burnham were able to cultivate markets which appreciated the firm's service orientation and capabilities. Argued one of them:

> Instead of specializing in any one market, perhaps we should specialize *within* each of them—with an "ultra-care" service for the movement of expensive furniture and equipment, for example. Or maybe we should cater only to executives and others willing to pay a premium for special attention.

Crowley believed that the advent of deregulation brought new urgency to the planning process for Burnham, stating,

> Deregulation has become a reality, and this will open up a lot of previously closed markets. Each moving company—be it an agent or national organization—has great flexibility in terms of what it will carry and how much it will charge. Some of our bigger competitors will be aggressively pursuing every possible op-

portunity, similar to Braniff's strategy after the airlines were deregulated. Others will focus their efforts on moves between certain areas or involving certain types of loads.

We have to preempt these efforts by being willing to change the game. This means upgrading our network of agents and truck operators and strongly considering new operating schemes. Where we focus, how we operate, and how we market will be our major concerns for quite some time.

NOTES

1. Vans were the large enclosed trailers in which goods were transported; some shipments traveled in containers on flatbed trailers. Both types of trailers could be detached from the power vehicle (tractor) which hauled them.

2. Storage-in-transit referred to shipments held in an agent's warehouse awaiting pick-up by a moving company or delivery acceptance by a customer.

3. In addition to the Columbus facility, there were Burnham branches in Austin and Houston,* Texas; Cheverly* and Laurel, Maryland; Buffalo, Poughkeepsie,* and Vestal, New York; Charlotte and Raleigh, North Carolina; Atlanta, Georgia; Boca Raton,* Florida; Cincinnati, Ohio; San Jose,* California; and Tucson, Arizona. (Branches marked with an asterisk were located close to plants operated by IBM, a major customer.)

EXHIBIT 1

Financial Highlights 1974–1979

	1974	1975	1976	1977	1978	1979
Revenues	$23,086[a]	$21,451	$22,441	$26,604	$31,475	$38,474
Profit (loss) before tax	(289)	298	742	1,260	1,560	3,619
Net income (loss)	(181)	150	519	674	862	2,090
Total debt	2,482	1,622	634	525	595	
Stockholders' equity	1,006	1,156	1,675	2,261	3,059	5,005
Total debt to stockholders' equity	247%	140%	38%	23%	20%	
Net return on beginning stockholders' equity		15%	45%	40%	38%	68%
Net return on beginning capitalization		7%	19%	29%	29%	54%
Additions to property and equipment	150	200	461	872	1,701	2,607

[a] All figures in thousands of dollars.
SOURCE: Company records

EXHIBIT 2

Ranking of National Motor Carriers by Annual Operating Revenue and Other Statistics

1979 versus 1978

Carrier	1979				1978			
	Revenue ($ millions)	Operating Ratio[a]	Miles Operated (millions)	Tons Transported	Revenue ($ millions)	Operating Ratio[a]	Miles Operated (millions)	Tons Transported
Allied Van Lines	268.5	99.2%	135.6	685,998	228.2	100.5%	126.0	661,069
North American V.L.[b]	220.5	96.3	125.2	503,852	170.0	96.9	108.0	450,993
United Van Lines	199.6	100.6	101.0	497,097	158.1	100.7	93.4	437,483
Aero Mayflower Transit.	169.7	99.0	85.8	402,889	140.0	98.6	86.5	376,095
Bekins Van Lines[c]	109.7	99.6	56.1	252,612	97.3	101.9	52.8	248,373
Atlas Van Lines	102.9	97.9	52.8	273,054	82.7	98.0	49.5	242,369
Global Van Lines	67.2	98.1	34.0	170,196	56.3	97.2	31.8	162,918
Burnham Van Service	34.3	90.3	14.5	85,089	27.0	94.5	14.5	82,748
Wheaton Van Lines	34.2	95.1	16.4	80,606	27.4	94.3	16.1	74,008
Lyon Moving & Storage	30.4	104.7	11.3	72,581	27.6	96.8	12.9	65,494

[a] Operating ratio equals total operating expenses divided by total operating revenue (interest costs, nonoperating income and expenses, and income taxes are excluded for this calculation).

[b] Does not include special products.

[c] Does not include Bekins Moving & Storage of Los Angeles, Dallas, or Seattle.

SOURCE: Household Goods Carriers Bureau

EXHIBIT 3

Typical Division of Revenues for an Investor-Owned Van Line

HOUSEHOLD GOODS	Percent Paid to Booking Entity (Either Agent or National Van Line)	Percent Paid to Hauling Entity (Could Be Agent or National Van Line)[a]	Remaining Percent (Always Paid to National Van Line)
TYPE OF MOVE			
A National Account and COD—500 miles and over and 1,500 pounds and over	20%	65%	15%
B Military—500 miles and over and 1,500 pounds and over	19	65	16
C Under 500 miles	15	70	15
D Under 1,500 pounds	15	70	15
E Quotations requiring a rate reduction:			
0%–10% rate reduction	15	69	16
11%–15% rate reduction	12½	71½	16
16%–20% rate reduction	10	74	16
21%–25% rate reduction	7½	76½	16
Over 25% rate reduction	5	79	16
SPECIAL PRODUCTS			
A 18,000 pounds and over, or exclusive use of van	20%	57%	23%
B Under 18,000 pounds	15	61	23
AGENTS BOOK AND HAUL			
Agents both booking and hauling a shipment under 1,500 pounds and moving less than 500 miles	90%		10%

PACKING FEE

	Percent Paid to Packing Entity (Either Agent or Branch)	Percent Retained by National Van Line
A National Account and COD	90%	10%
B Military	80	20

UNPACKING FEE

	Percent Paid to Unpacking Entity (Either Agent or Branch)	Percent Retained by National Van Line
A National Account and COD	90%	10%
B Military	15	8

OTHER SERVICES[b]

PICK UP AND DELIVERY SERVICES FOR NATIONAL VAN LINE[c]

A Pick up
1. Household Goods—$1.50/100 pounds
2. Special Products—5% of hauling commission

B Delivery
1. Household Goods—$1.50/100 pounds
2. Special Products—10% of hauling commission

[a] This percentage was paid to the *organization* which hauled a move. Independent truck operators were usually paid 53% of the total revenue, which meant that the hauling organization they contracted with retained from 4% to 26%.

[b] Fees for these services were charged separately from the moving fee itself and were split according to this schedule.

[c] These amounts were paid to an agent by the national van line, if it required one of these services to be performed.

EXHIBIT 4

Burnham Van Service, Inc., Shipment Origins and Destinations by State

(1978)

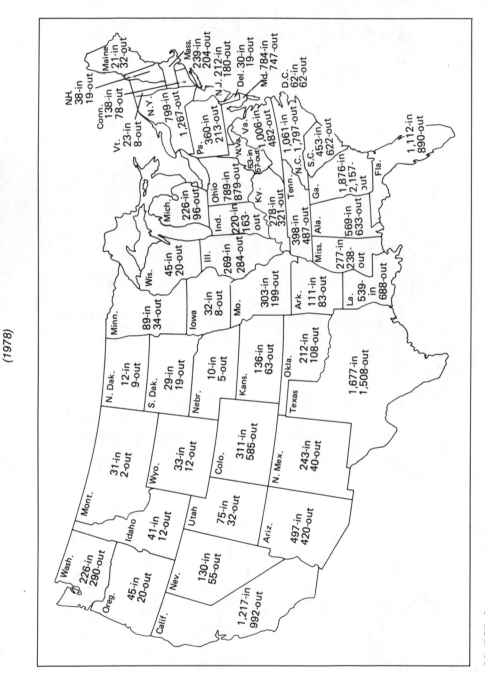

EXHIBIT 5

Distribution of Dollar Value of Household Goods Business by Market Category for Burnham and Six Major Carriers
1975–1979

MARKET	YEAR	BURNHAM	ALLIED	NORTH AMERICAN	UNITED	MAYFLOWER	BEKINS	ATLAS
NATIONAL ACCOUNT[a]	1975	32%	46%	38%	45%	31%	33%	44%
	1976	38	48	41	45	35	35	48
	1977	34	47	40	45	44	35	48
	1978	28	48	35	48	39	34	52
	1979	30	49	40	46	35	40	53
COD	1975	18	45	51	39	59	55	32
	1976	22	44	50	41	58	58	33
	1977	23	46	50	42	47	57	33
	1978	23	47	52	42	55	58	34
	1979	22	45	53	42	55	52	34
GOVERNMENT (DEPT. OF DEFENSE)	1975	50	9	11	16	10	12	24
	1976	40	7	11	15	8	7	19
	1977	43	7	10	13	9	8	19
	1978	49	5	13	10	7	8	14
	1979	48	7	7	12	10	9	13

[a] Excludes special products business.
SOURCE: Company records (derived from industry data)

EXHIBIT 6

Long-Haul[a] Revenue Status Report Summary of 1979 Performance[b]

	AVERAGE DISTANCE TRAVELED (MILES)	AVERAGE WEIGHT OF SHIPMENT (POUNDS)	AVERAGE GROSS REVENUE PER SHIPMENT	GROSS REVENUES	PERCENTAGE BOOKED BY AGENTS	PERCENTAGE BOOKED BY BURNHAM (INCLUDES BRANCHES)
Household Goods						
COD	1,050	4,411	$1,045	$2,463,822	85.4%	14.6%
Government	1,171	4,985	1,179	5,346,950	76.2	23.8
National Account	876	7,852	1,854	3,285,624	54.8	45.2
Other						
Container Shipments[c]				1,146,884	2.2	97.8
Other Carriers[d]				941,974	0	100.0
Special Products	678	4,439	752	12,355,873	10.3	89.7
Total Long-Haul Traffic				$25,541,127	39.7%	60.3%

[a] Long-haul indicates that the shipments traveled under Burnham operating authority from one city to another. This does not include shipments handled exclusively by one of Burnham's agents.

[b] Burnham's total revenue for 1979 was $38,474,000. The $12.9 million not accounted for in this exhibit was received for accessorial services performed by Burnham branches (packing, storage, etc.), shipments by branch trucks within their city of operation, international shipments, fees from the rental of unused headquarters office space, etc.

[c] A small percentage of household goods were shipped in containers on flat-bed trucks instead of in vans. This concept had never become popular in the industry because of the difficulty of keeping track of the containers.

[d] Occasionally Burnham would carry loads for other moving companies which their own trucks could not handle.

SOURCE: Company records

EXHIBIT 7   Extract from Consumer Brochure

We have the equipment, the people and the experience to handle your move right!

QUALITY PERSONAL SERVICE IS A HALLMARK AT BURNHAM VAN SERVICE!

WE ARE PLEASED TO OFFER YOU:

- **A pre-moving Survey-**
  A trained Burnham representative will come to your home and go over in detail all that is necessary to get ready to move. During this pre-move survey, the Burnham man will help you decide which items you will want to move, what you might pack yourself and offer other helpful moving tips.

- **"Moving Made Easy" Packet-**
  The Burnham representative can provide a handy packet containing checklists, moving tips, Change of Address labels for the post office and subscriptions, and many other valuable ideas on how and what to do to make your move as painless as possible.

- **We Do It All-**
  At Burnham, we start and we complete your move. No dealing with two different moving

services. Burnham has a nationwide network of agents and branch offices that offer complete personalized service to the entire continental United States and all the countries throughout the free world.

- **The Most Modern Equipment Including Air-Ride Vans-**
  The Burnham "Commitment to Excellence" extends to every phase of your move. We have the latest, most modern equipment to insure that your furnishings will be handled with the extra care you expect from Burnham Van Service.

- **You're Always in Touch-**
  Our toll free Customer Service Telephone number can tell you where your belongings are at anytime during the move. This service helps relieve the anxiety of a move because you always know that the answer to any question you might have is just a toll-free call away.

In 50 years we've moved 3 million American families. Please call us and let us add yours to the growing list of satisfied Burnham friends.

EXHIBIT 8

Corporate Advertising, 1980

In just 60 seconds, I can show you why...

Burnham Van Service, Inc. is the moving company that's on the move.

It all begins with service. We and our agents are committed to giving every customer the very best service regardless of the size or destination of the shipment. We call this program "Commitment to Excellence." Because of it, Burnham has had the best customer satisfaction ratio of any of America's nationwide movers for three years in a row.

This top-flight service is the primary reason that our domestic volume increases have led the industry. In 1979, our domestic volume increased over 30%. And this was a balanced volume of National Account, COD Household Goods and Special Products.

Sound management of this growing volume resulted in the industry's best operating ratio.

This consistent superior earnings performance has enabled us to invest millions of dollars in new equipment while at the same time, reducing our outstanding debt.

We have also dramatically improved our national coverage. This was accomplished by opening new branches and licensing strong agents in key cities. As a part of this continuing process, we have a few openings for selected, strong agents to help us complete this program.

Our fleet of independent contractors has also shown substantial growth. These independent businessmen appreciate a carrier who helps them reach their earnings potential with a sound compensation program built on a solid, balanced traffic mix.

There are many other things I could cite, but sixty seconds is about up. So, let me summarize by saying, "Commitment to Excellence" in all we do is the reason . . .

We're the moving company that's on the move.

1-800-241-8274

Ray Crowley
President
Burnham Van Service, Inc.

BURNHAM VAN SERVICE, INC.
ICC NO. MC 682

— READINGS —

Look to Consumers to Increase Productivity

CHRISTOPHER H. LOVELOCK

ROBERT F. YOUNG

In many services, attempts to improve productivity are likely to fail unless the support of consumers can be secured. This is particularly

Christopher H. Lovelock is associate professor of business administration at the Harvard Business School, and Robert F. Young is associate professor of marketing at Northeastern University. Reprinted by permission of the *Harvard Business Review.* "Look to Consumers to Increase Productivity" by Christopher Lovelock, and Robert F. Young (May/June 1979). Copyright © 1979 by the President and Fellows of Harvard College; all rights reserved.

true when management is trying to change the ways in which consumers interact with the organization. This article suggests several marketing strategies that service managers might employ to change consumer expectations and behavior and to encourage them to become a more integral part of the service delivery process.

Most people agree that low productivity is a major contributor to inflation. Lagging productivity gains are particularly a problem for the service sector of the economy, which now accounts for close to two-thirds of the GNP in the United States.[1]

Low productivity afflicts all three categories of service organizations—for profit, public, and nonprofit. In private companies, managers worry about their ability to maintain profits, yet fear that passing on higher costs in the form of higher prices might draw away consumers. Many public agencies find themselves with rising deficits at a time when taxpayers are angrily demanding tax cuts; yet a strategy of service cutbacks could have serious consequences for the welfare of disadvantaged citizens and the quality of life in general. Some nonprofit organizations that have relied unrealistically on increased donations or higher user charges have been hit particularly hard, some even to the point of collapse.

People usually think that improving productivity is a task for the R&D department, for the finance committee, or for operations and personnel management. Economists tell us that the three ways to increase productivity are (1) to improve the quality of the labor force, (2) to invest in more efficient capital equipment, and (3) to automate tasks previously undertaken by labor.

In this article, we are going to argue that there is a fourth component to improving productivity in service industries—that is, to change the ways consumers interact with service producers. This is a task that marketing—the art of demand management—can tackle best. Service managers can use marketing tools to encourage consumers to modify their behavior so that services can be delivered in a more productive and economically efficient manner. Our primary focus will be on what Richard B.

Chase has termed "high contact" service systems, where there is a high level of interaction between service producers and their customers.[2]

One can divide services into two broad categories: those that do something for consumers themselves—such as transporting them to distant locations, cutting their hair, and healing their bodies; and those that do something for consumers' possessions—such as transporting their mail, cutting their grass, and repairing their cars. The former, of course, involve a higher level of personal contact than the latter, but consumer behavior is important in both instances, and we will consider both here. Understanding consumer behavior is the first step in determining how to change it.

IMPACT OF CONSUMER ON SERVICES

Why is consumer behavior a particularly critical factor for productivity gains in the service sector of the economy? Three basic reasons come to mind.

First, service industries typically involve the consumer in the production process. A haircut requires you to sit in the barber's chair; a stay at a hotel requires that you check in and enter your room in person; to mail a letter requires that you address, stamp, and deposit it. If you fail to complete your bank withdrawal slip correctly and argue with the teller, then you will slow down the service and delay other customers as well.

Second, service industries are typically labor-intensive, with the service being part and parcel of the overall "product" being purchased. Sometimes, though, consumers can do some of the work themselves, replacing all or part of that previously done by the service employee. Consumers now serve themselves at buffets in restaurants and dial long-distance telephone calls directly instead of going through the operator.

Third, a service industry's product tends to be time-bound: It cannot be stockpiled. Thus the opportunity to sell an empty seat on the 9:00 p.m. flight to Boston is lost once the aircraft takes off. Conversely, theatergoers turned away by "house full" signs cannot be relied on to wait for the next available show. Because of the time-bound nature of service, managers place a heavy emphasis on capacity utilization. The productivity goal is to smooth the peaks and valleys of demand to avoid both excess demand (which cannot be satisfied) and excess capacity (which represents unproductive use of resources).[3]

In services where there is a great deal of personal contact, managers can increase productivity by changing procedures at point of delivery. But these changes, such as replacing a bank teller or a waiter with machines, directly affect consumers, and their acceptance of the change cannot be assumed.

Sometimes, as Chase points out, the "technical core" or "back room operations" of a service can be separated from the personal service aspect. In recent years, many of the productivity gains made by service organizations have been achieved within the technical core. Computers now handle accounting procedures and hotel/airline reservation systems; larger, faster, and more efficient aircraft fly more passengers; and partially automated mail-handling procedures speed up postal services.

But changes in the technical core may still affect consumers, requiring them to accept changes in bank statement formats, include ZIP codes when addressing mail, or accustom themselves to computer-generated reservation confirmations for seats on new kinds of aircraft. While many of these innovations offer benefits to customers—such as greater accuracy, faster service, more comfortable flights—service managers cannot take consumers' acceptance of change for granted.

FIVE CAUTIONARY TALES

In our experience, attempts to improve productivity in service industries all too often demonstrate a lack of sensitivity to consumer needs and concerns. Consider the following situations:

• In the early 1970s, the Universal Product Code made its appearance. By 1978, it appeared on some 170 billion packages. Yet it is estimated that only 2 billion of those packages actually passed through scanners. Less than 1% of U.S. supermarkets have installed registers that can read the code, in part because consumers distrust them.

• Between 1967 and 1974, the British Post Office introduced sophisticated alphanumeric postal codes. These identify mailing addresses down to a specific city block or even to a single dwelling. But a majority of Great Britain's consumers are still not bothering to include these "postcodes" when addressing their mail.

• Though many banks have installed automatic tellers, some of their customers are refusing to use them. As a "once bitten" consumer reports: "Well, I tried that machine just once, and it ate my card. The card came back in the mail, but I didn't bother using it again."

• In an effort to reduce crowding on its trains during the rush hour, Boston's transit system introduced "Dime Time," which offered a 60% discount on travel between 10:00 a.m. and 2:00 p.m. But because most consumers must travel during rush hours, Dime Time had only a modest impact on travel patterns and was finally abandoned as too costly.

• Despite the fact that self-service gas stations are quicker and cheaper, many people express a dislike for them. "I'm not going to slosh around in gas to save a penny" was a typical response to a recent research study.

The common thread linking these attempts by five major service industries to improve productivity is that consumers resisted the change, and the anticipated gains have yet to be fully achieved. In most instances, management has scaled down its expectations and has even abandoned some specific efforts for the time being. Let us look briefly at each situation in turn, and then consider what can be learned from them.

Universal Product Code

When they first introduced the concept in the early 1970s, marketers of the Universal Product Code had high hopes. They expected it to reduce labor costs, eliminate errors, and provide better information for retail management. In 1973, the UPC symbols began appearing on thousands of mass-merchandized consumer items. Why has so little progress been made in the past five years? Equipment costs are one reason; union resistance a second, and consumer opposition a third.

Some supermarket executives now concede that they did a poor job of preparing the public for the scanners. "Consumer groups raked us over the coals," admitted a senior executive of Giant Stores, "because we didn't bring them into the decision-making process two or three years earlier."[4]

Consumers' concerns centered around the fact that items would no longer be price marked (a potential source of labor costs savings for food stores). Consumer organizations expressed fears that, if items were not individually marked, surreptitious price hikes would result. In response to lobbying, six states—including California and New York—have passed laws forcing stores to retain item pricing.

Nevertheless, recent experience in those stores that have UPC scanners suggests that consumer reception for the new technology has been generally positive. Customers have accepted the clear price labeling on the shelves as a substitute for item marking (where it is not mandated by law), and like the faster checkout and itemized receipts.

The future of the UPC is now beginning to look a little brighter. Equipment costs have recently been cut and union opposition has eased. But any retailer who hopes to take advantage of this innovation will have to respond to consumers' concerns and make sure that they understand the new checkout procedures as well as the benefits of the system.

Postal Codes

Several years ago, Great Britain completed introduction of a sophisticated postcode designed to improve productivity through major advances in automated mail handling. In most developed countries postal codes, like the U.S. ZIP code, are limited to the "outward sort" at the origin sorting office. From there mail is directed to a specific destination sorting office where the "inward sort" into letter carriers' routes is done manually. By contrast, the British codes allow for a mechanized inward sort as well, which breaks down the incoming letters according to particular buildings or groups of houses on a mail-delivery route.

Conceptually, the system is brilliant, and the assignment of the codes represents a triumph of operations research. But consider the nature of the codes themselves. A typical British code looks like this: PL20 6EG; the first half of the code represents the outward sort and the second, the inward sort.

Now we come to the marketing problem. There are 1.5 million postcodes in Britain. People find it hard to remember the alphanumeric combinations; and since there are 114 postcode directories nation-wide, there is no ready means of finding out a complete code for a specific address unless one is responding to an incoming letter that already includes it as part of the return address. Moreover, delays in implementation of the program have left people skeptical about its value. While many Britons, not surprisingly, resist using these postcodes, U.S. citizens now almost universally use the simpler ZIP code.

Of course, the United Kingdom has experienced other setbacks associated with mail mechanization, including machine problems and union resistance; yet the fact remains that the Post Office can never achieve full productivity savings until mail users cooperate by including postcodes when addressing letters. And the needed cooperation will be that much harder to obtain because the original design was poor from a user's perspective and also because consumers perceive a lack of commitment to this program by the Post Office.

But perhaps a lesson has been learned. Since the mid-1970s, the British Post Office has adopted a much stronger marketing orientation, which accounts for some of its success in running all major facets of the service—including mail—in the black for the past three years.

Recently, the U.S. Postal Service announced its intention to add another four numerals to each ZIP code to facilitate inbound sorting. The numerals avoid the complications imposed by alphanumeric combinations, but consumers will still have to remember nine-digit codes. How the Postal Service markets the enlarged ZIP codes will be an important determinant of the extent to which consumers will use them.

Automatic Bank Tellers

The American Productivity Center has singled out banking as a particularly poor productivity performer. One strategy for improving this situation is to replace human tellers with machines for routine transactions.

In 1967, 24-hour cash dispensing machines were first installed in British banks; by 1969, the innovation had spread to the United States. In the early 1970s, a few banks began to experiment with automatic teller machines (ATMs) capable of performing the same range of transactions as a human teller.

A growing number of banks are now using ATMs, but with varying degrees of success. Some consumers resist the machines because they represent a new and strange approach to banking, others because the machines cannot replace the human contact tellers provide. The greatest success in introducing ATMs is en-joyed by banks that invest time and effort to develop carefully thought-out introductory programs. Typically, these programs emphasize deployment of specially trained staff to help customers learn how to use the machines and assist them if they have any problems.

In addition to personal selling, another important factor in consumer acceptance has proved to be the design of the machines. Some ATMs swallow the customer's magnetically coded card at the beginning of the transaction, returning it when all is completed. If a customer punches in the wrong personal identification code more than a predefined number of times (typically three), then the machine retains the card as a security measure. Sometimes, ATMs malfunction and refuse to return valid cards, which is very disconcerting to consumers, especially ones who are new to the ATM concept and possibly apprehensive about it. ATMs are also often out of order, leaving people with no access to their accounts. Both these problems make people distrustful of machines and reluctant to use them.

Significantly, some of the newer (and most successful) ATM installations are equipped with a telephone, staffed 24 hours per day, with which a customer can call for assistance in case of difficulties. One kind of machine does not swallow the cards, valid or not, so that it is impossible for a customer to lose one. Finally, some banks install clusters of two or three machines in a single location, so that even if one is down, there is a good chance that the others will still operate.

Each of these strategies reflects an understanding of consumers needs and concerns, the acquisition of which may have taken intensive consumer research by the marketers.

Transit Services

Travel demands during the rush hours determine the number of vehicles and personnel a public transportation system should have, but outside peak periods productivity is low. During nonpeak periods, equipment either lies idle or runs half empty, and many employees have time on their hands. If travel demands could be distributed evenly throughout the day, less staff and fewer vehicles would be needed to transport the same total number of passengers.

The Massachusetts Bay Transportation Authority experimented recently with a program called Dime Time. Between 10:00 a.m. and 2:00 p.m., the normal 25-cent fare on the rapid transit lines serving Boston was reduced to 10 cents. Although the MBTA attracted some new riders, it eventually discontinued the experiment because only a small percentage of rush-hour commuters switched to off-peak hours.

Why was the MBTA's strategy unsuccessful? Two explanations suggest themselves. First, people are not likely to change their behavior because of a financial incentive that amounts to only a 15-cent savings (albeit a 60% one) on the cost of the journey. Second, most people who travel at rush hours are traveling to and from work and have relatively little control over their working hours. So even if they had wanted to save money by traveling during Dime Time, their work schedules would not have permitted it.

The MBTA has not given up its efforts to improve productivity by smoothing out the peaks and valleys of travel demand. In the summer of 1978, armed with a better understanding of consumer behavior, it cosponsored a major conference, focusing on the benefits of staggered and flexible working hours and how to implement them, for Boston-area employers. As a result, a number of state agencies and private companies are moving to change their traditional working hours.

Self-Service Gasoline Stations

The main benefit to retailers of self-service gasoline stations is obvious. Because only a single attendant (a cashier) serves the station, labor costs are sharply reduced. And, because there is an obvious spread of self-service stations in the United States (consumers now pump about one-third of all gasoline marketed to the public), one might wonder why we include this service in our list of underachievers.

Success is relative. One might turn the sit-uation around and ask, why is twice as much gas still pumped by attendants as by consumers? Restrictive ordinances by local communities are one reason, but there is evidence that many consumers who have the choice resist the self-service option. Some perceive pumping gas as dangerous, dirty, and unduly complex; as simply a tiresome hassle. As the remark cited in the "cautionary tale" about self-service gas stations suggests, the price differential per gallon must provide a sufficient incentive to make the perceived difficulties worth enduring. If retailers want to change consumer behavior, which makes the savings possible, they must be willing to pass on some of these savings.

Also, successful gasoline retailers have found that good equipment and station design, proper weather protection, clear instructions, and a clearly visible cashier all help to reduce the anxieties consumers feel and thus to encourage self-service usage. But not all self-service stations meet these criteria.

AVOID INSENSITIVITY TO CONSUMERS

What can one learn from these five examples? It is clear that consumer resistance to changes in familiar environments and long-established behavior patterns can thwart attempts to improve productivity in service organizations. And all too often, management's failure to look at productivity-related changes from the customer's standpoint actually causes the resistance. Managers of service operations can, and should, avoid such insensitivity toward their customers. Seven possible steps suggest themselves:

1. Develop customer trust. It is harder to introduce productivity-related changes when people are basically distrustful of the initiator, as they often are in the case of large, seemingly impersonal service organizations. One group of shoppers even picketed a supermarket that had introduced scanners with signs reading "The Giants Are Out to Get Ya!" Service managers need to recognize the importance of maintaining the customers' goodwill, since their willingness to accept change may depend on it. Creating an atmosphere of mutual trust and respect requires a long-term strategy, not a superficial, short-term program that is switched on and off like an electric light.

If an organization does not have a strong positive relationship with its customers, the latter may be able to block productivity improvements that benefit nearly everyone by keeping down costs. For instance, in an effort to decrease unnecessary use of a costly and labor-intensive service, some U.S. telephone companies have been successful in introducing charges for information calls. (Typically, the plan allows customers three free calls per month, with continued free service for the handicapped and for customers calling from pay phones, hotels, motels, hospitals, and nursing homes.) However, other telephone companies with poor customer relations have found these moves blocked by regulatory agencies.

2. Understand customers' habits. In introducing the UPC, most retailers seem to have ignored the typical shopper's habit of examining price markings on packages and then watching the cashier punch in the prices on the cash register. Retailers made little effort to prepare consumers for the change and how it would affect them, let alone to explain the rationale for this innovation or promote its benefits.

3. Pretest new procedures and equipment. Before bringing out a new product, especially one representing a substantial investment, most manufacturers engage in careful testing of alternative product designs to determine probable consumer response. These efforts may include concept and laboratory testing, using representative samples of consumers, and/or field testing in one or more sites. Service organizations should do the same.

The British experience with postal codes is an example of overlooking the consumer at the product design stage. The Post Office did not test alternative post code designs with customers under actual (as opposed to laboratory) conditions, resulting in the selection of a needlessly complicated design.

When replacing service personnel by automatic equipment, it is particularly important for an organization to develop machines that consumers find easy to use. Some self-service equipment looks as if it has been designed by engineers, for engineers.

For instance, both automatic tellers and multiple-value ticket-issuing machines will be used by a very wide range of customers, of different ages and educational backgrounds, and of different physical characteristics—including height, eyesight, and manual dexterity. Even the phrasing of the instructions for use needs careful thought. Ambiguous, complex, or authoritarian phrasing may discourage customers with limited command of the language or poor reading skills, as well as people used to personal courtesies from the service personnel whom the machine replaces.

4. Understand the determinants of consumer behavior. Why do consumers behave as they do? Is it by choice, force of habit, or does some external factor control their behavior? Service managers who are thinking of smoothing out fluctuations in demand from one time of day, week, month, or year to another should first evaluate the reasons that demand for their service is so uneven. The timing of demand could be constrained by third parties, and these—rather than consumers—might be the logical targets for marketing efforts.

5. Teach consumers how to use service innovations. Simply installing self-service machines and providing printed instructions may not suffice to win over many customers, especially those resistant to change. Experience with ATMs shows that service personnel who can demonstrate the equipment and answer questions, providing reassurance as well as educational assistance, are a key element in successful introduction of new procedures and technology. Adding and training staff do increase installation costs, but managers can offset these by spreading the costs over a period of months in a multiple-outlet operation and by moving staff from one site to another as the innovation spreads to new locations.

6. Promote the benefits and stimulate trial. Introduction of ATMs and self-service gasoline pumps requires consumers to perform part of the task themselves. Although this additional "work" typically yields such benefits as extended service hours, time savings, and (in the case of gasoline) monetary savings, these benefits are not necessarily obvious— they have to be promoted. Part of the problem with consumer resistance to UPC scanning was that, in most instances, management never clarified the benefits to customers of faster checkouts and itemized receipts.

The critical, challenging phase in winning consumer acceptance of service innovations, especially those based on new technology, is the introduction period. Unless the benefits of the new approach are clearly obvious, many consumers prefer to stick to the tried and true. A marketing orientation can help here. Useful strategies may include use of mass media, on-site, and personal communications that inform people of the innovation and arouse their interest in it. Promotional incentives and price discounts may also serve to stimulate initial trial. Some banks have given away free ice cream or other gifts to customers who participate in a demonstration of how to use an ATM.

7. Monitor and evaluate performance. Introducing productivity improvements is not a static process but a dynamic one which occurs over time. For instance, a service manager at a bank might ask: Is ATM usage increasing, or are customers returning to use of the human tellers? Is the ratio of ATM to human teller usage the same for all branches? If not, why not? What distinguishes high ATM-usage branches from low-usage ones?

The same types of questions could be asked of any of the services we have discussed. The important thing is for a manager to learn from experience (both good and bad) and take corrective action where needed—whether it in-

volves redesign of facilities and procedures, better communications and educational activities, more dramatic promotional efforts, or more attractive incentives.

ADOPTING A MARKETING PERSPECTIVE

Efforts to improve productivity by "industrializing" personal service, as suggested by Theodore Levitt,[5] or by separating consumers from the technical core, as discussed by Chase,[6] tend to emphasize an operations management view of the world. We hope that, by now, readers are convinced of the need to adopt a marketing perspective as well.

Given the emphasis devoted to productivity in the manufacturing sector of the economy where production is totally separated from consumption, the fact that productivity issues should be dominated by operations specialists is not surprising. In services, however, consumers are involved in the production process. Consequently, they are also an input to production. The thoughtful service manager should ask: How can our customers become more productive inputs to the creation of the services that we produce for them? And what marketing strategies can we use to influence their behavior?

Let us review three strategies for changing customer behavior or expectations to increase productivity:

- Change the timing of customer demand.
- Involve customers more in production.
- Ask customers to use third parties.

Change the Timing of Customer Demand

Customers often find that the services they use are crowded and congested, reflecting seasonal (or time of day, week, or month) fluctuations in consumer demand. In such "crush" conditions, equipment and facilities may be strained, service employees harried and over-

- Do your customers have time on their hands as they wait for service? Is there something *they* could do to speed the service delivery process?

- Are your customers and service personnel meeting face-to-face unnecessarily? Could such contacts be handled instead by mail, phone, or computer terminal?

- Are there significant peaks and valleys in the demand for your service? If so, what is the *root* cause? Can you do anything to change or modify these demand patterns?

- Are your employees doing mechanical, repetitive work that could be done by customers themselves or by customer-operated machines?

- Are your customers trying to bypass service personnel and doing the work themselves? (One sign of this may be a reluctance to use the services of personnel who traditionally expect to be tipped.)

- Are customers asking your personnel for information that is readily available elsewhere (e.g., in a directory)? If so, why is this?

- Are your customers being subjected to needlessly bureaucratic forms and requests for personal data? Are such data necessary to your operations? Could they be gathered and recorded through alternative means?

- Is the efficiency of your operations being impaired by a minority of customers who appear ill-informed about the nature of your service and how to use it? If so, is there perhaps something wrong with your information dissemination efforts?

- Do customers show a high level of interest in the knowledge about the tasks being performed by your service personnel? Perhaps they would like to do some of these tasks themselves?

- Is there any reason, other than tradition, why you should provide certain personal-service "extras"? Which would do most for your competitive position—to continue offering these extras or to eliminate them and share the savings with your customers?

- Could you efficiently delegate all or part of your service functions—especially information, reservations, and payment—to third-party organizations already used by your customers (e.g., travel agencies, banks, supermarkets)?

---

worked, and customers disappointed by a deterioration in service (if indeed they receive any at all).

A straight "operations" solution to meet existing consumer needs and maintain service standards might be to add capacity by employing additional staff and expanding facilities. It is not always feasible, however, to add capacity during peak periods *only*. Letting extensive excess capacity lie idle outside the peak time reduces overall productivity and results in great expense to the organization.

An alternative approach is to develop marketing strategies to manage the timing of demand. Here the goal is to get customers to consume services at different times. But first the question must be asked: What determines consumer schedules?

In situations where consumers control the timing of their demand for services, the marketing problem is to encourage consumers themselves to change. This may be achieved by marketing strategies involving the service itself, pricing, communications, or the format and place of service delivery.

For instance, a perennial problem for the U.S. Postal Service has been the inefficiencies created by the enormous flow of mail at Christmas time. Despite hiring extra personnel and renting additional vehicles (at considerable expense), the collection, sort, and delivery system is often unable to cope with the volume. The inefficiencies and bottlenecks this crush causes can lead to reduced productivity. Yet, by simple procrastination, the general public causes much of the problem.

Through extensive advertising and promotional efforts, the Postal Service has convinced many people that it is beneficial for them and their addressees to "mail early." Notable among the goals of the Bureau of Planning and Marketing was "to structure services and products and the things that we do to meet the needs of our customers, and, on the other hand, *to induce customers to do the things that accrue to our mutual benefit*" [our italics].[7] As a result of this campaign, the U.S. Postal Service has achieved substantial savings.

Theater, restaurant, and airline managers among others have found that a reservation system smooths out consumer demand. And experience shows that consumers are willing to plan their other activities to fit the reservation time.

But to be successful, the reservation system must be capable, first, of taking and confirming reservations and, second, of delivering the desired product at the time and place promised. Also, prospective consumers have to know about the availability of reservations and how to make them, be willing and able to make them for the service in question, and then show up at the agreed time and place. Marketing communications can play an obvious role in helping consumers adopt the desired behavior.

Involve Customers More in Production

One often hears complaints to the effect that "there's no personal service any more." True, some individuals like to be waited on at every opportunity and have both the leisure time and the money that receiving such service may require. But this is not true for everybody. Many people prefer an active role to a passive one, particularly when taking it offers the potential for time and cost savings. If customers assume a more active role in the service production and delivery process, they effectively remove some of the labor tasks from the service organization. There may be benefits for both consumers and service organizations.

Following the installation of long-distance dialing throughout the country, AT&T possessed the technology to increase productivity substantially. Yet in 1970, almost half of all long-distance calls were still being placed with the operator and usage was increasing at the rate of 2% yearly. So in 1971, AT&T launched a major marketing program to change the way its subscribers placed their long-distance calls. In addition to introducing substantial price discounts for direct calls, the company also initiated a $9 million advertising campaign to encourage callers to dial direct. The ads said, "We have two reasons for urging you to dial long-distance calls direct. You save and we save too."

From 1970 to 1972, usage went up 14%. By the end of 1973, after about three years of marketing effort, directly dialed calls represented almost 75% of all long-distance calls. AT&T estimated that its marketing campaign for long-distance dialing resulted in productivity savings of about $37 million per year.

Hotels and restaurants, which traditionally have had a high labor component and relatively low productivity, provide other examples of making consumers do more of the work. In recent years, many restaurants have introduced self-service buffets or salad bars where patrons fill their own plates instead of being waited on. This reduction in personal service has, however, been promoted as a beneficial innovation that lets patrons select what they want of attractively displayed foods, in the quantities they desire, and without delay. While the customer receives an interesting new dining experience at a reasonable cost, the restaurant management has reduced its labor cost associated with preparing and serving individual portions of salad or other dishes.

A number of modestly priced hotels no longer offer morning coffee as part of their room service. Instead, rooms are equipped with an electric water heater, packets of tea, coffee, creamer, and sugar, and guests are encouraged to make their own. These facilities are typically promoted as a complimentary offering "for your convenience and enjoyment," as if one were getting some of the comforts of home free of charge. Consequently, staff time is freed up for more substantive tasks, and the hotel restaurant is less likely to be crowded at a busy time of day with guests wanting only a cup of coffee.

In many instances, management has shifted tasks from the service organization to the consumer in response to rising costs or shortage of properly trained staff. Customers often respond enthusiastically to changes of this nature. If asked, they might also generate some surprising insights about how to further replace personal service with customer-initiated actions, and we urge service managers to solicit their opinions.

Sometimes, of course, changing consumer behavior requires changing consumer expectations. Not many years ago customers assumed that, except in institutional cafeterias, a busboy or waitress would take away the dirty plates. Now at McDonald's and similar restaurants it is accepted behavior for people to clear off their own tables. The productivity implications are obvious. Making this change required the introduction of disposable plates and cutlery (another helpful innovation). Marketing communications were needed to facilitate such behavior changes, by explaining the rationale (reduced costs), promising a benefit (keeping prices down), and asking for customers' cooperation.

But implementing a reduction in personal service should not be approached lightly. In order to make the new procedures simple and as foolproof as possible, managers need a good understanding of consumer needs and characteristics. And they have to explain the new procedures carefully to consumers, highlighting the rationale and advantages from the latter's perspective. Even so, it may still be necessary to have personal service on call for customers who need or prefer it.

Ask Customers to Use Third Parties

We have already mentioned the need to enlist support of third parties, such as employers, in changing travel behavior by staggering working hours. In some instances managers can improve service productivity by delegating one or more marketing support functions to third parties. From the consumer's standpoint, the purchase process for services often breaks down into four components: information, reservation, payment, and consumption.

This division of activities has particular significance for distribution policy. The consumption of the service may occur in a single, possibly inconvenient location (e.g., an airport or train station, a theater, a stadium, or a dis-

tant city). However, the reservation and payment transactions can occur at numerous conveniently located outlets of retailers that act as ticket agents for a range of services.

Mail-order, telephone information, and reservations service are additional conveniences one can offer. From a service delivery standpoint, these may smooth the work flow, especially in situations where nonurgent requests for information can be recorded and responded to later. Computerized reservation systems are particularly useful; they give each retail outlet rapid access to a central file and, sometimes, provide terminals that print out tickets or reservations on the spot—another plus for customers.

Because of the economies of scale, such retail distribution agencies may be able to provide better ancillary services to consumers at lower cost than the client organization can. Also, important secondary services have sometimes been developed around agencies that handle reservations and sales for producers of the primary service. For instance, travel agencies represent an important service in their own right, offering the consumer a degree of expertise in certain areas that often exceeds that of the airlines, railroads, and hotels that they represent.

Although the demand for these secondary services is a derived one, such agencies may play a key role in stimulating primary demand for the basic service by creating and promoting "packages" of complementary services. Development of innovative, appealing packages may help to stimulate demand in off-peak periods when excess capacity exists, and thus contribute significantly to productivity improvements for the client services.

CONCLUDING THOUGHT

In their search for operating efficiency, there is a risk that managers of service organizations may come to see consumers as a nuisance, a constraint, and even as a barrier to productivity. The reductio ad absurdum of a mindset that stresses operating efficiency at the expense of the consumer is pungently illustrated in this newspaper report from the Midlands of England:

"Complaints from passengers wishing to use the Bagnall to Greenfields bus service that 'the drivers were speeding past queues of people with a smile and a wave of the hand' have been met by a statement pointing out that 'it is impossible for the drivers to keep their timetable if they have to stop for passengers.' "[8]

NOTES

1. *Authors' note:* This article grew out of our involvement in an ongoing research project on the marketing of consumer services that is being conducted at the Marketing Science Institute. A preliminary report on this project is *Marketing Consumer Services: New Insights* (MSI: December 1977).

2. Richard B. Chase, "Where Does the Customer Fit in a Service Operation?" *HBR*, November–December 1978, p. 137.

3. See W. Earl Sasser, "Match Supply and Demand in Service Industries," *HBR*, November–December 1976, p. 133.

4. Roger B. May, "As Costs Fall and Incentives Rise, Supermarkets Begin to Install Computer Checkouts on Counters," *Wall Street Journal*, June 13, 1978.

5. Theodore Levitt, "The Industrialization of Service," *HBR*, September–October 1976, p. 63.

6. Chase, "Where Does the Customer Fit in a Service Operation?"

7. Cited in T. V. Greer and J. G. Malcolm, "The U.S. Postal Service: A New Marketer?" *MSU Business Topics*, Winter 1973, p. 49.

8. Patrick Ryan, "Get Rid of the People and the System Runs Fine," *Smithsonian*, September 1977, p. 140; reproduced in C. H. Lovelock and C. B. Weinberg, *Readings in Public and Nonprofit Marketing* (Palo Alto, California: The Scientific Press, 1978).

The Employee as Customer

LEONARD L. BERRY

The same marketing tools used to attract customers can also serve to attract and retain the best employees, who can be thought of as "internal customers," that is, those within the service organization. Marketing research, segmentation strategies, and communication efforts should be directed toward employees and intermediaries, as well as toward external customers in order to get the former group to deliver the best possible performance and to increase their productivity.

There is a tendency to assume that the quality of personnel performance in retail banking will become a less important issue as electronic funds transfer (EFT) becomes more pervasive. In fact, nothing could be further from the truth. As more and more consumers use automatic teller machines, in-store check verification systems, telephone bill payment, and other EFT alternatives, the provision of personalized, competent, helpful service in the retail bank will become crucial. There are several reasons why this is so.

Leonard L. Berry is professor of marketing at Texas A & M University. Reprinted with permission from the *Journal of Retail Banking* (Vol. 3, No. 1). © 1981 by The Consumer Bankers Association. All rights reserved.

First, electronic banking by definition means fewer face-to-face encounters between the bank and many of its customers. Accordingly, when the bank does have the customer face-to-face, or on the telephone, it is important to handle the situation well. In short, in an EFT era there will be fewer opportunities to cross-sell, or build an image of personal service, and hence the "costs" of not capitalizing on the opportunities that do present themselves are greater.

Second, EFT is a homogenizing force in what is already a relatively homogeneous industry. With similar service, rates, advertisements, buildings, and even names, competing banks are frequently indistinct from the consumer's perspective. Electronic funds transfer—especially when systems are shared among several institutions—creates even more sameness. In such a homogeneous environment, one of the principal opportunities for a bank to distinguish itself, to be different and better than its competitors, lies in the quality of its people. The rise of EFT makes richer the opportunity for a bank to position itself as one that has good people, not just good machines.

One theme of this paper is that the eighties in retail banking will be the decade of the employee. Most of the key challenges facing retail banking touch the employee: competition, the need to sell, productivity, unionization, affirmative action, inflation, and, as noted, electronic banking. Moreover, changing social and economic conditions are producing a tougher, more demanding, harder-to-please consumer who will have to be served by an employee whose wants are broadening and escalating as well. In the eighties, America's best-managed retail banks will be run by executives who understand that it is difficult to have a strong service business when the service is lousy.

A second theme of this paper is that the philosophy and tools of marketing can be of genuine value to bankers as they address the human resource management challenge. Thinking like a marketer doesn't have to stop at the boundary of the external marketplace. The people who buy goods and services in the role of consumer, and the people who buy jobs in the role of employee, are the same people.

And the exchange that takes place between employees and employers is no less real than the exchange that takes place between consumers and companies. Whereas consumers exchange economic resources for goods and services, employees exchange human resources for jobs that provide, among other things, economic resources. Just as consumers can choose Honda automobiles over Ford automobiles, so can employees choose to work for an airline rather than a bank, or for one bank instead of another.

What bank executives think of when they think of marketing—consumer surveys, new service introductions, premium campaigns—is really external marketing. In the eighties, America's best-managed retail banks will also devote considerable attention to internal marketing.

INTERNAL MARKETING

There are several forms of internal marketing. What they all share in common is that the "customer" is inside the organization. In this article our interest is in employees as customers. We can think of internal marketing as *viewing employees as internal customers, viewing jobs as internal products, and then endeavoring to offer internal products that satisfy the needs and wants of these internal customers while addressing the objectives of the organization.*[1]

The rationale for internal marketing is straightforward. Banks are service businesses, which means they sell performances. Despite the evolution of EFT, these performances are still in large measure provided by people. For reasons already noted, the quality level at which these people perform is becoming increasingly important. Internal marketing can help a bank attract and retain the best possible employees and get the best possible work from them. Stated differently, by satisfying the needs and wants of its internal customers, a bank upgrades its capability for satisfying the needs and wants of its external customers.

The application of marketing research,

market segmentation, and advertising to internal markets illustrates the potential of thinking like a marketer when the task at hand is managing people.

MARKETING RESEARCH

Marketing research can be used to identify employee needs, wants, and attitudes just as it can be used to identify consumer needs, wants, and attitudes. Regularly surveying personnel concerning perceptions of supervision quality, working conditions, compensation and benefits, company policies, and other job-related matters provides several important benefits.

First, management receives direct feedback concerning the degree of satisfaction internal customers have with the internal product for which they are exchanging resources. Such feedback helps isolate components of different jobs that need to be improved. Second, personnel surveying provides a means for identifying policy violations or other organizational breakdowns. For instance, a question asking employees if they believe bank rules and regulations are enforced fairly and consistently and a follow-up question requesting an explanation if the answer is "no" will frequently identify policy violations. Because managers know this type of surveying is regularly conducted, the survey itself discourages policy violations.

The Marriott Corporation provides an example of a firm that systematically researches its employees. At Marriott, trained personnel representatives visit each hotel property and conduct a meeting of all employees. At the meeting, the survey is explained and candid participation by everyone is urged. Employees do not sign the questionnaires that require "yes" or "no" responses to a series of questions, e.g., "I get paid for all the hours I work," "I have been properly trained to do my job," "Our work load is reasonable." In addition, employees may add anonymous comments about each statement in subsequent interviews with personnel representatives. The survey responses are compiled and several weeks later a second employee meeting is held to discuss the results and to solicit additional comments. Later, still another meeting takes place to announce any actions that will occur in response to the survey.[2]

"Deep Sensing"

In addition to survey research, bank management may find helpful a process sometimes referred to as "deep sensing." Deep sensing concerns efforts by senior management to find out face-to-face what is on the minds of small groups of employees and to address concerns raised. The format for sensing meetings can vary widely from company to company. Some involve meals (for example, lunch) while others are held in conference rooms. Some firms select attendees randomly while others use specific criteria such as length of service or job classification. A typical meeting would involve 10 to 15 employees and one or several representatives from senior management. Among the companies that have used deep sensing are Minnesota Power and Light, Lockheed, TRW, General Electric, GEICO, and Kaiser Aluminum.[3]

Whether it is by deep sensing or other methods, it is useful for a bank's senior management to reach out beyond the inner circle of executives with whom they have regular contact and communicate with people from all levels of the organization. Doing so allows management to acquire information they might not otherwise acquire (even with formal surveying), address problems at an early stage, better assure that the bank's mission, objectives, strategies, and policies are understood, and demonstrate by deeds that what employees think matters.

Regardless of whether the focus of marketing is external or internal, its central purpose remains the same: the attraction and retention of patronage through the satisfaction of needs and wants. Satisfying the needs and wants of employees requires that management first understand what these needs and wants entail. The tools of the marketing researcher—questionnaires, personal interviews, group discussions—provide a means for understanding employee needs and wants.

MARKET SEGMENTATION

Marketers segment external markets because people in the same market can be quite heterogeneous. In the time-keeping market, for example, some consumers prefer very accurate watches, others inexpensive watches, others watches with multiple functions, and so forth. In the apparel market, some consumers willingly pay more for designer jeans, others insist on traditional national brands like Levis, others are content with store brands, and some refuse to wear jeans of any type. Such heterogeneity is just as real for internal markets. People are just as different when they are in the employee role as when they are in the consumer role.

Internal employee markets can and should be segmented. Indeed, it is the accommodation of individual differences that is behind such personnel concepts as "flexible work hours" and "cafeteria benefits." These concepts reflect internal market segmentation in action.

Flexible Work Hours

Flexible work hours (or flexitime for short) provide employees with greater freedom in selecting work hours than is customary in the eight-to-five type of workday. Although still working the expected number of total hours, employees on flexitime may vary starting and finishing times within certain prescribed boundaries. Typical flexitime systems involve "core time" (when all employees must be present) and "flexible time" (when work schedules are discretionary). Core time generally corresponds with peak work load patterns.

In Germany, where flexitime got its start, a quarter of the workforce was on flexitime by 1977. In the U.S., it has been estimated that about 6 percent of the nonprofessional labor force was on flexitime in 1977.[4] Among the

banks that have used flexitime are First National Bank in Seattle, First National Bank of Boston, The First Bank in New Haven, State Street Bank, and The First National Bank of Maryland.

Flexitime benefits both employees and employers. Benefits frequently reported for employers include increased job satisfaction, increased productivity, the elimination of punctuality as an issue, less personal business conducted on company time, less absenteeism, reduced personnel turnover, additional recruiting leverage, and lower unit labor costs. Half or more of all user companies experience economic gains; few experience net losses.[5]

Among the benefits frequently reported for employees on flexitime are increased job satisfaction, shorter commuting times, more time for leisure, personal business, and family activities, and added cross-training opportunity. Perhaps the outstanding characteristic of flexitime is that it shifts some control over working time to the employee and the job gains in dignity. In reporting on the experience at First National Bank of Maryland, Cottrell and Walker wrote.[6]

> One other major benefit from the system was the creation of a more adult atmosphere. No longer did employees have to ask for time off for doctor or dentist appointments. Missed rides, traffic jams, or late babysitters no longer brought the pressure and frustration as they had with the traditional nine-to-five schedule. Without question, employees responded in a positive manner when given some control over their lives.

The vast majority of employees who participate in flexitime programs prefer them to standard work schedules. Following State Street Bank's initial trial experiment with flexitime, participating employees voted 119 to 3 for its continuance.[7] At First National Bank of Maryland, a survey indicated that 90 percent of the employees and 100 percent of the supervisors wished to continue with flexible working hours.[8] Well over 90 percent of all organizations that have started flexitime programs have continued them.[9]

Flexitime is not a panacea and may prove

unworkable for certain types of banking jobs. Nevertheless, as a means for more precisely tailoring jobs to the people holding them (for example, working mothers or "morning persons"), flexitime is a potent concept that can be expected to grow in America throughout the eighties.

Cafeteria Benefits

Another segmentation-type response to the reality that people at work are heterogeneous is "cafeteria" fringe benefit programs. Under these programs, employers provide minimum coverage in life and health insurance, vacation days, and pensions. Employees then select additional benefits to suit their own circumstances and preferences, using credits based on salary, service, and age.[10] The net effect is that, within certain boundaries, employees put together their own package of benefits rather than employers doing it for them.

The appeal of a cafeteria benefits approach stems from research indicating that what is a valued benefit to one employee is not necessarily a valued benefit to another. Factors such as age, marital status, and family size influence which benefits are preferred.[11] Married women in particular find uniform benefit plans biased against them because of the duplication of certain benefits the husband receives, such as health insurance.[12]

Among the organizations that have adopted a cafeteria benefits approach are the American Can Company, TRW, and Educational Testing Service. During the seventies, unresolved tax liability issues and high administrative costs inhibited widespread adoption of such programs. Recent tax legislation defining guidelines under which cafeteria plans may be offered, and adopter experiences showing that administrative costs drop significantly once a program is established, should contribute to a growth pattern for cafeteria programs during the eighties.[13] The most compelling stimulus to growth, however, is that the advantages of a benefits system that accommodates individual differences are too important to ignore. As researcher Daniel Yankelovich writes:[14]

Increasingly, we will need a cafeteria concept of incentives, tailoring the incentive package to each individual. Throughout our history . . . American individualism stopped at the workplace door. Now it's knocking the door down . . . demanding entrance.

In a period of demographic upheaval (more working women, more single adults, an aging population) the time is right for a concept of fringe benefits that embraces the heterogeneity of the labor force rather than denies it. As Drucker states: 'The choice as to which benefits are the right ones for this or that individual is . . . best made by the individual alone."[15]

ADVERTISING

Marketers design advertising programs to influence customer-prospects to behave in desired ways, for example, to buy a product the firm sells. Advertising can also be used to influence employees to behave in desired ways. Many executives fail to realize that employees are a possible "second audience" for advertising. They do not consider that advertising designed for the external customer can also be designed for the internal customer.

When well conceived, advertising can have very positive effects on employees. It can involve them, motivate them, educate them; it can shape their perceptions about the company and about their jobs. A recent Delta Airlines print advertisement encompasses employees with the headline: "You never hear a Delta professional say, 'that's not my job.'" Underneath the headline, six Delta employees are pictured in work situations and identified. Smaller copy then reads:

You'll find a Delta Marketing Representative handling calls for reservations when the lines get hot. And a Line Mechanic lending a hand with the baggage to get a flight out on time. And a Passenger Service Agent rushing a wheelchair to the gate when all the Skycaps are busy.

Delta is people helping other people help you. It's family feeling. It's a spirit of service that just won't quit. It's men and women who know their jobs and love their work. And Delta has more than 34,000 of them.

Next trip go with the Delta professionals and have a great flight . . . Delta, the airline run by professionals.

The Delta advertisement, although ostensibly meant for the consumer, is also clearly meant for Delta personnel. This advertisement not only shapes the perceptions and expectations of consumers by promising helpful, professional service, it also defines for employees management's perceptions and expectations of them, i.e., "We think of you as professionals and expect you to perform as professionals."

Indiana National Bank's "person-to-person banking" advertising campaign provides another example of advertising directed internally as well as externally. In this campaign, bank employees were featured in radio and television spots explaining in their own words what person-to-person banking meant. In follow-up research on this campaign, over 90 percent of the bank's contact employees reported paying attention to the advertising. Just under 90 percent felt the promise of personal service in the advertising set a job performance standard for them to follow. Nearly 75 percent said that as a result of the campaign they had become more concerned with pleasing the customer and were more likely to go out of their way for customers.[16]

Sasser and Arbeit write: ". . . the successful service company must first sell the job to employees before it can sell its services to customers."[17] Advertising is an important tool for "selling" jobs in service businesses like banks. In consumption circumstances in which the performance of people is what customers buy, the advertiser should be concerned not only with encouraging customers to buy but with encouraging employees to perform.[18]

CASE HISTORY: INTERNAL MARKETING AT DISNEY WORLD

Achieving and maintaining high quality employee performance is never easy, but it can be done. It is a question of priorities and management attitude. It is no accident that the Dis-

ney Corporation consistently achieves high quality performances from thousands of cheerful, neatly groomed, competent employees at its theme parks. Disney is the classic internal marketer. Here is what they do at Walt Disney World.[19]

Recognizing the entertainment character of its business, Disney uses show business terminology. Instead of Personnel there is Casting. Those "cast members" who interact with the public are "onstage." Other cast members work "backstage." One is not better than the other, an attitude that is emphasized—it takes both types of employees to "put on the show." In addition, all employees in the theme park area have the word "host" in their job titles. There are security hosts rather than policemen, custodial hosts rather than street cleaners, food and beverage hosts rather than soft drink servers. Disney has no customers at its theme parks, only guests.

New cast members, once hired, are provided written information concerning the preparation-for-work stage, e.g., when and where to report, what is expected in terms of personal appearance, the length of each training phase. Everyone from entry-level, part-time employee to a new vice-president must attend Disney University and pass Traditions 1 before receiving more specialized training. Traditions 1 is an all-day experience in which new employees learn the Disney philosophy of doing business, the Company's history, and how the various park division—Operations, Food and Beverage, Entertainment, and so forth—relate to "the show."

The group attending a Traditions 1 session has its picture taken. When the Traditions 1 day is over, each participant is given a copy of the weekly employee newspaper featuring the group photograph on the front page. Called *Eyes and Ears*, the newspaper provides news on employee activities, educational offerings, special benefits, a classified section, and numerous pictures of cast members.

Every Disney employee wears a "first name only" name tag. Disney's policy is everyone uses first names regardless of rank in the organizational hierarchy. Annually each executive-level manager at Disney World participates in a week-long program called "cross-utilization" in which they work in the park selling tickets or popcorn or loading and unloading rides. The cross-utilization program is designed to give management a better insight into the cast member's and guest's perspective.

At the end of the summer season, each nonpermanent employee completes an anonymous questionnaire concerning reactions to hiring practices, the orientation program, the training given, organizational communications, wages, fairness of treatment, etc. There is a private recreation area with a lake and a library for the exclusive use of employees.

In sum, Disney World places a high priority on attracting good people to the jobs it has available, rigorously preparing them to perform these jobs well, and then motivating them to want to do them well. Disney World is at the same time a generous employer and a no-nonsense employer. They are in the people business and they know it. As Norwood Pope writes:[20]

> How Disney looks upon people . . . handles them, communicates with them, rewards them is, in my view, the basic foundation upon which its . . . success stands.

THINKING LIKE A MARKETER

If Disney can insist on and receive quality work from thousands of employees, banks can do the same with hundreds or dozens of employees. Thinking like a marketer can help. Here is a sampling of ideas readers can begin right away to institute in their banks:

• Consider whether the right people are interviewing job applicants at the bank. Are they sufficiently professional? Are they enthusiastic? Do they make a good first impression for the bank?

• Develop a first-rate orientation program for new employees. Involve senior management as presenters and use professionally produced audio-visual aids. Include coverage of the bank's history, philosophy, objectives, and organization. Conduct a tour of the bank's facilities explaining each department's function.

Provide comprehensive take-home information on bank policies and procedures.

• Conduct an employee attitude survey early enough each year so that the results can feed into the annual planning process. Find out what employees like most and least about their jobs. Do something about those aspects of the job they like least.

• Develop career paths for all job levels in the bank, including the teller position. The teller career path could include such steps as teller trainee, associate teller, senior teller, and head teller. This career path could be part of a broader system so that advancement beyond the teller position could occur for employees with the necessary desire, ability, and training.

• Emphasize team-building within the bank. For example, instead of developing a staff sales incentive program pitting individual against individual, develop one that pits branch office against branch office or department against department. Take advantage of the many integrating approaches available, for instance, weekly staff meetings, ad hoc task forces, staff retreats, joint business calls, in-bank training and education seminars, and brainstorming sessions. When there is a significant accomplishment, hold a celebration.

• Publish two annual reports, one for stockholders and the other for employees. The employee report can include a letter from top management, a statement of the bank's philosophy and objectives, a readable overview of the bank's financial performance, and a listing of noteworthy employee accomplishments.

• Provide sales training, sales kits, and personalized business cards to all employees of the bank. Proof operators, secretaries, night shift employees, tellers, guards—everyone in the bank would be asked to participate in the bank's selling effort and would be recognized and rewarded for doing so.

CONCLUSION

Marketing's scope has traditionally been restricted to the exchange that takes place between customers and organizations. Yet marketing is just as applicable to the exchange that occurs between employees and organizations. Employees are simply internal customers rather than external customers. Although executives are not accustomed to thinking of marketing in this way, the reality is that people do buy and quit jobs and therefore it is useful to think of jobs as "products" and attempt to design them to encourage buying and performance and discourage quitting.

Internal marketing is especially important in labor-intensive service industries because in these industries employee performance is the "product" the external customer buys. To the bank customer, a rude or incompetent teller is a rude or incompetent bank.

Competing banks face many homogenizing restrictions concerning the services they offer. In such a homogenizing environment, one of the key opportunities for a bank to distinguish itself rests with the quality of its people; there are no regulatory restrictions on people quality. This paper has been about investing in people quality. Investing in people quality, in a service business, is investing in "product quality."

NOTES

1. This definition and several other passages in the paper are based on material that first appeared in Thomas W. Thompson, Leonard L. Berry, and Phillip H. Davidson, *Banking Tomorrow—Managing Markets Through Planning* (New York: Van Nostrand Reinhold, 1978), Chapter 12.

2. G. M. Hostage, "Quality Control in a Service Business," *Harvard Business Review*, July–August 1975, p. 104.

3. "Deep Sensing: A Pipeline to Employee Morale," *Business Week* (January 29, 1979), pp. 124–128.

4. Stanley D. Nollen, "What Is Happening to Flexitime, Flexitour, Gliding Time, the Variable Day? And Permanent Part-time Employment? And the Four-Day Week?" *Across the Board* (April 1980), p. 9.

5. Nollen, p. 10.

6. Charles A. Cottrell and J. Mark Walker, "Flexible Work Days: Philosophy and Bank Implementation," *The Journal of Retail Banking* (December 1979), p. 80.

7. Warren Magoon and Larry Schnicker, "Flexible Hours at State Street Bank of Boston: A Case Study," *The Personnel Administrator* (October 1977), pp. 34–37.

8. Cottrell and Walker, p. 79.

9. Nollen, p. 10.

10. "Companies Offer Benefits Cafeteria-style," *Business Week* (November 13, 1978), p. 116.

11. Edward E. Lawler III, "New Approaches to Pay: Innovations That Work," *Personnel* (December–October 1976), p. 12.

12. Peter F. Drucker, *Managing in Turbulent Times* (New York: Harper and Row, 1980), p. 123.

13. "Companies Offer Benefits Cafeteria-style," pp. 116 and 121.

14. Daniel Yankelovich, "We Need New Motivational Tools," *Industry Week* (August 6, 1979), p. 65.

15. Drucker, p. 124.

16. Franklin Acito and Jeffrey D. Ford, "How Advertising Affects Employees," *Business Horizons* (February 1980), pp. 58–59.

17. W. Earl Sasser and Stephen P. Arbeit, "Selling Jobs in the Service Sector," *Business Horizons* (June 1976), p. 64.

18. William R. George and Leonard L. Berry, "Guidelines for Advertising Services," *Business Horizons*, in press.

19. This section is based on material appearing in N. W. Pope, "Mickey Mouse Marketing," *American Banker* (July 25, 1979), pp. 4, 14; and "More Mickey Mouse Marketing," *American Banker* (September 12, 1979), pp. 4, 5, 10, 14.

20. Pope, "Mickey Mouse Marketing," p. 4.

V

Managing Demand

Many people tend to associate marketing with strategies for increasing the volume of sales. But in recent years, the advent of resource shortages—particularly those brought about by various energy crises—has generated a broader awareness of marketing's role in dampening as well as stimulating demand.

Imbalances between supply and demand in the manufacturing sector are usually irregular and temporary phenomena, since inventories can generally be employed as a buffer between the two. But this is not necessarily true for services. The problem is worst, of course, for capacity-constrained organizations that face significant variations in demand levels. When demand is low, productive capacity is wasted, since a service business cannot normally store its product as inventory. And when demand is so high that it exceeds the organization's ability to meet it, potential business is likely to be lost.

MANAGING CAPACITY VERSUS MANAGING DEMAND

One solution to the demand problem that falls within the province of operations is to tailor *capacity* to meet variations in demand.[1] Possible actions at peak periods in-clude adding part-time staff and renting extra facilities. Reductions in capacity during periods of low demand may be achieved by laying off staff, scheduling employee vacations, renting out surplus equipment and facilities, or taking them out of service for periodic maintenance and renovation.

Another solution that should logically be entrusted to marketing is tailoring *demand* to match available capacity. (Many service organizations, of course, seek to manage both demand and capacity.) As we shall see, a variety of possible strategies can be employed to increase demand during periods of excess capacity and to reduce demand—known as demarketing—when it exceeds capacity.[2] Economists have long recognized the role of the price mechanism in bringing demand and supply into balance, but marketing communications and modifications to the product and distribution elements of the marketing mix can also help to smooth the peaks and valleys of demand.

Understanding the Patterns and Determinants of Demand

The search for demand management strategies should start with an understanding of what factors govern demand for a specific service at a given point in time. Among the questions to be asked are the following:

279

1. Does the level of demand for the service follow a regular predictable cycle?
   a. If so, is the duration of that cycle
      (1) One day (varies by hour)?
      (2) One week (varies by day)?
      (3) One month (varies by day or by week)?
      (4) One year (varies by month or by season; or reflects annually occurring public holidays)?
      (5) Some other period?
   b. What are the underlying causes of these demand variations?
      (1) Employment schedules?
      (2) Billing and tax payment/refund cycles?
      (3) Wage and salary payment dates?
      (4) School hours and vacations?
      (5) Seasonal changes in climate?
      (6) Occurrence of public holidays and so forth?
2. Are changes in the level of demand largely random in nature?
   a. If so, what are the underlying causes?
      (1) Day-to-day changes in the weather affecting relative use of indoor and outdoor recreational or entertainment services?
      (2) Health events whose occurrence cannot be pinpointed exactly? For example, heart attacks and births affecting the demand for hospital services.
      (3) Calls for assistance resulting from accidents, acts of nature, and certain criminal activities requiring fast response by emergency services?
3. Can demand for a particular service over time be disaggregated by segment to reflect such components as
   a. Use patterns by a particular type of customer?
   b. Use patterns for a particular purpose?

Generally, marketing efforts can do little to smooth out *random* fluctuations in demand over time, since these are usually caused by factors beyond people's control. But detailed market analysis may sometimes reveal that a predictable demand cycle for one segment is concealed within a broader, seemingly random pattern, and can thus be addressed by marketing strategies. Likewise, it may also be found that part of the demand for a particular service is undesirable, for instance, calls to emergency services to rescue cats from trees. These can be discouraged by marketing campaigns or eliminated by screening procedures. Getting rid of undesirable demand in this way won't eliminate random fluctuations in the remaining demand, but it may bring the peaks of that demand within the service capacity of the organization.

When demand for a service fluctuates widely but follows a predictable pattern over a known cycle, it may be economically worthwhile to develop marketing strategies designed to smooth out major fluctuations over time. However, no strategy is likely to succeed unless it is based on an understanding of *why* customers seek to use the service when they do. Consider the following examples:

- It is difficult for most hotels to convince business travelers to remain on Saturday nights since few executives do business over the weekend. (Instead, hotels should consider promoting use of their facilities for other purposes, such as conferences or pleasure travel.)

- Attempts to get commuters on public transportation to shift their travel to off-peak periods will probably fail since the timing of most commute travel is determined by people's employment hours. (Instead, marketing efforts should be directed at employers to persuade them to adopt flexitime or staggered working hours.[3])

- There are limits to the extent to which restaurants can persuade potential patrons to change the times when they eat, since eating habits are strongly conditioned by social convention and are reinforced by employment hours and body rhythms. (Instead, a restaurant might try promoting other product lines such as snacks, bar services, and entertainment.)

STRATEGIES FOR MANAGING DEMAND

At any given point in time, a fixed-capacity service organization may be faced with one of four conditions (see Figure V–1):

- Demand exceeds maximum available capacity, and potential business may be lost.
- Demand exceeds the optimum capacity level; no one is turned away, but all customers are likely to perceive a deterioration in the quality of service delivered.
- Demand and supply are well balanced at the level of optimum capacity.
- Demand is below optimum capacity, productive resources are underutilized, and (in some instances) customers may find the experience disappointing or have doubts about the viability of the service.

Note the distinction between *maximum available* capacity and *optimum* capacity. When demand exceeds maximum capacity, some potential customers may be disappointed because they are turned away, and their business may be lost forever. But when demand is operating between optimum and maximum capacity, there is a risk that all customers being served at that time may receive inferior service and may decide not to return in the future.

The optimum level of capacity is likely to vary from one service business to another and even from one market segment to another. Sometimes optimum and maximum capacities are the same. For instance, at a live performance in a theater or sports arena, a full house is generally regarded as very desirable, since it stimulates the players and creates a sense of excitement and audience

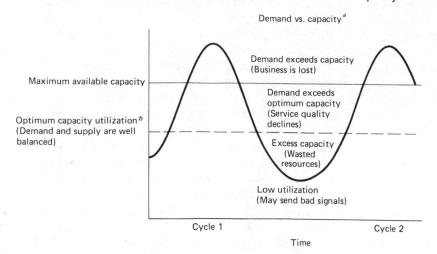

FIGURE V–1

Implications of Cyclical Variations in Demand Relative to Capacity

Demand vs. capacity[a]

Maximum available capacity

Demand exceeds capacity
(Business is lost)

Demand exceeds
optimum capacity
(Service quality
declines)

Optimum capacity utilization[b]
(Demand and supply are well
balanced)

Excess capacity
(Wasted
resources)

Low utilization
(May send bad signals)

Cycle 1   Cycle 2

Time

[a]For simplicity, this diagram assumes no variations over time in the amount of capacity available. In practice, however, some service organizations do seek to manage the level of capacity over the duration of the product-demand cycle.

[b]The optimum capacity is that level of utilization above which the perceived quality of service begins to deteriorate due to crowding. In some services, such as theaters and sports arenas, optimum and maximum capacity may be one and the same.

participation, thereby enhancing the service experience. But in other cases, customers may feel that they get better service if the facility is not operating at full capacity. The quality of restaurant service, for instance, often deteriorates when every table is occupied; passengers traveling alone in aircraft with high density seating usually feel more comfortable if the seat adjacent to them is empty; and delays may result at repair and maintenance shops when their capacity is fully scheduled, due to lack of surplus labor or machine time to cope with unexpected difficulties in completing jobs. So, smoothing demand to the optimal level may be a desirable goal even for service organizations that rarely encounter demand in excess of maximum available capacity.

Moreover, as emphasized in the section entitled "Managing the Customer Mix," making optimal use of capacity requires looking at the *mix* of business obtained as well as at the total volume. Some market segments may be more desirable because the customers in question fit particularly well with the ambiance that the service organization is trying to create, or they are willing to pay higher rates and are thus more profitable. Hence, there is a need for marketing managers to look at the components of overall demand and to stimulate or discourage demand from particular segments on a selective basis.

Five common approaches to managing demand are identified in Table V–1. The first, which usually reflects the absence of any strategy, involves taking no action and leaving demand to find its own levels. This approach has the virtue of simplicity: Eventually customers may learn from experience or word-of-mouth at which times they can expect to stand in line to use the service and when there will be space available. The second and third strategies involve taking active steps to reduce demand in peak periods and to increase it when demand is low, respectively. The fourth and fifth approaches come under the heading of inventorying demand. This can be accomplished either by introducing a reservations system, by adopting a formalized queuing system, or a combination of the two.

Table V–1 links these five approaches to three alternative demand/capacity situations and offers a strategic commentary on each of the 15 resulting cells. To achieve the best results over the duration of the demand cycle, many service organizations should consider using a combination of two or more of the options described.

Inventorying Demand for a Service

Service businesses, for the most part, can rarely inventory supply, but they can often inventory demand.[4] This can be done by asking customers to take their turn by waiting in line on a first-come, first-served basis (queuing), or by offering them the opportunity of reserving space in advance.

A marketing approach to queuing involves determining the maximum amount of time that people are willing to wait for service and then finding ways to ensure that this waiting time passes quickly and pleasantly. In addition to providing such features as comfortable surroundings (and, if possible, a seat), strategies to pass the time in a holding location might include dissemination of information on the service, promotion of other products offered by the organization, or provision of supplementary services such as entertainment, use of reading materials, or food and drink.

Usually goods requiring servicing can be kept waiting in line longer than people can. But sometimes their owners do not wish to be parted from them for long. Households with only one car, for example, often cannot afford to be without it for more than a day or two. So a reservations system may be necessary for service businesses in fields such

TABLE V–1

Capacity Situation Relative to Demand

STRATEGY	INSUFFICIENT CAPACITY (EXCESS DEMAND)	SUFFICIENT CAPACITY[a] (SATISFACTORY DEMAND)	EXCESS CAPACITY (INSUFFICIENT DEMAND)
Take no action	Unorganized queuing results. (May irritate customers and discourage future use.)	Capacity is fully utilized. (But is this the most profitable mix of business?)	Capacity is wasted. (Customers may have a disappointing experience for services, such as theater.)
Reduce demand	Pricing higher will increase profits. Communication can be employed to encourage usage in other time slots. (Can this effort be focused on less profitable/desirable segments?)	Take no action (but see above).	Take no action (but see above).
Increase demand	Take no action (unless opportunities exist to stimulate and give priority to more profitable segments).	Take no action (unless opportunities exist to stimulate and give priority to more profitable segments).	Price lower selectively. Try to avoid cannibalizing existing business; ensure all relevant costs are covered. Use communications and variation in products/distribution (but recognize extra costs, if any, and make sure appropriate trade-offs are made between profitability and usage levels).
Inventory demand 1. Reservation system	Consider priority system for most desirable segments. Make other customers shift (a) outside peak period or (b) to future peak.	Try to ensure most profitable mix of business.	Clarify that space is available and that no reservations are needed.
2. Formalized queuing	Consider override for most desirable segments. Seek to keep waiting customers occupied and comfortable. Try to predict wait period accurately.	Try to avoid bottleneck delays.	Not applicable.

[a] Note: *Sufficient capacity* may be defined as "maximum available capacity" or "optimum capacity," depending on the situation.

as repair and maintenance. By requiring reservations for routine maintenance, management can keep space free for handling emergency jobs that will be able to command a much higher contribution margin.

Increasing and Reducing Demand

The periodic cycle influencing demand for a particular service—what may be termed the *product demand cycle*—may

FIGURE V–2
Identifying Variations in Demand by Time Period

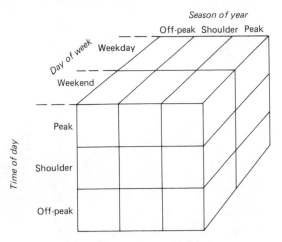

vary in length from 1 day to 12 months. In many instances, there may be multiple cycles operating simultaneously. For example, demand levels for public transportation may vary by time of day, day of week, and season of year. Thus, the level of demand for service during the peak period on a Monday in summer may differ from that during the peak period on a Saturday in winter, reflecting day-of-week and seasonal variations jointly.

Figure V–2 shows how the combination of three time-of-day periods, two day-of-week periods, and three seasonal periods can be combined to create 18 different demand periods. In theory, each of these might have its own distinct demand level (at a particular price) and customer profiles. But in practice, there would probably be close similarities between many of the demand periods, making it possible to collapse the framework into a total of perhaps three to six cells, each requiring a distinct marketing treatment to optimize the use of available capacity and to obtain the most desirable customer mix.

Each of the elements of the marketing mix has a role to play in stimulating demand during periods of excess capacity and in decreasing it (demarketing) during periods when insufficient capacity is available. In the next section, we'll look at each in turn.

MODIFYING MARKETING MIX
ELEMENTS TO MANAGE DEMAND

Although price is often the first variable to be considered when the issue of balancing supply and demand is raised, product and distribution modifications can also play an important role, as may communication efforts. The relative effectiveness of each depends in part on the underlying causes of demand variations and in part on the nature of the demand cycle. Our focus here will be on modifying demand for services where customers have at least some flexibility in the timing of their demand.

Communication Efforts

Even if the other variables of the marketing mix remain unchanged, communication efforts alone may be able to help smooth demand. Signing and advertising messages can remind prospective customers of the peak periods and encourage them to avoid these in favor of the uncrowded, off-peak times when service is, perhaps, faster or more comfortable. Examples include postal service advice to "Mail Early for Christmas," public transportation messages urging non-commuters such as shoppers or tourists to avoid the crush conditions of the commute hours, and so forth. In addition, management can ask service personnel or intermediaries, such as travel agents, to encourage customers with discretionary schedules to favor off-peak periods.

If there are changes in pricing, product characteristics, and distribution, it is vital to communicate these clearly to the target markets. Obtaining the desired response to variations in marketing mix elements is, of course, dependent on customers' being fully informed of their options.

Product Variations

An important way to influence demand levels is to change the characteristics of the product. This is illustrated in Table V–2, which shows examples of service offerings that remain unchanged throughout the year and those that undergo significant modifications according to the season. Examples of a variable product strategy can be divided into single item versus product-line offerings. In summer, a ski hill cannot be used for skiing, but by installing an Alpine slide (wheeled toboggans running down a curving concrete or plastic ramp), management can attract visitors to use the chair-lift capacity, which would otherwise remain idle. Similarly, a resort hotel can sharply alter the mix and focus of its peripheral services, such as dining, entertainment, and sports to reflect customer taste in different seasons.

Variations in the product offering can even take place during a 24-hour period. Restaurants provide a good example, marking the passage of the hours with changing menus and levels of service, variations in lighting and decor, opening and closing of the bar, and presence or absence of entertainment. The objective may be to appeal to different needs within the same group of customers, to reach out to different customer segments, or both, according to the time of day.

Different versions of the same service can also be offered simultaneously in response to variations in customer preferences and ability to pay. Examples include first-class, business class, and tourist-class service on airlines; different room and service categories in hotels; and different seating categories in theaters and concert halls. To reflect variations in demand between different customer groups over the course of the product-demand cycle, some service marketers vary the mix of capacity allocated to the different product categories, for instance, by adding or removing first-class seats from an airliner. But when the capacity mix is fixed—as it is in hotels and concert halls—changes in category allocations are tantamount to price increases or decreases, for instance, charging only the price of a regular room for a suite.

TABLE V–2

Examples of Alternative Strategies Over the Product-Demand Cycle

NUMBER OF PRODUCTS OFFERED AT ONE TIME	CONSTANCY OF PRODUCT OFFERING OVER THE DEMAND CYCLE		
	Unchanging	*Variable*	
		Summer	*Winter*
One	Golf Course	Alpine Slide	Downhill Skiing
Two or More	Hospital Emergency Room Surgical Services In-Patient Food Services Out-Patient Clinic	Hotel Rooms Outdoor Restaurants Golf Tennis Children's Program	Hotel Rooms Indoor Restaurants Skating Cross-Country Skiing Dancing

TABLE V-3

Variations in Distribution Strategy for Services by Time and Place

LOCATION(S) WHERE SERVICE IS AVAILABLE	SCHEDULE (HOURS/DAYS) OF SERVICE AVAILABILITY	
	Same Schedule	*Different Schedule*
Same Location(s)	1	2
Different Location(s)	3	4

Variations in Distribution

Rather than seeking to modify demand for a service that continues to be offered at the same time in the same place, it may be worthwhile to alter demand by modifying the time and place of delivery.

Table V-3 illustrates the four basic options available. Box 1 represents a strategy of "no change." Box 2, by contrast, involves varying the times when the service is available to reflect changes in customer preference by day of week, season, and so forth. For instance, theaters often offer matinees over the weekend when people are free during the day. In hot climates, banks may close for two hours at midday in summer when people take a siesta, but may remain open later in the evening when commercial establishments are still active. Box 3 involves taking the service to the customer at a new location. Some libraries have mobile units that visit different locations. In this strategy, the schedule should reflect an understanding of when patrons in these various locations are likely to use the service. Box 4, the most complex strategy, involves simultaneous variations in both scheduling availability and location. One New England airline, for instance, operates between Boston and Cape Cod in the summer; in winter, the aircraft go to Florida and operate a different route network and schedule.

Pricing

Although this is the most commonly advocated method of balancing supply and demand, it is not quite as universally feasible for services as for goods. Consider the respective problems of a ski manufacturer and a ski slope operator during the summer. The former can either produce for inventory or try to sell skis in the summer at a discount. If the skis are sufficiently discounted, some customers will buy ahead of the ski season in order to save money. However, no skiers in their right mind would buy ski lift tickets for use on a midsummer day at *any* price. The only hope for the owner to encourage use of the lifts is to change the product by installing an Alpine slide or by promoting the view at the summit to summer visitors.

For price to be effective as a demand management tool, the marketing manager must have some sense of the shape and slope of the demand curve for the product *at a particular point in time*. As shown in Figure V-3, the aggregate demand curve for a specific service is likely to vary sharply from one time period to another. In the hypothetical example shown in Figure V-3, significantly different prices would be needed to fill capacity in each time period.

To complicate matters further, there may be separate demand curves for different segments within each time period, reflecting variations between various customer groupings in the need for the service or in the ability to pay for it. Figure V-4 shows a hypothetical example of how such demand curves might vary by segment for two separate time periods.

One of the most difficult tasks facing service marketers is to determine the nature of

FIGURE V–3

Variations In Demand Curves by Time Period
(Hypothetical Example for a Transportation
Service)

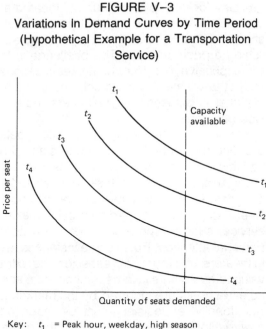

Key: t_1 = Peak hour, weekday, high season
       t_2 = Peak hour, weekday, low season
       t_3 = Peak hour, weekend, high season
       t_4 = Off-peak hour, weekend, low season

all these different demand curves. Research, trial and error, and analyses of parallel situations in other locations or in comparable services are all ways of obtaining an understanding of the situation. This information is needed not only for demand management purposes, but also to maximize the asset revenue-generating efficiency (ARGE) of the business (see the discussion in Section IV, "Managing the Customer Mix") or to optimize the social value of a public or nonprofit service.

Developing a Pricing Matrix

Many service businesses explicitly recognize the existence of different demand curves for different segments during the same time period by establishing distinct classes of service, each priced at levels ap-

propriate to the demand curve of a particular segment. In essence, each segment receives a variation of the basic product, with value being added to the core service in order to appeal to the higher paying segments. The objective, of course, is to maximize the revenues received from each segment.

Various usage conditions may also be set to discourage customers willing to pay top-of-the-line prices from trading down to less expensive versions of the product. Airlines, for instance, may insist that excursion tickets be purchased 21 days in advance and that the passenger remain at the destination for at least one week before returning—conditions that are too constraining for most business travelers.

An important task for service marketers is to develop a framework for establishing pricing policy and capacity allocation decisions by both value category (service class) and time period.

FIGURE V–4

Differing Demand Curves for
Different Segments in Two Time Periods
(Hypothetical Transportation Example)

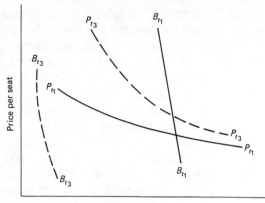

Key: B = Business travelers
       P = Pleasure travelers
       t_1 = Peak hour, weekday, high season
       t_3 = Peak hour, weekend, high season

FIGURE V–5

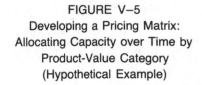

Developing a Pricing Matrix:
Allocating Capacity over Time by
Product-Value Category
(Hypothetical Example)

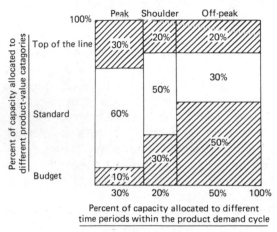

Figure V–5 shows a hypothetical example in which three service classes—top-of-the-line, standard, and budget—have been combined with three time periods—peak, shoulder, and off-peak—to form a matrix of nine price cells. The size of each cell reflects the percentage of total capacity allocated to it over the duration of the product-demand cycle. For instance, top-of-the-line/peak has been assigned 9 percent (30 percent × 30 percent) of total capacity. Accurate demand forecasting and understanding of customer behavior are important to this process. Fine tuning can be achieved by monitoring results and then changing capacity allocations and prices for future demand cycles.

This type of exercise may need to be performed separately for each operating unit, such as each motel in a motel chain or each route in a transportation system. Relevant criteria include strength of market demand, competitive price levels, quality of product relative to the competition, and variations in cost structure. Alternatively, individual units can be clustered into similar

groups—for example, restaurants located at airports versus those located in suburban shopping malls—for the purpose of establishing a pricing matrix. The challenge is to be responsive to individual market situations yet not to create a pricing scheme so complex that it confuses both customers and service personnel.

In order to ensure that profitability goals are met, the marketer must understand the variable cost per sales unit, such as a seat, a room, a specific repair task, and so forth. This cost is likely to increase, for instance, when extra value is added by providing extra service, such as more floor space or more personal attention. But in some instances, as in theaters with identical seat sizes, the extra value to customers is in better locations, and no extra costs are incurred by the marketer. Additionally, a decision must be made on how to allocate fixed costs among the different price cells. When the marketer wants to keep the price close to variable cost in order to stimulate off-peak demand for budget-class service, it may be appropriate to allocate no fixed costs to that cell at all. (However, all fixed costs must be allocated and recovered *somewhere* within the matrix!) The final issue is to recognize that 100 percent utilization may not be achieved in each cell. Hence, cost allocations per sales unit must reflect the anticipated utilization rate in each cell. Again, this places a premium on accurate forecasting.

CONCLUSION

Service marketers often face the problem of balancing demand against available capacity, especially when the level of demand varies sharply over a reasonable, predictable time cycle. Marketing strategies for managing demand to match capacity include taking steps to increase or decrease demand or introducing procedures such as reservations and customer-oriented queuing procedures. Each element of the marketing mix has a role to play in helping the service organization make optimum use of its capacity, and often the best results are achieved when several elements are used in conjunction with one another.

NOTES

1. See W. Earl Sasser, "Match Supply and Demand in Service Industries" (reprinted in Section V of this book).

2. See Philip Kotler and Sidney J. Levy, "Demarketing, Yes, Demarketing," *Harvard Business Review*, (November–December 1971), 74–80.

3. For further insights, see Christopher H. Lovelock and Robert F. Young, "Look to Consumers to Increase Productivity" (reprinted in Section IV of this book).

4. Inventorying the supply of a service is usually only possible for repair and maintenance services involving interchangeable goods. For instance, an industrial service shop may handle large numbers of identical electric motors. Regular customers who bring in such a motor for repair can be given a substitute motor, already serviced and sitting on the shelf, then billed subsequently for the work on their own motor, which will be offered later to another customer bringing in a similar piece of equipment at some future point in time.

CASES

THE 911 EMERGENCY NUMBER IN NEW YORK

The communications center at police headquarters in New York City is being flooded by calls to the 911 emergency number. More than half the calls are not true emergencies and are slowing police response to genuine emergencies. The police department, the mayor's office, and the New York Telephone Company are debating what to do about this situation.

The calls were pouring in at an unusually high rate at police headquarters yesterday about how hot it was, how the water wasn't running, how a big dog was after a cat again, and, occasionally, about a shooting or a suicide.

It was the fifth anniversary of the 911 system, the consolidation of the police, fire department, and ambulance services through a

single phone number, and it appeared that city residents, by the thousands, were ignoring Mayor Lindsay's appeal last week not to dial 911 except in a true emergency.[1]

So began a news story in the *New York Times* in July 1973 describing some of the problems surrounding New York City's 911 emergency telephone number. Flooded with calls which were often quite inconsequential, the

This case was prepared by Jeffrey S. Kahn, Harvard MBA Class of 1975, and Christopher H. Lovelock.

police department found itself unable to respond promptly to genuine emergencies.

Rising public criticism of such delayed responses had convinced Mayor John V. Lindsay and his advisers that a public education campaign should be developed to discourage use of 911 for nonemergency calls. The problem was how to devise a campaign which would differentiate emergencies from nonemergencies without reducing citizen confidence in the 911 system. As the Mayor stated, "We're suffering from success."

DEVELOPMENT OF THE 911 CONCEPT

In March 1967, the President's Commission on Law Enforcement and Administration of Justice recommended that, "Wherever practical, a single [emergency] number should be established, at least within a metropolitan area and preferably over the entire United States." By dialing a simple, easily remembered series of digits, any citizen would be able to summon a quick response to an emergency.[2]

At that time, most American cities had innumerable different numbers for fire, police, and ambulance service. The St. Louis telephone directory listed 161 emergency numbers on a single page; Washington, D.C., had at least 45 emergency numbers; and Los Angeles County had 50 numbers for police alone. The existing numbers were hard to memorize and rarely duplicated in other cities.

Hence the suggestion was made for a simple, universal emergency number. The concept was not new, having already been implemented in a number of other countries. Great Britain had used the number 999 ever since 1937 to call police, fire, or ambulance service. Although skeptics argued that the services desired could be reached just as simply by dialing 0 for the operator, studies showed that going through the operator took longer and that every second counted in achieving an effective response to emergencies.

The rising crime rate and civil unrest of the late 1960s lent urgency to the Presidential Commission's recommendation. The American Telephone and Telegraph Company announced in January 1968 that it would make the digits 911 available as the single emergency telephone number throughout the nation.[3] However, the decision whether or not to use this facility was left up to individual local governments.

IMPLEMENTATION IN NEW YORK

In New York City, which was often regarded as a magnification of the good and bad points of American city life, the 911 concept seemed ideal to the city administration and the police department. Mayor Lindsay's promise of a "Fun City" depended to a great degree on removing the fear of crime which affected both resident and visitor alike. Although New York had had a single emergency police number since November 1964, the seven digits (440-1234) were less easily remembered than 911 and took longer to dial.

The idea of easy access to police protection and emergency help was viewed not only as a solution to lawlessness, but also as a cure for citizen alienation. Inspector Anthony Bouza (later assistant chief and commander of the Police Communications Division) pointed out that 911 was to be ". . . a police-extended offer to participate in the solution of a citizen's problems . . . to overcome cultural and psychological barriers to these contacts" [between citizen and police officer].[4]

This reduction in citizen alienation was especially important to the New York City Police Department, the largest municipal police force in the nation. With 32,000 officers protecting eight million New Yorkers in five boroughs, the department provided one of the highest police-to-citizen ratios in the world. The organization of the force was divided along both functional and geographical lines. Functionally, there were detective, public affairs, communications, and other divisions; geographically the department split into 75 precincts and seven field-service-area commands (the five boroughs, plus Manhattan and Brooklyn divided north/south). Over the years, the NYCPD had been responsible for a number of innovations in police methods and technology, and at this time (summer 1968) New York was the first major American city, and only the third city in the nation, to initiate the 911 system. Nevertheless, the city continued to be regarded as a crime center.

The same commission that advocated 911 had also produced a report which showed a significant relationship between police response time to a crime and the probability of an arrest. By instituting 911, the police hoped to increase citizen participation in crime detection, speed police response time, and reduce crime. Reducing crime would increase public confidence in the force and, it was hoped, produce greater community support for the police—thus improving the probability that even more citizens would use 911 to notify police of emergencies.

The Emergency Communications Center

A centralized communications system had been recommended several years earlier, but it was only after several "hot" summers and AT&T's announcement of 911's availability that the mayor gave the go-ahead for the multimillion-dollar project.

Technologically the project was almost totally handled by the New York Telephone Company in coordination with the police. Previously there had been five separate "communications centers" in each of the city's five boroughs. Each answered calls to the "old" police emergency number, 440-1234, dialed from its portion of the city, and each had its own method for dispatching officers to the scene. Now there was to be one communications center handling all emergency calls via "automatic call distributors" (ACDs), which would continuously and evenly feed incoming calls to 48 switchboard positions.[5] These positions would in turn be linked by a 12-channel, color-coded conveyer belt to the radio dispatch consoles for each borough. An ACD operator would receive a call, fill out the appropriately colored dispatch form,

and place it on the belt, via which it would be whisked to the appropriate dispatcher.[6]

The dispatchers were linked to more than 500 radio motor patrol (RMP) cars and to an increasing number of walkie-talkie–equipped foot patrol officers. Each dispatcher covered about a dozen precincts with a separate radio frequency for that area.

Planning the Communications Campaign

The complex task of informing New Yorkers about 911 was shared by the Mayor's office, the New York Telephone Company, and the police department. The Mayor would be in charge of the operation and would provide press releases at timed intervals. The police would distribute the message on all department forms and stationery and the large mobile "billboards" provided by the doors and trunks of their radio cars. The New York Telephone Company would, in coordination with its advertising agency, develop and disseminate the marketing message.

The Mayor wanted the 911 campaign to be a highly visible symbol of his administration. Even more important, if the system were to succeed, it would have to be understood and used by a population which represented a wide range of educational and ethnic backgrounds. A message simultaneously bold and simple was required, and after some discussion the campaign slogan became: "DIAL 911." This logo, with the number written large inside a square frame, was to be endlessly repeated throughout the city, often in conjunction with an additional message (Exhibit 1).

Most critical was the timing of the campaign. To create the maximum awareness desired, it was felt that the campaign had to peak all at once, but if it were premature and people began using the system before it was ready, then they might quickly condemn it as simply another publicity flop. And so, on the week of June 24, 1968, after the last of a series of publicity releases on the forthcoming project had been reprinted in the *Times*, *News*, and *Post*, a publicity blitz covered the city. All telephone booths[7] received a bright red decal; police cars sported the symbol; subways and billboards urged the message, too. Newspapers carried advertising and end-of-the-month telephone bills displayed the logo. It was a saturation campaign.

Inauguration of the System

The following Monday, on July 1, 1968, Mayor Lindsay made the first "official" call inaugurating the system. After several false starts, caused by dialing 911 on an inside line, the Mayor finally got through, identified himself, and suggested that a squad car be sent to lock up the City Council. In his dedication speech, Lindsay said,

> This is, perhaps, the most important event of my administration as mayor. The miraculous new electronic communications system we inaugurate this morning will affect the life of every New Yorker in every part of our city, every hour of the day. No longer will a citizen in distress risk injury to life or property because of an archaic communications system.[8]

After fewer than four weeks of operation, the police department reported that emergency telephone calls had risen from 12,000 daily under the old 440-1234 number to 18,000 (including 2,000 for ambulances and 200–300 for fire emergencies) for 911. "The big thing we're doing is building up the public's access to us," commented Deputy Chief Inspector William J. Kanz of the Communications Division. Officials claimed that police cars typically arrived at the scene of a complaint within two minutes of a telephone call, more than a minute faster than under the previous system.[9]

Despite several complaints of slow response, the initial reaction was generally one of jubilation and acclamation. It was felt that 911 was bringing about a better relationship between citizen and government by overcoming the reluctance of many people to call the police. As Inspector Bouza pointed out,

> The implication of . . . [overcoming inhibitions] is tremendous because it reveals that the police are not dealing with a known volume of work, but rather with a flexible volume, the size of which depends on the accessibility and efficiency of the police.[10]

Concern Over Delayed Responses

Yet this "accessibility and efficiency" were the very points which soon began to trouble both citizen and policeman alike, not to mention Mayor Lindsay. The original criteria for 911 operations had emphasized speed in answering: 90 percent of all calls were to be answered within 15 seconds of the first ring, and 95 percent within 30 seconds. At first these standards were met and exceeded. However, as 18,000 calls per day began pouring in, the 5 percent acceptable delay rate meant that almost a thousand calls took longer than half a minute to answer, during which time many people hung up in frustration and lost confidence in the system.

Articles began appearing in the city's three dailies questioning the efficacy of the 911 system, or more pointedly, the efficiency of the New York City Police Department itself. 911 became the butt of some "New York City life" jokes, drawing guffaws from local TV and radio personalities as they called the emergency number on the air for the amusement of their viewers and listeners.

In response, the police department and telephone company consultants turned to improving the mechanics of the system. They eliminated the secondary pool of operators which handled overflow calls in order to increase the number of operators to answer primary demand. Since there was an unexpectedly large number of Spanish-speaking callers, more bilingual operators were put on the line. Yet even as goals for fast response were met and exceeded, the press and public continued to criticize the police.

Much of the souring of public response resulted from people's perception of the success or failure of the police in terms of visible response, which meant prompt arrival "on the scene." Unfortunately, the rising volume of calls at peak times (such as Saturday nights) placed a heavy strain on the NYCPD's squad-car resources. Too often police responded to a call only to discover that the "emergency" actually did not demand a squad car and two officers. Fewer such problems had arisen when an experienced precinct sergeant had handled calls; he might know that Mrs. Smith's "missing" husband was in fact sitting in the bar on the corner and be able to calm Mrs. Smith over the phone. Now Mrs. Smith called 911 with her problem and operators, answering within 15 seconds, dispatched a patrol car to her door.

Facing these difficulties, the department first requested additional patrol calls from the Mayor. Communications also set up a screening process which identified those calls which, in the operator's judgment, did not require a dispatch. A computer system was installed to direct reception and dispatching. All these improvements meant that calls were answered faster and patrol cars arrived sooner.

Yet as crime in the country at large—and in New York City in particular—continued to rise, more and more people dialed 911. In 1972 the police department, having made continuous use of technology to keep up with demand, now began to wonder if perhaps another approach was needed. In particular, many involved with 911 felt that there should be some way of cutting down on the nonemergency calls which were entering the system; not only the "Mrs. Smith's husband" type of calls which ought by rights to go still to the precinct, but also those which the police had never handled and were not equipped to handle.

HOW TO ELIMINATE NONEMERGENCY CALLS?

The situation finally came to a head in the summer of 1973, when hot weather helped push the total number of calls to well over 20,000 a day. Many of these calls were relatively inconsequential, such as requests for policemen to fix a malfunctioning airconditioner. "What may be an emergency for a lot of people," said Sergeant Albert Lucci, a supervisor in the communications center, "isn't necessarily an emergency for the police. A lot of people just don't realize this."

As a result, the 48 emergency phone circuits were often jammed with nonemergencies. "Sometimes," added Sergeant Lucci, "it takes a while for people with real emergencies to get through to us." Out of a daily average of 18,000 calls, studies had shown that only 7,100 were real emergencies to which police cars were dispatched. Other calls concerned such diverse problems as Medicaid information, marriage licenses, open hydrants, street potholes, and even VD information.

The rising volume of complaints about slow police response to the initial 911 call (delays of 5 to 45 minutes were cited) and subsequent tardy follow-up were a matter of serious concern to both the police and the city administration. The problem was particularly acute on weekends and on weekday evenings.[11]

The question was, what to do? An appeal by Mayor Lindsay in early July not to dial 911 except in a genuine emergency had no apparent impact. A New York Times editorial noted that "it is too easy for New Yorkers to make use of the emergency system, it costs too little in time and trouble, and therefore the temptation to dial 911 for trivial reasons has apparently become more irresistible." The editorial thereupon suggested that dialing 911 be made "a little more bothersome"—perhaps by turning it into a seven-digit number like 911-1000.[12] Others argued that the problem could be resolved by charging for 911 calls from pay phones.

After discussions between the police department, the telephone company, and the Mayor's office, it was eventually decided that some form of educational campaign was needed. At issue was the form the campaign should take. What organization(s) should sponsor it? At whom should it be directed? What media should it use? And what should the message say?

Watching the situation in New York City with some interest was adjacent Nassau County on Long Island, which was about to introduce its own 911 service. The Nassau County Police Department was very anxious to avoid a repetition of the problems which had plagued New York City and wondered which strategy it should employ.

NOTES

1. "Calls to 911 Show That One Man's Vexation Is Another Man's Dire Emergency," by Pranay Gupte, *New York Times*, July 10, 1973, pp. 43, 83.

2. "911—A Hot Line for Emergencies," by J. Edward Roush, *Readers Digest*, December 1968, pp. 211–219.

3. "AT&T Units Plan '911' Emergency Number Nationwide: Cost Will Exceed $50 Million," *Wall Street Journal*, January 15, 1968, p. 3.

4. "911 = Panacea or Nostrum?" by Anthony V. Bouza, *Bulletin* (Associated Public Safety Communications Officers), March 1972, pp. 8+.

5. "Electronics in Law Enforcement," by Marce Eleccion, *IEEE Spectrum*, February 1973, pp. 33–40.

6. "Police Emergency Center Dedicated by Mayor," by David Burnham, *New York Times*, July 2, 1968, p. 43.

7. Pay telephone booths were converted to make it possible to dial 911 without first inserting a dime.

8. "Police Emergency Center Dedicated by Mayor," by David Burnham, *New York Times*, July 2, 1968, p. 43.

9. "911 Busy Number, Police Here Find," *New York Times*, July 27, 1968, p. 25.

10. "911 = Panacea or Nostrum?" by Anthony V. Bouza, *Bulletin* (Associated Public Safety Communications Officers), March 1972, pp. 8+.

11. "Delays Are Cited on Calls to 911," by Pranay Gupte, *New York Times*, July 23, 1973, p. 1.

12. "Emergency Calls . . ." *New York Times*, August 14, 1973, p. 32.

EXHIBIT 1

911 Symbol as Used in Print Advertising,
Summer 1968

Now...
in New York City
for POLICE and
AMBULANCE
EMERGENCY

DIAL:
911

SOUTHWEST AIRLINES

A new airline begins service between three Texas cities. Despite vigorous competition from two larger carriers, Southwest quickly establishes itself as a force in the marketplace. After 18 months of operation, it has achieved a strong market share on the Dallas–Houston route, but it is doing less well elsewhere. To boost traffic between Dallas and San Antonio, it halves all fares on that route, with dramatic results. But then Braniff counterattacks with a price war on its Dallas–Houston service.

"BRANIFF'S 'GET ACQUAINTED SALE': HALF PRICE TO HOUSTON'S HOBBY AIRPORT" trumpeted the headlines on the full-page advertisement in the February 1, 1973, edition of the *Dallas Morning News*.

Lamar Muse, president of Southwest Airlines, held up the advertisement for members of the airline's management team and advertising agency executives to see, commenting as he did so,

> OK, at least we now know what Braniff's response to our San Antonio promotion will be. They are hitting us hard in our only really profitable market. Every decision they have made to date has been the wrong decision, so how can we turn this one to our advantage?

SOUTHWEST AND ITS COMPETITION

Southwest Airlines Co. had been organized as a Texas corporation in March 1967 with the objective of providing improved quality air service between the cities of Dallas/Fort Worth, Houston, and San Antonio. These cities, each 190 to 250 miles apart, formed a triangular route structure in eastern Texas. Southwest had been certified as an intrastate carrier on these routes by the Texas Aeronautics Commission in February 1968, but lawsuits by Braniff International Airways and Texas International

Airlines (TI) had delayed initiation of service by Southwest until June 1971.

The Dallas–Houston market, the largest of the three, was dominated by Braniff, which carried some 75 percent of the local traffic on that route during the first half of 1971 (Exhibit 1). A major international carrier with an all-jet fleet of 74 aircraft, Braniff reported systemwide revenues in 1970 of $325.6 million and carried 5.8 million passengers. Southwest's other principal competitor, Texas International, served the southern and southwestern United States and Mexico. In 1970 TI had a fleet of 45 aircraft, carried 2.2 million passengers, and generated $77.8 million in total revenues.

There was considerable public discontent with the quality of service provided by these two carriers on intrastate routes within Texas—a fact which Southwest hoped to exploit. Among other things, their local flights typically represented segments of longer, interstate flights, and it was often hard for local passengers to get seats.

After carefully assessing costs, Southwest settled on a $20 fare for each route. This compared with existing Braniff and TI coach fares of $27 from Dallas to Houston and $28 from Dallas to San Antonio. Management hoped that Southwest could anticipate an initial price advantage, although Braniff and TI would probably reduce their own fares promptly.

Southwest executives had calculated that

This case was prepared by Christopher H. Lovelock.

an average of 39 passengers per flight would be required to break even. They considered this level of business (and better) a reasonable expectation in light of the market's estimated potential for growth and the frequency of flights which Southwest planned to offer. Nevertheless, they predicted a period of deficit operations before this break-even point was reached.

OPERATING EXPERIENCE

Southwest inaugurated scheduled revenue service with a blaze of publicity on June 18, 1971. The airline offered all coach-class flights and introduced a number of innovations and attractions, including new Boeing 737 twin-jet aircraft, fast ticketing, glamorous hostesses, and inexpensive, exotically named drinks.

Despite extensive promotion, initial results were hardly spectacular. Between June 18–30, 1971, Southwest had an average of 13.1 passengers per flight on its Dallas–Houston service and 12.9 passengers on the Dallas–San Antonio route; passenger loads during the month of July showed only marginal improvement. Both competitors had met Southwest's lower fares immediately, as well as improving the frequency and quality of their services on the two routes served by the new airline, and heavily promoting these changes.

Management concluded that it was essential to improve schedule frequencies to compete more effectively with those of Braniff and TI. This became possible with the delivery of the company's fourth Boeing 737 in late September 1971, and on October 1 hourly service was introduced between Dallas and Houston and flights every two hours between Dallas and San Antonio.

Surveys of Southwest passengers departing from Houston showed that a substantial percentage would prefer service from the William P. Hobby Airport, 12 miles southwest of downtown Houston, rather than from the new Houston Intercontinental Airport, 26 miles north of the city. Accordingly, arrangements were completed in mid-November for 7 of Southwest's 14 round-trip flights between Dallas and Houston to be transferred to Hobby Airport (thus reopening this old airport to scheduled commercial passenger traffic). Additional schedule revisions included elimination of the extremely unprofitable Saturday operation on all routes.

These actions contributed to an increase in transportation revenues in the final quarter of 1971 over those achieved in the third quarter, but Southwest's operating losses in the fourth quarter fell only slightly, from $1,001,000 to $921,000 (Exhibit 2). At year's end 1971, Southwest's accumulated deficit stood at $3.75 million (Exhibit 3).

Although the majority of ticket sales were made over the counter at airport terminals, sales were also made through travel agents and to corporate accounts. Travel agents received a 7 percent commission on credit card sales and 10 percent on cash sales. Corporate accounts—companies whose personnel made regular use of Southwest Airlines—received no discount but benefited from the convenience of having their own supply of ticket stock (which they issued themselves) and of receiving a single monthly billing.

Between October 1971 and April 1972, average passenger loads systemwide increased from 18.4 passengers per flight to 26.7 passengers. However, this was still substantially below the number necessary to cover total costs per trip flown, some components of which had been tending to rise (Exhibits 2 and 4). It had become evident that the volume of traffic during the late morning and early afternoon could not realistically support flights at hourly intervals. It was also clear that most Houston passengers preferred Hobby Airport to Houston Intercontinental and the decision was made to abandon the latter airport altogether.

On May 14, 1972, Southwest reduced the total number of daily flights between Dallas and Houston from 29 to 22. Eleven flights daily continued to be offered on the Dallas–San Antonio route and six between San Antonio and Houston–Hobby. (Braniff quickly retaliated by introducing its own service from Dallas to Hobby and promoting it extensively.) The new schedule made it possible for the company to dispose of its fourth Boeing 737. Southwest had no trouble finding a ready buyer for this aircraft and made a profit of $533,000 on the resale.

CHANGES IN PRICING STRATEGY

June 1972 saw Southwest Airlines celebrating its first birthday. This provided an opportunity for more of the publicity stunts for which the airline was already becoming renowned. Posters were hung inside the aircraft and in the waiting lounges, the aircraft cabins were decorated, and there was an onboard party every day for a week. This activity, promoted by newspaper advertising, generated considerable publicity for the airline and, in management's view, reinforced Southwest's image as the plucky, friendly little underdog which had now survived an entire year against powerful, entrenched competition.

At this point, Southwest management decided it was time to take a hard look at the fare structure and its relationship to costs and revenues. For some months, Southwest had been experimenting with a $10 fare on Friday evening flights after 9:00 p.m. In May this reduced fare was extended to post-9:00 p.m. flights on a daily basis. The result was sharply higher load factors on these discount flights relative to the average achieved on full-fare flights (Exhibit 5). But management soon concluded that the airline could no longer afford a $20 fare on daytime flights. New tariffs were therefore filed with the Texas Aeronautics Commission, effective July 9, 1972; these raised Southwest's basic one-way fare from $20 to $26; established a round-trip fare of $50; and offered a $225 Commuter Club Card, entitling the purchaser to unlimited transportation on all routes for 30 days.

One problem was how to break the news of the increased fares to the public. At a strategy session with representatives of the advertising agency, it was suggested that Southwest announce a new Executive Class service on all full-fare flights, offering passengers improved amenities. The idea was quickly refined: two rows of seats would be removed from the aircraft, reducing its capacity from 112 to 104 seats but increasing legroom; additionally, passengers would be offered free drinks (it was felt that the hostesses would not have time to serve more than two drinks per passenger on such short flights). Full-page newspaper advertisements were then run, announcing Southwest Airlines' new Executive Class service, with first-class legroom for everyone and free cocktails. The $26 fare also absorbed the security check charges introduced the previous month.

The key consideration was how the competition would react. "For a few days," admitted the vice-president of marketing, "we were really sweating." Braniff's initial response was to devote an additional aircraft to its Dallas–Hobby Airport flights on July 11, thus permitting on-the-hour service most of the business day. However, on July 17, Texas International increased its fares to the same level as Southwest's; then on July 21 Braniff met all aspects of the fare and on-board service changes, also adding a $10 "Sundowner" flight to Hobby at 7:30 p.m. As a result of Braniff's increased service and the higher fares, Southwest's patronage fell back by 2 percent between the second and third quarters, but transportation revenues increased.

During September new advertising was launched, based on the slogan "Remember What It Was Like Before Southwest Airlines?" which the agency saw as a war cry to rally consumers. The principal media used in this campaign were billboards and television. TV commercials cited the advantages of flying Southwest, notably its dependable schedules.

At the end of October, another major change was made in pricing strategies. The $10 discount fares, which had never been advertised, were replaced by half-fare flights ($13 one way, $25 round trip) on the two major routes each weekday night after 8 p.m. Saturday flights were reintroduced, and *all* weekend flights were offered at half-fare. An intensive three-week advertising campaign accompanied these new schedules and price changes, using one-minute radio commercials on country and western, top 40 (popular rock music stations), and similar stations (Exhibit 6). The response was immediate, and November 1972 traffic levels were 12 percent higher than those in October—historically the best month of the year in Southwest's commuter markets.

In the new year, management turned its attention to its largest single remaining problem. The company was now actually making money on its Dallas–Houston flights but still incurring substantial losses in the Dallas–San Antonio market. Southwest offered only eight flights a day on this route, versus 34 by its major competitor (Exhibit 7), and in January was averaging a mere 17 passengers on each full-fare flight. The Dallas–San Antonio market had not grown as rapidly as had Dallas–Houston, and Southwest held a smaller market share (Exhibit 8).

Management concluded that unless a dramatic improvement in patronage was quickly achieved on this route, they would have to abandon it. They decided to make one last attempt to obtain the needed increase and on January 22, 1973, announced a "60-Day Half-Price Sale" on *all* Southwest Airlines flights between Dallas and San Antonio. This sale was promoted by TV and radio advertising. If successful, it was Lamar Muse's intention to make this reduced fare permanent, but he felt that by announcing it as a limited-period offer, he would stimulate consumer interest even more effectively while also reducing the likelihood of competitive response. Exhibit 9 shows a sample radio script.

The impact of these half-price fares was even faster and more dramatic than the results of the evening and weekend half-price fares introduced the previous fall. By the end of the first week, average loads on Southwest's Dallas–San Antonio service had risen to 48 passengers per flight and continued to rise sharply at the beginning of the following week.

On Thursday, February 1, however, Braniff employed full-page newspaper advertisements to announce a half-price "Get Acquainted Sale" between Dallas and Hobby on all flights, lasting until April 1 (Exhibit 10). However, fares on Braniff's flights between Dallas and Houston Intercontinental remained at the existing levels.

Lamar Muse immediately called an urgent management meeting to decide what action Southwest should take in response to Braniff's move.

EXHIBIT 1

Southwest Airlines and Competitors: Average Daily Local Passengers Carried in Each Direction
(Dallas–Houston Market)

	BRANIFF[a]		TEXAS INT.[a]		SOUTHWEST		TOTAL LOCAL MARKET[b]
	Passengers	Percent of Market	Passengers	Percent of Market	Passengers	Percent of Market	One-Direction Passengers
1967	416	86.1	67	13.9			483
1968	381	70.2	162	29.8			543
1969	427	75.4	139	24.6			566
1970							
First half	449	79.0	119	21.0			568
Second half	380	76.0	120	24.0			500
Year	414	77.5	120	22.5			534
1971							
First half	402	74.7	126	23.4	10	1.9	538
Second half	338	50.7	120	18.0	209	31.3	667
Year	370	61.4	123	20.4	110	18.2	603
1972							
January	341	48.3	105	14.9	260	36.8	706
February	343	47.6	100	13.9	277	38.5	720
March	357	47.5	100	13.3	295	39.2	752
April	367	48.3	97	12.8	296	38.9	760
May	362	48.5	84	11.3	300	40.2	746
June	362	46.8	81	10.5	330	42.7	773
First half	356	48.0	93	12.5	293	39.5	742
July	332	48.1	74	10.7	284	41.2	690
August	432	53.7	56	6.9	317	39.4	805
September	422	54.9	55	7.2	291	37.9	768
October	443	53.1	56	6.7	335	40.2	834
November	439	50.6	55	6.3	374	43.1	868
December	396	52.1	56	7.4	308	40.5	760
Second half	411	52.1	59	7.5	318	40.4	788
Year	384	50.1	77	10.0	306	39.9	767
1973							
January [c]	443	51.5	62	7.3	354	41.2	859

[a] These figures were calculated by Lamar Muse from passenger data which Braniff and TI were required to supply to the Civil Aeronautics Board. He multiplied the original figures by a correction factor to eliminate interline traffic and arrived at net totals for local traffic.

[b] Excludes figures for another carrier which had about 1% of the local market in 1969 and 1970.

[c] Projected figures from terminal counts by Southwest personnel.

SOURCE: Company records

EXHIBIT 2

Southwest Airlines' Quarterly Income Statements

	1971		1972			
	Q3	Q4	Q1	Q2	Q3	Q4
Transportation Revenues[a]	887 [b]	1,138	1,273	1,401	1,493	1,745
Operating Expenses						
Operations and Maintenance	1,211	1,280	1,192	1,145	1,153	1,156
Marketing and Gen. Admin.	371	368	334	366	313	351
Depreciation and Amortization	311	411	333	334	335	335
Total	1,893	2,059	1,859	1,845	1,801	1,842
Operating Profit (Loss)	(1,006)	(921)	(586)	(444)	(308)	(97)
Net Interest Revenues (Costs)	(254)	(253)	(218)	(220)	(194)	(204)
Net Income (Loss) Before Extraordinary Items	(1,260)	(1,174)	(804)	(664)	(502)	(301)
Extraordinary Items	(571)[c]	(469)[c]		533 [d]		
Net Income (Loss)	(1,831)	(1,643)	(804)	(131)	(502)	(301)

[a] Includes both passenger and freight business. Freight sales represent 2% of revenues in 1972.
[b] All figures in thousands of dollars.
[c] Write-off of preoperating costs.
[d] Capital gain on sale of one aircraft.
SOURCE: Company records

EXHIBIT 3

Balance Sheet at December 31, 1972, 1971, and 1970

	1972	1971	1970
ASSETS			
Current assets			
Cash	$ 133,839	$ 231,530	$ 183
Certificates of deposit	1,250,000	2,850,000	
Accounts receivable:			
Trade	397,664	300,545	
Interest	14,691	35,013	
Other	67,086	32,569	100
	479,441	368,127	100
Less allowance for doubtful accounts	86,363	30,283	
	393,078	337,844	100
Inventories of parts and supplies, at cost	154,121	171,665	
Prepaid insurance and other	75,625	156,494	31
Total current assets	2,006,663	3,747,533	314
Property and equipment, at cost			
Boeing 737–200 jet aircraft	12,409,772	16,263,250	
Support flight equipment	2,423,480	2,378,581	
Ground equipment	346,377	313,072	9,249
	15,179,629	18,954,903	9,249
Less accumulated depreciation and overhaul allowance	2,521,646	1,096,177	
	12,657,983	17,858,726	9,249
Deferred certification costs less amortization	371,095	477,122	530,136
	$15,035,741	$22,083,381	$539,699
LIABILITIES AND STOCKHOLDERS' EQUITY			
Current liabilities			
Notes payable to banks (secured)	$ 950,000	$	$
Accounts payable	124,890	355,539	30,819
Accrued salaries and wages	55,293	54,713	79,000
Other accrued liabilities	136,437	301,244	
Long-term debt due within one year	1,226,457	1,500,000	
Total current liabilities	2,493,077	2,211,496	109,819
Long-term debt due after one year			
7% Convertible Promissory Notes		1,250,000	
Conditional Purchase Agreements—Boeing Financial Corporation			
(1½% over prime rate)	11,942,056	16,803,645	
	11,942,056	18,053,645	
Less amounts due within one year	1,226,457	1,500,000	
	10,715,599	16,553,645	
Stockholders' equity			
Common stock, $1 par value, 2,000,000 shares authorized,			
1,108,758 issued (1,058,758 at December 31, 1971)	1,108,758	1,058,758	372,404
Capital in excess of par value	6,062,105	6,012,105	57,476
Deficit	(5,343,798)	(3,752,623)	
	1,827,065	3,318,240	429,880
	$15,035,741	$22,083,381	$539,699

Notes to Financial Statement not shown here.
SOURCE: Southwest Airlines Company annual reports, 1971, 1972

EXHIBIT 4

Incremental Costs per Flight and per Passenger, 1971–1972[a]

	LAST HALF 1971	FIRST HALF 1972	LAST HALF 1972
INCREMENTAL COSTS PER FLIGHT			
Crew pay	$ 46.62	$ 50.61	$ 56.82
Crew expenses and overnight	5.28	4.24	4.93
Fuel	93.50	93.35	94.91
Airport landing fees	10.44	12.87	12.37
Aircraft maintenance	69.98	69.51	75.19
Totals	$225.82	$230.58	$244.22
VARIABLE COSTS PER PASSENGER			
Passenger-handling personnel	$1.09	$ .88	$ .80
Reservation costs[b]	.92	.11	.10
Ramp, provisioning, and baggage handling[c]	.98	.40	.29
Baggage claims and interrupted trip expenses	.01	.01	.01
Passenger beverage and supplies	.25	.13	.43
Traffic commissions and bad debts	.61	.62	.74
Passenger liability and insurance[d]	.90	.38	.43
Totals	$4.76[e]	$2.53	$2.80

[a] Includes all costs treated as variable by Southwest management for the purposes of planning and analysis.

[b] Initially, Southwest contracted out its reservation service to American Airlines; after October 1, 1972, SWA's own employees handled this task.

[c] Initially contracted on a minimum cost-per-flight basis, subsequently used own employees on a phased schedule as facilities permitted.

[d] During the last half of 1971, SWA paid a minimum total premium for passenger liability insurance due to the low number of passengers carried.

[e] Comment by management: "The high figures for costs per passenger during the last half of 1971 represent the effect of minimum staffing with very few passengers. The minimum staffing effect declines substantially in later periods, and begins to represent a true variable."

EXHIBIT 5
Monthly Flights and Passenger Counts on Each Route by Type of Fare

| | DALLAS–HOUSTON | | | | DALLAS–SAN ANTONIO | | | | SAN ANTONIO–HOUSTON | | | | GRAND TOTALS | |
| | Full-Fare | | Discount | | Full-Fare | | Discount | | Full-Fare | | Discount | | | |
	Passengers	Flights	Passengers	Flights	Passengers	Flights	Passengers	Flights	Passengers	Flights	Passengers	Flights	Passengers	Flights
1971														
June[b]	3.6	273			1.9	148							5.5	424
July	10.3	642			5.2	346							15.5	988
August	11.3	672			4.8	354							16.1	1,026
September	11.7	612			4.8	327							16.4	939
October	14.6	764			6.5	382							21.0	1,146
November	14.0	651	0.1	3	4.2	240			0.9	72			19.1	966
December	14.5	682	0.2	5	4.0	165			1.7	134			20.4	986
Total	80.0	4,299	0.3	8	31.4	1,962	—	—	2.6	206	—	—	114.0	6,475
1972														
January	16.0	630	0.2	4	2.8	141			2.0	128			20.9	903
February	15.9	636	0.2	4	2.8	142			2.1	134			20.9	916
March	17.9	664	0.4	5	3.9	204	0.3	5	2.8	146			25.4	1,024
April	17.4	601	0.3	4	4.3	185	0.3	4	2.3	130			24.7	924
May	17.1	554	1.5	30	3.5	177	0.7	21	2.5	138			25.3	1,020
June	16.5	474	3.3	47	3.8	170	1.4	31	2.6	140			27.6	862
July	13.6	447	4.0	47	3.3	162	1.8	31	2.1	131			24.7	818
August	15.7	496	4.0	50	3.2	177	1.8	31	2.4	146			27.0	900
September	13.7	436	3.8	53	3.1	154	1.6	30	2.2	127			24.4	800
October	16.0	474	4.8	71	3.4	173	1.8	27	2.5	139			28.5	884
November	15.1	403	7.4	104	2.4	122	4.2	77	2.3	123	0.5	16	32.0	845
December	12.8	377	6.3	91	2.4	117	3.9	69	2.0	110	0.5	16	27.8	780
Total	187.7	6,192	36.2	510	38.9	1,924	17.8	326	27.8	1,592	1.0	32	309.2	10,676
1973														
January[c]	15.1	404	6.8	101	1.4	75	6.3	122	2.4	120	0.5	16	32.5	838

a All passenger figures are in thousands
b Part month only
c Estimated figures
SOURCE: Company records

EXHIBIT 6

Sample Radio Commercial for Half-Fare, Off-Peak Flights, Fall 1972

NUMBER:	98-23-2 LENGTH: 60 secs. (Dallas version) DATE: 10/13/72
MUSIC:	Fanfare
ANNCR:	Southwest Airlines introduces the Half-Fare Frivolity Flights.
HOSTESS:	Now you can afford to fly for the fun of it.
SFX:	LAUGHTER OF ONE PERSON BUILDING FROM UNDER, WITH MUSIC
ANNCR:	Now you can take any Southwest Airlines flights any week night at eight o'clock and all flights on Saturday or Sunday for half-fare. Just $13 or $25 round trip.
SFX:	LAUGHTER. MUSIC OUT. STREET SOUNDS UNDER.
MAN:	You mean I can visit my uncle in Houston for only $13?
ANNCR:	Right
MAN:	That's weird. My uncle lives in St. Louis.
MUSIC:	MEXICAN FIESTA SOUND
CHICANO:	Take your wife or lover on a Southwest Airlines Half-Fare Frivolity Flight to San Antonio this weekend. Float down the river while lovely senoritas strum their enchiladas and sing the beautiful, traditional guacamoles.
SFX:	ROCKET BLASTING OFF
ANNCR:	Take a Southwest Airlines Half-Fare Frivolity Flight to Houston and watch the Astronauts mow their lawns.
SFX:	FOOTBALL CROWD NOISES
ANNCR:	Take a Southwest Airlines Frivolity Flight to Dallas and watch the Cowboys hurt themselves.
SFX:	OTHERS OUT. RINKY-TINK MUSIC UP.
HOSTESS:	Half-Fare Frivolity Flights, every week night at eight o'clock and *all* weekend flights. Only $13. Almost as cheap as the bus. Cheaper than your own car. So relax with me, and stop driving yourself.
ANNCR:	Southwest Airlines' Half-Fare Frivolity Flights.
HOSTESS:	Fly for the fun of it.

EXHIBIT 7

Analysis of Weekly Flight Schedules by Southwest and Competing Carriers

January 1973

	DALLAS–HOUSTON[a]						HOUSTON[a]–DALLAS						TOTAL NUMBER OF FLIGHTS (Both Directions)	
	Mon–Fri		*Sat*		*Sun*		*Total Week*	*Mon–Fri*		*Sat*		*Sun*		*Total Week*	*Full-Fare*	*Discount*
	I	H	I	H	I	H		I	H	I	H	I	H			
Braniff	80	35	8	5	12	7	147	70	45	9	7	12	7	150	297	
Texas International	45		6		9		60	49		6		10		65	125	
Southwest		55		2		5	62		55		3		4	62	100	24
Total	125	90	14	7	21	12	269	119	100	15	10	22	11	277		

	DALLAS–SAN ANTONIO				SAN ANTONIO–DALLAS					
	Mon–Fri	*Sat*	*Sun*	*Total Week*	*Mon–Fri*	*Sat*	*Sun*	*Total Week*	*Full-Fare*	*Discount*
Braniff	85	16	15	116	85	14	17	116	232	
Texas International	10	1	2	13	5	1	1	7	20	
American	10	2	2	14	10	2	2	14	28	
Southwest	20	1	3	24	20	2	2	24	30	18
Total	125	20	22	167	120	19	22	161		

	SAN ANTONIO–HOUSTON[b]				HOUSTON[b]–SAN ANTONIO					
	Mon–Fri	*Sat*	*Sun*	*Total Week*	*Mon–Fri*	*Sat*	*Sun*	*Total Week*		
Braniff	5		1	6	10	2	1	13	19	
Texas International	10	2	2	14	15	3	3	21	35	
American	5	1	1	7	5	1	1	7	14[c]	
Continental	45	9	9	63	45	9	9	63	126[c]	
Eastern	20	4	4	28	20	4	4	28	56[c]	
Southwest	15	1	1	17	15	1	1	17	30	4
Total	100	17	18	135	110	20	19	149		

[a] I = flights to/from Houston Intercontinental, H = Houston-Hobby
[b] Southwest flights on this route used Houston-Hobby Airport; all other airlines used Houston Intercontinental.
[c] Some flights offered thrift or night fares with savings of $3 to $5 over regular fare.
SOURCE: *World Airline Guide,* North American edition, January 1973

EXHIBIT 8

Estimated Market Size, Dallas–Houston and Dallas–San Antonio Routes[a]

	LOCAL PASSENGERS CARRIED ANNUALLY (BOTH DIRECTIONS)			
	1969	*1970*	*1971*	*1972*
DALLAS–HOUSTON				
Braniff	268,630	265,910	246,170	300,780
Texas International	91,690	70,950	69,790	51,010
Other	4,390	4,790	1,830	1,910
Southwest			80,187	223,581
	364,710	341,650	397,977	577,281
DALLAS–SAN ANTONIO				
Braniff	144,010	124,690	135,660	177,020
Texas International	10,400	15,040	5,290	1,800
American	4,100	4,120	3,600	2,580
Other	520	560	380	330
Southwest			31,302	56,653
	159,030	144,410	176,232	238,383

[a] These estimates were made by Southwest Airlines' economic consultant in New York.
SOURCE: Company records

EXHIBIT 9

Sample Radio Advertising
for Half-Fare San Antonio Flights
(January 1973)

NUMBER:	118-23-2 LENGTH: 60 secs. (Dallas version) DATE: 12/21/72
WOMAN:	Harold, this is your mother in San Antonio talking to you from the radio, Harold. I want you to know that Southwest Airlines is having a half-price sale, Harold. For 60 days you can fly between San Antonio and Dallas for half price. Only $13, Harold. I expect to see a lot of you for those 60 days. Are you listening, Harold? Harold! (STATION WIND) I'm talking to you!
MUSIC:	LIGHT, HAPPY
HOSTESS:	Southwest Airlines half-fare flights. Every flight between San Antonio and Dallas every day. Only $13.
SFX:	STREET NOISES
IRATE MALE VOICE:	Hey! You people fly Southwest Airlines during this half-price sale. You're gonna have a lonely bus driver on your conscience. Take the bus. It only costs a little more, but it's four hours longer! You'll have a lot more time with me, won't you? (FADE) Well, won't you?
SFX:	STREET NOISES
MAN:	There is a cheaper way than Southwest Airlines. Put on roller skates, tie yourself to a trailer truck. . . .
MUSIC:	LIGHT, HAPPY
HOSTESSES:	Fly Southwest Airlines. Half price between Dallas and San Antonio on every flight every day. Why pay more?
VOICE:	Half price? Can they do that?
SECOND VOICE:	They did it!

Braniff's 'Get Acquainted Sale'

Half-price to Houston's Hobby Airport.

$13 Coach $17 First Class

To Hobby			Back to Dallas-Fort Worth		
Leave		Arrive	Leave		Arrive
7:30 a.m.	Non-stop	8:20 a.m.	8:00 a.m. (Ex. Sun.)	Non-stop	8:50 a.m.
9:30 a.m.	Non-stop	10:20 a.m.	9:00 a.m. (Ex. Sun.)	Non-stop	9:50 a.m.
11:30 a.m.	Non-stop	12:20 p.m.	11:00 a.m.	Non-stop	11:50 a.m.
2:30 p.m.	Non-stop	3:20 p.m.	1:00 p.m.	Non-stop	1:50 p.m.
3:30 p.m. (Ex. Sat.)	Non-stop	4:20 p.m.	4:00 p.m.	Non-stop	4:50 p.m.
5:30 p.m.	Non-stop	6:20 p.m.	5:00 p.m. (Ex. Sat.)	Non-stop	5:50 p.m.
6:30 p.m. (Ex. Sat.)	Non-stop	7:20 p.m.	7:00 p.m. (Ex. Sat.)	Non-stop	7:50 p.m.
			9:00 p.m.	Non-stop	9:50 p.m.

Sale lasts 'til April 1

From now until April 1, all Braniff International flights to Houston's Hobby Airport are priced to go. Half price to be exact. 50% off.

A one-way ticket in coach is $13.00. Round-trip is an even better bargain at $25.00. And in first class, $17.00 one-way, $34.00 round-trip.

We believe we have the best service to Hobby Airport. But not enough people know about it. So, we're offering you a chance to sample our big 727 Wide-Body jets to Houston's Hobby at half the regular price. We call it our "Get Acquainted Sale."

Half price and a reserved seat, too. Call Braniff International at 357-9511 in Dallas; 335-5811 in Fort Worth.

You'll like flying Braniff Style.

BRANIFF

U.S. MAINLAND   HAWAII   MEXICO   SOUTH AMERICA

MARRIOTT'S RANCHO LAS PALMAS RESORT

The management of a luxury hotel resort is planning its strategy for the "shoulder" and off-seasons when demand is lower. Will attempts to boost demand in the off-season by heavy discounting and appealing to less affluent customers negate the resort's attempts to win a five-star rating?

The electric tram hummed across the golf course, winding its way between groups of tall palms. Adjoining the greens, an artificial lake reflected the palms against a backdrop of shimmering brown mountains and cloudless sky. Robert I. Small, the driver of the tram, waved his free hand towards a cluster of buildings with white stucco walls and red tile roofs fronting the golf course. "There are just 11 five-star resort hotels in the United States," he said to the visitor accompanying him on an October day in 1979, "and we aim to make Rancho Las Palmas the twelfth!

"We're right in the middle of the desert resort area," continued the general manager of Marriott's Rancho Las Palmas Resort, "just 15 minutes from Palm Springs Airport and surrounded by country clubs, restaurants, and fashionable shops." He swung the tram around the side of the hotel complex, between green lawns and brilliant banks of flowers. "But like most resort areas, business here is highly seasonal," he went on. "Right now, we're in the shoulder season. The prime season starts with the Bob Hope Classic in January and lasts through April. Then there's another shoulder season before the summer."

Mr. Small parked the tram near the main entrance to the resort and climbed out. "Most hotels down here close from mid-June through mid-September," he added. "This was our first year and we decided to stay open during the summer. But you know, attracting guests to a resort when the temperature's over a hundred almost every day is quite a challenge. I thought we did pretty well! Now we're busy working on our strategy for 1980."

This case was prepared by Christopher H. Lovelock.

THE MARRIOTT CORPORATION

From modest beginnings in 1927—when J. Willard Marriott and his wife Alice opened the first two A&W root beer franchises in Washington, D.C.—the Marriott Corporation had grown into what was considered the most diverse company in the hospitality-leisure industry.

It operated five groups of businesses: hotels, family and fast-food restaurants, contract food services (including airline catering), theme parks (not unlike smaller Disneylands), and cruise ships. Hotels were the most profitable group in 1978, accounting for 33 percent of corporate sales of $1.25 billion and for 49 percent of the corporation's $134 million operating profit.

The company had first entered the lodging business in 1957 with construction of a 370-room motor hotel on the outskirts of Washington. Responsibility for development of the motor hotel program was entrusted to J. W. Marriott, Jr., who succeeded his father as president in 1964. The hotel group grew rapidly thereafter as the company built or purchased many additional hotels. It purchased its first resort hotel in 1967. By late 1979, there were 47 Marriott hotels located in 31 cities of the United States, as well as in several foreign countries. There were also 18 franchised Marriott Inns, owned and operated by other parties.

The Marriott Corporation had traditionally been a very centralized organization, with the head office exercising strong control over operating units. But with continuing growth and broader geographic coverage came moves towards decentralization and regional control. Within each operating unit, the general manager had full responsibility for management and performance; all managers and department heads reported to that individual. Meantime, the regional team responsible for operating results within a geographic region had a staff relationship to each operating unit for coordination, communication, auditing, training, and manpower planning.

Industry analysts and observers paid tribute to Marriott management's pragmatism and marketing skills. *Forbes*, for instance, noted that,

> [Marriott's] analysis of its strengths and weaknesses is hard-headed and realistic. . . . Its strength basically is in its knowledge of the hotel and eating businesses, its legendary attention to the details of satisfactory food, motivating employees, keeping clean premises—and in the all-important detail of site selection.[1]

A review of the lodging industry by the *Wall Street Transcript* in fall 1979 noted that,

> Success at keeping hotel rooms booked comes about in part thanks to Marriott's marketing expertise. Analysts say the family has long known how to entice customers with group rates and other incentives when occupancy shows signs of sagging. The fact that the Marriotts have located most of their hotels in metropolitan areas and given them a convention focus also guarantees good business, especially from air travelers.[2]

Hotel Group Strategy

During the 1970s, the Marriott hotel group had moved away from ownership of hotels (which tied up great amounts of capital) toward operation of hotels owned by others. Some existing hotels were sold to investors and leased back. In 1978, 60 percent of Marriott's 18,000 hotel rooms were operated on a fee-for-service basis, and it was expected that some two-thirds of future expansion would be under management agreement.

Between 1973 and 1978, Marriott hotels experienced a 13 percent annual growth in the number of rooms. For the next five years, average annual growth was targeted at a 20 percent rate on an expanding base; almost 90 percent of future expansion was planned for North America.

By 1979, Marriott hotels ranked twentieth in the U.S. lodging industry in number of units operated and fourteenth in number of rooms. The company had one of the highest occupancy rates in the industry, with more than 80 percent of available room nights sold in 1978. It could also boast more "four-star" ratings in the *Mobil Travel Guide* than any other hotel chain; in the 1979 edition, 20 Marriott hotels were awarded this rating. Additionally, two of its hotels, the Camelback Inn and the Amsterdam Marriott, received "five-star" ratings.[3]

Company executives noted that five-star institutions enjoyed great prestige and commanded top-of-the-line rates. A few exclusive groups would only hold their meetings at a five-star hotel or resort. Achieving and maintaining such a rating had a very positive impact on employee morale at the facility in question, as well as enhancing the overall Marriott image. But Marriott executives recognized that a five-star rating entailed risks as well as bringing rewards. Guests tended to have very high expectations and, therefore, to be more easily disappointed. And losing its fifth star could be very damaging for the image of a hotel or resort.

The marketing strategy adopted by Marriott during the 1970s had been to reposition the company from a chain of motor hotels to a group of properties ranking in the top 10 percent of all hotels in the country. "Marriott isn't at the top of the scale in luxury or price," remarked J. W. Marriott, Jr. "We offer a consistently high-quality product at a fair price; we are not flashy." Recently constructed Marriott hotels in urban areas were relatively conventional in appearance, lacking the dramatic architecture of hotels in the competing Hyatt chain. Marriott advertising emphasized the quality of personal service at its hotels, using the slogan, "When Marriott does it, they do it *right*." Among the full-color magazine advertisements employed in 1979 were one showing guests arriving in a Rolls Royce and being met by the doorman, and a second showing two guests breakfasting under palm trees on an outdoor patio.

The company stated in its 1978 Annual Report that its hotel system would "continue to focus on business travelers and meetings groups at locations in downtown and suburban areas and near airports." But it also planned to expand selectively in luxury resorts, such as the 423-room Camelback Inn in Scottsdale, Arizona (acquired in 1967), and the new Rancho Las Palmas Resort near Palm Springs, California, which opened in January 1979.

THE PALM SPRINGS AREA

Located in Southern California, Palm Springs had been internationally famous as a desert resort for over half a century. The City of Palm Springs was the largest and best known of five municipalities and five unincorporated communities in the upper Coachella Valley (Exhibit 1). In mid-1979 these had a permanent population of approximately 90,000 people, a significant proportion of whom were retired. During the first quarter of the year, the peak visitor and tourist season, the population swelled by over 50 percent. A 1978 forecast projected continued growth in the numbers of both residents and visitors.

Further south were the cities of Indio and Coachella, oriented towards agriculture and light industry, plus some unincorporated areas. The lower valley had a permanent population of some 45,000, which increased by about 20 percent in the peak season. Many of the lower valley's residents were of Mexican descent and were Spanish-speaking or bilingual.

One of the appeals of the Coachella Valley to visitors was its warm, dry climate and clear skies. During the coolest months of the year, November through March, the average daily high ranged from 69°F–80°F; in April, May, and October, the average high was 87°F–93°F. But from June through September the average daily high exceeded 100°F, and some days in July and August the mercury went above 120°F. However, even in mid-summer, the desert cooled rapidly in the evening and the low humidity made night-time temperatures quite pleasant.

The valley was approached by a highway from Los Angeles through the San Gorgonio Pass, below the occasionally snow-clad summits of Mount San Gorgonio (11,485 feet) and Mount San Jacinto (10,831 feet). Mountain ranges extended down both sides of the valley, at the bottom end of which, 228 feet below sea level, lay the 30-mile-long Salton Sea. Twice as salty as the ocean, the sea was known for its good sport fishing. The mountain climate was significantly different from that in the desert on the valley floor. At the top of the Palm Springs Aerial Tramway, for instance, the temperature averaged 40°F lower than in the valley 8,500 feet below. Visitors could go skiing in the San Jacinto State Park in the winter and hiking, camping, and riding there in comfortable temperatures during the summer.

Palm Springs—the hotel, retail, and financial center of the upper Coachella Valley—was approximately 110 miles east-southeast of downtown Los Angeles, 500 miles southeast of San Francisco, and 275 miles west of Phoenix. Its airport was served by eight airlines offering direct service to most major western and southwestern cities in the United States. During the peak season, the number of available flights increased to accommodate demand (Exhibit 2). But travel to Palm Springs from eastern and midwestern cities was more expensive and time-consuming than going to other sunbelt resorts such as Miami and Phoenix, often requiring intermediate changes for connecting flights.

South of Palm Springs, many new country club-style condominium projects were being developed around golf courses or other recreational facilities. Condominium units were often purchased as second homes by residents of other states (or Canadian provinces), who limited their stay in the Palm Springs area to less than six months per year in order to avoid legal residence in California with its obligation to pay the relatively high state income tax.

In the view of many observers, the popularity of the Palm Springs area as a resort was enhanced not only by its climate and magnificent natural setting, but also by the large and growing number of entertainment, recreational, retailing, and dining facilities available. The various unofficial titles bestowed on the area reflected its glamorous reputation: Golf Capital of the World (37 courses), Playground of the Stars, and even Swimming Pool Capital of the World (6,600 in the city alone).

For some visitors, however, their first exposure to the Palm Springs area was a disappointment. A *New York Times* story, written in 1977 when former President Gerald Ford and his wife took up residence in Rancho Mirage, noted that many easterners considered Palm Springs to be hot, dull, and provincial—even during the peak season—and were unimpressed by the desert landscape and bare mountains.

The Convention and Visitors Bureau

The economic growth of the area had been aided by vigorous promotion from the Palm Springs Convention and Visitors Bureau (CVB) and the Chamber of Commerce. In 1979, as in previous years, the CVB focused on promotion of tourism and conventions within the city limits of Palm Springs. Its annual funding of approximately three-quarters of a million dollars came entirely from hotel room tax revenues collected by the city; unlike similar bureaus in many other cities, the CVB sponsored no membership program for local airlines, car rental agencies, restaurants, or tourist attractions. It confined its promotional efforts to Palm Springs, neither seeking financial contributions from hotels and visitor attractions located outside the city limits, nor promoting such operations.

Although the magazine *Palm Springs Life* and other local publications liked to refer to the entire Coachella Valley as the "Desert Empire," no formal regional promotional program existed to attract visitors and tourists to the valley. Some observers pointed to the successful "Valley of the Sun" promotional program in the Phoenix/Scottsdale/Tempe area of

Arizona as a model that the Coachella Valley communities might seek to copy, but no one had yet been able to come up with funding.

THE HOTEL MARKET

In 1979, most hotel and motel rooms in the Coachella Valley were located within the City of Palm Springs. The city boasted 177 hotels and motels offering a total of some 6,300 rooms. One-third of these rooms and more than half of all room tax revenues were accounted for by eight major hotels: the Canyon, the Spa, the Hilton Riviera, the Gene Autry, the Ramada International, the Westward Ho, the TraveLodge, and the 7 Springs (Exhibit 3).

The three major hotels outside Palm Springs were Marriott's Rancho Las Palmas Resort in Rancho Mirage, the Erawan Gardens in Indian Wells, and the La Quinta Hotel in La Quinta. A number of small- and medium-sized hotels and motels were located in several of the other towns and unincorporated areas in the valley, notably Indio. While most had swimming pools, relatively few offered such resort facilities as golf and tennis.

Because of the seasonal nature of the demand for rooms, many hotels and motels were closed during the summer. Those that remained open—usually medium-sized, middle quality facilities—offered substantial discounts. Knowledgeable observers estimated that room rates during the "shoulder seasons" of May 1–June 30 and September 15–December 15 were approximately 70 to 80 percent of the peak season rates charged between December 15–April 30; during July and August rates were often as low as 50 to 60 percent of the rack rate.[4] Room tax revenue figures in Palm Springs published by the CVB demonstrated sharp seasonal fluctuations in total room sales income on a month-by-month basis (Exhibit 4). Contributing to this situation was the greatly reduced number of conventions held in Palm Springs during the warmer months (Exhibit 5).

The demand for hotel rooms had grown

significantly over the years, reflecting a rapid increase in the number of visitors to the Palm Springs area. In the quarter century between 1950 and 1975, convention attendance in the City of Palm Springs rose from 8,330 to 117,850. Two years later it topped 150,000, falling back to 140,968 in 1978, although the total number of conventions held continued to rise, reaching 1,317 that year.

A recent survey of Palm Springs hotel visitors showed differences in the visitor profile according to the season. Forty-five percent of visitors during the peak winter season came from out of state as opposed to only 12 percent during the summer. As compared to those who came during other seasons, winter visitors were somewhat more likely to be making their first visit to the area, to stay longer, to be older, and to have higher incomes (Exhibit 6). Not all visitors stayed at hotels or motels. Many owned second homes in the valley; others found that they could rent condominiums from absentee owners.

RANCHO LAS PALMAS

In 1975, Marriott Hotels Inc. and Sunrise Corporation joined forces to develop a major resort hotel and country club on 27 acres 12 miles south of Palm Springs. The hotel was subsequently named Marriott's Rancho Las Palmas Resort.[5] It was arranged that Marriott would manage the adjoining Rancho Las Palmas Country Club in addition to operating the hotel, and that hotel guests would be entitled to use the club's golf course and tennis courts on payment of a fee.[6]

The hotel, completed in early 1979, consisted of a central complex, constructed in a style reminiscent of early Spanish-Californian architecture, and 348 guest rooms and suites located in a series of free-standing, two-story villas. The central buildings housed the guest reception area, executive offices, a gift shop, barber and beauty shops, a grand ballroom (capable of seating over 1,100 diners and also divisible into eight smaller rooms), other meet-ing rooms, three restaurants, and a cocktail lounge.

The interior of the main buildings echoed the Spanish California theme, with exposed wood beams, rough textured stucco, tiled floors, wrought iron grillwork, hand-painted murals, and Spanish-style furnishings. The guest rooms, by contrast, were furnished in contemporary style and equipped with many accessories. There were 316 deluxe rooms, 24 smaller rooms called parlors, and eight suites. All rooms featured a patio or balcony; some overlooked small artificial lakes, others the golf courses of the adjoining Rancho Las Palmas Country Club. Most rooms were within a few minutes' walk of one of the hotel's two swimming pools and hydrotherapy pools.

The country club consisted of 864 condominium units built around three nine-hole golf courses, a clubhouse (containing restaurant, bar, and two pro shops), and a 25-court tennis center; eight of the tennis courts were lit for night use.

The main entrances to both hotel and country club were on Bob Hope Drive in Rancho Mirage, a rapidly growing resort community. The hotel was approximately half a mile from Highway 111, along which were located many expensive restaurants, giving the Rancho Mirage section of Highway 111 the nickname "Restaurant Row." An exclusive new shopping complex, scheduled for opening in late 1979, was under construction at the corner of Highway 111 and Bob Hope Drive. Two miles further south, the town of Palm Desert offered a wide choice of specialty shops and businesses.

The hotel opened for business on January 10, 1979, as construction workers and landscape gardeners hurried to complete the final touches. Many Hollywood celebrities attended the official grand opening the following month, and comedian Bob Hope broke the ribbon with a smashing golf drive.

By early October, Rancho Las Palmas had been open for ten months and the hotel's executive committee was reviewing progress to date as it worked on developing a plan for 1980. Occupancy rates and average room revenues for the first ten periods of 1979 are shown in Exhibit 7, as are projections for the balance of the year.

Hotel Management

Robert I. Small, general manager of Rancho Las Palmas, reported to the Marriott Hotel Division's vice-president–western region, who was located in Washington, D.C. Small headed an executive committee consisting of himself; the hotel's resident manager; the directors of marketing, food and beverage (F&B), and personnel; the chief engineer; and the controller. This committee met weekly, although the general manager often met separately with individual managers as the need arose.

Small's first exposure to the food and hospitality business had come 23 years earlier from working in his uncle's butcher shop in Tarrytown, N.Y. During college, he had worked summers at various resorts in the Catskills, a popular mountain resort area in central New York State. From the very beginning, he told a visitor as they walked into the cool of the hotel lobby, he had planned his career to get exposure to all facets of the food and lodging industry. After college, he had worked for Restaurant Associates in New York City, then for the El San Juan Hotel in Puerto Rico. He also worked for Fairmont Hotels and the Arizona Biltmore before joining Marriott in 1973 as resident manager at the Essex House in Manhattan. Next, he became general manager of the Saddlebrook Marriott in New Jersey, from which he went to the Netherlands for three years as general manager of the Amsterdam Marriott. He had taken up his appointment as general manager of Rancho Las Palmas in June 1978.

Small paused for a moment in the red-tiled lobby to exchange brief pleasantries with a uniformed hotel staff member and to introduce his visitor. An old stone fountain splashed in the center of the lobby, surrounded by groups of lush potted plants, including a 20-foot palm tree. Wrought iron candelabra hung from the beams of the three-story ceiling. Beyond some rounded archways, several guests were checking in at the reception desk. The staff member excused herself to see if she could assist them.

"Look around you!" said Small. "We set a tone at Rancho Las Palmas and first impressions are very important to our guests. We want to develop a relaxing holiday atmosphere here and have the guests enjoy themselves," he continued. "Our people, our facilities, and our food all contribute to that tone." Warming to his theme, Small led the way across the lobby and out to the terrace overlooking the swimming pool and the golf course. "This is a very personalized business," he emphasized,

You've got to take care of the guests and take care of the employees, too. It takes a lot of little things in both instances. There are 400 employees here at Rancho Las Palmas during the peak season—it's very labor intensive. As general manager, I like to train all my key personnel myself, so that they understand where I'm coming from and what my criteria are. If they don't understand, I'm in trouble!

How involved I am is how involved my managers are going to be. It's a matter of leading by example. Each of the components in this resort has got to come together—you have to have consistency. You also have to establish standards—standards which employees can relate to and take pride in. We're trying to make this a five-star resort, which involves offering guests exceptional facilities and exceptional service, with lots of little extra touches and amenities. I can't do that alone—it's got to be a team commitment. And everyone on my team understands where I stand on that.

One of our goals is to obtain a very high level of rebookings among our guests, both individuals and groups. The marketing people are expected to deliver the bookings, but if the guests are going to come back again, I've got to hook them by making sure the product is right.

Small saw Rancho Las Palmas as the prototype for new Marriott resorts. Unlike Camelback Inn, which had been purchased by the corporation as a going concern, Rancho Las

Palmas had been built by Marriott from the ground up. However, the general manager felt that being part of a chain imposed some constraints for his hotel.

Although the Marriott chain is positioned high, it's underpositioned for Rancho Las Palmas. We've had to deviate from the Marriott way at times. We've needed extra touches, extra amenities, extra services. I'm always looking for added components. That's the only way we'll ever get five stars.

The Marketing Organization

Immediate responsibility for marketing activities at Rancho Las Palmas rested with James K. Lopez, Director of Marketing. Lopez supervised a staff of eight, including the director of sales and three sales managers. Although Lopez's immediate superior was Bob Small, he also had a formal relationship with the regional director of marketing in Los Angeles and, through him, the vice-president–marketing for Marriott Hotels in Washington. The regional director was seen as providing a support system. "He works to establish goals for each of the five hotels in this region," said Lopez. "He's very experienced and can provide me with valuable insights and information. But he doesn't dictate."

Lopez, like the director of marketing at each Marriott hotel, was responsible for developing a marketing plan in the fall for the following fiscal year (beginning, at Marriott, at the end of December). Lopez noted that the company divided its fiscal year into thirteen 28-day "periods." Each one of those periods, he said, had its challenges and its holidays, not only in the rooms segment but also in food and beverage. The marketing plan addressed several areas—the rooms, F&B as it related to the restaurants and cocktail lounges, F&B as it related to banquets, and other smaller profit centers like the gift shop.

Lopez had joined Marriott on graduation from college as a part-time doorman at the company's hotel in Houston, intending to allow himself plenty of time for professional ten-

nis playing. "I had no idea of going into the hotel business," he admitted, "but I found I enjoyed the people aspects of the job." Soon he was offered a full-time position and later moved into sales. His work had taken him to four different Marriott hotels, including Camelback. Lopez had joined Rancho Las Palmas in August 1979 when his predecessor began a period of food and beverage training to enable him to take over the position of resident manager at the resort (a lateral move that would eventually put him in line for a general manager's job).

Marketing Activities

In addition to planning and supervising the work of the marketing department, Lopez devoted time to solicitation of major conventions and to advertising and public relations. The hotel employed a local public relations firm which reported to Lopez and was responsible for press releases.

National advertising for Marriott hotels was handled by Ogilvy and Mather, Inc., of New York. Rancho Las Palmas had been assessed some $43,000 in its 1979 budget (Exhibit 8) as its contribution to national advertising efforts.[7] This advertising, designed to gain national exposure for Marriott hotels as a group, appeared primarily in print media in 1979, notably inflight airline magazines, *Time*, *Newsweek*, and *Sports Illustrated*. The agency also put out a book of "stock" advertisements which any Marriott hotel could use to promote a wide range of services and events (e.g., Mother's Day lunches). Although Lopez felt that these stock ads worked well for Marriott's corporate hotels in urban areas, he believed that the distinctive nature of Rancho Las Palmas made it more appropriate for the hotel to design its own advertising for promoting its lounges and restaurants.

The budget for advertising and brochures at Rancho Las Palmas was set at $252,000 in 1979. Advertising accounted for approximately two-thirds of this total. Brochures ranged from small folders to lavish four-color booklets printed on expensive stock. They were employed for direct mail, as sales aids for the sales force, and for use by travel agents. Advertising was placed in travel industry publications, and in general interest magazines and newspapers targeted primarily at affluent readers in selected western and midwestern markets. Advertisements and listings in Palm Springs area publications emphasized the hotel's restaurants and cocktail lounges.

Group business was projected to account for 65 percent of total room nights in 1979. Exhibit 9 identifies group bookings at the resort during four representative periods of that year. Lopez noted that tough negotiation was often necessary to obtain satisfactory group rates: "You have to say no sometimes," he remarked. Personal selling efforts included work by Lopez, the director of sales, three sales managers, and supporting staff members. The 1979 budget for sales promotion and public relations was $263,000.

The director of sales (who also supervised the work of the three sales managers) was responsible for selling group bookings to national associations and major insurance companies. The national association segment was viewed as a prime source of group business and was projected at two-fifths of total group sales at Rancho Las Palmas. It was, said the director, a highly sophisticated market and involved dealing with professional meeting planners who were very demanding, familiar with major resorts around the world, and willing to pay top rates.

The Palm Springs area did not, Lopez added, have as strong a reputation with these planners as such resort areas as Hawaii, Phoenix, and Miami, each of which boasted a big convention center and a large number of major hotels, and was also promoted by regional or statewide convention and visitor bureaus. Lopez noted that both Miami and Hawaii had been successful in attracting foreign visitors (Europeans and Japanese, respectively) during their off-seasons. Although the Phoenix area lacked an ocean setting, it had been able to attract domestic visitors and conferences during the summer by offering substantial discounts, emphasizing the low humidity of its climate, and promoting the opportunity for early morning and evening recreational activities at outlying resorts.

Another major source of group business was represented by the corporate market, particularly as it related to incentive-type sales meetings or bonus vacations.[8] This market was very strong in the Palm Springs area. The third market, state and regional associations, was also quite large. Although the sales staff recognized that Rancho Las Palmas was too expensive for many of these associations, they were still optimistic about their ability to attract business from this segment. One of the sales managers was responsible for contacting corporations and state and regional associations, while a second focused on selling to corporate incentive houses (which arranged incentive packages for corporate customers).

The third sales manager was responsible for tour and travel business and directed her efforts primarily towards travel agencies and airlines, which produced both group and transient (individual) business for the hotel. Her job requirements included attendance at major travel agent conventions, work with airline sales personnel, and sales calls on travel agents in key markets (especially major West Coast cities in the U.S. and Canada).

The target for transient business in 1979 had been set at 35 percent of total room nights. This segment was reached primarily through advertising, direct mail, and travel agents. Transient guests paid full rates ($110 for double occupancy in a deluxe room, more for a suite) in the prime season, but could obtain major savings during the shoulder and summer seasons.

In addition to the personal selling efforts undertaken by each hotel, national sales efforts were directed by the Washington headquarters and national sales offices in New York, Chicago, and Los Angeles. These were targeted at existing major acounts or prospects that might be expected to make use of a number of different Marriott facilities. All Marriott hotels participated in what was known as the "Waygify" lead program, whereby organizers of group meetings at a particular hotel were asked, "Where Are You Going in Future Years?" Information on probable locations for each group were then relayed to the national sales offices. The 1979 budget at Rancho Las Palmas included an allocation of some $68,000 toward national sales expenditures.

The general manager had high expectations of the marketing group at Rancho Las Palmas and clear ideas of the role it should play.

> I want the marketing people to critique every aspect of this resort, including competition, and I expect to use them as the conscience of the hotel. They know what the guests are getting and they understand that word-of-mouth is a very strong recommendation. They're listening to the guests, they're doing the booking, and they're responsible for handling the groups when they come to the resort. We have to have an understanding here about what product the guest is going to get. I've known hotel people who just think that the guest is a nuisance.

Competition

It was Bob Small's opinion that no other hotel in the Coachella Valley could match the range and quality of amenities offered by Rancho Las Palmas nor the freshness of its physical facilities. The one area of competitive weakness that he saw concerned his hotel's lack of a health club and spa. Construction of such a facility, if done on a first class basis, would cost about $1.5 million. Although the general manager had been disappointed by the initial performance of the hotel's restaurants, he felt that weaknesses there had been corrected as a result of physical changes in the kitchen design and a change of management in the food and beverage department.

Small believed that the only significant local competition facing Rancho Las Palmas was the Canyon Hotel, a couple of miles from downtown Palm Springs. Built in 1962 and enlarged in 1973 by the addition of a large annex across the street, the Canyon complex was constructed in contemporary style with flat roofs and a white exterior. The Canyon Hotel had changed ownership and management more than once. It was presently managed by Pick Hotels, Inc., which also operated resort hotels in Pennsylvania and Florida.

The Canyon had an excellent private golf course, ten tennis courts, three swimming pools, and a spa. Its top-of-the-line restaurant, Hank's, was highly regarded by visitors and valley residents alike. However, some observers of the local hotel scene felt that the Canyon's physical facilities were somewhat "tired" looking and that its lobby did not create the ambiance of a luxury resort. Although the Canyon had previously always closed during the summer, it was rumored that management was considering keeping the hotel open during summer 1980. However, there was no mention of a summer season in the Canyon's newly published 1979–1980 brochure.

Lopez ensured that his staff monitored competitors on a regular basis. He pointed out that Rancho Las Palmas competed with a number of local hotels and resorts for certain types of business. "For instance," he remarked, "The Gene Autry competes with us for smaller meetings. Although I think we have a superior product, they're less expensive, closer to Palm Springs, and do a good job." Exhibit 10 summarizes characteristics of a number of leading hotels in the Coachella Valley.

Management saw the principal competition as coming from other leading resorts around the country, such as the Broadmoor in Colorado Springs, the Arizona Biltmore and Camelback Inn in the Phoenix area, and major resort hotels in California, Florida, and the south. "We are a destination resort," declared Small, "and we must sell the destination." However, some five-star resorts, such as the Greenbrier in West Virginia, were felt to be less directly competitive because their prime season was later in the year than Palm Springs'.

Experience During 1979

Despite a difficult period immediately following the opening in January—caused primarily by construction delays—and disappointing weather in February, the executive committee felt that Rancho Las Palmas's first prime season had been a success. Occupancy rates had averaged in the 80s and 90s, guest response to the facilities had been enthusiastic, and the percentage of rebookings had been very high. A majority of the transient guests had been affluent middle-aged couples. Small recalled,

> Initially we got a lot of ideas and advice from our colleagues at Camelback. Once we'd established ourselves as a premier, destination type of resort, that took care of the easy part—the prime season guest who can afford our rates. The shoulder and summer seasons are more difficult.

In the spring shoulder season, both occupancy and rates had declined somewhat, but business had still been brisk. The transient guests then had tended to be slightly younger than those during the peak season, Small recalled, and some couples brought their children with them.

During the summer, a period when most of the larger hotels and resorts in the Coachella Valley had traditionally closed, Rancho Las Palmas had elected to stay open. Some Marriott executives had questioned the wisdom of this policy, pointing out that Palm Springs was not a popular destination in summer and that demand would be limited.

The decision to remain open during the summer simplified, but did not resolve, an employment problem facing hotel management. The work force of 400 employees required in the prime season had to be reduced to half that number during the summer. The executive committee worked hard to minimize any resulting hardship. Jobs were found for a number of employees at other Marriott properties; for instance, 97 went to the Tan-Tar-A resort in Osage Beach, Missouri, where the prime season occurred during Palm Springs' off-season. A number of other employees who wished to take the summer off were granted leaves-of-absence, and only 11 actually went on unemployment. Those employees who remained were cross-trained so that they could work on more than one job; thus pool waiters and waitresses doubled as front desk clerks.

A number of other operating economies were made. These included reduced hours for the laundry, gift shop, and certain restaurants; removal or replacement of certain guest room amenities (such as expensive soap, bathgel,

and sewing kits); and discontinuance of room service except for continental breakfast.

The 1979 Summer Marketing Strategy

The marketing plan adopted for fiscal periods 7, 8, and 9, extending from mid-June through early September, contained three major elements. First, the basic transient rate was set at less than 40 percent of the prime season rate; substantial additional discounts were offered as part of weekend package deals, family packages, golf and tennis packages, and concessionary rates for airline and military personnel.

Second, extensive advertising was placed in local Southern California media, including *Los Angeles* magazine and the *Los Angeles Times*. A full-page color advertisement in the former urged readers to "Experience Marriott's Rancho Las Palmas Resort this summer at a cool 60 percent reduction in rates" (Exhibit 11).

Third, brainstorming sessions were held among the hotel's sales staff to identify groups that might be interested in meeting at the hotel at inexpensive rates, and to create special promotional events and packages that might attract transient business. A total of 36 ideas emerged from a preliminary screening; execution of each was assigned to a specific member of the sales staff, who was expected to do further research and then follow up through personal calls, direct mail advertising, and so forth. These ideas ranged from college and university seminars to religious retreats to outings for fraternal groups and sports fans; from a disco weekend package to a billboard campaign to bargain rates for members of the California Teachers Association; and from bridge tournaments to midnight tennis clinics to a running marathon.

Summer Results

Overall, the executive committee was pleased with the hotel's performance during the difficult summer season. Occupancy rates, budgeted for 44 percent, had remained in the vicinity of 55 to 60 percent during each of the three summer fiscal periods (Exhibit 7), although most patronage was concentrated at weekends. There were more young, single adults—many of them military personnel or airline employees—and more families with young children than at other times of the year.

Success in winning group business had been limited, especially during period 9 when transients accounted for over 80 percent of room nights. Many of the groups and "mini-markets" contacted had expressed no interest; none of the group bookings received had been large and the biggest—a church-related group of 75 persons one weekend—proved not to have been a recipient of one of the mailings sent out to 150 church and religious groups in early May.

Many of the 36 promotional ideas initially suggested had quickly been abandoned after further investigation. The running marathon idea, noted the sales manager responsible for follow-up, "was cancelled due to the lack of interest on anyone's part of having a running marathon in the desert in 110 degrees. The American Heart Association mentioned it would not consider sponsoring such an event."

Jim Lopez had spent his time since arriving at Rancho Las Palmas in reviewing the Hotel's operating experience during its first ten fiscal periods and looking for marketing insights.

> We know that in the prime season we can expect plenty of business, mostly from affluent, middle-aged couples who'll stay here for four or five days and then go on to San Diego or Phoenix. There's a lot of demand for our kind of product and these people will pay our rates. We're right in line with all the best resorts in the country. But in the summertime, it gets awfully hot, so we've tried to turn this around. The weather in L.A. is often smoggy and overcast in the summer; in San Diego it can be cool, damp, and foggy. So we offer "Day in the Sun" type of promotions which enable people to come out here for the weekend at very reasonable rates, get a good tan by the pool, and play golf and tennis in the morning and evening when it's cooler. We filled up every weekend

this summer—every one! But weekdays were tough, with occupancy rates in the 30s and 40s. One of the reasons it's so tough is that we're just not in a location where there's a lot of corporate business.

Groupwise, there aren't a whole lot of meeting planners who want summer meetings here, because of the heat. And for the most part, the organizations that think they can afford us don't meet in the summer anyway. So a majority of our summer guests will probably continue to be transients. Rancho Las Palmas is definitely a destination for weekend value seekers who want to experience a beautiful resort and look for reduced rates to do so. But they're a different mix of people. They tend to wander through the lobby in swimsuits, and experience has taught us to remove the upgraded guest amenities from the rooms since they seem to disappear at a rapid pace during the summer months.

But the summer's not our only problem: We've got to work really hard on drawing business in the shoulder seasons, too. One difficulty is that people in this part of the country just don't think of Palm Springs until after the first of the year. January through April is the prime season and then everyone just seems to bail out.

APPROACHING 1980

By October 1979, as the Palm Springs area entered the autumn shoulder season, cumulative financial results became available showing that Rancho Las Palmas was 4.2 percent ahead of its budgeted revenue figures for the first 10 periods of the year, but 8.6 percent ahead of budgeted costs, resulting in a very narrow profit margin. The executive committee was busy developing plans for 1980, as well as working hard to increase bookings for the months through Christmas. Preliminary indications were that the fall market was going to be a more difficult one to crack than originally anticipated; transient business, in particular, was not as strong as had been forecast, and projections for periods 11, 12, and 13 had been scaled back accordingly (Exhibit 7).

Financial projections for 1980 prepared by

the controller's office included a cost budget for each of the 13 periods in the fiscal year. The makeup of this budget varied somewhat from one period to another according to season. Exhibit 12 shows projected costs for period 3 (prime season), period 6 (spring shoulder season), and period 8 (off-season). The budget for the summer periods provided for an increased employment base over 1979, since the executive committee had concluded that the hotel had been understaffed then. To demonstrate the impact on costs of closing during the summer, an alternative budget had been prepared for each of the three summer periods. Although many employees could be laid off if the hotel closed, the resort could not be put into mothballs for the duration. About 65 personnel would have to be retained for the summer, including most of the engineers and gardeners, and some of the administrators and security officers. The adjoining country club and its recreational facilities would, of course, continue to operate during the summer, but these costs were separate from those of the resort.

As they reviewed the experience of the resort's opening year to date, Mr. Small addressed the question of the summer season. "Are we going about marketing the summer season in the right way?" he asked the other members of the executive committee. "Should we be approaching the problem differently or should we even be opening at all?" After reviewing the experience of the spring and considering the latest projections for the fall, he also suggested that the executive committee should devote greater emphasis to attracting transient business in the shoulder seasons.

Finally, he stressed again his goal of a five-star rating for the resort. "All of us at Rancho Las Palmas have got to think five stars," he urged, "and our operating and marketing plans for 1980 should reflect this goal."

NOTES

1. "Out of the Clouds, Back into the Kitchen," *Forbes*, 5/15/78, pp. 181–88.

2. "Lodging Industry: A TWST Roundtable Discussion," *Wall Street Transcript*, 10/1/79.

3. The *Mobil Travel Guide* rated more than 20,000 hotels, resorts, and restaurants each year. These ratings, ranging from one of five stars, were determined by field inspectors, a Mobil committee, local and regional consultants, and an evaluation of letters from the public. Criteria for rating hotels and motels included cleanliness, maintenance, quality of furnishings, scope of facilities and services, and degree of luxury. Standards for resorts were similar, but extra recreational services had to be available. Four stars, signifying "outstanding," were awarded to properties with larger than average bedrooms, good furniture, a high ratio of well-trained, courteous service people to guests, and an array of high-quality services and amenities, including restaurants. The distinction between a four- and a five-star resort, Mobil executives stated, lay in "luxury and a consistently superior level of performance." For a resort to be rated as "one of the best in the country," the quality of furnishings, decorations, and personal services should be perceived as not merely deluxe but unique; all guests had to be shown a uniformly high level of attention from a friendly, helpful, competent staff, with twice-daily maid service being standard; the grounds should be meticulously landscaped and maintained; a wide selection of recreational facilities, maintained and staffed by skilled instructors, should be available—as should special entertainment programs and the services of a social director.

4. The rack rate was the maximum daily charge for a room as established by hotel management.

5. For brevity, Marriott's Rancho Las Palmas Resort will subsequently be referred to here simply as "Rancho Las Palmas," "the resort," or "the hotel."

6. In 1979, tennis fees were $8.00 per court hour. A round of golf (18 holes) cost $18 per person, and rental of an electric golf cart cost $14. Tennis fees were reduced by 50 percent during the summer months and golf fees by 33 percent.

7. Each Marriott hotel was assessed a percentage of its total sales revenues as its contribution to national advertising and national sales activities.

8. Incentive meetings were often arranged by a company to reward its successful salespeople or dealers.

320

EXHIBIT 1

Visitor Map of Palm Springs and Vicinity

Note: The location of Marriott's Rancho Las Palmas Resort is marked RLP, slightly right of the center of this map. Reprinted by permission of *Palm Springs Life* Magazine. Copyright © 1981, Palm Springs Life Magazine.

EXHIBIT 2

Passenger Arrivals at Palm Springs Airport
1978–1979 versus 1973–1974

	1973–1974	1978–1979
July	3,931	13,589
August	3,918	13,945
September	6,728	15,220
October	12,347	20,824
November	14,060	26,558
December	16,389	27,741
January	18,475	34,916
February	23,944	42,309
March	25,322	45,539
April	19,242	33,354
May	11,571	24,744
June	7,904	17,130
Total	163,831	315,869

SOURCE: Palm Springs Convention and Visitors Bureau

EXHIBIT 3

Number of Hotels in City of Palm Springs by Size
(June 30, 1979)

CATEGORY NO. OF UNITS (ROOMS)	NO. OF HOTELS[a]	TOTAL NO. OF UNITS	PERCENT OF TOTAL HOTELS	PERCENT OF TOTAL UNITS	PERCENT OF TOTAL ROOM TAX RECEIVED BY CITY FOR FY 1978–1979
1 to 10	65	515	36.7%	8.2%	2.6%
11 to 25	57	935	32.2	14.9	7.5
26 to 50	27	883	15.2	14.0	7.8
51 to 100	10	630	5.7	10.0	9.3
101 to 150	10	1,240	5.7	19.7	20.7
Over 150	8	2,089	4.5	33.2	52.1
Totals	177	6,292	100.0%	100.0%	100.0%

a Hotels over 150 units are Riviera, Canyon Hotel, Ramada International, Palm Springs Spa, Westward Ho, Gene Autry, TraveLodge, and Hotel 7 Springs.
SOURCE: Palm Springs Convention and Visitors Bureau

EXHIBIT 4

City of Palm Springs:
Monthly Transient Occupancy Tax Collections as Percentage of Annual Dollar Total

YEAR	JAN.	FEB.	MAR.	APR.	MAY	JUN.	JUL.	AUG.	SEP.	OCT.	NOV.	DEC.	TOTAL TAX REVENUE ($000)
1966[a]	8.7%	14.9%	15.2%	14.5%	9.2%	4.6%	2.8%	2.1%	3.0%	8.5%	7.8%	8.8%	443
1970[b]	10.9	14.3	15.5	11.3	9.4	4.7	3.1	2.5	3.8	8.2	8.3	8.1	779
1975[c]	8.8	12.9	15.5	11.5	11.0	5.4	3.3	3.3	3.5	7.6	9.0	8.0	1,424
1976	9.7	13.8	13.1	12.7	10.2	5.1	3.1	3.0	3.7	8.0	8.7	8.8	1,648
1977	9.8	13.3	13.4	13.1	9.2	5.8	3.4	2.7	4.2	7.9	9.2	8.0	1,983
1978	9.5	12.7	13.8	11.8	9.5	4.4	3.4	3.0	5.0	8.2	10.0	8.8	2,249

[a] Tax rate 4%.
[b] Tax rate 5%.
[c] Tax rate 6%.
SOURCE: Palm Springs Convention and Visitors Bureau

EXHIBIT 5

Number of Conventions Held in Palm Springs in Each Month of 1978

	SIZE OF GROUP								
MONTH	0–49	50–99	100–199	200–499	500–999	1,000–1,499	1,500–1,999	2,000 and Over	TOTAL
January	66	37	23	15	2	1			144
February	83	47	21	7	4				162
March	51	30	16	12	3	1			113
April	62	44	16	13	7				142
May	48	35	20	14	4	3			124
June	32	19	15	6	2		1	1	76
July	29	7	1	2	1				40
August	28	8	2	2	1				41
September	40	19	12	10	4		2		87
October	55	32	26	12	4			1	130
November	69	46	34	12	2		1		164
December	45	27	9	9	3	1	–	–	94
Total	608	351	195	114	37	6	4	2	1,317

SOURCE: Palm Springs Convention and Visitors Bureau

EXHIBIT 6

City of Palm Springs
Seasonal Analysis of the Palm Springs Hotel Visitor, 1976

	VISITORS IN THE			
	Spring	*Summer*	*Fall*	*Winter*
1. Visitor Origin				
Southern California	75%	84%	70%	48%
Northern California	11	4	6	7
Illinois	1	1	3	5
New York	0	0	3	5
Oregon/Washington	2	2	4	9
Arizona/Colorado/Nevada	2	3	0	4
Michigan/Minnesota	0	1	2	6
Canadian Provinces	1	1	4	4
Other	7	4	10	15
2. Frequency of Visits				
First visit to Palm Springs	16%	10%	15%	23%
Repeat visit to Palm Springs	84	90	85	77
3. Average No. of Visits per Year (among repeaters)	2.3	3.2	3.9	1.9
4. Main Purpose of Visits				
Pleasure/vacation	70%	76%	66%	67%
Vacation and business	8	6	8	13
Convention	9	5	10	9
Business	5	7	8	6
Therapeutic	3	4	4	4
5. Average Size of Visitor Party	2.9	3.0	2.5	2.7
6. Transportation to Palm Springs				
Car	82%	90%	78%	66%
Air	10	4	13	26
Car and Air	4	4	6	8
Bus	0	0	1	0
7. Age of Visitors				
0–20 years	15%	21%	11%	11%
21–35	38	42	28	28
36–50	24	20	29	26
51–65	14	11	22	20
Over 65	4	1	4	9
8. Average Length of Stay (Nights)	3.1	3.0	4.5	6.0
9. Annual Family Income				
Under $10,000	9%	9%	6%	6%
$10,000–19,999	27	27	19	19
$20,000–29,999	25	24	24	22
$30,000–39,999	14	16	20	12
$40,000–49,999	7	6	10	11
$50,000 and over	13	11	16	20

SOURCE: Palm Springs Convention and Visitors Bureau

EXHIBIT 7

Marriott's Rancho Las Palmas Resort's Room Occupancy Statistics
January–December 1979[a]

			NUMBER OF ROOMS OCCUPIED			
PERIOD[b]		OCCUPANCY RATE (%)	Group	Transient	Total	AVERAGE RATE ($)
1[c]	12/30–1/26	84.3%	2,349	1,465	3,814	$55.34
2	1/27–2/23	78.1	5,886	2,737	8,623	83.30
3	2/24–3/23	90.9	6,470	2,689	9,159	83.84
4	3/24–4/20	80.9	4,917	3,132	8,049	84.30
5	4/21–5/18	63.5	6,840	1,744	8,584	69.99
6	5/19–6/15	61.2	3,363	2,756	6,119	57.35
7	6/16–7/13	57.5	2,819	3,008	5,827	31.10
8	7/14–8/10	55.8	2,408	3,624	6,032	29.56
9	8/11–9/07	60.4	915	5,360	6,275	27.78
10	9/08–10/15	55.6	3,537	1,884	5,421	48.44
11	10/16–11/12	79.4	6,162	1,578	7,740	67.18[d]
12	11/03–11/30	78.7	4,651	3,016	7,667	70.19[d]
13	12/01–12/29	54.8	3,156	2,186	5,342	68.83[d]

[a] Actual data for periods 1–10; projected data (as of 10/1/79) for periods 11–13.
[b] The fiscal year was divided into 13 periods of four weeks each.
[c] The hotel opened on January 10, 1979, so there were only 13 operating days in Period 1. During this period, 50% discounts were offered on all room rates since the hotel was still in the final construction stages.
[d] Projected.
SOURCE: Company records

EXHIBIT 8

Marriott's Rancho Las Palmas Resort's
Operating Budget
1979

	$000
SALES REVENUES	
Rooms	$ 5,252
Gift Shop	407
Food and Beverage	4,825
Other	242
Total	$10,726
DEPARTMENTAL EXPENSES	
Rooms	$ 1,198
Gift Shop	313
Food and Beverage	3,253
Other	597
Total	$ 5,361
DEPARTMENTAL PROFIT	$ 5,365
UNIT EXPENSES	
General and Administrative	$ 629
Credit Card Discount	125
Heat, Light, Power	306
Repairs and Maintenance	391
Sales Promotion	252
Local Advertising and Brochures	263
National Advertising Allocation	44
National Sales Allocation	68
Other	210
Total	
House Profit	$ 3,076
Total Investment Factors	$ 2,219
Profit Contribution	$ 857

SOURCE: Company records

EXHIBIT 9

Profiles of Selected Hotels and Resorts in the Coachella Valley
1979

HOTEL	NUMBER OF ROOMS	PUBLISHED DAILY ROOM RATES 1979–80		SPECIAL FEATURES
Spa Hotel**** Palm Springs	230	Double: Suite:	9/15–12/20 $90–$105 $100–$320 12/21–4/30 5/01– 6/30 $75– $90 $100–$250	2 swimming pools, natural spa with 24 therapy pools. Golf and tennis by arrangement at local clubs. A short walk to Palm Springs shops and restaurants. Facilities for small conferences.
Hilton Riviera**** Palm Springs (1½ miles NW of city center)	500	Double: Suite:	9/16–12/15 $70– $90 $130–$235 12/16–4/30 5/01– 6/30 $45– $65 $115–$215	5 tennis courts (all night-lit). Olympic-size pool; therapy pools. Golf by arrangement at local clubs. Convention Center can seat 2,500.
Canyon Hotel**** Palm Springs (2½ miles SW of city center)	450	Double: Suite:	9/14–12/20 $108–$128 $160–$375 12/21–4/30 5/01– 6/30 $75– $95 $140–$375	18-hole private golf course, 10 tennis courts (3 night-lit), 3 swimming pools, 3 therapy pools. Excellent reputation for dining. Conference Center separate from main hotel building.
Gene Autry Hotel*** Palm Springs (3 miles SE of city center)	161	Double: Suite:	10/01–11/30 $70–$100 $120–$165 12/01–4/30 5/01– 5/30 $55– $85 $120–$135	3 swimming pools, 2 therapy pools, 6 tennis courts, golf by arrangement.
La Quinta Hotel*** La Quinta (19 miles SE of Palm Springs)		Double: Suite:	9/01–6/30 $155–$185 $165–$250	2–4 room bungalows in 35-acre park-like setting, 1 swimming pool. 6 tennis courts (night-lit). Golf by arrangement at local clubs (own course under construction). Rates are full American plan and include all meals.
Erawan Gardens*** Indian Wells (15 miles SE of Palm Springs)	223	Double: Suite:	9/01–6/30 $49– $55 $96–$105	Two-story, Cambodian architecture. Mini-health club—jacuzzis, sauna, executive room. Two pools. Golf and tennis by arrangement. Head-quarters for Bob Hope Desert Classic Golf Tournament.

Note: Stars denote rating in 1979 *Mobil Travel Guide*.
SOURCE: Company records and hotel brochures

EXHIBIT 10

Advertising by Rancho Las Palmas in Los Angeles Area Magazines[a]
Summer 1979

Experience Marriott's Rancho Las Palmas Resort this summer–at a cool 60 percent reduction in rates.

Rancho Las Palmas, the centerpiece of the desert playground, keeps on sparkling all summer long.

And from June 15 to September 15, it can be yours at remarkable savings. A full 60 percent less than during prime season.

You'll be right in the middle of the desert's excitement – surrounded by fashionable shops, restaurants and country clubs, just 15 minutes from the Palm Springs Airport by courtesy shuttle.

A country club itself, Rancho Las Palmas has been expanded by Marriott into the area's finest luxury resort – with the addition of 348 oversized rooms and suites, 3 restaurants, and a discotheque.

You can enjoy your entire vacation right here.

Golf. There are 27 holes on site – the most in the area. And all were designed by noted golf architect Ted Robinson. Our professional is Warren Smith Jr.

Tennis. 25 courts, 8 lighted for night play. Bill Smith Jr. is Tennis Dir.

Swimming. Two pools to splash in, two hydrotherapy pools to relax in.

Wining, Dining and Dancing. The three restaurants are *Cabrillo*, a 200-seat multi-level international restaurant. *Fountain Court*, a family style restaurant. And for buffets, the *Sunrise Terrace* – a delightful patio.

For cocktails, dancing and entertainment, there's *Miguel's* lounge.

All in all, we think your visit here will be one of the memorable experiences of a lifetime.

Because on top of everything else, Rancho Las Palmas is staffed by Marriott people ready to prove: when Marriott does it, they do it *right.*

To reserve, call a professional, your travel agent, or toll-free 800-228-9290. Direct: (714) 568-2727.

Marriott's.
RANCHO LAS PALMAS RESORT

41000 Bob Hope Drive
Rancho Mirage, California 92270
(714) 568-2727

[a] Original in color

EXHIBIT 11

Rancho Las Palmas—Budget Revenues and Operating Costs by Representative Seasonal Periods[a]

1980

DEPARTMENTAL REVENUES	PERIOD 3 (PRIME SEASON)	PERIOD 6 (SHOULDER SEASON)	PERIOD 8[b] (SUMMER SEASON)
Rooms	863	416	142
Gift Shop	62	43	24
Food and Beverage	611	334	182
Other[c]			21
DEPARTMENTAL COSTS			
Rooms	139	111	74
Gift Shop	42	31	21
Food and Beverage	415	280	179
Other[c]	33	31	24
UNIT COSTS			
General Administrative	62	60	51
Heat, Light, Power	25	32	37
Repairs and Maintenance	40	41	40
Sales Promotion	22	22	20
Local Advertising and Brochures	12	12	12
National Advertising Allocation	6	4	2
National Sales Allocation	13	7	3
Other[d]	35	35	20

[a] All figures are in thousands of dollars.

[b] Management estimated that if the hotel were to close during the three summer periods, there would be a savings of $50,000 in unit costs over the duration of the summer season. But operating expenditures would continue to be incurred for departmental costs at the rate of $50,000 per period.

[c] Telephone and Recreation Center.

[d] Includes on-the-job training and accident insurance.

Note: Period 3 would run from February 22 to March 21. Period 6 would run from May 17 to June 13. Period 8 would run from July 12 to August 8.

EXHIBIT 12

Group Meetings Booked by Rancho Las Palmas in Periods 3, 6, 8, and 11, 1979

PERIOD	TYPE OF GROUP	HOME STATE	TYPE OF MEETING	GROUP SIZE	ROOM NIGHTS
3	Fast Food Co.	Illinois	Incentive Sales	150	200
3	Trade Association	Oregon	Annual Regional Assn.	250	800
3	Electronics Company	Illinois	Sales	125	175
3	Trade Association	Canada	Annual Regional Assn.	50	135
3	Trade Association	D.C.	Annual	24	48
3	Oil Company	California	Transportation Div.	50	110
3	Trade Association	California	Annual Nat. Assn. Conf.	220	550
3	Medical Center	California	Medical	200	400
3	Insurance Company	Wisconsin	Nat. Sales Incentive	250	550
3	Insurance Company	Connecticut	National Sales Incentive	200	670
3	Company	Pennsylvania	Annual Conference	250	480
3	Company	California	Management	32	112
3	Insurance Company	Illinois	Sales Conference	500	950
3	Trade Association	California	Board of Directors	70	105
3	Auto Company	California	Sales Conference	140	360
3	Medical Firm	California	Medical Conference	250	250
3	Construction Company	New Jersey	Sales	24	48
3	Consulting Firm	California	Seminar	200	320
3	Drug Company	California	Sales	75	81
3	Foundation	California	Seminar	60	70
3	Sporting Goods Company	Colorado	Sales	24	59
6	Trade Association	D.C.	Annual Conference	300	525
6	International Bank	California	International	100	150
6	Service Firm	California	Annual Review	25	100
6	Agric. Trade Association	California	Regional Assoc.	20	70
6	Gas Company	California	Corporate	22	72
6	Trade Association	California and New York	Regional	30	30
6	Trade Association	California	Regional Assoc.	175	235
6	Insurance Company	California	Insurance Sales	35	105
6	Company	California	Sales	300	300
6	Trade Association	California	State Assn.	200	500
6	Professional Association	California	Pre-Convention Conference	25	36
6	Broadcasting Company	New York	Programming	40	120
6	Insurance Company	Illinois	Annual Sales Conference	350	635
6	Food Company	California	Golf Outing	100	130
6	Company	Washington	Award Trip	36	55
6	Company	California	Western Regional Sales	90	300
8	Bank	California	Employee Outing	200	200
8	Company	California	Sales	200	200
8	Airline	California	Sales	300	200
8	Dance Professional	California	Dance Clinic	400	300
8	Lay Religious Group	California	Conference	300	200
8	Tour Group	New York	Youth Bus Tours	40	140
8	Life Insurance Company	California	Sales	22	27
8	Beauty and Talent Pageant	California	Youth Beauty Pageant	400	300
8	Company	California	Sales	300	300
8	Foundation	California	Annual/Fraternal	100	100
8	Franchise Bottling Co.	California	Sales	60	60
8	Company	California	Sales	500	250
8	Company	California	Sales	55	56

(continued)

EXHIBIT 12 (continued)

PERIOD	TYPE OF GROUP	HOME STATE	TYPE OF MEETING	GROUP SIZE	ROOM NIGHTS
8	Airline	California	Sales	60	75
11	Nonprofit Organization	California	Regional	300	800
11	Trade Association	California	Annual Assn. Conference	350	800
11	Professional Association	D.C.	National	80	150
11	Company	Illinois	Sales	150	550
11	Professional Association	California	Annual Regional Conference	350	950
11	Trade Association	Illinois	Annual	80	160
11	Trade Association	California	Annual	400	675
11	Professional Association	New York	Fall Annual	150	475
11	Hospital	California	Medical Conference	200	200
11	Nonprofit Research Assn.	California	Annual Conference	150	212
11	Company	New York	Sales Conference	300	660
11	Auto Dealer	California	Sales Incentive	54	120
11	Electronics Firm	California	Corporate	14	65
11	Moving and Storage Company	California	Corporate	50	55
11	Security Firm	California	Regional Conference	40	50
11	Company	California	Sales	70	120
11	Electronics Company	California	Corporate	20	40
11	Insurance Company	California	Sales Incentive	40	80

READING

Match Supply and Demand
in Service Industries

W. EARL SASSER

What makes service industries so distinct from manufacturing ones is their immediacy: the hamburgers have to be hot, the motel rooms exactly where the sleepy travelers want them, and the airline seats empty when the customers want to fly. Balancing the supply and demand sides of a service industry is not easy, and whether a manager does it well or not makes all the difference. This article discusses several ways service managers can alter demand and influence capacity.

CHARACTERISTICS OF SERVICES

The literature on capacity management focuses on goods and manufacturing, and many writers assume that services are merely goods with a few odd characteristics. Unfortunately, these researchers never fully explore the implications of these strange traits:

W. Earl Sasser is professor of business administration at the Harvard Business School. Reprinted by permission of the *Harvard Business Review.* "Match Supply and Demand in Service Businesses" by W. Earl Sasser, Jr. (November/December 1976). Copyright © 1976 by the President and Fellows of Harvard College; all rights reserved.

1. Services are direct; they cannot be inventoried. The perishability of services leaves the manager without an important buffer that is available to manufacturing managers.

2. There is a high degree of producer-consumer interaction in the production of service, which is a mixed blessing; on the one hand, consumers are a source of productive capacity, but on the other, the consumer's role creates uncertainty for managers about the process's time, the product's quality, and the facility's accommodation of the consumer's needs.

3. Because a service cannot be transported, the consumer must be brought to the service delivery system or the system to the consumer.

4. Because of the intangible nature of a service's output, establishing and measuring capacity levels for a service operation are often highly subjective and qualitative tasks.

MANAGING SERVICE CAPACITY

Whereas the consumption of goods can be delayed, as a general rule services are produced and consumed almost simultaneously. Given this distinction, it seems clear that there are characteristics of a service delivery system that do not apply to a manufacturing one and that the service manager has to consider a different set of factors from those that would be considered by his or her counterpart in manufacturing. And if one looks at service industries, it is quite apparent that successful service executives are *managing* the capacity of their operations and that the unsuccessful are not. So, the "odd characteristics" often make all the difference between prosperity and failure.

Consider the following service managers' actions, which resulted in fiasco:

Increasing the wrong kind of capacity. In studying the battle statistics in the war for market share among airlines, competitors observed that an air carrier in a minority position on a particular route would often get a smaller proportion of the total passengers

flown on the route than the share of seats flown.[1] Conversely, the dominant airline would carry a disproportionately larger share of the total passengers flown. The conclusion was obvious: Fly the seats, and you get the passengers.

In an effort to fly more seats, the airlines lined up to purchase jumbo jets. However, when competitors began flying smaller planes more frequently on the same routes and reaping a good number of passengers, it became painfully apparent to many airlines that frequency (and, to some extent, timing) of departures is the key to market share. Consequently, the airlines "mothballed" many of the jumbos or sold them if they could.

Not increasing all-around capacity. A resort operator decided to increase the number of rooms in a lodging facility and not to expand the central services required to support the additional guests. The fact that room rentals contribute up to 90% of total revenue and that tennis courts, swimming pools, meeting rooms, parking areas, and so on contribute next to nothing, or nothing, convinced the operator to create an imbalance in favor of revenue-producing activities. However, the number of guests adjusted itself to the level of occupancy that the central services could support, not to the level of room capacity. The room capacity beyond the level supported by the central services was wasted.

Not considering the competitive reaction. The Orlando, Florida, lodging industry's response to the announcement of Disney World's opening is a classic example of this type of service management fiasco. Disney executives had learned well the lessons of Orange County, California, and Disneyland, where revenue is limited to on-site entertainment, food, and souvenir dollars. However, businesses besides Disney have made large profits in lodging, restaurant, and recreational facilities. Correctly perceiving that the same thing would happen in Florida, Disney purchased 200,000 acres south of Orlando, eight times the number owned in Anaheim.

When news broke that Disney would buil in central Florida, however, everybody with hotel or motel in his or her portfolio began plans for Orlando units, even though Disney had preempted all the land within two miles of the Magic Kingdom. The subsequent over-building has been well documented. More than 30,000 rooms were built to service a market estimated to need only 19,000. As an Orlando lender moaned, "We had a great little 200-room property there, the only one at the inter-section. In less than a year, there were 5,000 rooms either built, under construction, or planned within a quarter mile of that intersec-tion. We had to foreclose, and our occupancy has been running at only 35%."

Undercutting one's own service. A new entrant in the overnight air freight trans-portation industry discovered that attempts to capture market share by adding to the existing number of planes and branch offices increased costs faster than revenues. Still looking for market share, the company then offered lower rates for second- and third-day deliveries. Be-cause it had excess capacity, however, the com-pany always delivered packages on the next day. As consumers discovered this fact, the mix of business shifted dramatically to the lower-priced services. So although there was an in-crease in volume, the resulting lower margins pushed the break-even volume even higher.

These pitfalls are not inevitable. Successful service executives do avoid them, and there are enough examples of well-managed service businesses from which to glean some wisdom on how to match demand for services with capacity to supply them. There are two basic capacity-management strategies available to most companies and a number of ways open to executives to manage both the demand and the supply sides of their businesses. I will discuss the strategies and choices in turn.

TWO BASIC STRATEGIES

Consider the national operations group of the XYZ brokerage firm. The group, housed in an office building located in the Wall Street area, handles the transactions generated by registered representatives in more than 100 branch offices throughout the United States. As with all firms in the brokerage industry, XYZ's transactions must be settled within five trad-ing days. This five-day period allows opera-tions managers to smooth out the daily volume fluctuations.

But fundamental shifts in the stock mar-ket's volume and mix can occur overnight, and the operations manager must be prepared to handle extremely wide swings in volume. For example, on the strength of an "international peace" rumor, the number of transactions for XYZ rose from 5,600 one day to 12,200 the next.

However, managers of XYZ, not unlike their counterparts in other firms, have trouble predicting volume. In fact, a random number generator can predict volume a month or even a week into the future almost as well as the managers can.

How do the operations managers in XYZ manage capacity when there are such wide swings? The answer differs according to the tasks and constraints facing each manager. Here's what two managers in the same firm might say:

Manager A: The capacity in our operation is currently 12,000 transactions per day. Of course, what we should gear up for is always a problem. For example, our volume this year ranged from 4,000 to 15,000 transactions per day. It's a good thing we have a turnover rate, because in periods of low volume it helps us reduce our personnel without the morale prob-lems caused by layoffs [The labor turnover rate in this department is over 100% per year.]

Manager B: For any valid budgeting procedure, one needs to estimate volume within 15%. Cor-relations between actual and expected volume in the brokerage industry have been so poor that I question the value of budgeting at all. I maintain our capacity at a level of 17,000 trans-actions per day.

Why the big difference in capacity man-agement in the same firm? Manager A is in charge of the cashiering operation—the han-dling of certificates, checks, and cash. The per-sonnel in cashiering are messengers, clerks, and supervisors. The equipment—file cabinets, vaults, calculators—is uncomplicated.

Manager B, however, is in charge of handling orders, an information-processing function. The personnel are key-punch operators, EDP specialists, and systems analysts. The equipment is complex—cathode ray tubes, key-punch machines, computers, and communication devices that link national operations with the branches. The employees under B's control had performed their tasks manually until increased volume and a standardization of the information needs made it worthwhile to install computers.

Because the lead times required to increase the capacity of the information-processing operation are long, however, and the incremental cost of the capacity to handle the last 5,000 transactions is low (only some extra peripheral equipment is needed), Manager B maintains the capacity to handle 17,000 transactions per day. He holds to this level even though the average number of daily transactions for any month has never been higher than 11,000 and the number of transactions for any one day has never been higher than 16,000.

Because a great deal of uncertainty about the future status of the stock certificate exists, the situation is completely different in cashiering. Attempts to automate the cashiering function to the degree reached by the order-processing group have been thwarted because the risk of selecting a system not compatible with the future format of the stock certificate is so high.

In other words, Manager A is tied to the "chase-demand" strategy, and his counterpart, Manager B in the adjacent office, is locked into the "level-capacity" strategy. However, each desires to incorporate more of the other's strategy into his own. A is developing a computerized system to handle the information-processing requirements of cashiering; B is searching for some variable costs in the order-processing operation that can be deleted in periods of low volume. The characteristics of these two vastly different strategies are outlined in Exhibit 1.

Service managers using the chase strategy are usually responsible for unskilled employees performing jobs with little or no discretion for low pay in a relatively unattractive environment. Managers use the level strategy most often where more highly skilled people perform jobs for high pay, with some or a lot of discretion in a relatively pleasant environment.

Because the skill-level requirement for "chase" is lower than that for "level," the training cost per employee will also be lower for "chase." However, the annual training costs in a department using the chase strategy could be much higher than for one using the level strategy. The chase strategy requires more employees, and those employees exhibit a

EXHIBIT 1

Comparison of Chase-Demand and Level-Capacity Strategies for the XYZ Brokerage Firm

	CHASE DEMAND	LEVEL CAPACITY
Labor-skill level required	Low	High
Job discretion	Low	High
Compensation rate	Low	High
Working conditions	Sweatshop	Pleasant
Training required per employee	Low	High
Labor turnover	High	Low
Hire-fire costs	High	Low
Error rate	High	Low
Amount of supervision required	High	Low
Type of budgeting and forecasting required	Short-run	Long-run

higher rate of turnover because of the job characteristics just described.

The chase strategy is usually more costly than the level strategy for other reasons as well. The high turnover rate and the use of unskilled employees both contribute to a high error rate, which means that more supervisors are needed to ensure that jobs are performed according to specifications.

For the chase strategy, the lead times required to attract and train new employees in periods of increased volume and to reduce the work force in periods of contraction are so short that forecasting and budgeting is needed only for the short run. However, because managers using a level strategy need a longer lead time to acquire or dispose of equipment and trained personnel, for them, forecasting and budgeting is a long-run process.

Although the chase-demand strategy has many negative connotations for enlightened managers, there are some service delivery systems, such as amusement parks and resort hotels with highly seasonal or random fluctuations in demand, that survive only as a result of its successful application.

MANAGING DEMAND AND SUPPLY

Besides electing to adopt one of the strategies just described, the service executive may select one or another additional way to cope with a fluctuating demand schedule. To understand how one business did it, see Exhibit 2.

Altering Demand

The manager can attempt to affect demand by developing off-peak pricing schemes, nonpeak promotions, complementary services, and reservation systems. Let's look at each of these demand-leveling options in turn.

Pricing. One method managers use to shift demand from peak periods to nonpeak ones is to employ a differential pricing scheme,

which might also increase primary demand for the nonpeak periods. Examples of such schemes are numerous. They include matinee prices for movies, happy hours at bars, family nights at the ball park on week nights, weekend and night rates for long-distance calls, peak-load pricing by utility companies, and two-for-one coupons at restaurants on Tuesday nights.

Developing nonpeak demand. Most service managers wrestle constantly with ideas to increase volume during periods of low demand, especially in those facilities with a high-fixed, low-variable cost structure. The impact of those incremental revenue dollars on the profitability of the business is tremendous. Examples of attempts to develop nonpeak demand are not hard to find. Hamburger chains add breakfast items to their menus, and coffee shops add dinners to theirs. Urban hotels, which cater to the business traveler during the week, develop weekend "minivacation" packages for the suburban population in their geographic areas, while resort hotels, jammed with pleasure travelers during school vacations, develop special packages for business groups during off-seasons.

However, caution must be used in developing plans to increase demand for the underused periods of the service facility. Many companies have made costly mistakes by introducing such schemes and not seeing the impact they would have on existing operations. As Wickham Skinner has noted, for manufacturing companies, there are some real costs associated with "unfocusing" the service delivery system, which is exactly what market-expanding activities have a tendency to do.[2] New concepts often require equipment and skills not currently found in a service delivery system. The addition of these skills and equipment may require a new type of labor force, a new layout, or more supervision.

Even if the new concept succeeds in creating demand in nonpeak periods, the effects are not always positive. Managers often use slack time productively as a time to train new employees, do maintenance on the equipment, clean the premises, prepare for the next peak, and give the workers some relief from the frantic pace of the peak periods. A new concept,

EXHIBIT 2

Finding a Creative Solution

A southeastern U.S. resort had a problem: in all probability, the demand for its tennis facilities would be very high in July and August, higher than it had the capacity to serve. Management knew it could build extra courts, at a cost of $12,000 each, but since those courts would only be used during the vacation months, they would cause a net loss to the company.

The managers agreed that each guest who wanted to play tennis should get the chance to play at least once a day for an hour. Agreeing on a service level established a base line for the number of court hours needed. The resort estimated that twice the number of courts it had was needed, and because there was no room for the additional courts at the existing location, it decided to build a new tennis clubhouse and a shop at a new site, all of which would be costly. When balanced against the costs associated with not having enough courts for guests at a resort that had heavily promoted its tennis facilities in the national media, however, the projected costs seemed small. Management saw the prospect of losing contributions if guests did not return in the future because of inadequate tennis facilities as a real cost, and the prospect of losing a real estate deal as a catastrophe. To cope with its capacity problem, management made several new moves.

To manage the demand, the resort managers made sure that all promotional literature carried a warning to prospective guests that the courts would be crowded in July and August. A reservation system made it possible to allocate court time and to steer demand to times when the courts were often not in use. Changing the court fees increased the attractiveness of doubles play (four could play for the same price as two). Recognizing that the real deterrent to doubles was not the money but available partners, the resort set up tennis mixers and round robins. These were held at the beginning of each week to enable the new group of vacationers to meet and size up each other's tennis game. Finally, by promoting activities that were not filled to capacity, such as surfing, sailing, and nature walks, management reduced the tennis demand and shifted some of it from peak hours.

The resort was just as innovative in managing capacity. First, it added lights to a number of courts so that tennis play could continue after dusk. Second, the resort opened the courts at 6 a.m., two hours earlier than before, and provided complimentary coffee and doughnuts to the "early birds." Finally, management built a few new courts but neither a clubhouse nor a tennis shop at the new site. Instead, a tent was set up to house someone to check reservations, collect fees, and sell balls. The original shop and clubhouse served the other needs. The overflow tennis area was opened only in the peak months and was staffed mainly with college students on summer vacation.

The combined effect of these moves was that the total investment in the new courts and facilities turned out to be much less than the original estimate. In fact, the moves helped make tennis a profitable operation.

335

therefore, may have a tendency to reduce the efficiency of the present system at best, or, at worst, to destroy the delicate balance found in most service delivery systems.

Developing complementary services. Another method managers use to shift demand away from peak periods is to develop complementary services, which either attract consumers away from bottleneck operations at peak times or provide them with an alternative service while they are in the queue for the capacity-restricted operations. For example, restaurant owners have discovered that on busy nights most patrons complain less when sitting in a lounge with cocktails than when standing in line as they wait for tables in the dining area. Also, the profitability of restaurants with bars can more than double.

A diversion can also relieve waiting time. A hotel manager installed mirrors on each floor's central lobby so that customers could check their appearance while they waited for the elevator. Banking by mail or by automated tellers are other ways to cut down customer waiting time.

Creating reservation systems. Service executives can effectively manage demand by employing a reservation system, which in essence presells the productive capacity of the service delivery system. When certain time periods are booked at a particular service facility, managers can often deflect excess demand to other time slots at the same facility or to other facilities at the same company and thereby reduce waiting time substantially and, in some cases, guarantee the customer service.

For instance, if a motel chain has a national reservation system, the clerk can usually find a customer a room in another motel of the chain in a fairly close proximity to his or her desired location if the first-choice motel is full.

In a similar manner, airlines are often able to deflect demand from booked flights to those with excess capacity or from coach demand to first class, especially if their competitors do not have seats available at the consumers' desired flight time.

However, reservation systems are not without their problems, the major one being "no-shows." Consumers often make reservations they do not use, and, in many cases, the consumer is not financially responsible for the failure to honor the reservation. To account for no-shows, some service companies oversell their capacity and run the risk of incurring the wrath of customers like Ralph Nader, who do show. Many service companies have made it a policy to bill for capacity reserved but not used if the reservation is not cancelled prior to a designated time.

Controlling Supply

The service manager has more direct influence on the supply aspects of capacity planning than he or she does on the demand side. There are several things a service manager can do to adjust capacity to fluctuating demand.

Using part-time employees. Many service companies have found that it is more efficient to handle demand whenever it occurs than it is to attempt to smooth out the peaks. The peaks vary by type of business—during certain hours of the day (restaurant), during certain days of the week (hair styling), during certain weeks of the month (banking), and during certain months of the year (income tax services). These service businesses usually maintain a base of full-time employees who operate the facility during nonrush periods but who need help during peak periods. One of the best-known resources is part-time labor pools, especially high school and college students, parents who desire work during hours when their children are in school, and moonlighters who desire to supplement their primary source of income.

Maximizing efficiency. Many service managers analyze their processes to discover ways to get the most out of their service delivery systems during peak demand periods. In effect, such analyses enable the service company to increase its peak capacity for little additional cost. For example, during rush periods employees perform only the tasks that are essential to delivering the service. If possible, managers use slack periods for doing supporting tasks, which in essence they are inventorying for peak periods.

To maximize efficiency, managers examine even peak-time tasks to discover if certain skills are lacking or are inefficiently used. If these skills can be made more productive, the effective capacity of the system can be increased. For example, paramedics and paralegals have significantly increased the productive time of doctors and lawyers. Even rearranging the layout of the service delivery system can have a major impact on the productivity of the providers of the service.

Another way to attack the peak capacity constraint is by cross-training. The service delivery system is composed of various components. When the system is delivering one service at full capacity, some sections of the system are likely to be underused. If the employees in these sections are able to deliver the peak service, they add capacity at the bottleneck. When the demand shifts and creates a bottleneck in other components of the system, the employees can shift back again.

Increasing consumer participation. The more the consumer does, the lower the labor requirements of the producer. Bag-'em-yourself groceries, salad bars at restaurants, self-service gas pumps, customer-filled-out insurance information forms, and cook-it-yourself restaurants are all examples of increased consumer participation in the production of services.

There are, of course, some risks to increasing consumer input: consumers might reject the idea of doing the work and paying for it too; the manager's control over delivery of the service is reduced; and such a move can create competition for the service itself. A cook-it-yourself restaurant customer might just stay at home.

Sharing capacity. The delivery of a service often requires the service business to invest

in expensive equipment and labor skills that are necessary to perform the service but that are not used at full capacity. In such cases, the service manager might consider sharing capacity with another business to use required, expensive, but underused resources jointly.

For example, a group of hospitals in a large urban area might agree that it is unnecessary for each to purchase expensive medical equipment for every ailment and that they ought to share capacity. One would buy cardiac equipment, another gynecological and obstetrical equipment, another kidney machines. Participating doctors would have admitting privileges at all hospitals. By sharing equipment, hospitals would not only better use expensive resources, but as groups of trained and experienced specialists developed at each facility, hospitals would also deliver better medical care.

The shared-capacity concept is possible in the airlines industry in several forms. Several airlines with infrequent flights in and out of a particular airport share gates, ramps, baggage-handling equipment, and ground personnel. In fact, some domestic airlines flying different routes with different seasonal demands exchange aircraft when one's dip in demand coincides with another's peak.

Investing in the expansion ante. Wise service managers often invest in an "expansion ante." When growth occurs, it sometimes becomes clear that some of the new development could have been done when the facility was originally constructed for much less cost and disruption. A careful analysis before the facility is built will show what these items are. For instance, for a small investment, a restaurateur can build his kitchen with extra space in order to service more diners later on. Contractors can run wiring, plumbing, and air conditioning ducts to the edge of the building where the expansion will take place. The manager can inventory enough land for the expansion and additional parking requirements. These actions will allow the restaurant manager to increase capacity without having to renovate the kitchen, redo the wiring, plumbing, and air conditioning systems, or purchase adjacent land at much higher prices.

SEEKING THE BEST FIT

Managing demand and supply is a key task of the service manager. Although there are two basic strategies for capacity management, the enlightened service manager will, in almost all cases, deviate from these two extremes.

The challenge to the service manager is to find the best fit between demand and capacity. In order to manage the shifting balance that characterizes service industries, managers need to plan rather than react. For example, managers should try to make forecasts of demand for the time periods under question. Then he or she should break the service delivery system down into its component parts, calculate the present capacity of each component, and arrive at a reasonable estimate of what the use of each component will be, given the demand forecast.

Because each system cannot handle infinite demands, the manager needs to question how much of the peak demand the system must handle. Just what is the appropriate level of service for the delivery system to provide?

Once the manager can approximate the answer to these questions and has decided which of the basic strategies to employ, he or she is ready to experiment with the different options to alter demand and capacity. Each plan and option a manager arrives at can be costed, and the best fit for the particular service selected.

Ultimately, of course, on the demand side, a manager's true aim is to increase revenues through an existing service delivery system of given capacity. Once the true variable costs are subtracted out, all revenues flow to the bottom line. On the supply side, the manager aims to minimize costs needed to increase or decrease capacity.

When facing increased demand, the business raises its revenues with minimal investment. In times of capital rationing, small investments are often the only ones available to the company. When facing contracting demand, the manager needs to select the best way to adjust the system's capacity to a lower volume.

In following the ideas outlined in this article, service managers need to think creatively about new ways to manage demand and supply. The most important thing to recognize is that they both can be managed efficiently and that the key to doing so lies in planning.

NOTES

1. See William E. Fruhan, Jr., *The Fight for Competitive Advantage: A Study of the United States Domestic Trunk Air Carrier* (Boston: Division of Research, Harvard Business School, 1972).

2. See Wickham Skinner, "The Focused Factory," *HBR*, May–June 1974, p. 113.

VI

Managing
the Service Marketing
System

Marketing and operations are more closely intertwined in service organizations than in manufacturing firms. Manufacturing often takes place far away from the points of purchase and consumption and substantially in advance of both. In many instances, the customer is able to draw a clear distinction between the identity of the manufacturer and that of the retail outlet where the product is sold. But in services, the final elements of the service "assembly" process usually take place simultaneously with consumption, so that the customer is much more likely to encounter the service production process in operation. Purchasers of goods rarely see the factory where the product is manufactured; purchasers of services, by contrast, often have to visit the factory to consume the product.

SERVICE BUSINESS AS A SYSTEM

As suggested in Figure VI–1, the service operation can be thought of as a *system*. Parts of this system are visible (or otherwise apparent) to customers; other parts are hidden from view and the customer may not even know of their existence. Many service organizations offer a product line of services; customers using one service—a room in a hotel, for instance—may be exposed to other services, such as a restaurant in the hotel, even though they make no use of these.

The visible components of the *service operations system* can be divided into those relating to service personnel and those relating to physical facilities and equipment. Customers may find themselves interacting with either or both of these and also, possibly, with other customers.

Variations in Visibility
of the Service Operations System

The proportion of the overall service operation that is visible to customers varies according to the nature of the service. Those services, such as airline travel, hairdressing, and hospitals, that are delivered to the physical person of the customer require customers to enter the "factory," although there may

FIGURE VI–1
The Service Business as a System

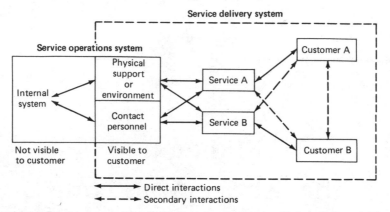

SOURCE: Adapted from Eric Langeard, John E. G. Bateson, Christopher H. Lovelock, and Pierre Eiglier (1981), *Services Marketing: New Insights from Consumers and Managers,* Cambridge, Massachusetts: Marketing Science Institute

still be many behind-the-scenes activities that these individuals do not see. Services that result in tangible actions to customers' physical possessions, such as repair and maintenance, may require the customer to drop off the item at the factory door and then pick it up again later when the work is completed. Alternatively, some services provide pickup and delivery at the customer's own home, office, or plant. For service to large or immovable items, such as a house, the service personnel may perform the work on-site—essentially bringing portions of their factory with them. In these instances, the visible component of the service operations system tends to be proportionately smaller than for services delivered at the factory.

Intangible service transactions such as broadcasting, insurance, information, and legal services that are delivered either to customers' minds or to their intangible assets, can often be conducted at arm's length by mail, telephone, or other electronic media. There may be no operational reason at all for the customer to see the "factory" where the work is performed.

Getting the Customer Out of the Factory

Traditionally, the interaction between service organizations and their customers has been a close one. But for reasons of both operational efficiency and customer convenience, customers seeking nonpersonal services, that is, services not requiring their *physical* presence, are finding that the level of direct contact they have with the service organization is being reduced. In short, the visible component of the service operations system is shrinking.

This situation has both advantages and disadvantages for service customers. Electronic media communications offer greater convenience than face-to-face communications. Self-service equipment, such as automatic teller machines, is often more conveniently located and available 24 hours a day, seven days a week. But the disadvantages are twofold. First, a change from personal service to self-service may intially be disconcerting. Hence, management of such changes requires careful attention to consumer education, responsiveness to consumer concerns, and possibly even some initial incentives. For example, gasoline at self-service pumps is usually several cents a gallon cheaper than gasoline pumped by attendants. Similarly, some retail banks may offer customers free ice cream or other small gifts as inducements to participate in a demonstration of how to use an automatic teller machine.

The Service Delivery and Service Marketing Systems

In Figure VI–1, the right-hand two-thirds of the diagram is enclosed in a large dotted rectangle. It comprises both the visible aspects of the service operation plus the customers themselves (assuming that they are visible to each other). This area can be thought of as the customer's view of the *service delivery system.*

But there are other components, too, that may contribute to the customer's overall view of the service organization. These include the communication efforts of the advertising and the sales departments, telephone conversations with service personnel (some of them located within the internal organiza-

tional system), billings from the accounting department, news stories and editorials in the mass media, word-of-mouth comments from current or former customers, and even exposure to market research studies.

Collectively, the components cited above—plus those in the service delivery system—add up to what may be called the *service marketing system* (Figure VI–2). In essence, this represents all the different ways in which the customer may encounter or learn about the service organization in question. Since services are experiential, each of these elements offers clues about the nature and quality of the service product. Inconsistency between elements may weaken the organization's credibility in the customers' eyes.

Identifying the components of the service marketing system. The following list provides a summary of all these components and can serve to identify the nature of the service marketing system for a specific organization.

1. Service personnel (Contacts with these may be face-to-face, by telephone, or by mail)
   a. Sales representatives
   b. Operations

FIGURE VI–2
Three Overlapping Systems: Service Operations, Service Delivery, and Service Marketing

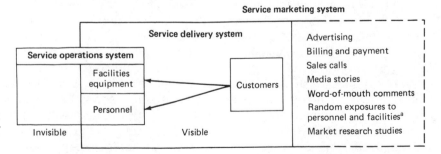

*May include exposure to service operations elements that are not normally visible during service delivery.

c. Customer service

d. Accounting/billing

2. Service facilities/equipment

   a. Buildings

   b. Vehicles

   c. Other equipment

3. Nonpersonal communications organization

   a. Letters

   b. Brochures/catalogues

   c. Advertising

   d. News stories/editorials in the mass media

4. Other people

   a. Customers encountered during service delivery

   b. Word-of-mouth comments

The significance of this approach is that it represents a customer's view of the service organization, looking at it from the outside, rather than from an internal operations perspective. Managers should remember that it is how customers *perceive* the organization that determines their decisions to select one service rather than another.

The scope and structure of the service marketing system will inevitably vary sharply for different types of organizations. Try using the list given above to develop a profile of the service marketing system for a variety of services—a hospital, an airline, a college, a hotel, a dry-cleaners, a bank, an automobile service shop, and the postal service. Recognize, though, that interactions with many of the components listed may be random rather than planned. For instance, what impression does it create in a prospective customer's mind to see a truck belonging to an express delivery service broken down by the side of the road? Or to be buying stamps at the post office and observe a uniformed employee (say a doorman) from a nearby hotel shouting rudely at the postal clerk at the adjacent window? Or to visit a friend in a hospital where the grounds and buildings are scru-

pulously clean and well maintained, the interior decor cheerful rather than institutional, the staff friendly and efficient, and the friend full of praise for the personal care he or she has been receiving and even for the quality of the food?

In short, service businesses can be divided into three overlapping systems, as shown in Figure VI–2. The *operations system* consists of the personnel, facilities, and equipment required to run the service operation and create the service product; only part of this system is visible to the customer. The *delivery system* incorporates the visible service operations' elements plus the customers, who may often be called upon to take an active role in helping create the service product, as opposed to being passively waited upon. The *marketing system* includes not only the delivery system, which is essentially composed of the product and distribution elements of the marketing mix, but also the many other ways in which customers may be exposed to the service firm and thereby form an impression of it. These additional components may include billing and payment systems, exposure to advertising and personal sales visits, word-of-mouth comments from other people, and random exposures to visible aspects of the service operations systems as well as to elements that would normally be invisible.

Although it is clearly the function of operations to run the service operations system, it is marketing's task to ensure that it is run in ways that balance satisfaction of customer needs and concerns against considerations of operating efficiency. Much operations work is done behind the scenes and is only of relevance to marketing inasmuch as it results in creation and delivery of a good product. But the visible elements of the operation must be seen in the perspective of the broader service marketing system. In short, there's an overlap between the marketing and operations spheres of influence, and managers on both sides must try to understand the others' perspectives.

THE SEARCH FOR QUALITY AND CONSISTENCY IN THE MARKETING SYSTEM

Not every component of the service marketing system is under the organization's direct control. Attempts must be made to manage customers (who often have a choice of alternative suppliers) to ensure that they use the service at the right time and know how to do so properly. If customers are ill-informed about how to use the service, they may damage equipment, waste employees' time, or behave in ways that will discourage other customers from making a repeat purchase. Hence, the need for ongoing efforts to educate customers, keep them informed, and correct them tactfully when they make an error or fail to behave in the desired manner.

Word-of-mouth comments are also outside the organization's direct control, but it may be possible to influence their content. ("If you liked our service, tell your friends; if not—tell us!") Among the functions of a good publicity-PR department are to ensure that the information circulated to the mass media puts the organization in a positive, but not inaccurate, light and to see that inaccurate rumors or misleading stories are quickly corrected. Maintenance of good media relations and a reputation for honesty in dealing with editors and reporters may allow off-the-record briefings and consultations, which, under some circumstances, may minimize the risk of subsequent misrepresentation.

The other components in the service marketing system may be under the direct control of the service organization or contracted out to intermediaries. Federal Express, for example, has a totally "closed" operations system: The vehicles, aircraft, facilities and personnel are all its own. Other organizations may find it cost effective to delegate certain tasks. For instance, airlines rely heavily on travel agents to handle many customer interactions in such areas as giving out information, taking reservations, accepting payment, and ticketing. Some banks have developed point-of-sale banking services at booths in supermarkets and department stores, which are operated by the store's employees. Trucking companies regularly make use of independent agents rather than having their own branches in each of the different cities they serve; they may also choose to contract with independent "owner-operators," who drive their own trucks, rather than buying trucks and hiring drivers as employees. Colleges often offer evening or weekend extension programs in local high schools as well as at the main campus, in order to make access more convenient to students; to supplement full-time faculty, they may also hire part-time adjunct faculty members to teach these courses.

The disadvantage of delegating activities to intermediaries is that it entails some loss of control. Ensuring that an intermediary adopts exactly the same priorities and procedures in delivering services to customers is difficult. Even if an intermediary performs well, there may still be a risk that customers will perceive inconsistencies between the intermediary's approach to the task and the overall positioning sought by the primary service organization. For instance, the use of high schools as satellite campuses by a college extension division may lead prospective users to perceive the product as inferior, regardless of the quality of the facilities and teaching.

And even within a "closed" service delivery system, in which all elements but the customers themselves are controlled by the organization, consistency of service quality is likely to remain an elusive goal. Customer-contact employees differ from one another and have good days and bad days. Quality control in a manufacturing plant can be interposed between the production process and subsequent sale of the product. Often this is impossible in a service business where consumption and final production take place simultaneously. Service procedures and execution can be standardized, but it is very hard to "clone" the desired output. The problem is compounded when services are being delivered through multiple outlets.

Two strategies can be adopted to help resolve this problem: (1) the creation of a professional, centralized *customer service function,* and (2) the use of what may be termed *internal marketing,* which embraces a variety of internally focused efforts, including training programs.

The Rise of the Customer Service Function

A majority of the activities performed by the organization in the service marketing system have traditionally been under the control of operations. The activities explicitly assigned to marketing usually centered on communication efforts such as advertising and sales management. In both instances, these activities may be performed by either regular employees or intermediaries who serve as subcontractors.

Because of the high degree of continuing interaction between customers and the service business, operations and sales personnel often find their energies diluted by the need to respond to a wide range of customer queries and complaints. They may also have to perform an order-taking function in the case of frequently purchased services offered in numerous different formats, for example, freight and passenger transportation or car rentals. Such services entail a multiplicity of possible destination pairs, variations in price by time period, level of service and/or type of shipment; they also involve a strong desire for effective execution on the part of customers.

Since complex services are particularly prone to Murphy's Law—"If something can go wrong, it will"—managers need to plan procedures for handling complaints, responding to requests for assistance, and providing information on how quickly the problem will be rectified.

New technology has made it possible to centralize certain activities that do not require face-to-face contact between customers and the organization. Reservations and simple inquiries can be handled over the phone, free of charge to the caller. Specially trained personnel in a central location can have access to needed information on a computer or can transfer the caller to an experienced supervisor for difficult queries and complaints. Information concerning orders and reservations can then be transmitted directly to the appropriate field operations location for action. Formalization and centralization of these customer service activities are creating a new function, *customer service,* which is separate from both operations and sales yet interacts closely with both.

Figure VI–3 shows how a centralized customer service department (CSD) can take over certain functions from both operations and sales, so that they may focus on making the best use of the specialized skills in their respective functions. In addition, the data collected in the CSD central computer can be used to generate valuable data for both operational and marketing planning purposes.

An interesting organizational question is whether the customer service department should be independent of both the marketing and operations functions, whether it should report directly to general management, or whether it should report at a senior level to either marketing or operations. The

FIGURE VI–3
Role of the Customer Service Function

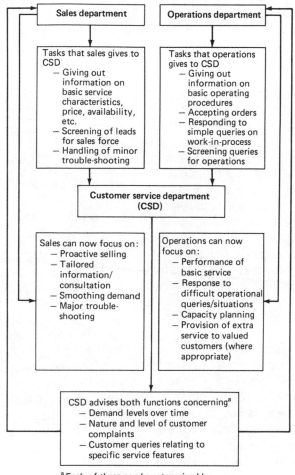

[a] Each of these can be categorized by type of customer.

approach used at one major corporation, which has pioneered the professionalization of the customer service function, is to have the CSD report to the senior vice president for marketing and customer service, who also oversees sales and advertising. The rationale here is that customer service deals directly with customers and is the corporation's most immediate link to the marketplace.

The net result of adopting such an approach is twofold. First, it reduces the visibility to the customer of the local operations system. Second, it helps to standardize, at a high level, the quality and consistency of customer service activities.

Service organizations that use intermediaries to execute selling or operational tasks obtain an additional advantage. By centralizing customer service activities, the organization regains a degree of control over interactions with its own customers. Moreover, the flow of orders, requests for information, and (perhaps) complaints to a centralized facility can be recorded and used to monitor the performance of the intermediaries.

Internal Marketing

Employees and intermediaries who work for the service organization can also be thought of as having a customer-like relationship with it. From a long-term perspective, at least, the relationship is a voluntary one. There are benefits to working for the organization, but there are also associated costs. If the costs, which may include the hassle and pressure of certain performance standards, exceed the benefits (earnings, friendships, job satisfaction, and so forth), then one of three things is likely to happen: The employee/intermediary either demands better terms, quits, or else seeks to reduce the costs, perhaps by not complying with all the prescribed standards.

Large service organizations can use a number of marketing tools, similar to those directed at external customers, to motivate employees and intermediaries to adhere to desired standards. This is particularly important when employees are in contact with customers and thus are a part of the product, or in time-sensitive services when the quality of employee actions at the time of the performance is difficult to control. Research may be needed to identify employees' and intermediaries' concerns and preferences relative to the work environment and to the execution of work-related tasks. This information should help management identify ways of improving the quality of the employment or subcontract "product" and of reducing the associated "costs." Communications to explain policies or to seek cooperation with procedures can take place on a personal basis (as in personal selling) or through some form of impersonal medium, such as a company magazine, direct mail, or videotaped presentation.

The use of internal marketing strategies is particularly appropriate when significant changes are taking place in how specific services are created and delivered, or when new services are being introduced. Following are some of the steps involved in developing, implementing, and monitoring an internal marketing program under such circumstances:

1. Undertake research to determine the perceived costs and benefits of proposed changes in operating procedures for the following:
   a. Operations personnel
   b. Sales personnel
   c. Other customer-contact personnel
   d. Intermediary organizations

2. Research findings may suggest the need for actions by management to reduce the perceived costs and to increase the perceived benefits for employees and intermediaries. Such actions might include
   a. Tailoring procedures to fit existing skills and preferences
   b. Changes in the physical operating environment (service facilities and equipment)
   c. Retraining of personnel (new skills)
   d. Changes in the financial reward structure
   e. Creation of new benefits and incentives

3. Subsequently, personal selling may be needed to
   a. Communicate the rationale for change
   b. Motivate employees and intermediaries to accept the importance of change
   c. Educate and train them in new procedures
   d. Respond to questions and resolve problems
   e. Receive feedback for fine tuning

4. Audio-visual or printed messages may be appropriate to
   a. Communicate the rationale for change
   b. Motivate

c. Show employees that previously expressed concerns are recognized and have been incorporated into planning

d. Educate and train in new procedures

e. Remind

5. Additional research may subsequently be needed to monitor the situation on an ongoing basis.

CONCLUSION

Services are often described as intangible, ephemeral, and experiential. This is true inasmuch as one cannot buy all the elements of a service, wrap them up, and take them home for later consumption. But a whole host of features in a service business are quite evident to one or more of a customer's senses. Collectively, they add up to what has been described here as the *service marketing system,* and they represent all the ways in which the service organization, or information about it, touches current and prospective customers.

Marketers should recognize that a customer's or a prospective customer's evaluation of a service is often based on a multiplicity of impressions that are not confined to performance of the core service. One progressive firm has explicitly defined the service product as consisting of "all the actions and interactions that customers perceive they have purchased." An important task for service marketers is to understand how customers actually perceive all the different service elements. Their views may be based not only on their experiences during planned service transactions, but also on chance encounters with specific elements away from the main service facility.

Sometimes it is difficult to get customers to recognize the work that is done—often behind the scenes—to make a service perform well. So it may be necessary to dramatize elements of the service in some tangible way. Examples include putting employees in uniforms that emphasize their functions, sealing newly cleaned hotel fixtures with some form of protective wrapping, or polishing shoes that have been repaired to make them look newer and more serviceable.

A major problem in service businesses, from both the marketing and operations perspective, is maintaining consistent standards of service. The problem is compounded when a service is delivered at multiple sites, or when certain tasks are delegated to intermediaries. Quality control standards can be laid down for each step in the service process, but because of the human element involved and the real-time environment of simultaneous production and consumption, it is much harder to standardize services than it is manufactured goods. One approach, when there are certain repetitive interactions between customers and sales or field operating personnel, is to centralize all telephone interactions through a professional *customer service function,* backed up by computer support. Another approach involves using the tools of marketing to develop *internal marketing strategies,* designed to win the understanding and cooperation of employees and intermediaries. If the needs and concerns of these groups can be identified and addressed, it may be possible to motivate them to behave in ways that will maintain and improve service standards, thereby increasing customer satisfaction.

CASES

MITCHUM, JONES AND TEMPLETON, INC.

A brokerage firm wants to introduce new personal financial-planning services to its product line. However, the firm is meeting opposition from its brokers, who are concerned about their lack of expertise in this area and who do not wish to endanger their relationships with their clients.

In the early part of 1973, Robert Phillips, senior vice-president of Mitchum, Jones and Templeton, Inc. (MJT), a West Coast investment banking and brokerage firm, was considering the long-term marketing strategy for his Retail Marketing Department. A major consideration was the viability of including personel financial planning among MJT's retail services. Financial planning, which was defined as personal estate planning and management, had recently aroused considerable interest in the brokerage industry. Phillips had to decide to what degree, if any, a commitment should be made to this area.

Another important consideration, which would be a major factor in any decision relating to financial planning services, was that of expanding the sales force. Two major issues were raised by the possibility of sales force expansion: first, compensation of branch managers and account executives (brokers), and second, training brokers in-house at MJT versus recruiting brokers from other firms. (Despite a NYSE ruling against "piracy," recruiting from other firms was a common practice in the industry.) The resolution of these two issues could have a major impact on MJT's retail operations.

COMPANY BACKGROUND

Mitchum, Jones and Templeton, Inc., established in 1920, was considered to be one of the largest regional brokerage firms and one of the smaller full-service investment banking and brokerage firms in the country. It offered retail and institutional brokerage, market making and underwriting services, distribution of corporate, municipal and mutual fund securities, investment advisory, and other security services. MJT held six seats on the New York Stock Exchange and was a member of the American and Pacific Coast Stock Exchanges, among others. Its 19 branch offices were located primarily in and around Los Angeles and San Francisco. In early 1973, corporate expansion into the Pacific Northwest was being considered.

Although MJT was a regional firm, and therefore somewhat smaller than many of the New York–based firms such as Merrill Lynch and Dean Witter, it did not seem to be hampered by its size. A *Wall Street Journal* article on the "Most Profitable Brokerage Firms in 1971" placed MJT twelfth on the "Most Profitable" list (on the basis of 1971 profit margins).

This case was prepared by Roberta N. Clarke, assistant professor of marketing at Boston University, and Martin V. Marshall, the Henry R. Byers professor of business administration at Harvard Business School.

Competition

MJT was generally regarded as one of the largest regional securities firms in the country in terms of revenues and number of employees; it was the second largest in terms of dollar value of underwritings managed. Because of its size, MJT found itself positioned between the smaller West Coast regional firms and the larger New York–based companies that had branch offices on the West Coast. This resulted in competition with both groups. The smaller regional firms generally had less breadth of services and lacked the underwriting capabilities of MJT. The New York–based firms usually had greater underwriting capabilities and often provided a range of services competitive with those of MJT; however, a substantial segment of the local population was thought to be attracted to MJT's regional image, resulting in a customer preference for the regional firm.

It was believed that the four securities firms with the largest shares of market in the West Coast were, in order, Dean Witter, Merrill Lynch, E. F. Hutton, and MJT, the first three firms being New York–based. None of the four—which were all considered "large" firms because they grossed greater than $20 million in commission revenue annually—were thought to have greater than a 10 percent share of the market.

MJT executives had recently taken a strong competitive interest in the large firm/small firm distinction vis-à-vis advertising. Large firms' advertising budgets averaged 1.1 percent of retail revenues and small firms' averaged 0.9 percent; MJT's advertising/retail revenues ratio was 0.3 percent as of late 1972. At that point, the only advertising which MJT ran was a single full-page advertisement in every other issue of the *Institutional Investor*.

A higher advertising budget was being considered at MJT, partially because the recent Merrill Lynch "We're bullish on America" advertising campaign had indicated that advertising could increase the firm's name awareness and improve broker credibility. The possibility of increased advertising led to such questions as: What type of advertising (lead generating or coupon advertisements versus image advertising); how much to spend on advertising; and whether or not to compete with Merrill Lynch's advertising expenditures in MJT's geographic region.

Retail Operations

MJT's retail operations—the area that would be affected by Phillips' decision on introduction of financial planning and/or the expansion of the sales force—were conducted at 19 branch offices through 260 registered brokers. Each branch office was supervised by a branch manager who had overall responsibility for all activities of the branch. Brokers were compensated on a commission basis.

Almost 60 percent of MJT's revenue was accounted for by retail operations. The retail (or commission) business was characterized industry wide as being a low margin, low-profit business compared to underwriting, which was a high-margin business. However, most of the industry's higher margin businesses were dependent upon the distribution power of retail operations for their success. For example, Merrill Lynch had built its powerful status in almost all segments of the industry, including underwriting, with the merchandising policy that it had implemented through its extensive retail network.

In order to underwrite an issue successfully, a firm had to be able to sell a large portion of the issue to a broad clientele, making necessary a large number of brokers; it also had to syndicate most of the issue to other firms which were not generally anxious to take part in the original firm's syndication unless that firm had a history of participating in their syndications. Taking part in another firm's syndication required substantial distribution power, which meant successful retail operations with many brokers. Because they were so strongly interrelated with the success of underwriting and many other aspects of the brokerage and investment banking business, retail operations, with their low margins, tended to be grossly undervalued. However, they were considered to be the keystone of MJT's product mix. Long-term plans for MJT included growth in the higher margin areas, which would further dictate a strong retail sales force and capability.

BROKERS—THE EXISTING OPERATION

The job of a broker was to open accounts, to offer each client (the account) expertise in the stock market, and to maintain the account by making wise investments for the client. Since many sophisticated clients had more than one stockbroker in order to keep their lines of information and product flow open, brokers were in essence fighting with other brokers for market share. A broker could increase his/her market share by winning more accounts (clients), by gaining a larger proportion of an individual client's investments, or both.

The relationship between broker and client was viewed as being a personal one, based on the personal credibility of the broker. The broker was generally the only link between the brokerage firm and the client, so that the latter's view of the firm was based predominantly on the broker. The importance of this relationship had resulted in a phenomenon called "hip-pocket" accounts, whereby brokers moving from one firm to another took most of their accounts with them. This reflected the fact that the client's loyalty lay more with individual brokers than with brokerage firms. As one broker said: "A client does not invest in a company; he invests in a person." This situation often spurred competition among brokerage firms to offer large bonuses to productive brokers to switch firms.

Recruiting and Training Brokers

The majority of MJT brokers were internally trained in the company's training program. Most people selected for the training program were aged 25 to 31 and had prior sales experience. Many prospective trainees were recruited through personal contacts with other brokers or MJT clients. There was also limited use of newspaper advertisements and employment agencies for recruitment.

Those without previous brokerage experience entered MJT's six-month training program, which cost MJT $10,000 to $12,000 per trainee. Trainees, who were paid $750 to $1,000 per month, attended one month of classes, and spent five months in observation, study, and readings in the MJT offices. The first month consisted of a formal training program covering the essentials of stock exchanges, regulations, operations, securities, selling skills, and insights into how to build one's business. The other five months were spent in a branch office, where the branch manager familiarized the trainee with branch procedures, various product flows, and the economic area in which the branch was located. The branch manager also assisted the trainee in comprehending the material contained in numerous correspondence courses and literature dealing with the industry. Although a common complaint about the training program was that it was too long, it could not be shortened because of a New York Stock Exchange requirement that brokers attend a six-month training period before they could be registered and were allowed to deal with the public.

According to one of MJT's top executives, whose responsibilities included sales force (broker and branch manager) administration, the training program was primarily oriented toward learning selling techniques. He believed that MJT's training program was of above-average quality; he knew that trainees complained about lack of sufficient knowledge about product and market, but stated that MJT was taking steps to correct the situation.

The alternative to training brokers was to "buy" them. This was a common practice in the industry, although not employed aggressively by what were regarded as the better firms since it violated NYSE rules. When a fully registered producing broker was bought, no training costs were incurred. Furthermore, a "bought" broker brought the firm "instant gross" or immediate new business because of his/her hip-pocket accounts.

Although brokers could be bought, such individuals had to be offered higher-than-average compensation for at least the first few months to induce them to leave their present firms. "Instant gross" brokers tended to be viewed as being more disloyal than internally trained brokers, because they could often be bought with the offer of even more money elsewhere.

Broker Compensation

The compensation schedule for MJT's existing services was somewhat confusing. Different types of securities and mutual funds merited different percentage commissions. The size of the commission was also affected by the size of the transaction and by the monthly gross of the broker involved. The commission structure encouraged emphasis on higher-margin products and larger transactions.

This confusion was compounded by the fact that brokers had operated under three different compensation schedules in the past year. The first reflected a $15 surcharge that was in effect in early 1972, of which the brokers received nothing. When the NYSE eliminated the surcharge, a new schedule came into effect to maintain MJT's profitability. However, the payout to the brokers had been miscalculated and turned out to be too low, so it was changed in response to broker pressure.

According to Mr. Phillips, the company's brokers were very well compensated. The average industry percentage commission on a transaction to a broker was 32 percent, but MJT's brokers averaged 37 percent. Merrill Lynch, by comparison, paid out only 26 to 28 percent in commissions. If MJT's commission rates had been comparable to Merrill Lynch's, MJT would have saved $2.16 million pre-tax net. (See Exhibit 1 for additional data on MJT broker compensation and gross transactions.) Alternative methods of compensation, such as treating a broker like a profit center, or paying brokers a base salary with a bonus based on the volume of gross transactions, were receiving consideration as was an across-the-board cut in percentage commission.

Phillips felt that a change in the compensation schedule would have to be well researched before action could be taken, because any cut in compensation might lead MJT brokers, especially the big producers, to seek positions at other firms. Since the average payout to brokers in smaller firms ran somewhat higher than industry average, brokers had an incentive to forsake their present positions for smaller firms.

BRANCH MANAGERS—SELECTION, COMPENSATION, AND TRAINING

MJT's 19 branch managers were responsible for the recruiting, hiring, development, and firing of brokers, and for their branches' gross and net revenues. Branch managers were usually selected from among the company's highest producing brokers, because they had credibility with the brokers they were supposed to manage. Additionally, three years of experience in the brokerage business was required before the New York Stock Exchange would allow someone to become a branch manager. The effect of this method of selection was that, as branch managers, they earned less than they had as brokers. This situation was widespread; the industry as a whole was unwilling to compensate solely for management. For performing management functions, a branch manager would receive 2 percent of the branch gross plus 5 to 10 percent of the net; this averaged out from $20,000 to $25,000 per year for management activities, although it could vary significantly from office to office. The Los Angeles office, for example, had 36 brokers and $2.7 million in gross transactions, while the Redlands office had only 8 brokers and $350,000 in gross transactions.

Because of this compensation system, most (15 of the 19) branch managers continued to spend their time primarily on brokerage activities in order to maintain a high level of income. Said Ron Glazer, one of MJT's better regarded branch managers,

> Most branch managers do not spend enough time in management; they are too interested in carrying out their brokerage activities. And there is no assurance that the limited time they spend in management will be spent in good management because a good broker, which is what most branch managers are, is not necessarily a good manager.

Phillips recognized that there would be major problems in reorienting branch managers to direct themselves toward management rather than toward brokerage production. A basic problem was monetary incentives. For instance, the Reno, Nevada, branch manager earned over $100,000 per year from his brokerage production, and one of the company's two division managers—branch managers reported to division managers—made more than $60,000 per year from commissions. Present compensation for management activities did not approach these figures. However, it was pointed out that a branch manager with good management capabilities could raise the brokerage production per broker by $500 to $1,000 per month, in addition to improving the recruitment, selection, and development of brokers.

Very few of MJT's branch managers had progressed entirely through the MJT organization from trainee to manager. Many had served as branch managers in other organizations before coming to MJT, so that they had a track record in branch management. The few who strictly relied on salaries for income were from outside MJT, and had learned to manage in firms that did not allow their managers to produce commissions. All of the branch managers who had "grown up" in MJT, however, still relied on commissions to provide 50 percent or more of their income.

Phillips was considering starting a branch manager's training program, but hadn't decided on how to do it or how much to spend on it. In general, he would probably have to replace two or three managers in existing branches, in addition to hiring new managers for any new branches he decided to open.

Expansion of the Retail Sales Force

Expansion of the company's retail sales operation could occur in two ways: (1) through growth in the current operating branch offices and (2) by opening new branch offices. Mr. Phillips could foresee the possibility of opening three new branch offices in 1973 with 7 to 8 brokers each; all other growth in that year was expected to be internal.

Phillips felt that certain economies were to be gained by increasing the number of brokers at a branch. Beyond 25 brokers, however, the manager seemed to become less effective in managing the office and developing brokers' skills because the span of control was too great. With the exceptions of the Los Angeles office, which already had 36 brokers, and the Redlands, Santa Rosa, and Napa offices, which had insufficient potential to support 25 brokers, existing MJT branches were each located in a marketing area that was thought to be capable of supporting a 25-broker office.

One MJT executive felt that the financial burden of increasing the number of brokers from 13 to 25 should be easily absorbed by MJT. He estimated that a new broker had to achieve only $18,000 per year in gross revenues to cover the incremental costs involved (i.e., communications, secretarial, supplies, travel, entertainment, etc.); in fact, the average broker grossed $72,000 per year. He further suggested that if, over the next three years, a branch manager acquired one broker every three months, that branch would be doing $864,000 added gross at the end of three years (12 new brokers × $72,000 average gross = $864,000). Since the contribution was approximately 35 percent of gross, this addition of new brokers would result in $302,400 additional net income per branch to the company.

It was also believed that a good branch manager could lessen turnover of brokers by one-third, and therefore speed up expansion. Given MJT's present annual broker turnover rate of 15 percent, and the expectation of training half the new brokers and "buying" the other half, a branch manager would have to add an additional two brokers per year in order to maintain the present size of the branch sales force. Taking into consideration both the expansion plans and the turnover rate, the branch manager would have to hire a total of six new brokers per year over the next three years. Yet several branch managers had not hired a trainee in many years.

FINANCIAL PLANNING

Phillips also had to make a decision as to whether to introduce personal financial planning as a new product into MJT's retail operations, and if so, how much of a commitment to make to it. Financial planning, which was defined as personal estate, tax, and investment planning and management, involved handling all the phases of an individual's investments: stocks, bonds, mutual funds, trusts, insurance, wills, real estate, and tax shelters. The availability from one company of all these financial services allowed the individual to do what some MJT executives referred to as "one-stop financial shopping." Adding such services would allow MJT to compete for a greater percentage of the dollars a client spent on various financial services, since their present retail operations could bid only for the dollars which clients spent on brokerage investments.

A number of financial institutions had recently begun to enter the financial planning market. In 1973, Merrill Lynch, Pierce, Fenner and Smith—the world's largest securities firm—was offering the consumer "29 different ways to invest your money," and was developing specialized departments to handle the various aspects of asset management. A few firms had been offering personal financial planning, in addition to brokerage capabilities, for a number of years. Investors Diversified Services, for example, offered 19 different financial instruments or services. Nonsecurities financial firms were also beginning to extend their product lines to include financial planning products and services which had not traditionally been associated with their industries: Life insurance companies, for instance, were selling mutual funds; co-operative banks were selling life insurance; and banks, such as the Chase Manhattan, were selling real estate and trust funds. This apparent trend toward selling a multiplicity of financial services led one MJT executive to speculate that financial planning was "the wave of the future."

The Case of Ben Ivy

MJT first became interested in personal financial planning in 1967–1968, when a young Stanford MBA named Ben Ivy, who had recently finished the MJT training program, began to operate in a way unlike the typical MJT broker. Once a month, Ivy would send out approximately 5,000 engraved invitations to carefully selected groups of individuals (such as lawyers, doctors, recent purchasers of Mercedes, and members of a certain country club) to attend a seminar, which ran two hours on a Tuesday evening and two hours the following Thursday evening. In the seminar, which covered the complete range of personal financial planning, Ivy encouraged audience members to view themselves as individual financial entities and to look at their security needs, income needs, estate needs, and investments simultaneously.

Of the 50 couples or individuals (out of 5,000) who attended each seminar, approximately 60 percent expressed an interest in these suggestions. Ivy followed up by meeting interested individuals in his office. In this meeting, the individual would describe his/her entire financial situation; Ivy then recommended a strategy that reflected the person's needs and the services available to fit these needs. In 1972, Ivy earned $157,000 selling these services.

MJT was quite pleased with Ivy's performance since the contribution rate of financial planning services to the company was 40 to 4_ percent. The processing costs also tended to _ much lower for financial planning than for brokerage. Three other trainees also followed Ivy's lead, and in 1972, each earned $50,000 to $100,000 in personal income.

Reaction to Financial Planning

As a result of the success of Ivy and others, and also because of industry interest in personal financial planning, MJT attempted its first formal venture into financial planning in early 1972 in the area of insurance. This initial venture was not well received by most brokers. One branch manager noted a lack of enthusiasm for the insurance seminars by the brokers; of those who attended the seminars, less than half performed adequately on a subsequent insurance examination. Because this first attempt to expand MJT's services had met with such limited success—and had led some brokers to resist any further efforts to broaden the traditional role of the broker—top management believed that a more careful consideration was required of how to implement financial planning, if it were to be implemented at all.

Some brokers and branch managers—Glazer among them—ventured their opinion that, since product knowledge appeared to be the weak aspect of the training program, the addition of any new products to the training program would be unwise. They viewed the possible addition of financial planning to retail services with reservation.

Many branch managers, who spent much of their time on brokerage activities (an accepted practice at MJT because even top management continued to maintain their own clients), felt that adding financial planning to the services already provided by the broker would be more than they, as managers, could handle. All the branch managers knew the brokerage business and felt that they could manage it. Very few, however, had had more than superficial contact with the various aspects of financial planning and were uncomfortable with the prospect of adding these services to MJT's retail business.

On the other hand, the four younger brokers previously mentioned (each with less than five years in the business), had mastered much of the broad range of products and were deeply involved in financial planning. All four ranked in the top five for volume of gross transactions among MJT brokers who had been in the business less than five years. One of them was in the running for the firm's top producer of the year. Financial planning was attractive to MJT because it was a highly profitable business and could help smooth the cyclical nature of revenues and earnings, which currently mirrored stock market fluctuations.

Plans for Implementation of Financial Planning

One suggestion for incorporating financial planning services into MJT's retail business was to have separate specialized departments for each type of financial service, which would then be staffed with experts in that particular field (i.e., lawyers in the trusts and wills department, insurance experts in the insurance department). The company had already added one in-house expert in insurance. The idea was that the brokers, upon finding a need for some type of financial planning in some of their brokerage clients, would refer the clients to the relevant specialist department.

Criticism of this suggestion by brokers reflected fears that this system might upset their relationship with their clients. Some brokers believed that their clients might not receive as expert advice from in-house departments at MJT as they might from outside companies specializing in those specific financial planning areas. The brokers did not want to endanger their brokerage relationships with clients, for it was the number and the productiveness of these relationships that was the measure of their success. Many brokers were unwilling to demonstrate a lack of knowledge in these areas to their clients, fearing lest it also reflect negatively in the clients' minds upon their knowledge of the brokerage business.

A second suggestion for implementation of financial planning was that each broker be trained as a financial planning expert with limited backup support from a few in-house experts in each area. The insurance seminars for brokers had been a first step in this direction. Some individual brokers had already taken it upon themselves to become experts in one of the many financial planning areas and to give seminars to the public in these areas, from which they would gain additional clients in both the specific financial planning area and in the brokerage area.

Many brokers resisted this idea because they did not want to diverge from their traditional role. They thought that it would threaten their credibility, even as brokers, if they were to ask clients to believe that one person (their broker) was capable of performing all these functions. As one broker said,

> You cannot be all things to all people. If you try, you will dilute your effectiveness. I do not think that financial planning is the responsibility of a brokerage firm. We are in the brokerage business. If we go beyond our primary business, we will find legalities and regulations involved in almost every area. Are we prepared to deal with these? And is the client willing to deal with a broker trying to sell him everything from insurance to tax shelters to trust funds?

Another source of resistance to financial planning came from brokers who were highly successful in their brokerage activities. These individuals, who were considered expert salespeople, were very highly compensated and could conceive of no reason why they should abandon their lucrative profession for what they perceived was likely to be a less profitable, less sales-oriented venture. Attempts to induce them to become involved in financial planning services by cutting back their brokerage commission were unlikely, since no brokerage firm wanted to lose its most productive brokers, which is what might happen if commissions were decreased.

This situation did not seem to bother Jim Norris, who was in charge of financial planning at MJT. He believed that the type of person best suited to be a financial planner might have a very different personality from that of a good broker. He envisioned a change in MJT recruiting practices, whereby a small stream of people interested in the broad range of personal financial services would be fed into the organization to be developed as financial planners. With respect to training existing personnel, he hoped to isolate and train only those brokers who expressed a reasonably strong interest in financial planning. He hoped that the brokerage community as a whole would be powerful in educating the public to the need for financial planning.

EXHIBIT 1

MJT's Broker Compensation and Gross Transactions

GROSS PER MONTH	PERCENT OF MJT BROKERS IN THIS CATEGORY	PERCENT OF MJT GROSS DONE BY THIS CATEGORY
Less than $3,000	32.0	12.0
$3,000–$4,000	16.5	10.0
$4,000–$5,000	15.0	13.0
$5,000–$6,000	10.0	10.0
$6,000–$8,000	12.0	15.0
$8,000–$10,000	3.0	5.0
$10,000–$12,000	5.0	10.0
Greater than $12,000	6.5	25.0
	100.0%	100.0%

Note: Approximately 35% of a broker's gross was take-home pay. The average gross per year = $72,000. The average take-home pay per year = $25,000. The median take-home pay per year = $15,000–$16,000. The highest gross by an individual broker in the month of September 1972 was $90,000, from which he took home in pay 45% to 50% before tax.

FEDERAL EXPRESS: CUSTOMER SERVICE DEPARTMENT, I

A rapidly expanding air freight business specializing in the transportation of small packages is trying to improve the quality of customer service. Various technological solutions have been proposed, including a central, computerized order-entry system. But operations and sales personnel are concerned about losing contact with their customers.

By the end of 1978, the five-year-old Federal Express Corporation, which had lost approximately $29 million in its first 26 months of operations, was being hailed by the business press as one of the great success stories of American entrepreneurship. The Memphis-based air freight company had become the nation's premier carrier of small packages requiring overnight delivery, controlling approximately 30 percent of the market. Volume had grown from the 15 packages carried when operations began on April 17, 1973, to over 43,000 nightly. On the average, revenues had been increasing at a rate of over 50 percent per year since 1974.

Pleased as they were by Federal's phenomenal expansion, several of the company's marketing executives expressed concern about its effect on customer service. Market research commissioned privately revealed that more than one customer felt that Federal was paying a high price for its growth. The shipping manager for one industrial parts distributor complained:

I don't think they're as congenial as they were when they first broke open the door, rushed in, and promised you the world. They did try for the first year and a half. But since they established themselves, it's been downhill. Before, they were willing to come in and talk to you once in a while. Now I've had to wait over six weeks for someone to come out and they said they were shorthanded.

I have no real complaint against them, because percentage-wise, it's just unreal, the service they've given me. But as far as getting anyone to answer a question, it's part of every big company and I call it growing pains.

COMPANY BACKGROUND

Federal Express was incorporated in 1971 by Frederick W. Smith, Jr., the 27-year-old heir of the founder of Dixie Greyhound Bus Lines. Borrowing a concept developed by United Parcel Service, he designed a nationwide air service network to resemble the spokes of a wheel, with Memphis, Tennessee, as hub. Each night, after packages had been collected from customers by the company's pickup vans (deadlines ranged from 7:00 p.m. in New York City to 4:30 p.m. on the West Coast), Federal Express aircraft stationed throughout the U.S. were loaded with cargo and then flown to Memphis, where the packages were unloaded onto an 800-foot-long conveyor system. As huge clocks overhead counted down the minutes till deadline, the loading crews sorted packages according to destination and reloaded them. The planes then flew to their destination cities, where the packages were delivered by Federal Express couriers by noon of the following day.

Federal Express began operations with six aircraft and 150 employees, serving 18 cities. By November 1978 the company served 148 markets (including Canada) and employed 4,600 people. Although initial losses were staggering, Federal Express passed the breakeven

This case was prepared by Penny Pittman Merliss, research associate at the Harvard Business School, and Christopher H. Lovelock.

point in mid-1975 and cleared $3.6 million in fiscal 1976, its first profitable year. By the end of fiscal 1978, profits exceeded $20 million (Exhibit 1).

Station/Customer Interface

Through field stations located near 120 airports, Federal Express served over 10,000 communities—reaching, according to company estimates, about 80 percent of the nationwide demand for air express services. By fall of 1978, it was estimated that about 18 percent of Federal's customers used the company's services each day. To accommodate this demand, Federal's fleet of pickup and delivery vans had been increased to over 900. Station clerks were receiving over 15,000 "on-call" pickup requests per day, in addition to the 2,200 customers who had arranged for permanent daily pickups. Approximately half of the company's employees worked in stations outside the Memphis headquarters.

Stations were classified according to package volume. An "A" station like Boston might handle 1,500 packages nightly and employ 15 people; Peoria, Illinois, a "D" station, employed 5 people and handled 50 packages or fewer. Because orders for service were made by telephone, customers almost never visited a station; "on-call" customers were linked to the company through their courier, and larger customers with standing pickup orders were visited by sales representatives as well. By the same token, dispatchers and station agents rarely met their customers. Station managers, on the other hand, often accompanied couriers or salespeople on their rounds.

Services

Federal Express offered three primary services to its customers: Priority One, Courier Pak, and Standard Air Service (Exhibit 2). Incremental services available at extra cost included Restricted Articles Service, providing special handling for hazardous cargo; Signature Security Service, a special-handling pro-

cedure that included signed receipts from everyone having custody of a package; and Saturday Delivery Service. The decision to use Federal Express as a carrier could be made by any of a variety of people, varying somewhat according to the service chosen. A traffic manager, mailroom supervisor, or shipping clerk usually placed Priority One and Standard Air Service orders; executives or their secretaries were more likely to call for Courier Pak pickups. Similarly, standing orders were customarily handled through company traffic or mailrooms, and on-call, intermittent requests for pickup usually came from managers, clerks, or secretaries.

All Federal Express shipments were originally transported in small Dassault Falcons (converted executive jets), which had a cargo capacity of 6,200 pounds. Smith had chosen the Falcon in order to escape federal regulation by the Civil Aeronautics Board (CAB); the CAB controlled the rates, routes, and services of all aircraft carrying over 7,500 pounds of freight. But by mid-1976, the same regulatory loophole which had made Federal Express possible was limiting its growth and inflating its costs. Unable to use large aircraft, the company was sending as many as six fully loaded Falcons nightly to a single city, wasting $25,000 a night as well as thousands of gallons of fuel. Smith and his associates took their case to Congress, lobbying heavily for a bill that would permit Federal Express to buy bigger jets. What they won, in November 1977, was a much greater victory: the total deregulation of the air freight industry.

AIR FREIGHT SHIPPING IN THE UNITED STATES

The U.S. air cargo industry was estimated at $1.2 billion in 1978. Although air freight was the most expensive way of shipping small packages, users considered it a good value. One study revealed that fast delivery, reduced probability of loss, and protection of fragile items were the three major incentives that moved shippers to choose air freight. Most air shi ments were small; 90 percent were composed of individual pieces weighing less than 70 pounds.

Originally dominated by the scheduled passenger airlines ("trunk carriers"), the air freight industry opened up in 1974–1975 as rising fuel costs led the trunks to substitute more profitable passenger traffic for freight. Although freight continued to be carried in the bellies of passenger aircraft, by fall 1978, only five major U.S. airlines continued to fly all-cargo freighters; 81 percent of their capacity was concentrated among four cities: New York, Chicago, Los Angeles, and San Francisco.

COMPETITION

Federal Express was not the only company to move into this breach. In September 1976, Connecticut-based Emery Air Freight, the nation's leading air freight forwarder,[1] opened a network covering 21 cities. Service was provided by 16 chartered aircraft, ranging from four-engine jets to small single-engine aircraft. Within two years Emery's revenues had risen from $305 million to $413 million. In September 1978 the company began to offer, in addition to its heavy-cargo shipping, a one-day small-package service called Emery Express. This service was available to 35 cities initially, and the company planned to reach 100 within a year. Emery promised later pickup (7:30 p.m.) and earlier delivery (11 a.m.) than Federal, as well as 5 to 10 percent lower rates. "Our unique selling proposition is that Emery is the only company a shipper can turn to for all weights, all markets, and same-day service," an Emery marketing executive explained.

Other significant competitors included Seattle-based Airborne Freight, also cheaper than Federal, which handled about 2.2 million pieces in its express service during 1978, and the U.S. Postal Service's Express Mail, which handled 7.7 million pieces in 1978 and projected 12 million for 1979. Express Mail, limited to material under 70 pounds, was considerably cheaper than either Federal Express or Emery, but delivery beyond the destination post office was promised only by 3 p.m. the following day. The Postal Service also charged extra for pickup. According to some users, avoiding the pickup charge often meant waiting in long lines to drop off shipments at the post office; however, consignees willing to pick up their packages at the post office could receive them by 10 a.m. of the day after shipment. USPS offered a full refund on any delayed packages.

Smith felt that the impact of competition on Federal Express remained minimal and that his rivals' promotion of their express services benefited the entire industry. Annual unit growth rates for the air express package market were averaging 15 to 20 percent. Since users of air express services were predominantly fast-growing, service-oriented businesses, it was anticipated that rapid growth would continue. Indeed, some industry analysts felt that Federal's quality service was creating its own demand, leading some companies to develop business strategies based on Federal's performance capabilities. The firm's package volume increased 34 percent in the fiscal year ending in May 1978; the number of Federal Express customers increased 66 percent in the same period.[2] New users accounted for 83 percent of the company's increase in revenues in fiscal 1978, and no single customer represented more than 2 percent of Federal's business.

Developments after Deregulation

Contrary to predictions, deregulations of the air freight industry led only a handful of new competitors to enter the field, most of them regional charter and air taxi services. Industry observers noted that unlike the trucking industry, where capital requirements were low and new operators could easily obtain financing, the airline industry was very capital-intensive. For instance, a new Boeing 747 jet freighter cost more than $50 million. There were few markets, if any, that could support the

250,000-pound capacity of a jumbo jet freighter that were not already being served by existing airlines.

Immediately following deregulation, Federal arranged to augment its fleet of Falcons with 10 secondhand Boeing 727s, a move designed to increase its service to cover 300 U.S. cities. The 727s, costing a total of about $40 million, had a freight capacity of 40,000 pounds each. In April 1978 the company went public, increasing equity from $25 million to $49 million, and began planning to enlarge the Memphis hub to a capacity of 120,000 packages per night. (Projections of future volume are presented in Exhibit 3.) In addition, Federal Express had begun to expand its network of downtown convenience centers in major market areas. These locations allowed customers to drop off packages in the late afternoon and early evening, after regular pickup deadlines had passed.

CUSTOMER SERVICE AT FEDERAL EXPRESS

As the company's growth continued and field operations became more and more efficient, Smith and his associates began to turn their attention to marketing and, particularly, customer service, a relatively neglected function within the corporation. J. Vincent Fagan was given responsibility for marketing and quickly developed advertising campaigns that came to be acknowledged as the most successful in the industry. In order to coordinate promotion and sales, Smith assigned the sales department to Fagan in 1975, and in 1977 Fagan also assumed responsibility for customer service, with the title of senior vice-president–marketing, sales, and customer service. Summarizing this integration, Fagan explained,

> The thinking was that marketing and sales were responsible for price, promotion, and product. Customer service was the one remaining function that looked as though it had overall control over product and a need for con-

sistency. When customer service consisted of a local station with a battery of busy phones, no one knew what kind of service the customer was getting—there was no control. We knew how good our package delivery was, we knew whether planes were arriving on time, but we had no overall way to measure or control customer service.

Early Customer Service Structure

From the beginning, Federal Express had made the assumption that the group of people moving the shipments—the field personnel— should also provide information and assistance to customers. According to one senior company executive, this assumption was rooted in Federal's anonymous paperwork and control system, derived from United Parcel Service. As he explained package tracking by the "exception" system,

> The logic is that since we are a wholly controlled entity—since we own the trucks as well as the planes and the package never leaves our hands—then once we have the package, it can't get lost on another carrier's airplane (as Emery's can) or go to another trucking company. In essence, it's got to be somewhere in the system. Thus we can make the assumption that if we know all the packages which didn't get to where they were supposed to go, then everything else will arrive on time. So if a package that was supposed to go to Des Moines ends up in Detroit, it's the responsibility of the people in Detroit to call up Des Moines and let them know about it, so they'll be ready when the customer calls in.

Since there was no way anyone could be certain of where a package was in the system on any given day, requests for information had been transferred to field personnel "because they probably have as good an idea of what's going on as anyone else." Once the source of operational information was transferred to the field, it appeared to be a logical and cost-effective step to make the station also responsible for informational tasks, answering questions on rates and features of service.

Initially, customer service was provided both locally and through Memphis headquarters. In the field, telephone clerks (known as station agents) took orders for service, traced missing packages, and answered questions about rates, delivery, and insurance. The great majority of traces were handled by contacting the other station involved in the shipping; only rarely did a package have to be traced through Memphis. Complaints were dealt with by station managers in the smaller stations or by station agent supervisors.

The Memphis service group, known as Customer Service Agents (CSAs), performed the same functions handled by station agents: taking orders, answering questions, tracing packages. Memphis CSAs were reached through a toll-free number, which according to one station manager was used "mostly by people who don't know or don't want to look up their local station. They seem to feel that if they call the corporate office they'll get faster service." Orders taken in Memphis were relayed electronically to the local stations via Datacom, a system similar to Telex.

Need for Turnaround

Although Federal's customer service structure appeared acceptable on paper, by 1977 it was considered a problem by almost everyone in the company. Fagan recalled,

At the station level, there was no consistency whatsoever. Customer service was an ad hoc, local option system; training consisted of a single sentence—"answer the phone as best you can." Station managers were using customer service people for all kinds of jobs—unloading trucks, sluicing down floors, grabbing the phones.

Recognizing the depth of the problem, Fagan assigned responsibility for the customer service department to Heinz Adam, who had joined the company in 1976 as director of marketing administration and supervised the strategy which led Courier Pak's average daily volume to increase by over 500 percent in two years. Adam took the job of vice-president—customer service under protest in March 1978, well aware of the challenges he faced.

Corporate customer service has traditionally been a very defensive function—a bunch of far from dynamic older people usually drawn from the secretarial ranks, sitting in a back room trying to make nice-nice for everyone else's screw-ups. Their usual job is to try to compensate for salesmen who make big promises that the company can't keep; customers complain that orders aren't arriving, and customer service people try to speed up production. When I took over this job, that's exactly what I found: 45 Florence Nightingales who spent most of their time tracing lost orders, listening to complaints, and giving out information. A very defensive bunch of people.

Adam felt that the group handling written communications needed at least as much improvement as the other agents.

When I took over, the answering of written complaints was essentially being handled by women who worked in the sales department. A customer would write in to Fred Smith, say, complaining about a bill or a lost package or a goofy courier, and he would be answered by the sales manager and his secretary. It was one girl typing on the typewriter, one guy dictating letters, and the financial department saying, whatever you do, apologize but don't give any money back. The typography was bad—even Xeroxed letters were used—the language was bad, and there was no system at all. I inherited eight boxes of correspondence that was nine months old and hadn't been answered because they couldn't get to it.

Problems in customer service were also affecting Federal's sales force. Jack McHale, a corporate sales executive, recalled:

Back in fall of 1977, we had just reorganized sales and set up a system where we had about 110 sales representatives, working in local stations, who reported to regional sales managers, who reported to the regional vice-president of operations. Each sales rep, as is true now, had a goal of 25 calls weekly, and at that time any account was fair game—even shippers who only used us three times a year would get a sales call if they wanted one. Now, of course, personal calls are restricted to high-volume and potentially high-volume accounts.

The problem was that every time there was any sudden change in volume, resulting from a strike at United Parcel Service, for instance, customer service just couldn't handle it, and we'd be pulled inside. The reps would have to answer the phones and, before you know it, they'd be trying to sell over the phone, not just addressing the customer's information request, and the call backup would only get worse. Sometimes we were not only answering the phones but helping the couriers make pickups and deliveries.

Within the station, pickup orders for dispatchers as well as telephone messages for sales reps were recorded by station agents on preprinted cards. Adam explained,

> They simply had phones with push buttons, and when a call came in, a light would go on, and the agent would take the call. If it was an established customer, she'd then go over to a big tub file and pull the customer's card for company data—otherwise, she'd take the information over the phone. When she was done, assuming it was a pickup order, she gave it to the dispatcher. It was like the airlines 25 years ago. They too had a tub file and they'd just check off seats till the plane was booked up.

The flow of paperwork thus generated was growing steadily, especially in major markets. The New York station, for example, handled 1,600 dispatch orders and messages daily by mid-1978.

CENTRALIZING CUSTOMER ORDERS AND REQUESTS

As early as May 1975, before Adam even joined the company, Federal Express management began to realize that their present customer service system was not equipped to handle an order volume growing by 50 percent a year. Recalling his initial approach to the problem, Sydney Tucker Taylor, vice-president of operations for ten Southern states, illustrated the company's predicament by sketching an hourglass:

> On one side you have demand—20 million packages a year, 50 million, one day 100 million; on the other is our ability, through the expansion of our transportation network, to meet that demand. The bottleneck is the finite number of phone lines that link the two.

> We had enough trucks, we had enough people, but we didn't have enough phone lines. We had all these planes and couriers, but we still couldn't meet demand, and the reason was, people couldn't get through to us.

Adam saw the problem as a reflection of company priorities:

> Initially there were three major objectives at Federal Express. First, the establishment of an airline: hiring the pilots and mechanics, buying the planes, and so forth. Second, the establishment of a reliable pickup and delivery service, which meant building up a trucking company. Third, in 1976, the decision to tell the world we're in business—build up our marketing and communications program.

> We got a lot of customers that way, but the problem was that they couldn't communicate with us. There were 120 separate order entry points, one for each city, with no communication between them. Customers got different answers to their questions—assuming they didn't get a hold or a busy signal.

> It was a system built on moving packages; the people in the field were hired because they had the ability to run trucking operations.

Taylor summarized,

> We had placed primary communication and customer service responsibility on the field, and the net effects were no improvement whatsoever in operational communications (same-day tracing); skyrocketing field communications costs (for which we tended to blame field discipline); and total confusion in communications—we had inside sales reps, outside sales reps, CSAs, station agents, supervisors, service clerks, and trainers, all giving the customers inconsistent messages.

Assigned by Fred Smith to break up the service bottleneck at Federal Express, Taylor examined the ordering and reservations systems of a variety of service organizations: commercial airlines, car rental agencies, hotel chains. "There were two elements to the problem," he recalled. "One, to get the customer in to call you, to open up access to the system, and two, once you've got the information, getting it to the courier so he can make a pickup." Thus the airline model was only partially useful, since airlines simply stored reservations in a computer and waited for passengers to appear at the airport. Avis and Hertz had a task more similar to that faced by Federal Express—taking a reservation, and then, through instant communication with the right branch office, making sure that a car was ready.

In December 1976 Taylor presented his findings to Smith and the company's senior executives, making the following recommendations:

- that service at Federal Express be redefined as all actions and reactions which customers perceived they had purchased;
- that these actions include providing documentation and information on shipments as well as delivering them;
- that customers' needs for information be served through a centralized telephone system to handle all orders and requests.

Potential Benefits

A central order-entry system, Taylor believed, offered significant benefits to Federal Express as well as to customers. It would not only be a more efficient source of information for dispatchers than the tub-file method, but would also give station managers and supervisors more time for planning, executing, and supervising station operations. According to Taylor's estimates, the average manager spent two to two and one-half hours per day on the phone with customers discussing tracing, billing, and service problems which eventually had to be solved in Memphis.

Moreover, centralizing the order-taking process would facilitate more rational and realistic personnel planning in the stations. As Taylor put it,

One of the critical problems of field productivity rests with the company's inability to plan field staffing requirements. If those requirements were solely a function of volume, the task would be straightforward. The fact is that the "telephone answering" aspect of Federal Express is a function of service level, not volume. Anyone who has ever been in a city station when the morning's aircraft is three hours late, or the previous evening's departing flight missed the sort, needs no convincing of this.

The aggregate service level at Federal Express, Taylor noted, was predictable, even though specific service problems in a given station were impossible to anticipate. Centralized order entry and customer service, he felt, would allow the local station to staff for volume, and the customer service department to staff for predictable aggregate service level.

Taylor also predicted that the centralized system would give the local sales reps time to make the phone calls (on a private line) required to keep in touch with their 250 to 300 assigned accounts. He pointed out,

Since its inception, the local field sales program has floundered. The major reason rests with the physical impossibility of coming anywhere close to achieving the desired number of sales calls when the sales reps are in the local office answering the phone.

Furthermore, a computer-based order-entry system would provide specific data, to be used for management planning, regarding the nature and number of phone calls received by the stations. By learning exactly how many calls an agent should be able to handle and by forecasting staffing needs more precisely, Taylor felt the company would realize substantial productivity gains—possibly as much as $7 million annually.

To centralize the order-entry process, Taylor envisioned a network of four or five regional call centers distributed around the country. When the system was fully developed, he argued, it could operate as follows:

> A prospective customer calls a local number, wanting information on Federal Express. The call is answered at any one of five service centers and routed to a CSA by an automatic call distributor. The CSA, seated at a video terminal, can call up rate and service information and relay it to the customer. If the customer asks for a pickup, the CSA will press a key and an "order blank" will flash onto the screen. After the CSA types in the order, it is immediately transmitted by the computer to a printer in the local station, and the dispatcher receives the request for pickup. If an established customer calls, the CSA can display and confirm all information required to make the pickup, and provide the local dispatcher with the same information.

Testing the New Service Concept

Taylor's new service concept, christened "Project Sydney," was first tested in April 1977. Data processing personnel designed a software package which utilized Federal's existing Burroughs computer to link the telephone lines of the Newark, New Jersey, station to a central answering facility in Memphis. Taylor and his associates prepared for the test with painstaking care. Afraid lest Newark customers be taken aback by the Southern accents of the Memphis CSAs (a problem described in internal memos as the "ken-ah-hep-ya syndrome"), they circulated exhaustive lists of New Jersey town and street names and drilled the CSAs in proper pronunciation. Letters were sent to customers explaining the change; heavy-volume shippers received personal calls from salespeople.

Focus group interviews conducted before the test revealed consistent opposition among customers, all of whom felt it was important for customer service to be available locally. One woman commented,

> When I come to work in the morning, I do two things: I make a cup of coffee, and I call my Federal Express station to check on my packages.

Yet, probing further, the interviews also revealed that what was really important to customers was a responsive answer to their questions, not geographic proximity.

The strongest objections came from Federal's own station personnel. Taylor recalled,

> The people out in the field thought it was the dumbest thing they ever heard of. For a very valid reason: One of the things you lose when you centralize this operation is the personal touch. The problem is that with Federal Express growing the way it is, you can't keep that anyway. Eventually the New York City market, for example, gets so big that you can't talk to Debbie every time even if the phone's being answered locally. In many places those good old days were dead already, but people out in the field were reluctant to recognize that. They didn't want some strange woman with a Southern accent in Memphis talking to their friends in Newark.

To many people's surprise, customer reaction to the test of the new system was favorable. Federal Express had spared no expense training the 27 CSAs in Memphis who took over the Newark phones; customers sensed a new aura of professionalism and responded to it. Surveys conducted shortly after the test revealed that even the "ken-ah-hep-ya-syndrome" had turned out to be a nonissue; almost two-thirds of those surveyed had been unaware that they were talking with CSAs outside Newark, not even noticing the Southern accents. Forty-four percent of respondents had observed a difference in service and praised Federal's speed and courtesy, as well as the drop in busy signals. Within 12 weeks, volume in the Newark station had risen 4 percent— and station personnel had changed their minds about the new system. One sales rep remarked: "I love it. The phones don't ring."

Encouraged by these developments, Taylor and the Project Sydney team added Chicago to the system. This time difficulties arose, particularly in the dispatching of orders; the fault lay not in the CSAs nor in the program but in the Burroughs computer, which had reached the limits of its capacity. (In addition to the order-entry tests, the computer was also handling flight scheduling and the company's accounting functions.) Management then decided to abandon Taylor's original concept of four or five large call centers in favor of 20 to 30 smaller ones, which could also be spread across the country but would use mini-computers. Accordingly, Federal Express arranged to lease the new equipment—only to be informed by the manufacturer a few days before the scheduled delivery date that part of the necessary hardware had not yet been developed.

RECOMMENDATIONS AND DEBATE

By this time, Federal's data processing executives had become convinced that the Burroughs computer would not be able to handle the company's continued growth, even without the burden of Project Sydney. They urged that the company set up a data processing "think tank," charged with developing a totally new software package to satisfy all Federal's data processing and customer service needs.

The data systems division also recommended that Federal Express purchase the recently introduced IBM 30XX System. Designed for scientific computation and business data-communication networks, the 30XX System offered up to 16.8 million characters (megabytes) of main memory and included two IBM 3033s and two 3031s. The package, which cost $7.5 million, also included communications units, operator consoles, and power and cooling units.

Several Federal Express executives were concerned by the long waiting period required for delivery of the 30XX. First deliveries were scheduled for the third quarter of 1979, and there was already a waiting list. Even IBM salespeople had initially expressed doubt as to whether the company needed such extensive processing capacity; as one remarked, "a lot of

agencies in the U.S. government don't use two 3033s." When IBM learned of the proposed new application of the 30XX System, however, they encouraged Federal Express to obtain the equipment and proposed several ways to obtain delivery early enough to start developing the new software package as planned.

At the same time that Data Systems presented its recommendations, Fagan, Taylor and Adam urged that Taylor's original plan for four to five regional call centers controlling all Federal Express customer service functions be implemented as soon as possible. In a memo to the company's senior information systems executive, Fagan and Taylor declared,

> The fact is that we are rapidly reaching a point in our major cities where we cannot handle any more on-call pickups. At a point somewhere between 900 and 1,200 on-call pickups per day, the combination of our need to answer the telephone intelligently and politely, our need to access relevant customer information, and our need to communicate with the driver puts an absolute limit on our volume growth.

Internal Resistance

The most immediate opposition to both the data processing expansion and the call centers came from the company's financial officers. Reviewing the initial plans for Project Sydney, which forecast a total net cash requirement of almost $10 million between 1979 and 1984, Federal's manager of financial analysis had commented,

> Regardless of the merit of the proposal, the financial implications are nothing less than astounding: Since the origination of Federal Express, no capital expenditure program, with the exception of aircraft fleet additions, has required more funding.

The financial analyst had insisted that a joint research project be undertaken by Operations Research and Finance to define the exact correlation between increased profitability and increased service level. He also wanted to see concrete evidence of predicted productivity improvements, warning that "gut feel and intuition no longer should suffice in a corporation of our sophistication." These studies were not carried out. However, in October 1977, in response to the financial division's continued requests, the operations research and planning division, working with Taylor and Fagan, produced a detailed projection of the costs for a centralized order-entry system using four call centers.

Unfortunately, Taylor's initial vision of a $7 million annual productivity savings had proved impossible to substantiate. He had simply guessed that station personnel could answer only about 65 calls per person per day, as compared to 110 for a CSA at a call center. But in reality, it appeared that a station clerk could handle at least the same amount of calls as a call center agent, although the former's accuracy was considerably less reliable. The new projections indicated an increase in net operating cost, after tax of $1,301,961 in FY 1981, declining slightly to $1,252,441 for FY 1983 (Exhibit 4). These figures did nothing to allay the misgivings of Federal's financial executives.

Company executives opposed to the project also pointed out that simply adding personnel and a Collins Automatic Call Distributor to each of Federal's six major markets (New York, Chicago, Los Angeles, San Francisco, Boston, and Washington, D.C.) would remove much of the order-taking burden from present employees—at a fraction of the cost required in the same period for a network of four call centers.

The productivity problem was complicated by the fact that both Fagan and Adam felt it would be a major mistake in labor relations to lay off any personnel. Federal Express employees were not unionized, and the company made it a point to keep relations smooth through profit sharing, opportunities for stock purchase, tuition refunds, aircraft jumpseat privileges, and heavy internal promotion. Heinz Adam described the dilemma,

Management is saying to me—okay, are the call centers going to save people? And I have to say no, people are currently answering all these phones, but we're not going to just get rid of

them with the new system, we're going to find other work for them. Firing these people is absolutely not an option—misgivings about the new system are causing attitudinal problems anyway.

Any reduction in the labor force, Adam felt, should come through attrition and the hiring of temporary workers to replace those who left a station within six months before it went online. He added,

Besides, when a company is growing as fast as Federal Express is, finding adequately trained people to support that growth is one of management's biggest problems. We have these people, and if Project Sydney were implemented we could divert them to other jobs.

Doubts from the Field

Federal Express salespeople expressed the greatest opposition to Project Sydney; as they saw it, their carefully cultivated contacts would be turned over to a faceless person in another state. One sales rep in Boston worried,

What about the big customer who usually calls in past our formal cut-off time and always gets service because of his account status? What about anyone who calls in past the deadline? Are those customers just going to be referred to a downtown convenience center, even if they're out in the sticks? How can somebody in Memphis who doesn't know the area, doesn't know where the trucks are, make judgments like that?

The anonymity of the new system provoked other fears. Customers who were known to the local stations were never asked to repeat details about themselves or their companies when placing orders; Memphis CSAs would be required to review at least some of this information with each call. Moreover, despite favorable customer reaction to the Newark test, many station personnel wondered how shippers would respond to an impersonal, faraway voice on the phone. Pointing to the success in Newark, Fagan insisted that this was an invalid concern.

People will give up the luxury of personal contact and the security of the local operation, the mom and pop thing, if instead they get a very professionally run organization. They may be on guard because of the previous bad service record of computers, but we'll just have to prove ourselves.

In an attempt to allay the fears of sales and station personnel, Taylor drew up another list of the new system's operational advantages. As he saw it, Project Sydney could generate a tentative invoice that could be altered when the packages were picked up, if they were different than described. These invoices would provide advice to flight scheduling, indicating unusual peaks and valleys in the system (outbound and inbound) prior to departure. By calling up records on their video screens, CSAs could keep "call for pickup" time under 60 seconds for established customers and could also check credit risks on the first call for billable service. Finally, the computer could generate constantly updated customer mailing lists for marketing purposes.

Additional Concerns

Other executives argued that the new system might make Federal Express dangerously dependent upon the telephone company. As even Taylor admitted, the phone company did string cables across bridges—and a bridge washout could paralyze a call center for six hours or more. The short-term answer to this problem, he felt, was an elaborate overflow and diversion system that would direct other call centers to pick up the slack. Long term, Taylor visualized an independent satellite communications system for Federal Express.

Adam refused to see the company's reliance on AT&T as a significant problem,

We will depend on them to some extent, but we're not unique in this respect—so do the car rental agencies, the airlines, the credit card companies. Suppose some lines do go down—through coordinated effort and a good backup system we can handle it. For a good commercial company like Federal Express, the phone

company will break their backs to get the repairs done. There's a certain paranoid quality to too much of this "what if that happens" thinking. The key to the whole problem is good, sane, nonoverreactive management.

GOING TO THE BOARD

As the time to present Project Sydney to the board drew nearer, Federal Express financial executives remained unconvinced of the system's ultimate value and skeptical of its forecast costs (which had assumed 6 percent annual inflation). To many minds, the opportunity costs of the new system were almost as unsettling as the debatable financial data. A decision to go ahead with Project Sydney would seriously retard the development of a larger data processing and operational software package for the company—perhaps by as much as two years.

Since the vast majority of customer complaints concerned tracing, Federal Express was particularly interested in the development of an optical scanning system for packages to ensure a reliable documentation and tracking process and to simplify package loading and manifesting operations. The company also hoped to improve dispatcher-to-courier communications, possibly by installing computer-linked printers or video terminals within delivery vans. These projects would have to wait if Project Sydney were implemented.

Time to Act

No other company within the air freight industry had developed anything similar to Project Sydney. Emery had attempted to computerize its tracing process, with mixed results. Yet Adam felt that adoption of Taylor's concept was essential, not only for meeting customer needs but for maintaining Federal's positioning as the leader in the industry. Facing a pile of memos asking for more data on the new system, Adam was ready to blow up,

So many people want a black-and-white solution to this problem, but how many times in the real world do you have that situation? Once you know you have the money to do something, it comes down to politics, proper interpretation of attitudes, and crystal ball gazing. These guys keep saying to me—Heinz, put together some numbers and show us that this will make fiscal sense. I can't—there isn't any way. I can show that the online city stations are growing faster than the others, but this incremental growth is only marginal—1 to 2 percent.

In Fagan's view, one of the greatest benefits of the new system would be consistency,

Centralized order entry creates quality control assurance—you know your product's the same everywhere in the country. It's like McDonald's—you get the same hamburger everywhere you go. What if it is cheaper to have customer service in the field? Can you measure that trade-off in dollars?

Adam was even more vehement. Gazing up from his desk at the large map of the U.S. tacked on his wall, where a constantly multiplying stream of red pins gave visual proof of the extent of Federal's growth, he argued,

Most decisions are based on return on invest-
ment—if we spend this money, it's a good investment because we're going to make money. Well, in this case, if we *don't* spend the money, we aren't going to grow. Look at it this way—it's only going to cost us a nickel a package to ensure that we go from 35,000 packages to infinity. That's different than saying if we buy a DC–10 instead of flying three 727s wingtip to wingtip, we can save money because it's less expensive to operate the DC–10.

We've got another problem here. Within the corporation, there's a very negative attitude about customer service, and there has been for as long as I've been here. The reasons for that are very complex, but they boil down to the tremendous difference between what our own people expect of us and what we are in fact able to do. At one time, I'll admit, the customer service department wasn't very reliable—but it's improved tremendously in the past year. My people can handle the order processing job—the tests have proved it.

There's never been an emphasis on customer service here, just a policy that if all else fails, give it to customer service. The fact is, if the service problems were simple we would never get involved. The station managers and sales force and billing office would take care of things themselves.

NOTES

1. Freight forwarders, the wholesalers of the industry, arranged pickups and delivery for customers as well as retailing cargo space on commercial aircraft.

2. Each one of an organization's branches and offices using FEC's services was considered a separate account by Federal Express.

EXHIBIT 1

Federal Express Corporate Financial Summary
1974–1978

	FISCAL YEAR ENDING MAY 31,				
	1974	*1975*	*1976*	*1977*	*1978*
OPERATING RESULTS					
Operating revenues	$17,292 [a]	$43,489	$75,055	$109,210	$160,301
Operating expenses	26,137	47,613	65,210	95,608	134,024
Operating income (loss)	(8,845)	(4,124)	9,845	13,602	26,277
Other charges, net	(4,521)	(7,393)	(6,210)	(5,390)	(5,693)
Income (loss) before income taxes	(13,366)	(11,517)	3,635	8,212	20,584
Income taxes			(2,032)	(4,243)	(6,980)
Income (loss) before tax benefit of loss carryforward	(13,366)	(11,517)	1,603	3,969	13,604
Tax benefit of loss carryforward			1,982	4,185	6,425
Net income (loss)	($13,366)	($11,517)	$3,585	$8,154	$20,029
FINANCIAL POSITION					
Current assets	$ 7,891	$ 9,481	$14,725	$ 20,349	$ 30,370
Property and equipment, net	59,701	59,276	55,297	53,616	71,813
Total assets	70,697	70,193	71,229	75,321	106,291
Current liabilities	9,136	11,818	12,954	18,658	22,741
Long-term debt	51,605	59,892	56,186	46,229	30,825
Stockholders' investment	9,956	(1,517)	2,089	10,434	52,725

[a] All figures in thousands of dollars.
SOURCE: Company records

EXHIBIT 2

Federal Express Primary Services

Fiscal Years 1974–1978

	ARRIVAL TIME	WEIGHT LIMITATION	RATES[b]		AVERAGE DAILY VOLUME					AVERAGE VARIABLE COSTS/ PACKAGE	
			1976	1978	1974	1975	1976	1977	1978	1976	1978
Priority One	Noon of day after pickup	70 lbs.	$23.56	$28.12	2,467	6,159	10,301	13,947	17,684	$10.60	$12.27
Courier Pak[a]	Noon of day after pickup	2 lbs.	12.50	14.00	187	549	1,077	2,632	6,759	4.25	4.75
Standard Air Service	Second business day after pickup	300 lbs. per shipment; 70 lbs. per item	12.62	14.75	1,456	4,356	3,214	5,352[c]	5,073	9.21	10.13

a Shipped in a waterproof, tear-resistant envelope, provided by Federal Express.
b Rates for Priority One and Standard Air Service varied according to package weight and distance carried; figures shown here are systemwide averages. Priority One rates were discounted, based on the total number of Priority One packages tendered to Federal Express from one shipper on any single business day.
c Inflated by United Parcel Service strike.
SOURCE: Company records

EXHIBIT 3

Federal Express Average Daily Package Volume[a]

FISCAL YEAR	VOLUME
1974	4,110
1975	11,064
1976	14,592
1977	21,931
1978	29,516
1979[b]	45,000
1981[b]	65,000
1983[b]	104,000

[a] Based on five-day weeks.
[b] Projections.
SOURCE: Company records

EXHIBIT 4

Project Sydney Projected Profit and Loss Statement
(All Dollars Expressed in Annual Terms)

	FY 1981	FY 1983
OPERATING DOLLARS SAVED		
CSA salaries and fringe	$ 8,235,000	$12,060,000
Overhead	480,718	627,635
Total (1)	$ 8,715,718	$12,687,635
Operating dollars saved/package	.53	.48
OPERATING COSTS		
Depreciation and amortization		
Equipment	$ 22,488	$ 30,172
Software development	260,000	260,000
Computer installation	10,000	10,000
Personnel Costs		
Fixed	660,000	660,000
Variable	6,318,100	8,723,100
Computer personnel	350,000	350,000
Supporting costs		
Data conversion	47,803	62,461
CRT installation	22,860	19,209
Computer hardware	594,615	594,615
Automatic call distributor	292,318	371,648
Rent and utilities	334,862	415,540
CRTs	391,166	544,839
Supplies	80,153	110,888
Line cost	2,281,147	3,373,048
Total operating cost (2)	$11,292,653	$15,156,310
Total operating cost/package	.68	.57
Imputed interest (3)	26,986	36,206
Net cost before taxes [(2) + (3) − (1)]	$ 2,603,921	$ 2,504,882
Income tax savings	1,301,961	1,252,441
Net cost after tax savings	$ 1,301,961	$ 1,252,441
Net after-tax cost/package	.08	.05

SOURCE: Company records

FEDERAL EXPRESS: CUSTOMER SERVICE DEPARTMENT, II

The management of Federal Express has decided to adopt a comput-erized system to improve the handling of customer orders and enqui-ries. Sales representatives are concerned because they see the newly enlarged customer service department coming between them and their customers, and failing to give special treatment to large customers.

"Let me be blunt about it," declared Jack McHale, manager of strategic sales planning for the Federal Express Corporation (FEC), "customer service is the scourge of sales."

THE IMPACT OF COSMOS

By the late spring of 1980, it was clear that relations between FEC's sales and customer service departments, frequently somewhat strained, were being further taxed by the intro-duction of a centralized, computer-based order-entry system named COSMOS (Con-sumer Oriented Services and Management On-line Systems).

Customers who had previously placed pickup orders with local station clerks now conducted their business through toll-free calls to customer service agents (CSAs) in regional call centers located in Somerset, New Jersey, and Memphis, Tennessee; a third center was scheduled to open in Sacramento, California, in August. The CSAs also provided general in-formation on Federal Express service and re-ceived tracing requests.

COSMOS, installed in 1979 at an initial cost of $5.6 million, offered distinct benefits to the company (greater operational efficiency, great-ly expanded capacity for growth) and also to its customers (standardized, faster, more con-sistent response to calls). The main working room of each call center was specially designed to reduce noise; it held approximately 180 CSAs and 14 supervisors. CSAs worked in brightly colored hexagonal "pods," each equipped with six individual working bays. In addition, the Memphis call center contained 84 agents who specialized in tracing and 14 "executive desk" assistants who handled calls requiring more follow-up, such as complaints.

CSAs were trained to use their own judg-ment in deciding whether to hand a difficult caller over to a supervisor or executive as-sistant. But only a tracing agent, working with FEC's invoice adjustment department, could authorize a refund. Requests by customers for late pickups were passed to station dis-patchers, who decided whether or not couriers' schedules could accommodate last-minute calls.

J. Vincent Fagan, senior vice-president–marketing, sales, and customer service, felt that COSMOS had increased FEC's consis-tency in training and service, as well as creat-ing checks and balances for the operating de-partments. "For example," he noted, "if we find through customer input to CSAs that a certain station can't handle its volume, the company can correct that." Although company market research had not revealed that customers per-ceived substantial differences between COS-MOS and the earlier, fragmented system, Fagan was convinced that the adoption of COSMOS had been operationally imperative.

Yet many Federal Express salespeople still had misgivings about the new system, which was being progressively introduced in FEC's 141 stations. In areas already on-line, custom-er-station telephone contact had been elimi-nated almost entirely by COSMOS. Station

This case was prepared by Penny Pittman Merliss, a former research associate at the Harvard Business School, and Christopher H. Lovelock.

phone numbers were now unlisted, and employees were instructed not to give the numbers to customers.

"At first," commented Fagan, "the sales reps were worried that having agents answering the phones from a central location might confuse customers in another part of the country. That fear turned out to be groundless, but there's still a problem, because now customer service has become a middleman between the sales force and the customers. Since customers can't call stations directly anymore, they have to leave a message at one of the call centers if they want to reach a sales rep."

Differing Perspectives on Customer Service

It was generally agreed at Federal Express that customer service had been a relatively inefficient, unprofessional function prior to March 1978, when Adam assumed control of the department and its 45 employees. But corporate surveys of Federal's sales representatives in late 1979, when CSAs numbered almost 400, indicated that the sales force's opinion of customers service was still very low. McHale noted,

> Any salesman will look at customer service and tell you—dammit, they just don't react like I would react to my customer. We're really a little worried about all these calls going through the call centers. When a customer calls just to give a message or to discuss what looks like an easy problem, he may still want to see a sales rep personally. What's happening now is that a lot of these problems are being handled in the call centers, without our even knowing about them. The customers can get a little irritated because the sales rep never returns their calls— and the sales rep is really irritated because he never knew the customer had a problem.

> It's very tough selling service. You're only as good as your performance on the last shipment. Some people in the company say, "Gee, we've got advertising and customer service; we don't need sales reps. What are they doing?" Well, we're doing this: We're maintaining the business. A lot of sales reps make service calls on

customers who've demanded to see them, who don't want to talk to the customer service center. They'll tell you: "I give you ten packages a day, I want to see a sales rep."

Adam, vice-president of customer service, saw the situation from a different perspective.

> We're helping the sales reps by taking their calls, not hurting them, because we've trained our agents to screen customers and try to determine an account's potential volume before passing the call on. A lot of people call up and say, "I'd like to see a salesman." Well, see a salesman for what reason? Have you got 20 packages a day to give us, or do you want a free lunch?

> Quite frankly, what happened before was that the field people would take messages and the salesmen would run out and make calls and find out that a lot of messages were really questions like, "Hey, could you tell me, do you serve Albuquerque?" Our agents have cut the sales reps' message volume by 75 percent, and now the calls they're getting are, in fact, real problems. The recession is also something that's cutting into their calls, which they don't seem to recognize; their assumption, their paranoia, is that we're not allowing customers to contact the sales force.

> The other thing that's really interesting here is that now the salesmen have to work. They can't spend eight hours returning calls and giving out rate information—they've got to get out and hustle. We're not held in the highest esteem because we're taking away their cotton candy.

Federal Express sales managers tended to respond to Adam's comments by pointing out that CSAs, many of whom had come up through the secretarial ranks, received only three weeks of training before assuming their new jobs (reservations agents for the airlines, in contrast, received approximately eight weeks of training). Summing up the situation, McHale declared,

> Customer service does a heck of a job taking orders. Even the tracing function, which still needs work, is improving. Heinz is really turning the department around, and it's only natural for him to want to expand the CSAs' respon-

sibilities. But with a recession in sight, our salesmen are under a lot of pressure to perform, and the last thing we should have to worry about is some kind of middleman standing between us and our customers.

Adam, on the other hand, was convinced that the CSA's expanded role would benefit Federal Express. He wondered how to bring the sales department around to his point of view.

RESPONDING TO THE RECESSION

In addition to dealing with sales department concerns over the role of customer service agents, Heinz Adam also found himself at odds with the other department over a plan to use COSMOS to give preferential treatment to high-volume customers.

As summer drew closer, it was becoming clear that the deepening U.S. economic recession, which had already resulted in the layoff of over 200,000 auto workers and caused a sharp decrease in consumer spending, would cast its shadow over Federal Express as well.

Only a few months earlier, company management had felt that Federal's business was largely recession-proof, and announced plans to add 8 used DC–10s and 23 used 727s to its existing fleet of 15 secondhand 727s, 5 new 737s, and 32 Falcons. By June, 2 DC–10s and 2 additional 727s had already joined the fleet. Average daily package volume now exceeded 68,000, a 48 percent increase over the past fiscal year; annual revenues for the fiscal year ending May 31, 1980 reached $415 million, a 61 percent increase over fiscal 1979 (see Exhibit 1). But, as Adam admitted,

> We've had an average 50 percent annual growth in revenues since 1974, and suddenly we're facing a slowdown in certain segments of our business. The customers that we call "on-call" customers, who use us irregularly and place their orders through our central computerized system—COSMOS—are increasing at a good rate. These are professional service and high-technology firms. But the big industrial

shipper—who arranges a standing pickup order through our sales department—is giving us less business.

During 1979–1980, the company's advertising in the business media had emphasized the simplicity of using Federal Express (Exhibits 2 and 3) and the value of this service for emergency shipments (Exhibit 4). A new print advertising campaign, scheduled to begin in business publications at the end of June, focused instead on the importance of not keeping people waiting for vital documents and supplies; it suggested that Federal Express was a new business tool that companies could use to improve their productivity (Exhibit 5).

Preferential Treatment Plan

As Federal's sales department received more and more pressure to meet goals, Jack McHale had devised a way to use the capabilities of COSMOS to boost sales revenues. Examining the "order blank" (Exhibit 6) that appeared on the video terminals used by customer service agents, McHale felt that COSMOS could be programmed to identify high-volume customers. In his words,

> Right now, when the customer data come up on the screen, there's no way for the CSA to know whether this person has been shipping two packages a year or 500. At present, we have about 4,000 key accounts which represent less than 2 percent of the total account numbers, and they account for almost 45 percent of the business. It's very important that the customer service people realize that these accounts deserve special treatment.

> I don't know what the phraseology would be, but I'd like to hear a CSA say something to a big customer like, "We recognize that you're a very good customer of ours, one of the better customers in the Hartford area. And I'm going to let your sales representative"—we may be able to put his name in the COSMOS file—"I'm going to let Joe Smith know about your problem (or your order) and I'll continue working on it too."

Adam was totally opposed to the plan, though he admitted that the programming required to implement it should be minimal. Shaking his head, he stated firmly,

If we're doing our job right, that kind of system should be totally unnecessary. I believe we should have service levels so high that we don't need to differentiate between the large and the small, between Leibowitz and Katz and General Motors or IBM.

The sales department is getting beaten on by everybody because the big accounts are suffering, and I would love to help them. But let me point out a few other problems with this idea, aside from my personal objections.

First, when you're dealing with 400 agents, it's difficult to teach them double standards in three weeks of training. It's a logistics problem, and it's also a very dangerous step. I certainly don't want them to start thinking they only have to try hard when one of these "special" guys comes on the screen. Besides, how do you set up this treatment in the first place? How do you tell an agent, "Hey, make your voice sound nicer if it's IBM versus Leibowitz and Katz"?

McHale was aware of Adam's objections, but he still felt his plan held potential. "Federal Express has invested millions of dollars in the COSMOS system," he observed, "and right now the onus is still on sales to identify preferred customers, because the COSMOS file contains no package volume or revenue data.[1] Our present daily call volume is about 50,000, and CSAs are handling almost half those calls.[2] Many customers even have to go through a CSA to reach a sales rep. I see no reason why those agents shouldn't have a much clearer idea of what kind of potential business they're dealing with."

NOTES

1. Volume and revenue data were generated by the financial department's data processing system, separate from COSMOS: There were no plans to make financial files available to Adam's CSAs.

2. One hundred of the 141 Federal Express stations were not yet on-line to COSMOS; it was expected that all stations would be on-line by 1983. Adam estimated that by the end of May 1981, 85 percent of Federal Express orders would be processed through call centers.

EXHIBIT 1

Federal Express Operating Results and Financial Position
1976–1980

	FISCAL YEARS ENDING MAY 31				
	1976	*1977*	*1978*	*1979*	*1980*
OPERATING RESULTS					
Air freight revenues	$75,055[a]	$109,210	$160,301	$258,482	$415,379
Operating expense	65,210	95,608	134,024	216,330	346,416
Operating income	9,845	13,602	26,277	42,152	68,963
Other expense (net)	6,210	5,390	5,693	6,329	7,628
Income before income taxes	3,635	8,212	20,584	35,823	61,335
Income taxes	2,032	4,243	6,980	14,400	22,605
Income before tax benefit of loss carryforward	1,603	3,969	13,604	21,423	38,730
Tax benefit of loss carryforward	1,982	4,185	6,425		
Net income	$ 3,585	$ 8,154	$ 20,029	$ 21,423	$ 38,730
FINANCIAL POSITION					
Current assets	$14,725	$ 20,349	$ 30,370	$ 48,975	$ 85,454
Property and equipment (net)	55,297	53,616	71,813	123,844	277,702
Total assets	71,229	75,321	106,291	179,823	398,127
Current liabilities	12,954	18,658	22,741	40,067	58,775
Long-term debt	56,186	46,229	30,825	45,729	145,562
Common stockholders' investment	(16,561)	(8,216)	38,294	76,789	171,589

[a] All figures in thousands of dollars.
SOURCE: Company records

EXHIBIT 2

Advertising in *Wall Street Journal,* August 1979

FEDERAL EXPRESS CAN TAKE THE STUFF OFF YOUR DESK

AND SEND IT CLEAR ACROSS THE COUNTRY TO SOMEBODY ELSE'S DESK, OVERNIGHT.

Announcing a novel solution to the paper explosion. It's called Federal Express COURIER PAK? and it comes in three sizes: envelope, box and tube.

Here's what you do. When you have some documents, artwork, contracts, reports, print-outs or any papers that absolutely, positively have to be somewhere else overnight, just pick up the phone and call us. We come to your office and give you a supply of boxes, tubes, and envelopes to put them all in, and we take them off your back.

That night we fly them in our own planes and we deliver them in our trucks right to the other person the morning of the next business day.

That's all there is to it. It's simple, safe, convenient, and it's absolutely, positively overnight.

Our Courier Pak service is exactly the same as our regular overnight package service: same trucks, same planes, same reputation for delivering on time.

And we don't charge a fortune for it either. For example, one Courier Pak envelope with up to 2 lbs. of paper, picked up, flown, and delivered to any of more than 10,000 cities and towns coast to coast is only $16.00. And if we pick up more than one, you're entitled to discounts of up to $6.00 per Courier Pak.

We're in the white pages under Federal Express, or call our toll-free number (800) 238-5355.

Give us a call the next time the paper explosion starts to blow you away.

WE'LL EVEN GIVE YOU THE CONTAINER TO SHIP IT IN, FREE OF CHARGE.

FEDERAL EXPRESS
WHEN IT ABSOLUTELY, POSITIVELY HAS TO BE THERE OVERNIGHT.

EXHIBIT 3

Advertising in *Wall Street Journal,* April 1980

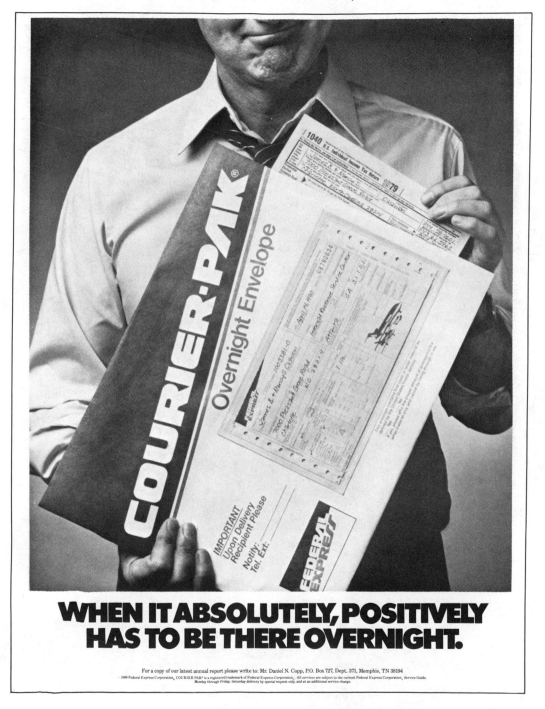

WHEN IT ABSOLUTELY, POSITIVELY HAS TO BE THERE OVERNIGHT.

For a copy of our latest annual report please write to: Mr. Daniel N. Copp, P.O. Box 727, Dept. 371, Memphis, TN 38194

1980 Federal Express Corporation. COURIER PAK® is a registered trademark of Federal Express Corporation. All services are subject to the current Federal Express Corporation. Service Guide. Monday through Friday. Saturday delivery by special request only, and at an additional service charge.

EXHIBIT 4

Advertising in *Wall Street Journal,* April 1980

FEDERAL EXPRESS IS SO EASY TO USE, EVEN A CHAIRMAN OF THE BOARD CAN DO IT.

Even if you're way above the day-to-day details of business, you can still use Federal Express.

Because even a big shot uses the telephone, and that's all it takes to use Federal Express.

All you do is pick up the phone and we come to your office or mailroom and pick up the envelope or package.

Then we fly it overnight in our own planes and deliver it door to door the next morning to any of more than 10,000 cities and towns in the U.S. and Canada.

It's as simple and easy as that. No complicated forms, red tape or shipping lingo involved. What we've done is taken the mystery and complication out of air express and made it available to anyone in the company with an urgent problem.

The cost is reasonable too. Our prices start at only $16.00, including pickup and delivery.

So the next time you have something that absolutely, positively has to get somewhere overnight, just pick up the phone and call your mailroom supervisor or call us direct.

We're listed in the white pages under Federal Express. Or call our toll-free number at (800) 238-5355.

If that's easy enough for the chairman of the board, you can handle it too.

FEDERAL EXPRESS
WHEN IT ABSOLUTELY, POSITIVELY HAS TO BE THERE OVERNIGHT.

© 1979 Federal Express Corp. Federal Express overnight air service is a door-to-door service with packages scheduled to be delivered to the consignee's address by 12:00 noon the following business day after pickup by or tender to Federal Express

For a copy of our latest annual report please write to: Mr. Daniel N. Copp, P.O. Box 727, Dept. 371, Memphis, TN 38194

EXHIBIT 5

Advertising Planned for Business Publications—June 1980

WAITING IS FRUSTRATING, DEMORALIZING, AGONIZING, AGGRAVATING, ANNOYING, TIME CONSUMING, AND INCREDIBLY EXPENSIVE. IT'S ALSO UNNECESSARY.

Waiting.

It's another cost of doing business today. Because business is spread out all over the country.

And it takes time to get things from one part of the country to the other, sometimes days and days.

And that gets expensive.

For instance, every time an executive sends a letter, a document, or a report to another city, someone has to wait for it.

This slows down the whole project which affects productivity, which affects profit, which affects the entire performance of the company.

And when you're talking about skilled labor waiting for a part for a machine or computer, you're talking big money for each day of waiting.

Fortunately, there is an alternative.

Next time, instead of waiting for something from somewhere else, tell them to send it Federal Express and you'll have it overnight.*

For as little as $19.00, the report you called Phoenix for on Monday can be in your hands on Tuesday.

The part sitting on a shelf in Pittsburgh on Thursday can be in your assembly foreman's hands in Los Angeles on Friday.

With Federal Express you don't have to wait for anything anymore.

Imagine what that could do to this country's productivity figures if everyone used Federal Express to eliminate waiting.

Imagine what that could do to your profit statement if you used Federal Express more and more.

Look at Federal Express as not just a service to use in an emergency, but also as a way to eliminate the frustration, the annoyance, and the expense of waiting, and you'll start to see Federal Express the way we envisioned it in the first place.

Federal Express is really a new tool that can and is revolutionizing the way America does business, as did the phone, the copy machine, the computer, and jet travel.

In a very real sense, it's the next tool that's needed now that we can pick up the phone and talk to anyone and now that we can get on an airplane and go meet with anyone.

Thanks to Federal, you can now have things sent to you from practically any place in the country overnight.

So pick up the phone and call us at 800-238-5355 and we'll pick up, fly and deliver your package or envelope overnight.

With no waiting, and all the mental and physical problems that go with it.

After all, why wait when you don't have to?

FEDERAL EXPRESS
WHY WAIT WHEN YOU DON'T HAVE TO?

EXHIBIT 6

Federal Express Information and Dispatch Request Form

Pickup Information and Dispatch Request[1] Station Identification

---

★★★★★Customer Detail Information★★★★★

Shipper # _____ Shipper _____ Zip Code _____

Pickup Address _____ City _____ State _____ Company Closing Time _____

Contact [Name] _____ Area Code _____ Phone _____ Extension _____ Status _____

List Ret[2] _____ Collect Cash _____ Type of Commodity[3] _____ Type Req (A/C/D/S)[4] _____

★★★★★Customer Request Information★★★★★

Rate _____ Dispatch _____ Cust/Svc[5] _____ FEC Account # _____ Cust Sply[6] _____

                                                                   Missed Pickup

★★★★★Package Information★★★★★

Time Package to Be Ready _____ Package Rate _____ Type of Service _____

Destination Zip Code _____ Total Number of Packages _____ Total Weight _____

Next Day Pickup? _____ Cust Supplies[7] _____ CSA Remarks _____

Dispatch # _____ Area _____ Courier Route #[8] _____ Pickup Date _____

---

[1] The caller was first asked for an FEC account number. When this was typed in, the bulk of the other information (excepting details of the specific shipment to be picked up) was automatically retrieved from the computer's memory, displayed on the screen, and double-checked by the CSA with the customer.

[2] Agent file search tool.

[3] Papers, machinery, art work, etc. Foodstuffs and poisons could not be carried on the same day of the week.

[4] (a) Add to record; (c) change record; (d) delete record; (s) show (display) record.

[5] Customer request to see sales representative.

[6] Bulk supplies (e.g., 100 airbills, 50 service guides) to be sent to customer.

[7] Unit supplies to be brought by courier.

[8] Automatically displayed.

SOURCE: Federal Express Corporation

BUFFALO SAVINGS BANK

A large, aggressive savings bank has developed electronic distribution channels to extend the availability of its services to customers as they shop in supermarkets and other retail stores. Currently it is using two such "point-of-sale" (POS) systems—one shared with other banks, the other restricted to its own customers. How will consumers and retailers react if the bank drops the shared POS system?

Robert W. Ramsey, chairman and chief executive officer of the Buffalo Savings Bank, was discussing marketing strategy with his four most senior officers. Glancing around the conference table on June 17, 1977, he began,

Gentlemen, we're here to make a decision on whether or not to continue Buffalo Savings Bank's simultaneous participation in two point-of-sale terminal networks. As you know, the bank presently operates its own group of 16

This case was prepared by Penny Pittman Merliss, a former research associate at the Harvard Business School, and Christopher H. Lovelock.

POS terminals in the Buffalo area; we also participate in eleven outlets of the Metroteller POS system, developed by Erie Savings Bank. My understanding of the situation is that our own POS network is highly reliable and has become very popular with our customers, but Metroteller is giving everybody problems. Warren, can you elaborate?

Warren E. Emblidge, Jr., group vice-president for marketing and banking services and the officer charged with overseeing the POS project, responded:

Let me begin with some bad news. From the start, through no fault of our own, we've had problems getting our customers' daily Metroteller transactions logged into our computer on time every night. Every delay in sending us data on Metroteller's end guarantees dissatisfied customers on ours. But what happened last night was much worse than a simple delay: I've just found out that Metroteller fed us the same magnetic tape two nights in a row, and we ran thousands of transactions twice.

Pausing as a murmur of surprise and displeasure ran around the room, Emblidge shook his head and continued,

That kind of disaster can cast a blight over even the best reputation for customer service. We've got to reevaulate the entire rationale behind our decision to participate in Metroteller, from the customer's perspective as well as our own—and we've got to reestablish the credibility of our own POS banking before our customers begin to distrust any and all innovations in our delivery of financial services.

THE BANK

Chartered in 1846, BSB was the tenth largest savings bank in New York State, with total assets of some $1.9 billion in January 1977 (see Exhibit 1). BSB was the leading regional source of financing for home buyers, and allocated more than $100 million for local residential mortgages in 1976. The bank's depositor base comprised over 500,000 checking and savings accounts, half of which had balances un-der $1,000; the average savings balance was $4,000. Over $104 million was paid out in dividends to depositors during 1976.

Buffalo Savings Bank defined its trading area as the entire Niagara Frontier, a 1,587-square-mile area extending from the Canadian border at Niagara Falls, 20 miles north of the city, to Hamburg, New York, ten miles south. This region comprised approximately 1,750,000 people. The City of Buffalo was a community of approximately 450,000 on the shores of Lake Erie, some 360 miles northwest of New York City. The leading U.S. inland port, Buffalo was almost equidistant from New York, Boston, Philadelphia, and Chicago and handled over 20,000,000 tons of cargo annually.

Five commercial banks and four other savings banks constituted BSB's primary competition within the Niagara Frontier. The most significant competitors were Marine Midland Bank and Manufacturers and Traders Bank (both commercial banks), and Erie County Savings Bank (Exhibit 2). In recent years, BSB's share of consumer accounts had been rising as Marine Midland's slipped. According to projections by an independent market research firm, Buffalo Savings Bank's account share, which was 14.9 percent in 1977 as compared to Marine Midland's 24 percent, would equal Midland's at about 20 percent in 1981, making BSB one of the two leaders in the Niagara Frontier.

Use of banking services within the Buffalo market was extensive. Over 88 percent of all households used checking accounts; over 80 percent held savings accounts (Exhibit 3). Approximately 55 percent of all savings accounts and 22 percent of all checking accounts were located in savings banks. BSB held approximately 26 percent of savings accounts in the Buffalo area, and 13 percent of personal checking accounts. Erie Savings, BSB's closest rival among savings banks, held about 18 percent of savings and 11 percent of personal checking accounts.

The bank's headquarters was an imposing granite building constructed in 1899, located on the fringe of Buffalo's reviving downtown area. Its gilded dome, a local landmark, was 54 feet in diameter; the dome's interior was decorated with elaborate renditions of the signs of the zodiac, below which were huge murals depicting life in nineteenth-century Buffalo. In addition to its main office, the bank had ten branches located within a 58-square-mile area along the Niagara Frontier. BSB also either directed or participated in 27 point-of-sale facilities, located in supermarkets, drugstores, and department stores within a 30-mile radius of Buffalo (Exhibit 4). The bank had no automatic teller machines.

Branches ranged in size from the newest in Amherst, New York, open three weeks with 5,000 accounts and $2 million in deposits, to the main office, with over $500 million in deposits. Commercial banks, which had unlimited branching privileges in New York State, often established numerous small branches, some under 2,000 square feet. Manufacturers' and Traders' Bank of Buffalo, a commercial bank with $200 million less in assets than BSB, had 64 branches to BSB's 11. Savings bank branches, on the other hand, were much larger, at least 6,000 square feet, and contained significantly more deposits. "Commercial banks may have only $5 to $10 million in a branch," one Buffalo officer commented, "but we're very disappointed if we don't have $10 million within the first 30 days after we open." The locations and opening dates of all BSB branches are listed in Exhibit 4.

Banking in the State of New York

All savings banks in New York State (as well as all savings and loan associations) were mutual institutions; that is, they paid out all their net earnings to depositors as interest and dividends, retaining only those portions of earnings legally required for invested surplus and reserve funds.[1] Savings banks had been founded in the early nineteenth century, in order to encourage thrift among the working classes created by the Industrial Revolution. The banks took in the savings of individuals and families and invested them in low-risk home mortgages and government bonds. Commercial banks, by contrast, had been founded to serve the needs of trade and were in business to earn a profit.

Consumer services offered by New York State savings banks varied widely, including bank-by-phone and individual retirement plans as well as several different types of savings accounts. Loans, when secured by real estate, were available to commercial accounts as well as private individuals. Following an act by the New York State legislature in mid-1976, checking accounts could also be offered by savings banks, providing no charge was assessed for the standard check-processing service.

In 1977, there were 118 savings banks in New York State, with assets totaling $73 billion. All were chartered by the state and regulated by the state banking department. Federal regulation of interest rates for all savings accounts gave savings banks a 0.25 percent advantage over commercial banks (5.25 percent was the maximum annual interest rate allowed for passbook savings).

Marketing

Marketing at the Buffalo Savings Bank was directed by Edward K. Duch, Jr., assistant vice-president–marketing, who had joined the bank five years earlier after obtaining his M.B.A. from SUNY Buffalo. Duch reported to Warren Emblidge, who held the position of group vice-president—marketing and bank services. Emblidge had joined the bank in 1965 on graduation from college, left to pursue graduate studies at The Wharton School, but returned in 1969 after obtaining his M.B.A. Emblidge had assumed responsibility for the marketing department in 1972 and had been promoted to his present position in 1976.

Appraising Buffalo Savings Bank's internal marketing environment, Duch stated,

> Marketing in the banking industry, especially savings banking, has traditionally been thought of as public relations. A lot of marketing decisions in the past have been made directly by a bank's president, working in conjunction with an ad agency. Buffalo Savings Bank is an exception, and I think the competitive environment in Buffalo has a lot to do with that. We have very aggressive, very innovative competition, and that has stimulated our own development. We view marketing within this bank not as a staff function but as a catalyst which can bring about change based on research and numbers.

But Duch noted that regulation placed strict restrictions on many areas of bank operations.

> If you look at the four p's of the marketing mix—price, place, product, promotion—we're limited on almost every one that we can offer. "Price"—our interest rate—is fixed by law. Our "place" or distribution is limited to the opening of only one new branch a year. Similarly, we can offer a major promotion like a giveaway only once a year, and thus we usually reserve it for the opening of a new branch. And, of course, almost every product or service we devise is subject to intense regulatory scrutiny, particularly if it has the potential to draw business away from commercial banks. It took years of lobbying, and extensive advertising, before savings banks were allowed to offer checking accounts in this state.

BSB had a long tradition of leadership in new product development; the bank had instituted direct employer deposit of payroll checks in 1928, the first financial institution in the country to do so. Duch observed,

> We have to look hard for opportunities within the current law to offer new services, and basically, they all hinge on our interpretation of what's permissible. Recently we developed a depositor discount plan which allowed customers making a $2,000 or greater deposit to get a 20 percent discount on merchandise in one day of shopping at a major local department store. We also created an Instant Refund Savings plan which gave customers immediate interest on their expected federal income tax refund, even though the refunds wouldn't reach us for three months.

Creating new products could be difficult, but the decision to offer them was usually not. According to one Buffalo Bank executive,

> We offer every single product or service that we legally can. We're so regulated that we've never had the problem of choosing from a wide variety of potential products.

Duch also directed the bank's extensive market research program, which included regular shopping surveys of the competition to determine prices and services as well as "mystery shopper" inspections of Buffalo's own branches. Each branch was monitored quarterly by an independent market research firm to survey the quality and consistency of its customer service. Researchers measured the quickness of service at teller stations and customer service areas and checked to see how hard the customer service representatives tried to sell other bank services to new customers opening checking or savings accounts. The friendliness, courtesy, and even degree of eye contact exhibited by all bank personnel were monitored. "Too often banks have a paternal relationship with their customers," Emblidge explained. "We want to treat our customers as knowledgeable adults."

Research into demographics, derived from telephone interviews with 729 randomly selected Niagara Frontier households, showed that 37 percent of Buffalo Savings Bank's customers were college graduates and 39 percent were high-level white collar workers; Erie percentages on these categories were similar. Twenty-seven percent of Buffalo customers and 23 percent of Erie customers had household income exceeding $25,000.

In a second independently conducted survey of consumer attitudes toward banking, a panel of 660 Buffalo area residents was asked to fill out a 32-page questionnaire and return it by mail; a 74 percent response rate was obtained. These respondents rated Buffalo Savings Bank first in the area (32 percent), followed by Erie Savings (24 percent) and Marine Midland (22 percent). Current customers of Buffalo Savings Bank were most impressed by its "good reputation" and "financial responsibility."

NEW APPROACHES TO RETAIL BANKING

Banking alternatives to human tellers had been gaining in popularity since the 1960s, when bank-by-mail systems achieved wide use. These plans allowed customers to mail in their deposits (or drop them in a locked box at the bank) and receive a confirmation by return mail, thus avoiding long lines at tellers' windows. The first automatic teller machines (ATMs) were introduced in Britain in 1967 and reached the U.S. in 1969, with increasingly sophisticated models being introduced during the 1970s. These automated banking consoles, usually built into one of a bank's exterior walls, allowed customers to make limited withdrawals, deposits, and account transfers 24 hours a day, seven days a week, using a specially coded magnetic card. Some would even print account balances on request. By mid-1977 over 6,000 ATMs were operating in the U.S., many functioning as "mini-branches" in high-traffic areas like shopping centers and airports.

At the same time, about 11,000 point-of-sale (POS) electronic banking terminals were being used in retail stores, mostly to verify checks. POS systems ranged from rudimentary check verification devices, operated by punching an identification number into the machine, to sophisticated terminals using magnetic cards as well as identification numbers to contact a central computer for approval of deposits, withdrawals, and transfers. Few POS systems operated on "real time"; in most cases an account was not debited or credited for a transaction until the next business day.

Telephone bill-paying had also been introduced. In 1973 a Seattle bank offered customers with touch telephones a package of services (recordkeeping, reminders, bill-paying) for $6.50 monthly—but was forced to withdraw the service after a few months when fewer than 1,000 customers subscribed. Subsequent systems in other cities enjoyed somewhat more success.

Remote Electronic Banking

Remote electronic banking facilities (as distinct from automatic teller machines located on bank premises) made their first appearance in the U.S. in January 1974, when First Federal Savings and Loan of Lincoln, Nebraska, set up electronic terminals in two Hinky Dinky supermarkets. The extension of banking hours made possible by the terminals attracted consumers immediately, and First Federal began opening more than 100 new accounts per week—some of them from neighboring Iowa. By the end of 1976 this POS network, now called TMS-Nebraska, was shared by seven savings and loan associations, a credit union, and a bank and operated at 92 merchant locations (five supermarket chains, a mass merchandiser, and a clothing store).

In early 1977, 32 banks in neighboring Iowa joined to form the Iowa Transfer System (ITS), the nation's first statewide electronic bank network; it offered customers a mixture of 69 ATMs and POS terminals in 20 cities and towns. Other sizeable POS networks were located in Minneapolis, Columbus, and Florida. "Store" banking was most successful in areas like Iowa and Nebraska, where banks' relatively small size encouraged them to share the sometimes heavy capital expenditures which a POS system required (a single terminal could cost up to $3,000; ATMs ran up to $50,000).

The expansion of POS networks was inhibited by regulation in some states. The McFadden Act of 1927 prevented banks from establishing branches outside their home states and required them to obey state branching laws—and several state courts had decided that POS terminals did constitute branches, even though the U.S. Comptroller of the Currency had ruled otherwise. Since the Supreme Court had declined to review these state decisions, electronic expansion of bank services in Colorado, Michigan, Minnesota, and Missouri had been halted. In Illinois, rural independent banks feared that POS banking would allow large Chicago banks to take over their territory, and successfully lobbied against electronic branching bills in the state legislature.

Controversies over shared systems had also slowed expansion. Sixteen states had passed laws requiring financial institutions to make their terminals available to other banks, usually on a "fair and equitable" basis. Yet it also appeared possible that the Justice Department could judge shared systems anticompetitive—the seeds of a nationwide banking system that could one day choke off small institutions. This view was shared by many, but some analysts argued otherwise, insisting that terminals spread throughout the country would enable small banks to retain the loyalty of their customers.

The high costs of extensive electronic banking systems led many to believe that all but the wealthiest banks had no choice but to participate in shared systems. Although both branches and consumers were pleased by the extended hours of service which the terminals allowed, the new equipment was often difficult to cost-justify. One banking executive observed,

> Every attempt to cost-justify electronic delivery systems tends to be a function of the personality of the company. Aggressive marketers cost-justify based on new account acquisition and related values of market share and image. Cautious conservatives justify terminals as substitutes for the live teller and other direct and indirect labor expenses. Aggressive, geographic competitors justify on the basis of cost avoidance vis-à-vis conventional brick-and-mortar offices.[2]

The same analyst noted that "any terminal which fails to sustain 3,000 to 3,500 transactions per month is a disaster. Some of the most costly and highly visible programs would qualify as disasters."[3] His reservations were borne out by the collapse of a large Southern California POS network in March 1977. This system, consisting of 137 POS terminals in 20 Southern California supermarkets, was still losing money after two years of operation and a $400,000 investment. Bank officials complained that customers simply cashed their checks and paid their bills without making big deposits. As was the case in most places, consumer resistance to the concept of electronic banking per se had not been a problem; customers had merely not chosen to deposit their cash at the POS branches.

Metroteller

Remote electronic banking reached Buffalo in January 1976, when the Erie Savings Bank opened a pilot remote banking station in a local supermarket. This facility, the first in New York State, had been planned since early 1974 and consisted of a single terminal adjacent to the supermarket's service booth. In accordance with state banking regulations, the teller was an employee of the retailer rather than the bank. Four supermarket employees were trained for two days at the bank to operate the POS machine, which resembled a large, complicated typewriter.

A customer began a transaction by filling out a one-part deposit/withdrawal ticket, then presented this ticket and plastic "EZ Banking" card at the customer service booth, where a clerk ran the card through a reader attached to the terminal (Exhibit 5). The customer then entered a four-digit Personal Identification Number (PIN), and the store operator next keyed in the dollar amount of the transaction, a function key, and a transmit key which sent all the data to the computer. The transaction was logged for subsequent processing in remote computers, and teller totals were updated. Finally, a message was sent back to the store to validate the deposit or withdrawal ticket. In addition to making deposits and withdrawals, customers could, with the teller's assistance, cash personal and payroll checks and make monthly mortgage payments. Withdrawals were limited to $300 daily.

According to an Erie marketing officer, public acceptance of this pilot facility was "immediate and enthusiastic." The service was available throughout daily supermarket hours, 8 a.m. to 11 p.m., Monday to Saturday; it attracted 97 transactions during its first week of business and averaged 250 transactions weekly after six weeks. During this time $10,000 in new deposits was attracted and $25,000 in mortgage payments collected. Erie made no secret of its plans to expand the remote banking network, beginning in the latter part of summer 1976 with 15 more locations in supermarkets across the Niagara Frontier. The name chosen for this POS system was Metroteller. A large sign above the service booth identified it as a Metroteller location and also carried the names of participating savings banks.

Metroteller was administered by the Consum-R-Serv Systems Corporation, an entity established by Erie Savings Bank. Erie had no intention of restricting Metroteller to its own customers; on the contrary, it sought to enroll as many Niagara Frontier savings banks as possible under the Metroteller umbrella. All banks sharing a specific Metroteller facility were listed by name on the large sign above the terminal. Consum-R-Serv obtained retail locations, provided computer systems and equipment, and trained retail store employees to operate the terminals. By June 1976, the Niagara County Savings Bank of Niagara Falls had announced its intention to participate in Metroteller; savings banks in Rochester and Schenectady had also expressed interest; and Buffalo Savings Bank had agreed to share in the operation of eleven Metroteller facilities within Buffalo area supermarkets.[4]

In deciding to join Metroteller, Emblidge and his colleagues had been impressed by independently conducted marketing surveys which showed that 27 percent of western New York householders would make deposits and withdrawals to their checking and savings accounts at retail establishments where they shopped, if facilities existed to handle such transactions. Consumers listed supermarkets as a first choice for this activity, followed by department stores and drugstores. Furthermore, the more frequently someone shopped, the higher that person's perceived need for the store banking service. The most likely user was found to be a woman under 35 who wrote about 20 checks a month. Merchants, too, were interested in the new system as a potential traffic builder for their stores.

Bank-and-Shop

Following passage in May 1976 of a state law permitting savings banks to offer checking accounts, the concept of remote electronic branches became even more attractive, and near the end of June 1976, Buffalo Savings Bank signed an agreement with the Wm. Hengerer Co. to open "Bank-and-Shop" facilities in Buffalo's five Hengerer department stores. In addition to competitive pressure, Warren Emblidge saw four major reasons for Buffalo Savings Bank's own entry into what he called "store banking." It would permit the bank to expand its locations; to extend banking hours; to reduce customer traffic at existing branches; and to increase its penetration of the customer and retail marketplace.

The need for extended service had been underscored by an analysis of the bank's current transactions. On average, checking account customers made three transactions per month, substantially more than savings account customers. BSB had opened 45,000 checking accounts since May 1976; these accounts added 1.6 million transactions annually. The conventional branches, with 475,000 savings accounts, processed about three million transactions annually already. Thus, when the number of checking accounts reached 80,000, the number of transactions would more than double to over 6 million, putting severe pressure on the distribution system's capability to service customers. Emblidge believed that store banking would be an economic way of diverting some of the projected traffic and transaction flow without costly branch expansion or a decline in service quality.

Having made the decision to go into store banking, Emblidge and his colleagues began the search for proper equipment. Since the system would be operated by retail clerks, simplicity was thought to be a key requirement. Emblidge recalled the bank's needs:

> We wanted a banking system that required minimum operator training, and was simple for the merchant to use. One recurring complaint about store banking is that bankers design their systems for other bankers, instead of for the merchant. Most important, we required a low upfront capital investment.

Emblidge's choice was AT&T's Transaction I Telephone, essentially a Touchtone telephone with a plastic-card reader on top (Exhibit 5). Installed and maintained by the New York Telephone Company, each Transaction Telephone could be leased for $40 per month, after a one-time $50 installation charge.[5] It occupied about one square foot of space. Both the equipment and procedures were different from those used by Metroteller, and it was not feasible to add other banks to the same unit. A large sign above the service booth carried the BSB symbol and the words "Buffalo Savings Bank Service Center."

Using the Transaction Telephone, a customer could make a deposit or withdrawal or cash a check in 30 seconds. As Emblidge described the process,

> The terminal operator (a retail clerk) "dials" the bank at the start of each business day by passing a magnetically encoded card through the reader slot in the Transaction Telephone. To process an individual transaction, the customer's own magnetic card is passed through. The operator then enters a two digit transaction code, plus the amount of the transaction. Next, the customer enters a four-digit confidential PIN. A computer-generated voice response then provides the necessary account information, and the transaction is completed.

Retail employees could be trained to operate the Transaction Telephone in half a day. As time passed, Emblidge noted that store employees familiar with the terminal operation frequently trained new personnel themselves.

Bank-and-Shop locations within retail stores handled only deposits, withdrawals, check cashing, and provision of account balances. No mortgage or small loan payments were accepted and state regulation did not permit the opening of new accounts there. Withdrawals were limited to $300 daily, and the maximum number of daily transactions was three. Cash to operate the system was supplied by the individual merchants. Store accounts were struck daily by the bank, and a fee of $.20 per transaction was paid monthly to the merchants. One service representative was on call at the bank between 8 a.m. and 11 p.m. to handle questions and problems; other service reps visited each location at least once a week. Metroteller also had a service rep on call, but site visits were considerably less frequent.

Contrasting Metroteller and Bank-and-Shop

Both Consum-R-Serv and Buffalo Savings Bank employed sales representatives to market their respective systems to store owners. In both instances, their task was to convince merchants that terminals in their stores would stimulate traffic and generate fee income without significantly increasing expenses.

BSB sold Bank-and-Shop on the basis that this bank had the largest number of customers in the area and that, by promoting its system to these customers, it could bring depositor/purchasers into participating retail stores. BSB representatives emphasized the compact size of the terminal, its ease of operation, and the simplicity of training new personnel. Metroteller, by contrast, was presented as a shared system, available to all savings banks in the area, which the stores could use to generate the maximum customer traffic.

BSB's initial contract with a merchant was for one year, with several two-year options to extend—if initiated by the bank.

From the start, in Emblidge's opinion, Buffalo Savings Bank's proprietary system enjoyed two great advantages over Metroteller: It was on-line and real-time, and it clearly announced to customers that they were dealing with BSB. "Let me give you an example," he explained.

> A customer can go to a supermarket location identified by Buffalo Savings Bank signs and make a deposit, which is immediately credited to her account through our computer. Five minutes later, her husband can withdraw the money at another location. Half an hour later, she can stop at a neighborhood branch, get her new balance, make another deposit, and get her latest balance again. Both the customer and her husband were able to use Bank-and-Shop just as they'd use a neighborhood BSB branch, and they perceived that they were, in fact, dealing with Buffalo Savings Bank.

Under Erie's Metroteller system, in contrast, the customer might also visit a supermarket POS location, but information on account balances would not be available, nor could users draw on their deposits until some time during the next business day. At the conclusion of each day's processing, transactions generated in the Metroteller network were sent via magnetic tape to member banks like BSB, which then updated their own account records. Member banks in turn sent Metroteller any updates generated through conventional branch or internal activity.

The Metroteller system thus required the maintenance of duplicate account data—one set at Metroteller, one set at the member bank. Because account activity was not entered into the computer until evening, no one could be certain during the day how much money was really in a Metroteller account; withdrawals were automatically screened according to a customer's credit record and any other standards which a member bank desired to establish. Nor could merchants be sure at the end of the day how much money they owed to (or were owed by) Metroteller.

Emblidge explained his bank's use of two separate POS systems. "Since the startup and incremental costs of our own system were so low," he remarked, "We thought we could afford to experiment with the higher fixed-cost Metroteller network—and gain valuable experience by participating in two dramatically different systems."

Introductory Promotions

Both Metroteller and Bank-and-Shop were heavily promoted by their sponsoring banks. To introduce its first 15 Metroteller locations, opening in August–September 1976, Erie mailed 100,000 magnetic cards to its checking, savings, and mortgage customers, followed by a second mass mailing of PIN codes. Erie also launched an ambitious regional marketing campaign that featured a nationally known television and radio star as sponsor for all the new "Easy Banking" services. Television, radio, and print advertising, in addition to billboards, bus cards, and point-of-sale signs, promoted Metroteller's availability, services, and convenience. Letters and statement inserts repeated the message. After two weeks, the 15 new Metroteller locations were handling a weekly average of 1,800 transactions.

Buffalo began its campaign by promoting the introduction of POS banking to its customers and listing at its branches all the retail locations where POS service—either Bank-and-Shop or Metroteller—was available. Subsequently, in a specific promotion of Bank-and-Shop, BSB mailed 15,000 "Cashmate" cards to checking account customers, inviting them to visit the bank to select a PIN code. Approximately 50 percent of checking customers re-

sponded. The bank then turned to its savings accounts. Noting that the 55,000 payroll savings customers were less likely to draw on their savings accounts than passbook or "statement" savers, Emblidge decided to insert information about POS in the bank's quarterly account statement to depositors. Statement savers were asked to show their interest in POS service by completing and returning a postcard attached to a brochure which had been enclosed with the statement (Exhibit 6). The 5,500 customers responding received a plastic "Statement Savings" card.

All BSB cards, store banking facilities, and advertisements were built on a red, white, and blue color scheme; Metroteller's cards, facilities, and promotion were predominantly orange and brown. Buffalo Savings Bank customers who wanted to use both systems required only one card.

Buffalo's marketing strategy also included hostesses at both branch and retail locations, who demonstrated how to use the new system, answered customers' questions and, at branches, opened new accounts. Hostesses and bank personnel stressed to these new customers the advantages of making transactions at a Bank-and-Shop location. Additionally, monthly statement stuffers encouraged existing customers to use Bank-and-Shop. Promotional incentives included inexpensive cooking spatulas and four-color prints of the Buffalo hockey team, both available free at all Bank-and-Shop locations. Unlike Erie, BSB made no effort to promote Bank-and-Shop to the general public. This concerned some of Bank-and-Shop's merchant sponsors, who thought more publicity would build more traffic for their stores.

Emblidge had heard that Erie spent approximately $300,000 to launch and promote Metroteller. Expenses for introductory promotion of Bank-and-Shop facilities during their first 12 months of operation totaled $75,000.

ASSESSING THE EXPERIMENT

Initial consumer reactions to the new POS services were favorable to both Metroteller and Bank-and-Shop. In August 1976, personal interviews with 50 households living within one mile of a selected Metroteller supermarket facility shared by Erie and BSB showed that 84 percent of respondents were aware of the service; 38 percent stated that they intended to use it. Both Buffalo and Erie were equally associated with the Metroteller service by respondents, 70 percent of whom identified it with one or both of the two banks. BSB transactions through Metroteller rose rapidly, reaching 6,535 by the end of 1976—more than double the number of transactions made through Bank-and-Shop.

By January 1977, however, operational difficulties with Metroteller had begun to cast doubts on the value of a shared service network. In a memo to Emblidge, Buffalo's auditor noted several problems. Cash settlements from Metroteller were running up to a week late, and representatives of both Metroteller and Erie Savings Bank appeared relatively unconcerned about Buffalo's complaints. The auditor also noted the difficulties of attempting to operate a POS network through an intermediary, in this case the Consum-R-Serv Corporation (CRS). He commented,

> CRS managers seem to think that they act only as an intermediary that settles with us after they settle with the supermarkets. Transactions that are obviously wrong are not credited to us until the funds are straightened out with the supermarkets, most often after a great length of time. But we feel that we are doing business with CRS, and that it is our contract with them that should be honored.

Despite these concerns, Emblidge and his colleagues believed that the advantages of staying with Metroteller outweighed the risks. However, BSB did not significantly expand its participation in Metroteller as that network grew; its ties to Metroteller remained limited to eleven supermarkets, giving Metroteller time to improve its operational performance. During the first six months of 1977, Buffalo Savings Bank continued to expand its Bank-and-Shop network, adding five drugstores in January, five Bells supermarkets in February and March, and one Bells supermarket in early June (Exhibit 4).

By mid-June 1977, Emblidge thought the time had come for an exhaustive reassessment of Buffalo's experiment in simultaneous shared and proprietary POS operations. Operational difficulties with Metroteller had not abated. Robert D. Weiss, assistant vice-president and manager of the POS network, observed to Emblidge,

> We've always known that our on-line, real-time capability offers better customer service by instantly updating accounts. But as POS banking becomes more familiar to consumers, I see another problem—a lot of customer confusion over the name Metroteller, which isn't directly associated with any bank. The fact is that customers have difficulty understanding why they get a higher level of service at Bank-and-Shop than they get at Metroteller, when they're making transactions with the same bank. Frankly, some of our Metroteller customers are having fits.

Bank-and-Shop had suffered occasional operational problems, but never any continuous difficulties.

In using Metroteller, Weiss pointed out, BSB was forced to adopt the operational procedures set by Consum-R-Serv. In its proprietary system, on the other hand, BSB could clearly identify itself and its product and provide service consistent with that provided at its branches. Some bank officials believed that Metroteller's chief goal was to penetrate the market as rapidly as possible and enroll all types of financial institutions from throughout the state; removing operational flaws and maintaining a high level of customer service, they thought, were somewhat less important concerns for Metroteller. Bank-and-Shop's primary objectives in contrast were to relieve the load of transactions on BSB branches and to provide good service to customers; expansion of the network to other institutions was secondary.

Transaction data prepared by the BSB marketing department further revealed that Buffalo's share of Metroteller transactions at shared locations had been steadily increasing (Exhibit 7), leading Weiss to comment, "I think Metroteller may need us more than we need them." By May 1977, Metroteller had ex panded to 31 POS facilities, up from 21 in January. Several local banks now shared all or part of the Metroteller network. Metroteller transaction volume for April was 42,683, as compared to 21,692 in January.

Emblidge next looked at cost data. Discussing the problems involved in cost accounting for a POS system, he noted the near impossibility of attributing the production of new, profitable accounts directly to Buffalo's proprietary POS system, simply because of the difficulty inherent in determining why a customer opened an account. In evaluating the cost-justification for POS, Emblidge used what he called "the cost-indifference point"—the point at which it would cost the same to service an account in a retail store as it cost at a bank office. Using the accounting department's costing studies, he calculated that the cost of a POS transaction would approximate the cost of a conventional branch transaction by the end of 1978.

A key factor in Emblidge's analysis of the comparative costs of future participation in Metroteller and Bank-and-Shop was his estimate of Buffalo Savings Bank's checking account and transaction growth. These calculations are reproduced in Exhibit 8. He also assembled a list of the major costs that would accrue if the bank decided to drop Bank-and-Shop and expand its Metroteller participation from eleven outlets to 50 (Exhibit 9). For purposes of comparison he then assembled similar costs to accrue if BSB left Metroteller and expanded Bank-and-Shop (Exhibit 10). From these figures, Emblidge believed he could produce for BSB senior officers a comparison of the total projected costs associated with each strategy.

Emblidge was particularly pleased that Bank-and-Shop's deposit dollars outnumbered dollars withdrawn by a ratio of 9 to 1. He attributed this phenomenon to the bank's decision to emphasize the use of store banking services to checking rather than savings account customers. "Additionally," Emblidge noted, "we chose to limit distribution to a single terminal located at a store's courtesy booth, rather than placing one terminal at the end of each checkout line. The latter approach is an expensive solution which encourages customers to pay for their groceries but make few deposits."

DISCUSSION

Ramsey and the bank's other officers listened in silence as Emblidge presented his findings. When the floor was open for discussion, John Gilbert, group vice-president, commented,

Warren, a lot of your findings would seem to point toward a break with Metroteller. Bob Weiss may be right—they may need us more than we need them. But let me bring up a number of problems you haven't addressed.

How real *is* customer dissatisfaction? What we've got at the moment is a lot of hearsay. If Metroteller is so inefficient, why was it used for over 12,000 BSB transactions last month—more transactions than we processed through Bank-and-Shop? And assuming that we do withdraw from Metroteller, how can we take those 12,000 transactions with us? Have we figured out whether we can convince a shopper to change supermarkets so we can cash her checks?

Another point. Are we prepared to collide head-on with Metroteller in a fight for the remaining potential POS outlets in this area? Right now our research shows that about 60% of the prime locations for POS on the Niagara Frontier have already been signed up. You'll have a hard time trying to convince Metroteller merchants to switch to a Bank-and-Shop facility. What kind of inducements are we prepared to offer an undecided merchant to make him choose us instead of them?

And what about the future? You know we're in a fight with commercial banks for market share. Our industry needs to stick together. Let's not hurt each other and let the commercial banks beat us both. A lot of experts think that merchant demands and economic pressure will make it impossible for any proprietary network to survive against a shared system. What makes you think Bank-and-Shop will be an exception?

Gilbert leaned back in his chair and pursed his lips. "I'm sorry," he concluded, "but right now I think we should be directing our efforts toward getting better service from Metroteller, not toward breaking away from it. We're accounting for over half their transactions now at the outlets we use; we must have some clout with their organization."

Before Emblidge could respond, Ramsey cut into the discussion. "Warren," he commented, "I share your misgivings about Metroteller, but John has brought up some good points. Why don't you give the whole situation some more thought over the weekend?" He continued,

On Monday, I'd like to see a memo reviewing all the relevant data and making concrete recommendations as to how we should proceed on this question. Assuming you decide that we should withdraw from Metroteller—and I'll admit I share some of your misgivings about that system—I want you to address John's objections specifically. In particular, I want a detailed comparison of the costs associated with participation in each system, and I want to see a strategy for taking those 12,000 Metroteller transactions with us in the event that we do decide to withdraw.

NOTES

1. Savings banks and savings and loans were very similar in New York State. Savings banks were oriented more toward depositors, whereas savings and loans were designed to serve the needs of borrowers. Their deposits were insured by different federal agencies.

2. "Why Put a Teller Station Here?" *Savings & Loan News*, August 1976, p. 45.

3. Ibid.

4. State regulation prohibited commercial banks from sharing a POS system with savings banks. As of mid-1977, no commercial bank in the Niagara Frontier had attempted to start its own POS system.

5. The fully allocated costs to Buffalo Savings Bank of opening a new Bank-and-Shop outlet were estimated at $5,000.

EXHIBIT 1

Buffalo Savings Bank
Statement of Assets and Liabilities

JANUARY 1, 1977

ASSETS	
Cash and Due from Banks	$ 18,535,964
United States Government Obligation	299,993,060
United States Government Corporations and Agencies	55,092,063
Obligations of States and Political Subdivisions	65,782,874
Other Bonds, Notes, and Debentures	
Public Utilities	69,431,735
Industrial	6,446,131
Other	15,265,716
Common Stock	35,377,016
Preferred Stock (Less Reserves)	47,898,357
Real Estate Mortgage Loans (Less Reserves)	1,190,853,569
Other Loans	29,877,154
Other Assets (Less Reserves)	54,074,107
Total Assets	$1,888,627,746
LIABILITIES AND NET WORTH ACCOUNTS	
Savings Deposits	$ 923,595,018
Time Deposits	817,239,280
Checking Accounts	7,399,082
Other Demand Deposits	14,039,815
Borrowed Funds	7,811
Other Liabilities	5,079,730
Net Worth Accounts	121,267,010
Total Liabilities and Net Worth Accounts	$1,888,627,746

SOURCE: Buffalo Savings Bank Annual Report

EXHIBIT 2

Household and Account Coverage by Major Banks in the Buffalo Area
1972–1979

	HOUSEHOLD COVERAGE				
	1972–1973	*1975*	*1977*	*1978[a]*	*1979[a]*
COMMERCIAL BANKS					
Marine Midland	51.3%	53.4%	55.2%	45.4%	44.7%
Mfrs. & Traders	34.0	35.2	32.8	38.0	33.3
Liberty National	15.5	16.8	15.0	14.0	14.5
Citibank		4.9	6.4	9.9	7.8
Bank of New York	7.9	9.6	12.3	8.2	6.7
SAVINGS BANKS					
Buffalo Savings	22.9	28.0	33.9	35.9	37.5
Erie Savings	21.9	24.7	28.8	27.0	28.7
Western NY Savings	10.5	14.4	13.0	15.9	14.1
Permanent Savings	1.8	4.6	6.3	5.0	5.0
Niagara County Savings	1.7	2.0	3.0	5.0	4.7
	SHARE OF ACCOUNTS				
	1972–1973	*1975*	*1977*	*1978[a]*	*1979[a]*
COMMERCIAL BANKS					
Marine Midland	30.8%	27.1%	24.0%	21.0%	21.9%
Mfrs. & Traders	21.4	17.9	15.2	15.2	14.9
Liberty National	8.9	7.3	6.8	5.3	5.9
Citibank		1.7	2.2	3.0	2.5
Bank of New York	4.2	4.1	4.5	3.1	2.6
SAVINGS BANKS					
Buffalo Savings	9.6	11.1	14.9	16.7	17.6
Erie Savings	8.6	10.0	12.3	12.0	11.5
Western NY Savings	4.1	4.9	4.7	6.4	5.6
Permanent Savings	0.8	1.4	2.3	2.0	1.8
Niagara County Savings	0.7	0.8	1.2	2.0	2.3

[a] Projected.
SOURCE: Independent market research commissioned by Buffalo Savings Bank

EXHIBIT 3

Use and Market Share of Banking Services in the Buffalo Market
1975–1977

	PERCENTAGE OF HOUSEHOLDS USING SERVICES		ACCOUNTS PER HOUSEHOLDS WITH SERVICE		ACCOUNTS PER HOUSEHOLD IN THE MARKET		COMMERCIAL BANK ACCOUNT SHARE			SAVINGS BANK ACCOUNT SHARE		
	1975	1977	1975	1977	1975	1977	1975	1976	1977	1975	1976	1977
Total Households	84.3%	88.3%					91.1%	88.6%	88.0%	57.7%	60.7%	62.9%
Total Accounts					4.11	4.65	65.3	60.9	59.2	27.7	33.5	34.2
Total Checking			1.11	1.19	0.93	1.05	94.6	80.4	76.2	4.4	19.2	22.2
Savings Account	82.2	86.6	1.45	1.60	1.19	1.39	40.4	37.4	36.8	51.4	55.3	55.1
Savings Club	12.8	9.9	1.13	1.12	0.15	0.11	64.0	60.1	64.8	23.9	30.1	27.9
Savings Certificate	14.6	18.4	1.35	1.45	0.20	0.27	25.9	20.6	21.0	62.1	67.5	64.4
Auto Loan	15.9	16.8	1.04	1.06	0.17	0.18	88.6	95.6	94.3	5.2	2.2	3.6
Personal Loan	14.7	12.7	1.06	1.05	0.16	0.13	72.0	78.8	74.5	23.1	19.1	21.7
Extra Cash	7.4	12.9	1.06	1.08	0.08	0.14	99.7	79.4	77.0	0.3	20.6	21.5
Credit Card	48.1	54.4	1.25	1.25	0.60	0.68	99.8	100.0	98.2	0.2		1.8
Mortgage	42.7	44.5	1.01	1.02	0.43	0.45	21.9	22.9	21.7	52.1	56.3	54.1

SOURCE: Independent market research commissioned by Buffalo Savings Bank

EXHIBIT 4

Locations of BSB Branches, Bank-and-Shop, and Metroteller Facilities

	LOCATION IN NEW YORK	DATE OPENED
BSB CONVENTIONAL OFFICES (11)		
Headquarters	Buffalo	1846
Branch	Buffalo	6/47
Branch	Buffalo	4/48
Branch	Kenmore	10/60
Branch	Cheektowaga	6/67
Branch	Amherst	6/68
Branch	Williamsville	10/72
Branch	West Seneca	6/73
Branch	Williamsville	5/74
Branch	Orchard Park	6/75
Branch	Amherst	12/76
BANK-AND-SHOP		
Supermarkets (6)		
Bells	Hamburg	2/77
Bells	Hamburg	2/77
Bells	East Aurora	2/77
Bells	Buffalo	2/77
Bells	Cheektowaga	3/77
Bells	Buffalo	6/77
Department Stores (5)		
Hengerers	Buffalo	9/76
Hengerers	Amherst	9/76
Hengerers	Amherst	9/76
Hengerers	Kenmore	9/76
Hengerers	West Seneca	9/76
Drugstores (5)		
Rite Aid	Amherst	1/77
Rite Aid	Amherst	1/77
Rite Aid	West Seneca	1/77
Rite Aid	Wheatfield	1/77
Rite Aid	Tonawanda	1/77
METROTELLER FACILITIES SHARED BY BSB		
Supermarkets (11)		
Bells	Williamsville	8/76
Wehrle Super Duper	Amherst	8/76
Bells	Cheektowaga	8/76
Super Duper	Amherst	8/76
Bells	Cheektowaga	8/76
Bells	West Seneca	8/76
Super Duper	Depew	8/76
Bells	Amherst	8/76
Bells	Tonawanda	9/76
Bells	Tonawanda	9/76
Bells	Buffalo	9/76

SOURCE: Company records

EXHIBIT 6

The Metroteller and Bank-and-Shop Terminals

Metroteller Terminal

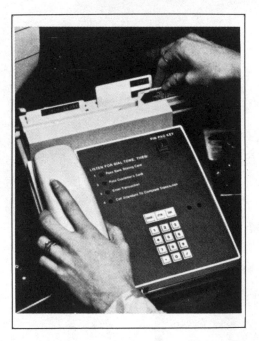

Bank-and-Shop Transaction Telephone

EXHIBIT 6

Direct Mail Promotional Brochure

BANK AND SHOP IS EASY TO USE!

BANK WHERE YOU SHOP

DETAILS ON ALL SAVINGS ACCOUNTS AVAILABLE AT ANY OFFICE.

UP TO 15 HOURS A DAY, SEVEN DAYS A WEEK...

BUFFALO SAVINGS BANK

SERVICE CENTER

To cash a check, just:
1. Hand the check and your ID card to the clerk.
2. Key-in your private security code.
3. Your transaction is complete.

To make a deposit or withdrawal, just:
1. Fill out a deposit or withdrawal slip (they're located right at the Bank-and-Shop counters).
2. Hand the slip and your ID card to the clerk.
3. Key-in your private security code.
4. Your transaction is complete.

You need a card
Your identification card and private security code are necessary for all Bank-and-Shop transactions. Passbooks CANNOT BE USED at these locations.

Bank-and-Shop Locations
For a complete list of department stores, supermarkets and retail businesses where you can bank-and-shop, call 847-5800.

YOU CAN BELIEVE IN BUFFALO

BUFFALO SAVINGS BANK Member FDIC

Phone 847-5800

Reorder 0180 - 200M

Mail this card today!

Banking where I shop sounds good to me. Please send me the necessary forms to open the following account:

☐ Absolutely Free Checking
☐ Statement Savings
☐ Interest-on-Checking

Name

Address

City _____ State _____ Zip

Telephone

(Please use ball point pen.)

397

EXHIBIT 7
Bank-and-Shop and Metroteller Transaction Data
(1976–1977)

	BSB TRANSACTIONS AT SHARED METROTELLER FACILITIES	ERIE TRANSACTIONS AT SHARED METROTELLER FACILITIES	TOTAL BSB/ERIE METROTELLER LOCATIONS[a]	BSB TRANSACTIONS AT BANK-AND-SHOP	TOTAL BANK-AND-SHOP LOCATIONS	TOTAL BSB POS TRANSACTIONS	PERCENT OF BRANCH ACTIVITY
1976							
August	193	N/A	8	0	0	193	0.1
September	1,115	1,570	11	220	5	1,335	0.8
October	3,233	6,269	11	1,171	5	4,404	1.7
November	4,686	7,458	12	2,314	5	7,000	2.0
December	6,535	8,427	12	3,132	5	9,667	3.8
1977							
January	6,352	7,552	12	2,568	10	8,920	3.7
February	7,799	9,142	11	3,580	14	11,379	4.5
March	10,078	11,569	11	6,307	15	16,385	5.0
April	11,886	12,392	11	8,651	15	20,537	6.2
May	12,759	N/A[c]	11	10,004	15	22,763	7.2
June[b]	14,418	N/A[c]	11	12,037	16	26,455	7.9

[a] One of the stores containing a Metroteller outlet shared by BSB subsequently went out of business.
[b] Projection.
[c] Metroteller stopped supplying competitive transaction data in April 1977.
SOURCE: Company records

EXHIBIT 8

BSB's Estimated Checking Account and Transaction Growth

YEAR ENDING	NUMBER OF CHECKING ACCOUNTS	PERCENT OF CHECKING ACCOUNTS ACTIVE AT POS	MONTHLY TRANSACTIONS AT POS	ESTIMATED NUMBER OF POS LOCATIONS
12/31/77	55,000	12	2.5	30
12/31/78	70,000	18	2.7	50
12/31/79	83,000	23	2.9	70
12/31/80	93,000	27	3.1	90

Note: For every four checking account transactions at a POS, it was estimated that one statement savings account transaction would occur. In addition, for every five account transactions, it was expected that there would be one transaction where the customer would simply ask to cash a payroll (or other) check without actually making a deposit. Such a transaction at a POS incurred the same costs as any other.

SOURCE: Company records

EXHIBIT 9

Representative Components of Metroteller Pricing Schedule[a]

STORE ORIENTATION CHARGES[b]	
Year 1	$10,000 per store
Year 2	7,000 per store
TRANSACTION FEE[c]	
Less than 10,000 transactions per month	$1.15
10,000–20,000 transactions per month	1.05
20,000–30,000 transactions per month	0.95
30,000–40,000 transactions per month	0.85
40,000–50,000 transactions per month	0.75
Over 50,000 transactions per month	0.65
INTERCHANGE FEE	
Per active account per year	$0.90
DATA PROCESSING FEE	
Per account per month	$0.01
New account set up	0.10

[a] Data are disguised.

[b] These charges were paid to Consum-R-Serv by Buffalo Savings Bank for the first two years that it was associated with each Metroteller location.

[c] This fee was paid to Consum-R-Serv by Buffalo Savings Bank for each Metroteller transaction made by a BSB customer. The sliding scale related to the total number of BSB transactions through all Metroteller outlets in a given month.

SOURCE: Buffalo Savings Bank

EXHIBIT 10

Representative Components of Buffalo Savings
Bank Internal POS Cost Allocation System[a]

STORE OPENING CHARGE				
Per Store				$5,000
TRANSACTION COST				
Merchant fee and line charge				$0.29

MONTHLY DEPARTMENTAL COSTS

	TRANSACTIONS PER MONTH (THOUSANDS)			
	10–40	40–70	70–100	100+
Administration[b]	$0.53	$0.35	$0.27	$0.20
Computer Center	0.12	0.10	0.08	0.05
Total	$0.65	$0.45	$0.35	$0.25

[a] The data which are disguised refer to costs incurred by Buffalo Savings Bank.
[b] Includes depreciation, merchant account reconciliation, location servicing, and plastic card production. Marketing not included.
SOURCE: Buffalo Savings Bank

--- READINGS ---

Where Does the Customer Fit in a Service Operation?

RICHARD B. CHASE

What does management have to give up in order to let customers "have it their way"? This article suggests that the less direct contact customers have with the service system, the greater the potential of the system to operate at peak efficiency. And, conversely, where direct customer contact is high, the less the potential that exists to achieve high levels of

Richard B. Chase is professor and head of the Department of Management at the College of Business and Public Administration, University of Arizona. Reprinted by permission of the *Harvard Business Review*. "Where Does The Customer Fit in a Service Operation?" by Richard Chase (November/December 1978). Copyright © 1978 by the President and Fellows of Harvard College; all rights reserved.

efficiency. This distinction between high- and low-contact systems provides a basis for classifying service production systems that can enable management to develop a more effective service operation.

With the recently legislated increase in the minimum wage law in the United States and the current economic downswing in Europe, service system managers in Western economies can look forward to continued pressure to run their operations more efficiently. While most managers are aware of the success stories of companies in a few industries (notably fast foods), there is little in the way of theory to help them decide how far they should go in altering their products, technologies, work forces, and work methods in attempting to achieve the nebulous goal of an efficient production system for services.

To appreciate the nature of the problem, consider the following stereotypical comment from the operations vice president of a finance company:

> I just don't understand it—the branch managers of our company never seem to run their offices in an efficient fashion. They rarely have the right match between lending personnel and clients demanding their services; they need more typists and clerks to do essentially the same amount of clerical duties that we perform in the home office. In my opinion, what we need is more work out of our methods department to get these branches as efficient as my home office operations. After all, we are in the same company providing the same general service to our customers.

Much has been written about improving service company operations, and many useful distinctions have been drawn among different kinds of service operations. In this article, I wish to propose still another way of looking at service organizations, a method of analysis that can be very helpful to managers. The essential features of this method are a classification scheme for service systems and a list of leading questions to be used in developing a production policy for the service system at hand.

EXTENT OF CONTACT

Service systems are generally classified according to the service they provide, as delineated in the Standard Industrial Classification (SIC) code. This classification, though useful in presenting aggregate economic data for comparative purposes, does not deal with the production activities through which the service is carried out. What the manager needs, it would seem, is a service classification system that indicates with greater precision the nature of the demands on his or her particular service system in terms of its operating requirements. In manufacturing, by contrast, there are fairly evocative terms to classify production activities (e.g., unit, batch, and mass production), which, when applied to a manufacturing setting, readily convey the essence of the process.

It is possible, of course, to describe certain service systems using manufacturing terms, but such terms, as in the case of the SIC code, are insufficient for diagnosing and thinking about how to improve the systems without one additional item of information. That item—which I believe operationally distinguishes one service system from another in terms of what they can and cannot achieve in the way of efficiency—is the extent of customer contact in the creation of the service.

To elaborate, *customer contact* refers to the physical presence of the customer in the system, and *creation of the service* refers to the work process that is entailed in providing the service itself. *Extent* of contact here may be roughly defined as the percentage of time the customer must be in the system relative to the total time it takes to serve him. Obviously, the greater the percentage of contact time between the service system and the customer, the greater the degree of interaction between the two during the production process.

From this conceptualization, it follows that service systems with high customer con-

TABLE 1

Classification of Service Systems
by Extent of Required Customer Contact
in Creation of the Service

High contact	PURE SERVICE	Increasing freedom in designing efficient production procedures
	Health centers	
	Hotels	
	Public transportation	
	Restaurants	
	Schools	
	Personal services	
	MIXED SERVICE	
	Branch offices of:	
	Banks	
	Computer companies	
	Real estate	
	Post office	
	Funeral homes	
	QUASIMANUFACTURING	
	Home offices of:	
	Banks	
	Computer companies	
	Government administration	
	Wholesale houses	
	Post offices	
	MANUFACTURING	
	Factories producing durable goods	
	Food processors	
Low contact	Mining companies	
	Chemical plants	

tact are more difficult to control and more difficult to rationalize than those with low customer contact. In high-contact systems, such as those listed in Table 1, the customer can affect the time of demand, the exact nature of the service, and the quality of service, since he tends to become involved in the process itself. In low-contact systems, by definition, customer interaction with the system is infrequent or of short duration and hence has little impact on the system during the production process.

Technical Core

One way to conceive of high- versus low-contact business is that the low-contact system has the capability of decoupling operations and sealing off the "technical core" from the environment, while the high-contact system does not. As one researcher has pointed out, "The technical core must be able to operate as if the market will absorb the single kind of product at a continuous rate, and as if inputs flowed continuously at a steady rate with specified quality."[1] Indeed, decoupling production from outside influences (for example, via inventory buffers) is a common objective in designing manufacturing systems.

Several industries provide examples of shifts in customer contact through two or more of the stages given in Table 1:

• Automatic banking tellers, with their 24-hour availability and their location for easy access, illustrate pure service; branch offices, with their provision of drive-in tellers, coordinated waiting lines, and often visible back offices, illustrate mixed service; and home offices, designed for efficient receipt, processing, and shipping of bank paper, illustrate quasimanufacturing.

• Airlines exhibit mixed service characteristics at their terminals (high-contact ticket counters and low-contact baggage handling), pure service characteristics within the planes, and quasimanufacturing characteristics in their billing and airplane maintenance operations.

• Blood collection stations provide an obvious example of pure service—they are (or should be) operated with the psychological and physiological needs of the donor in mind and, in fact, often take the "service" to the donor by using bloodmobiles. The blood itself is processed at specialized facilities (blood-banks) following "manufacturing" procedures common to batch processing.

• Many consulting firms switch back and forth between pure service and quasimanufacturing. Pure service takes place when data are gathered at the client's facility, while quasimanufacturing takes place when data are analyzed and reports are prepared at the firm's home offices. Other firms, of course, have facilities designed for mixed service operations;

their client waiting areas are planned in detail to convey a particular image, and back offices are arranged for efficient noncontact work.

Effect on Operations

Of course, the reason it is important to determine how much customer contact is required to provide a service is that it has an effect on every decision that production managers must make. Table 2 is a list of some of the more interesting decisions relating to system design. The points made in this exhibit lead to four generalizations about the two classes of service systems.

First, high-contact systems have more un-certainty about their day-to-day operations since the customer can always make an input to (or cause a disruption in) the production process. Even in those high-contact systems that have relatively highly specified products and processes, the customer can "have it his way." Burger King will fill special orders, TWA will (on occasion) delay a takeoff for a late arrival, a hospital operating room schedule will be disrupted for emergency surgery, and so on.

Second, unless the system operates on an appointments-only basis, it is only by happenstance that the capacity of a high-contact system will match the demand on that system at any given time.[2] The manager of a supermarket, branch bank, or entertainment facility

TABLE 2
Major Design Considerations in High- and Low-Contact Systems

DECISION	HIGH-CONTACT SYSTEM	LOW-CONTACT SYSTEM
Facility location	Operations must be near the customer.	Operations may be placed near supply, transportation, or labor.
Facility layout	Facility should accomodate the customer's physical and psychological needs and expectations.	Facility should enhance production.
Product design	Environment as well as the physical product define the nature of the service.	Customer is not in the service environment so the product can be defined by fewer attributes.
Process design	Stages of production process have a direct immediate effect on the customer.	Customer is not involved in the majority of processing steps.
Scheduling	Customer is in the production schedule and must be accomodated.	Customer is concerned mainly with completion dates.
Production planning	Orders cannot be stored, so smoothing production flow will result in loss of business.	Both backlogging and production smoothing are possible.
Worker skills	Direct work force comprises a major part of the service product and so must be able to interact well with the public.	Direct work force need only have technical skills.
Quality control	Quality standards are often in the eye of the beholder and hence variable.	Quality standards are generally measurable and hence fixed.
Time standards	Service time depends on customer needs, and therefore time standards are inherently loose.	Work is performed on customer surrogates (e.g., forms), and time standards can be tight.
Wage payment	Variable output requires time-based wage systems.	"Fixable" output permits output-based wage systems.
Capacity planning	To avoid lost sales, capacity must be set to match peak demand.	Storable output permits setting capacity at some average demand level.
Forecasting	Forecasts are short-term, time-oriented.	Forecasts are long-term, output-oriented.

can predict only statistically the number of people that will be in line demanding service at, say, two o'clock on Tuesday afternoon. Hence employing the correct number of servers (neither too many nor too few) must also depend on probability.

Low-contact systems, on the other hand, have the potential to exactly match supply and demand for their services since the work to be done (e.g., forms to be completed, credit ratings analyzed, or household goods shipped) can be carried out following a resource-oriented schedule permitting a direct equivalency between producer and product.

Third, by definition, the required skills of the work force in high-contact systems are characterized by a significant public relations component. Any interaction with the customer makes the direct worker in fact part of the product and therefore his attitude can affect the customer's view of the service provided.

Finally, high-contact systems are at the mercy of time far more than low-contact systems. Batching of orders for purposes of efficient production scheduling is rarely possible in high-contact operations since a few minutes' delay or a violation of the law of the queue (first come, first served) has an immediate effect on the customer. Indeed, "unfair" preferential treatment in a line at a box office often gives rise to some of the darker human emotions, which are rarely evoked by the same unfair preferential treatment that is employed by a distant ticket agency whose machinations go unobserved by the customer.

Implications for Management

Several implications may be drawn from the foregoing discussion of differences between high-contact and low-contact systems.

To start with, rationalizing the operations of a high-contact system can be carried only so far. While technological devices can be substituted for some jobs performed by direct-contact workers, the worker's attitude, the environment of the facility, and the attitude of the customer will determine the ultimate quality of the service experience.

Another point to keep in mind is that the often-drawn distinction between for-profit and not-for-profit services has little, if any, meaning from a production management standpoint. A not-for-profit home office can be operated as efficiently as a for-profit home office, and conversely, a high-contact for-profit branch is subject to the same inherent limitations on its efficiency as its not-for-profit counterpart.

Clearly, wherever possible, a distinction should be made between the high-contact and low-contact elements of a service system. This can be done by a separation of functions: all high-contact activities should be performed by one group of people, all low-contact activities by another. Such an adjustment minimizes the influence of the customer on the production process and provides opportunities to achieve efficiency where it is actually possible to do so.

Finally, it follows that separation of functions enhances the development of two contrasting classes of worker skills and orientations—public relations and interpersonal attributes for high-contact purposes and technical and analytical attributes for low-contact purposes. While some writers have urged mixing of duties under the general rubric of job enrichment, a careful analysis before doing so seems warranted when one recognizes the considerable differences in the skills required between high- and low-contact systems.

POLICY DEVELOPMENT

Applying the foregoing concepts for developing a production policy for services entails answering several questions:

What kind of operating system do you have?

Is it a pure service, mixed service, or quasi-manufacturing? What percentage of your business activity in terms of labor hours is devoted to direct customer contact?

A good indication of where a production system falls along the contact continuum can be obtained by using the industrial engineering technique of work sampling. This approach involves taking a statistically determined random sample of work activities to find how much time is being spent in customer-contact work. The Pacific Finance Company has regularly used this method to determine if a branch office is properly staffed and if some of its paperwork activities should be shifted to the home office. Another industrial engineering technique, process charting, has been used successfully to help specify the proper balance between front-office and back-office capacity in the mixed services operations of the Arizona Auto Licensing Bureau.

Are your operating procedures geared to your present structure?

Specifically, have you matched your compensation system to the nature of the service system—for example, high-contact systems based on time and low-contact systems on output? Are you appropriately allocating contact and no-contact tasks? Are you using cost or profit centers where these two measures are subject to control by the on-site managers?

Obviously, paying service workers according to the number of customers served tends to speed up service in the high-contact system. However, with the exception of extremely simple standardized operations, such as toll booths, mailing a package from a post office, and supermarket checkouts, speed of processing is not the most important element of service to the customer. Indeed, if the customer feels rushed in a hospital, bank, or restaurant, he is likely to be dissatisfied with the organization.

Further, it makes little sense for a seller of any service that can be at all customized to measure system effectiveness in terms of total number of customers served when in fact one should be giving more leisurely attention to a smaller number of "big spenders." (The reader may verify this point by comparing the attention accorded the casino bettor at the $2 blackjack table with the amenities observed at the $25 table.)

Can you realign your operations to reduce unnecessary direct customer service?

Can tasks performed in the presence of the customer be shifted to the back office? Can you divide your labor force into high-contact and no-contact areas? Can you set up plants within plants to permit development of unique organizational structures for a narrower set of tasks for each subunit of the service organization?[3]

The idea of shifting operations to the back office has recently become popular among tax preparation companies that now take a client's tax records and prepare a computer-processed return in his absence. Likewise, word-processing centers prepare documents in the absence of the customer, who provides original copy.

Managers have long recognized the desirability of having "attractive" personnel greet the public in such job classifications as receptionist, restaurant hostess, and stewardess, while being more concerned with technical skills on the part of those individuals removed from customer contact, such as typists, cooks, and those in maintenance positions. Plants-within-plants are typical in hospitals (e.g., labs, food service, and laundry), in insurance companies (e.g., underwriters, pool typists, and records), and in restaurants (e.g., cooking, table service, and bar).

Can you take advantage of the efficiencies offered by low-contact operations?

In particular, can you apply the production management concepts of batch scheduling, forecasting, inventory control, work measurement, and simplification to back-office operations? Can you now use the latest technologies in assembling, packaging, cooking, testing, and so on, to support front-office operations?

The production management literature offers numerous applications of the foregoing concepts to low-contact systems. One interesting example concerns the improvement of the forecasting procedure used to determine manpower requirements at the Chemical Bank of New York.[4] Daily volume of transit checks (checks drawn on other banks and cashed at Chemical Bank) averages $2 billion a day, often with a $1 billion variation from day to day. The new forecasting method employs a two-stage approach using multiple regression followed by exponential smoothing to forecast daily loads in pounds of checks per day. This approach yields significant improvement in forecast accuracy over the previous intuitive methods and thereby provides a basis for effective production planning.

Can you enhance the customer contact you do provide?

With all nonessential customer-contact duties shifted, can you speed up operations, by adding part-time, more narrowly skilled workers at peak hours, keep longer business hours, or add personal touches to the contact you do have?

The key to employing this step lies in recognizing the implications of Sasser's and Pettway's observation: "Although bank tellers, chambermaids, and short-order cooks may have little in common, they are all at the front of their employers' public images." If the low-contact portion of a worker's job can be shifted to a different work force, the opportunity exists to focus that work force on critical interpersonal relations.

For example, store sales personnel are frequently called on to engage in stocking activities, which often must take precedence over waiting on customers. However, since the salesperson's central function is as a personal representative within the store, it may be better to hire more stock clerks and free the salesperson to fulfill that personal function.

Can you relocate parts of your service operations to lower your facility costs?

Can you shift back-room operations to lower rent districts, limit your contact facilities to small drop-off facilities (à la Fotomat), or get out of the contact facilities business entirely through the use of jobbers or vending machines?

Unless it is an essential feature of the service package, or an absolute necessity for coordination purposes, managers should carefully scrutinize back-office operations before appending them to customer-contact facilities. As advocated throughout this article, high- and low-contact operations are inherently different and should be located and staffed to maximize their individual as well as joint contribution to the organization. The notion of decentralizing service depots as indicated by my examples is, of course, a well-understood marketing strategy, but it deserves additional consideration as an alternative use of service "production" facilities.

APPLYING THE CONCEPT

Going through the process of answering the policy questions should trigger other questions about the service organization's operation and mission. In particular, it should aid management to question whether its strength lies in high contact or low contact, and it should encourage reflection on what constitutes an optimal balance between the two types of operations relative to resource allocation and market emphasis.

Also, the process should lead to an analysis of the organization structure that is required to effectively administer the individual departments as well as the overall organization of the service business. For example, it is quite probable that separate managements and internally differentiated structures will be in order if tight coordination between high-contact and low-contact units is not necessary. Where tight coordination is necessary, particular attention must be paid to boundary-spanning activities of both labor and management to assure a smooth exchange of material and information among departments.

NOTES

1. James D. Thompson, *Organizations in Action* (New York: McGraw-Hill, 1967), p. 20.

2. For a detailed discussion of capacity planning in services, see W. Earl Sasser, "Match Supply and Demand in Service Industries," *HBR*, November–December 1976, p. 132.

3. See Wickham Skinner, "The Focused Factory," *HBR*, May–June 1974, p. 113.

4. Kevin Boyd and Vincent A. Mabert, "Two Stage Forecasting Approach at Chemical Bank of New York for Check Processing," *Journal of Bank Research*, Summer 1977, p. 101.

5. W. Earl Sasser and Samuel H. "Case of Big Mac's Pay Plans," *HBR*, July-1974, p. 30.

Guidelines for the Advertising of Services

WILLIAM R. GEORGE

LEONARD L. BERRY

Advertising intangible services performed by fallible and inconsistent human beings is quite a different thing from advertising physical goods. When customers are buying the performances of service personnel, the advertising should not only be concerned with encouraging customers to buy, but also with encouraging employees to perform well. Other considerations include providing tangible clues, making the service more easily understood, and promising only what can be delivered.

Despite the growth and importance of service industries, there has been little work published specifically on the advertising of services. Given this lack of attention, one might conclude, incorrectly, that the problems of services advertising are no different from the problems of goods advertising. But, in some basic ways, goods and services are different and the advertising of each must reflect these differences.

This article presents six guidelines for services advertising based on some of the special characteristics of services. Service industries are of course quite heterogeneous and the intention is to present guidelines that will have relevance to a wide range of service industries, but not necessarily to all of them.

ADVERTISING TO EMPLOYEES

The most fundamental difference between a good and a service is that a good is an object and a service is a performance. When the performance is people-based (for example, real estate sales) rather than equipment-based (for example, telephone communications), the quality of the service rendered is inseparable from the quality of the service provider. A rude or slow waiter or a careless cook can ruin what otherwise might have been perceived as a fine meal. A testy stewardess means a testy airline to the consumer.

Not unlike goods advertising, services advertising will normally be directed towards one

William R. George is associate professor of marketing at Rutgers University, and Leonard L. Berry is professor of marketing at Texas A & M University.

or more target markets. In addition, customer-contact personnel are a potentially important "second audience" for services advertising. This is especially true for people-based service organizations. When the performances of people are what customers buy, the advertiser needs to be concerned, not only with encouraging customers to buy, but also with encouraging employees to perform.

When well conceived, advertising can have quite a positive effect on employees. A recent advertising campaign of a large bank promised "person-to-person" banking. Bank employees were featured in radio and television commercials explaining in their own words what person-to-person banking meant. In follow-up research, over 90 percent of the bank's contact employees reported paying attention to the bank's advertising. Just under 90 percent felt that the personal service advertising set a job performance standard for them to follow. Nearly 75 percent said that they had become more concerned with pleasing the customer and were more likely to go out of their way for customers.[1]

A recent Delta Airlines print advertisement includes employees in its audience with the headline: "You never hear a Delta professional say, 'That's not my job.'" Underneath the headline, six Delta employees are pictured in work situations and identified. Smaller copy then reads:

> You'll find a Delta Marketing Representative handling calls for reservations when the lines get hot. And a Line Mechanic lending a hand with the baggage to get a flight out on time. And a Passenger Service Agent rushing a wheelchair to the gate when all the Skycaps are busy.

> Delta is people helping other people help you. It's a family feeling. It's a spirit of service that just won't quit. It's men and women who know their jobs and love their work. And Delta has more than 34,000 of them.

> Next trip go with the Delta professionals and have a great flight. . . . Delta, the airline run by professionals.

The Delta advertisement, although ostensibly meant for the consumer, is also clearly aimed at Delta personnel. This advertisement not only shapes the perceptions and expectations of consumers by promising helpful, professional service, it also helps define for employees management's perceptions and expectations of them—namely, that "We think of you as professionals and expect you to perform as professionals."

Sasser and Arbeit write: "The successful service company must first sell the job to employees before it can sell its service to customers."[2] Advertising is an important tool for "selling" jobs; it is a tool for motivating, educating, or otherwise communicating with employees.

CAPITALIZING ON WORD-OF-MOUTH

The labor intensiveness of many services introduces a degree of variability in the service provided, which is not present when equipment dominates the production process. Such variability occurs because people providing services differ in their technical and customer relations skills, in their personalities, and in their attitudes towards their work; moreover, one individual worker may be inconsistent in the quality of service he or she provides.

The ever-present potential for variability in the provision of labor-intensive services is well understood by those who consume services, and contributes to the important role word-of-mouth communication plays in the selection of service suppliers.[3] When the consequences of buying a lower quality service are perceived to be important, service consumers can be expected to be especially receptive to word-of-mouth communications. In brief, to find the right doctor, hairdresser, attorney, real estate agent, college professor, or automobile mechanic, the consumer is often interested in the opinions of others with appropriate previous experience.

The importance for word-of-mouth communications in many service markets suggests the opportunity to use advertising (and other forms of promotion) to capitalize on this pro-

prim-
2nnd y and -" "expectations of service become
stds of performance"

fx are approached
Personalitable approaches

pensity. Making a conscious effort in advertising to leverage word-of-mouth might involve persuading satisfied customers to let others know of their experience, developing communication materials for customers to make available to noncustomers, targeting advertising to opinion leaders, or guiding prospective customers in soliciting word-of-mouth information. Yet another approach involves featuring the comments of satisfied customers in the advertising itself, a strategy which in effect merges conventional and word-of-mouth advertising.

Marketers of management development programs sometimes ask satisfied program participants for permission to reprint their comments in future advertisements. At the University of Wisconsin, Madison, each participant in a management development workshop receives a "You can be a name dropper . . . and do a friend a favor" postcard asking for the names and addresses of up to three people who would be interested in receiving a catalog listing of the various programs offered. The recommender is given the choice whether or not to be identified in the cover letter. A successful Richmond, Virginia, hairstylist prominently displays the following sign in his shop: "If you like our service, please tell a friend; if you don't like it, please tell us." E. F. Hutton emphasizes the importance of word-of-mouth recommendation with its advertising message, "People stop and listen when they know your broker is E. F. Hutton."

What is important to glean from these examples is that it may be possible to design nonpersonal communications that capitalize on the service consumer's receptivity to more personal, word-of-mouth communications.

PROVIDING TANGIBLE CLUES

Because goods are tangible and can be seen and touched, they are generally easier to evaluate than services. Consumers perceive service purchases to have a higher risk than goods purchases and to be a less pleasant buying experience.[4]

Word-of-mouth communication is prevalent in service consumption because it is a means to reduce risk. For the same reason, consumers tend to be attentive to tangibles associated with a service for "clues" about the service's quality. Although a service is intangible in the sense that a performance rather than an object is purchased, there are tangibles associated with the service offered (for example, the facilities in which a service is performed), and these tangibles can provide meaningful evidence concerning the service itself.

Thus, one way advertisers can help lower the consumer's perception of uncertainty and risk-taking is by using tangibles in advertising in such a way as to convey appropriate signals about the service. Shostack has written about the need to use tangible clues in services advertising:

> It is clear that consumer product marketing often approaches the market by enhancing a physical object through abstract associations. Coca-Cola, for example, is surrounded with visual, verbal and aural associations with authenticity and youth. . . . A high priority is placed on linking these abstract images to physical items.
>
> But a service is already abstract. To compound the abstraction dilutes the "reality" that the marketer is trying to enhance . . . reliance must be placed on *peripheral* clues.[5]

Prior to his death, actor John Wayne was successfully used as advertising spokesman for California's Great Western Savings and Loan Association. Well known for his strong personal views as well as for his film characterizations of a rugged and honest cowboy who always stood tall against evil, Wayne represented tangibility and credibility in Great Western's advertising. The service conglomerate, Trans-America, features prominently its large, pyramid-like headquarters building in its advertising. Merrill Lynch signifies its "bullishness" on America through the continuing use of bulls in its advertising. Allstate and State Farm insurance companies, among others, have emphasized in advertising the tangible relationship between the insurance consumer and the insurance agent who "is presented as an all-around concerned counselor for the family."[6] Some service advertisers rely on the tangibility of numbers in their advertising—for example, "in business since 1910," or "70 percent of the people taking this course pass the state exam."

What these examples share in common is a visual concreteness that is often absent from services advertising. The tangibles used implicitly provide evidence about the service that the service itself cannot provide.

MAKING THE SERVICE UNDERSTOOD

One of the problems arising from the intangibility of services is that they are often difficult to define or grasp mentally.[7] Stephen Unwin captures the creative challenge intangibility presents services advertisers when he writes: "The service advertiser . . . is often left with describing the invisible, articulating the imaginary and defining the indistinct."[8] As suggested in the previous section, one method for dealing with intangibility is to use tangibles in advertising as evidence of the service's quality. Sometimes, however, it is possible to use tangibles for a different purpose: to make the service more easily understood.

Again, the insurance industry provides interesting examples. The insurance industry has made it easier for consumers to understand what is being sold by associating the intangible of insurance with relevant tangible objects more easily understood.

The following advertising themes illustrate:

- *"You are in good hands with Allstate."*
- *"Under the Travelers' umbrella."*
- *"The Nationwide blanket of protection."*

Insurance advertisers are using the images of hands, umbrellas, and blankets to communicate more effectively the benefits of buying insurance. Tangible objects representing what consumers seek from insurance are used to better define and communicate the service.[9]

ADVERTISING CONTINUITY

With the exception of radio, all advertising media are visual media; that is, readers or viewers see pictures. Services, however, are non-visual by nature. American Airlines can picture its planes in advertising, or the planes' destinations, but not the service itself.

The intangibility of services undoubtedly adds to the frequent difficulty competing service firms have in differentiating themselves.[10] Whereas goods can often be made physically distinctive on the basis of design, packaging, and branding, services have no physical appearance. Moreover, physically distinctive goods can be shown in advertising and associated with various forms of imagery.

Although differentiation is not easily attained by service firms, its achievement is by no means impossible. Advertising continuity is an important strategy in this regard because it involves the continual use in advertising of certain distinctive symbols, formats, and/or themes to build and reinforce the desired image, regardless of any changes in specific advertising campaigns.

A master of advertising continuity is McDonald's, which while using television advertising for different specific purposes (Big Macs, breakfast, special promotions, etc.), invariably uses the same image-reinforcers in all advertisements: memorable tag lines, theme music, and pictures of upbeat, energetic employees and spotless facilities. Whatever the specific item advertised, McDonald's advertising consistently sends out the same signals: "We are fast and efficient, we are friendly, we are superclean, we offer value, we are a family restaurant."

The concept of advertising continuity is also epitomized by Harris Trust and Savings Bank in Chicago, which has used its cartoon lion mascot, Hubert, in its consumer advertising since the 1950s. Research shows that Hubert is one of Chicago's most recognized celebrities. Hubert is a device for tying Harris' past advertising efforts to its present campaign; Hubert is a means for "branding" Harris' advertising, and, in the process, for helping the bank attain a distinctive image.

Advertising continuity gives a company's advertising a recognizability which continually communicates and reinforces its image. Ideally, consumers should be able to associate a specific firm with its advertising even if the firm's name is inadvertently left off a specific advertisement. If a tax-shelter annuities ad features a bull standing inside a cave, Merrill Lynch would immediately come to mind, even if the advertisement were anonymous.

PROMISING WHAT IS POSSIBLE

Since service buyers have only fulfilled promises to carry away from the service transaction, it is especially important that service firms deliver on advertising promises. Yet, as discussed earlier, the labor intensiveness of many services introduces variability into the service offering. Accordingly, when making promises in services advertising, prudence and caution should rule.

When Holiday Inn's advertising agency used consumer research as the basis for a television campaign promising "no surprises," top management accepted it while operations executives opposed it. Operating personnel knew that "surprises" frequently occur in a complex company like Holiday Inn in which thousands of people are involved in the operations of facilities spread throughout the country and

world. When it was aired, the campaign raised consumer expectations and provided dissatisfied customers additional grounds on which to vent frustrations. It is not surprising that the "no surprises" advertising had to be discontinued.

In advertising in general, and services advertising in particular, it is better to promise only that which can be delivered a very high percentage of the time. It is better to foster realistic expectations than unrealistic expectations.

The six guidelines for more effective services advertising are based on certain special characteristics of services, most notably that services are performances rather than tangible objects and that frequently these performances are labor-intensive. Services advertisers can use these guidelines to make a checklist of considerations in designing effective advertising programs.

- Does the advertising have positive effects on contact personnel?
- Does the advertising capitalize on word-of-mouth?
- Does the advertising provide tangible clues?
- Does the advertising make the service more easily understood?
- Does the advertising contribute to continuity?
- Does the advertising promise what is possible?

NOTES

1. Franklin Acito and Jeffrey D. Ford, "How Advertising Affects Employees," *Business Horizons,* February 1980, 58–59.

2. W. Earl Sasser and Stephen P. Arbeit, "Selling Jobs in the Service Sector," *Business Horizons,* June 1976, 64.

3. Eugene W. Johnson, "Are Goods and Services Different? An Exercise in Marketing Theory," Unpublished Doctoral Dissertation, Washington University, 1969, 166, 201; and Duane Davis, Joseph P. Guiltinan, and Wesley H. Jones, "Service Characteristics, Consumer Search, and the Classification of Retail Services," *Journal of Retailing,* Fall 1979, 3–23.

4. Johnson, p. 166; and William F. Lewis, "An Empirical Investigation of the Conceptual Relationships Between Services and Products," Unpublished Doctoral Dissertation, University of Cincinnati, 1976, 82.

5. G. Lynn Shostack, "Breaking Free from Product Marketing," *Journal of Marketing,* April 1977, 77.

6. James H. Donnelly, Jr., "Service Delivery Strategies in the 1980s—Academic Perspectives," in *Financial Institution Marketing Strategies in the 1980s,* Leonard L. Berry and James H. Donnelly, Jr., eds. (Washington, D.C., Consumer Bankers Association, 1980), 148.

7. Leonard L. Berry, "Service Marketing Is Different," *Business*, May–June 1980, 25.

8. Stephen Unwin, "Customized Communications: A Concept for Service Advertising," *Advertising Quarterly*, Summer 1975, 28.

9. Donnelly, 147–148.

10. Pierre Eiglier and Eric Langeard, "A New Approach to Service Marketing," in *Marketing Consumer Services: New Insights*, Pierre Eiglier, et al., eds. (Cambridge, Mass.: Marketing Science Institute, 1977), 39.

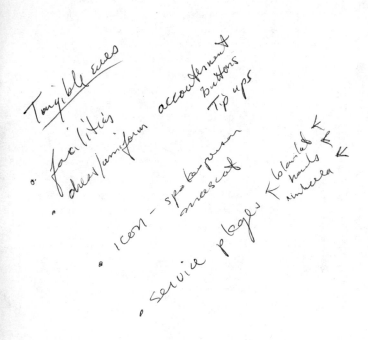

VII

Planning, Organizing, and Implementing the Marketing Effort

Marketing managers who move from manufacturing to service industries are sometimes shaken to discover how different the managerial environment is between their current and former jobs. This is particularly true for individuals whose previous position was in a consumer packaged goods firm, where the marketing function tends to occupy a central role in the organization.[1] Because the concept of a formalized marketing function is still relatively new to most service businesses, it is often difficult to define where marketing specialists should be positioned in the organizational structure, what their responsibilities and authorities should be, and precisely what should be expected of them beyond a somewhat reactive advertising or public relations role.

In the increasingly competitive environment facing service industries today, one of the motivations for creating a marketing department is to guide the future direction of the business. Without a broad strategic framework that identifies the current position of the firm and sets goals for where it should be headed one, three, or five years from now, marketing efforts are likely to be simply tactical and reactive in scope. Hence the need for skills in strategic market planning to set the business on the right course.

However, a marketing plan in itself is a blueprint for action, nothing more. Implementing such a plan requires resources—people (labor and know-how), money, equipment, and physical facilities. A critical issue is how the tasks allocated to the human elements should be structured. This, in turn, requires consideration of what organizational framework is most appropriate for marketing personnel and how they should relate to other management functions.

Marketing organizations have been described as the houses in which marketing strategies live,[2] raising such questions as: What floor plan is most appropriate for a particular company (or nonbusiness organization)? How should that floor plan be changed as the company evolves? These questions are particularly timely for service businesses in view of the major changes taking place in the service sector environment.

PLANNING, ORGANIZATION, AND IMPLEMENTATION

Planning can be described as a method for achieving an end. If a service business wishes to survive and prosper in a competitive environment, it needs to establish a set of marketing goals that explicitly recognizes where the organization is now, where it would like to be, and how it proposes to get from here to there. The following list[3] summarizes the key elements in a marketing plan, beginning with an analysis of the current situation and identification of problems and opportunities:

1. *Situation analysis* ("marketing audit")
   Where are we now?
2. *Identification of problems and opportunities*
   What does the future hold?
3. *Marketing program goals*
   Where do we want to go? And by when?
4. *Marketing strategies*
   How are we going to get there?
5. *Marketing budget*
   What financial, human, and capital resources will we need to get there?
   How should these resources be allocated?
6. *Marketing action plan*
   How should our people be organized?
   Who is going to do what, and when?
7. *Monitoring system*
   Are we progressing on schedule toward where we want to go?
   Do we need a course correction?

A good marketing plan does more than identify goals and strategies that are based upon facts and current assumptions; it also provides a plan of action for accomplishing the mission, using existing or readily available resources. Among the requirements for effective implementation are

- Establishment of the necessary organization

- Definition of responsibilities in terms of who should do what at specific points in time
- Procedures and control systems that allow the general manager (and subordinates) to delegate authority without losing strategic control
- Provision for continuity of execution over the full operating period of the plan, avoiding ad hoc decisions, yet allowing enough flexibility for contingencies
- Coordination of many different but related activities over an extended time period
- Good communication between managers so that all know what each is trying to achieve and how he or she intends to accomplish specific tasks

These are, of course, generalized characteristics of a good marketing plan. So what, if anything, is distinctive about marketing planning in the service sector? The key distinctions have to do with coordination and implementation, which must reflect the nature of the interactions between marketing and operations in many service businesses.

Marketing Function in Service Organizations

Production and consumption tend to be clearly separated in manufacturing firms. In most instances, a physical good is produced in a factory in one geographic location, shipped to a retailer or other intermediary for sales in a different location, and consumed or used by the customer in a third location. As a result, it is not usually necessary for production personnel to have any direct involvement with customers, especially where consumer goods are concerned. In such firms, marketing acts as a bridge between producers and consumers, providing the manufacturing division with guidelines for product specifications that reflect consumer needs, as well as projections of market demand, information on competitive activity, and feedback on performance in the marketplace. In its bridging role, marketing also works with transportation and logistics specialists to develop strategies for distributing the product to prospective purchasers.

The situation in service firms, however, tends to be sharply different. As noted in Section VI, "Managing the Service Marketing System," customers are often directly involved in service production, or at least in final "assembly" of the service product. Many service operations are literally a "factory in the field," which customers enter at the specific time that they need the service in question. In situations where the completed service is consumed as it is produced, there has to be direct contact between production (operations) and consumers.

The simultaneous nature of final production and consumption in many service businesses poses problems for marketing management in terms of how this function should relate to operations. Unlike their counterparts in manufacturing firms, service marketers do not assume full responsibility for the product once it leaves the production line. Contact between operations personnel and customers is the rule rather than the exception—although the extent of this contact varies according to the nature of the service. In many instances, operations management is responsible for running service distribution systems, including retail outlets. Yet none of this reduces the need for a strong, efficient marketing organization to perform the following tasks:

- To select service product characteristics that are tailored to the needs of the target market segments and that are equal or superior to those of competitive offerings
- To set prices that reflect costs as well as competitive strategies and consumer sensitivity to different price levels
- To tailor location and timing of service

availability to consumer needs and preferences
- To develop an effective communication strategy to inform prospective customers about the service and to promote its use

The net result is that the marketing function in service businesses finds itself closely interrelated with—and dependent upon—the procedures, personnel, and facilities managed by the operations function. To a greater degree than in manufacturing, marketing and operations in service operations must work together on a day-to-day basis.

Operations Function in Service Organizations

Although marketing has assumed greater importance in recent years, the operations function still dominates line management in most service institutions. This is hardly surprising, since operations has traditionally been the central function in most service firms, and effective management of operations remains the most important requirement for success in a service business.

Operations is typically the largest department in a service business. Operations managers are responsible not only for operating equipment and procedures behind the scenes, but also for retail outlets and other facilities used by customers. In labor-intensive services, operations managers are likely to direct the work of large numbers of employees, including many who serve the customers directly. The following list,[4] based upon interviews with managers in several different types of service businesses, illustrates some of the common stereotypes of the marketing and operations functions held by service sector managers.

Operations function
"Well established"

"Big"

"Line management"

"Hub of organization"

"Makes the business tick"

"Understands how the business works"

"In the field"

"Direct contact with the customer"

"Controls customer-contact personnel"

Marketing function

"New" (to many services)

"Starts off small but usually grows"

"Initially a staff function"

"An add-on to the organization"

"Located in headquarters or regional office"

"Understands customer motivations, habits"

"Identifies opportunities"

"Tells the customers"

"Indirect contact with customers through research and media"

"Historically, little or no control over customers"

"Moving to matrix organizational structure" (in some instances)

Operations managers like to point out to marketers that it is the former's department, not marketing, that has direct contact with customers. Almost by definition, operations managers are likely to have been with the organization longer than their marketing colleagues and to understand it better. Yet there is growing recognition of the contributions that marketers can make in terms of understanding customer motivations and habits, identifying opportunities, and telling customers about the product.

Even among operations managers who feel that marketing should not become directly involved in line management, there is recognition that marketing specialists may be able to provide useful inputs to designing the characteristics of the augmented product. This perspective is illustrated by the following comment from a senior operations manager in a quick service restaurant chain:

The customer evaluates your total product—the store, the product, the price, the courtesy and service of the employees, and the convenience. So you can turn off the customer very easily by falling down on any one of those variables. That's not so true in packaged goods. Marketing doesn't have any direct line authority at the store level [in our firm]. That's operations. But the rules have to be followed so that service standards are adhered to, and marketing has an input to these standards.[5]

Evolution of the Marketing Function

There is much evidence to suggest that marketing is moving up the learning curve in the service sector and, in the process, is acquiring more management clout in many service organizations. One possible evolutionary sequence can be described as follows:

1. An advertising and PR staff function is formalized at head office.

2. A field sales organization is developed, reporting to operations.

3. A marketing research staff function is introduced at head office.

4. An experienced marketing manager is hired to manage and expand the strategic planning function at head office.

5. A senior vice-president–marketing position is created, with responsibility for advertising, sales, PR, and marketing research and planning.

6. Marketing personnel become involved in decisions on pricing, service features, and location of service outlets.

7. General managers and operations managers participate in marketing seminars to improve their understanding of the marketing function.

8. In multiproduct service firms, the marketing organization shifts its focus from a product-centered to a market-centered emphasis.

9. Marketing managers help establish consumer-oriented standards and procedures for customer-contact personnel, and are in-

volved in internal marketing efforts to orient operations people to consumer and competitive dynamics.

10. A professional customer service function is established, taking over tasks formerly assigned to sales and operations; this new function is placed under marketing.[6]

11. Operating divisions (and sometimes operating units) are transformed from cost centers into profit centers as the strategic business unit concept is pushed down the organization; in each instance the responsible manager assumes general management (as opposed to operations management) status.

12. In large organizations, marketing plans are formulated at the divisional or unit level, and marketing personnel are assigned at one or both levels to help the general manager to plan, implement, and monitor the marketing strategies thus developed.

INTERFUNCTIONAL CONFLICT: MARKETING VERSUS OPERATIONS[7]

As service organizations change and devote more emphasis to proactive marketing efforts, there is increased potential for conflict between the marketing and operations functions. Marketing managers are likely to see the operations perspective as narrow and one-sided; even if they recognize the dominance of operations, they may not accept it. Alternatively (and representing the opposite extreme), marketing may be content to accept a passive staff role in which it assumes no initiative whatsoever.

How comfortably do the two functions coexist, and how are their relative roles perceived within a service organization? One executive in a service firm commented,

> Marketing's role is typically seen as constantly adding superiority to the product offering so as to enhance its appeal to customers and thereby increase sales. Operations sees its role as paring these elements back to reflect the reality of service constraints—

staff, equipment, and so forth—and the accompanying need for cost containment.

Revenue versus Cost Orientation

Because of the ways in which they are evaluated, operations managers tend to be concerned with improving efficiency and keeping down costs, whereas marketers look for opportunities to increase sales. Although a marketing idea may have potential with customers and offer the likelihood of increased sales, the financial and opportunity costs may sometimes be too high. As one senior executive in a quick-service restaurant chain remarked,

> One pitfall that marketing falls into in fast-food companies is that the marketing people can't relate to the realities of the marketplace. They may design a product or a promotion that boosts sales but doesn't increase net revenues. Marketing people are often very creative but should concentrate more on being total business managers. Operations people tend to rate the marketing folks on how well they understand the operation.

Different Time Horizons

Marketing and operations often have different viewpoints on the need to expedite a new service. For instance, marketers may be oriented to current concerns and anxious to achieve an early competitive advantage (or to regain competitive parity) by introducing a new product. The operations division may prefer to adopt a longer time horizon in order to develop and refine a new technology or new operating procedure.

Perceived Fit of New Products with Existing Operations

Another problem relates to compatibility: How well does a new product that may be very appealing to existing and prospective customers fit into the operation? An executive in a quick-service restaurant chain related the operational problems attending the introduction of a new menu item:

> It was a big mistake. Our stores are small. They didn't have space for the new equipment that was needed. It really didn't fit with our existing business and was just a square peg in a round hole. Of course, just because it wasn't right for us doesn't mean it wouldn't have been a great success in another quick-service restaurant company. It was really popular with our customers, but it started to mess up the rest of our operation.

In short, if a new product is incompatible with existing production facilities and operating skills, good-quality execution may be infeasible. There is, of course, a difference between a permanently bad fit and short-term start-up problems. Resistance by operating personnel is one such start-up problem. There is often a natural tendency on the part of low-level operations people to want to make the job as easy as possible. Supervisors may be reluctant to disturb existing patterns by imposing new procedures on employees. This mindset can be summed up as, "Somebody 'up there' has come up with a new-fangled operation, which they expect me to learn. But it's going to complicate my life, so it's a threat to me."

REDUCING ORGANIZATIONAL STRESS BETWEEN MARKETING AND OPERATIONS

As more service firms develop a strong marketing orientation, the risk of conflict between marketing and operations is likely to increase. The challenge for top management, therefore, is to develop organizational structures and procedures that harness the energy of managers in different functional areas, rather than allowing it to be dissipated in interfunctional disputes or permitting one functional area to dominate (and thereby frustrate) the other. Fortunately, there are a number of ways in which service firms are seeking to reduce interfunctional stress.

Interfunctional Transfers and Task Forces

One approach is to transfer managers from one functional department to another to ensure better understanding of differing perspectives. Another approach is to create a task force for a specific project—such as planning the introduction of a new service—made up of those individuals in each functional area who are most attuned to the others' viewpoints. In operations, this means looking for what one manager has termed "field hands"—personnel who are practical and understand how to deal with people, rather than being totally systems- and technology-oriented. In marketing, a task force requires an orientation toward operating systems and what is involved in making them work from both a staffing and technical perspective; it does not necessarily require detailed technical training or an understanding of the inner workings of technology.

Task forces offer a way of integrating functional viewpoints into an environment that is at least partially insulated from the pressures and distractions of day-to-day management activities. The participants create a microcosm of the organization in order to focus attention on the task at hand. Properly planned and managed, the task force environment provides a forum for discussion and resolution of many of the problems likely to occur during the development and commercialization of an innovative service. There needs, of course, to be an external mechanism for settling any disputes which members of the task force cannot resolve among themselves.

Whenever a marketing manager is assigned the leadership role on a task force, the commitment of top management to this individual must be explicit, since it flies in the face of the traditional seniority system of operations.

New Tasks and New People

Bringing about organizational change requires that new relationships be developed, jobs redefined, priorities restructured, and existing patterns of thought and behavior modified, often sharply. There are two schools of thought here. One involves taking the existing players and redirecting them. The other calls for switching the people.

The extent to which the second approach is feasible depends not merely on institutional policies and procedures, but also on the availability of an appropriate pool of new people—either outside or inside the firm. Larger firms obviously have a bigger pool of people on whom to draw; they have managers and specialists in other divisions or regions who have not been "contaminated" by close exposure to the activity in question, yet are sufficiently knowledgeable about the organization that they can quickly be productive in a new project. One difficulty is the limited availability of skilled marketing managers in service organizations.

DEVELOPING A MARKETING ORIENTATION AT THE FIELD LEVEL

A key objective of integrating the marketing and operations functions is to enable the firm to compete more effectively. Many service firm managers see the major integration problem as developing a marketing orientation at the field or unit level. Often, this is viewed as the key to competitive success, since local operating units such as hotels, branch banks, or industrial repair shops are often in direct competition for the customer's business with other units in the same locality.

Among the approaches to making the unit managers more consumer-oriented are: (1) decentralization of revenue responsibility; (2) use of internal marketing; and (3) standardization of control through procedures manuals. These approaches are more often used in combination than separately. Each has its advantages and disadvantages, as discussed below. The appropriateness of each depends, of course, on the nature of the unit being managed and the caliber of the management in each instance. Does the service concept in, say, a lodging chain call for a standardized motel that offers the same experience in Texas as in Ohio, or for a distinctively different hotel that reflects the needs and characteristics of the local marketplace? The answers to such questions help determine which approach is most suited to the situation at hand.

Decentralizing Revenue Responsibility

Among the reasons why unit managers may lack a consumer orientation is that, as part of the operations function, they have traditionally been subject to evaluation on cost rather than revenue criteria. In cost centers, managers and staff are likely to be driven inward to focus on their operation rather than outward to reach toward their customers.

Some large service firms have restructured their traditional functional organizations into strategic business units (SBUs), with a view to pushing profit responsibility down to the field level. The impact of this approach on traditionally minded branch or unit managers can be traumatic; they are suddenly faced with a need to understand where their revenue stream comes from! The most obvious result of such a move is typically a growing awareness of the consumer and of the need for proactive marketing at the unit level. There is evidence from research to suggest that managers in SBU organizations tend to be more concerned with consumers and to allocate a greater fraction of their time to customer-related issues than do managers of cost centers operating under tight control by centralized management.[8]

Internal Marketing

Service innovations targeted at existing and potential customers must be designed with customer needs and concerns in mind. This requires a strong orientation toward the marketplace. But there is also an *internal* marketplace, in the sense that innovations usually affect service employees, too. Sometimes innovations involve just minor changes in operating procedures; at other times, they may require major procedural changes, and retraining or displacement of employees. This poses a need for internal marketing which, as noted in Section VI, may be as important for success as externally focused efforts.

Gaining acceptance of service innovations among management and staff members is a human relations problem. Formation of a task force is one way of moving the project off the drawing board and into the development phase—"dimensioning the dream." But final implementation requires that members of the task force interact with operating personnal in the field. Winning the cooperation of operating managers requires that they be represented on the task force itself. Winning the acceptance of unit or branch personnel requires that senior field management sell the project to the staff.

In one bank, selling an innovation to the staff was accomplished by making a pilot introduction in one region of a service that would eventually be offered systemwide.

The new service—the automatic teller machine (ATM)—was tested in just two branches; then ATMs were installed in each branch in the region. As the regional vice president, who worked closely with the task force, described the situation, "We became the business foil against which new ideas were tested." He estimated that for some 15 months he spent between 60 and 75 percent of his time on internal marketing.

One of the major risks that we identified early on was that the ATM, once installed, would become like an appendage added to the bank by other people [that is, by top management], sometimes unrealiable, just like an adding machine. It would never become *their* responsibility.

So, about six months into the exercise, I took the branch managers away for two or three days. We gave them the problem and asked for their ideas. They all came up with plans. They were not very useful, but we took as much as we could even if it meant spending more money. It worked very well and gave them the beginning of a sense of commitment to the project; it started to become *theirs*.

We worked on the pride aspect—how wonderful it was that our region had been chosen! To build on this, the first two trial branches were called "flagship branches." We gave a lot of cocktail parties. The flagships were really prototypes.

Once they were up and running, we brought other branch managers and tellers to see and touch. I would literally take a teller's hand and put it on the machine: "I want to show you something: Why don't you do it? See how easy it is!" The next thing we knew, we had managers asking to be moved up in the schedule. There are two branches that are really too small to have the machines—boy, were those managers upset!

Another variant of internal marketing can be seen in the approach to training adopted by many airlines. Training in operating tasks has been supplemented by efforts to develop appropriate attitudes among reservations, terminal, and cabin staffs toward customers. In these and many other service firms, necessary education often includes sophisticated training films whose message content has been developed with as much care as any advertisement seen by the customers.

Control by Procedures Manuals

One of the commonest documents found in service firms is the procedures manual, which lays down detailed procedures and systems for performing virtually every operating task. This manual is the operations department's standard control document. When a service firm finds itself faced with the need to adopt a stronger consumer orientation, one of the ways to achieve this is through the medium of its procedures manual. Through research, the firm can identify the "key success factors" from a consumer perspective. These factors can then be incorporated into standard procedures to be followed by operating personnel.

For instance, a number of service firms have expanded their manuals to include procedures for how service personnel should interact with customers. The new versions specify such factors as the maximum time that customers should be allowed to wait before being served, key phrases that should be used in conversing with customers (often including an attempt to cross-sell another service), and the need for service personnel to make eye contact with the customer and, where appropriate, to smile. Such manuals require a control system to ensure that the prescribed procedures are, in fact, followed. One control system takes the form of a "mystery shopper," who visits service outlets in the guise of a customer to evaluate the qualitative and quantitative aspects of the service provided to consumers. In order to score maximum points from the mystery shopper, field managers are obliged to make sure that their subordinates act in ways corresponding to the requirements of the procedures manual, thereby controlling the quality of the service they deliver.

DEVELOPING A MARKETING ORGANIZATIONAL STRUCTURE

Earlier, marketing organizations were characterized as the houses within which marketing strategies live and are implemented. Because a business and its strategies are constantly evolving, marketing organizations need to evolve, too. This requires creative thinking about what size of marketing "house" and what "floor plans" are most appropriate to a particular type of service business. Attention must also be given to how the marketing function relates to other management functions, particularly operations. Should marketing be located in an isolated little house away from both operations and top management, should it be housed within the operations organization and subservient to it, or should marketing and operations coexist side-by-side with equal access to general management?

Staff versus Line

The most fundamental organizational distinction lies between staff versus line positions. In service businesses, with an established marketing function, the division of marketing responsibilities often looks something like this:

Staff
  Advertising and public relations
  Marketing research and analysis

Strategic planning

Product development

Pricing studies

Specialists in specific areas such as distribution, franchising policy and site evaluation (real estate)

Internal marketing and training programs

Line

Product execution (including management of retail facilities)

Sales management and execution

Customer service (both centralized and field)

Franchise development and recruitment

Execution of promotional programs in the field

Staff positions are typically located centrally or in regional offices. Line positions involving execution need to be located in the field, although senior line managers may be based in regional or central offices. Most line marketing tasks have historically been assigned to operations-oriented managers, but new organizational structures often give marketing managers direct control over elements such as sales and customer service. Almost by definition, product execution remains the responsibility of operations; after all, the operation *is* product creation and delivery. However, a new breed of unit and divisional general managers is emerging, who have the skills needed to understand and balance operating and marketing considerations.

Focusing the Marketing Effort

Just as a variety of different floor plans may be possible within a given size and shape of building, so can a marketing group be organized in several different ways. The complexity of the tasks facing marketing managers are, of course, related to the size

and scope of the operation. It is relatively simple to market a single-product service delivered from a single service location to a homogeneous market. Here the organization is likely to be relatively small, with both staff and line managers housed together in the same office. Far more difficult is marketing a broad product line of services through multiple service units dispersed across a wide geographic area, while seeking to appeal to numerous different market segments.

To bring order and focus to marketing planning and execution, the marketing function can be structured along four dimensions:

1. Functions (organized by functional marketing tasks)
2. Product (organized by individual products in the line)
3. Geography (organized by geographic regions or territories)
4. Markets (organized by market segments that transcend geography)

These four dimensions are by no means mutually exclusive. In fact, some large, complex service organizations include elements of all four. For instance, functional and market specialists may be found in staff positions at the head office, and service units may be organized into geographic areas with sales representatives in each territory specializing in different products.

Most large service firms need functional, in-house specialists. Thus, a large advertising budget cannot be administered effectively simply by delegating the advertising task to an outside agency. A firm whose marketing strategy places heavy emphasis on direct sales will benefit from centralized direction of recruiting, training, compensation policies, goal setting, and monitoring, as well as from the presence of sales managers in the field. Similarly, in-house skills may be needed on an ongoing basis at headquarters in such areas as new product development, market research, pricing studies, and site selection for new service outlets.

In small firms, one manager, aided perhaps by a few staff assistants, may have to handle all of these marketing functions. This is sometimes a problem in service businesses that have previously defined marketing as advertising and public relations. Sometimes, top management recognizes the need for a broader marketing perspective, yet expects to achieve this by promoting the director of advertising and public relations to a new position of vice president—marketing. Without additional training or resources, the new vice president is a prime candidate for early demonstration of the Peter Principle in action.

The larger the marketing organization, the more explicit the choices between further specialization on a functional basis and specialization on a product, geographic, or market basis. In multiunit, multiproduct service businesses, operations have traditionally focused on a product-geographic market organizational structure. As marketing is expanded within the organization, there is a natural tendency to suggest that marketing management should adopt a similar perspective.

Although an in-depth understanding of their products and the geographic markets in which they are sold is important to managers in service businesses, such an organizational structure often ignores the specific needs and concerns of different market segments. As service markets become more competitive, a carefully formulated product positioning strategy becomes more important for success. But this requires an emphasis on tailoring product attributes to the needs of a limited number of carefully selected market segments.[9] An essential prerequisite for such an approach is understanding what customers want and how they feel about current offerings, so that the prod-uct (and other marketing mix strategies) can be tailored to selected segments.

Reflecting the increased competition in the service sector, many service institutions are beginning to move from product-centered to market-centered organizational structures. Success in making this move requires that marketing managers understand the needs of individual segments as they relate to several different services. A key advantage of a market-centered approach is that it facilitates cross-selling and packaging of products to the same segments. However, persuading product-oriented sales personnel to shift their focus can be difficult. The securities industry provides a good example, in that older brokers are often quite reluctant to sell new products (such as cash management accounts or IRA/Keogh accounts) to existing customers; they would rather sell their specialty—stocks and bonds—to new customers. Retraining or even replacement of existing sales personnel is often necessary in such situations. Or product specialists can be appointed to whom sales or customer-contract personnel can turn for in-depth advice or assistance when selling an unfamiliar product to a customer.

Marketing Activities at Different Levels in the Organization

Large, dispersed, multisite service businesses are usually divided into operating regions, and sometimes subdivided into territories. In such instances, four different levels exist—headquarters, regions, territories, and units. An important issue is what marketing tasks should be undertaken at what levels. Much depends on the degree of autonomy assigned to each level of operating management: Is the product standardized or do unit (or territory or regional managers) have authority to customize? Even if the product is standardized, are regional, territorial, or unit variations in pricing, delivery locations, and communications permissible and appropriate?

Staff marketing functions are most commonly associated with the head office. But in large service businesses where marketing strategies and markets must necessarily vary widely from unit to unit, certain staff functions may be performed at the regional, territorial, or even unit level. The trade-off is one of responsiveness to local conditions versus the operating efficiencies and greater depth that can be obtained from centralization.

Where line marketing functions are concerned, another important issue is whether it makes sense to focus on geographic market segments served from the closest operating unit as opposed to market segments served across a broader geographic area. The more specialized the product, the greater the distance (in many instances) that the customer may be willing to travel to obtain it.

Some multiunit, multiproduct service businesses, such as industrial repair and maintenance shops, have found that they can offer better service by having each shop in a territory specialize in certain tasks, rather than attempting to offer "one-stop shopping" at all service shops. In the former instance, the sales function is probably best organized on a territorial basis, with sales representatives specializing by type of customer (which probably means that they only have to understand a subset of all available services). In the latter instance, sales representatives should be organized by unit, with each representative trying to understand the needs of a broad cross section of customers served by that unit. Clearly, however, sales management and training are likely to be more focused and more professional when undertaken at the territorial level.

A significant issue for all marketing organizations is the extent to which individual managers and staff should develop functional specializations keyed to the different elements of the marketing mix—such as product policy, pricing, advertising, sales, and distribution—as opposed to specializing by product or market and making all marketing mix decisions for a specific product or market. The risk of the latter approach is that it may lead to a lack of consistency in the overall marketing posture of the firm and to a lack of professionalism in fields (such as advertising) requiring in-depth experience for cost-effective decisions. Very large organizations can avoid this problem by having a matrix organization at headquarters, structured on both a functional and a product-market basis.

As a generalization, the more distinctive the product supplied by an individual operating unit and the greater the variations between market environments faced by each unit, the stronger the argument for local autonomy in advertising, sales, and pricing decisions. On the other hand, there are important advantages to be gained from centralized design of advertising campaigns and purchase of space in national media; further, a national sales force may be the most economic and professional way to reach major corporate and institutional buyers.

The advantages of centralization include economies of scale, greater professional expertise, and consistency of quality and image. The advantages of delegation to the unit level concern the ability to tailor marketing decisions to the characteristics of each local marketplace. But centralization and delegation of marketing authority are not necessarily incompatible. Many large service chains resolve the dilemma through the following procedures:

• Head office develops and executes national and major regional advertising campaigns, assessing each unit a percentage of its operating revenues toward the cost of these efforts. They also develop libraries of print, TV, radio, and direct mail advertisements for use on local media and containing space for insertion of the individual unit's name, address, phone, and other relevant information. Unit management is allowed to use these professionally prepared advertisements as it sees fit, perhaps using a local advertising agency to select an appropriate media schedule and add artwork containing the appropriate local information.

• Head office develops and executes national sales campaigns targeted at major corporations and associations that might use the firm's services in a number of different locations. (Similar regional campaigns might be conducted out of regional offices.) Again, local units may be assessed a charge to help pay for these campaigns. Individual units maintain a local sales presence through sales representatives operating out of the unit (or through sales representatives based in a territory office that represents a cluster of units in the same geographic area).

• Pricing guidelines are established at head office, but managers of individual units are allowed some flexibility within these guidelines to enable them to meet local competitive practices and market expectations.

• Some promotions (for example, discount coupons) are designed at head office to be accepted by all units. But individual unit management is allowed to develop additional local promotions as it sees fit.

• Market research into national or regional trends and opportunities is conducted at head office. Experts from head office assist unit managers to conduct and analyze specialized local studies as needed. Standardized questionnaires are assigned for local use to measure such variables as customer satisfaction with the service at each unit.

• The marketing manager at each unit reports to the general manager of that unit, who, in turn, reports through regional and/or territorial general managers to top corporate management. A parallel marketing organization exists at the head office and at regional and territorial levels to provide marketing support and consultancy. Although regional marketing managers have merely a "dotted line" relationship to unit marketing managers, the regional marketing offices provide a forum for all marketers to get together, share ideas and insights, and coordinate marketing efforts on a regional basis.

Delegation of marketing responsibilities to the local unit level is not appropriate when (1) product standardization is a key element in the service concept; (2) there are only minor differences between the market environments of each unit; (3) little or no selling to local corporate purchasers is required; (4) competition is also relatively standardized; and (5) requiring local management to become actively involved in organizing or supervising marketing efforts would dilute their effectiveness in managing a tightly prescribed and cost-efficient operation.

However, in national (or major regional) service chains, there may still be a need for an intermediary level of marketing management between the head office and the units. This is particularly necessary when there are major differences between units in different geographic areas in terms of either level and timing of demand for the service (perhaps reflecting life-style or climatic variations) or in the nature and extent of competitive activity.

CONCLUSION

As marketing becomes more widely accepted in the service sector, greater attention is being given to planning, organizing, and implementing marketing efforts. The scope and shape of the marketing organization tend to evolve over time as marketing moves from a reactive to a proactive role within the firm and acquires responsibilities relating to all elements of the marketing mix.

Within any given service institution, marketing has to develop a means of coexisting with operations—traditionally the dominant function—whose concerns tend to be cost- and efficiency-centered rather than customer-centered. One of the responsibilities of the general manager is to act as arbiter in disputes between marketing and operations, balancing the concerns of both sides. Clearly, this requires that the general manager have a good understanding of both functions.

A continuing challenge for any service firm is to organize its marketing efforts in ways that give efficient leverage to its competitive standing in the marketplace. Decisions on whether to structure the marketing organization by marketing function, products, markets, or geographic areas (or a combination of these) should reflect an understanding of the key success factors that underlie the positioning strategy selected by the firm.

The approaches to stimulating a consumer orientation at the field or unit level discussed in this chapter represent two alternative philosophies of managing multisite operations. One advocates control from the center, implying that head office management knows best. The problem here is getting field management and staff to perform in desired ways, requiring the use of internal marketing and control procedures. The other approach is characterized by a belief that field managers are in the best position to recognize and meet their customers' needs. Holders of this viewpoint tend to advocate profit or revenue centers at the field level and individual service outlets also set up on such a basis.

Deciding which perspective to adopt is difficult. The advantage of being a large service organization is based on the ability to standardize procedures and products at a large number of sites. The rental car, motel, and fast-food industries, for instance, are predicated on this capability. Standardization can be reassuring to the consumer, as well as allowing economies of scale to be derived from centralized research, development, purchasing, and marketing programs. On the other hand, a standardized system can also result in consistent mediocrity of service delivered by "robot-like" contact personnel. This can be the end-product of training films and control systems that allow no latitude for individual initiative. It is a debatable point whether "Have a nice day" or "Thanks for flying Action Airlines," delivered in a lifeless monotone, is meaningless to customers or actually negative. Similarly, standardized advertising or pricing promotions, while simple to execute, may be unresponsive to local market conditions and may make it difficult for individual service units to compete effectively against other service firms that take a more flexible approach.

In short, the organizational structure and procedures to be adopted should reflect the nature of both the service institution and its environment. In many instances, the most appropriate solution may be to employ a mix of centralization and initiative at the unit level. No service firm can afford to allow its organization to be cast in concrete. As the role of marketing matures and becomes more widely accepted, and as changes take place in products, markets, and the competition, so organizational frameworks should be allowed to evolve in response.

NOTES

1. See Gary Knisely's interviews with service marketers who previously worked for packaged goods firms, reprinted in Part I of this book under the title, "Comparing Marketing Management in Package Goods and Service Organizations."

2. See E. Raymond Corey, Christopher H. Lovelock, and Scott Ward (1981), *Problems in Marketing*, 6th ed., New York: McGraw-Hill, 716–18.

3. For further insights into the process of developing a marketing plan, see Philip Kotler, William Gregor, and William Rodgers (1977), "The Marketing Audit Comes of Age," *Sloan Management Review*, Winter, 25–43; and (1981), *The Marketing Plan*, New York: The Conference Board.

4. Source of this list is Eric Langeard, John E. G. Bateson, Christopher H. Lovelock, and Pierre Eiglier (1981), *Services Marketing: New Insights from Customers and Managers*. Cambridge, MA: The Marketing Science Institute, p. 101.

5. Ibid., p. 85.

6. See the discussion of customer service in Section VI.

7. This discussion and the one that follows are based closely on Langeard, et al. (see Note 4 above), 87–95. All quotations are taken from this study.

8. This research is reported in Langeard, et al., (see Note 4 above), 66–80.

9. See Section III, "Positioning the Service Organization."

CASES

UNITED STATES POSTAL SERVICE, I

One of the world's largest service operations is the United States Postal Service. The Postal Reorganization Act of 1971 made USPS more like a business than a government agency and stimulated the establishment of a formal marketing function within the organization. Executives hired from private industry have brought a product management focus to the broad array of services offered by USPS.

The Post Office has always been operated as if it were an ordinary government agency. . . .

In what it does, however, the Post Office is a business: Its customers purchase its services directly, its employees work in a service-industry environment, it is a major communications network, it is a means by which much of the nation's business is conducted.[1]

When the President's Commission on Postal Organization submitted its report, *Towards Postal Excellence*, in June 1968, it emphasized the need for a full-time marketing function. "Only a Post Office quick to identify and meet market needs," it said, "can successfully serve a changing economy." By 1974, many postal executives believed that significant progress had been made in introducing marketing to an

---

This case was prepared by L. Frank Demmler, research assistant at the Harvard Business School, and Christopher H. Lovelock.

organization with no previous experience of this function.

HISTORICAL BACKGROUND OF THE POSTAL SERVICE

The post office made its first appearance in the American colonies in 1639, when the General Court of Massachusetts appointed one Richard Fairbanks of Boston to take charge of letters arriving from, or destined for, overseas. Subsequently, many other postal arrangements were instituted by the individual colonies over the next century or so.

In July 1775, the Second Continental Congress, meeting in Philadelphia, established a post office system and appointed Benjamin Franklin as postmaster general. Profitability in operations was prohibited, and it was stipulated that any "deficit shall be made good by the United Colonies."

The Post Office Department

The Post Office Department was established as an agency of the federal government in 1789. This agency was part of the Executive Branch, and from 1829 to 1971 the position of Postmaster General was at the cabinet level. In the years shortly before 1971, Congress had control over postal rates and the salaries of postal workers. Although the Post Office was one of the nation's largest businesses, it was not run as a business, but as a cabinet agency of the U.S. Government.

Discussing the special nature of the Post Office Department and its successor agency, a senior USPS executive commented,

> The Post Office was, historically, a political play child of both the executive and legislative branch. The Postmaster General was the chairman of the winning national party, Larry O'Brien being the most recent example; James Farley probably being the most famous. Local postmasters were appointed based on party affiliation.

In the past, the post office had offered new services or expanded existing ones by just adding them on to the structure which existed at the time. With no overall planning or coordination at the highest levels, the Post Office Department had become a conglomerate of parts by the mid-1960s, and operational problems continued to mount as new parts were tacked on.

The role of Congress further accentuated these problems. Pay scales and fringe benefits were set by Congress. The interplay of Congressional politics determined postal rates and it was alleged that, due to lobbying efforts, rates reflected the views of some sectors of business rather than the interests of the general public. Revenues went directly to the Treasury, and the Post Office Department was dependent upon annual appropriations which, while covering the rising deficit, provided decreasing amounts for capital investments. (The Post Office Department operated at a deficit in 48 of its last 52 years.) Finally, Post Office Department jobs were a primary source for repaying political favors. This sometimes resulted in selection of managers without regard to their training or experience relative to the jobs involved. This factor and the relatively rapid turnover of personnel (reflecting, in part, changes in Administrations) were major obstacles to any long-range planning or programs.

The Reform Movement

These conditions created a movement for postal reform in both the public and private sectors. Although growing in strength, the catalyst which mobilized the forces was the total breakdown of the Chicago Post Office in October 1966. Ten million pieces of mail sat immobile for almost three weeks until a special task force appointed by the Postmaster General, vested with special authority, could gradually restore order.

Investigation into what had occurred revealed that the breakdown was caused by a lack of management authority, personnel problems, extremely low productivity, a poorly designed physical plant, and breakdowns in this plant. These revelations fanned the embers of the reform movement into flame.

Political pressure was exerted and in April 1967 President Lyndon B. Johnson established the President's Commission on Postal Organization (Kappel Commission). The Commission submitted its findings in June 1968, with its primary recommendation the creation of the United States Postal Service as a federal government corporation. The report stated that the infusion of professional management and a move to more "business-like" operations could reduce costs by at least 20 percent while improving service.

Not long after submission of the report there was a change of Administration. The new Administration lent its support to the effort to draft and pass enabling legislation quite similar to that recommended in the report. In addition, the new Administration made the difficult decision to forego using the patronage system to fill postal positions. The Postmaster General at the time, Winston M. Blount, also took the first step in reorganization on June 5, 1969 by establishing the Bureau of Marketing and Planning. This bureau was comprised of three formerly independent divisions of the Post Office Department and allowed for a more coordinated management effort, while also providing a vehicle for long-range planning.

FORMATION OF THE UNITED STATES POSTAL SERVICE

On August 12, 1970, President Richard M. Nixon signed the Postal Reorganization Act (Public Law 91–375). The fact that the original Presidential Commission had been formed by one Administration, and the legislation signed by another Administration of a different political party, served to underscore the bi-partisan recognition that reform was needed. The subject at issue was, on one hand, an American tradition and, on the other, a giant public utility affecting the daily commercial life of the nation. The Act became effective on July 1, 1971, and the Postal Service was born.

The Postal Reorganization Act clearly reinforced the special public service responsibilities of the new organization. The Act stipulated, for example, that the Postal Service had "the obligation to provide postal services to bind the nation together through personal, educational, literary, and business correspondence of the people." In addition, "the costs of establishing and maintaining the Postal Service shall not be apportioned to impair the over-all value of such service to the people."

Two very basic changes took place, however, as a result of the Act. One change dealt with the financing of the Postal Service. The cost of services was to be borne by users, not taxpayers, and a series of fiscal objectives culminating with a breakeven position in 1984 was established. These financial changes made the Postal Service more like a business than a government agency.

The second basic change was that the Law really made the Postal Service responsible for the planning, development, promotion, and provision of adequate and efficient postal and other services at fair and reasonable rates. In order to carry out this responsibility intelligently, it was necessary for the Postal Service to establish a marketing organization, which heretofore had not been considered necessary. The law also required in part that it provide types of service responsive to customer needs. Historically, decisions had been made largely on the basis of operational or legislative considerations.

The Act also contained other features aimed at ensuring the Postal Service's independence. First, a rational rate-making procedure was dictated. The keystone of this procedure was the creation of a Postal Rate Commission, composed of five technically qualified persons appointed by the President to serve staggered six-year terms. The Postal Service would propose rate changes to the Rate Commission. The Commission would hold public hearings, then develop a recommendation for submission to the Governors for final decision. Rates previously had been set by Congress.

The Board of Governors was an 11-person body including the postmaster general and the deputy postmaster general. The remaining nine members were appointed by the President and approved by the Senate for staggered nine-year terms. These nine selected the postmaster general in addition to making important decisions. The 11-person Board has final authority in all the Postal Service's other decision-making areas, and the nine governors were not legally bound to accept the recommendations of the Postal Rate Commission.

The Act empowered the Postal Service to raise capital funds through bond issues. The limit to such funding was $10 billion with a maximum of $2 billion in any one fiscal year.

The Postal Service and the four postal unions were directed to initiate collective bargaining with each other. Additionally, promotion and appointment on merit was specified for full-time postal employees, replacing the former procedure under which major postmasterships and top management positions had been political appointments. By October 1974, over 10,000 postmasters (out of a total of over 33,000) had been appointed on merit.

In order to carry out the mandates of the Postal Reorganization Act of 1970, Postmaster General Blount announced a reorganization of the Post Office Department on May 12, 1971, which marked the dawning of the Postal Service era. The new organization had three goals. First, operating responsibilities were to be decentralized to the regional and district levels. Second, the organization was to be such that it was possible to focus on the major businesses of the Postal Service. Third, the organization was to acknowledge the special postal management requirements of large metropolitan areas.

The organization in late 1974 was as shown in Exhibit 1. The Executive Committee operated as an internal policy level review body. Virtually all major finanical or marketing proposals were presented to this group for approval prior to discussion with the Postal Service Board of Governors. Each region had an organization which was basically similar to that of headquarters with the exception of such functions as government relations, planning, etc.

Basic Statistics

As of June 30, 1974, the magnitude of the Postal Service could be reflected in a series of numbers. The Postal Service employed 710,433 people. The annual budget was $11.3 billion, of which 85 percent represented labor expenses. During the fiscal year, 90 billion pieces of mail were moved, which translated into an average 297 million pieces per day. Over the past ten years this figure had increased at a rate averaging 2.5 percent annually. The Postal Service operated 31,000 post offices, ranging in size from one corner of Seward's General Store in Menemsha on the island of Martha's Vineyard in Massachusetts, to Chicago's main post office, the biggest in the world. The latter's 21,000 employees worked on nine floors of a 13-story, 60-acre building, and received, sorted, and dispatched 15 million pieces of mail a day. The Postal Service's fleet of almost 100 thousand vehicles made it the country's largest consumer of fuel outside the military. As a result, each one-cent increase in the price of gasoline and diesel fuel increased annual operating costs by $3.5 million. Exhibit 2 summarizes key financial statistics from 1970–1974.

An indication of the degree to which the Postal Service was labor-intensive was provided in a 1968 study. The ratio of net fixed assets to employee was found to be $1,145. This could be compared to $35,630 in the leading companies of the telephone and telegraph industry, $7,170 in manufacturing, and $2,836 in merchandising.

The actual transportation of the mail between post offices cost over $707 million in 1972. This included a complex network of 15,000 contract truck routes, 8,000 commercial air flights, 169 air-taxi routes, and 154 passenger and freight trains.

The handling of mail was also complex. It was comprised of six steps: collection, culling, canceling, sorting, transportaion, and delivery. Although there had been a movement toward mechanization, a study showed that one letter might be handled by up to 43 different individuals. Thus the chance for error was very great.

Prior to postal reorganization, no service standards had ever been defined. Standards were therefore issued in 1972. These were set by top management and subsequently validated by market research. The most desired quality for mail delivery was found to be consistency of service, with consumer expectations being highest for local mail. In the case of first-class mail, objectives were delivery of local mail in one day, nonlocal but within 600 miles in two days, and beyond 600 miles in three days. The goal of the Postal Service was to meet these objectives for 95 percent of all pieces. However, meeting that goal would have still meant that almost two and one-half billion first-class letters (5 percent of total) arrived late in 1974.

THE CUSTOMER SERVICES DEPARTMENT

The Kappel Commission report strongly recommended that the new organization be firmly based on the concept of meeting customers' needs through a marketing approach. The Postal Reform Act provided the means for the establishment of a true marketing function.

Marketing activities within the USPS were centered in the Customer Services Department, under the direction of the Assistant Postmaster General (APMG) for Customer Services, William D. Dunlap. Dunlap, 36, had joined the Postal Service in May 1969 from the Procter and Gamble Company, where he had previously held the position of new products marketing manager. After assignments as special assistant to the postmaster general responsible for press relations, development of new philatelic programs, and special assignments, he was appointed as APMG for Product Management in 1971 and named to his present position in June 1973. He reported directly to the senior assistant postmaster general for administration.

Partly at Dunlap's urging, several other Proctor and Gamble "graduates" had joined him in the Customer Services Department, among them James L. Schorr, 32, director of advertising, and Robert F. Jordan, 33, director of product management. Jordan, who held an MBA from the University of Connecticut, had previously worked in the Advertising Department of the Packaged Soaps and Detergents Division at Procter and Gamble, where he had held product management responsibility for several nationally distributed, branded products. He had joined the USPS in April 1972.

The mandate provided by the 1970 Act, Dunlap said, gave the USPS the flexibility to make major changes in the structure of the system.

> In our particular area, our job is to develop and market new products and services while doing a better job of making our current services more customer oriented.

However, Jordan presented a warning concerning the overall impact of the Act:

> Just because there is a law written, it does not change the inertia of operating in a certain way and the value systems that are present in any large, established organization.

> I think that people coming from the outside, like I did, really didn't appreciate that. I think there was some confusion between a legislative act and a divine miracle. There's a great gap between the two. The only thing, I think, that can be said is that because it has the strength of law, the Postal Service has an advantage over organizations that don't have that catalyst.

The Act also had specific marketing implications. For example, it stated that, "In determining all policies for postal services, the Postal Service shall give the highest consideration to the requirement for the most expeditious collection, transportation, and delivery of important letter mail." Jordan reflected,

> That doesn't make much sense from a marketing point of view. It incorrectly equates speed of delivery with service. It also suggests that the cost of providing faster and faster service would have to be borne by all users when only a small fraction really need expedited delivery.

The Structure of the Marketing Organization

With the mandate of the Postal Reform Act, a marketing organization was developed within the Customer Services Department which evolved over time to the structure in Exhibit 3, comprised of two divisions and six offices.

The Special Events Division had several responsibilities. Postal Forum, Inc., a wholly owned, separate corporation, ran a national convention. A primary objective of the Division was to operate the Postal Forum, a national meeting of some 3,000 postal customers, conducted annually. Additionally, the Division was responsible for all industrial conference relationships, such as trade show activities.

The Planning and Management Division acted in a service relationship between Dunlap and the Offices, in terms of the planning and implementation of the management-by-objectives system which had been instituted in the Customer Services Department.

The Office of Stamps was responsible for both the regular stamps and the entire philately operation. It had both product and marketing responsibility for its own products.

The Office of International Postal Affairs represented the U.S. Postal Service in the Universal Postal Union. Established in 1874, the UPU consisted of 152 member countries dedicated to the basic goal of creating one "international postal community." Even when nations were at war, the UPU saw to it that mail was delivered between them. This office also negotiated bi-lateral agreements with other countries on postal matters, such as the recently concluded agreements on International Express Mail. Within the U.S. Postal Service, the Office served as a focal point for contacts with foreign administrations and interpreted the Universal Postal Union regulations for operating officials.

The Office of Advertising had functional responsibility for all measured media advertising. This included three areas of advertising. Public service advertising, such as for ZIP codes, was designed and then broadcast at no charge. Corporate advertising consisted of paid advertising messages responsible for attitude shifts and image building, not dollar volume, and included such campaigns as "There Is No Such Thing as Junk Mail." Product advertising—promotion of special postal products and services—was the functional responsibility of this office, but had to have the concurrence of the managing office or product manager.

The Office of Product Management (discussed in greater depth later in the case) was responsible for the overall management of all elements and activities related to USPS products.[2] Additionally, this Office had market research responsibility for the entire Postal Service.

The Office of Customer Marketing was formed to consolidate the "field marketing" functions into one office. This office had the responsibility for sales training, sales planning, and evaluation of field sales performance. Lobby design, point-of-purchase materials, self-service equipment, and window merchandizing were main functions in the retail area.

The Office of Consumer Advocate acted as a liaison between the Postal Service and its customers. It handled an average of 500 complaints a week. The Consumer Advocate had the authority to call any postmaster in the country and find out what was right and what was wrong and get any problems seen to immediately.

Organizational Problems

The marketing organization faced some important problems resulting from the overall organization of the Postal Service and from the newness of marketing within the Postal Service. These problems were primarily concerned with the interaction of marketing and operations.

The first problem was that all field activities were under Operations and thus marketing had no line authority over the "salesmen" (customer service representatives) or the postmasters and their activities. This complicated coordination of all the elements in a marketing program.

Second, individual post offices were treated as cost centers, and thus postmasters resisted any changes which would increase costs. The impact of changes on revenues was institutionally overlooked at this level.

To overcome this institutional inertia, marketing had to go to great efforts—in the form of market research, operations research, and detailed marketing plans—in order to ensure that its recommendations received careful consideration at all levels.

THE OFFICE OF PRODUCT MANAGEMENT

The Office of Product Management had overall responsibility and authority for product marketing within the U.S. Postal Service. Upon assuming the newly created position of Director of Product Management on July 1, 1973, Jordan realized that he had to develop an organizational structure that was appropriate for the Postal Service as a whole and the Customer Services Department in particular.

Starting from the mandate in the Reorganization Act that said we should provide services based on customer needs, we have asked ourselves: What is the proper business of the Postal Service?

Our answer is that, first, we are in the communications business with our message transfer services like first-class mail. Second, we're in the media business by using the mails to deliver advertising messages. Third, we're in the materials handling business with products and services like parcel post. Fourth, we're in the financial business. We're the number one money order brand in the United States, for example, and have a very high cash flow and a lot of financial expertise. And we run a large retail business. I think the number of outlets is ten times greater than the A & P chain, for example.

Goals, Objectives, and Responsibilities

The primary goal underlying creation of the Office of Product Management was the development of an organizational structure compatible with the existing range of services and able to permit addition or appropriate new products and services. A secondary goal was to provide flexibility for the organization to evolve, expand, and contract over time in response to a changing environment and product line. Jordan particularly wanted to avoid a structure "carved in granite."[3]

A key element of product management is to be as flexible as possible. I change things as the needs of the business require. I do not want the organization to get carved in granite in some kind of civil service personnel department because if the thing works I'll go from two to fifty people and if it doesn't work I'll go from two to zero people. I also need the flexibility to move resources from declining to growing businesses.

He defined the objectives of the Office of Product Management as twofold. First, to increase the technical performance, customer acceptance, and revenue contribution of current postal services and products, except philatelics. And second, to improve service and build revenues through the development and marketing of new postal services and products.

As director of product management, Jordan had prepared the following written statement of the basic responsibilities of Product Management within the Postal Service:

1. Establish policy, objectives, and priorities regarding the development and sales of assigned products and services.

2. Determine customer needs, customer acceptance, and technical performance. Develop new services or standards, or modify existing services and standards as required.

3. Develop and approve marketing plans and programs for assigned products and services. Be

accountable for the volume and revenue results of these activities.

4. Develop and approve marketing budgets for assigned products. Be accountable for the net contribution of products assigned.

5. Provide market research services to other Customer Services and USPS organizations.

6. Work closely with others in carrying out the responsibilities of the Office of Product Management. Receive creative and media services from the Office of Advertising. Receive implementation support from the Sales and Retail Divisions. Coordinate with other Headquarters and Regional groups as required. Select, manage, and evaluate the performance of assigned contractors.

Organization

In designing a product management organization which would meet the above objectives, Jordan drew heavily on his previous experience at Proctor and Gamble. Product-related divisions were based on three principles:

1. *Marketing*—The organization should mirror the way the customer views our business and the structure of the markets where we do business.

2. *Operations*—The organization should have a natural, common link to the way the Postal Service provides products and services to the customer.

3. *Priorities*—The organization should provide maximum focus against key products.

By October 1974, after several interim designs, the organization had been refined to that shown in Exhibit 4. Jordan commented,

> . . . Taking the results of our analysis, and adding postal nomenclatures with an eye for the need to communicate and be able to relate to the rest of the Postal Service, we came up with this particular array. I could think of about three other ways of doing it, which might be as good or better, but this has worked very well. We'll change it again as the needs of the business require.

The Office of Product Management was structured into six divisions, titled Letter Mail, Parcel Mail, Retail Products, Special Services, Electronic Mail, and Market Research. Each division was headed by a general manager, and in some cases supported by a group product manager. Responsibility for individual products rested with the product manager, who would provide technical direction to assistant product managers and product assistants assigned to the product. Titles in the Market Research Division differed due to the nature of the business; however, the positions were similar in level and responsibility.

The five product-related divisions were a rational grouping of the numerous USPS products and services. The divisional structure provided an umbrella under which new lines could be added and weak ones phased out. Each division represented a product line, and thus a coordinated effort across a group of products could be effected.

DIVISIONS IN THE OFFICE OF PRODUCT MANAGEMENT

Letter Mail Division

The Letter Mail Division had primary responsibility for first-class mail, airmail, and special delivery—products producing more than 55 percent of postal mail revenues annually. These were the only USPS products protected from competition by private express statutes.

First-class mail contributed approximately half the volume and revenue of the Postal Service. It represented the cornerstone of the business. Volume had grown 36 percent in the last ten years, from 38 billion pieces in 1964 to over 51 billion pieces in 1974, putting extraordinary demands on processing techniques. Revenue more than doubled in that period, from $2,109 million to $5,019 million.

Airmail volume was 1,334 million pieces in 1974 and revenue was $234 million. Special delivery volume was 82 million pieces, which produced $52 million revenue in 1974.

These letter mail products held a 20 percent share of the domestic, private-message communications market. Telephone, telegraph services, and, to a very small degree, TWX, telex, telegram, and courier services constituted the primary competition in this market.

Retail Products Division

In late 1974, the responsibilities of the division, which some felt might more aptly be titled "financial products," were being shared among several other divisions. The responsibility for money orders was placed with the Letter Mail Division, since most were sent through the mail. In FY 1974, the Postal Service sold 165 million money orders, which generated fee revenues of $52 million. Registered and certified mail were with the Special Services Division. Responsibility for products and product development related to the emerging area of electronic funds transfer was with the Electronic Mail Division. Long-range plans were to form a complete division devoted exclusively to financial products.

Parcel Mail Division

Products under this division were parcel post, priority mail and express mail, and other fourth-class mail.

Fourth-class had FY 1974 revenue of $732 million with volume of 859 million pieces. Over half of the revenue came from zone-rated parcel post, which competed primarily with the service offered by United Parcel Service and, to a lesser extent, with those of other private carriers such as freight forwarders.

Priority mail consisted of first-class mail over 12 ounces, airmail over 9 ounces, and air parcel post and accounted for $394 million revenue in FY 1974 with a volume of 222 million pieces.

Express mail was a new service designed to provide fast inter-city delivery of information, merchandise, and other materials of 50 pounds or less, with a money-back guarantee if performance standards were not met. This service took two forms. First, programmed service was provided to companies, such as banks, which had regularly scheduled needs between specific cities. Special service agreements were individually custom-tailored, typically calling for a 12-hour delivery. Second, regular service was provided to those with unpredictable needs at designated counters in specific post offices. This service guaranteed next day delivery by 3 p.m. to the addressee or to a specified post office to be picked up by 10 a.m.

Revenues from express mail increased from $1 million in FY 1972 to more than $3 million in 1973, and $6 million in 1974. By October 1974 the network included over 400 cities in the United States and abroad.

Special Services Division

This division managed products and services which met the special needs of select customers. Organizationally, the division was divided into the Security Mail Group and the Advertising Mail Group. The Security Mail Group included registered, certified, insurance, and COD mail, as well as a new service, Controlpak. The Advertising Mail Group was comprised of direct mail advertising (first-class, third-class, and fourth-class catalogs) and second-class mail (primarily magazines).

Security mail products were additional, value-added options available for the basic requirement categories of mail. These products generated $140 million in postal revenue through 240 million transactions in 1973. Controlpak was a new service designed for the valuable letter market. The service was positioned between registered and first-class mail. Controlpak traveled through the registry system in heat-sealed plastic bags until it reached the office of delivery. At this point, the individual pieces entered the first-class delivery network. By October 1974 more than 50,000 shipments had been made with none lost or stolen.

Advertising mail was one of the most important revenue producers. In FY 1974, advertisers sent over 22 billion pieces of advertising mail, spending over $1 billion in postage to generate an estimated $50 billion in the sale of goods and services. This product, 93 percent of which was bulk-rate third-class, faced extreme and continuing competition. Ad mail was an important component of the direct mail industry. In 1973, national expenditures for direct mail were $3.7 billion, a 14.7 percent share of total U.S. advertising expenditures. Major competition was from newspapers, television, radio, magazines, private postal operations, and hand-delivery firms.

Electronic Mail Division

This division was organized primarily to explore and develop new services in the area of telecommunications. Rather than physically transporting the hard message, these services electronically transmitted the information content of the message to its destination where a hard copy was recreated and delivered. Some of this division's work involved products which were not expected to reach the marketplace until 1980. Others, such as urgent message service and mailgram, were already operational.

The *urgent message service* provided for electronic transmission of visual images between specified cities. This service made it possible for a customer in one city to transmit the image of, say, an engineering diagram, and have a facsimile copy generated by receiving equipment in a distant destination. There was guaranteed one-hour lobby pick-up or four-hour door delivery. The average cost per page was $4.

Mailgram, initiated in 1970, was a joint venture between the USPS and Western Union. The service, first proposed by Western Union, involved first transferring a message by Western Union equipment and then delivering a printed copy the next day through the Postal Service's regular mail network. By October 1974, 450,000 mailgrams per week were being sent as compared with an average of 265,000 in the last quarter of 1973. Postal revenues during the first six months of 1974 were $2.9 million, up from $1.3 million during the same period in 1973. By year end 1974, mailgram volume surpassed telegrams.

Market Research Division

In discussing the role of market research, Jordan noted that the Office of Product Management had market research responsibility for the entire Postal Service. This had the advantage of insuring the marketing activities of the regular divisions took full advantage of research, but required special management skills.

The market research manager and myself have to insure other Postal clients get fair, confidential treatment. One of our own product managers can get pretty upset if he or she has to wait for research because someone from another office or department was in line first or has higher priority work.

PRODUCT MANAGEMENT STAFFING

Jordan regarded the product manager as "the focal point around which everything turns. He's the guy who is supposed to make everything happen. I'm 'overhead' by comparison."

The product manager typically headed a small group consisting of one or more assistants. Some assistants were called product assistants, which was the entry-level position. Others were called assistant product managers, more experienced and only one step away from being promoted to manage their own product. The size and composition of one of these groups varied by the requirements of a particular business. They ranged from one to six people, with a group of three being most typical.

There was also provision for a group product manager position,

We are just beginning to actually fill these positions. On one hand, we favor the idea because it provides additional depth, focus, and opportunities for professional growth. On the other hand, it is not needed until individual product clusters are implemented, and too many in number for the division manager to handle well.

Creating an organization on paper and activating it with qualified people were two different things, Jordan stated.

We have been able to attract some good people from within the Postal Service, but the talent base is too thin for our needs. There was no marketing in a professional sense in the old Post Office, so people with the skills and instincts we need are few in number.

This has made it necessary to recruit heavily from the outside. Before we started, we trained ourselves in interviewing, conducted salary and job surveys, and got help from experts in the private sector. The job is worth doing, very challenging, and we think, competitive from a compensation view.[4]

Still, we've had some difficulty. First, there is a general skepticism toward government among people in private companies. Second, few have thought of the Postal Service as a business.

We're also pretty picky and would rather live with a vacancy than fill it with someone about whom we may have a doubt. Initiative and perseverance are two essential characteristics in a good product manager, especially here since we're creating new programs out of whole cloth. So we tend to look more at the psychology of a person, rather than focus on *years of experience* and the like. A common denomina-

tor is that the candidate should demonstrate capacity, fluency, and independence in his or her thinking. Leadership ability, results orientation, communications skills, and goal motivation are some of the things we look at before examining technical skills in detail.

Candidates are pre-screened by the outside consultant and our own personnel people before being scheduled for an interview. Even with tight requirements and the pre-screening, we don't make offers to the majority of people we interview.

In net, we've done pretty well so far. Six of the last nine product managers we've hired have MBAs, and two of the last three market research specialists have PhDs. Interestingly enough, two of our more successful managers are attorneys.

Long term, we hope to get to the position where most of our hires are at the entry-level position, and we promote from within for manager positions.

In November 1974, there were 52 authorized management-level positions in the Office of Product Management, of which 34 had been filled. Only 6 of the present managerial staff had been employed by the old Post Office Department prior to postal reorganization, the remaining 28 having been hired from outside. Most of these had previous business experience.

NOTES

1. *Towards Postal Excellence*, Report of the President's Commission on Postal Organization, June 1968, page 1.

2. Henceforth the term *product* is used in the generic sense to denote service offerings as well as physical goods.

3. This was *literally* true for the former Post Office Department. At the old Post Office Building on Washington's Pennsylvania Avenue (which the

USPS had recently vacated for newly constructed offices in L'Enfant Plaza), the names of the services offered by the Department were actually carved into the stone frontage of the neo-classical building.

4. In late 1974, salary ranges were: group product manager, $25,767–$34,603; product manager, $21,500–$28,831; assistant product manager, $16,908– $22,617; and product assistant, $13,830– $18,409.

EXHIBIT 1

Headquarters Organization Structure of United States Postal Service, 1973

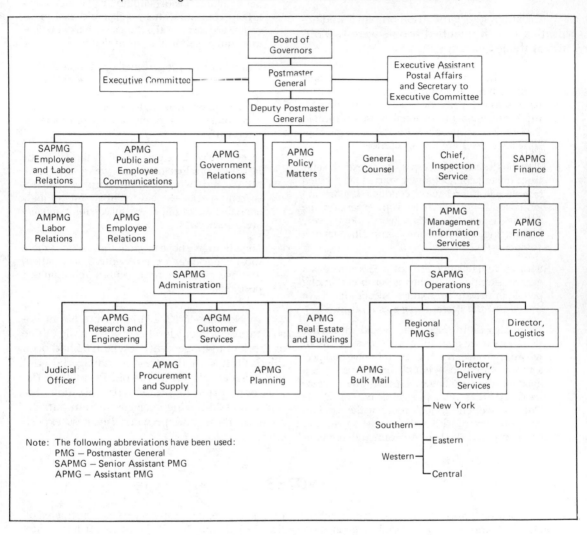

Note: The following abbreviations have been used:
PMG — Postmaster General
SAPMG — Senior Assistant PMG
APMG — Assistant PMG

Note: The following abbreviations have been used: PMG—Postmaster General; SAPMG—Senior Assistant PMG; and APMG—Assistant PMG.
SOURCE: *U.S. Postal Service*

EXHIBIT 2

United States Postal Service Financial History Summary (Fiscal Years 1970–1975)

(All Figures in Thousands of Dollars)

	JUNE 30				
	1974	1973	1972	1971 ᵃ	1970
STATEMENT OF OPERATIONS					
Operating revenues	$9,008,314	$8,338,945	$7,884,188	$6,664,988	$6,346,655
Government appropriations	1,750,445	1,485,595	1,424,191	2,086,496	1,355,040
Total income	10,758,759	9,824,540	9,308,379	8,751,484	7,701,695
Salaries and benefits	9,641,557	8,450,914	8,145,538	7,467,036	6,524,819
Other expenses	1,653,782	1,475,527	1,439,831	1,488,228	1,342,450
Total operating expenses	11,295,339	9,926,441	9,585,369	8,955,264	7,867,269
Operating loss	536,580	101,901	276,990	203,780	165,574
Other income, net	98,221	88,937	101,555		
Net loss	$ 438,359	$ 12,964	$ 175,435	$ 203,780	$ 165,574
BALANCE SHEET					
Assets					
Current assets	$1,718,458	$1,950,676	$2,059,829	$1,989,212	$1,501,827
Property plant and equip. and other assets	5,115,850	3,674,005	2,676,796	1,415,466	1,259,405
Total assets	6,834,308	5,624,681	4,736,625	3,404,678	2,761,232
Liabilities					
Current liabilities	$2,167,925	1,483,665	1,437,929	1,346,165	890,314
Reserves	3,254,618	2,325,464	1,500,390	372,796	333,368
Long-term debt—USPS Bonds and Mortgages	264,983	250,000	250,000		
Equity	1,146,782	1,565,552	1,548,306	1,685,717	1,537,550
Total liabilities and equity	$6,834,308	$5,624,681	$4,736,625	$3,404,678	$2,761,232
ANALYSIS OF CHANGES IN EQUITY					
Beginning balance	$1,565,552	$1,548,306	$1,685,717	$1,537,550	$1,149,834
Deduct:					
Retroactive adjustments recorded at July 1, 1971				(243,678)	
Balance July 1	1,565,552	1,548,306	1,685,717	1,293,872	1,149,834
Net loss	438,359	12,964	175,435	203,780	165,574
	1,127,193	1,535,342	1,510,282	1,090,092	984,260
Add:					
Capital contributions	21,235	27,403	32,539		
Government appropriations—capital				486,825	380,000
Buildings and other transfers to/from government agencies	(1,646)	2,807	5,485	108,800	173,290
Ending balance	$1,146,782	$1,565,552	$1,548,306	$1,685,717	$1,537,550

ᵃ The United States Postal Service was established July 1, 1971. Financial statements prior to that date are those of the Post Office Department. Such statements for 1970 and 1971 have been restated above to be in a format generally consistent with 1972–1974.
SOURCE: Annual Report of the Postmaster General, 1973–1974

EXHIBIT 3

United States Postal Service: Organization of Customer Services Department

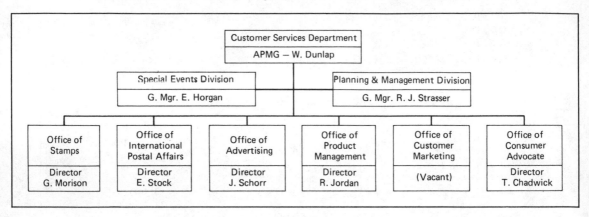

EXHIBIT 4

United States Postal Service: Organization of Office of Product Management.

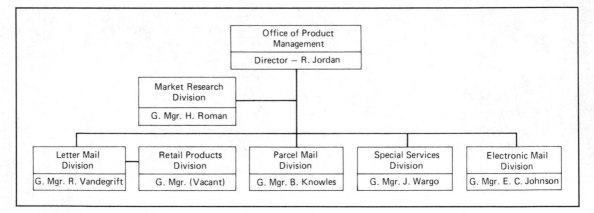

UNITED STATES POSTAL SERVICE, II

A new assistant postmaster general—customer services is appointed. He undertakes a major reorganization of the Customer Services Department.

From substitute clerk to assistant postmaster general of the United States—John Applegate thought back on those 30 years as he looked at the flags, the fountain, the Capitol dome from his new Washington office.

His postal career had started in Champaign, Illinois, in 1945. There had been assignments as an inspector, an installation manager, and a manager of delivery services. The last assignment had been assistant regional postmaster general for Customer Services in the southern region. This included directing sales, retail services, delivery, and fleet management. It also included implementation of national marketing programs generated by Postal Headquarters in Washington.

Applegate had been in his office in Memphis when the news came of his promotion to assistant postmaster general—Customer Services. The promotion reflected, he knew, a new policy of greater emphasis on advancement of career employees. It also was an opportunity to be sure future national marketing programs reflected more field and operations input. He felt that some of the programs from Headquarters he had had to implement in the past might have been "okay" for a Procter and Gamble or an IBM, but just weren't always practical in the real postal field environment.

REORGANIZATION—1976

A major reorganization of the Customer Services Department took place in May 1976. Applegate, in announcing the change, noted the need to cut costs and streamline the organization. For one thing, he felt there were too many positions at higher-grade levels. And he knew from eight months' firsthand experience that there were too many managers reporting directly to the APMG. The new Customer Services organization chart and functional statement are attached as Exhibits 1 and 2.

The Office of Product Management was one of the elements within Customer Services that was most affected by the reorganization. The existing product-type divisions were regrouped and combined into three new divisions. Responsibility for philatelic marketing was added as a fourth division. A Marketing Services Division was also created to provide internal market research, service analysis, and advertising services.

The result was a wholly new Office of Marketing Programs. An organization chart and functional statements are attached as Exhibits 3, 4, and 5.

This case was prepared by Christopher H. Lovelock.

EXHIBIT 1

Organization Chart of Customer Services Department

(May 1976)

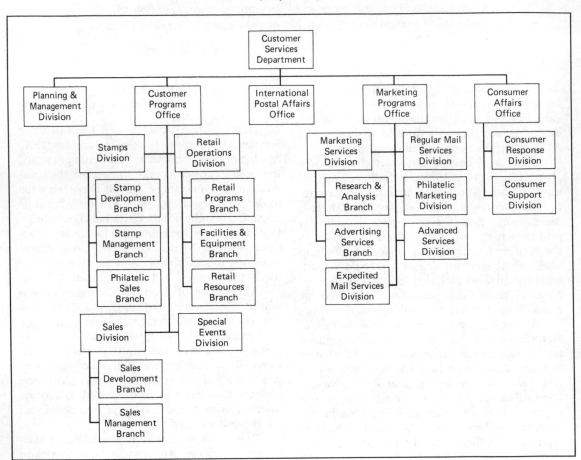

EXHIBIT 2

Customer Services Department

The Customer Services Department is responsible for

- Analysis, development, adjustment, and marketing of all postal products and services.
- Establishment of policy and the functional management of the Postal Service's retail and sales operations. Provision of functional guidance to the Regional Customer Services Department.
- Management of the design, production, and distribution of postage stamps and postal stationery.
- Representation of the interests of individual consumers, responding to consumer needs and problems.
- Liaison with postal systems of other countries and representation of the United States in the Universal Postal Union and the Postal Union of the Americas and Spain.
- Conduct of market research and diagnostic service analysis.
- Liaison with postal customers, including the planning and implementation of the National Postal Forum.
- Development and execution of the Postal Service's advertising and promotion programs.

SOURCE: USPS records

EXHIBIT 3

Organization Chart for Marketing Programs Office

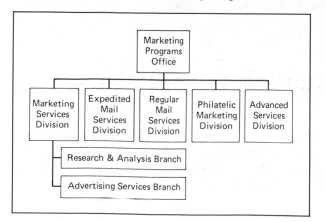

EXHIBIT 4

EXHIBIT 5

Office of Marketing Programs

The Office of Marketing Programs is responsible for

- Development and execution of all marketing programs within the Postal Service.
- Provision of market analysis and research and diagnostic service testing and analysis.
- Establishment of policy and objectives for promotion and advertising programs within the Postal Service.
- Comprehensive review and analysis of Postal Service products and services; including technical performance, customer acceptance, financial performance, and market performance.
- Collaboration with other departments and offices to insure a free flow of information regarding those product features which affect postal services in the marketplace.
- Provision of information and projections on products and services to the Offices of Operational and Strategic Planning for both long- and short-range planning efforts.
- Provision of analyses and recommendations to Rates and Classification Department regarding rates.
- Recommendation to management of adjustment to existing products/services and institution of new products/services.
- Provision of policy interpretation and program guidance on marketing programs to the regional Customer Services Department through the Assistant Postmaster General, Customer Services Department.

SOURCE: USPS records

OFFICE OF MARKETING PROGRAMS

Scope of Division Assignments

- *Expedited Mail Services Division*—Assigned marketing programs, involving high speed, and/or above-normal delivery frequency mail services, such as express mail, priority (heavy pieces) mail, mailgram, and special delivery.
- *Regular Mail Services Division*—Assigned marketing programs involving regular mail services (basic services, normal delivery frequency), such as first class, advertising mail, fourth class, and associated special services.
- *Philately Marketing Division*—Assigned marketing programs for philatelic products and services, domestic and international.
- *Advanced Services Division*—Assigned marketing programs for future technology new services.
- *Marketing Services Division*—First, to provide market research, service analysis, and creative counsel to internal clients. Second, to develop and implement public service advertising programs such as ZIP Code and Christmas Mail Early.

SOURCE: USPS records

CUNNINGHAM INC.: INDUSTRIAL SERVICE GROUP

Cunningham Inc. is an example of a major manufacturing firm that has diversified into services. Its Industrial Service Group provides repair and maintenance services on a wide array of electrical and mechanical equipment. ISG management is evaluating the results of an

This case was prepared by Penny Pittman Merliss, a former research associate at the Harvard Business School, and Christopher H. Lovelock.

experiment involving the clustering of service centers on a territorial basis for the purposes of planning, sales management, and service execution. Sales are up in the test region, but there are concerns that territorial clustering will undermine the initiative of individual unit managers.

Adam Newman, director of strategic planning for Cunningham's Industrial Service Group, felt a mixture of nervousness and suspense as he tapped on the open door of his general manager's office on a February day in 1981. "We've finally got it," he thought, "the territorial organizational blueprint that's going to carry this division through the 1980s. But is Paul McDonald going to buy all these new ideas?"

The answer was not long in coming. Glancing up from his paper-strewn desk, McDonald waved Newman to a chair, leaned forward, and declared,

> Adam, I'm concerned about some of the implications in this latest plan to reorganize our field operations. There's no question that our marketing management in the field is weak, and with the prospect of 15 percent annual earnings growth, we've got to do a better job of training and directing our sales force. We've got a national network of 15 large service centers that can service just about any kind of mechanical or electrical equipment, and 50 smaller ones with more limited capabilities. And, of course, each center has its own salesmen.

McDonald tapped a thick binder on his desk.

> You've got a plan here that integrates the sales effort for both large and small service centers at the territorial level. I know Tom Simmons has had some success trying it out in his region, and you're telling me now that this is the way of the future for ISG.

Newman watched as the older man walked over to a corner window and surveyed the busy industrial scene four stories below. Finally, McDonald turned and continued,

> What worries me about this reorganization is its effect on management development. Tradi-

tionally, our small-center managers have been one of our best sources of talent. We need better marketing, all right—but if you take control of the sales function away from a small-center manager, you're taking away a good chunk of his control over his own work flow. You're weakening his autonomy and cutting into his decision-making powers. And is that really going to help the group in the long run?

SERVICE BUSINESSES AT CUNNINGHAM INC.

Cunningham Inc. reported approximately $7 billion in sales and $430 million in net income in 1979. It offered a wide range of manufactured goods and services to its customers, including motors, generators, and power delivery equipment, as well as a broad line of consumer and defense products. The company had entered the service business more than half a century earlier by providing after-sales equipment repair for its own products. As Cunningham's line of manufactured products had grown, so had the range and scope of services. Over time the company came to offer its repair and maintenance services to customers who operated equipment produced by other manufacturers as well.

By 1981, service businesses, including financial services, broadcasting, and industrial maintenance and repair made up an increasing share of the company's income. All the service operations, like those in manufacturing, were measured as independent profit centers, not as contributors to other divisions of the corporation, and all were managed with an aggressive invest-grow strategy. Cunningham's chairman drew attention to the success of the service groups in the company's latest annual report:

Today, the management and stockholders of Cunningham Inc. can take pride in an organization which has grown far beyond its original area of expertise—the manufacture of high-quality electrical equipment. This is still our key business, but earnings in our service businesses are growing too, at about 13 percent annually. Services now account for 25 percent of our revenues.

Industrial Service Group

The Industrial Service Group (ISG) was among the fastest-growing groups of the company; sales more than doubled between 1974 and 1979 (Exhibit 1). ISG was one of the leading domestic and international suppliers of high-quality repair and maintenance services for all manufacturers' electrical and mechanical equipment. Through its extensive geographic coverage—service centers existed within 100 miles of 83 percent of potential business—the group had established a strong position in a field where fast turnaround was considered extremely important. In 1981, ISG had 65 domestic service centers; the national network included 15 large centers capable of repairing the largest transformers (20 feet high) and motors (20 tons), and 50 smaller centers where technicians spent much of their time rewinding electric motors of less than 200 horsepower.

Structurally, the ISG organization was divided between five headquarters departments and three field regions. The headquarters organization consisted of directors of service programs, strategic planning, employee relations, and finance, plus legal counsel and their staffs. The field organization consisted of three regional general managers who had profit center responsibility for the service centers in their regions. Each of these eight individuals reported directly to the group general manager, Paul McDonald (Exhibit 2).

The key to the complex central organization was the service programs department, a matrix within which were located five program managers, each of whom had nationwide responsibility for marketing and technical direction (with measurements tied to the results of their segment sales and earnings in the service centers) and five functional managers specializing in sales, communications, pricing, manufacturing,[1] and training.

The five program managers and their supporting staffs each interacted with regional management and the service centers, as did the five functional managers and their staffs. Likewise, staff from the strategic planning, employee relations, finance, and legal departments also provided specialized assistance to the regions and the service centers.

ISG had no marketing manager. As Newman explained from his vantage point as director of the Strategic Planning Department,

> In this kind of matrix, what you've really got is a kind of double integration—both groups of managers within the headquarters staff, plus the field territories. The person charged with bringing together field marketing and headquarters sales, communication, and pricing people is our group general manager.

Market research was handled centrally by ISG's strategic planning department. The division's planners and program managers worked closely with field service center managers and ISG's general manager to review sales and performance data from the field and set each center's sales goals for the upcoming year.

The field operating group was composed of three geographically dispersed regions. Each region contained 4 to 6 large service centers, whose managers reported directly to the regional general manager, and 14 to 20 smaller centers, which were often clustered about the larger ones. The average annual sales volume for large centers, most of which occupied about 50,000 square feet in floor space, was approximately $10 million; small centers occupied 10,000 to 12,000 square feet and averaged about $4 million each year in sales. In 1980, the seven sales reps assigned to each large center had an annual sales quota of $1.5 million per person. Small centers averaged three salesmen each, and their individual quotas were $1.3 million. Small-center managers reported to a manager of development and operations (MDO), who was responsible for opening new shops and expanding existing shops as well as overall supervision. The MDO, like the managers of the large centers, reported directly to the regional general manager. It was ISG's goal to make field management responsible for all service segments in a geographic area.

Service Segments

Equipment serviced by ISG was divided into five major categories or service segments: base electrical, large transformers, transit equipment, installation and field service, and mechanical apparatus (Exhibit 3). Each required different equipment and service skills and faced different kinds of competition. All ISG customers performed some of their own maintenance, but many lacked capacity for major overhauls or repair. Some firms operated their own maintenance facilities, known as "captive shops." These could be huge; the Consolidated Edison shop in Astoria, New York, for example, had about 400,000 square feet of floor space (ISG's nearest large service center had about 80,000).

Yet the competitive threat posed by captive shops, ISG managers felt, was becoming less and less significant. Although unions often resisted sending out work, it was difficult for the captives to keep pace with technological developments. The division's sales reps stressed that since customers' work volumes often did not justify investment in specialized equipment and training, captive shops were inherently inefficient, misapplying resources that could be better spent elsewhere in the customer's company.

ISG's major competitors were Morison Electric, with a national network of 70 service centers, and Marlborough-Fuchs. Despite Morison's long-standing reputation as a major manufacturer of electrical equipment, ISG market research showed that Cunningham was preferred by slightly more customers than Morison in three of the five major service segments (Exhibit 4). Marlborough-Fuchs was potentially a more significant competitor. It owned Republic Electric Inc., with a substan-

tial but smaller network of electrical centers, and had recently acquired the Katz-Hartley Corp., which controlled a national network of mechanical service centers.

Privately owned, independent service shops could be substantial regional competitors in motor and generator repair. Many specialized in electric motors; because of their proximity to customers, they could frequently offer faster turnaround time than Cunningham.

Other customers might turn to an independent or to an original equipment manufacturer (OEM) for service because they were unaware that ISG serviced all brands of equipment, not just Cunningham's.

Prospects for Growth

Management considered ISG's growth prospects excellent. The market growth rate was expected to average 12 percent annually during 1980–1984. Sales growth had reached 12 to 15 percent annually. Appraising the future, Newman commented:

> In a world of limited resources and continuing economic stress, ISG is going to thrive. We've been hit by the recession, of course, but not as much as the new equipment businesses. Our business has always lagged recessions by three to six months. The first thing that's shut off in a recession is capital investment—while repair is continued, although at a somewhat lower level. Also, inflation is pushing up the prices of new equipment right now faster than productivity improvements can offset costs. That's another reason why repair and modernization, as compared to new purchase, will be more and more attractive to our customers.

Equally important to Newman and the division's other planners was ISG's favorable strategic environment. According to Newman's analysis of the market for industrial service—which included captive shops—ISG had only a 3.2 percent share of the domestic market in 1979, though it was among the market leaders worldwide. ISG sales were about 80 percent those of Morison, its nearest rival; corporate planners saw no serious roadblocks to expansion.

Customers and Markets

ISG's customers and markets varied widely from segment to segment. In recent years, the division had concentrated on diversification in those shops that were highly dependent on any single customer segment. Frank Mays, manager of ISG's large New Mutley center, recalled,

> After the oil crisis of 1973–1974, it occurred to us that the utilities represented a very high percentage of all our revenues in New Mutley. We suddenly woke up and said, "Hey, maintenance is the only cost that they can control—and they could cut us off at any time." So I put together a plan stating that no segment was to represent more than 25 percent of the shop's business, and no single customer was to account for more than 10 percent. The point is not to cut back on our service to utilities, but to broaden our offerings as we expand and to concentrate on high-growth segments.

Nationally, ISG categorized its customers by industry, as indicated in Exhibit 5. ISG was required to match the delivery time, quality, and price offered by its competitors when it went after a Cunningham job, and internal accounts were treated much the same as any others, receiving regular calls from ISG salesmen. "If they get preferred service when they're down," one manager commented, "it's because they're big, regular customers, not because they're Cunningham."

A VISIT TO A SERVICE CENTER

The New Mutley service center was one of ISG's largest facilities, with sales exceeding $14 million in 1980. Like most of the other centers, it was located in a commercial and light-industrial area on a heavily traveled suburban road. Staff offices were small and functionally furnished; the heart of the operation was out on the floor.

"Don't forget your safety glasses," directed Steven Meyers, the center's assistant manager, as he led visitors into the first of the service areas, where motors were rewound. Electric motors of all shapes and sizes in various stages of cleaning and assembly were neatly ranked around the work space. Sunlight filtering through the service center's windows gleamed on bright copper wire as a 6-foot technician stepped out of a 30-foot-high cylindrical machine.

"Ever seen one of these before?" Meyers asked. "It's a ball mill drive motor. A ball mill is like a giant tin can rotating its side, with a number of large metal balls inside. You insert chunks of stone or cement and start to rotate the mill. As it revolves, the balls drop down and crush the stone into small pieces. The motor on this mill is about 6,000 horsepower—Bill's just finished rewinding it.

"We employ about 200 men here," Meyers continued, gesturing toward another area where a technician was welding a connection on a high-pressure descaling pump. "Our people work in two shifts. You're probably surprised to see how few technicians are out here on the floor—well, this is a job shop operation, not a production line, and a single group of employees will usually do the whole job on this piece of equipment."

Moving to the transformer repair area, Meyers pointed to an oven the size of a small garage: "We can bake just about anything in there. We usually use it for curing the transformer's insulation system, after the equipment is rewound and ready to go back in its tank. Maximum temperature is about 600°F. Over there," he continued, pointing to a tank 12 feet in diameter, "is the second-biggest vacuum pressure impregnation tank on the East Coast. The VPI tank is what we use to provide the new insulation to a motor or transformer like the one I just mentioned. It takes a lot of maintenance to keep this tank ready for use—we've got to keep 10,000 gallons of resin in a separate tank, chill it, and stir it off and on so it won't harden. The VPI tank is idle right now, and it may be idle for weeks. But when we need it, it'll be there."

Meyers' comment was overhead by Anthony DiGrazia, the center's sales manager, also making his way across the floor to check on a job. "That's true for a lot of our most important equipment," DiGrazia explained. "When we approach a customer, we emphasize that we're selling capability—the ability to help him when he's down, at any time, night or day. Our electric utility customers may need that large lathe over there only once a year—but when they do need it, they want it right away."

Stepping aside to make way for a trolley loaded with pump casings, DiGrazia led the way to a hydroturbine generator rotor approximately seven feet in diameter. "Take a look at this thing," he directed, and scraped it carefully with his fingernail, revealing over two inches of caked-on sludge. "This rotor was struck by lightning recently. We're repairing its burned-out stator coils and we're trying to talk the plant foreman into letting us clean the rest. It's costing $17,000 just to disassemble the thing and transport it to and from this shop; it'll cost $20,000 to repair it, and it would take another $25,000 to give the rotor the cleaning it needs. I doubt that it's been properly cleaned since it was first installed 60 years ago. On the other hand, without proper maintenance the rotor could fail, and fail catastrophically—ruining associated equipment and causing upward of $400,000 worth of damage."

The group continued to another work space, stopping to inspect a structure that resembled a square tent pitched on the shop floor. "Here you're looking at a little ingenuity," Meyers remarked, smiling. "We're doing a lot of fluorescent penetrant black-light work these days—testing components like turbine nozzle boxes for defects that are invisible in natural light." He turned to point to another technician across the floor. "That fellow working on the 50-ton crane over there is using a device similar to a Geiger counter to do magnetic particle testing, looking for surface cracks that could disable the equipment later. Nondestructive testing in general is becoming a very big area for us; it lets the customers know where trouble's developing *before* their equipment goes down."

Just before leading his visitors back to the front office, Meyers paused to point out a vertical file of job orders. Many had a photograph clipped to the front page. "That picture is for our protection, as well as the customer's," he explained. "The customer can show us just what he wants done—and we can prove to him that we're returning what he gave us. Makes it a little more difficult for a guy to point to a part that 'we' must have broken while it was here in the shop.'

MARKETING

ISG's marketing function was decentralized. Headquarters program managers for sales planning, communications, pricing, and market research constituted a planning and teaching force, but the actual marketing was executed at the centers themselves.

ISG employed 255 salesmen, of whom 105 were associated with large centers and 150 with small centers. Those at the large centers reported to a sales manager based at the center; the others reported to the small center managers. Each facility was considered a profit center and encouraged to pursue all segments of business; each salesman, with only a few exceptions, called on accounts representing every segment the center serviced. It was a divisional policy that any small center, if aggressively managed and marketed, could become a large one.

Almost by definition, however, large centers could service more segments than small centers, which did not encounter enough business in some areas to justify investment in expensive specialized equipment. Yet even though the small centers frequently uncovered business too complex for their own facilities to handle, they did not go out of their way to send it along to their larger neighbors. As Mays of the New Mutley center put it,

> That small-center manager is measured for his center alone. The salesmen work on straight salary, no commission, and unless their center can do the job, they don't really have the incentive to go out there and represent everybody else.

Sales

ISG sales representatives were recruited from a variety of sources—colleges, other Cunningham operations, the service centers themselves. Although many had an engineering background, advanced technical expertise was not considered a requirement for the job. In Mays's opinion, recruitment had historically been less than selective: "Too many people felt that the Cunningham name alone would bring in 60 to 70 percent of our business." The group policy of individual performance measurement for all centers, added to the fact that small-center salesmen reported to small-center managers, created other problems. Small-center managers had been known to use salesmen as replacements for foremen, or as on-site job supervisors—taking them off the road for as long as six months.

On the other hand, the small-center manager's close involvement with the sales force could constitute a real advantage, according to Mark O'Hara, manager of one of ISG's small centers:

> My salesmen cover all the accounts except for one big customer, which I handle; I also cover all problems and questions coming into the office from customers. That way we've got salesmen out knocking on doors, and the manager in the office. I'm always on the phone with customers; the most important thing for them—in some ways even more important than the work itself—is feeling free to get back in touch with the center easily, knowing that someone's watching over the job.

The ISG sales force received little formal training, after a one-week course in salesmanship. Some follow-up training was available in the form of three-day courses introducing new services. Large-center salesmen could consult their sales manager when problems came up—although the manager also received relatively little training in sales direction and had only occasional contact with other sales managers in the division. Small-center salesmen rarely saw their colleagues in other centers and received sales direction from their center managers, whose sales experience varied widely.

Near the end of each calendar year, salesmen began planning for the next by filling out a budget sheet for each account, stating available and target business. These figures were checked and adjusted by the sales or center manager and given to the regional general manager, who compared them with projected figures drawn up at headquarters. If the regional figures appeared too low, they were increased, and the center was faced with the burden of deciding whether to spread the new quotas out, hire new sales representatives, or seek out new markets.

Newman and other ISG planners held strong opinions concerning the need for effective sales management within ISG. According to Newman,

> The job of time management is much more important here than it is in selling something like a steam turbine where you can work for three years on the same job before it closes. ISG selling means repetitive calls, often keen competition, and a diligent effort to diversify services.

It was difficult to measure sales effectiveness, although each member of the sales force did make out a weekly call plan to be reviewed by the sales or center manager after calls were finished. Because calls were often made under emergency conditions, sales representatives were expected to use their own judgment in allocating their time. As Carl Hoffenberg, sales manager for a large service center, pointed out, this could be risky.

> Think of the case where you've sent out a salesman to cultivate a potential $100,000 maintenance contract—and he suddenly hears that a $1,000 motor has broken down somewhere else. We do have guys who will cancel the contract meeting to go look at the motor.

About 25 to 30 percent of sales calls were made under emergency conditions at customer request. To keep business growing, the ISG sales force knew it was necessary to schedule calls at other times also—when some of them found it difficult to know what to talk about.

Mark O'Hara, who had joined ISG as a service technician and spent six years in sales for the New Mutley center before moving up to management, felt that even a routine sales call required a carefully planned presentation tailored to a customer's specific needs. Sales brochures with color pictures were essential tools in introducing customers to ISG's capabilities; but even the brochures, O'Hara told his sales force, were not as effective as case histories and examples related to the customer's own equipment.

It was a group sales goal to move ISG along a continuum that ran from emergency repair to regular maintenance, toward "turnkey maintenance"—a contract to maintain equipment either during its scheduled maintenance shutdowns, or continuously all year long.

A Sales Manager's Comments

Tony DiGrazia, sales manager for the New Mutley service center, had come to ISG from new equipment sales and considered his current job a particular challenge. "You're really selling an intangible," he noted, "capability, manpower, yourself, your organization. It's a job that has real room for creative selling, because you can't demonstrate your product in place and working." He added,

> You're usually directing your selling effort to first line supervision and middle management—the foreman, sometimes his superintendent or general foreman, or the manager of maintenance. Some of these people are very cautious—they've often worked their way up from the floor—and it can be extremely difficult to convince them to spend $25,000 on maintenance to keep a $500,000 generator from breaking down.

DiGrazia saw one of the hardest sales tasks as "selling away from the OEM"—convincing a satisfied user of Morison equipment, for example, to try Cunningham service. He described his approach as "flexible":

> On one hand, for Cunningham equipment we have all the drawings and the background and we know how it works and so forth, so we're

the ideal service supplier. When we're competing for another manufacturer's equipment, we sell our Cunningham expertise. Also important is our centralized matrix support and ability to replicate what we learn at one center across many centers, which is a real strength in servicing virtually all manufacturers' electrical and mechanical equipment.

Hoffenberg saw even more challenging difficulties in the sales job.

> I think the hardest problem is getting work out of captive shops—fighting unions and getting public agencies to spend money. Depending on the segment we're talking about, captive shops do 25 to 70 percent of the total maintenance work available. It can also be extremely frustrating trying to persuade customers to order maintenance work that they can put off—even though their faulty equipment could malfunction, possibly causing extensive damage and downtime.

Advertising and Promotion

Advertising and promotion at ISG were divided between headquarters and the field. National media purchases were planned by the group's communications manager, who had budgeted $1.5 million for sales promotion of all kinds in 1981. Because most potential buyers were not thought to be print-oriented, ISG had traditionally spent little money on newspaper or magazine advertising, usually limiting ads to industrial magazines such as *Plant Engineering* rather than the general business press.

It was up to a center's sales manager to put together a local marketing strategy—in small centers, the center manager handled the job. Investments in promotion varied widely; some large centers spent several thousand dollars a year on local promotion, and some small ones spent $100. The most common promotional tool, outside personal selling and brochures, was direct mail addressed to a plant's maintenance superintendent, and sometimes composed by a local sales manager (Exhibit 6).

Pricing

The repair industry as a whole was characterized by wide price flexibility. Markets were local, with local competition; moreover, the cost of emergency repair for any customer was usually insignificant compared to downtime costs. Company research indicated that speed of delivery and quality of repair were valued most highly by customers in selecting service suppliers (Exhibit 7). Accordingly, ISG positioned itself as a price leader whose technical expertise and excellent facilities would ensure the speedy turnaround and high craftsmanship that customers valued over price.

Routine repairs such as the rewind of small motors were included in a pricing handbook published by headquarters; such jobs accounted for approximately 30 percent of ISG's sales. The field retained authority to change prices when it appeared advisable to do so— for instance, to meet competition. For less routine work, pricing calculations were facilitated by the use of an estimating sheet, which allowed sales representatives or service technicians to identify the operations required for a particular job, then estimate the cost of labor, materials, and equipment. To this, Cunningham added a target margin which took into account the nature of the job and the technical and scheduling risks it involved. "Each job is unique; each situation is different," observed one center manager.

Hoffenberg, discussing pricing at a meeting with DiGrazia, commented,

> What this all comes down to is an opportunity to be fully paid for value given. We had a call last week from a ship with a broken pump shaft, and we were there within an hour and got the shaft right into the service center.

DiGrazia cautioned,

> If you're smart, you darned well better give *some* kind of estimate to make sure the customer understands the magnitude of the job. During an emergency, price is not important, but later they can get irritated if you didn't give them some notion of what was coming. I look at a job and say, "You've got about a $10,000 job here on this shaft"—and try to estimate and anticipate all the work that will be required. It's a very delicate thing—you should give the guy a feel for the job, but not to the point where he latches onto the number and won't negotiate later. You've really got to know the value of your service, which is why face-to-face negotiation is one of my favorite parts of this job. Where's the challenge in carrying a price book around all the time?

Also important in pricing negotiations, as one service center manager put it, was the fact that "we have a total capability for service which many of our competitors don't have, and that costs us every day whether we use it or not." Hoffenberg amplified,

> We've got a 350-ton wheel press in the Dorset center that nobody else has got. Now suppose a customer finds he has some expensive piece of large equipment with a bad wheel. Without a press of that tonnage, he can't separate the wheel from the shaft and save the shaft—he'll have to replace them both. What do we charge him? Well, he saved $5,000 to $10,000 on a replacement shaft, if not more, so he ought to be willing to pay a few bucks.

The relative costs of repair versus new purchase, as Hoffenberg pointed out, were essential in pricing negotiations. A small coupling, for instance, might be repaired for less than half its replacement cost, in which case the customer's savings over replacement would affect pricing. When a replacement wouldn't be available for six months, the value of ISG's service was even greater. DiGrazia noted,

> The whole situation is so totally up in the air that it really puts the onus on the salesman, and the sales manager and the center's organization, to be fair, because these are continuing relationships that we have with these customers.

Added Hoffenberg,

> We try to get it through to customers that we're in the service business, not the business of selling machine time. Particularly in the mechan-

ical area, a lot of work has traditionally been done on a machine-time basis, involving the replacement of a part rather than the overhaul of a whole piece of equipment. You can get into a fight with customers where they'll say, "Gee, that machine only took so many hours to work" and so forth and we keep telling them we're in the business of performing repairs and doing overhauls, not of selling a machine operator. We're selling capability, readiness to serve, and expertise—and we're saving money and production time for our customers.

One of the sales force's most important duties was pointing out to customers the quality difference that lay beneath very different competitive estimates for the same job—the fact that, as Hoffenberg put it, "one guy's metallizing with platinum and the next is metallizing with lead." The key was to sense the customer's needs—"to find out whether he doesn't want the extra benefits, or just doesn't know about them." For a brand new account the center might do a "Cadillac job" at no extra charge, calling its quality to the customer's attention at intervals and trying to sell the same job next time.

Although much pricing was left to individual discretion, the group did place limits on the size of the jobs which each rank in the selling hierarchy could approve. Sales representatives were limited to $10,000; sales managers and small-center managers, to $25,000; and large-center managers, to $100,000. "It's important to keep in mind that competition and customer relations do keep pricing within reasonable limits," Newman commented. "The group's ratio of net income to sales is considerably less than 8 percent, which is typical of most industrial service industries."

PLANNING FOR GROWTH

Newman and a few other ISG planners and managers had come to feel that ISG's field organization needed improvement if it was to support continuing growth during the 1980s. They were concerned about ISG's failure to provide marketing direction to its sales force, as well as the group's lack of what Newman called "rationalized capacity between centers." Ideally, he felt, even salesmen working for a small center should be able to offer customers access to all ISG services. Others felt that fragmentation of the marketing effort was seriously affecting sales. Said Mays, "We really aren't serving all the markets because of the boundaries we've set up."

Past Changes in Organizational Structure

ISG had gone through several reorganizations in the past as its potential became more widely recognized. For many years after Cunningham's founding, the service centers had handled only Cunningham products and had reported to regional selling organizations. In 1960 came the first major change, as the service centers were joined together into a national organization with a national general manager. Subsequent growth came from increased geographic penetration as well as the addition of new services. In 1975 the service centers were given corporate group status; soon afterward the three field service regions were set up, and a manager of development and operations (MDO) appointed in each region to supervise managers of the smaller centers (Exhibit 2).

Because the backgrounds of small-center managers varied widely—some had degrees in engineering or business administration, others were foremen who had worked their way up from the floor—it was thought that these centers needed special senior management attention. ISG prided itself on the entrepreneurial spirit of the small-center managers, and gave them a chance early in their careers to handle almost all the functions of running a business. In Newman's words, "The concept was that the MDO would be a senior person (usually a former large-center manager) who really knew how to run service centers, and he could teach the small-center managers." But Mays believed that these expectations had not been fully realized.

As we've continued to grow, the demands on the MDO's time have shifted from operations to business development. Almost 50 percent of his time is now devoted to acquiring new accounts and identifying new service offerings, and about 50 percent to operating the centers. The attention that the small-center managers is getting has been slipping, and when that happens, growth in the small centers slows down.

Newman disagreed; he thought the MDOs devoted substantial time to the small centers. However, because they were measured on the success of the small centers, the MDOs tended to keep as much work there as possible, ignoring the resources of the larger centers. Yet Newman, like Mays and other ISG managers, felt the MDO concept was a step in the right direction. The problem was, what should come next? Several ISG managers urged that the group be broken up nationally by segments, rather than geographically. Newman had different ideas.

> If you look at market share performance, you'll see a great difference between the large and the small centers. The large centers are doing more large, specialized work, and relatively few smaller, repetitive jobs. The small centers are doing a lot of general service and repair, but fewer specialized projects. To take full advantage of both capabilities, the centers will have to work together—and that means we need an integrated geographic organization and a regional sales force.

The Regional Experiment

Thomas Simmons, who had been appointed regional general manager for one of ISG's three regions in 1978, agreed with Newman's assessment. Simmons subsequently broke his region into four geographic sales territories, placing experienced, aggressive sales managers in his four biggest centers. As before, seven local sales representatives reported to the sales manager of each large center. Now, however, for the first time, all small-center salesmen also reported to a sales manager, located at a large center (Exhibit 8), receiving professional sales planning help and direction from this individual. Small-center managers reported to the MDO as before. Sales was the only function reorganized during this experiment.

The need for centralized, professional direction of the work of each center was one of the key motivators to the experiment, according to Newman. He felt it was very easy for ISG salesmen to become reactive, following current jobs through the center rather than developing new business.

> One of our centers, for instance, was inundated with work during the Vietnam war, doing ship conversions. Business surged and we really didn't pay enough attention to what the mix of that business was. When the war ended, the center manager found that he had lost the customers for the base service business in his territory.

When Newman and his colleagues analyzed Simmons' experiment after one year, they discovered mixed reactions. Many were enthusiastic. One sales manager noted that for the first time, sales managers were being encouraged to discuss their problems with other sales managers, and salesmen in small centers were getting coordinated, professional sales direction. Mays added,

> Walls are definitely breaking down. Now the small-center manager is really interested in the New Mutley center because the salesmen are bringing some of his customers to us. Since the work flow is more directed, each center is beginning to develop an expertise. We're sending all the centrifuge work to Devonville, for example. It's still a local business, but it doesn't have to be as local for some services as for others. Customers are not reluctant to ship some major pieces of equipment a few hundred miles—for good work.

Throughout the experiment, however, MDOs continued to be compensated based on the profits of the centers reporting to them, and thus had a strong incentive to keep as many big jobs as possible in small centers. The fact that the large-center sales manager, who was now directing small-center sales, reported to the large-center manager, led to built-in conflict with the MDOs. Despite these constraints, sales figures supported Mays's optimistic impression of the territory concept; it was considered largely responsible for an annual rate of sales growth in Tom Simmon's region averaging 15 percent from 1978 through 1980, up from 12 percent between 1972 and 1977.

The greatest opposition to the experiment came from small-center managers. Newman himself sympathized with their fears, commenting that, "You won't find anywhere else in Cunningham Inc. a situation where a young person can take on as much responsibility so early in his career." One small-center manager added,

> You don't have to be a genius to look at this new type of organization and figure out that if we're not very careful down the road, my small center could be only a specialty arm of the territory and not a complete service organization. And what about the impact on customers? How can my salesmen prove to customers that they're keeping a close eye on a job several hundred miles away?

Mark O'Hara had even more misgivings. Although he favored more group help with time management, he felt his sales force had a greater need for down-to-earth personal assessment of the way they handled sales calls. Even under the territorial experiment, he believed, salesmen lacked the personal attention they needed; instead, they were invited to meetings and given general tips on how to sell technical service. Shaking his head, he added,

> Under the territorial plan, my center will be in the New Mutley territory, and Joe Green's center—which is only 100 miles away from mine—will be in a separate territory. Well, this means Joe is not supposed to send me any more of his business, and I'm supposed to send my overflow to New Mutley, where they have all kinds of guys running around—unit managers, foremen, project managers—who all have different interests. If I send a job to New Mutley, I've got to call the foreman myself and tell him. Mays and the unit manager aren't going to

know about it. But when I sent my jobs to Joe, I knew he was going to be involved in them—and if he sent me one, I told my foreman and production people, it's Joe's job, let's get on it.

Internal Consultants' Study

It seemed logical to some planners that if the territorial concept were extended, service centers should no longer be measured as individual profit centers. Yet a corporate consulting team assigned to the problem detected much support for maintaining the small centers on an independent, full profit-and-loss basis. ISG did have excellent geographic coverage, as the consultants' report noted, and small centers were still capable of servicing a variety of customers; but because of their limited capability, small-center market share was not as large as it could be. Moreover, large centers tended to favor the bigger, more specialized jobs in their area and therefore had lower market share for smaller, more general service work. One consultant added privately to Newman,

> We're troubled by the parochial concerns of some small-center managers and salesmen. They have been seen to take business first, and worry later about how to do it. Small centers don't even have the capacity to handle large mechanical work, one of our biggest growth segments.

THE NEXT STEP

As he cleared his desk for the weekend, Newman was still brooding over McDonald's objections to the territorial reorganization. Maybe, he thought, the chief's fatherly feeling for the small-center managers is getting the best of his judgment. Or is it really impossible to implement this plan without hurting the small centers?

At that moment, the phone rang. "Any more ideas on what we talked about this morning, Adam?" McDonald asked.

"Well, nothing new right now," Newman replied. "As I see it, we have several choices. We can continue the territory experiment in Tom's region, maybe with some changes to keep small-center managers happy. We can extend the experiment to another region. We can drop the whole idea and run the group nationally, by service segments. Or maybe . . ."

McDonald interrupted:

Or maybe we still haven't found the solution.

Adam, I've directed this group for many years, and I've seen it grow very fast. As far as I'm concerned, we've grown because we've got a lot of service centers out there run by venturesome guys who'll take on any job they can get and somehow use their resources and ingenuity to get it done. I know our marketing and our field organization can be improved, but those entrepreneurial managers are the backbone of our business—and I'm not going to approve any change that lessens their enthusiasm for the job.

NOTES

1. The manufacturing manager had staff responsibility for new repair technology, new plant construction, safety, and environmental programs.

EXHIBIT 1

Cunningham Inc.: ISG Sales and Earnings

YEAR	SALES	NET INCOME	PERCENT RETURN ON SALES[a]
1974	$148.3[b]	$10.1	6.8%
1975	200.5	15.6	7.8
1976	225.4	18.0	8.0
1977	251.9	19.9	7.9
1978	302.3	21.8	7.2
1979	356.7	25.7	7.2
1980 (est.)	406.7	27.7	6.8

[a] Includes income going to international joint venture partners.
[b] All figures are in millions of dollars.
SOURCE: Company records

EXHIBIT 2
Cunningham Inc.: Organization Chart

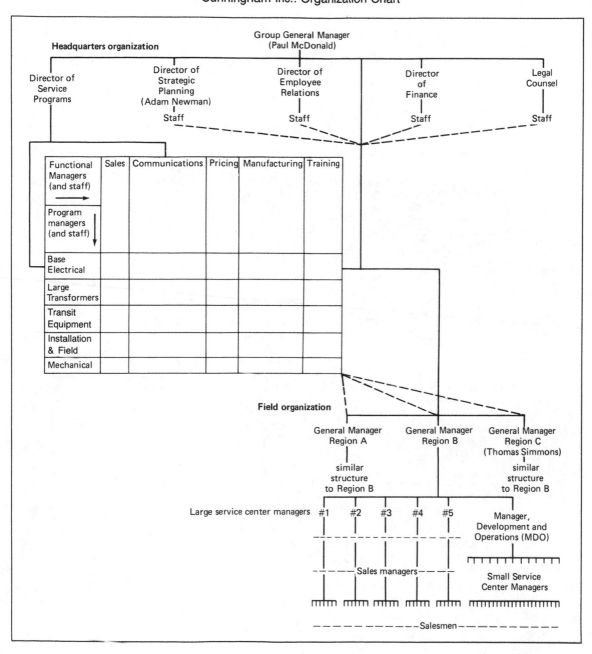

EXHIBIT 3

Cunningham Inc.: ISG Service Segments

EQUIPMENT SERVICED	MAJOR COMPETITORS	SHARE OF ISG REVENUES	
		1976	1980[a]
Base electrical (motors and generators, switchgear, small transformers)	Independent service shops—6,000 in U.S.	46%	42%
Large transformers	Morison Electric	12	11
Transit equipment (traction motors, generators, electrical auxiliaries)	Captive shops	8	8
Installation and field service (electrical on-site service, management, inspection)	Captive shops, some specialized independents	14	12
Mechanical (pumps, fans, blowers, compressors, valves, centrifuges, mining equipment)	OEMs, independent machine shops	13	21
Other		7	6

[a] 1980 figures are estimated.
SOURCE: Company records

EXHIBIT 4

Cunningham Survey of Major Supplier Standing[a]
1976 to 1978

PERCENT OF TOTAL CENTERS IN FIRST PLACE

	Cunningham	*Morison*	*Independent 1*[b]	*Independent 2*[b]
Base electrical	30%	28%	32%	10%
Large transformers	38	36	24	
Transit equipment	40	45	15	
Installation and field service	45	49	5	1
Mechanical	20	18	52	10

[a] Fifty-five service centers were surveyed and classified by number of mentions as a preferred supplier. The data here indicates how frequently Cunningham, Morison, or an independent was mentioned as the leading supplier. The mentions for preferred supplier of total electrical service have been weighted by size of the product markets.
[b] Independent 1 refers to the leading independent in each geographic region surveyed. Independent 2 refers to the second most popular independent in that region. Many service organizations classified as independents were centers managed by OEMs, such as Katz-Hartley.
SOURCE: Cunningham Inc. Market Research Department

EXHIBIT 5

ISG Customers by Industry and Location

INDUSTRY	PERCENT OF CUSTOMER BASE	PRIMARY LOCATION
Steel and other metal producers	17%	Midwest
Refineries	6	Southwest
Chemical manufacturers	7	East and Gulf Coast
Pulp and paper	12	Northwest, New England
Utilities	15	National
Transportation	12	National
Mining	11	Midwest and Rocky Mountains
Other	20	National

SOURCE: Company records

EXHIBIT 6

Cunningham Inc.: Direct Mail Promotion

Cunningham Inc.

Industrial Service Group

Dear Customer:

A penny  for your thoughts - your maintenance thoughts that is! If you are like most organizations these days, you are trying to solve repair problems and maintain your equipment while staying within an ever-shrinking maintenance budget. As the penny in our letter illustrates, our money-buying power is getting smaller daily, especially in these times of high inflation.

The Cunningham Service Center can help you with this maintenance dilemma with sound advice and excellent service. Take a moment and ask yourself a few questions. Are you able to stretch your pennies to cover all your pressing maintenance needs? Are you really getting your money's worth on repair service? Is your present equipment service a good value for the money spent? What areas can be improved by new ideas?

As part of our standard capabilities, we have values that can help you with each of these questions and would like to share our ideas with you.

Our service capabilities include:

-Base electrical service for motors and switchgear
-Transit equipment repair and maintenance
-Transformer testing and repair
-Mechanical repair of all types
-Installation and field service

All of these capabilities can be performed within our center or on-site at your plant.

Send back the enclosed reply card and we'll share our maintenance ideas with you. You have nothing to lose, but you can gain more value for the money spent by your company.

It's as simple as a penny - we want to be your maintenance vendor.

We are ready to put our people in touch with your organization at a moment's notice - are you ready?

Best regards,

Anthony DiGrazia

Anthony DiGrazia
Sales Manager

ARG:im

EXHIBIT 7

Cunningham Profile of the Ideal Service Supplier[a]
1978

	Base Electrical	Large Transformers	Transit Equipment	Installation and Field Service	Mechanical
			PERCENT OF MENTIONS		
Delivery-related: good, fast service; fast delivery, etc.	43%	32%	34%	35%	36%
Quality and competence: quality of workmanship; reliability and dependability; past performance and experience	30	39	33	33	29
Cost	18	19	12	15	11
Location/facilities	7	7	9	9	10
Preference for OEM	1	2	10	6	12
Other factors	1	1	2	2	2
Total	100%	100%	100%	100%	100%

[a] Respondents to the Cunningham survey (see Exhibit 4) in each of the product categories were asked on an unprompted basis why their current supplier(s) were preferred. This exhibit reflects the ideal service offering for each product category.

SOURCE: Cunningham Inc. Market Research Department

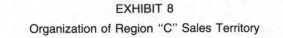

EXHIBIT 8

Organization of Region "C" Sales Territory

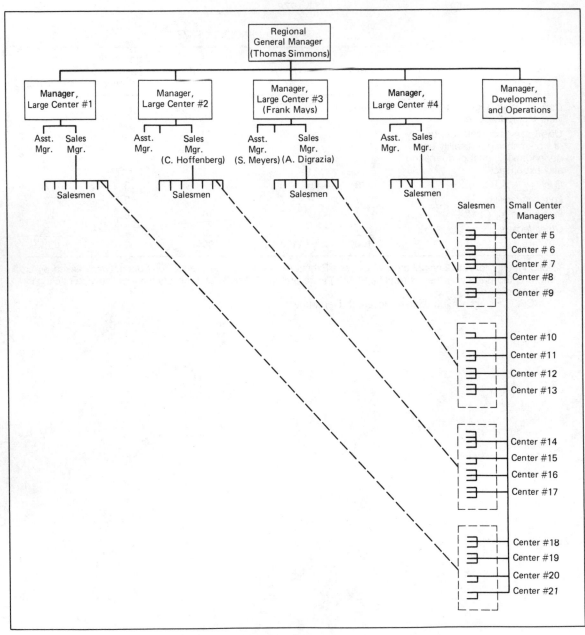

DUNFEY HOTELS CORPORATION

The president of a chain of 22 rather dissimilar hotels has developed procedures for standardizing the marketing planning process employed by each hotel. A concerted internal training and educational effort is needed to get managers to understand and employ this process.

THE DUNFEY CHAIN: A SAVIOR OF DYING HOTELS ran the headline above a half-page story in the financial section of the Sunday *New York Times* for June 22, 1980. The story began,

> Suburban motor hotels. Sprawling convention hotels. Small and elegant city hotels. Foreign hotels. At first glance, the collection of properties under the Dunfey name seems an unmanageable mishmash.
>
> Yet the Dunfey Hotel Corporation, which within the last year and a half has put together such a chain of unlikely properties, is getting to be known as a comer in the lodging industry, with a knack for taking over aging hotels and returning them to profitability. In fact, Dunfey is a success story on top of a success story.
>
> Success Story No. 1 goes back to the 1950s and features the Dunfeys, an Irish-American family of eight brothers from Hampton, New Hampshire. The Dunfey boys, who started with a hot dog stand at Hampton Beach, built a multi-million-dollar New England hotel and restaurant chain.
>
> Success Story No. 2 stars Jon Canas, brought in by the Dunfeys as chief operating officer and executive vice president in 1975. Mr. Canas . . . is a marketing man who is not afraid to step in to operate a hotel where others have faltered. With Mr. Canas on board, Dunfey has become one of the nation's fastest growing hotel chains.

COMPANY HISTORY

After being discharged from military service shortly after World War II, John and William Dunfey opened a clam and hot dog stand on the boardwalk at Hampton Beach, New Hampshire. Soon John and William were joined in the business by four younger brothers. In 1954, the six brothers formed a partnership with their mother, and purchased Lamie's Tavern in Hampton, 3 miles from the original business in Hampton Beach.

In 1958, the family business headed in a new direction when a 32-room motor inn was constructed adjacent to Lamie's Tavern. Further acquisitions followed. By 1968, Dunfey Family Corporation, as the firm was then known, either owned or managed 18 hotels in the eastern U.S. Many of these properties, including the original Lamie's Motor Inn, were operated as franchises of Sheraton Hotels, the nation's largest hotel corporation.

In 1969, Dunfey Family Corporation made two new moves. First, Dunfey's Tavern Restaurants were opened in four of the company's New England properties. Second, the company acquired its first downtown hotel by purchasing the historic Parker House in Boston. The experience gained in succeeding years in renovating and repositioning the Parker House was to play an important role in shaping the future growth strategy for the Dunfey hotel business.

Injection of New Capital and Management

To finance further expansion following the purchase of the Parker House, the Dunfey family sold the company to the Aetna Life Insurance Co. in 1970. Six years later it was acquired from Aetna by Aer Lingus, the national airline of Ireland. But throughout these changes in ownership, the Dunfey family maintained managerial control over the business, with Jack Dunfey continuing on as the chief executive officer.

During the early 1970s, a number of professional managers were hired. They included Jon Canas, who joined the company in 1975 as vice-president of sales and marketing. Canas, a Frenchman by birth, had been educated at the Cornell School for Hotel Administration and also held an MBA from Northeastern University; he had worked for six years with the Hotel Corporation of America and, subsequently, four years with the Sheraton Corporation, where his most recent position had been vice-president of sales and marketing for Sheraton's two international divisions—Europe/Africa/Middle East and Hawaii/Far East/Pacific.

A New Approach to Planning

Canas recalled how his experience with Sheraton had led him to develop a planning approach based on market segmentation for marketing widely diverse hotels.

> About four years before coming to Dunfey, I was assigned the position of sales director of Sheraton's Hawaii Division, consisting at that time of seven hotels. Since I had no previous experience in the day-to-day operation of the selling function as such, I decided to approach the job from a planning point of view. I began immediately to ask those questions, the answers to which would result in a better understanding of the market: Why do people come to Hawaii? What kind of hotel experience are they looking for? What does competition currently offer? Are there segments of consumers who differ in their needs for the level and quality of service? The more I worked on it, the more I could see practical solutions evolving out of this approach.

> In Hawaii, at that time, virtually the only thing standardized about the Sheraton properties was the Sheraton name. The individual hotels varied widely in terms of size, age, location, rates, and types of customers. Faced with marketing such a diverse portfolio of properties, I was forced into understanding market segmentation. In the hotel business, this translates into offering different types of hotels for different types of customers . . . the idea really isn't revolutionary but you must remember that it ran against the tide of an industrywide move toward standardization of the "product"—a move which was clearly at the heart of the corporate strategies of most chains. . . . We were very successful in Hawaii. Not only did current properties perform well, but two years later our territory was expanded to include several new and existing hotels in the Far East and Pacific.

> When the Dunfey opportunity came up, a friend of mine in the industry told me that, as a group, the Dunfey properties were "a mixed bag" of hotels, widely diverse in location and service level. Several had generally reached the end of their life cycle. I could see some similarities with the Hawaii situation. I took the job partially to see whether the planning approach I had developed was really successful or whether I had just been lucky in Hawaii.

Dunfey Hotel Properties

Since purchasing the Parker House, the Dunfeys had continued to acquire additional properties and management contracts as the opportunities presented themselves.[1] In 1972, for instance, when Aetna Life Insurance acquired Royal Coach Motor Inns, Dunfey was hired to manage four units of this chain, each located on a major suburban highway in Atlanta; Dallas; Houston; and San Mateo, California, respectively. Each was built in an exterior style reminiscent of sixteenth-century English Tudor, set off against a round, stonefaced, castellated tower; while the hotel interiors were decorated in a Scottish clan theme. The previous owners had gone bankrupt.

By mid-1980, Dunfey Hotels fully or partially owned, leased, or managed 22 properties in the United States and Europe, containing a total of 8,950 rooms (Exhibit 1). Fourteen of these properties had been part of the Dunfey organization for six years or more. Each hotel was managed by a general manager who headed an executive operating committee (EOC) of department heads.

The Dunfey inns and hotels were divided into four groups, each directed by a group director of operations (Exhibit 2 shows a corporate organization chart). These groups were as follows:

1. Dunfey Classic and Luxury Hotels (four properties: the Parker House, Boston; the Ambassador East, Chicago; the Berkshire Place, New York; and The Marquette, Minneapolis).
2. Dunfey Major Meeting and Convention Hotels (seven properties, located in Atlanta, Dallas, Houston, Cape Cod, San Mateo, New York, and Washington).
3. Dunfey Inns and Airport Hotels (nine properties located in New England and Pennsylvania).
4. International Hotels (two properties, located in London and Paris).

Some of the airport hotels and motor inns were affiliated, for marketing purposes only, with another chain (Sheraton or Howard Johnson). Although this affiliation had the advantage of linking the inns to national advertising campaigns and toll-free telephone reservation numbers, it did nothing for the visibility of the Dunfey organization.

Between 1974 and 1979, average occupancy, systemwide, increased from 56 to 72 percent. A financial summary, showing total revenues and operating profits for all U.S. units in the Dunfey organization, both owned and managed, appears below.

Dunfey Hotels Corporation Financial Summary
(U.S. Units Only)

YEAR	TOTAL REVENUES	OPERATING PROFIT
1976	$ 58 million	$ 7 million
1977	72 million	9 million
1978	88 million	16 million
1979	120 million	21 million
1980 (est.)	165 million	34 million

Jon Canas and the Dunfey "System"

When Canas joined Dunfey in May 1975, the company had a marketing staff, but not an organized marketing effort. Recalled Canas,

The operation was characterized by extremely tight cost control, declining occupancy, and declining market share. Internally, many units were perceived to be at the end of their life cycle. We moved quickly to take some specific actions which paid off, and we were helped along by an improving economy beginning in 1976. Group sales doubled in three years, and occupancy went from below the industry average to above.

In reviewing the specific areas of the business that the company had concentrated on, Canas divided the years 1975–1980 into three distinct periods:

Our greatest need during 1975 and 1976 was to build occupancy. I don't have to tell you that profit in the hotel business comes from selling rooms, and we did everything possible to "keep the lights on" as they say in the industry. This meant going after any and all types of business, including lower rated (in terms of revenue-per-room night) market segments. As an example, we found early success in attracting what we call "training and destiny" business. This is primarily in-residence programs centered around training sessions, often lasting five to eight weeks. One example would be a flight attendant training program by an airline. Such programs are typically repeated many times over the course of a year by the same company, and effectively amount to an extended rental of space in the hotel. The meetings are planned far in advance and don't require elaborate arrangements such as banquet facilities; demand is fairly price sensitive. Of course, as occupancy began to improve, we instituted a policy of actively pursuing higher rated segments and gradually substituted this new business for the lower rated segments.

During 1977 and 1978, we embarked on a major program to improve the overall appearance of our properties. In most cases this involved renovating, restoring, repositioning, and re-marketing individual properties. Basically, we made the decision to *reject* the life cycle assumptions which prevailed in the firm at the time. The Parker House in Boston is a good example of this philosophy. The Parker House was an old property which had a deteriorating and outdated physical plant, declining occupancy, and had been given up on by the previous management. We saw an opportunity in the hotel's heritage—and the fact that it occupied an excellent location in a metropolitan area where quality lodging was in short supply. The result of this renovation was dramatic increases in occupancy and profitability.

Now as room occupancy rates topped-out on a companywide basis, we sought revenue in other departments. We went into a very creative period where new restaurants and lounges were created. We didn't just open a room, we created a *concept*. A key product of our "creative period" is the Tingles lounges and discotheques located in several of our hotels; these discos were unique in that the sound, loud over the dance floor, but softer at surrounding tables, allowed people to sit, relax, and converse. As an example of the impact on revenue, the conversion of the lounge in the Atlanta Hotel to a Tingles, took food and beverage revenue from $8,000 to $9,000 per week to over $25,000 weekly in that room.

In 1979 we entered a new phase. With both room and food and beverage (F&B) revenues peaking, we turned our attention to better cost management to maintain profit growth. We brought in an outside consulting firm to help us develop a rather sophisticated cost management/payroll efficiency system. The system was tested at the Parker House in 1977–1978 and was expanded to our other units in 1978–1979. In addition, we sought cost savings in centralized purchasing and in better heat, light, and power management.

So in looking back, I suppose you could say we concentrated our efforts on different areas of the business at different times. We were consciously trying to improve the "state of the art" in all areas of the hotel business, and I think the results show that we succeeded.

The situation facing Dunfey in 1975 was surprisingly similar to that of the Sheraton situation in Hawaii when I became sales manager: The mixed bag of food and lodging businesses grouped under the Dunfey corporate name ran the gamut from small, outlying motels to larger urban hotels. In fact, unlike Sheraton, the Dunfey group lacked a common name and identity—There were Sheratons, a Howard Johnson's, a group of four hotels purchased from Royal Coach renamed Dunfey Hotels, as well as several properties which stood alone in terms of identification. Thus, it was out of a need to simplify the management task that the Dunfey Planning Process and the Dunfey Management Approach evolved.

In essence, our approach to marketing planning is based on the belief that there exists a unique strategy or market position for each property which will maximize revenues in the long term. While other hoteliers were focusing on product efficiency and standardization, at Dunfey our commonality became the planning process. Of course, we've come a long way since 1975. In particular, we have grouped our hotels in a way where we can take advantage of some economies of scale in marketing. However, our basic approach is still at the individual hotel marketing level.

THE DUNFEY PLANNING PROCESS

As a first step towards development of a management system for all the Dunfey properties, Canas had drafted a series of internal documents. "The Dunfey Management Approach" and "The Way We Work" enunciated a management philosophy based on the conviction that each hotel had to recognize and satisfy certain needs from its customers, owners, and employees. The third document, titled "The Dunfey Planning Process," laid out a clearly defined system of annual and quadrimester (four-month) planning, dealing with objectives and strategies relating to customers, owners, and employees.

Canas believed that the planning system for any given unit must begin with the needs of one or more clearly identified customer segments, which, when related to the nature and extent of competition, served to determine the positioning the hotel would have in the marketplace. Time and again, remarked Canas, he had seen chains which had standardized their offerings against certain market segments expand unsuccessfully into geographic areas that already had an excess of hotel rooms serving those same segments.

He emphasized that profitability in the hotel business was primarily based on the revenue side and stressed the importance of good rooms merchandising through a specific planning process which was evaluated with the help of a performance measure he called Room Sales Efficiency (RSE).[2] "The key to good rooms merchandising and to good cost control," he said, "was accurate forecasting of demand at all times of the week and all seasons of the year."

Every year, the management of each Dunfey hotel had to prepare both an annual plan and a series of three quadrimester (four-month) plans, referred to as Q-Plans. The planning process for each hotel proceeded through four basic steps, supported by appropriate documentation.

1. Assess supply-demand relationship—by examining the type (e.g., conventions, tourists, business travelers, etc.) and quantity of customers available in a given geographic market. A careful evaluation was made of the positioning of competitive hotels against each segment.
2. Determine where Dunfey *should be* in terms of the market position of the hotel as a whole, and each food and beverage outlet within that hotel.
3. Identify the gap between where the hotel is currently positioned and the desired position.
4. Structure the measures required to move the hotel and F&B outlets toward the desired market position. Requests for capital expenditures—to add to or improve facilities—were a key element of Step 4.

The outcome of Steps 2, 3, and 4 was a "Mission Statement" for each hotel which had as its input the supply-demand relationship and as its output a set of specific operating objectives for all members of the field operations team.

Exhibit 3 summarizes the planning process. In essence, broad strategic goals embodied in the Mission Statement were "stepped down" into key result areas (KRAs)—specific action steps to be undertaken in support of unit or departmental objectives—via a series of annual planning forms referred to as Y1s (unit objectives and strategies), Y2s (departmental objectives and strategies), and Y3s (specific goals for each unit and department objective). These goals formed the basis for the employee's incentive plan. Similar planning efforts, with a shorter-term focus, were undertaken each quadrimester; these were referred to as "Q-Plans."

The planning process for each unit (hotel) was carried out by that unit's executive operating committee (EOC) with the participation of the corporate planning committee (CPC). The unit EOC usually consisted of the general manager (GM), assistant general manager or resident manager, sales director, rooms manager, food and beverage (F&B) manager, and personnel director. The CPC comprised Jon Canas, the controller, and five vice-presidents in charge of operations, staff support, product design, profit planning, and marketing. The CPC was assisted in its review of individual unit plans by the vice-president–sales, the corporate F&B director, and the relevant group director of operations.

Each group director of operations was responsible for coordinating the preparation of key planning documents by each of the unit EOCs in his group of hotels. The various documents were submitted to the corporate planning committee for approval in a succession of steps carried out from July 1 to November 1 of each year. Units were required to submit an outline of their preliminary thinking in July in order that the CPC could provide early feedback on the appropriateness of tentative plans.

Based on these early submissions, the CPC had, by early August, classified individual hotel plans as

- "green," signifying that the unit was on track and should not change direction
- "yellow," signifying that the unit was on track except for certain items (outlined) which should be corrected (no major direction change)
- "red," indicating that the unit was seriously

off track—corporate staff would be assigned to assist in making major direction changes

Each unit EOC, working with their group director, was required to prepare a Mission Statement addressing the following questions:

- What type of customer are we aiming for?
- Where do we stand versus the competition?
- What are we trying to be?
- Where should we focus our efforts to satisfy targeted customers, as well as dealing with owners/corporate needs and also employees' needs?

The hotel business, noted Canas, was operations oriented, involving a multitude of basic activities that must be carried out over and over again, yet could be done in a number of different ways. He continued,

We believe that people carry out functions in different ways depending on the purpose they have in mind. The GM may have one purpose, the F&B manager another—and neither may be in concert with the corporation. So, as simplistic as it sounds, the Mission Statement integrates the activity of unit and corporate management. Any management team that has succeeded in crystallizing and communicating the mission of the hotel will find the various departments pulling together, in the same direction, to create the sought-after hotel experience for the customer. It provides more fulfillment for the employees and better results for the owners and the corporation. Also, the process helps achieve agreement between corporate and unit management.

The Ideal Business Mix

"The most important part of the mission," Canas noted, "deals with what we call the IBM—ideal business mix. This defines the customer segments we will direct our sales efforts toward at various times of the year." He elaborated:

There are many ways to segment the market. The first, of course, is the way we categorize business on our control reports, for instance,

pure transient, regular corporate group, bus tours, and so forth. In addition, we segment our marketing effort by geography and by industry, and we assign sales coverage to whatever groupings seem to make sense for a particular area.

The point is that, once we identify our desired segments, it becomes a simpler task to set objectives for the operating departments—such as sales, rooms, and food and beverage. We've found that certain segments of the market tend to have common needs—or "reason to buy." Very often the marketing challenge is to define these needs: Is the customer primarily interested in price, in location, in facilities, in social status—or is he just looking for a hotel consistent with his personal tastes in furnishings and food?

The ideal business mix also carries implications for our capital spending and renovation and maintenance decisions. We often say, "We could reach this segment *if* we had certain facilities." The *if* here is important: We may have an intended market position, but we must have programs and facilities to reach it. The restoration and revitalization of the Parker House taught us a lot about repositioning—a lesson we have been able to apply to other properties in the chain.

After we have outlined our goals by type of customer, number of room nights, period of year and rates, then we ask two further questions: (1) How do we market—how do we reach these customers? And (2) how do we deliver? (And delivery at a *profit?*)

Our Rooms Merchandising Plan and the supporting Account Coverage Program guide our sales efforts. As part of the Rooms Merchandising Plan, you have your ideal business mix prioritized by segments and by lead time in their respective buy decision. If, for example, a convention cancels 9 months ahead of time, then you go after alternative segments. It's like starting all over again. But, at least you will have identified in advance where you are going to go to make up that business.

Most hotels hire a sales manager and tell him or her to "fill the rooms." This usually works in the short term, but is not a good business approach in the long term. Customers contribute to the atmosphere or hotel experience; you should choose your clientele selectively to match your market position. In our system we specify: (1) a certain kind of customer at (2) a certain time of year at (3) a certain rate.

With the Rooms Merchandising Plan you know what to ask sales and reservations people to do. In general, in the industry, salespeople often don't know who to see, they don't know how many rooms are available, and they don't know what rate to charge. At Dunfey we provide these guidelines as closely as possible in order to maximize our profitability and productivity.

In general, we find there is an inverse relationship in the lead time between the buy decision and consumption by various market segments and the rate we can get. In other words, the farther in advance groups book, the cheaper the rate usually is. So, most hotels used to book business way in advance, without consideration of more desirable business which could be booked later on.

So, the moral for the periods of time where we anticipate strong demand—and since we have a limited supply of rooms—is that we shouldn't sell on a first-come, first-served basis. For better profits, we plan the IBM proportion which is set aside for long lead time groups and for shorter lead time groups, and then save some capacity for higher rated walk-in business.

When business for the future begins to pick up, we try to monitor whether we're attracting our target customers. We want to build our business with the correct market segments—not just fill rooms—because we're building an image for the future and the profile of customers we take in has a tremendous impact on the position of the hotel. Of course, when occupancy is very low, oftentimes we will sell rooms to less desirable segments, but as we build occupancy, we can become more selective in our marketing.

Now, talking about the Account Coverage Program, in a lot of cases we find that 20 percent of the accounts give us 80 percent of our business. Therefore, it is important to identify, qualify, and quantify all our accounts to set proper sales priorities. It also allows us to know what accounts we'll have to approach to get what business. Moreover, we identify what "buy decisions" exist for each individual account. For instance, for corporate groups it's usually either a "price buy," a "location buy," or a "facilities buy."

Also, our sales department provides a significant amount of information and feedback on our supply-demand studies. Through the direct salespeople we know what to sell, to whom, and at what rates. We truly use "need satisfaction" as a sales approach to sell and get repeat sales.

A MANAGEMENT ISOLATION MEETING

An isolation meeting—so designated because the participants were isolated from the interruptions of the home office—was held in the early fall of 1979 to discuss the status of the 1980 planning process and to reinforce understanding of Dunfey management philosophies among the top 15 corporate operations and marketing executives.

Jon Canas opened the meeting by reiterating some of the basic precepts of the Dunfey Management Approach:

The Dunfey Management Approach is companywide. It includes not only the concepts inherent in the way we look at our business, but also includes the process and the systems through which we operate. We must have agreement at top on our philosophies. That means amongst all of us. And then we must attempt to achieve concurrence at lower levels.

What we're saying is that the traditional "get results and we don't care how you do it" doesn't work at Dunfey. We *do care* how you do it! We're concerned with the manner in which results are obtained.

The mission becomes the point of reference for the selection of unit objectives and strategies. The process to be followed by the EOC is to ask: "If we were totally successful in reaching our mission, what are the desirable things that would happen, or desirable conditions that would prevail (positive indicators of success), and what are the undesirable conditions that should be eliminated (negative indicators of success)?"

It's here that we should use the scenario approach: That is, take any aspect of the operations—such as the guest experience at the front desk—and talk through what would happen if we were successful. Each department and facet of the business should be able to visualize what the operation would look like if fully successful. Out of this come the specific action steps that we can focus on as our key result areas—KRAs.

Each department must understand what was expected of it, continued Canas, and how it contributed to the whole. "Sometimes," he observed, "we move too fast from the mission to our planning structure without understanding the implications of what we're doing."

Pushing the Dunfey Approach Down the Organization

Following a brief discussion of the basic approach, Canas turned to his area of principal concern.

Overall, I think you will agree we have been successful in establishing the Dunfey business philosophy among members of the organization down through the level of the EOCs of each hotel. The challenge I want to discuss with you today is in modifying the behavior of people farther down in the organization. In order to convey our philosophy and our approach to the customer, we must push a commitment to our management style down to the very lowest levels of the organization. This is a particular problem when, like us, you take on many new people during the year.

Also, we have had some areas of confusion, such as in defining KRAs. When we talk about key result areas, we're talking about the 20 percent of items against which we can devote effort which will account for 80 percent of the success in reaching our goals. A good selection of KRAs requires a narrow focus and clear delineation of those few key areas which will make the biggest difference in our results at the end of the year.

Now, for instance, if the food and beverage manager gives us 36 things he wants to do, these are *not* KRAs. Most of these are just doing his job; after we get through those, there are probably one or two KRAs which we can identify which will really make a quantum improvement in his operations. If he works 14 hours a

day and doesn't accomplish his KRAs, he has failed. But if a manager has a list of 17 KRAs, he just doesn't understand our planning process!

Yervant Chekijian, at the time group director of operations for the three Dunfey Classic Hotels, caught Canas's eye and offered an illustration:

I can point to an example of this at the Ambassador East. The engineers had many KRAs but I noticed the stoppers in the sinks weren't working. I asked them to get to the basic problems like stoppers in the sink before they submitted a bunch of lofty KRAs. And I mentioned to them that they shouldn't just say they're going to fix the stoppers, they should propose an action plan as follows:

1. Inspection.
2. Locate the problems.
3. Define the scope of work.
4. Allocate man-hours.
5. Commit to having the job completed by a specific date.

Canas nodded agreement and added,

What we need is a scenario documented for each member of the operating team. We need to describe a certain level of service, start setting some standards of guest expectations, and relate the scenarios to these. Otherwise, the people we are dealing with at the lower levels easily forget the basics that we are expecting from them.

Canas turned towards the group directors of operations. "I guess you could say that our planning process and programs have given Dunfey people a common language. It also means we can transfer people from property to property and they will know the system." He went on to say, "One of the things I need to know is how well this planning process is actually being implemented by the EOC in each of our hotels."

Chekijian answered,

At the Parker House, the EOC meets on a weekly basis to go through the Q-Plan and review benchmarks. At the Ambassador East, on the other hand, they work with it, but they have a tendency to be overwhelmed by what happens during the day—putting out fires, if you will. They usually "intend" to use the plan when things are "normal." One general manager did the plan three times—over and over again—threw up his hands, and asked me if he should get back to work. My answer was, "How can you work without a plan?"

A regional director of sales observed that in some ways the plan was "sophisticated—even scary—but it's very natural when you get into it." Chekijian responded that the plan would not get used if its content wasn't real. The group directors, he said, must be responsible for ensuring that individual hotels not only understood the plan but had also proposed realistic goals and action steps.

Canas then turned the discussion toward the question of contingency planning:

> We didn't predict the slowdown in business resulting from the 1979 gasoline shortages until nine months into the year. Very frankly, the oil crisis just wasn't predicted, so we didn't have a "Plan B" in marketing. However, we had one in cost control, which is a lot easier to implement. Another question is, how do you build in sales flexibility when rooms merchandising calls for such advance bookings?

Jurgen Demisch, group director of operations for Dunfey's Inns division, offered a solution: "If sales aren't coming in, we can go to the sales force and ask them to use their account coverage program and get more business from the segments lower down the list."

"So, what you're saying" responded Canas, "is that we already have a system. We have sales action plans, pricing flexibility, ability to cut costs over a 30-day period, and an account coverage program. What we need now is to fully learn to use these things."

"Overall, I see our planning as an evolutionary process," remarked Demisch. "As people learn to work with the plan, they become Dunfeyized, and then when these people are promoted, they can get into the plan from day one at any new property."

"We must get the planning process down to the third level: to restaurant managers, engineers, etc.—down the organization," Canas emphasized. "What I think we need for your division, Jurgen, is a simplification of The Way We Work. All the ingredients must be there and we don't want to shortcircuit it—but Jurgen, we must find a way to have a simplified planning process for a division like yours where you take in so many new people in a short period of time. After all, the basis objective is to be professional innkeepers."

Chuck Barren, group director of operations for several medium-sized hotels, entered the discussion:

> At Hyannis we have a very structured, Dunfeyized team. They are using the planning process and they're moving on without looking back to where they were. We've had a new sales manager in there for 10 days and he already has an excellent plan for the first quarter. The planning system was readily applied here and worked very well.
>
> Baltimore was initially a distress property, and we said, "Do we really want to work from a checklist?" After three months, we went into the planning process. The owners sat in at our planning meetings, and it really helped *them* understand our side of the business and to set mutual objectives.
>
> It's clear that the planning process tends to break down where we don't have Dunfeyized people. And where this occurs, we should have a checklist or a simplified version of the plan to use in situations like takeovers.

Conclusion of Meeting

In answer to a question from one participant, Canas conceded that Dunfey had indeed developed its own management language, which made it hard to acculturate new people, and especially to bring in top management people at the operations level. On the other hand, he felt that the Dunfey process still allowed individual styles to come through, and in fact, called on the creativity of each manager. "The process provides no solutions," he stated, "only managers do!"

Before the meeting adjourned, Canas reiterated the essence of the corporate operating mission, which he read to participants:

To create and/or maintain the structure that provides for the appropriate satisfaction of specifically defined needs of targeted customers, owners, and employees.

He added,

The key here is that we're talking about a structure—and a structure has strength. It has durability. It's an entity which must be full and self-supporting. The structure is our management philosophy and our planning process which, when implemented properly, will provide for the needs of owners, employees, and customers.

NOTES

1. Between 1975 and 1980, the company had discontinued its relationship with 12 units. This turnover included properties that no longer fitted in with the Dunfey product line, either because of product, market, or owners' objectives. The properties replacing them tended to be larger and more important hotels.

2. RSE equals the total room sales revenue received during a period divided by the total revenue that could have been obtained if all available rooms had been sold at the maximum price.

EXHIBIT 1

Properties Owned or Managed by Dunfey Hotels
October 1980

GROUP	TYPE	PROPERTY	LOCATION	YEAR ACQUIRED	STATUS[a]	NUMBER OF ROOMS
1	Classic Hotels	Ambassador East	Chicago, IL	1977	P	300
		Berkshire Place	New York, NY	1978	P	500
		Marquette	Minneapolis, MN	1979	M	270
		Parker House	Boston, MA	1969	F	550
2	Meeting and Convention Hotels	Dunfey Atlanta Hotel	Atlanta, GA	1971	F	400
		Dunfey Dallas Hotel	Dallas, TX	1971	F	650
		Dunfey Houston Hotel	Houston, TX	1971	L	450
		Dunfey San Mateo Hotel	San Mateo, CA	1971	F	300
		Dunfey Hyannis Resort and Conference Center	Cape Code, MA	1972	F	250
	Other Metropolitan Hotels	New York Statler	New York, NY	1979	P	1,800
		The Shoreham	Washington, DC	1979	P	900
3	Inns	Howard Johnson's Motor Inn	Newton, MA	1970	L	275
		Sheraton Inn and Lamie's Tavern	Hampton, NH	1958	F	30
		Sheraton Lexington	Lexington, MA	1967	F	120
		Sheraton N.E. Philadelphia	Philadelphia, PA	1973	F	200
		Sheraton, Tobacco Valley	Windsor, CT	1968	F	130
		Sheraton Wayfarer	Manchester, NH	1962	F	200
	Airport Hotels	Sheraton Airport Inn	Philadelphia, PA	1974	M	350
		Sheraton Inn	South Portland, ME	1973	F	130
		Sheraton Airport Inn	Warwick, RI	1973	F	125
4	International Hotels	London Tara Hotel	London, England	1976	F	850
		Hotel Commodore	Paris, France	1979	L	170
Total		22 Hotels				8,950

[a] Key: F = fully owned by Dunfey Hotels; P = partially owned by Dunfey Hotels (joint venture with management contract); L = leased by Dunfey Hotels; M = strictly management contract.
SOURCE: Company records

EXHIBIT 2

Dunfey Hotels Corporation: Corporate Organization Chart
(December 1980)

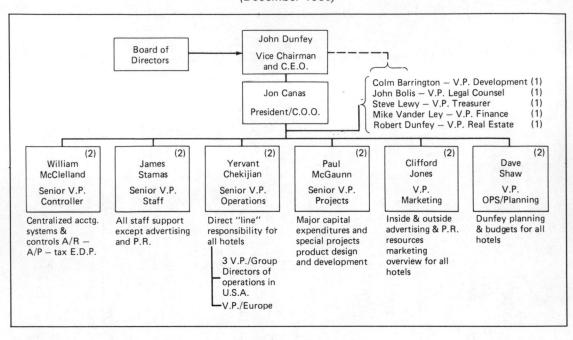

(1) Member of the Finance Review Committee, which also includes the vice chairman, president, and Dave June, vice-president–financial services.
(2) Member of the Corporate Executive Operating Committee, which also includes the president.
SOURCE: Company records

EXHIBIT 3

Dunfey Hotels Unit Planning Process

OBJECTIVE: Corporate Planning Committee (CPC) to provide corporate input and direction for each unit's 1981 Mission and Annual Plan; the CPC includes the Corporate Executive Committee (see Exhibit 2) plus, as appropriate, vice-president–sales, corporate food and beverage director, and the relevant group director of operations (GDO).

A. *For the CPC to do this, it needs*
  1. *Marketing Assessment which includes*
    a. One- to three-page summary of supply/demand analysis.
    b. One-page report to indicate if S/D calls for a significant change in strategies or product.
    c. Historical and proposed (1981) market segmentation and F&B and total revenues.
  2. *Financial Assessment which includes*
    a. One page, outlining
      1) Corporate objectives for the unit
      2) Are we meeting corporate objectives? (If not, why?)
    b. Historical financial summary for 3 to 5 years showing financial results and key statistics.
  3. *Outside Owners' Assessment[a]*
    a. Page outlining outside owners' objectives.
    b. Assessment of current results.

EXHIBIT 3 (continued)

B. The CPC will review the above material resulting in a memorandum to the GDO and Unit EOC outlining
   1. Unit is on track and should not change direction. O.K. to proceed to items C and D.
   2. Unit is on track except for certain items (outlined). O.K. to proceed to items C and D.
   3. Unit is off track seriously—people will be assigned to assist in making major direction changes. Do not proceed to items C and D.
C. The director of marketing and GDO will then write the Unit Mission Statement and send it to the units (after CPC has approved the wording).
D. Unit EOC will then prepare Y–1, Y–2, and Y–3 (GDO and Corporate Staff must review and approve).
E. CPC will have final approval on Item D.

^a For properties managed by Dunfey Hotels for outside owners.

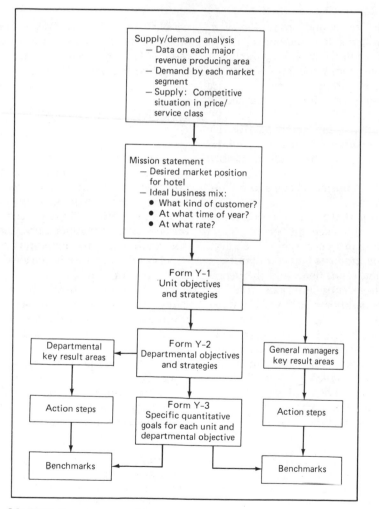

SOURCE: Company records

READINGS

How to Succeed in a Service Industry:
Turn the Organization Chart Upside Down

DAVID S. DAVIDSON

The secret of success in running a good service business is to recognize that customer-contact personnel are the key people in the organization. Friendly, polite, and well-trained customer contacts are as important as sound management.

With an advertising and promotion blitz, Super Parking Systems, Inc., announces that it is opening a new central city parking facility. A personal message from Super's president assures the public of prompt, courteous service and tender, loving care for cars parked at Super.

Not only is the parking facility aggressively and expensively promoted, but it is genuinely needed, and the public responds favorably. Then something goes wrong. After the initial influx of customers, business begins to fall off. What's the problem?

The problem is that Super's president and other dedicated management people don't park cars, issue claim checks, make change, answer telephone inquiries and complaints, or sweep the waiting room floor; and the people who do have these entry-level jobs don't see why they should bend over backward to make customers happy.

Super Parking System isn't a real company, but this story can accurately be called a composite case history of service companies that have failed, or at least failed to realize their full potential, because of shortcomings at the bottom of the organization chart.

Think how many times you have heard people say, "I'll never deal with that outfit again. The employees are rude and indifferent." How many times have you said something like this yourself?

MANAGEMENT TOOLS

It is easy enough to put the blame on customer-contact employees. In the final analysis, however, the blame falls on people at the top for failing to use management procedures that should be routine. Those procedures are: careful selection of contact personnel; proper indoctrination and motivation; constant, vigilant supervision; and speedy removal of those who don't measure up.

In a service industry, the secret of success is recognition that customer-contact personnel are the key people in the organization.

As one chief executive puts it, "In a successful service organization, the organization chart is turned upside down, with the customer-contact personnel at the top."

This is not to say that sound, imaginative management is less important than properly trained service personnel. It does mean, how-

At the time of publication, David S. Davidson was president of ITT Services Industries Corporation and group general manager of the Education, Building, and Transportation Services Group of International Telephone and Telegraph Corporation. This article appeared in *Management Review* (April 1978) and is reprinted by permission of the publisher. © 1978 AMACOM, a division of American Management Association. All rights reserved.

ever, that the most efficient management can be meaningless if not counterbalanced by well-trained, courteous customer-contact personnel.

AIRLINE SUCCESS STORY

Some service companies have learned the lesson well—United Airlines, for example. An airline is about as consumer-oriented as any business can get. From ordering a ticket, to having luggage checked at the air terminal, to being served food and drink aboard the plane, to getting luggage back, the passenger deals with company people entirely at the customer-contact level.

United has recognized the importance of properly trained public-contact employees, and the airline's consumer affairs department had played an important role in recent company history. After Edward E. Carlson moved into the president's office in 1970, one of his first official acts was to have consumer affairs report directly to a senior vice-president, who reports to the president. Carlson is now chairman, but his successor as president, Richard Ferris, has continued this practice.

A company spokesman says that attention paid to customer relations by top executives has played a major part in an upsurge of United's fortunes. The company is a leader in its industry in profitability.

Baggage mishandling, one of any carrier's biggest headaches, was dramatically cut in relatively short order, thanks to a beefing up of personnel and procedures. Unsolicited passenger compliments exceeded complaints for the first time in United's history.

United did not stop with its initial improvement of baggage handling. Last summer it became the first airline to use a computerized system for tracing mislaid luggage. The system dramatically speeds up the reuniting of a passenger with his luggage when, say, the passenger flies to Chicago and his luggage is flown to Washington.

Customer complaints that do not call for immediate action are answered as rapidly as possible anyway. Consumer affairs gives itself a deadline of seven days, at the outside, to answer customer complaints. If a complaint seems serious—and, to consumer affairs, any complaint is serious until proved otherwise—it is traced back to its source. If investigation shows an employee to be at fault, the likelihood that the employee will err again is slim.

TRAINING AT AVIS

Avis, Inc., is another company whose management feels that proper attitude on the part of customer-contact employees is essential to success in a service industry.

"Every cent of revenue that this company receives is touched by our prime service people," says Russell L. James, Avis Rent-A-Car System vice-president of corporate training. "I take the attitude that they are out there paying my salary, because if they weren't there doing a good job, then I wouldn't be here."

Avis believes that all personnel should receive training before they have any communication with the customer. When employees are hired, they spend the first day being introduced to the offices where they will be working. They are then flown to one of five major training centers for ten days of instruction dealing with Avis services and the standards of performance that Avis attaches to those services.

Instruction includes heavy use of role-playing in the classroom, where real-life situations are duplicated.

The progression of the student from one learning plateau to another is constantly monitored, and employee attitude is evaluated.

When customer-contact employees return to Avis offices from the training centers, they are then considered able to cope with 90 percent of the situations with which they will have to deal in the first two or three weeks of counter work. Monitoring of the employees continues once they actually begin to function as Avis representatives.

Avis's current instruction program was made mandatory in 1970 when the company installed a central computer control system and was forced to standardize procedures.

One benefit from mandatory training was a greatly decreased turnover in service personnel. In the years before mandatory training, many people who had not been given the opportunity to learn the skills necessary for their jobs at Avis became frustrated and left.

MANAGEMENT MEETS CUSTOMERS

Another aspect of Avis's concern over customer contact is the company's "visible management" program. Every manager, including the chairman and president of Avis, must spend some time each year working the counters or servicing cars. James, who has been with Avis for 13 years, spends three weeks a year working with first-line customer-contact personnel. "This company believes that I should know what it is all about," he says.

When Avis takes on a new corporate officer or second-line manager, he or she must go through rental agent training and serve time on the counter before being allowed to function in the Avis management offices.

Avis has grown over the years, and it feels its personnel training activities have played a large part in that growth.

STEPS YOU CAN TAKE

The managements of many large national organizations throw up their hands in despair over the shortcomings of customer-contact employees who are far removed from corporate headquarters. Many a consumer blames the company itself for incompetence, say, on the part of a salesperson at one of the company's retail outlets. This certainly poses a difficult problem, but it is not an insuperable one if the proper steps are taken.

Having reviewed the records of service companies, large and small, successful and unsuccessful, I would like to offer a system for ensuring that the right personnel are in place. There are additional intermediate steps, but these cover the main points.

• *Select and train.* Select carefully for the particular job. This can best be done by drawing up a very specific job description. If you carefully interview the job-seeker, you usually will find it easy to determine whether the applicant really fits the job. Job training to ensure an understanding of the needs of the customer and of how to satisfy those needs is equally important. In my own field, insurance, I have successfully used videotaping during training sessions. The videotape permits the trainee to actually see himself experiencing the service process and permits the manager to determine if corrective action is necessary before the trainee is put on the job.

• *Detect.* What this boils down to is close supervision. Don't hesitate to use spotters posing as customers, as many insurance companies do. The companies aim at making sure applicants for insurance are properly informed and that the sales methods used are, in general, proper. You are looking for weak spots in dealings with the public. Finding them in time can avoid development of negative public attitudes toward the company. I have found that, by checking up with applicants for insurance, the insurance company can detect problems and correct them before they create later policyholder service problems.

• *Correct.* With a quick, eager worker, this may entail simply pointing out shortcomings due to inexperience. Retraining may be needed. On occasion it may be necessary to correct company policies or practices which cause customer dissatisfaction. For example, if an insurance sales representative is deviating from the prescribed sales presentation, and this results in misleading applicants for insurance, a retraining session by the employee's managers may get him or her back on the track. However, if such sales presentation problems are found to be frequent among representatives, the presentation itself should be examined for possible revision.

• *Reject.* When, despite other steps to improve customer contact, you still have a square peg in a round hole, it may be necessary to remove an employee from his job. This does not mean the employee must be discharged. For example, someone who doesn't do well in face-to-face dealings with the public may be quite suitable for other kinds of work. Your experience should be fed back to your selection-training program to ensure future avoidance of this problem.

I have had several experiences where insurance sales representatives were not successful because of an inability to prospect for clients and to close sales. The same people were very effective in telephone solicitation, in fact-finding, or in setting up appointments for other representatives to make the actual sales presentations.

It goes without saying that a good complaint department, or whatever you want to call it, is essential for success in any service business. The department should be responsive to complaints and diligent in finding out the facts.

I asked a friend, who is an executive of a large service company, whether customer complaints are a burden on management's time. His unhesitating response was: "Complaints tell us what we're doing wrong. If we didn't get any, I would solicit them."

Why Marketing Management Needs to be Different for Services

CHRISTOPHER H. LOVELOCK

Services often compete with goods to offer similar core benefits to customers, but this does not mean that the marketing management tasks are the same. There are currently both generic and contextual differences between goods and services marketing. Although the latter are likely to narrow over time, the former will remain, requiring service marketers to play a number of roles not usually expected of their counterparts in manufacturing industries.

Let me start with an immediate concession to those who argue that the similarities between goods and services marketing outweigh the differences: I make no claim that the marketing of services is uniquely different from that of physical goods. If the two *were* uniquely different this would raise serious doubts as to the coherence of marketing as a functional area of management. My contention is simply that a different management approach is needed in services marketing.

Services, of course, often compete in the marketplace with goods that offer their users the same (or broadly similar) core benefits. For instance, buying a service may be an alternative to doing it yourself: examples range from lawncare and babysitting to janitorial services and industrial equipment maintenance. Too, using a rental service is frequently an alternative to owning a good. The Yellow Pages in any large city includes listings for a wide array of rental services, ranging from trucks to typewriters and from furniture to formal wear.

But just because a good and a service may be close competitors does not mean that the marketing management tasks for each are the

Christopher H. Lovelock is associate professor of business administration at the Harvard Business School. Reprinted with permission from *Marketing of Services*, eds. James H. Donnelley and William R. George, the American Marketing Association (Chicago, 1980).

same. A packaged foods marketer is likely to come to grief using similar strategies to market fast food restaurants; a successful automobile marketer will not necessarily find it easy to replicate that success in the rental car business; a marketing executive for a manufacturer of heavy electrical equipment will need to develop a new managerial style—as well as new strategies—if transferred to the same company's equipment servicing division.

It's my contention that marketing management tasks in the service sector can be differentiated from those in the manufacturing sector along two dimensions. The first relates to the generic differences between service products and physical goods products. The second concerns the management environment or context within which marketing tasks must be planned and executed. Let's look at each in turn.

GENERIC DIFFERENCES BETWEEN GOODS AND SERVICES

Five generic differences can be identified that separate goods from services marketing. These involve the nature of the product itself, how that product is created, the marketer's ability (or inability) to stockpile the product, the nature of the distribution channels for the product, and the relative ease of determining costs for pricing purposes.

1. Nature of the Product

"A good," writes Berry (1980), "is an object, a device, a thing; a service is a deed, a performance, an effort." Admittedly, goods are sometimes an integral part of a particular service, especially where rentals are concerned. But even in such an explicitly goods-oriented service as the car-rentals business, the relevant product attributes extend far beyond those normally associated with owning one's own car, including such elements as pick-up and drop-off locations (often in different cities), inclusive

insurance, maintenance, free connecting airport shuttle buses, long-distance reservations, and speedy, courteous customer contact personnel.

From the customer's perspective, three distinctive characteristics of most service products are: their ephemeral, experiential nature; the emphasis on time as a unit of consumption; and the fact that people—both service employees and other customers—are often part and parcel of the service product. As we shall see, the relative importance of these characteristics varies according to whether the *target* of the service is the customer in person or the customer's possessions.

2. Different Production Methods

Producing a service typically involves assembling and delivering the output of a mix of physical facilities and mental or physical labor. Sometimes the customers' role is relatively passive, more often they are actually involved in helping create the service product. These factors make it hard for service organizations to control for quality and to offer customers a consistent product. As a former packaged goods marketer, turned hotel marketer, observed: We can't control the quality of our product as well as a P&G control engineer on a production line can. . . . When you buy a box of Tide, you can reasonably be 99 and 44/100 percent sure that this stuff will work to get your clothes clean. When you buy a Holiday Inn room, you're sure at some lesser percentage that it will work to give you a good night's sleep without any hassle, or people banging on the walls, and all the bad things that can happen in a hotel." (Knisely, 1979a)

3. No Inventories for Services

Because a service is a deed or performance, rather than a tangible item, it cannot be inventoried. Of course the necessary equipment, facilities, and labor can be held in readiness to create the service, but these simply represent productive capacity, not the product itself. Unused capacity in a service organization is rather like a running tap in a sink with no plug: The flow is wasted unless customers (or possessions requiring servicing) are present to receive it. As a result, service marketers must work to smooth demand levels to match capacity.

4a. Lack of Physical Distribution Channels for Most Services

The marketer's task in manufacturing firms includes developing distribution strategies for physically moving the product from the factory to the customer. Typically, this involves the use of one or more intermediaries. Because services delivered to the person of the customer are consumed as they are produced, the service factory, retail outlet, and consumption point are often one and the same. Hence distribution strategies in service organizations emphasize the *scheduling* of service delivery as much as the locations. And unlike manufacturers, most service organizations have direct control over the service delivery outlet, either through outright ownership or tightly written franchise agreements.

However, physical distribution channels do exist for certain services performed on customers' goods. Examples include film processing, off-site equipment repair and maintenance, certain specialty cleaning services, and so forth. But these instances—involving drop-off at a convenient retail location, and shipment to a plant where the necessary servicing is done—are the exception rather than the rule in the service sector.

4b. Availability of Electronic Distribution Channels for Some Services

A rapidly growing approach to service distribution is through electronic distribution channels. Physical goods and people cannot yet be "teleported," as science fiction writers predict that some day they will. But services directed at the customer's mind—such as advice, education, entertainment, and information—

can be telecommunicated through such channels as radio, television, the telephone, telecopying, or microwave relays. Moreover, the use of remote printers, video recorders, and telecopiers even makes it possible for such services to produce a hard copy at the receiving end—the closest we have yet come to "teleportation." Services directed at the customer's intangible assets—such as banking, insurance, and stockbroking—can also be distributed, faster than a speeding bullet, through telephone-based authorizations or automated electronic transmission systems.

Theaters, hotels, and transportation operators have long used travel and ticket agencies as intermediaries to handle inquiries, reservations, and ticket sales. Telecommunications now make it possible to deliver certain service products through independent retail intermediaries. One example is the availability in some cities of on-line banking services at supermarkets and department stores (Merliss and Lovelock, 1980). A second is the ability of libraries to sell on-line, computerized information services connected to data banks thousands of miles away. While marketing managers in such organizations face such traditional distribution problems as selecting outlets and determining commission structures (see, for instance, Davis and Star, 1977) they have some novel advantages over their manufacturing industry counterparts. Demand can be smoothed by use of variable, time-of-day pricing; supplies can be cut off instantly as an extreme form of sanction; and new products can be made available spontaneously at many different locations, since there are no lengthy "pipelines" to fill.

5. Determining Costs for Pricing Purposes

Relative to manufacturing firms, it is much more difficult for service businesses to determine which fixed and operating costs are associated with which products—especially when several services are being produced concurrently by the same organization (Dearden, 1978). If a marketer does not know the average cost of producing a unit of service, it is hard to determine what the selling price should be.

The variable cost of selling one additional unit of service (e.g., an extra seat on an aircraft, an extra room in a hotel) is often minimal. Since demand may fluctuate widely by time of day (or week, or season), this gives service marketers much greater flexibility than goods marketers to offer similar products at different prices to different market segments. The challenge is to ensure that the weighted average of all prices charged exceeds the average costs, thus looping the problem back to the tasks of cost determination and allocation.

Summary

Taken as a broad product class, services are distinguished from goods by several generic differences that have important implications for marketing management. Services are not homogeneous, of course; there are many different types (Lovelock, 1980). Yet although the generic differences described above may be more or less pronounced for a specific type of service, and although some goods may share certain features with some services, these generic differences will continue to require distinctions in marketing practice between the manufacturing and service sectors.

CONTEXTUAL DIFFERENCES BETWEEN GOODS AND SERVICES MARKETING

Service marketers whose previous job was in the manufacturing sector—and particularly those who came from consumer packaged goods—often note sharp differences between their current and previous working environments. These differences presently include a narrow definition of marketing by other managers, limited appreciation for marketing skills, a different organizational structure, and a relative lack of competitive data. In addition, many service industries are experiencing a loosening of both government regulations and

professional restrictions on management practices, with important strategic implications for marketing. Finally, there are special constraints and opportunities facing marketers in public and nonprofit organizations.

1. Narrow Definition of Marketing

Professional marketing management is still relatively new to the service sector. Many service industry executives, who tend to be operations oriented, still define marketing as simply advertising and public relations; others extend this definition only as far as sales and market research. Decisions in such areas as new product development, retail site location, pricing, and product line policy have traditionally been excluded from marketing's domain in the service sector. This situation is changing, but many service organizations still have a long way to go before they can be said to have adopted the marketing concept and implemented it across a broad range of managerial activities.

2. Lack of Appreciation for Marketing Skills

The comedian, Rodney Dangerfield, whose perennial complaint is that "I don't get no respect," would probably feel very much at home as a marketing manager in most service firms. Knisely (1979b) records an interview with a Lever Bros. executive who had spent some time as a senior marketing manager in a large service organization; the latter observed: "You feel less loved and less needed. . . . In a service company which has perhaps been built on skills and disciplines that have not included large doses of marketing, you're selling— you're saying 'listen to me' as opposed to 'tell me, tell me.'"

Limited appreciation for marketing skills among other managers makes the service marketer's job just that much more difficult. Lack of clout limits his/her ability to win acceptance of new strategies—particularly if they require deviation from current practice; it may also constrain the amount of resources allocated to marketing.

3. Different Organizational Structures

As noted by Lovelock et al. (1981), service organizations frequently include a general management-type position at both corporate and field levels. Example of the latter would be a branch bank manager, a station manager for an airline or trucking company, or the general manager of a hotel.

These "field general managers," who usually report to operations, are engaged in marketing management tasks whether they recognize them as such or not. In particular, they are usually responsible for managing service personnel in regular contact with customers.

As noted earlier, service organizations generally control service outlets, the service equivalent of a retail store. But much of this benefit is lost if the "store" is not run in a way that balances marketing considerations against operational ones. This means that marketing managers at the corporate level must either develop an organizational structure, such as a matrix, that provides them with access to customer contact personnel, or they must ensure that "field general managers" possess marketing skills and are rewarded for good marketing practice. As noted by Czepiel (1980), most service businesses have some distance to travel before they achieve an organizational structure that integrates marketing and operations in ways calculated to deliver consistently high levels of service quality and customer satisfaction.

4. Lack of Data on Competitive Performance

One of the differences felt most keenly by consumer goods marketers who have moved to the service sector is the lack of market data on their "brands." In many packaged goods businesses, historical data is available on brand performance extending back for many years; and detailed new Nielsen reports (or other retail audits) are published at regular intervals. However, in most service industries, as one bank marketing executive complained to Knisely (1979c), "there is an almost complete lack of historical competitive data. . . . Therefore, the product manager and his (advertising) agency are not able to monitor the results of their marketing efforts as tightly."

Because service organizations rarely use third parties to sell their products to customers, development of an independent retail audit similar to Nielsen would be difficult. (Ticket sales through travel agencies probably do not constitute a representative cross-section of the total sales base.) Many service businesses—from colleges to hotels—share sales information with similar institutions, but there is always the problem that some organizations may decline to participate or else supply deliberately biased information. And although some regulated industries are obliged to supply customer usage data to state or federal agencies, such data is usually highly aggregated for publication purposes.

5. Impact of Government Regulation and Deregulation

Many service industries have traditionally been highly regulated in the United States. Regulatory agencies have mandated price levels, constrained distribution strategies by limiting transportation route structures and banking service areas, and, in some instances, prescribed product attributes. Additionally, self-imposed "professional ethics" have prohibited or restricted advertising in such fields as health care and the law.

Since the late 1970s there has been a trend toward complete or partial federal deregulation in several major service industries. Changes in the regulatory environment are taking place at the state level, too. Meantime, the Federal Trade Commission has achieved removal or relaxation of bans on advertising in certain professional service industries. These moves have frequently served to stimulate competition and to unfetter such key strategic elements as pricing, distribution, and advertising. As a result of deregulation, marketing will undoubtedly assume greater importance as a management activity in the industries in question.

6. Constraints and Opportunities for Nonbusiness Marketers

The past decade has seen greater application of marketing to public and nonprofit services. But marketers need to be aware of the special context in which those services operate. In the public sector, priorities are often established externally by politicians, not management. Externally imposed constraints may include limiting the use of advertising, confining service delivery within established political boundaries, mandating service to "uneconomic" segments, establishing pricing policies, and even defining specific product attributes. Nonprofit marketers, meantime, may have to defer to the wishes of volunteer boards (Selby, 1978) and make compromises to retain the support of important donors.

On the other hand, many public and nonprofit services can be offered at prices well below the full costs of producing them; some are even offered free of charge. Free advertising time and space may be available in the form of public service announcements. And volunteers may offer their services free of charge for such marketing-relating tasks as personal selling and customer-contact at the point of service delivery.

Conclusion

The context within which many service marketers must work is often sharply different from that facing their counterparts in the manufacturing sector (especially in consumer packaged goods firms, where marketing expertise has achieved a high level of sophistication).

But as service businesses become more familiar with the contributions that marketing management can make, there will be greater acceptance of this function. This, in turn, will facilitate development of new organizational structures that give marketing a more equal status with operations in managing the business. Greater competition in service markets will spur efforts to develop more detailed, reliable market data. Finally, public and nonprofit service organizations, faced with greater financial stringency in the years ahead, are likely to develop more market-oriented operating strategies than they have historically, and to charge prices which cover a higher proportion of total costs.

ROLES FOR SERVICE MARKETERS

Reflecting the generic differences between goods and services, the life of a service marketer is, in my view, more varied than that of a goods marketer. To round out this paper, I'd like to look at some of the many roles played by service marketers—using the term "marketer" in its broadest sense to include all service managers with responsibilities that include managing customer relationships.

The Service Manager as Admissions Director

With a few exceptions, usually confined to potentially dangerous products, the only qualification required of an adult wishing to buy a specific good is the ability to pay for it. By contrast, service marketers are much more likely to screen their customers against nonfinancial criteria before agreeing to sell their products. Since the customer is often part of the product and in close contact with service personnel, it may be very important for service businesses to ask: "Which types of customers will we agree to serve?"

In higher education, would-be college students must apply for admission to the college of their choice, and may be rejected if they fail to meet certain minimum aptitude standards laid down by the institution. Other types of services may or may not have a formal admissions process, yet they still employ screening procedures. The hospitality industry, for instance, recognizes that for any one customer, other guests are part of the product experience. Hence a service manager must ask: "How will the appearance and behavior of different types of customers affect the nature of the product experience? Should we set explicit (or implicit) standards and discourage patronage by those who fail to meet them?"

The proprietors of professional practices are often as concerned with the psychic satisfaction they obtain from their job as with the financial income they obtain. Once business exceeds a certain volume, they may start to become very selective about which jobs they accept, seeking to focus on those projects that will be challenging and satisfying; they may prefer more leisure time to obtaining additional income from a boring project.

The strategic questions here for service marketers are: How do we attract the customers we want, *when* we want them? And what procedures do we employ for evaluating prospective customers and tactfully screening out those whose business fails to meet our criteria?

In some instances, acceptance of a customer results in a long term relationship, during the course of which numerous transactions take place. This results in an important role for . . .

The Service Marketer as Club Secretary

Many service businesses have much in common with clubs. You have to "join" them before you may use their services. Using almost any form of public utility requires a formal turning on of the supply and (usually) paying a predefined, monthly subscription. To use most bank services requires that you first open an account. Although credit-worthiness is frequently a necessary criterion for admission to "membership" in a service organization, other criteria may include possession of specific types or models of physical equipment, residence within defined political boundaries, evidence of intellectual aptitude, attainment of a certain age, and even personal chemistry between marketer and customer.

"Membership" can also be *de facto* rather than *de jure:* Regular users of a specific service outlet can often obtain preferential treatment over casual, one-time customers, reflecting personal recognition by the service provider.

The service manager's role as club secretary requires attention to such tasks as (1) setting monthly dues and supplementary fees, (2) admission procedurs; (3) membership rights and privileges (these may have to be spelled out in contractual form in some instances); and (4) publication of the "club newsletter" (unlike many goods marketers, service marketers are much more likely to know their customers' names and addresses for billing and legal purposes; this greatly facilitates use of direct mail promotions, which can be included with the periodic financial statements sent to "members"). Finally, there must be established procedures for updating membership lists and handling resignations and terminations. This leads us to the role of . . .

The Marketer as Police Officer

Because customers are frequently involved in the service production process and often interact with other customers, service marketers may have to lay down formal rules for customer behavior. Sometimes such rules are required by law for safety purposes (consider how tightly your behavior is prescribed every time you take a commercial airline flight); at other times they are laid down by the service organization and relate to such behaviors as form of dress (e.g., restaurants, sailing schools), level of permitted noise (e.g., hotels), physical activity (e.g., health care), accurate completion of documents (e.g., banking), and avoidance of dangerous or inconsiderate activities (e.g., smoking in a nonsmoking area).

This raises the problem of how to get customers to conform to the desired standards, how to enforce behavior when exhortation fails, and how to discipline disobedient customers.

When violations are nonlegal in nature, a mixture of tact and firmness may be needed to achieve the desired effect without generating bad feelings and even an embarrassing "scene." If worst comes to worst, the disobedient customer can be escorted to the door. In practice, the marketer's role as police officer can be made much easier by effective implementation of the role of . . .

The Service Marketer as Teacher

All but the simplest physical goods are accompanied by a set of instructions describing how to use the product. Dollar for dollar, services tend to be much more complex for first-time purchasers to buy and use than are goods. Compare using the bus system in a new city—perhaps a 50 cent purchase—with buying and using a new brand of soap (or soft drink). And compare buying a room and breakfast at a hotel—perhaps a $50 purchase—with buying and using a common household appliance of similar value. As a broad generalization, I think it's fair to say that the service purchase and usage process is considerably the more complex of the two. Typically it involves a sequence of steps, each of which must be successfully negotiated (usually in the presence of other people) before proceeding to the next.

Customers who fail to use a physical good correctly seldom cause problems for other users of the same product (car drivers are an exception). But, customers who misuse a service product may also interfere with the smooth running of the service operation, delay service personnel, and irritate other customers who are seeking service at the same time. This places a great premium on effective education of customers, through printed materials, retail signage, and assistance from customer contact personnel.

The information to be transmitted may include instructions on where and when to seek the service, what operating procedures to follow, how to identify and interact with customer service personnel, how to tender payment, how to dress, how to interact with other customers, and what to do (and what *not* to do) if problems arise.

Contributing to the need for effective education is the fact that the customer is frequently participating in a carefully stage-managed process, designed to achieve both operational efficiencies and creation of a desirable atmosphere. This, in turn, emphasizes the role of . . .

The Service Marketer as Dramatist and Choreographer

Among the tasks faced by many service organizations are designing the service setting and costuming the service personnel; employee uniforms may be necessary not only for practical purposes, but also to simplify customer recognition of relevant personnel. When customers arrive at the service outlet, they may be left to find their own way; alternatively their progress may be carefully stage managed. Service personnel often have a prepared script to deliver to customers, perhaps combining an introductory welcome with some information about how to use the service itself and some discreetly phrased guidelines concerning required or desired behavior.

The delivery of the core service is sometimes carefully choreographed, especially in more complex services that involve the presence of several specialist personnel, require cooperative behavior from customers, and employ a carefully sequenced delivery system. Examples range from good restaurants to airlines to dentists' offices.

Customer complaints tend to be more frequent and more emotional in service businesses, because quality control is harder to maintain and the customer is usually more immediately involved. Effective handling of such complaints is an important marketing task because, if done well, considerable good will may result, whereas if done badly the outcome may be permanent disaffection on the customer's part. Either outcome is likely to result in word-of-mouth advertising, the one positive and the other negative.

The final opportunity for theatrical action in the service transaction might be described as ringing down the curtain—closing out a specific customer contact in ways that leave good feelings on both sides and increase the likelihood of repeat usage.

The Service Marketer as Demand Engineer

Demand levels, as we have noted, often vary widely over time in a service business. Yet without warehouses to store the product, how can service managers bring supply and demand into balance?

Although supply cannot be inventoried, there may be opportunities for operations managers to adjust capacity levels and for marketing managers to smooth demand levels (Sasser, 1976). Successful demand management requires increasing demand in slack periods and decreasing demand on occasions when it would otherwise exceed capacity. It may entail such strategies as product enhancement in off-peak periods, selective pricing, and use of communications for both informational and persuasive purposes.

Another strategy is to inventory demand at times when it exceeds capacity. The service firm's ability to do this depends in part on the target of the service: it is difficult to keep people waiting in line for long unless a truly exceptional service is being offered. But if the target of the service is one of the customer's assets (such as an appliance to be repaired), then that item can be put in a holding area for days or even weeks. An alternative is to introduce a reservations system that establishes a mutually agreed time when the customer shall receive the service (or deliver a possession to be serviced). These may sound like operational procedures; the marketing task consists in designing and promoting them to be acceptable to customers.

The Service Marketer as Manufacturer and Product

Those who create the service product are often perceived by customers as part of the product. The higher their level of contact with customers, the more likely they are to be evaluated by customers as an attribute of the service. From an operational perspective, flight attendants are a much less important aspect of the airline product than flight crew and mechanics; but the marketing role played by the former is usually much more significant, since they are in much closer contact with customers.

The salesforce and the production team are sometimes one and the same in service organizations—particularly in professional service firms such as consultants. Unfortunately, the fact that they are good service manufacturers does not necessarily make them convincing salespeople.

For some personal services, there is a veritable "service trinity," with a single individual running the service operation, seeking to market the service, and being equated by customers with the product. Few people have the skills to play all three roles successfully; marketing specialists can help such service professionals to understand the customer's viewpoint better and to develop an effective outreach strategy.

SUMMARY AND CONCLUSION

In this paper I've emphasized a management perspective in contrasting goods and services marketing.

It's my contention that the contextual differences between goods and services marketing are currently quite significant in many service businesses; but I believe they will become progressively less pronounced as service marketing evolves and moves up the learning curve.

On the other hand, I expect certain generic differences between services and goods marketing to remain. For many services, these differences will always require distinctive marketing strategies that cannot be transferred directly from goods marketing. As a result, service marketers will continue to play a wide variety of roles that, in certain respects, are richer and more interesting than those played by goods marketers.

I hope, in conclusion, that I have convinced you "why marketing management needs to be different for services."

REFERENCES

BERRY, L. L. (1980), "Services Marketing Is Different," *Business* (May–June), 24–29.

CZEPIEL, J. A. (1980), "Managing Customer Satisfaction in Consumer Service Business." Cambridge, MA: Marketing Science Institute.

DAVIS, N. and S. H. STAR (1977), "The Information Bank." In S. H. Star et al., *Problems in Marketing.* New York: McGraw-Hill, 551–580.

DEARDEN, J. (1978), "Cost Accounting Comes to Service Industries," *Harvard Business Review* 56 (Sept.–Oct.), 132–40.

KNISELY, G. (1979a), "Greater Marketing Emphasis by Holiday Inns Breaks Mold," *Advertising Age*, 1/15.

——— (1979b), "Listening to Consumer Is Key to Consumer or Service Marketing," *Advertising Age*, 2/19.

——— (1979c), "Financial Services Marketers Must Learn Packaged Goods Selling Tools," *Advertising Age*, 3/19.

LOVELOCK, C. H. (1980), "Towards a Classification of Services." In C. W. Lamb and P. M. Dunne, *Theoretical Developments in Marketing.* Chicago: American Marketing Association, 72–76.

———, E. LANGEARD, J. E. G. BATESON, and P. EIGLIER (1981), "Some Organizational Problems Facing Marketing in the Service Sector." In J. H. Donnelly and W. R. George, *Marketing of Services.* Chicago: American Marketing Association, 168–71.

MERLISS, P. P. and C. H. LOVELOCK (1980), "Buffalo Savings Bank," 9–581–065. Boston, MA: Intercolleg. Case Clearing House.

SASSER, W. E. (1976), "Match Demand and Supply in Service Industries," *Harvard Business Review*, 54 (Nov.–Dec.), 133–40.

SELBY, C. C. (1978), "Better Performance from 'Nonprofits,'" *Harvard Business Review*, 56 (Sept.–Oct.), 92–98.

APPENDIX

Studying and Learning from Cases

The cases featured in this book represent real-world problems that managers in different service organizations have had to face and resolve. Although designed principally for use in classroom discussions, many of these cases can offer valuable insights to the individual reader.

The comments that follow are directed primarily at students, or participants in executive education programs, who have been assigned one or more of these cases to prepare for subsequent class discussion. Dealing with these cases is very much like working with the problems that men and women encounter in their jobs as managers. In most instances, you will be identifying and clarifying problems facing a service organization, analyzing qualitative information and quantitative data, evaluating alternative courses of action, and then making decisions about what strategy to pursue for the future.

Reflecting the uncertainty of the real-world managerial environment, the information presented in a case is often imprecise and ambiguous. The goal in using the case method is not to develop a set of "correct" facts, but to learn to reason well with available data. You will find—and perhaps be frustrated by the fact—that there is no single "right" answer or "correct" solution to a case. Instead, there may be a number of feasible strategies management might adopt, each with somewhat different implications for the future of the organization, and each involving different trade-offs.

As a teaching approach, the case method can only be successful if you accept the role of an involved participant in the case, as opposed to that of a disinterested observer. Unlike lectures and textbooks, the case method of instruction does not present students with a body of tried and true knowledge about how to be a successful manager. Instead, it provides an opportunity to learn by "doing."

If you are using this book in a course, you will be exposed to a wide range of different management situations within the space of just a few months. Yet these cases collectively provide a much broader exposure than most marketing managers experience on the job in many years. Recognizing that the problems with which managers must deal are not unique to a particular institution (or even to a specific field, such as hotels, banking, or transportation) forms the basis for a professional sense of management.

CASES AND THE REAL WORLD

In spite of the realism that casewriters try to build into their cases, it's important to recognize that they differ from "real-world" management situations in several important respects. First, the information is "prepackaged" in written form. By contrast, practicing managers accumulate their information through such means as memoranda, meetings, chance conversations, research studies, observations, news media reports, other externally published materials, and, of course, rumor.

Second, cases tend to be selective in their reporting because most of them are designed with specific teaching objectives in mind. Each must fit a relatively short class period and focus attention on a defined category of management problems within a given subject area. To provide such a focus—and to keep the length and complexity of the case within reasonable bounds—it may be necessary to omit information on problems, data, or personnel that are peripheral to the central issue(s) in the case.

In the real world, management problems are usually dynamic in nature. They call for some immediate action, with further analysis and decisions delayed until some later time. Managers are rarely able to wrap up their problems, put them away, and go on to the "next case." In contrast, a case discussion in class is more like a "snapshot" taken at a particular point in time. However, sometimes a sequel case provides a sense of continuity and recognition of the need for future decisions within the same organization.

A final contrast between case discussions and the realities of real-world management is that participants in case discussions are not responsible for implementing their decisions, nor do they have to live with the consequences. This does not mean, however, that you can be frivolous when making recommendations in class. Your instructor and classmates are likely to be critical if your contributions are not based upon a careful analysis and interpretation of the facts.

PREPARING A CASE

Just as there is no one right solution to a case, there is no single "correct" way of preparing a case. However, the following broad guidelines may help familiarize you with the job of case preparation. With practice, you should be able to establish a working style with which you feel comfortable.

Initial Analysis

First, it is important to gain a feel for the overall situation by skimming quickly through the case. Ask yourself:

- What sort of organization is the case about?
- What is the nature of the industry (broadly defined)?
- What is going on in the external environment?
- What problems does management appear to be facing?

An initial fast reading, without attempting to take notes or underline, should provide you with some sense for what is going on and what information is being presented for analysis. Then you will be ready to make a very careful second reading of the case. This time, seek to identify key facts so that you can develop a situation analysis and clarify the nature of the problem(s) facing management. Take some notes as you go along in response to such questions as:

- What decisions need to be made, and who will be responsible for making them?
- What are the objectives of the organization itself and of each of the key players in the case? Are they mutually compatible objectives? If not, can they be reconciled, and will it be necessary to redefine the objectives?
- What resources and constraints are present which will help or hinder attempts by the organization to meet its objectives?

You should make a particular effort to establish the significance of any quantitative data presented in the text of the case, or, more often, in the exhibits. See if new insights may be gained by combining and manipulating data presented in different parts of the case. But don't blindly accept the data. With cases, as in real life, not all information is equally reliable or equally relevant. On the other hand, casewriters do not deliberately misrepresent data or facts to "trick" you.

Developing Recommendations

At this point, you should be in a position to summarize your evaluation of the situation and to develop some recommendations for management. First, identify the alternative courses of action that the organization might take. Next, consider the implications of each alternative, including possible undesirable outcomes, such as provoking responses from stronger competitors. Ask yourself how short-term tactics fit with longer-term strategies. Relate each alternative back to the objectives of the organization (as defined or implied in the case, or as redefined by you). Then, develop a set of recommendations for future action, making sure that these are supported by your analysis of the case data.

Your recommendations will not be complete unless you give some thought to how the proposed strategy should be implemented. Consider the following questions:

- What resources—human, financial, and other—will be required?
- Who should be responsible for implementation?
- What time frame should be established for the various actions proposed?
- How should subsequent performance be measured?

Small Group Discussions

The best results in the early stages of case preparation are generally achieved by working alone. But a useful step, prior to class discussion, is to discuss the case with a small group of classmates. (In some instances, you may find yourself allocated to a small discussion group as an integral part of the program experience.) These small groups facilitate initial "testing" of the ideas and help to focus the discussion on the main considerations. Within such a discussion group, present your arguments and listen to those of other participants. The aim of such a meeting is not to reach a consensus, but to broaden, clarify, and redefine your own thinking—and to help others do likewise.

Effective management of the marketing side of a service business involves adjusting the organization's resources to the changing character of the marketplace; this is different from just applying knowledge about "what works" and "what doesn't work" in marketing. Accordingly, the focus of small group discussions should be on analysis and decision making: What are the facts? What do they mean? What alternatives are available? What specifically should management do, how, and when?

CLASS DISCUSSIONS

Role of the Instructor

In class, you may find that the role played by an instructor teaching the case method differs significantly from that of a lecturer. The instructor's role in case discussions is often similar to that of a moderator—calling on students, guiding the discussion, asking questions, and periodically synthesizing previous comments.

In most instances, the instructor will try to solicit insights, analysis, and recommendations from a broad cross-section of participants, rather than allowing a small number of them to dominate the discussion. Sometimes, he or she will encourage individuals with contrary views to debate their points with each other or even to role-play some of the characters featured in the case.

Responsibilities of Participants

Similarly, the role of participants is different from the usual student role. Instead of being a passive note-taker, you will be expected to become an active participant in class discussions. Indeed, it is essential that you participate; for if nobody participates, there is no discussion! If *you* never join in the debate, you will be denying the other participants the insights that you may have to offer. Moreover, there is significant learning involved in presenting your own analysis and recommendations and debating them with your classmates who may hold differing views or else seek to build on your presentation. But don't be so eager to participate that you ignore what others have to say. Learning to be a good listener is also an important element in developing managerial skills.

A few words of general caution may be helpful. Avoid indiscriminate "rehash" of case facts in your presentations—the instructor and the other participants have already read the case, too. Work toward building a coherent class discussion rather than making random comments. Before making a contribution, ask yourself if the points you plan to make are relevant to what has gone before, or if they will result in a significant redirection of the discussion.

Occasionally, it may happen that you are personally familiar with the organization depicted in a case. Perhaps you are privy to additional information not contained in the case, or perhaps you know what has happened since the time of the case decision point. If so, keep this information to yourself unless, and until, the instructor requests it. There are no prizes for 20–20 hindsight, and injecting extra information that nobody else has is more likely to spoil the class discussion than to enhance it.

Learning comes through discussion and controversy. In the case method of instruction, participants must assume responsibility not only for their own learning, but also for that of others in the class. Thus, it is important that you be well-prepared, willing to commit yourself to a well-reasoned set of analyses and recommendations, and receptive to constructive criticism. If you do not accept this challenge, you are likely to find the case method aimless and confusing. On the other hand, if you do accept it, you'll experience that sense of excitement, challenge, and even exasperation that comes with being a manager in real-world situations.